Why History?

Why History?

Why History?

A History

DONALD BLOXHAM

OXFORD
UNIVERSITY PRESS

OXFORD
UNIVERSITY PRESS

Great Clarendon Street, Oxford, OX2 6DP,
United Kingdom

Oxford University Press is a department of the University of Oxford.
It furthers the University's objective of excellence in research, scholarship,
and education by publishing worldwide. Oxford is a registered trade mark of
Oxford University Press in the UK and in certain other countries

First Edition published in 2020

Impression: 1

Published in the United States of America by Oxford University Press
198 Madison Avenue, New York, NY 10016, United States of America

British Library Cataloguing in Publication Data
Data available

Library of Congress Control Number: 2019957614

ISBN 978-0-19-885872-0

Printed and bound in Great Britain by
Clays Ltd, Elcograf S.p.A.

For Cordelia, Yasmin, and Zahra

Preface

With a young family I took this project on at entirely the wrong time, so my apologies, as well as my greatest debts of gratitude, are owed to three Beatties: Cordelia, Yasmin, and Zahra. For helpful discussions and references I thank Zubin Mistry, David Patterson, Natasha Wheatley, Tom Brown, Reinbert A. Krol, Thomas Ahnert, and Bill Aird. For the same things, and for their time and effort in reading and commenting on one or more chapters I thank Douglas Cairns, Felicity Green, Adam Fox, Lucy Grig, Jürgen Matthäus, Louise Jackson, Jane Caplan, Stephan Malinowski, Martin Shuster, Cordelia (again), Chris Given-Wilson, Fabian Hilfrich, Guy Halsall, Rick Sowerby, Michael Bentley, David Laven, and Colin Richmond. Steve Rigby read the entire manuscript with the most helpful rigour and generosity of intellectual spirit.

Contents

Introduction

On 'Modern Historical Consciousness'

The nineteenth-century French historian N. D. Fustel de Coulanges wrote that in order to relive a bygone epoch one must try to bracket all knowledge of what came subsequently. A classical education was misleading insofar as it rendered Greeks and Romans all-too-familiar. 'We have some difficulty in considering them as foreign nations...Hence spring many errors. We rarely fail to deceive ourselves regarding these ancient nations when we see them through the opinions and facts of our own time.' Best 'to study them without thinking of ourselves, as if they were entirely foreign to us; with the same disinterestedness, and with the mind as free, as if we were studying ancient India or Arabia.'[1]

Fustel cogitated on foreign worlds past around ninety years before L. P. Hartley's *The Go-Between*. For Hartley's narrator in 1952 the decades from childhood at the turn of the century, 'the most changeful half a century in history', separated the present from the 'foreign country' of the past. As we know from the novel's famous opening line, in the past 'they do things differently'. Ultimately, though, *The Go-Between* concerned the relationship between present and past. For his part, Fustel also wrote that 'the past never completely dies for man. Man may forget it, but he always preserves it within him. For, take him at any epoch, and he is the product, the epitome, of all the earlier epochs. Let him look into his own soul, and he can find and distinguish these different epochs by what each has left within him.'[2]

So Fustel provided manifestos for two different sorts of historical enquiry—two different answers to the 'why History' question with which this book is occupied. (Throughout, uppercase *History* denotes the discipline of studying the past, or works of such study, while lowercase *history*, historical, etc., refer to the past.) One was an empathetic examination of different, almost self-enclosed worlds past. This is the sort of thing medievalists get at when they invoke the 'otherness' or 'alterity' of the Middle Ages. The second was a study into relations between now and then, asking what the historian Arnold Toynbee later took to be the

---

[1] N. D. Fustel de Coulanges, *The Ancient City* (Kitchener, ON: Batoche, 2001 [orig. 1864]), 5–6.
[2] Ibid. 8; L. P. Hartley, *The Go-Between* (New York: New York Review Books, 2002 [orig. 1953]), 17, 313.

historian's 'elemental question': 'How has this come out of that?'[3] Insofar as this book makes no effort to forget what came afterwards in the study of any given historical 'epoch', perhaps it contravenes the spirit of Fustel's first sort of enquiry. Then again, perhaps he set an unnecessarily exacting standard. There is no contradiction between trying to take the inhabitants of a long and diverse past 'on their own terms' while also seeking to comprehend how their thoughts and actions contributed to changes that affected other, later inhabitants. Nor is there any reason that different approaches cannot be accommodated in the same book.

In combining the two approaches it becomes impossible to separate the elements of this enquiry that might be said to be of purely intrinsic interest from those that are of more utilitarian concern. When contemplating what of the past remains and what has been lost along the way, one is casting light, directly or indirectly, on the present. This can be done in such a way as to strew petals down the royal road to the here and now, or to show how fortuitous were the twists and turns of that route to the present, or to subject the present to critical scrutiny.

The present work surveys the development of historical thinking within the baggy, porous, and influential 'western tradition'. Its aims are to understand how earlier students of the past justified what they did and also to illustrate the functions of what they did, whether or not they recognized those functions. The study concludes with a lengthy critical reflection on History's purposes and functions today. The book does *not* seek to provide a comprehensive history of the evolution of the discipline over three thousand years. It does have to probe aspects of that general evolution to varying depths, but only insofar as is necessary for explaining the historical evolution of answers to the questions of what History is for, and why History matters.

Which aspects of the mainstream are relevant? On the whole, Histories of the discipline of History have emphasized the changes that have occurred between epochs, and two related sets of changes have preoccupied the lion's share of attention. One is in the area of technique and critical discernment. The other concerns changes culminating in what is sometimes called 'modern historical consciousness', which in this context means the idea that the past is wholly past, significantly different to the present, a foreign country with its own particular ways of knowing, being, doing, and valuing—a foreign country towards which the historian needs a mode of comportment different to any that she adopts toward the present.

None of this terrain is free from interpretative conflict, and what follows in this introduction is but a taste of the fine scholarship that has joined battle. Some historians trace the roots of a particularly 'modern' critical-contextual style of historical thought to the secularization of theological exegesis, others to

---

[3] Arnold J. Toynbee, *A Study of History*, abridgement of vols. VII–X ed. Robert Somervell (Oxford: Oxford University Press 1985), 353.

eighteenth-century aesthetic theory.[4] One sees 'Copernican' significance in the fourteenth-century poet Petrarch's sense of the past's difference, then locates the birth of the idea of anachronism in the later Renaissance period and its traditions of reading and seeing, while arguing that this idea is not incorporated fully into historical depiction until the Enlightenment of Montesquieu.[5] Some find 'the first traces of a critical historical method' and an associated 'historicism' in Guicciardini's sixteenth-century oeuvre. The significance of the French jurist, philosopher, and historian Jean Bodin (1530–96), and the 'French school' of legal-historical exegesis to which his work is indebted, is widely acknowledged in many accounts.[6] Others detect a 'historical consciousness' in the Islamic philosopher Ibn Khaldūn the century before and—in Europe—in the Italian philosopher Giambattista Vico only more than a century after.[7] A historically minded philosopher sees Machiavelli's moment and the late eighteenth- and early nineteenth-century period as two significant steps in approximately the same direction: the 'sublime' dissociation of the past from the present in light of ruptures that upset any sense of historical continuity.[8] Intellectual historian Reinhart Koselleck's work on the advent and protean nature of modern 'historical consciousness' characterizes it as a perception in which the future was open-ended, thus not foretold by any religious eschatology, yet expected to be markedly different from the present just as the present was different to the past. Koselleck arrives at 1850 as the time, roughly speaking, when the new frame of mind had fully crystallized. He sees the shift from previous conceptions of time occurring in the generations

---

[4] Amos Funkenstein, *Theology and the Scientific Imagination from the Middle Ages to the Seventeenth Century* (Princeton: Princeton University Press, 1986), part IV and the wider range of Funkenstein's work discussed in Samuel Moyn, 'Amos Funkenstein on the Theological Origins of Historicism', in Robert S. Westman and David Biale (eds.), *Thinking Impossibilities: The Intellectual Legacies of Amos Funkenstein* (Toronto: University of Toronto Press, 2008), 142–66; Allan Megill, 'Aesthetic Theory and Historical Consciousness in the Eighteenth Century', *History and Theory* 17 (1978), 29–62.

[5] Zachary Sayre Schiffman, *The Birth of the Past* (Baltimore: John Hopkins University Press, 2011), 144 ff.. Some of this draws on Peter Burke, *The Renaissance Sense of the Past* (London: Arnold, 1969). Further on classic examinations of the innovations of the Quattocentro in terms of conceptualizing the past, see the literature invoked in Gary Ianziti, 'Humanism's New Science: The History of the Future', *I Tatti Studies in the Italian Renaissance*, 4 (1991), 59–88, here 59.

[6] On Guiccardini, Jacques Bos, 'Renaissance Historiography: Framing a New Mode of Historical Experience', in Rens Bod, Jaap Maat, and Thijs Weststeijn (eds.), *The Making of the Humanities*, 2 vols (Amsterdam: Amsterdam University Press, 2010 and 2012), vol. 1, 351–65, here 362; on Bodin, Robert A. Nisbet, *History of the Idea of Progress* (New Brunswick, NJ: Transaction, 2009), 119–24; J. Samuel Preus, *Explaining Religion: Criticism and Theory from Bodin to Freud* (Oxford: Oxford University Press, 1996); also Schiffman, *Birth*, 183 ff. As to sixteenth-century France, see Donald R. Kelley, *Foundations of Modern Historical Scholarship: Language, Law, and History in the French Renaissance* (New York: Columbia University Press, 1970); Claude-Gilbert Dubois, *La Conception de l'histoire en France au XVIe siècle* (Paris: Nizet, 1977); Zachary Sayre Schiffman, *On the Threshold of Modernity: Relativism in the French Renaissance* (Baltimore: Johns Hopkins University Press, 1991).

[7] Bradley Nelson Seidel, 'Giambattista Vico and the Emergence of Historical Consciousness' (Marquette University: PhD thesis, 1996).

[8] Frank Ankersmit, *Sublime Historical Experience* (Stanford: Stanford University Press, 2005).

either side of the French Revolution's destruction of the ancien régime, and also as a result of industrialization and technological development.[9] With regard to that nineteenth-century context, another historian has identified a 'new' interest in older, written sources, as opposed to eyewitness accounts. He sees that development as commensurate with a shift away from the time-honoured tradition of History as contemporary History—but yet another historian sees the same shift occurring in Italian historianship of the fifteenth century.[10]

Historical events loom large in many explanations for shifting conceptualizations of the relation of past to present, but events are so many and various that we cannot look for much consensus there. The French Revolution was surely significant, but changes in historical thought were encouraged *inter alia* by: the Greco-Persian and Peloponnesian wars; the rise and fall of the western Roman empire; the Norman conquest of large parts of Britain; the withdrawal of the Holy Roman Empire from the Italian peninsula; what Guicciardini called *le calamità d'Italia* in the late fifteenth century; the Reformation and its theological and political aftermaths; nineteenth-century nation-state-building and industrialization; the World Wars; and decolonization. These and many more instances, often of upheaval and antagonism, have left their mark on conceptions of the present's relationship to the past, and thus on conceptualizations of the point of History.[11] So, too, have cross-cultural encounters of the sort that led the seventeenth-century philosopher René Descartes to compare foreign journeys to 'living in the company of the men of other times'.[12] From Herodotus to Herder via 'Marco Polo' and Montesquieu, other ways of life have been revealed, expanding the conceptualization of human difference across space and by extension time. The most self-serving and exploitative such instances include the invasion of the Americas, a.k.a the 'new world' as opposed to the Eurasian and southern Mediterranean 'old' one, but despite the attention lavished on that encounter, akin to the focus on the impact of the French Revolution, it was just one in a series of salient events. At the other end of the spectrum encounters have been more like awkward family reunions, as when Latin Christendom became more extensively reacquainted with certain ancient Greek traditions of thought and a tranche of classical historianship from the late fourteenth century.

Even on the more purely technical front it is very difficult to establish which of very many rich accounts most merits credence. The ancient Greek historian

[9] Reinhart Koselleck, *Futures Past: On the Semantics of Historical Time* (New York: Columbia University Press, 2004).
[10] Ianziti, 'Humanism's New Science', 64–5; cf. Jaap den Hollander, 'Beyond Historicism: From Leibniz to Luhman', *Journal of the Philosophy of History* 4 (2010) 210–25, here 220–1.
[11] On some of these moments, see Daniel Woolf, 'From Hystories to the Historical', in Paulina Kewes (ed.), *The Uses of History in Early Modern England* (San Marino, CA: Huntington Library, 2006), 31–68, here 35–6.
[12] René Descartes, *Discourse on Method*, trans. Andrew Wollaston (Harmondsworth: Penguin, 1960), 40.

Polybius wrote that each later historian 'makes such a parade of minute accuracy, and inveighs so bitterly when refuting others, that people come to imagine that all other historians have been mere dreamers…and that he is the only man who has made accurate investigations, and unravelled every account with intelligence'. The British historian of the classical world J. B. Bury credited Polybius's predecessors with being the first to apply genuine criticism to historical evidence. The nineteenth-century 'Whig' historian E. A. Freeman, however, found the twelfth-century William of Malmesbury to be the first properly critical historian—the sort of claim that has fallen out of fashion recently.[13] Renaissance historian Gary Ianziti claims a Copernican Revolution (analogies to scientific revolutions being popular in historiographical periodization) in source criticism in the work of fifteenth-century scholars like Lorenzo Valla and Flavio Biondo.[14] Anthony Grafton sees sixteenth-century historiographical disputes as comprising the forgotten crucible of much of the inheritance of the later professionalized discipline.[15]

Whatever the diversity of modern historiography, the most influential accounts of how the discipline got to where it is today are anchored in a conception of a cultural modernity that emerged in the sixteenth or seventeenth century and found its apotheosis in the nineteenth century. Sometimes such accounts draw on a symmetry of classical and/or patristic (early Christian) scholarship on one side and humanist-influenced History on the other.[16] Both tendencies have a great deal going for them, but they share an absence, or at least a much diminished, often caricatured presence: the 'medieval'. In the first set of accounts, the medieval world is that from which modernity has departed. In the second set the medieval is the absent point around which the symmetry is forged.

In exemplification of the first tendency, consider Koselleck's virtuoso accounts of the development in the early modern period of a 'new quality' of 'historical time'. He also dubs this novelty 'a temporalization [*Verzeitlichung*] of history' as opposed to the supposedly 'achronological' character of prior historical thought.[17] His insights on trends of thought between roughly 1500 and 1850 are less relevant

---

[13] Frederick J. Teggart, *Theory and Processes of History* (Berkeley: University of California Press, 1962), 12–14.

[14] Ianziti, 'Humanism's New Science', 65.

[15] Anthony Grafton, *What was History? The Art of History in Early Modern Europe* (Cambridge: Cambridge University Press, 2007).

[16] Dimitri Levitin captures the richness of the more recent of the two symmetries, and includes most of the relevant references: Levitin, 'From Sacred History to the History of Religion: Paganism, Judaism, and Christianity in European Historiography from Reformation to "Enlightenment"', *The Historical Journal* 55:4 (2012), 1117–60. Burke, *The Renaissance Sense of the Past*, creates a symmetry between Roman and Renaissance historiography. Anthony Grafton and Megan Williams, *Christianity and the Transformation of the Book: Origen, Eusebius, and the Library of Caesarea* (Cambridge, MA: Harvard University Press, 2006), Coda, considers relations between Renaissance palaeography and Hebraism and patristic scholarship. The title of Arnaldo Momigliano's *Classical Foundations of Modern Historiography* (Berkeley: University of California Press, 1990), is self-explanatory.

[17] Koselleck, *Futures Past*, 10, 11.

here than his characterization of what went before, notably his conception of the relationship between 'the' medieval sense of time and theologically influenced Christian philosophies of the historical process. Now Koselleck is writing on a grand scale, so large generalizations are inevitable, but his generalization tends towards caricature. Thus what is first described in one of his essays as 'the history of Christianity' becomes two pages later the History of 'the Church', as if these were co-extensive.[18] Even the former usage is ambivalent between the history of Christianity understood as ways of conceiving the historical process within Christian civilization or as an account of that civilization itself. One suspects the latter: we learn that Guicciardini's insights stem from his being 'in Italy, the land where modern politics originated', as if the practice of modern politics were coterminous with the sort of political theory that Machiavelli and others have some claim to have founded. For our nascent moderns, 'Weighing the probability of forthcoming or nonoccurring events in the first instance eliminated a conception of the future taken for granted by religious factions: the certainty that the Last Judgment would enforce a simple alternative between Good and Evil through the establishment of a single principle of behavior'. From this we can only infer that prior to Koselleck's chosen point in time, political leaders did not think about issues of probability in deciding on their action, that they could not distinguish between long-term prognoses and immediate situations, and so forth. Koselleck tells us that 'Prognosis produces the time within which and out of which it weaves, whereas apocalyptic prophecy destroys time through its fixation on the End. From the point of view of prophecy, events are merely symbols of that which is already known.'[19] Only post-medievals are apparently aware of the importance of 'foresight', as if, say, the thirteenth-century Dominican friar Thomas Aquinas had not thought long and hard on 'prudence', or that one should be prepared for 'surprise', with its implications of contingency planning.[20] There is a sense of a fine mind getting carried away by the logic of its own arguments when Koselleck suggests that various calculations of Frederick the Great around the First Partition of

---

[18] Ibid. 11, 13.   [19] Ibid. 18, 19.
[20] Ibid. Cf. Aquinas: 'The knowledge of singulars pertains to the perfection of the intellective soul, not in speculative knowledge, but in practical knowledge, which is imperfect without the knowledge of singulars, in which operations exist...Hence for prudence are required the remembrance of past things, knowledge of present things, and foresight of future things.' Thomas Aquinas, *Summa Theologica* (Raleigh, NC: Hayes Barton Press, 2006), 3790. Koselleck is obviously aware of some of the relevant literature on *gestae* (deeds) and events because he cites a few medieval instances in another important essay (*Futures Past*, 26–42), though again to illustrate the differences between medieval senses of continuity and modern senses of change, whereas the material could be used against the arguments cited in the main text here. Not only am I not convinced that some at least of the medieval justifications for exemplar History are so very different to the justifications for history suggested at the end of Koselleck's essay by 'moderns' like Theodor Mommsen and Henry Adams (*Futures Past*, 41–2), this literature clearly shows that 'events' could be used in medieval historical thought in a way other than in symbolic relationship to prophecy. See the discussions in Chapter 3 below.

Poland were 'clearly possible only in a particular historical situation'. Unless that statement is pure tautology, in which Frederick's actions are to be defined in terms of the precise situation against which he was reacting, it is a negative generalization which is not tested against any actions from the vast tracts of time outside of that 'situation'. Only one counter-case would be needed to falsify it, but counter-cases from outside the time in question are absent. Even when Koselleck rather erases some of the distinctions that he has himself forcibly made—'the distance separating the early modern political consciousness of time from that of Christian eschatology was nowhere near as great as it might seem'—the reductive association of medieval political consciousness with 'Christian eschatology' remains.[21]

Koselleck has no monopoly on such characterizations.[22] Even those like the medievalist Bernard Gunée who have protested in 'defence' of the medieval, and the historian of the Renaissance Peter Burke who has somewhat revised his influential views in light of such accounts, have ended up saying something to the effect that the medievals had their own historical sense—one that was historical in some meaningful fashion, but nonetheless different to Renaissance or high modern senses. This represents a conceptual advance, and after all one does not want to pretend that nothing changed across time, because a great deal did. But we still end up with a sort of relativism that maintains the hard periodizations already established and with them a misleading concept of different historical 'epochs' each with corresponding, discrete outlooks on the past.[23]

---

[21] Koselleck, *Futures Past*, 20, 21. See also Koselleck, *The Practice of Conceptual History: Timing History, Spacing Concepts* (Stanford: Stanford University Press, 2002), 111–12, and Koselleck 'Begriffsgeschichtliche Anmerkungen zur "Zeitgeschichte"', in Victor Conzemius, Martin Greschat, and Hermann Kocher (eds.), *Die Zeit nach 1945 als Thema kirchlicher Zeitgeschichte* (Göttingen: Vandenhoeck & Ruprecht, 1988), 17–31.

[22] Hanan Yoran, 'Florentine Civic Humanism and the Emergence of Modern Ideology', *History and Theory* 46 (October 2007), 326–44, also deploys the generic 'medieval' to perform the work of contrast, even as he ultimately recognizes the significance of a distinctly medieval trend—nominalist philosophy—in preparing the ground for what he sees as humanism's break with this medieval. Nor do I have any monopoly on contesting such characterizations. See for instance Judith Pollmann, *Memory in Early Modern Europe, 1500–1800* (Oxford: Oxford University Press, 2017), who on pp. 9–10 takes issue with Koselleck and others whose position is relevantly similar to his. My own analysis and accompanying corrective goes further back than Pollmann's.

[23] And this despite the evidence unearthed by the likes of Gunée that shows commonalities as well as differences across time: Bernard Gunée, 'Y a-t-il une historiographie médiévale?', *Revue Historique* 258 (1977), 261–75. For Burke's latter-day position which concurs with medievalist R. W. Southern that medievals had *a* sense of the past, one which was then replaced by a different such sense, see his 'The Sense of Anachronism from Petrarch to Poussin', in Chris Humphrey and W. M. Ormrod (eds.), *Time in the Medieval World* (Woodbridge: York Medieval Press, 2001), 157–73, here 162. (Southern's piece is 'Sense of the Past'.) Compare this to Burke's 1969 pronouncement (*Renaissance Sense*, 1) that 'during the whole millennium 400–1400, there was no "sense of history" even among the educated'. On the evolution of Burke's thought, see Margreta de Grazia, 'Anachronism', in Brian Cummings and James Simpson (eds.), *Cultural Reformations: Medieval and Renaissance in Literary History* (Oxford: Oxford University Press, 2010), 13–32, here 27.

Now the table of contents may suggest that at certain points this book has replicated a version of the epochal schema just criticized, but examination of the text itself will show merely that some familiar placeholders have been deployed in order to break down the account into digestible chunks. While a broadly chronological development underpins the volume's structure, cleaving to calendrical markers too rigorously would seriously blunt the argument. One reasons that is so is that some issues simply do retain their relevance for long periods; such themes are elaborated in the second part of this introduction. Another reason is that the moment of the translation and reception of certain ideas in certain places is often separated from the moment of their production in other places. There is a great deal of 'cross-hatching' between the 'horizontal' chronological arrangement of the chapters and the 'vertical' themes.

Amongst other things, this book attempts a new way to relate 'the medieval' to what went before and after. The purpose of the operation follows both of Fustel's lines. 'Medieval' and other instances of historical scholarship are placed in whatever are held to be the salient contexts of their writing at different junctures, in the attempt to 'do justice to them' by their own standards and according to their own purposes. But the aim is also to try to blur the distinctions between 'ancient', 'medieval', and 'modern' by illustrating powerful continuities as well as changes in historical thinking. This is an especially important task in relationship to the medieval and the modern because these two 'epochs' still stand as interdefined 'others', mutually constituted opposites.

One way of deconstructing the medieval–modern opposition is to trace the presence of some allegedly modern thought in the heart of the medieval 'other', whether that thought originated in the Middle Ages or was merely sustained or enhanced therein. Another way is to press the narrative of change forward well beyond whenever the medieval period is held to have ended. The coming contemplation of the development of 'modern' historical thought moves beyond even the concluding points that most detect in the eighteenth and especially nineteenth century and stretches the issue right up to, and through, the present. Looking backwards, alongside significant departures, some enduring conceptions may be traced back to the beginning of the western historiographical tradition. Along the way from that beginning to the present, newer justifications for History have only overlain their predecessors without always superseding them. We would do well to appreciate this when we talk about 'modern historical consciousness'. It will help us to understand the ongoing tensions elaborated in the final chapter in the way 'we' orient ourselves towards the past today.

The matter is more than a purely scholarly debate. It is not only scholars who are interested in the past, and History, as in the pursuit of reflection on the past, has a correspondingly significant social role to play. In social affairs evidence from the past is an important element in guessing at the social future, and attitudes to the past much of what we have in prescribing for the future.

Continuity and Change in Justifications for History

Judging by the historical scholarship that has survived, ancient Greek historians had at least eight justifications for History at their disposal. Most if not all of those were available from the very outset of Greek prose History in the 'Classical Period', the fifth and fourth centuries BCE.[24] The justifications appear here in no order of priority.

One was recreational, with an emphasis on evoking the romance and drama of the past through the performative tradition. This will be referred to as 'History as Entertainment'. As a justification it is partly *substantivist*, meaning that entertainment depends on the content of the past described, and partly *formalist*, in the sense that a tale requires authorial skill in organization or 'emplotment'. A vital element is *enargeia*, in Latin *evidentia*. Whatever connotations 'evidence' has now, *enargeia* referred then to vividness of depiction, the capacity to evoke audience feelings appropriate to the event under representation. If this History is not already being performed theatrically then the objective for the writer is to try to render readers or listeners into spectators. *Enargeia* 'is in the verbal realm the counterpart of verisimilitude in the visual arts'.[25]

A second justification appears in Herodotus's opening lines and again blends substantivism and formalism. His aim was 'preserving from decay the remembrance of what men have done, and of preventing the great and wonderful actions of the Greeks and the Barbarians from losing their due meed of glory; and withal to put on record what were their grounds of feud'. This justification is dubbed 'History as Memorialization'.

A third justification lies in much of Herodotus's subject matter and is more wholly substantivist. He is a founder member of an enduring tradition of studying other cultures in such a way that, as the poet G. K. Chesterton put it, one may finally 'set foot on one's own country as a foreign land'.[26] The project may be furthered by travel back in time as well as across place. The label for this justification is 'History as Travel'.

A fourth justification is equally substantivist. It is present in Polybius (*c*.200–*c*.118 BCE), who wrote in what is today called the Hellenistic period, which succeeded the Classical period, but it is there in Herodotus too. It involves tracing

---

[24] François Bédarida, 'The Modern Historian's Dilemma: Conflicting Pressures from Science and Society', *Economic History Review*, 2nd ser. XL:3 (1987), 335–48, here 340, mentions three. I take those and add some more.

[25] Andrew D. Walker, 'Enargeia and the Spectator in Greek Historiography', *Transactions of the American Philological Association* 123 (1993), 353–77, here 358; Stefania Tutino, *Shadows of Doubt: Language and Truth in Post-Reformation Catholic Culture* (Oxford: Oxford University Press, 2014) 67–8. On theatricality, Gregory Nagy, *Poetry as Performance: Homer and Beyond* (Cambridge: Cambridge University Press, 1996).

[26] G. K. Chesterton, 'The Riddle of the Ivy', *Tremendous Trifles* (London: Methuen, 1909), 203–10, here 204.

large-scale developments but also seeks to identify an underlying historical process that sweeps all superficial historical developments in some direction. If such a process does exist, is it linear, cyclical, spiralling, etcetera? Finally, and this question is especially important in Judeo-Christian historical thought, is there any meaning to the process? This modality of History is 'History as Speculative Philosophy'.

The fifth and sixth justifications are both matters of 'philosophy teaching by examples', in words once attributed to Dionysius of Halicarnassus (60–7 BCE). The real author of the expression attributed its gist to Thucydides.[27] The substance of the historical record was again vital. In a stronger version the past was mined for discrete transferable lessons; in a weaker version, historical events provided a sounding board for contemporary reflection, whether that be inspiration by great deeds, or solace or stoicism in the face of the vicissitudes of fortune. These justifications are hereafter called 'History as Moral Lesson' and 'History as Practical Lesson', and since the two have a close relationship especially but not only in classical historiography, it will sometimes be the case that they are both referred to by the moniker 'History as Lesson'.

A seventh justification is *proceduralist*. The methods of the historian are at the forefront, rather than any particular content of the past. In the logic of this justification there is an affinity between the mode of dispassionate, critical enquiry and a desirable disposition for the citizen or politician. Hence: 'History as Method'.

Of all of the rationales elaborated so far the seventh is the least problematic by the standards of the contemporary historical profession, but more than one of the seven may still be found in the framing of any work of History. Few historians would deny the need to observe some proceduralist principles, for example, and all historians try their best with form even when many baulk at the claims of strongly formalist accounts such as Hayden White's.[28] While propounding the benefits of 'universal' History, Polybius wished that the reader would 'derive from history' not just 'profit' but 'delight', i.e. entertainment.[29] Elements of superhuman, trans-historical direction, characteristic of History as Speculative Philosophy, could coexist on the same pages as more mundane History. That was true for the role of *tyche/fortuna* (in the Greek and Roman respectively) and it could be true for the Christian redemptive philosophy of the whole course of history. For much of the occidental history of History too, there was no opposition between History as Methodology and either species of History as Lesson.

[27] Dionysius of Halicarnassus, *On Thucydides*, ed. W. Kendrick Pritchett (Berkeley: University of California Press, 1975), 72.

[28] Hayden White, *Metahistory: The Historical Imagination in the Nineteenth Century* (Baltimore: Johns Hopkins University Press, 1973); White, *The Content of the Form* (Baltimore: Johns Hopkins University Press, 1987).

[29] Cited in Darryl W. Palmer, 'Acts and the Historical Monograph', *Tyndale Bulletin* 43:2 (1992) 373–88, here 388.

Dionysius wrote of the historian's 'obligation in the first place to choose a good subject of lofty character which will be truly profitable to the reader, and in the second place to devote the utmost care and industry to the task of providing himself with proper sources for his own composition.'[30] Memorial and didactic functions were often one and the same. Herodian of Antioch, writing in the first half of the third century CE, was surely not the first to fuse them with the further concern for 'scrupulous exactitude' and also the hope that his History, the *History of the Roman Empire after the Death of Marcus Aurelius*, was 'not without entertainment for future generations.'[31] With significant continuity in the fortunes of History as Entertainment and History as Travel, much of the relevant recent history of History concerns the mutation of the remits of History as Lesson.

The decline of History as Lesson—the discarding of the Roman rhetorician Cicero's belief that History was *magistra vitae*, the teacher of life[32]—is often taken to be one index of History's modernization. Decline there was but it was by no means total and in key instances what looks like decline can just as well be interpreted as revision according to intellectual circumstance. It is a matter of perspective whether the emphasis is on the changes or the unifying underlying conviction that the substance of the past has something to teach us. In any case, such is the prominence of substantivist rationales across large tracts of time that their evolution is one of the key thematic sinews connecting successive chapters in the book. A whistle-stop tour might help in the orientation.

Let us say that at some point it became embarrassing in intellectual circles to admit to consulting History books for advice on comportment. The reason may have been an appreciation of the difference of historical circumstances and/or cultures and/or the development of philosophies of politics and of the individual that sought a conscious break with the past. Some of the logic of didactic exemplarity could nonetheless be salvaged by an idea devised in classical antiquity. In the concept of *similitudo temporum* certain civilizations, epochs, and moments shared characteristics and dilemmas with earlier counterparts. Everything did not need to be the same, as long as some things were. Appropriately enough for an idea about periodic resurfacing, the idea resurfaced periodically, with especial vigour in the turmoil after the Reformation, but also well into modernity—it is still with us today in dilution.[33]

So much, then, for positive relevance, in the sense of resonances of the present in the past and vice versa. Negative relevance, or relevance by contrast, could be just as useful if we consider some of the ways in which eighteenth-century

---

[30] Dionysius, *The Ancient History of Rome*, Book I, ch. 1, repr. in Arnold J. Toynbee, *Greek Historical Thought* (New York: Mentor Books, 1952), 53.

[31] Book I, ch. 1, repr. in Toynbee, *Greek Historical Though*, 77.

[32] Marcus Tullius Cicero, *De Oratore*, II.ix.36, in *Cicero: On the Orator, Books 1–2*, trans. E. W. Sutton and H. Rackham (London: Heinemann, 1967), 224.

[33] A. Dwight Culler, *The Victorian Mirror of History* (New Haven: Yale University Press, 2009).

'enlighteners' referred to the past. Voltaire and Condorcet sometimes used History to denigrate, listing past errors in the service of a better future. That stance met in turn with another reaction.

Romanticism was more sympathetic to the medieval world not because it saw history as unchanging but because it saw the past as the root of the present. Studying the past was less useful in the sense of transferable lessons, more so in the sense that comprehending one's life story helped one to make sense of one's attitudes in the present. Furthermore, in the holistic, indeed essentialist way it conceived cultures and cultural difference, romanticism had strong relativist connotations across *place* even if it was more concerned with balances of change and continuity across *time*.

Especially after the world wars romanticism and its historical counterpart, *Historismus* (historicism), lost their lustre. Partly this was because of their German associations, partly because the wars themselves marked another of those ruptures in time that estranged the past 'within' what had previously been considered the same culture. The way was paved for a more decided relativism across time as well as place.

There was also a shift towards social History and, to varying degrees, the social scientific model. Here the sorts of 'lessons' in prospect were not generally in the form of examples. In some cases historians aspired to infer historical laws based on quantitative methods. Another substantivist goal was and remains the recovery of histories of the marginalized or the masses. This goal had presentist connotations at the joinder of the two different meanings of representation—one (in German *Darstellung*) meaning something like portraiture, the other (in German *Vertretung*) pertaining to a political voice.

The reaction to social scientific History was a cultural History that nonetheless evinced some of the concerns of social History in its demotic and everyday objects. On one hand, it pressed ever harder on the concept of human 'difference' across time and place, thus fortifying the substantivist rationale of History as Travel, with its implications for enhancing the sympathies. On the other hand, since the sorts of differences in which cultural historians were interested were cultural, i.e. non-natural, the message was: that which humans have made, they can unmake, and remake. The point seemed especially powerful when it came to showing that things that had once been thought natural and given were in fact changing cultural products. Here, in the project of 'de-reification', as prelude to emancipation, we see some coincidence between the aims of cultural historians and the Marxist historians whose fortunes had varied across the century with intellectual fashion as well as political circumstance. This justification for studying the past is 'History as Emancipation' and its most prominent recent proponents have tended to be those influenced by poststructuralism and postmodernism.

Since this book does not just consider change over time but also the coexistence of differing conceptions of History's utility, and what happens when one such conception periodically brings its arsenal of supporting assumptions to bear on another, one further 'Greek' rationale needs to be thrown into the mix. It is a conception at least as old as any of the candidates, and as enduring as any—indeed one can identify it in Herodotus despite his broad sympathies. It is History as Identity, the great chameleon. History as Identity is substantivist, concerned with the content of the past. It is primarily genealogical, in the sense of establishing causal relations and relations of identity between past and present, but as noted (p. 2) it can be enacted in different spirits. The more open-minded and potentially self-critical version involves understanding where the present has come from, in the knowledge that identity is historically conditioned. The alternative is more narcissistic and self-justificatory, involving the vindication of present identities and projects by retrospective legitimation—this brand can often avail itself of the Memorial tendency. Along with Entertainment Histories, Identity Histories of differing sorts are the ones that fill bookshops. They are the most consumed Histories in our societies and tell us a great deal about the nature of general interest in the past irrespective of the rationales academic historians come up with for their activities.

If in terms of *Geschichtsinteressen*—reasons for concerning oneself with the past—there is at least as much variation within any given period as across periods, is it too much to suggest that the same applies to 'historical consciousness'? Consider some examples from the study of geology. In the late eighteenth and early nineteenth centuries, which as it happens was a key period in the institutionalization of the discipline of History, geologists and other scientists established a substantial professional consensus about the great age of the earth, and its vast pre-human history, on the basis of evidence such as dinosaur fossils and sedimentary rocks. All this helped pave the wave for the reception of Darwin's theory of evolution, which, with the rise of geology and 'geo-history', marked a grand historical turn in the natural sciences just as parts of the occident at least were entering an especially historically obsessed period in terms of concepts of the nation.[34] Decades later, in 1872, the archaeologist George Smith rediscovered what came to be known as the *Epic of Gilgamesh*, a Babylonian story of 'Noah's' flood—written at least a millennium before the book of Genesis. A public stir ensued, leading a latter-day historian of the controversy to ask himself why that should have been so if 'the idea of deep time was more or less settled for "western" savants'? Most obviously, he concluded, because 'savants are not an entire culture'. Had the Victorians as a whole 'internalised ideas about deep time (the 4.55 billion

---

[34] Martin J. S. Rudwick, *Worlds before Adam: The Reconstruction of Geohistory in the Age of Reform* (Chicago: University of Chicago Press, 2008), with 'geohistory' at 389.

years of history in which we now believe)', then the rediscovery 'would have been of interest principally to antiquarian specialists rather than the newspaper- and periodical-reading masses'. As it stood, the diverse group of people that we call Victorians grappled protractedly over the shift from a shortish anthropocentric history, Garden of Eden and all, to a far more removed, impersonal origin tale of seas and sludge.[35] As for 'modern historical consciousness' in the study of human affairs, remember Fustel. When preparing his work on classical antiquity *The Ancient City* (1864), he encountered many who talked of the Greeks and Romans as if they were 'talking of the French or the English of their own time. They nearly always imagined these people as living in the same social conditions as we do and as thinking like us on nearly all issues.'[36] And this only a few generations after the grand historical rupture of the French revolution. Still today, politicians and cab drivers are prone to invoke the Lessons of History even when academics can see nothing but contextual variance.

The media of History vary as much as do historical interests and inferences. For all the attention justifiably devoted to the historiographical significance of Herodotus and Thucydides, these historians were but one of many tributary influences on historical thought in their time. Painted vases, relief sculpture, and epic poetry were as important then in creating an image of the past as historical novels and films and museums are today; legal and political ritual, ceremonies, drama, and civic space and architecture endure across the temporal divide. While matters of manageability and space prohibit examination of novels, films, museums, and other fora of popular historical engagement explored by the likes of Raphael Samuel and David Lowenthal, the final chapter nonetheless tries to grapple with some of the issues arising in the present at the interface of professional and popular reckoning with the past.[37]

Manageability still remains a problem since this is a historiographical enquiry in a broad sense, with a correspondingly eclectic base of primary and secondary sources. At many of the moments under consideration those people who are most identifiable as historians by today's lights were not the key influences on historical thought. Theologians, philosophers, jurists, political theorists, and social scientists often loom as large in this book even when the study of the past was not their

[35] Vybarr Cregan-Reid, *Discovering Gilgamesh: Geology, Narrative, and the Historical Sublime in Victorian Culture* (Manchester: Manchester University Press, 2013), 4.

[36] Fustel's inaugural lecture, 1862, repr. in Fritz Stern (ed.), *The Varieties of History* (New York: Meridian, 1956), 179–88, here 184.

[37] On some ancient Greek historical media, Lloyd Llewellyn-Jones, 'The Great Kings of the Fourth Century and the Greek Memory of the Persian Past', in John Marincola, Lloyd Llewellyn-Jones, and Calum Alasdair Maciver (eds.), *Greek Notions of the Past in the Archaic and Classical Eras: History without Historians* (Edinburgh: Edinburgh University Press, 2012), 317–46. On non-academic sources of History in the present, Raphael Samuel, *Theatres of Memory* (London: Verso, 1994), David Lowenthal, *The Past is a Foreign Country* (Cambridge: Cambridge University Press, 1985), and Lowenthal, *The Heritage Crusade and the Spoils of History* (Cambridge: Cambridge University Press, 1998).

primary interest. The principle of selection is that they provided intellectual articulation, whether in manifesto or by the logic of their works, of new investigative techniques and principles, or of particular strands of temporally and historically oriented thought. Its broader intellectual contextualization is one of the things that distinguishes this book from other works with much the same chronological span such as John Burrow's lucid masterpiece *A History of Histories*, the classics of Ernst Breisach and Donald R. Kelley, and fine newer surveys such as that by Jeremy Popkin.[38] It should go without saying that not all major relevant thinkers are considered here, and that is not just because there is no general agreement as to the size of that pool of intellectuals; the coverage is inevitably sometimes patchy, and other scholars would have had different emphases.

Often, at least as important for shifts in historical thinking as writing works of History was honing methods of reading existing texts, especially old ones, and especially sacred ones. Changes in the comprehension of the past have frequently been related to advances in philology and the art of interpreting meaning that is known as hermeneutics. Hermeneutics itself has a very long history, one intertwined in the occidental tradition with the monotheistic religions. In honour of its religious origins the relevant rationale is named 'History as Communion', and its fortunes have varied along with the state of faith. Its traces are all but absent in most of today's professional scholarship, but in previous centuries some of its logic fused with the logics of History as Travel and the Romantic variant of History as Identity.

History as Communion is the tenth rationale for historical enquiry to be named so far in this introduction, and it bears stressing that at least nine of those ten– the possible exception being History as Emancipation, though that may have relevant precursors—are at least two millennia old. Naturally other typologists might categorize differently, so the point ought not to be pressed too far, yet it is instructive as to the weight of continuity alongside all the change that only a few of the ten have been discarded as of today and that the one further rationale to be added to the list in modernity, namely 'History as Therapy' (see Chapter 8), has not been very successful.

[38] John Burrow, *A History of Histories* (London: Allen Lane, 2007); Ernst Breisach, *Historiography: Ancient, Medieval and Modern* (Chicago: University of Chicago Press, 2007); Donald R. Kelley, *Faces of History: Historical Inquiry from Herodotus to Herder* (New Haven: Yale University Press, 1998); Jeremy D. Popkin, *From Herodotus to H-Net: The Story of Historiography* (Oxford: Oxford University Press, 2015). As compared to these works, mine has more of the broad conceptualization of historiography manifest in Aviezer Tucker (ed.), *A Companion to the Philosophy of History and Historiography* (London: Wiley, 2009); Michael Bentley (ed.), *Companion to Historiography* (Abingdon: Routledge, 2007); and the five-volume *The Oxford History of Historical Writing* (Oxford: Oxford University Press, 2011–12) under the general editorship of Daniel Woolf.

1

Classical History between Epic and Rhetoric

Introduction

If choosing when to begin any History, including a History of History, is never free of prejudgement, the same goes for choosing where to start. The eastern Mediterranean point of departure flagged in the introduction makes sense given the occidental focus of this work. Nonetheless, very different cultural traditions— say *izibongo*, South African Nguni praise poetry—share functions and purposes with the themes examined here, be those functions the entrenchment of in-group identity, those purposes exemplarity or drama.[1]

The work of Confucius (551–479 BCE) has interesting parallels too. Ancestor-worship pre-dated him, and with it the preservation of genealogies, especially those of the royal families of the various Chinese states, but he channelled this convention into a continuous historiographical tradition sustained by scholar-bureaucrats. The concern with precedents in the resulting Histories occupied a place reserved in other cultures of the time for sacred texts. The first Chinese landmark work in the tradition was the *Spring and Autumn Annals*, the chronicle of the state of Lu from 722 to 481 BCE. It is thought to have been edited by Confucius, and a quality conventionally attributed to it is the subtle introduction of elements of moral evaluation, thus spawning emulators in the assignment of praise and blame over the next few centuries and, indeed, periodically until the end of the empire in 1911.[2]

More directly relevant in the coming narrative are traditions in what is often today called the Middle East. Jewish historical thought pertains, both in terms of speculative philosophy of the development of the 'overall historical process' and literalist depiction of past events and contexts. As with Christian interpretation of the Bible, these two tendencies need not be at loggerheads. The Torah in its narrow sense, as in the first five books of the Hebrew Bible (Pentateuch in Greek) was probably composed in the Persian period of Jewish history (*c.*520–*c.*320 BCE),

---

[1] Richard Whitaker, 'History, Myth, and Social Function in Southern African Nguni Praise Poetry', in David Konstan and Kurt A. Raaflaub (eds.), *Epic and History* (Chichester: Wiley-Blackwell, 2010), 381–91, here 386, 389.

[2] David Morgan, 'The Evolution of Two Asian Historiographical Traditions', in Bentley (ed.), *Companion*, 11–22, here 17–20.

with Persian authorization though not dictation. By establishing conditions of blood genealogy (descent from Abraham, Isaac, and Jacob) and social contract (upholding the Covenant) the Pentateuch defined membership in the community of Israel, a community of faith and obligation though not a politically independent entity. Its account of creation draws for some of its best-known motifs on cardinal Babylonian texts, which is perhaps ironic given the significance of the Babylonian exile as a symbol of punishment and dispersion in Jewish history.[3]

With Babylonian culture in mind, note that Homer's *Odyssey* has some similarities to the *Epic of Gilgamesh*, which in turn may have drawn on elements from the yet earlier *Atrahasis Epic*. There was also likely some influence of the Babylonian *Enuma Elish* on the *Theogony* of Homer's approximate contemporary, Hesiod. These epics are relevant because while convention suggests that a discussion of Greek historiography proceed from Herodotus (*c*.484–425 BCE) or Thucydides (*c*.460–*c*.395 BCE), we will instead begin with the two poets—Homer, if he was indeed an individual, and Hesiod—who lived earlier, probably in the first half of the Archaic Period, which runs from *c*.800 to *c*.480 BCE.[4]

The justification for this point of departure is that the epic poems have some of the characteristics of subsequent historical scholarship, as well as having exerted a great influence on popular historical thought. First, in Homer's *Iliad* XVIII, the noun *histor* appears, and this histor is an enquirer who takes testimony, 'less than a judge' but 'more than an arbitrator'.[5] Secondly, thinking to the identity function of History, the *Iliad* plays a central role in amplifying the collective 'memory' of the Trojan wars, which had a huge influence not just on Greco-Roman civilization but on many later origin myths in Christian Europe. Thirdly, the *Odyssey* in particular pits the human actor, armed only with his resourcefulness, determination, and counterproductive hubris, against capricious circumstance and indeed supernatural power. Today sociologists would parse the opposition as structure versus agency and elucidating the interaction of the two elements over time remains a central problem for historians, not least because it is intertwined with the balance of continuity and change. Not much less of a problem has been the recovery of voices inadvertently or deliberately silenced in what is quaintly called the historical record. Here too, and thus fourthly, the *Odyssey* represents and

---

[3] Kyong-Jin Lee, *The Authority and Authorization of Torah in the Persian Period* (Leuven: Peeters, 2011); Paula Gooder, *The Pentateuch: A Story of Beginnings* (London: T&T Clark, 2000), 30 ff.; 41ff.; Jean Louis Ska, *Introduction to Reading the Pentateuch* (Winona Lake, IN: Eisenbrauns, 2006) 225–8. On Babylonian influence see also the next note.

[4] Interesting comparisons and contrasts between different epic and epic-historical traditions are explored in Konstan and Raaflaub (eds.), *Epic and History*. Generally in this area, see John Marincola, 'Introduction', to Marincola et al. (eds.), *History without Historians*, 1–13. Further on Herodotus's antecedents and milieu, Nino Luraghi (ed.), *The Historian's Craft in the Age of Herodotus* (Oxford: Oxford University Press, 2001).

[5] Hannah Arendt, *The Life of the Mind* (New York: Harcourt, 1978), 216; G. J. Basile, 'The Homeric ἵστωρ and oath-taking', *Cuadernos de Filología Clásica. Estudios griegos e indoeuropeos* 28 (2018), 17–39, with quote at 25.

reinforces a norm. In the absence of his father, Odysseus' son Telemachus grows from boy to man, and part of the process of self-assertion is public rebuke of his mother Penelope. 'Speech', he says, meaning authoritative public utterance, 'will be the business of men'.[6] Even in this epic, which gives not insignificant attention to women, their speech can only be in the private sphere, which is at once to deni-grate it and to ensure it will not be recorded. (As the Athenian statesman and general Pericles pronounces in one of Thucydides' best-known passages, ideal was the woman who was not discussed between men in any terms, glowing or derogatory.) Fifthly, while for a long time many Greeks seem to have assumed that the period of heroes and gods portrayed by the poets was real and provided clues to 'the way the world works',[7] we may detect a different though not necessarily contradictory tendency in Homer. With the end of the heroic age, which is when the heroes ultimately return after the Trojan wars, the gods no longer intervene directly in earthly affairs and mortals are no longer so large or strong. This sense of qualitative difference across time may prefigure the 'historical consciousness', as we seem bound to call it, that is present in subsequent Greek historiography— and present in the historiography of all subsequent periods too, if with differing emphases.[8]

This opening chapter establishes the foundations on which the rest of the book is built since post-classical western scholarship largely develops from classical models or is shaped by its reaction against those models. The chapter addresses a series of conceptual issues that have recurring relevance, including: differing con-ceptions of the nature of historical truth; the relationship between History and ethnography; the relationship between rhetoric and historianship; the relation-ship between philosophy, poetry, and History; and the relationship between 'use-ful' and 'pleasurable' Histories. In a more empirical vein the chapter discusses the relationship between Greek and Roman historianship and accounts for different tendencies in the development of historiography in each culture—tendencies like a greater or lesser interest in the outside world, and a greater or lesser interest in individuals as opposed to power structures or the study of society and culture. The question of the consciousness of qualitative historical change is also discussed in the case of a number of historians. In the 900 or so years of historianship covered in this chapter no rationale for History that is present at or near the out-set was ruled out by the end, though of course many avenues of possibility were more fully explored. It is more than coincidence that the survey opens and closes

---

[6] On this and many later echoes in the occidental tradition, Mary Beard, 'The Public Voice of Women', *London Review of Books*, 20 March 2014, 11–14.

[7] Emily Baragwanath, 'The Mythic Plupast in Herodotus', in Jonas Grethlein and Christopher B. Krebs (eds.), *Time and Narrative in Ancient Historiography* (Cambridge: Cambridge University Press, 2012), 35–56, here 35; Charles Edward Muntz, *Diodorus Siculus and the World of the Late Roman Republic* (Oxford: Oxford University Press, 2017), 91.

[8] A proponent of the view is Strasburger, cited in Fleming A. J. Nielsen, *The Tragedy in History: Herodotus and the Deuteronomistic History* (Sheffield: Sheffield Academic Press, 1997), 33.

with species of History as Identity, beginning with the most elementary type of that genre: genealogy.

Genealogy, Ethnography, and Historical Consciousness

Hesiod's *Theogony* might be the first Greek genealogical work, understood as a systematic attempt to establish relations and lineages between actors. In this case the actors were the legendary heroes. Much later, during the fifth century BCE, a number of genealogies were produced in prose, which supplanted poetry as the primary form of expository discourse around that time. Some genealogies tried to tie local myths into the major myths. Hecataeus of Melitos (*c.*550–*c.*476 BCE) seems to have developed the distinction between a *spatium mythicum* and a *spatium historicum*—terms which can easily confuse a modern audience. The distinction did not pertain to a mythical time versus a real, properly historical one. Rather Hecataeus distinguished between times that could not be reliably reconstructed by the historian's enquiry and those that supposedly could, and tried to establish where the boundary lay. He was interested in establishing the relations between the heroes who lived around the time of the Trojan War as systematically as possible, treating them as humans with ordinary generational and familial relations. Historical research could then take over to flesh out what could be fleshed out down to the present. The widespread adoption of Hecataeus meant that Greek genealogists in subsequent centuries felt on secure ground as they established the deepest historical links between themselves and 'barbarian' peoples such as various Italians, including the Romans.[9]

Herodotus' younger contemporary Hellanicus of Mytilene (*c.*480–*c.*405 BCE) is a seminal figure in the development of two trends that relate to the genealogical project. He was probably the first Atthidographer, meaning a specialist in the history of the region of Attica which encompasses Athens.[10] At the end of the fifth century he devised a History spanning the supposed deep origins of Attica, the period of Athenian Kingship, and the Peloponnesian wars of his own time. He had already worked to establish a formal chronography that would help correlate different local Histories with each other, and which would also be used in future by Romans to synchronize their time with the time of the Greeks. In the 430s Hellanicus introduced a system that worked from the list of successive

---

[9] Charles William Fornara, *The Nature of History in Ancient Greece and Rome* (Berkeley: University of California Press, 1983), 4–12; Peter Hunt, 'Hecataeus of Miletos', *The Encyclopedia of Ancient History* (Wiley online library, 2012): https://onlinelibrary.wiley.com/doi/abs/10.1002/9781444338386.wbeah08075

[10] On these historians, see Charlotte Schubert, 'Formen der griechischen Historiographie: Die Atthidographen als Historiker Athens', *Hermes* 138:3 (2010), 259–75; Felix Jacoby, *Atthis: The Local Chronicles of Ancient Athens* (Oxford: Clarendon Press, 1949).

priestesses of Hera, and assigned noteworthy events to the nth year of the relevant priestess. The point of these exercises was to connect events and people and construct meaningful temporal frameworks around these connections, rather than inserting events into an already given frame.[11]

Herodotus adopted Hecataeus's distinction between the *spatium mythicum* and the *spatium historicum*, though he went far beyond the work of genealogies to study events in a way that is much more fully characteristic of subsequent History.[12] Naturally, events further in the past were apt to be more likely to fall into the *spatium mythicum*, but again clarification is needed. Herodotus did not think the *spatium mythicum* to be filled with what today we call myths, but rather that the recountability of genuine History in that 'space' had been compromised by the *mythoi* of poets who blended historical truth and fiction.[13] The existence of the distinction does not mean Herodotus was always correct in his claims for what was verifiable, or that his sense of historical likelihood was like those of twenty-first-century historians. With Hecataeus and Hellanicus, Herodotus believed that the *spatium historicum* went back to the time of the supposed reconquest of the Peloponnese by the Heracleidae (descendants of Heracles), after the Trojan War. He further believed that the Trojan War, dated to some time in what we would now call the twelfth or thirteenth century BCE, occurred in roughly the manner assumed in Greek collective memory, as opposed to there simply having been some sort of war at some point at a place dubbed Troy.[14]

In his view of what could be treated historically Herodotus was not arbitrary, even if we might sometimes think him incorrect. When investigating the deeper past he engaged with the engraved and written records of Egypt and the collective memory of its priesthood, which he saw as more historically reliable than the Greek epics.[15] It was precisely his enquiries among non-Greek sources that corroborated, to his satisfaction, parts of what were otherwise suspect Greek accounts of the Trojan War. Equally, those enquiries influenced his circumspection about what could be claimed about the causes of the war.[16] Further to the

---

[11] Kai Brodersen, 'Hellanicus of Mytilene' and Denis Feeney, 'Chronography', both in *The Encyclopedia of Ancient History* (Wiley online library 2012): https://onlinelibrary.wiley.com/doi/abs/10.1002/9781444338386.wbeah08076 https://onlinelibrary.wiley.com/doi/10.1002/9781444338386.wbeah08035

[12] Muntz, *Diodorus*, 90–3.

[13] Virginia J. Hunter, *Past and Process in Herodotus and Thucydides* (Princeton: Princeton University Press, 1982), 87.

[14] Ibid. 90; Nielsen, *The Tragedy*, 33–5; Fornara, *The Nature*, 9.

[15] In general terms official record-keeping, which was the function of 'the archive', and an important source of documented state memory, was better established in other, older Mediterranean societies, be they Hittite, Babylonian, Sumerian, or Egyptian.

[16] Suzanne Saïd, 'Herodotus and the "Myth" of the Trojan War"', in Emily Baragwanath and Mathieu de Bakker (eds.), *Myth, Truth and Narrative in Herodotus* (Oxford: Oxford University Press, 2012), 87–106, here 88–92. Also on Egyptian sources, see Hunter, *Past and Process*, 74. Note that while Herodotus lost faith in a Greek time of the gods, he still believed in a time of the gods, just a much earlier one, corresponding to Egyptian chronologies.

question of evidence, Herodotus evinced a preference for recent history where oral testimony was supposed to be most reliable; the great bulk of his focus is on the period from roughly 100 years before writing, especially from Cyrus's founding of the Persian Empire in 560 BCE.[17] All this, simply put, was a matter of source comparison and criticism.[18]

When Herodotus's contemporary focus is combined with his geographical and ethnographical range one can understand why Dionysius of Halicarnassus later put him in the category of historians who organized their work by *kata topous*, space, as opposed to those who organized by time, *kata chronous*.[19] While this categorization seems appropriate for the overall balance of Herodotus's *Histories*, he nonetheless often blended spatial and temporal organization. He thus brought together in one historical work two themes that had been separate in Hecataeus, who, in addition to his *Genealogies*, had produced a partly ethnographical narrative geography of the known world, the *Periodos Ges*.[20] Herodotus also recognized discontinuities in the identities and customs of other groups, which stands as corrective to those who see him as part of a longer trend of ethnographic enquiry that depicts 'others' in a timeless present—a characterization which is just as untenable as the one whereby Herodotus did have a sense of historical change but that that sense was exceptional in his period. Furthermore, there is a parallel between his 'sensitivity to epistemological limits due to time' and his 'sensitivity to the elusive nature of other kinds of knowledge, concerning geographically distant places', as expressed in the deliberately tentative nature of his reportage.[21]

Thus Herodotus has been called the father of anthropology as well as of History. (Sometimes he has been called the father of lies too, and in the nineteenth-century era of a professionalizing historical academy, that patronymic superseded others.)[22] More reticent than Thucydides in overt judgement, he expressed sentiments that are sometimes considered culturally relativist, albeit that his treatment of the polygamous and oppressive 'oriental despotism' of Persia indicated a hard parameter to his thought, which is more openly curious and tolerant about different

[17] T. James Luce, *The Greek Historians* (London: Routledge, 1997), ch. 3.

[18] On which see the defence by Hunter, *Past and Process*, 91–2.

[19] Carole Atack, 'The Discourse of Kingship in Classical Athenian Thought', *Histos* 8 (2014), 329–62, here 332.

[20] On Herodotus's blend, Baragwanath, 'The Mythic Plupast'; on Hecataeus's various contributions, see Fornara, *The Nature*, 4–14. On the different strands of historical writing, Felix Jacoby, 'Über die Entwicklung der griechischen Historiographie und den Plan einer neuen Sammlung der griechischen Historikerfragmente', *Klio*, 9:9 (1909), 80–123.

[21] Quotes and material from Baragwanath, 'The Mythic Plupast', 36. On alleged timelessness in Herodotus, Johannes Fabian, *Time and the Other: How Anthropology Makes its Object* (New York: Columbia University Press, 2014), 80, 196 n. 10.

[22] J. A. S. Evans, 'Father of History or Father of Lies: The Reputation of Herodotus', *The Classical Journal*, 64:1 (1968), 11–17; James Redfield, 'Herodotus the Tourist', *Classical Philology*, 80:2 (1985), 97–118. On the antiquity of the praise as well as the allegations, Momigliano, *Classical Foundations*, 39–40.

lifestyles than it is strictly relativist.[23] He was concerned with the synchronic description of forms of life as well as diachronic analysis, addressed a range of social and cultural issues, and had a marked and unusual concern for the study of women. He often deployed the first person to opine, though such admissions of perspectivalism, much rarer in Thucydides, did not always extend to critical interrogation of the oral opinion on which he sometimes relied. Nor did he explicitly profess the political utility of his work. That said, Herodotus was obviously interested in political and military matters. One point of describing cultural diversity was precisely to invalidate imperialism, specifically the Persian imperialism which had loomed in the Greco-Persian wars that occupied much of the first half of the fifth century BCE. Here Herodotus's own form of allegorical exemplarity came to the fore, as he hinted that Athens would succeed Persia in the cycle of hegemonic powers, and awarded excessive credit to Athens in the struggle against the Persians.[24]

In the intra-Hellenic Peloponnesian War of 431–404 BCE between Athens and its allies and Sparta and its allies, Thucydides was gifted a subject matter just as momentous as was Herodotus with the Greco-Persian wars. If the choice is between Herodotus and Thucydides, more straightforwardly politically minded successors then as now preferred the latter. His approach was certainly the more popular for many centuries, though this may be partly explained by his writing in Attic Greek, which became the standard classicizing Greek. (Herodotus wrote in Ionic.)[25] The success of his tradition may further be explained by the fact that Histories were quite widely consumed by policy-making elites with particular, corresponding interests.[26] Nevertheless, Herodotus continued to be held in high esteem, and Herodotean Histories continued to be written. Herodotean markers of temporality like 'until my time' and 'even still today' were quite often reproduced in subsequent Hellenic scholarship.[27]

Thucydides' latter-day label as a 'realist' implies, as 'realist' international relations theory still does, that, beneath the superficial cultural differences of humankind's sub-groupings there exists a basic similarity of attitudes towards material power and its sources, and Thucydides also writes as if he is encapsulating

---

[23] On relativist-sounding pronouncements: Herodotus, Histories, Book 3.38, cf. Book 7.152. See also the discussion of Egyptian customs in Book 2. On Persia, see Paul Cartledge, 'Historiography and Ancient Greek Self-Definition', in Bentley (ed.), Companion to Historiography, 23–42, here 29. On Herodotus as cultural pluralist, Thucydides as a monist, Lauren J. Apfel, The Advent of Pluralism: Diversity and Conflict in the Age of Sophocles (Oxford: Oxford University Press, 2011), Part Two.

[24] Jonas Grethlein, The Greeks and their Past: Poetry, Oratory and History in the Fifth Century BCE (Cambridge: Cambridge University Press, 2010), 204—and 135 on the deployment by Herodotus and Thucydides of techniques used in the epics.

[25] On dialect, Warren Treadgold, The Early Byzantine Historians (Basingstoke: Macmillan, 2010), 8.

[26] Arnaldo D. Momigliano, 'The Historians of the Classical World and their Audiences', Annali della Scuola Normale Superiore di Pisa, 3rd series, 8 (1978), 59–75.

[27] On Herodotus's influence, Christopher A. Baron, Timaeus of Tauromenium and Hellenistic Historiography (New York: Cambridge University Press, 2013), ch. 10; for the specific phrases, 237.

anthropological universals more generally. Style seemed to mirror substance: his writing has a quality of heroic literary realism to it. With the Homeric tradition as well as Herodotus in mind, he pronounced that his proofs would 'not be disturbed either by the lays of a poet displaying the exaggeration of his craft, or by the compositions of the chroniclers that are attractive at truth's expense'. He supposed that his approach would cost him some of his audience, but that this was a price worth paying were his History of the *Peloponnesian War* to 'be judged useful by those inquirers who desire an exact knowledge of the past as an aid to the interpretation of the future, which in the course of human things must resemble if it does not reflect' the past.[28]

In this last clause there is a small qualification, raising questions about how precise parallels can be, and, I would suggest, how far generalizations about human nature can go. In his introductory dip into Greek history 'from the earliest times', Thucydides thoroughly secularized the actors in the Trojan War and its aftermath. He concentrated on mundane cause, effect, and motivation in his observations on ancient political regimes, military preparedness, resources, and the conduct of conflict, and, except in their brevity, the depictions are much as they are when he moved on to discuss conflict in his own time.[29] Yet he also noted change in customs and attire over time, and these shifts are partly correlated with variations in custom between peoples. He posits an early time in which 'the same mode of life was...equally common to all', a mode of life with which Athenians were the first to break. Others, in Asia but also in parts of 'Hellas', had apparently not yet made that break. Thus 'there are many...points in which a likeness might be shown between the life of the Hellenic world of old and the barbarian of today'.[30] This attitude of superiority in difference, in which 'others' are viewed as primitive versions of the self, is a trope common to much subsequent anthropological and indeed imperial thought.[31] Albeit to a lesser degree than Herodotus, Thucydides evinced just that sense of change in ways of life and dress that are held by some to be innovations of Romans like Lucretius (c.94–55 BCE), Virgil (70–19 BCE), or Horace (65–8 BCE).[32] In his conception of other peoples as effectively living in stasis Thucydides was less acute than Herodotus, partly, one assumes, because he was just less concerned with non-Hellenes than Herodotus was; but such an attitude is only possible when one has a sense that one's own group has changed over time.

---

[28] Thucydides, *The Peloponnesian War: The Crawley Translation* (New York: Random House, 1982), Book I, 21–2.

[29] Ibid. 9–19. See also Rosario Munson, cited in Muntz, *Diodorus*, 92.

[30] Thucydides, *The Peloponnesian War*, I.5–6.

[31] The analytical philosopher of History Frederick Teggart long pre-empted Fabian's exposition of the point that for many Europeans, looking across to things like the transatlantic 'new world', different cultures were understood as primitive versions of the European. Teggart, *Theory*, 93–5; cf. Fabian, *Time and the Other*.

[32] On the Romans, Burke, *The Renaissance Sense*, 139–41.

What we may say is that one of the many ways in which Thucydides' work differed from Homer's, as from Hesiod's myth of the ages in *Works and Days*, is that in the epics the distinction between past and present is more greatly emphasized in virtue of the superiority of the denizens of the past, whether or not the heroes were actually depicted as godly.[33] Whether we understand this particular difference between History and mythic poetry as large enough to be a matter of nature as opposed to mere degree depends on one's yardstick of measurement. An argument for categorical difference is that while the poets and the historians all deployed *exempla* for didactic purposes, the epic established the exalted, indeed ideal(ized) standards set by its heroes, while History of the Thucydidean variety sought to endure through its relationship to its readers, who would be bound to each other across time by recognizing the constancy of key facets of their own nature.[34]

An argument that epic and History differ in degree only comes from the classicist Christopher Pelling. He writes that if the past of the poets provides 'a matrix for thought experiment', it does so 'because it allows moral issues to be addressed with a smaller encumbrance of circumstantial detail than they carry in real life, then encourages the reapplication of that thinking to make sense of the more confusing everyday world'. In this sense, epic poetry is more like philosophical abstraction than the thick description one is apt to encounter in the novel, or again historiography, which 'does engage with that mass of real-life circumstance'. Yet Pelling also writes that 'The historians themselves are also extrapolating and suggesting recurrent patterns to make sense of what-Alcibiades-did-and-suffered, and helping readers to disentangle the telling facts from the purely contingent to see how this might be a case study for broader truths about, say, Athens or democracy or individualism or rhetorical flair'. Each sort of author does 'part of the thought-experimental work; in some genres and authors they do more and in some they do less. But the rest is up to the audiences, both the immediate and the long-term, both them and us.'[35] At the junction of Homer with Thucydides, just as in epic-like *izibongo*, evaluation of the 'real' or imagined past is judgemental because it sees itself at some level as being commentary of general relevance.[36]

---

[33] Cf. Jonas Grethlein, who substantiates a sense of the difference of the past in Greek epics as opposed to its depiction in historical literature, but sees this difference as a somewhat different sort of difference to that discerned between present and past-as-foreign-country in modern historiography. See his and Christopher B. Krebs's 'The Historian's Plupast: Introductory Remarks on its Forms and Functions', in Grethlein and Krebs (eds.), *Time and Narrative in Ancient Historiography: The 'Plupast' from Herodotus to Appia.* (Cambridge: Cambridge University Press 2012) 1–16.

[34] Jonas Grethlein, '"*Historia magistra vitae*" in Herodotus and Thucydides? The Exemplary Use of the Past and Ancient and Modern temporalities', in Alexandra Lianeri (ed.), *The Western Time of Ancient History* (Cambridge: Cambridge University Press, 2011), 247–63; Grethlein, 'Homer and Heroic History', in Marincola et al. (eds.), *History without Historians*, 14–36, here 33.

[35] Christopher Pelling, 'Commentary', in Marincola et al. (eds.), *History without Historians*, 347–65, here 365.

[36] Observations I owe to Whitaker, 'History, Myth, and Social Function', 386.

Rhetoric, Purpose, Truth

Talk of general relevance brings us to the funeral oration by the statesman and soldier Pericles in Book II of Thucydides' *History*. The speech was a compelling piece of advocacy for the values of the Athenian *demos*, though like Pericles himself Thucydides was more oligarch than democrat. In this set-piece, Thucydides departed from strict reliance on 'proofs' and instead took licence to imagine the sort of thing that would have been said on such occasions, just as would distant successors such as the medieval Geoffrey of Monmouth. These moments of rhetorical flourish are not merely incidental, but are rather crucial for an understanding of the narrative structure of Thucydides' work. Specific examples like the speech highlighted the exemplary nature of the entire text. At the same time, undue focus on them can distract from the rest of Thucydides' prose where plain-speaking could produce its own seductions. The scholarly consensus has now moved more towards viewing Thucydides as an 'artful reporter'.[37]

What exactly is meant by describing someone as an artful reporter varies with what one expects of them in the first place; how one understands what they were trying to do, and how one understands contemporary audience expectations of works of that sort. This is immensely complex terrain given that we are dealing with the inception or very early development of a genre that existed in relations with more established literary forms and overlapped with them often to a considerable degree. Further, from fifth-century Greece through late antiquity, rhetoric was considered one of the highest arts and no historian could ignore that even if they desired to. They knew their audiences had literary expectations and wanted their works to be embraced as literature as well as History, which helps explain intertextual allusions as well as elegant digs at other historians. They pursued celebrity just as much as the actors whose deeds they recounted—indeed Thucydides and many of his successors had themselves been men of action (soldiers) earlier in life. The second-century CE *Anabasis of Alexander* by Arrian of Nicomedia recounts a story of Alexander the Great laying a wreath at the supposed tomb of his hero Achilles and noting Achilles' good fortune in having a poet—Homer—to celebrate his deeds and sustain his memory.[38] Happy for the historian that he was needed just as much as the hero! But he must be up to the task, and better qualified than potential competitors, as a researcher, perhaps, but also as a herald. Quite what doing justice to the achievements of an Alexander might mean is a good question, since recording them was apt to be inseparable

---

[37] Virginia Hunter, *Thucydides the Artful Reporter* (Toronto: Hakkert, 1973), and for an earlier emphasis on Thucydides' artistic side Francis MacDonald Cornford, *Thucydides Mythistoricus* (London: Edward Arnold, 1907).

[38] Arrian of Nicomedia, *The Anabasis of Alexander*, 1.12.1, at p. 53 of *Arrian* vol. 1, trans. E. Iliff Robson (London: William Heinemann, 1967).

from burnishing them in a way tailored to contemporary tastes and poetic convention. Given appropriate substitutions, the same went for describing villains, anti-heroes, and catastrophes. Let us try to take the bull by the horns and explore the question of historians and truth in the light of rhetorical, literary, and other concerns. That question has conventionally been at the forefront of comparisons and contrasts between ancient and modern historiography.

It is a blunder to conceive rhetoric as necessarily opposed to truth and to see it as illegitimate persuasion rather than effective communication. Of course rhetoric can be opposed to truth: the Roman master of rhetoric, Cicero, had to stipulate that while rhetoricians could stray from the path of truth when needed, historians ought never to do so. More important for present purposes is establishing the varieties of rhetoric's more 'positive' relationships to the truth. Some historians deployed the technique of *ecphrasis*, which combines their immediate, situated perspective as eyewitnesses to events, and their broader perspective as historians who have colligated other viewpoints and after-the-fact knowledge. Thus a historian might 'recall' things that he could not have been in a position to see at the moment he purports to have seen them—such as fine details of an army that was scores of miles distant—but this does not mean that such details were made up.[39] We can adapt the seventeenth-century historical theorist Agostino Mascardi's terms of the true verisimilar and the false verisimilar, with the former denoting what the apostles of Christ were up to, and the latter denoting something purely fictitious, which may include but is not limited to deceit.[40] As Mascardi himself saw, it is not easy even for the historian who wishes to portray things precisely as they were to avoid verisimilitude, but that would not have been a surprise or a problem for very many centuries' worth of historians. In Cicero's Latin (to which it is not illegitimate to refer at this stage given the debt of Roman rhetoricians to Greece), the skills of *elocutio* (style), *dispositio* (organization), combine with *inventio*, which Cicero considered the most important of the rhetorical arts, and is embedded in *ingenium*, which pertains to creativity and originality. *Inventio* means the 'discovery' of what 'needs' to be said, and is not to be confused with the arbitrariness or bad faith of modern 'invention'. Quintilian's *Institutio Oratoria* averred that it was never a question of truth itself, which was absolute, but of 'invented' judgements as to the nature of the truth. *Iudicium* is the faculty of judgement that most directly pertains to truth. *Enargeia* along with *concilium* (prudence), *kairos* (the capacity to discern what is appropriate as well as opportune), *ethos* (the establishment of credibility) and *pathos* (emotional connection with the audience, often established by bringing the audience into the

---

[39] Gavin Kelly, *Ammianus Marcellinus: The Allusive Historian* (Cambridge: Cambridge University Press, 2008), 83–6.
[40] Tutino, *Shadows of Doubt*, 66.

appropriate mode of receptivity for the message), can all augment *logos* (reasoned argument) as well as betraying it.[41]

Then there is the question of the sort of truth that is to be conveyed. The most common concept of historical truth today is something like accordance with particular facts about some bygone time. With Pericles' speech, however, Thucydides was depending by his own admission on a conception of truth as plausibility or likelihood, which is not so very different from Homer recounting what might have happened in the Trojan Wars.[42] A related concept, and one that can also be traced at least as far back as Hecataeus, was captured by Herodotus when he called *mythos* not just that which was 'incapable of proof' but that which was 'unintelligent', i.e. incompatible with evidence or reason. When it is not a question of specific sources at issue there may be an appeal to a sort of common-sense arbitration that can rely on the concept of a 'mythical' story as being one that seemed 'contrary to nature'.[43] Then there is the idea of general/universal rather than specific/particular truth—i.e. the desire to transmit the truth about wars as such, as well as (or even instead of) the particular war under scrutiny. Since at any point a historian might be using one of a range of rhetorical techniques to indicate one of a range of types of truth, we get a sense of the multiple layers at which works of History had to be read, the scope for confusion among those unaccustomed to the salient techniques and concepts, and the space for historians to introduce agendas of their own that might run contrary to this or that or every concept of truth.

How far any particular sort of truth might be manipulated or abandoned varies from case to case. One especially controversial instance emerges at the very end of the period with which this chapter is concerned: Ammianus Marcellinus' *Res Gestae*, written in the 380s CE. In his study of Ammianus, the historian Gavin Kelly nicely epitomizes his subject matter by declaring himself 'agnostic and non-committal on the question of veracity', partly because 'the question rarely admits of definite proof', but also because the veracity question is 'the wrong question'. I take Kelly to mean that it is wrong to ask if Ammianus was a 'romantic' or 'allusive' historian as opposed to a 'proper' or 'literalist' one, because these binaries are spurious ones within the context of classical antiquity—and, to some extent, even now. After all, one cannot say that Ammianus has no interest in reporting historical particulars as accurately as he can: frequently he does the mundane

---

[41] Michael Comber, 'Re-Reading the Roman Historians', in Bentley (ed.), *Companion to Historiography*, 43–56, here 49–54; Tutino, *Shadows of Doubt*, 67–8; on *inventio* in particular, Jody Enders, *The Medieval Theater of Cruelty: Rhetoric, Memory, Violence* (Ithaca: Cornell University Press, 1999), 29–32.

[42] Thucydides, *The Peloponnesian War*, I.22.

[43] Emily Baragwanath and Mathieu de Bakker, 'Introduction: Myth, Truth, and Narrative in Herodotus' *Histories*', in Baragwanath and de Bakker (eds.), *Myth, Truth and Narrative in Herodotus*, 1–58, here 11–14; Saïd, 'Herodotus and the "Myth" of the Trojan War'', 92; on Hecataeus, Muntz, *Diodorus*, 91; on Homer, Neilsen, *The Tragedy*, 32; on the rhetoricians, Fornara, *The Nature of History*, 10.

work of establishing chronologies, particular battle strategies, or statistics of soldiers and wounded.[44] The concept of historical reality in much the literal sense we
would understand it today is relevant in light of Ammianus' own terms: as Kelly
records, Ammianus described his own 'stretch[ing] reality' for performative
effect.[45] The adoption of standards in relation to some concept of truthfulness—
and implicitly therefore standards of the opposite, be that falsehood, deceit, bias,
or incompetence—is there in Herodotus and Thucydides and many of their most
important successors. Certainly the claim to particular trustworthiness was itself
a part of their rhetoric, a claim often buttressed by the rhetorical device of *autopsy*,
which means recounting something from one's own eyewitness experience, minor
details and all, to give the impression of authenticity. But we already know rhetoric is not 'just rhetoric': the claim to trustworthiness and authenticity cannot be
dissociated from the concept of truthfulness, even if the most trustworthy person
cannot be guaranteed to have found the truth. Likewise the longstanding classical
desire to allot praise or blame appropriately in one's History cannot be divorced
from some claim to establish the facts of the matter about motives and actions:
the Greek αἴτιον/*aítion*, in Latin *causa*, connoted (moral) responsibility and aetiology together. Such claims are thus open to contestation on evidentiary grounds.
Meanwhile, eyewitness reports are intrinsically evidential as well as serving a
rhetorical purpose and tended to be juxtaposed with reliance on questionable
past authorities. Indeed the general assumption amongst readers seems to have
been that the contemporary parts of any given History were the most historically
valuable precisely because of the availability of eyewitnesses, even when the
author started far earlier—which underlines how far historians' practices were
also embedded in social expectations and *savoir faire*.[46]

   For all of these reasons, whether or not any given historian was actually challenged about their truth claims, and many were, it is not anachronistic to conceive
them in relation to standards of truthfulness. It is just that in addition to establishing what the salient concept of truth was, one also needs to consider the
dimensions of any given History that cannot be accounted for under the rubric of
falsifiability and that may have been rather more important as selling points. Here
one can only hint at the range of performative functions that works of History
fulfilled. For instance, in relation to historical content, a historian might do
justice to some historical figure whilst really having within his sights some

---

[44] Kelly, *Ammianus*, 64–5, 94; Treadgold, *Early Byzantine Historians*, 76. In terms of the contro-
versy over Ammianus—basically whether he should be viewed as a truth-seeking historian or be read
as a work of literature—Kelly forges a third way (not a splitting of the difference) against
John F. Matthews, *The Roman Empire of Ammianus Marcellinus* (Baltimore: Johns Hopkins University
Press, 1989) and Timothy D. Barnes, *Ammianus Marcellinus and the Representation of Historical
Reality* (Ithaca: Cornell University Press, 1998).

[45] Kelly, *Ammianus*, 84.

[46] Ibid. 69–70. On Ephorus's much earlier preference for detail about contemporary events,
Fornara, *The Nature*, 9.

contemporary leader whom he wished to flatter or slight by allegory. Irrespective of substance, historical narrative may be indistinguishable from myth at the formal level, in the plots that each employ in the interests of giving coherence and meaning. The fact that the structure of Herodotus' work, like Thucydides', was informed by epic, especially tragic, traditions, is one important reason not to distinguish as clearly between the two 'fathers' as later historiographers often have.[47]

Each also had political purposes which helps explain their choices of topic at least as much as it explains their treatment of that which they chose. While Thucydides aimed more at instructing elites, Herodotus sought to encourage a pan-Hellenic consciousness. Then we might consider the burgeoning of 'local' Histories after Hellanicus. Some Atthidographers took advantage of the chronographies developed in the fifth century to establish ostensibly clear lines of descent from the mythical age to the present, in the process blurring, even erasing, any distinction between *spatium mythicum* and *spatium historicum*, and trying to render causal rather than purely genealogical accounts of relations between successive states of affairs. Mythical founder-kings, especially Theseus, were at once historically normalized and depicted as ideal exemplars of the virtues of citizenship at a time of ongoing political strife. Reference to the mythical age emphasized the historical primacy of Athens over Sparta, bolstering patriotic pride while distracting from recent failure. Political rhetoricians such as Isocrates (c.436–338 BCE) could then 'cite their heritage of kingship to position their democratic city as equivalent or superior to rising *ethnos* state monarchies such as Macedon'—like Sparta, Macedon already had its king-lists. In place of intra-Hellenic struggle, a common Athenian-shaped regional–cultural heritage could, indeed should, be the basis for common action against genuine enemies like the external Persians.[48]

Useful and Pleasurable History

In the generation after Thucydides, the most influential historian was Xenophon (c.430–354 BCE), a student of the great philosopher Socrates. While, like Thucydides, he was an eyewitness to many of the events he narrated, sometimes as a mercenary in Sparta's service, he was not quite a match for Thucydides in the quality of his research. His *Hellenica* continued Thucydides' History from 411 to 362 BCE, recounting Sparta's declining fortunes after its costly victory in the Peloponnesian wars. Xenophon was also party to an argument over the purpose of historical enquiry, a debate whose terms were shaped by the cultural environment at the waning of the 'golden age' (i.e. the Classical period), after the

---

[47] Jonas Grethlein, 'Homer and Heroic History'.
[48] Atack, 'The Discourse of Kingship', esp. 331–2, 339–40.

Peloponnesian wars and the defeat of the Athenian-led Delian League. In essence this historiographical controversy addressed the relative merits of 'pleasurable' History—History as Entertainment—as opposed to 'useful' history—especially History as Lesson. Concerns about accuracy and analysis were integral to the dispute.

Those demanding utility included Theopompus of Chios (c.380–c.315 BCE) and Ephorus (c.400–330 BCE), author of a partly thematic History from the time of the *Heraclidae* up to one of Philip of Macedon's later victories in 340 BCE.[49] Their targets tended to be the scholars charged with taking most poetic licence in their writing, prioritizing 'vividness' and the stimulation of emotion, such as Ctesias, who produced a History of Persia around the turn of the fifth–fourth centuries, and Duris of Samos (born c.350 BCE). In latter-day scholarship, owing probably to Polybius's insinuations, Phylarchus of the early third century is some-times thought of in the same category. Duris it was who responded to Ephorus and Theopompus that their work offered neither a portrait nor pleasure for the reader. History ought to depict life in the way tragedy does.[50]

A preliminary thought is that whatever Ctesias, Duris, and Phylarchus did or did not do, we ought not assume that they were breaking any implicit contract of trust with readers—nor that Ephorus et al. were themselves innocent of the 'faults' with which they charged others.[51] This is partly because of audience expectations, partly because what is pleasurable and what is useful are not mutually exclusive categories. The pre-Socratic philosopher Gorgias (c.485–c.380 BCE) influentially argued that the reader, observer, or listener might be improved by enjoyment of the sort promoted by arts like tragedy or poetry. This was a roundabout argument to utility. The same point from the other side, and this is the argument to rhetoric as broadly conceived, is that such utility as History was thought to have was best served by rendering historical accounts digestible, attractive, i.e. in some way pleasurable, by some combination of intelligent periodization and narration, leavened perhaps by interesting digressions.[52]

'Useful' meant didactic in some sense, whether in fostering the facility of pru-dence or in instructing the moral faculty more directly by use of moral examples.

---

[49] Frances Pownall, *Lessons from the Past: The Moral Uses of History in Fourth Century Prose* (Ann Arbor: University of Michigan Press, 2007).

[50] Jan P. Stronk, *Ctesias' Persian History: Introduction, Text, and Translation* (Düsseldorf: Wellem Verlag, 2010), concludes that whatever Ctesias said about his Persian royal archival sources, his infor-mation about them was oral and second-hand, and that rather than being assessed by the straightfor-ward standards of historianship, even Herodotus-like historianship, he should also or even instead be assessed by the standard of a novelist or a poet in the sense of a creative writer. Ctesias may well have seen himself as a tragedian, as Duris saw himself. See pp. 42–3 on the discussion of Ctesias and Duris together.

[51] On contracts and different sorts of truth, Tim Whitmarsh, *Beyond the Second Sophistic: Adventures in Greek Postclassicism* (Berkeley: University of California Press, 2013), 23.

[52] Frank W. Walbank, *Polybius, Rome and the Hellenistic World* (Cambridge: Cambridge University Press, 2015), 231–4.

In either case, the goal was to influence the *praxis* of the reader. *Praxis* is not any old action. It is 'action in the sense of a deed', something which, when done, one 'has' as one's work, or *ergon*. 'What do I keep having from this ergon? The hexis [habit] I have exercised in doing the praxis.'[53] Hence the idea that History can be a teacher of life: it is up to the student to live up to the lessons by actually living them.

At the same the subject matter of much 'useful History' tended to be the behaviour of states and militaries, or individuals *qua* commanders or representatives, and thus pertained to life in the *polis*, the public sphere. Obviously this does not mean the History was evacuated of moral content. Clearly different moral considerations might apply in public as opposed to public life, where such distinctions exist, but this is a far cry from saying that public life has ever been free of moral considerations.[54] Thucydides is in this sense bound together with the more obviously moral-didactic agendas of Ephorus and Theopompus, both of whom had been students of the sophist rhetorician Isocrates. Thucydidian international relations 'realism' is predicated upon moral characterizations of the nature of state actors and norms, as is abundantly clear in Thucydides' famous Melian dialogues.

The likes of Theopompus might also have common cause with the likes of Thucydides in opposition to the likes of Duris on those occasions when the 'pleasurable' did seem to come into tension with the 'useful', as when the deployment of vividness was considered not to aid or give point to moral reflection but to suborn it by sensationalization or prejudicial emotivism. Fear of subornment along these lines was prominent in Polybius's mind in the second century BCE, when targeting Phylarchus. Polybius was not uninterested in moral judgement and its attendant instruction, but he believed that such judgement must be impartial, in the sense of not being biased and not automatically favouring one party over another. We ought not 'shrink from accusing our friends or praising our enemies, nor need we be afraid of praising or blaming the same people at different times... We must therefore detach ourselves from the actors in our story, and apply to them only such statements and judgements as their conduct deserves.'[55] Judgement, explicit or tacit, must also be based on rigorous causal investigation in order that whoever is blamed or praised, the grounds are correct. Here emotivism may be an obstacle. So when discussing the Cleomenean War of 229/228–222 BCE between Sparta and the alliance of Macedon and the Achaean League, Polybius

[53] Jill Frank, *A Democracy Of Distinction: Aristotle and the Work of Politics* (London: University of Chicago Press, 2005) 34–5. On *praxis/praxeis* and *res gestae*, see Raoul Mortley, *The Idea of Universal History from Hellenic Philosophy to Early Christian Historiography* (New York: Edwin Mellen, 1996), ch. 2.

[54] Pownall, *Lessons from the Past*, describes many of the relevant relations and tensions.

[55] Polybius, *The Rise of the Roman Empire*, trans. Ian Scott-Kilvert (London: Penguin, 1979), editor's introduction 9–40, here 20–3; quotation from p. 55 (Book I.14 of Polybius's *Histories*).

was dismissive of Phylarchus, whose purpose he deemed to have been 'to emphasize the cruelty of Antigonus and the Macedonians and also that of Aratus and the Achaeans' in the victimization of the Mantineans. 'In his eagerness to arouse the pity of his readers and enlist their sympathy through his story', Phylarchus 'introduces graphic scenes of women clinging to one another, tearing their hair and baring their breasts'. While there is an implied call for a sort of dry History, as against Phylarchus's 'ignoble and unmanly' account, this does not mean that Polybius's primary objection was to the emotive element per se. Rather, Polybius believed that the Mantineans had brought their own misfortune on themselves, and as such did not deserve the pity which Phylarchus's description might elicit. Had Phylarchus devoted more energy to explaining the causes of the Mantineans' plight he would have realized this, Polybius was saying.[56]

In the period of Ephorus et al., one of the moments in which the political uses of History came to a head concerned the use of the written word by a group of aristocrats, Plato (420s–c.348/7 BCE) in their number, to combat the oratory of the Athenian democrats. Against earlier failures of oligarchy, and in the teeth of the more radical democratic order, the best way to try to retain some control over the future was to influence elite *paideia*, meaning, like German *Bildung*, a sort of rounded cultural education. Access to the realm of prose was perforce limited to men of a certain class, so textual historians could channel the past through the written word to inculcate aristocratic norms. At the same time Plato assailed the orators' 'abuse' of the historical record in pursuit of their democratic goals.[57] This is the context for his mockery of the likes of the Atthidographers as they stoked the fancy of the populace with tales of 'the genealogies of heroes and men…and the foundations of cities in ancient times' (*Hippias Major* 285d), and for his parody in *Menexenus* of the Thucydidean tradition of inventing speeches for performative effect.[58]

That Plato needed rhetoric too is beyond contestation—again, who and what rhetoric served was what was really at stake—as he acknowledged in his last work on the topic, the *Phaedrus*. Yet his attitude remained consistent with his animus towards the philosophy of Gorgias and thus towards poetry, in the broad sense of something created by the writer or speaker, as opposed to something found or identified in the present world or the historical record. In Plato's philosophy the entire sensible world was one of 'seeming' and 'becoming', a world of appearances, impermanence, and fallible 'common-sense' (*doxa*) in rude approximation to a realm of pure, eternal 'being' and *logos*, literally word, but here meaning pure reason or truth. For Plato, philosophical theory, *theoria* ('looking-on'), required

---

[56] Polybius, *Histories*, II.56 (Polybius, *The Rise of the Roman Empire*, 167–8); Cf. Walbank, *Polybius, Rome and the Hellenistic World*, 235–6. On pp. 231–41 Walbank has important observations to make on the question of utility versus pleasure.

[57] Pownall, *Lessons from the Past*, 38 ff.   [58] Atack, 'Discourse of Kingship', 338.

laying aside practical matters in order to face the *kosmos* without any distraction of contingent interest.[59] Only with such an attitude could the dimensions of the world beyond the mind be comprehended, and its well-ordered structure replicated in the philosopher's soul through the process of *mimesis*. Here the role of even the least 'fanciful' History is unclear, since although History need not be 'deceitfully' creative as poetry is, the best that it can aspire to is recording the world of becoming rather than the world of being, so it was already a diminished sort of knowledge. One use of History became apparent when Plato moved from the philosophical endeavour of ontology—a branch of metaphysics concerned with the nature of existence—to the more mundane matter of political philosophy and *social* science. His *Republic* and *Laws* are thus informed by data about the past organization of different Greek *poleis*. The third book of the *Laws*, for instance, shows the philosopher engaged in a comparative constitutional History. This was at once a form of negative exemplarity, showing what measures to avoid in the setting up of a new government from scratch, and an exercise in abstraction that produces the elements of the best conceivable social framework from the existing models. That best framework is the closest available thing to an ideal political arrangement.

From Greek to Roman Historiography

For all that Plato showed History could be deployed for the purposes of a social science, historiographical innovations were tending to focus more on individual political actors. Thus Xenophon's life of Agesilaus II of Sparta, Theopompus's account of the exploits of Philip of Macedon, *Philippica*, and then Callisthenes' slightly later *The Acts of Alexander*, wove together History as Lesson and biography, such that the lives became the exemplary acts.[60] It was perhaps appropriate to the monarchical nature of the Macedonian polity that Philip should be the prism through which one explored Macedon prevailing over Athens and then driving eastward. This personalization of history was the culmination of a trend begun by the Atthidographers with their focus on past kings. The trend was perpetuated by the continuators of Theopompus, whose works had in turn continued Xenophon's.

Two significant developments of third-century BCE historical scholarship were direct results of conquests by Philip's son, Alexander 'the Great'. One was an expansion of ethnographic literature, as in the early-century work of the Ionian Megasthenes on India. This sort of ethnography 'did not simply describe the

---

[59] On *theoria*, Eric Voegelin, *Published Essays, 1953–1965* (Columbia: University of Missouri Press, 2000), 115.

[60] On *Philippica*, see Cartledge, 'Historiography and Ancient Greek Self-Definition', 28, 34.

world as it was; it created an imagined sense of where the world had been, where it was now, and where it would be through the language of custom, habit, origins, discovery, and exchange.[61] It was also partner to a revived chronographic project of synchronizing timescales in ever more territories to provide the inclusive chronological framework for new synthesizing Histories.[62]

Ethnographic interests spurred the study of Rome by Timaeus of Tauromenium (*c.*356–*c.*260 BCE), a historian and chronographer best known as the butt of later criticism by Polybius, and perhaps the first historian to deploy the pan-Hellenic Olympic games as a yardstick with which to integrate multiple political histories. While only fragments of Timaeus's works remain, there is evidence to suggest that Polybius, in fact, had some respect for him, and was thus trying to discredit him as a rival. It has been both claimed and denied that Timaeus identified the growing significance of Rome, which would have made him the first Greek historian so to do. Irrespective, it is a mild coincidence that his probable date of death was only a few years into the First Punic War (264–241 BCE), which was the first of the Roman Republic's military engagements beyond the peninsula, into Timaeus's homeland of Sicily. Polybius (*Histories*, I.5.I) tells us that Timaeus ended his History in 264, when the Romans arrived in Sicily.[63]

As far as we know, although again we only have the work in fragments, the first major Roman prose History was written around the close of the third century by Quintus Fabius Pictor (born *c.*270 BCE).[64] A senator at the time of writing his History of Rome, Fabius had previously served in the army, and had seen some of the Second Punic War (218–201 BCE). He is generally assumed to have written in Greek, though there is some doubt on this, and a suggestion that he may have been translated from the Latin. In any case, his work evinces Greek literary influences as well as Roman civic pride by beginning the story at Rome's mythic point of Romulan origin. So many subsequent Roman works started *ab urbe condita*, 'from the founding of the city', and this was not true only of prose Histories. Thus Fabius's younger contemporary Quintus Ennius (*c.*239–169 BCE) penned an epic poem over eighteen books that spanned the fall of Troy and Marcius Porcius Cato's time as Roman censor, 184 BCE. It became one of the most influential texts on Roman history and was only supplanted as the canonical work of epic poetry

[61] Todd S. Berzon, *Classifying Christians: Ethnography, Heresiology, and the Limits of Knowledge in Late Antiquity* (Oakland: University of California Press, 2016), 34, 32.

[62] Feeney, 'Chronography'; Treadgold, *Early Byzantine Historians*, 11.

[63] On predictions about Rome, W. R. Connor, 'Historical Writing in the Fourth Century BC and the Hellenistic Period', in P. E. Easterling and B. M. W. Knox (eds.), *The Cambridge History of Classical Literature*, Vol. 1, Part 3: *Philosophy, History and Oratory* (Cambridge: Cambridge University Press, 1989), 46–59, here 55 and Walbank, *Polybius, Rome and the Hellenistic World*, 172–6; cf. Baron, *Timaeus*, ch. 3. See the final work more generally on Polybius's relationship to Timaeus's work, and Timaeus's ethnographic interests.

[64] On Fabius in general, and on all of the other nineteen major Roman historians of whom fragments remain prior to Livy, Julius Caesar, and Sallust, see Hans Beck and Uwe Walter, *Die frühen römischen Historiker*, 2 vols. (Darmstadt: Wissenschaftliche Buchgesellschaft, 2001, 2004).

by the *Aeneid* of the Roman Homer, Virgil (79–19 BCE), which provided a compelling vision of Rome's foundation, the moment of constitution of the political 'we', via the myth of the Trojan refugee Aeneas's arrival on Italy's shores.[65]

Fabius's History was also characteristic of later work in its elite political authorship which links author and author-ity (*auctoritas*) in the sense of position, qualification, and experience. Another theme common to both Fabius and later writers was the defence of Roman external policy. Fabius sought to blame the Second Punic War on a few of the Carthaginian leaders, and to justify the course and content of Roman action.[66] Internal Roman developments are more often the subject of criticism, albeit against the standards set by Roman traditional virtues. Accordingly, Cato's Latinate *Origines* criticized elements of the Roman political elite after the Second Punic War for sins including arrogance and the mistreatment of provincial subjects and allies, as measured against past achievements and the wisdom of the citizenry at large.

Philosophy, Poetry, History: A Greek in Rome

The 'universal' *Histories* of the Greek politician and soldier Polybius (203–120 BCE) stand in contrast to the particularist Roman narratives. He took up his story from Timaeuss' endpoint, 264 BCE, working through Rome's victory over Macedon in 168 BCE, and ending with the obliteration of Carthage in 146 BCE. Ephorus's heir in the scale of his canvas, Polybius rejected Ephorus's partly ethnographic approach to focus more exclusively on political and military affairs. He described the ascent of the Roman Empire with the purpose of instructing his fellow Greeks in the nature of the force that had superseded their dominion and gained Mediterranean hegemony in only a few generations. For all of his calls for impartiality in explanation and judgement, one imagines that the project was not disadvantageous to his personal prospects in Roman custody as a comfortable hostage. Indeed, while it would not be until the 50s BCE that Romans chronographers systematically aligned Roman consuls with Greek temporal markers, Polybius took some important steps from the Greek side in the symbolically important act of grafting the two timelines together.[67]

---

[65] Virgil was not the first to do this, merely the most influential, presumably because he himself was a Roman, giving Romans ownership of an idea once imposed upon them by the Greeks: he was preceded by several centuries by Hellanicus of Mytilene.

[66] For the orthodoxy on Fabius, and the characteristics of Roman historiography, Uwe Walter, 'Annales and Analysis', in Andrew Feldherr and Grant Hardy (eds.), *The Oxford History of Historical Writing: Beginnings to AD 600* (Oxford: Oxford University Press, 2011), 265–90, here 265–6. On the question of Greek vs Latin, see A. J. Woodman, *Lost Histories: Selected Fragments of Roman Historians* (Newcastle: Histos, 2015), 4–22. For an example of Polybian citation and contestation of Fabius on the Second Punic War, Polybius, *Histories*, III.8–9 (Polybius, *The Rise of the Roman Empire*, 185–7).

[67] On 50s BCE Roman chronography, Feeney, 'Chronography'.

Polybius's most famous contribution to the philosophy of history as an overall process—as opposed to the explanation of particular segments of history—is his *anacyclosis*. This was a conception of recurrent historical cycles that surely owes a debt to Hesiod. However, Polybius also deployed a notion of a more linear, progressive narrative with a teleological element, making his a species of History as Speculative Philosophy.[68] While competing in some ways, and by no means everpresent, these notions each served to divide an otherwise endless temporal continuum, whether homogeneous, heterogenous, or utterly random. They engaged with the Platonic view of the mundane world as one of becoming, rather than atemporal being, whilst also claiming for History a certain divinatory significance that went beyond mere *ex post facto* accounting for what had happened.

This enhanced significance also served as a rejoinder to one notable claim by Plato's pupil, Aristotle (384–322 BCE). Where Plato had seen poetry as the antithesis of philosophy, for Aristotle poetry was closer to philosophy than was History. At the outset of Book IX of his *Poetics*, Aristotle wrote that it is the function of the poet, whether tragedian or epic,

> to describe, not the thing that has happened, but a kind of thing that might happen, i.e. what is possible as being probable or necessary. The distinction between historian and poet is not in the one writing prose and the other verse—you might put the work of Herodotus into verse, and it would still be a species of history; it consists really in this, that the one describes the thing that has been, and the other a kind of thing that might be. Hence poetry is something more philosophic and of graver import than history, since its statements are of the nature rather of universals, whereas those of history are singulars. By a universal statement I mean one as to what such or such a kind of man will probably or necessarily say or do—which is the aim of poetry, though it affixes proper names to the characters; by a singular statement, one as to what, say, Alcibiades did or had done to him. In Comedy this has become clear by this time; it is only when their plot is already made up of probable incidents that they give it a basis of proper names, choosing for the purpose any names that may occur to them.... In Tragedy, however, they still adhere to the historic names; and for this reason: what convinces is the possible; now whereas we are not yet sure as to the possibility of that which has not happened, that which has happened is manifestly possible, else it would not have come to pass.[69]

Poetry performed a certain abstraction that gave it a more general utility than History—and 'general' is a good way to understand what Aristotle means by

---

[68] Walbank, *Polybius, Rome and the Hellenic World*, chs. 12 and 13.

[69] Aristotle, *Poetics*, IX, in Aristotle, *On the Art of Poetry*, trans. Ingram Bywater (Oxford: Oxford University Press, 1920), 43–4.

'universal'. The poet imposed a conceptual order on the interpretation of human affairs 'as such', or in general, that could not be established in the reportage of particular human affairs that had actually materialized. The poem evinces an inner logic by emplotment, i.e. the poet's deployment of plot; the key to poetry is, Aristotle wrote, 'plots rather than verses'.[70] Plots give the unity of a proper narrative with a middle and an end foreshadowed in the beginning, and a moral-of-the-story, as opposed to works of History where the chance intersection of rather haphazard causal chains might explain what happened to X in year Y, but had no wider significance. Aristotle also compares poetry to a 'living creature' in the sense that the animal is a physiological entity rendered full by the harmonious and necessary interrelationship of parts, as opposed to History where the relationships were merely contingent.[71] As one latter-day literary scholar puts it, Aristotle 'claimed that stories were truer than history because stories show principles while history shows sequence'.[72] By contrast with *this* one of Aristotle's accounts of History (we need always to bear in mind that elsewhere Aristotle found utility in historical reflection), in Polybius's claim that the historical chain of events under his narration also constituted a body, one whose wholeness and unity could be grasped by the historian's *sunopsis*, we see the historian propounding the general utility of his *pragmatikē historia*, responding to philosophers who distinguished the particular importance of their pursuit as the way to conform the self to the higher patterns of the universe.[73]

Polybius did not think every History comprised a unity in the organic sense, just that his did. His was, in his view, a universal/general History, because it had identified the force that unified all the other elements—Rome. From the beginning of the Second Punic War in the 220s, 'the affairs of Italy and of Libya have been interwoven (*sumplekesthai*) with those of Greece and of Asia, all leading up to one end'. One of the features of an account structured around periodizations— he used the period between Olympiads—was that in any given period one could easily move laterally, describing different elements in the overall picture across place, showing both causal relations between ostensibly disparate events and the ever-tightening connections that would ultimately bring unity out of diversity. There was thus an important difference between Polybius's conception of the universal and Aristotle's: the philosopher meant universal in the sense of generalizable, whereas the historian used it in the sense of all-encompassing. At the same

---

[70] Aristotle, *Poetics*, IX, in Aristotle, *On the Art of Poetry*, 44.

[71] Aristotle, *Poetics* VII and XXIII, in Aristotle, *On the Art of Poetry*, 39–41 and 79–80 respectively.

[72] Marshall Gregory, *Shaped by Stories: The Ethical Power of Narratives* (Notre Dame: University of Indiana Press, 2009), 89.

[73] François Hartog, 'Polybius and the First Universal History' and Peter Liddel, '*Metabole politeia* as Universal History', in Peter Liddel and Andrew Fear (eds.), *Historiae Mundi: Studies in Universal Historiography* (London: Duckworth, 2010), 30–40, esp. 35–6; M. F. Williams, 'Polybius' Historiography and Aristotle's Poetics', *Ancient History Bulletin* 21 (2007), 1–64.

time, Polybius had to keep something of Aristotle's sense of necessity (as opposed to accident) in order to address, beyond the question of interconnectedness, the question of plot—which is why there is such a teleological element in his 'all leading up to one end'. There had to be a 'tragic' element, and this came in the form of *tyche*, here meaning something like an overweening force of historical destiny. In detecting and reporting the operations of *tyche*, the work of the appropriately insightful historian—meaning Polybius himself—was promoted to the level of *theoria*, looking-on, rather than poetry, creation.[74]

As we shall see in the next chapter, *tyche* came in other manifestations than grand destiny. One point of Polybius's work, at the micro-level of practical instruction, was to show by example how the study of the past could help readers cope with capricious fortune rather than succumbing to fatalism. Another, at the meso-level of institutional arrangements, was to suggest that the Roman adoption of a mixed constitution could delay the operations of the historical cycle.[75] Finally, the grand explanatory exercise Polybius set himself presupposed the explicit investigation of cause, as opposed to the less obviously analytical narration of events as they occurred. Such explanation sometimes reached for the hand of *tyche*, but his fame as a causal historian would scarcely have endured if this were all there was to it.

Roman Historiography in the Late Republic

Historians Hans Beck and Uwe Walter credit Polybius's achievements in causal explanation as a key influence on what they call the 'modernization' of Roman historiography. Other factors included the growth of a more erudite reading public which demanded Latin imitation of Greek literary styles, and the extension of the Republic in terms both of its territorial conquests and its emancipation of non-Roman Italians. This modernization occurred in the period of the late Republic, which is generally dated from 147 to 30 BCE, and more precisely around the end of the second century BCE. Alas, the first wave of Roman historians that Beck and Walter categorize as modernizers have only come down to us fragmentarily. They include the likes of Coelius Antipater and Sempronius Asellio.[76]

The best-known of the Roman historians are renowned for their literary qualities and rhetorical facility, as Latin letters reached their golden age in the two

---

[74] Hartog, 'Polybius and the First Universal History', esp. 35–9.

[75] Connor, 'Historical Writing in the Fourth Century BC and the Hellenistic Period', 56–7; Walbank, *Polybius, Rome and the Hellenic World*, 185–6, 239–41.

[76] Beck and Walter, *Die frühen römischen Historiker*, 17 ff., and in connection with Lucius Coelius Antipater, discussed at 35 ff. Further on Polybius's impact and Greek borrowings more generally, Dieter Timpe, '*Memoria* and Historiography in Rome', in John Marincola (ed.), *Greek and Roman Historiography* (Oxford: Oxford University Press, 2011), 150–74, here 166–7.

centuries either side of the birth of Jesus. How far a commitment to truthfulness cohered with the demands of literary art varied from case to case, in the works of writers such as Julius Caesar (100–44 BCE), Sallust (86–35 BCE), Livy (59 BCE—CE 17), and Tacitus (c.56–c.120 CE).[77] It is a reasonable hypothesis that artistic and intellectual reflection was stimulated by the crises and military conflicts of the long first century BCE, corresponding to the period of the Late Republic. Putting aside the many external wars of the period, the evidence from within suggests that the institutions that might have been fit for a city state proved inadequate for the administration of an expanding empire: that evidence includes the failed 'Gracchan revolution' of 133–121 BCE, three slave wars up to 71 BCE, the Social War of 91–88 BCE between Rome and its Italian allies, the civil wars of 88–80 BCE culminating in Sulla's dictatorships, the Catiline conspiracy of 77 BCE, and the Triumvirate period and ensuing civil wars from 53 to 30 BCE. The developments of the long first century accentuated an existing tendency to venerate the distant Republican past as against the present and help to explain the sense of historical change that has been claimed as a feature of the work of those approximate contemporaries, variously poets, rhetoricians, and antiquarians, Lucretius, Virgil, Horace, Cicero (106–43 BCE), and Varro (116–27 BCE).[78]

History under Monarchy

If we also categorize as historians Suetonius (born c.69 CE) and the Greek Plutarch (46–120 CE), plus the first emperor himself (63 BCE–14 CE), author of the self-serving funerary inscription *Res Gestae Divi Augusti* (*Deeds of the Divine Augustus*), we notice the recurrence of a historiographical pattern. As Rome passed from Republic to Empire much the same historiographical shifts occurred as had occurred during the transition, roughly speaking, from Thucydides to Theopompus: a more pronounced emphasis developed on individuals at the power centre. That might mean the emperor alone, or the emperor in relation to senators, as in Tacitus, or, as in the case of Sallust, who did not live to witness the Principate, an emphasis on plotters and other actors in the internecine political warfare that presaged the downfall of the Republic. Plutarch wrote matched biographies of Greek and Roman luminaries, and Suetonius recorded the lives of twelve successive Julio-Claudian and Flavian caesars, beginning with Julius

---

[77] On Sallust's attitude see William Batstone, 'The Drama of Rhetoric at Rome', in Erik Gunderson (ed.), *The Cambridge Companion to Ancient Rhetoric* (Cambridge: Cambridge University Press, 2009), 212–27, here 221 ff.

[78] On whom see Burke, *Renaissance Sense*, 139–41. On the distance of Rome's 'golden age' and the claim that 'Recent history had for centuries been held to show a degeneration from this legendary ideal', see editor's 'Introduction', p. xxxi, in Tacitus, *Tacitus: The Annals and the Histories*, ed. Hugh Lloyd-Jones (New York: Washington Square Press, 1964).

Caesar. Writing thematically, in aid of comparison, each life was for Livy a form of History as Moral Lesson, as he deployed the range of rhetorical skills in *enkomium* or damnation.

Writing *ab urbe condita* ('from the birth of the city') up to 9 BCE, Livy's vastly popular and influential general *History of Rome* does not conform to this pattern. With the declared intent 'to record the story of the greatest nation in the world', his agenda was rather less subtle than that of Polybius, though like Polybius his conception of history had both linear and cyclical aspects.[79] As with almost all classical historiography Livy had ample space for prominent individuals, such as Hannibal and Scipio Africanus in his account of the Punic wars, but he also resembled Herodotus in his ethnographic concern to recreate the 'mood' of a time or place. A patriot writing in something of the spirit of Porcius Cato's *Origines*, the main object of Livy's admiration was the Roman past, not its present, and in this sense History had the task of holding up an improving mirror. In 'the study of history it is especially improving and beneficial to contemplate examples of every kind of behavior... From it you can extract for yourself and your commonwealth both what is worthy of imitation and what you should avoid because it is rotten from start to finish.' More specifically,

> I ask that each person pay close attention for himself to the following, namely what was the way of life and the traditions, through which men[,] and by what abilities, both civic and military, the empire was created and increased; next, let him mentally trace those traditions as first they slipped, together with the gradual decline of their proper inculcation, then collapsed more and more, and then began to tumble headlong, until we have come to our current straits.[80]

This was History as Lesson and a critical form of History as Identity, looking backwards for moral and practical inspiration as Virgil and Horace did. It was clearly not pro-monarchist but nor was it anti-monarchist, since the rot had set in during the Republican period whose earlier phase Livy venerated. Moreover, while his attitude towards Augustus is not entirely clear, and coming to an estimation on it is not helped by the fact that we do not know when he finished writing his work, Livy was not insensible to the order that Augustan rule produced since he wrote so much of his History in that context.

More than half a century ago one of Livy's translators noted that Livy's invitation to ponder the degradation of the world was indeed 'a solemn invitation; but most people enjoy being *collectively* scolded for their wickedness, and Livy's

---

[79] On Livy's cyclicism, see Gary B. Miles, 'The Cycle of Roman History in Livy's First Pentad', *The American Journal of Philology* 107:1 (1986), 1–33; on his linearity, Ianziti, 'Humanism's New Science', 71–2. Livy quote from the opening paragraph of Book I.1 of Livy's *History of Rome*, in Livy, *The Early History of Rome*, trans. Aubrey de Sélincourt (Harmondsworth: Penguin, 1960), 17.

[80] Translation from Adam, 'Annales and Analysis', 268–9.

contemporaries accepted it with ardour'. The work did indeed sweep all other accounts before it even if its length meant many people only encountered it in abbreviated form. The 'collective' element is key here, more particularly the element of collective memory, in light of Augustus's own determination to 're-awaken' Roman awareness of tradition. The conflicts under account were conflicts of the collective past by the time Livy wrote, while the values he venerated might be collectively renewed in modified circumstances. It was after all the people that were at the centre of Livy's thoughts, which may be explained by the fact that, unusually amongst the other historians mentioned here, Livy himself was not an active politician involved directly in power squabbles, but a more aloof *rhetor* or man of letters. He seems to have conceived the people almost as an organism that developed over time and had to adapt itself, but which still had a true nature to which it should adhere.[81]

Like Livy, and setting off in his *Annals* from where Livy finished, Tacitus (*c*.56–*c*.120 CE) engaged with the grand subject matter of warfare, but his abiding concern is the workings and psychology of power. He is one of the great stylists, though in the tradition of Sallust rather than Cicero or Livy.

Tacitus's epigrams are like the thrust of a knife, clean and wounding; they imitate, in their very unadorned economy, the terrible times they describe. Tacitus's antitheses are never pretty; they are images which contrast appearance and reality with almost brutal concision, and always at the expense of reality. The Romans are elegant in the forum and ruthless in the field: *Solitudinem faciunt, pacem appellant*—'They make a desert, and call it peace'. The Britons mistake the trapping for the essence of culture: *Humanitas vocabantur, cum pars serviutis esset*—'They called it civilization, when it was part of servitude'.[82]

These famous phrases come not from the *Annals*, which covered the period from the death of Augustus and Tiberius's ascension to Nero's death (14–68 CE), nor the earlier-written *Histories*, which went from 69 CE to Domitian's death in 96 CE, but from a yet earlier work written in 98 CE, a laudation of Tacitus's father-in-law Agricola, who was at the forefront of the conquest of Britain. The *Agricola* might as well have been written as a rejoinder to the recommendation in Sallust's *The War with Catiline* that 'men should strive with all their resources not to pass their lives unnoticed'.[83] It shuns vainglorious resistance to overwhelming force while

---

[81] On this and the previous paragraph see Adam, 'Annales and Analysis', 268–9, 271–2. For the quote on collective scolding, Livy, *The Early History of Rome*, trans de Sélincourt, 13: emphasis added. Further on the element of identity-construction, Andrew Feldherr, 'Livy's Revolution: Civic Identity and the Creation of the *Res Publica*', in Thomas Habinek and Alessandro Schiesaro (eds.), *The Roman Cultural Revolution* (Cambridge: Cambridge University Press, 1997), 136–57. On Livy's biography, popular focus, and the organism idea, see Timpe, '*Memoria* and Historiography in Rome', 169–70.
[82] Peter Gay, *The Enlightenment: An Interpretation* (New York: Norton, 1966), 158.
[83] Sallust quoted in Batstone, 'Drama of rhetoric', 221.

recalling how a good man tempering decency with prudence could endure even under bad rulers who sought to wield the imperial power structure as a tool for their designs. Like Tacitus's *Germania* (also 98 CE) with its 'noble savage' view of Germanic tribes, and with as little first-hand experience, *Agricola* also contains ethnographic reflections on Britain.

At first glance the *Annals* are straightforwardly anti-imperial, the latest instalment in a long tradition of decline literature. With the advent of the Principate 'the state had been revolutionized, and there was not a vestige left of the old sound morality. Stripped of equality, all looked up to the commands of a sovereign without the least apprehension for the present.' Yet while Tacitus did not share the opinion of Livy or the less well-known Velleius Paterculus (19 BCE–31 CE) that the imperial order could actually restore some Republican virtue, he nonetheless saw it as important in the establishment of peace within the empire, and in the return of law to corrupt provinces hitherto run by greedy governors. He was critical of the emperor Domitian (81–96) in *Agricola* and in such parts of the *Histories* as survive, but since Domitian was the last of his dynasty, the Flavian line, this was hardly a challenge to successive new emperors, Nerva and Trajan. Further ambiguity coloured Tacitus's estimation of the prospects for the influence of the senatorial class—of which he and Agricola were members—under an emperor. Yet, in the final analysis, there can be little doubt that his overall approach bears the imprint of senatorial class consciousness.[84] In insisting on writing with reference to the consular year, as against the periodization provided by the reigns of emperors, Tacitus was making a political as well as aesthetic choice.

In his claim to write *sine ira et studio*, without anger or partiality (*Annals* I:1), Tacitus was manifestly not promising to avoid evaluation, or to tell the story aperspectivally. He was declaring sufficient detachment from the affairs under scrutiny as to pass judgement where, and in the measure, due. This sentiment stands alongside Polybius's claim to avoid political bias, irrespective of the success of either in adhering to his own standards, which for Tacitus were the exalted norms of a class memory of yesteryear. Whatever we make of Tacitus's avowed judgementalism, it stands in as great a contrast to the moral exemplarity that provides a paean to current mores as it does to the History that purports neutrality. It was of a piece with Cicero's definition of historical truth as defined against sympathy or favour, and Sallust's refusal to be influenced by 'hope, fear, or political partisanship'.[85]

---

[84] Tacitus, *Annals*, I.4 (p. 5) and the editor's 'Introduction', pp. xxxi–xxxviii, in *Tacitus*, ed. Hugh Lloyd-Jones; Ellen O'Gorman, 'Imperial History and Biography at Rome', in Feldherr and Hardy (eds.), *The Oxford History of Historical Writing: Beginnings to AD 600*, 291–315, here 294, 300–8. Further on Tacitus's ambiguities, Momigliano, *Classical Foundations*, 117.

[85] On Sallust and Cicero, Walter, 'Annales and Analysis', 276.

Pre- and Anti-Christian Influences

Before the expanded presence of Christianity in the empire, Hellenistic culture remained the major non-Roman influence on Rome and actually expanded in the first and second centuries CE as Roman elites embraced the Greek cultural renaissance known as the Second Sophistic. Early Greek responses to the shock of Rome overrunning Greece had included the comforting conceit that Romans were really the protégés of the older civilization; Plutarch's later paired biographies continued the tradition of conjoining the two. In between, Dionysius of Halicarnassus, who wrote his *Antiquities of the Romans* in the late first century BCE, effectively claimed that Romans just were Greeks. Dionysius was also a major player in the Atticist movement, which adverted to the culture of the Athens-centred 'golden age' and promoted a linguistic style which was at once deliberately archaic—a clear affirmation of cultural change over time—and something of a lingua franca across the Greek cultural sphere. In the following centuries Atticism became a major strand in the Second Sophistic. Significant historians with Atticizing tendencies included Arrian (born *c.*86/89 CE), Appian of Alexandria (95–165), and Cassius Dio (*c.*155–235), all of whom were members of the Roman political hierarchy.[86] During the period spanned by these men the symbiosis was such that it was not just Greeks who wrote in Greek—Italians did too. The Atticizing tendency continued for centuries in the eastern—'Greek'—part of the Roman empire, and not until after the sixth century did any historians in that tradition adopt an obviously Christian position. Between Tacitus and the fourth-century Ammianus Marcellinus there is no record of a prose historian who wrote contemporary History in Latin, and evidence of only two who wrote in that tongue about Republican History.[87]

In the fourth century, Suetonius's influence is present in the last known biographical series emerging from the Roman empire, the *Historia Augusta*. This was written during the reign of Theodosius, the final ruler of both halves of the empire, east and west. Theodosius it was who effectively made Nicene Christianity Rome's official religion, three-quarters of a century after Constantine had pronounced tolerance of Christianity in 313. The *Historia Augusta* detailed emperors and pretenders from Hadrian to Carinus, thus covering the period 117–285. It also includes many fictional characters and invents historical sources and texts.

---

[86] David S. Potter, 'Greek Historians of Imperial Rome', in Feldherr and Hardy (eds.), *The Oxford History of Historical Writing: Beginnings to AD 600*, 316–45, here 316–17, 325, and 329 on the deliberate archaisms; Sulochana R. Asirvatham, 'Historiography', in Daniel S. Richter and William A. Johnson (eds.), *The Oxford Handbook of the Second Sophistic* (Oxford: Oxford University Press, 2017), 477–92. On Cassius Dio's Atticism, his archaisms, and his relationship to sophism and the Second Sophistic, Brandon Jones, 'Cassius Dio—*Pepaideumenos* and Politician on Kingship', in Carsten Hjort Lange and Jesper Majbom Madsen (eds.), *Cassius Dio: Greek Intellectual and Roman Politician* (Leiden: Brill, 2016), 297–315, here 297–9.

[87] Potter, 'Greek Historians of Imperial Rome', 328.

Another compendium of moral didactics, it was concerned amongst other things with the quality of the men surrounding successive emperors. The belief that advisers 'made a Syrian [Severus Alexander, r. 222–35] into a good emperor, just as their evil friends made Roman emperors the worst even to posterity' reveals a nice prejudice that, all else remaining equal, emperors of non-Roman extraction were a bad idea.[88] If the author was himself Gallic, as some suppose, this may be a further instance of the Tacitean syndrome of 'going native' towards Rome.

Finally, we come to Ammianus (c.320s–c.390s). Part of his choice of topic—its timespan—indicates a disregard for the other Histories of Rome since Tacitus, at whose endpoint Ammianus began. His work is influenced by advocacy of 'pagan' culture, which helps explain his disregard of ecclesiastical history and his solicitousness towards the emperor Julian (r. 361–3), the last non-Christian ruler of the Roman empire. Julian repays Ammianus in the text by being interested in History, good at learning its lessons. Ammianus wrote, too, in the interests of preserving the language and culture of Rome at a time of Greek cultural predominance: though he was as fluent in Greek, and indeed raised in the Greek-speaking east, his was the last major History in classical Latin. Trying to sustain the increasingly antiquated view that Rome really still had claim to the leadership of the Roman Empire, he prescribed a revival of moral vigour under an appropriate emperor. This would remedy the defeat of the eastern Roman emperor Valens by a confederated Gothic force at the Battle of Adrianople in 378, which closes the History. Ammianus did not live to see the sack of Rome by Alaric's Visigoth forces in 410.[89]

---

[88] O'Gorman, 'Imperial History', 292–312.

[89] Points on Ammianus variously from Kelly, *Ammianus*, 66, 71, 287 (and more generally 284–93), 316, 318–21 and Treadgold, *Early Byzantine Historians*, 68–79.

2
History, Faith, *Fortuna*

Introduction

Chronologically and conceptually, this chapter links classical antiquity to the middle ages. Most of its focus is on the second to sixth centuries, and especially the overlap of 'late antiquity' and the 'patristic era', or the era of the church fathers. It addresses historical thinking in Christianity in the context of Christianity's relationship to Greco-Roman and Jewish influences. It is a story of intellectual novelty, and of imposition, but just as much it is a tale of syncretism.

Of the rationales for History identified in the introduction, the two figuring largest in this chapter are History as Speculative Philosophy and History as Identity, the latter especially in its genealogical form. Along the way, attention is devoted to the relationship between grand conceptualizations of the overall historical process and the study of human choice and agency. That discussion illustrates similarities as well as contrasts in the way causal explanations can operate in disparate sorts of historical account, whether or not divine or quasi-divine forces are involved. The point looking forward is that at certain levels secular and non-secular Histories need not conflict.

Classical–Christian Fusion

It was common to find counterparts of the 'pagan' Ammianus Marcellinus in actual or former Roman territories: people who at once upheld Roman culture and the Christian religion. Mirroring Dionysius's claim that the Romans were really Greeks, the cultural elites of what was latterly called Byzantium considered themselves Romans to the end of the polity in 1453 CE, as well as sustaining a Christian church that was for hundreds of years more stable and secure than its equivalent to the west. In the west, we might consider proud Romans like Boethius (*c.*480–*c.*524) and Cassiodorus (*c.*485–*c.*585), successive heads of governmental and court services in the Ostrogothic Kingdom of Italy (483–553), who sustained the Aristotelian and Ciceronian rhetorical tradition and incorporated classical texts and techniques into Christian education. Cassiodorus also preserved and reproduced sacred texts under threat from the Ostrogothic armies which did not always act in accordance with the tolerant Arianism of their leaders.

As historiographer to the Ostrogothic king Theoderic, he also pleasingly united Goth and Roman antecedents in his *Chronica*.

On the doctrinal side, before Christianity was officially tolerated in the empire, let alone endorsed at the expense of paganism, Christian theologians and propagandists had established syncretic links with some of the foremost pre-Christian philosophical and rhetorical traditions. Classicizing language was adopted by evangelizers from the third century BCE in order to draw pagans to the new faith by means of a familiar cultural idiom, as in Eusebius's work. Much earlier than that, the biblical book Acts of the apostles by Luke seems to have drawn on Greco-Roman techniques and styles as well as Old Testament Histories like 1 Maccabees.[1] Cynic influence is detectable in Jesus's and Paul's teaching and rhetoric. Not far from Cynic thought, Stoic morality bore comparison with the austere morality of the church fathers, and the conception of conscience propounded under Christianity reflects the thought of Stoics like Cicero and Seneca. *Conscientia* was the word accurately used by Jerome in the fourth century when he translated the Bible into Latin; the corresponding Greek word was *syneidēsis*, connoting reflexive awareness (of, say, guilt) and it had a pre-Christian provenance.[2]

Theology and philosophy merged most explicitly in the Christian encounter with the Platonic tradition, in particular with middle Platonists such as the Hellenized Jewish philosopher Philo of Alexandria (*c.*20 BCE–*c.*50 CE), and late Platonists, latterly called Neoplatonists, most important among whom was Plotinus (204/5–270 CE). Plato's own thought was congenial to Christianity in positing an immortal soul made in a divine image, and a supersensible, extramental realm that constituted something like godly intelligence. Subsequent middle Platonist and Neoplatonist admixtures emphasized a tripartite ontology analogous to the Christian trinity—the first systematic Christian theologian, Origen Adamantius (*c.*185–*c.*254 CE), who leant on Philo amongst others, gave the names Father, Christ, and Holy Spirit to this triad. The triad of Origen's younger contemporary, Plotinus, comprised first the One, or the Good, which is a unitary first principle from which all else emanates, and which is thus a version of a principle to be found in some of the very oldest, pre-Socratic philosophy. Then there is Intellect, i.e. the realm of the eternal, unchanging, perfect forms. Then there is Soul, which acts in relation to the external natural world—that world whose material things are the 'image' of the forms from the realm of Intellect, and which includes the bodies of things that 'contain' souls. Soul also acts internally in relation to the realm of Intellect, which is Soul's highest, purest activity because it

---

[1] Palmer, 'Acts and the Historical Monograph', 373–5, 387–8.

[2] Cynic influence on Jesus and the early church: F. Gerald Downing, *Cynics, Paul and the Pauline Church* (London: Routledge, 1998), ch. 10; on Christian atticizers, Staffan Wahlgren, 'Byzantine Literature and the Classical Past', in Egbert J. Bakker (ed.), *A Companion to the Ancient Greek Language* (Chichester: Blackwell, 2010), 527–38, here 530; Glenn F. Chesnut, *The First Christian Histories: Eusebius, Socrates, Sozomen, Theodoret, and Evagrius* (Macon, GA: Mercer University Press, 1986), 190.

involves working in the direction of return to the One/the Good. In other words it is possible for human souls to gain some sort of access to the higher, spiritual–transcendental realm of Intellect (equivalent to the Platonic realm of Being, rather than the earthly realm of becoming), by a process of contemplation that rids itself, 'through quiet recollection, of deceit and of all that bewitches vulgar souls'. This contemplation is Plotinus's version of *theoria*.[3]

The Neoplatonic outlook was easily co-opted by Christianity, especially early, underground Christianity with its otherworldly, spiritual focus. Any attachment of the Soul to bodily or otherwise material things is an evil if it hinders the movement of return. And while none of the varieties of Platonism quite had an equivalent of the Christian incarnation—the word/*logos* being made flesh, as in John 1:14—the platonic idea of the body as a temporary container of the soul does come close. Indeed it was close enough for Augustine of Hippo (354–430 CE) to have subscribed to Neoplatonism for a while and still be taken as a Christian. Better put, there was a period in which Augustine's Neoplatonic and Christian beliefs overlapped with little tension, before the latter came to predominate. Christians even concocted a historical account to explain the synergy in terms favourable to themselves. Where Ambrose (Aurelius Ambrosius: *c.*340–397 CE) had claimed that Plato had gleaned his wisdom from the prophet Jeremiah, Augustine, who realized that Plato lived around a century too late to meet Jeremiah, nonetheless felt that Plato could have become acquainted with the Bible via Egyptian authorities.[4] Neoplatonism was compatible with the Christian distinction between the body, romantic love, and the outside world of laws on one hand, and the soul, spiritual love, and the realm of faith on the other. It is no coincidence that the man who wrote of salvation by faith alone, Paul the Apostle, was also one of the most prominent de-judaizers of Christian thought, scorning, as Augustine later would, the Jews' allegedly blind allegiance to the letter of the commandments, and their supposed neglect of the spirit that lay behind them.

Christianity and Judaism

Besides traducing the Jewish religion, one of the easiest ways for theologians to contrast Christianity with Judaism was to stigmatize Judaism's adherents, notably

[3] John Hermann Randall, *Nature and Historical Experience* (New York: Columbia University Press, 1958), 124–6; Rex Warner, *The Greek Philosophers* (New York: New American Library, 1958), 225–6.

[4] On the adoption of Platonism see Dermot Moran, 'Platonism, Medieval', in Edward Craig (ed.), *Routledge Encyclopedia of Philosophy*, vol. 7 (London: Routledge, 1998), 431–9. On Plotinus, Lloyd Gerson, 'Plotinus', *The Stanford Encyclopedia of Philosophy* (Summer 2014 edition), ed. Edward N. Zalta, https://plato.stanford.edu/archives/sum2014/entries/plotinus/ On Augustine, C. W. Wolfskeel, *De Immortalitate Animae of Augustine: Text, Translation and Commentary* (Amsterdam: Grüner, 1977), 10–20. On Origen, Edward Moore, 'Origen of Alexandria', *Internet Encyclopedia of Philosophy*: http://www.iep.utm.edu/origen-of-alexandria/#SH5b

with the allegation of deicide. This also helped divert responsibility for Jesus's death from Rome, facilitating coexistence with the worldly power and proselytization amongst the empire's peoples. At the same time the early propagandists of Christianity also needed to sustain the link with Judaism to which their own religion was said to be a successor. One contribution to the project of supercession was the manipulation of extant works of History, notably the work of the great Jewish historian Josephus (37–c.100 CE). Josephus's *Antiquities of the Jews* was prized for its wealth of material on early Christianity in the first century CE, such that Cassiodorus later included it on his influential list of suitable Christian reading alongside the major ecclesiastical historians of the fourth and fifth centuries.[5] Josephus supposedly said in his *Antiquities*, which was written around the early 90s CE:

> Now there was about this time Jesus, a wise man *if it be lawful to call him a man*, for he was a doer of wonders, *a teacher of such men as receive the truth with pleasure*. He drew many after him *both of the Jews and the Gentiles. He was the Christ.* When Pilate, *at the suggestion of the principal men among us* [that is, the Jews], had condemned him to the cross, those that loved him at first did not forsake him, *for he appeared to them alive again the third day, as the divine prophets had foretold these and a thousand other wonderful things about him*, and the tribe of Christians, so named from him, are not extinct at this day.
>
> (*Antiquities* 18:63–4)

The italicized sections were almost certainly inserted by subsequent Christian copyists, in order to substantiate Christ's divine nature, fortify charges of deicide, and insinuate Christian sympathies on Josephus's part.[6]

By claiming right of succession, Christianity also claimed inheritance of the framework of Jewish history, and by extension of established Jewish chronological linkages with other peoples. Thus Christianity was inserted into a deeper world history which was important for legitimation in the competition of faiths, even though the major warrant Christianity claimed was transcendent, not historical. In one expression of this historical tendency, Matthew's and Luke's gospels both claimed lineages from King David to the earthly family of Jesus. The Carthaginian Tertullian (160–225 CE) in the west and the Greek Clement of Alexandria (c.150–c.215 CE) in the east both made headway in annexing Jewish history, but the major steps were taken by Sextus Julius Africanus (c.160–c.240). On the basis

---

[5] For the reading list, Peter W. Edbury and John Gordon Rowe, *William of Tyre: Historian of the Latin East* (Cambridge: Cambridge University Press, 1990), 34. Alongside Eusebius of Caesarea, we encounter 'Paulus' Orosius, and the *Historia tripartita* which combined works of the Greek Christian historians Socrates, Sozomenus, and Theodoretus.

[6] David Patterson and Alan L. Berger, *Jewish–Christian Dialogue: Drawing Honey from the Rock* (St Paul, MN: Paragon House, 2008), 82–3.

of the timespan for the creation of the world in Genesis, and the claim in Psalms that a millennium was but a day in God's eyes, the world was said to be scheduled to last for 6,000 years after the creation plus another thousand years of rest to match the seventh, Sabbath day. Christ was apparently born precisely halfway through the world's last standard millennium, in 5,500. After the second coming of Christ, there would be a further, eighth 'day', a timeless, supramundane one.[7]

A complement to chronological synchronization was the way in which 'figural' readings of events and personages intimated religious succession, in keeping with the basic proposition that the coming of Jesus was a fulfilment of Old Testament prophecy. Tertullian again made notable developments in this line of thought. A *figura* is partly metaphor, partly allegory. Figural reading is best understood in its relation to the concept 'prefiguration', by which, for instance, Moses could be tied to Jesus by the imputation of a reciprocal relationship. Moses presaged Jesus and Jesus fulfilled Moses. Both were at once concrete historical individuals and gained their shared significance as expressions of God, infused with vital force and accorded special architectural powers by this shared essence.[8] So on one hand, as we have seen, Christians, like Romans, oriented their sense of time around key moments in the past, meaning that their sense of time was always historical in some fairly orthodox sense.[9] On the other hand, some of their 'historical' thinking pertained to a realm out of time: Moses and Christ could not be linked in any temporal, causal sense of one thing prompting another in 'horizontal', linear fashion—their relationship could only work if 'vertically' referred to the atemporal deity. According to the pivotal theorist of figural thought, Erich Auerbach, it was this fusion of real historical event and 'providential world-history' which gave Christianity its 'tremendous powers of persuasion', underpinning its medieval hegemony.[10]

Figural reading was but one strand of a rich patristic and medieval interpretative tradition. Indeed within occidental history we might say that while the great techniques of writing and speaking were elevated to a high level by the Greeks and Romans, the techniques of reading and interpretation collectively known as hermeneutics were honed to a finer point in the Christian world, as, amongst other things it drew on rich Jewish traditions of scriptural exegesis. Both

[7] Michael Whitby, 'Imperial Christian Historiography', in Feldherr and Hardy (eds.), *The Oxford History of Historical Writing: Beginnings to AD 600*, 346–70, here 347–8.

[8] David Dawson, *Christian Figural Reading and the Fashioning of Identity* (Berkeley: University of California Press, 2001), 88 ff., 163–4; Eric Auerbach, *Mimesis: The Representation of Reality in Western Literature* (New York: Doubleday, 1957), 73 ff.

[9] On historical as well as theological time, Rosamond McKitterick, 'Constructing the Past in the Early Middle Ages', *Transactions of the Royal Historical Society* 6th ser. VII (1997), 101–29, here 104. On foundational and original moments in ecclesiastical History, Momigliano, *Classical Foundations*, ch. 6.

[10] Terry Cochran, *Twilight of the Literary: Figures of Thought in the Age of Print* (Cambridge, MA: Harvard University Press, 2001), 58–60. Auerbach's text is 'Figura' in Eric Auerbach, *Scenes from the Drama of European Literature* (Minneapolis: University of Minnesota Press, 1984), 11–76.

monotheisms had sacred texts around which to orient their sense of past, present, and future, and to provide life rules and morality tales. Interpreting these texts 'correctly' was therefore a task of the highest importance, with the promise of nothing less than getting as close as possible to the thought of god.[11] Given the breadth of the texts' contents, hermeneutics came to bridge theology, philosophy, and law. As we shall see further in the next chapter, historical–critical study was increasingly important to the interpretative endeavour, whence 'History as Communion'.

Early in the third century CE, Origen had sketched a tripartite scheme of biblical exegesis, incorporating moral, literal, and allegorical levels of meaning. John Cassian (c.360–435) added a fourth level and his quadriga became the standard medieval reading scheme, though Cassian's contemporary Augustine practised a variation. The quadriga comprised (i) historical or literal, (ii) moral or tropological, (iii) allegorical, typological or analogical, and (iv) eschatological or anagogical readings. Figural reading is subsumed in the third of these category-groups. The meaning of each group was elaborated in the mnemonic *Litera, gesta docet; quid credas, allegoria; moralis, quid agas; quo tendas anagogia*; 'The letter teaches events, allegory what you should believe, morality what you should do, anagogy what mark you should be aiming for'.[12] One of the quadriga's purposes was to ensure that reading and learning were not passive exercises providing once-and-for-all comprehension, but rather comprised an arduous, interactive, and ongoing process.[13] At the same time, multi-layered readings permitted the circumvention of otherwise tricky contradictions, and the rationalizing of distasteful chronicle—not every level of interpretation needed to be applied together to every text. Such reading practices helped reconcile the New Testament with the Old. They also underwrote the legitimacy of separating some History from knowledge of God, including thus separating some biblical facts from theological interpretation.[14]

Early Christian Historiography

Alongside these reading practices, early Christianity produced its own written History, of which that of Eusebius of Caesarea (c.255–339 CE) stands out for its

[11] David R. Olson, *The World on Paper: The Conceptual and Cognitive Implications of Writing* (Cambridge: Cambridge University Press, 1996), 150.

[12] Quote from the Glossa Ordinaria, cited in Gianfrancesco Pico della Mirandola, *Pico della Mirandola: Oration on the Dignity of Man: A New Translation and Commentary*, ed. Francesco Borghesi, Michael Papio, and Massimo Riva (Cambridge: Cambridge University Press, 2012), 72 n. 16.

[13] Werner H. Kelber, 'The Quest for the Historical Jesus', in John Dominic Crossan, Luke Timothy Johnson, and Werner H. Kelber, *The Jesus Controversy: Perspectives in Conflict* (Harrisburg, PA: Trinity Press, 1999), 75–116, here 78 ff.

[14] Peter Van Nuffelen, 'Theology versus Genre? The Universalism of Christian Historiography in Late Antiquity', in Liddel and Fear (eds.), *Historiae Mundi*, 162–75; see also Momigliano, *Classical Foundations*, ch. 6.

influence. We should actually distinguish between two Eusebian contributions of different sorts, each buttressing the other. One was a chronography that he assembled as Book II, the *Chronological Tables*, of his two-part *Chronicle*. The other was his list of sources in Book I. In its final form the *Chronological Tables* ended in the year 326 CE; Jerome continued the story up to 378. The work is not notable for the novelty of the research, for almost all of its sources were themselves earlier compilations—today we would call them secondary sources. Its key purpose was linking biblical history with that of the pagan peoples of the Middle East and the Mediterranean, thus expanding outward from the basis provided in Julius Africanus's work.

The *Chronological Tables* were divided according to the kings of the different peoples. They began in what corresponds to our 2016 BCE, which was supposedly Abraham's birth year. Monotheists therefore had priority here even though, by Eusebius's own reckoning, that date was also the first year of Egypt's sixteenth dynasty, the year in which, amongst other things, King Ninus of Assyria founded the city of Nineveh. The monotheists had priority at the conclusion, too, though they shared it with Rome. Given that Eusebius's columns were allocated to kings, so it was that when non-monarchical governments appeared peoples lost their place in the table until they regained their royalty, if they did. This approach can be partly explained by the difficulty of dating periods without reigns to punctuate them, but there was also an ideological function to this particular assemblage of data. From 70 CE, when the Romans took Jerusalem, only one column remained in the *Chronological Tables* until the end: that of the Roman emperors whose rule united the known world and under whom, ultimately, and despite periodic persecutions, the Christian church had survived and expanded. Polybian assumptions about Rome's universal historical role were co-opted: the reduction of the table to a single point was also a way of pointing towards a future of Roman-Christian imperium. Unlike Julius Africanus, however, Eusebius did not believe it possible to infer the time of Christ's second coming from chronographical data.[15]

The *Chronicle* epitomized some of the subject matter of Eusebius's *History of the Church*, which was the first work to chart that path since the book of Acts and the gospels, especially Luke's gospel. As Eusebius said, his goals included tracing

> The successions of the holy apostles along with the times extending from our Saviour to our own day; the magnitude and significance of the deeds said to have been accomplished throughout the ecclesiastical narrative, how many governed and presided over these affairs with distinction in the most famous communities; how many in each generation served as ambassadors of the

---

[15] Treadgold, *Early Byzantine Historians*, ch. 2; Grafton and Williams, *Christianity and the Transformation of the Book*, ch. 3, which also shows continuities between the *Chronicle* and Origen's *Hexapla*.

Divine Logos [the word of God], either in unwritten form or through written compositions; the identities, number and dates of those who, thanks to a yearning for innovation, drove on to the heights of error and proclaimed themselves the introducers of what is falsely called knowledge and mercilessly attacked Christ's flock like vicious wolves; and in addition, what befell the whole Jewish people right after their plot against our Saviour; how many times and in what ways war was waged against the Divine Logos by the Gentiles during each time period; how great were the contests fought in each period on Its behalf, through blood and torture, and in addition the martyrdoms of our very own day, and the gracious and kind relief of our Saviour that came at last...[16]

The framing of divinely imposed punishment for Jews alongside Christian martyrdom and fortitude shows that this is far from a secular History in its purposes and meaning. Nonetheless there are many mundane elements to it, including the treatment of Jesus's human life. It is better researched than Eusebius's *Chronicle*, notwithstanding its use of the altered Josephus. It makes extensive use of quotations from works at Caesarea's great library, including accounts of the lifetimes of ancient writers (plucked 'like the flowers of verbal fields'[17]), and some Roman documentation as well as biblical sources.

If Eusebius's *Chronicle* and *History* intimated a favourable teleology by tracing the ascent of Christianity through Rome, the work of Augustine's student 'Paulus' Orosius (born c.380–5 CE) reflected the challenges to Christian Rome during its author's lifetime. Orosius complemented Augustine's theological treatise *Concerning the City of God against the Pagans* with a more explicitly historical tract aimed at the same target. His *Historiae adversum paganos* or (*The Seven Books of*) *History against the Pagans* served to counter the claim that Rome had fallen because it had weakened by embracing Christianity—a claim Gibbon wove into a wider explanation 1,400 years later. Orosius pointed to the extent of violence and disaster entailed in the expansion of republican Rome, arguing that it was greater than anything that had occurred since Rome's adoption of Christianity. He was especially scathing of Roman conduct in the Punic wars. At the same time the possibility of Christ's intercession, once he had revealed himself, paved the way for human improvement. More recent disasters could be rationally explained as just punishment for wrongs, but also as the result of the continued existence of pagans—and Jews. The sack of Rome was anyway mild in comparative historical terms. Alaric and his fellow 'Goths' (Visigoths) had respected the sanctity of the churches in Rome, and before long, by 417–18, so Orosius maintained, the city

---

[16] Eusebius of Caesarea, *The History of the Church: A New Translation*, ed. and trans. Jeremy M. Schott (Oakland: University of California Press, 2019), 39 (Book I, ch. 1, 1–2 of the original).

[17] Ibid. 40 (Book I, ch. 1, 4 of the original).

returned to normalcy. Above all else, this forced encounter with barbarians enabled the fulfilment of Christ's injunction (Matthew 24:14) to spread the gospel, in this case into the lands from which the barbarians came. Emblematic of the prospects for the future was the marriage in 414 between the Visigoth King Ataulf, and Galla Placidia, daughter of the former Roman Emperor Theodosius. Apparently Ataulf had thought to replace 'Romania' with 'Gothia' but had been persuaded by his wife to restore and enhance Rome.[18] Orosius's account was enduringly popular in medieval Europe perhaps because it fitted the conceits of later Christianized European 'barbarians' who formed the martial and demographic backbone of western Christendom.

Christian Philosophy of History

Orosius, Augustine, Julius Africanus, and Jerome all subscribed to some version of the theory that came to be known as *translatio imperii*, transfer of dominion. The most influential source of the idea of four successive dominant kingdoms is the dreams and visions recounted in the Old Testament book of Daniel with its apocalyptic overtones, whereby the end of the fourth kingdom brings the end of days and the advent of god's kingdom. In fact this is another motif that tied together both of the monotheistic religions with some pagan traditions. The four kingdoms idea may have originated in Persia and was certainly present in Greek tradition well before the composition of Daniel. Herodotus listed Assyria, Media, and Persia; after the successes of Alexander, Macedon or Greece could easily be added. Polybius appended fallen Carthage to the list of Assyria, Media, and Persia, which explains why Jerome thought Polybius necessary to interpret Daniel.[19] Most Jewish and Christian exegetes took Daniel to be alluding to the Babylonian empire, the Medio-Persian empire, the Greek empire, and the Roman empire. One can therefore imagine the significance attached to the seeming collapse of the Roman empire and, conversely, to Orosius's vision of Rome's endurance in a new form.

Looking forward from late antiquity and the fall of the western Roman empire, it was of vital symbolic import when the title emperor was revived in 800, when it was bestowed by Pope Leo III on the Christian Frank, Charlemagne. In 962, after a series of early tenth-century disputes in which the title was lost by the

[18] See especially David Rohrbacher, *The Historians of Late Antiquity* (London: Routledge, 2002), 135–49; also Richard Godden, 'The Medieval Sense of History', in Stephen Harris and Bryon L. Grigsby (eds.), *Misconceptions about the Middle Ages* (New York: Routledge, 2008), 204–12, here 206.
[19] George Wesley Buchanan, *The Book of Daniel* (Eugene, OR: Wipf and Stock, 1999), 68; Conrad Trieber, 'Die Idee der vier Weltreiche', *Hermes*, 27 (1892), 311–42. On Jerome and Polybius, Arnaldo Momigliano, *Essays in Ancient and Modern Historiography* (Chicago: University of Chicago Press, 2012), 79.

Carolingian line, the crown was given to the founder of the Ottonian dynasty, Otto I. The position of Emperor was constantly occupied until the Napoleonic wars and the dissolution in 1806 of what had by then long been known as the Holy Roman Empire. As the *translatio imperii* concept developed, it was contended, most influentially and perhaps originally by the chronicler and universal historian Otto of Freising (1114–58), that history's unfolding also involved a gradual east to west movement of civilization.[20] The 'evolution' from the Middle East through the eastern Mediterranean through to the Holy Roman Empire, and then by some estimates to France and then England, still has some pale echo today, in the rhetoric of manifest destiny in a certain westerly successor to Middle Eastern Christendom. By this account it is more than a literal observation that the sun rises in the east (the Orient, in German *Morgenland*, literally morning-land) and sets in the west (Occident; *Abendland*; evening-land). It is figuratively true.

Overall, Christian philosophies differed from most of their Greco-Roman predecessors in three ways. The first difference concerned the nature of divinity and the cosmos. As opposed to classical conceptions of the cosmos as possessing its own immanent purpose or teleology, in the Christian conception god was outside of the natural order entirely, though could intervene in it and even incarnate 'himself' within it. Neoplatonic metaphysics blurred this distinction somewhat with its conception of a sort of sliding scale of immaterial to material, divine to mundane.

The second difference concerned the shape or pattern of human history. If the most famous classical models depicted either constancy or a kind of cyclical or spiralling passage of rise and fall (Hesiod, Polybius, even Herodotus) or some sort of future recurrence-in-reverse-order of past events (as in Virgil[21]), then the Christian model, like the Jewish model before it, was predicated upon a more linear movement. The difference is certainly not absolute, given, on the one hand, the linear aspects of Polybius's and Livy's work, which offered an example helpful to smoothing over civilizational differences, and, on the other hand, that 'Christian time' could also be circular or liturgical, basing its calculations on both Hebrew lunar and Roman solar elements. The annual cycle of festivals was tied both to fixed points such as Christmas and the moveable feast that was Easter.[22]

The third difference between the two sets of philosophies is less a matter of pattern than of point, purpose, and meaning, as enshrined in what, for Christians,

---

[20] Samantha Zacher, *Rewriting the Old Testament in Anglo-Saxon Verse: Becoming the Chosen People* (London: Bloomsbury, 2013), 89; Marie-Dominique Chenu, *Nature, Man, and Society in the Twelfth Century* (Chicago: University of Chicago Press, 1968), 186–7, 195–6.

[21] Richard Jenkin, *Virgil's Experience: Nature and History; Times, Names and Places* (Oxford: Clarendon Press, 1998), 205.

[22] Ianziti, 'Humanism's New Science', 71–2; cf. McKitterick, 'Constructing', 104–6.

lay at the end of the historical process. Here we notice the particular continuity with the 'Old Testament' conception of History, a continuity implicit in twentieth-century historian Josef Yerushalmi's observation that while Herodotus was the 'father of History', the 'fathers of meaning in history were the Jews'.[23] Again, the difference between Judeo-Christian and Greco-Roman models is not absolute, because Christian universal History retained some of the assumptions of Platonic philosophy in its reliance on a fixed point of reference for whatever happened in the mundane realm. This very contrast with the atemporal realm concerned not just the mortal life of man but the life of the world. Time must, in other words, run out—this was the eschatological dimension of Christian thought, meaning its preoccupation with finality, with endings, and it was associated with the idea of divine interventions in history from beyond it, and figural readings. The questions of when and how time would run out, and who had authority to interpret its course, were of the essence in theological terms and increasingly, too, in terms of the church's worldly power.

Following the Protestant theologian Paul Tillich, we might divide the linear visions of Christian future-oriented history into prophetic and apocalyptic versions. Both the prophetic and apocalyptic versions had the clearest of origin stories, and were carried along by a sense of history as unfolding divine reason and improvement in consciousness of god's grace.[24] Both versions recognized *kairoi* (plural of *kairos*, meaning event-like interruptions of continuous human history around which it could be periodized) but the prophetic version was conservative in the sense that it claimed that the final major earthly event had already occurred, with Christ's advent. Following Julius Africanus, Augustine tended to the conservative stance, albeit with some particular interpretative differences. The historical process was, like the week, divided into seven stages, with earthly history comprising six, of which Augustine fancied that he lived in the last.[25] He anticipated the seventh, Sabbath stage of eternal rest, the end of time and the advent of the heavenly city that was prefaced by final judgement. Augustine's position may also be called ecclesiastical in a particular sense. *Ecclesia*, derived from the Greek *ekklesia*, the lawmaking assembly of Athenian citizens, means variously a literal church building and something like the assembly of the faithful. In practice, the claim to speak for this elect was arrogated to the church hierarchy, just as the Athenian assembly comprised a small elite. Since its authority was based on the view that history was in its final period, there was no ground for radical

---

[23] Samuel Moyn, 'Jewish and Christian Philosophy of History', in Tucker (ed.), *History and Historiography*, 427–36; analysis and quote from 428.

[24] Andrew Fear, 'Orosius and Escaping from the Dance of Doom', in Liddel and Fear (eds.), *Historiae Mundi*, 176–88.

[25] The concept of six earthly stages and the idea of four successive kingdoms, while apparently in tension, need not be so in fact. Both implied overall unity in the evolving experience of the known world, and the sixth age and fourth kingdom were of the Romano-Christian present.

critique of the order that it underpinned. The fourth-century church declared the competing apocalyptic vision a heresy.

In that apocalyptic or 'sectarian' vision, which came to have revolutionary connotations, the final event was yet to come. This vision borne by chiliasts, or millenarians as they are sometimes dubbed, entailed a utopia on earth before the end of days, a utopia of social justice in which the Holy Spirit was with everyone, and intermediary authorities unnecessary. Joachim of Fiore (c.1135–1202) was the most prominent high medieval sectarian, whose tripartite division of history characterized the Old Testament period as the age of the father and of law, i.e. the time of 'man's' obedience to the laws of God, the New Testament period as the age of the Son and of grace, with man as God's progeny, and the impending (from 1260) age of the Holy Spirit and of love, when man and God would be in direct contact. Joachim's lead was taken by a group of radical Franciscans known as the Spirituals, and his spirit endured through the Reformation and the English revolution in the bodies of Taborites, Anabaptists, and certain revolutionary peasants and Puritans.[26] Despite the anti-Judaism of chiliasts such as Tertullian, in some respects their beliefs accorded with Jewish theodicy conceived at a time of political weakness, with its concept of a coming fulfilment by revelation of what yet remained hidden.[27] Apocalypticism could in principle promote a more activist ethos than propheticism, and here too it bore some resemblance to Jewish thought as opposed to the conservative prophetic mode which could encourage a tendency simply to 'mark time' until the end.[28]

If in the vastly influential Augustinian theology the past comprised a text communicating God's message to man—with the 'Old Testament' not only being history, but also constituting 'the shadow of the future'[29]—then, at the same time, doctrinal disputes and the very refusal of history to come to an end prompted growing contestation about timings and meanings on all sides. It also prompted some to give up on the prediction game in line with Eusebius's doubts about the predictive value of chronology. In but one example from the central middle ages,

[26] Paul Tillich, *The Protestant Era* (London: Nisbet, 1955), 25–7; Marjorie Reeves, *The Influence of Prophecy in the Later Middle Ages: A Study of Joachimism* (Oxford: Oxford University Press, 2000).

[27] On Jewish theodicy, Moyn, 'Jewish and Christian Philosophy of History', 428–9.

[28] On Jewish philosophies of History, see chapter 3 of Berger and Patterson, *Jewish–Christian Dialogue*, esp. 72. Note—and here I draw also on correspondence with the author of that chapter, David Patterson—that 'Israel' means 'one who strives with God', implying interaction of the temporal and eternal realms, where one 'lives God', as it were, by one's comportment towards other people, as commanded in the Torah. The holy Jewish calendar works not from the first day of creation but the sixth, the day of the creation of the first human. In Judaism, one's acts in this world towards others are also actions towards God. And this world is a changing one, an unfolding, developing one, in much the same way relationships—among humans and with god—unfold and develop.

[29] Marc Bloch, *Feudal Society* (London: Routledge, 1989), 88–102, 'the shadow of the future' at 90; Peter Haidu, *The Subject of Violence: The Song of Roland and the Birth of the State* (Bloomington: Indiana University Press, 1993), 16.

Henry of Huntingdon's (1088–1157) epilogue to his *History of the English People* dated his present moment as the

> thirty-fifth year of the reign of the glorious and invincible Henry, king of the English. The sixty-ninth year from the arrival in England, in our own time, of the supreme Norman race. The 703rd year from the coming of the English into England. The 2,265th year from the coming of the Britons to settle in the same island. The 5,317th year from the beginning of the world. The year of grace 1135 ... We are leading our lives, or—to put it more accurately—we are holding back death, in what is the 135th year of the second millennium.

Henry reflected on the inhabitants of the corresponding year in the first millennium and then spoke to the people of the year 2135, asking them to pray for him: 'In the same way, may those who will walk with God in the fourth and fifth millennia pray and petition for you, if indeed mortal man survives so long.' Against those who would ask 'Why do you talk in this way about future millennia when the conclusion of Time will come in our own epoch and we are in daily and trembling expectation of the end of the world?' Henry provided his own reasons for the great endurance of the 'truth promised for many ages', but he also noted that 'no one knows the extent of Time except the Father of all'.[30]

The obstinate determination of time to carry on was a problem in different ways for the prophetic Histories and their apocalyptic competitors, though Histories of both sorts continued to be produced. Not long before Joachim of Fiore made his intervention, Henry of Huntingdon's younger contemporary Otto of Freising restored an eighth era to Augustine's model. Variations on both sides continued to be written for centuries, and recognition of variation gets us away from the idea of two pure and purely opposed types of theological history. Even Augustine's theology, which was on the prophetic side of the divide, concerned elements of interaction between God and man that were present in Jewish theology and in Origen's increasingly disfavoured thought. This ambiguity had connotations for understanding the course of human history as well as divine intervention. If one's metahistorical outlook was still shaped by a sense that men could influence the destiny of humankind, history was open to reinterpretation in light of earthly events as observers strained to locate the present in relation to the moment of salvation.[31] Amongst other things, this meant that 'ordinary' historians were not irrelevant to the great philosophers of the historical process.

[30] Henry of Huntingdon, *The History of the English People 1000–1154*, ed. and trans. Diana Greenway (Oxford: Oxford University Press, 2002), 119–20. See also p. 146 for the editor's note on the problematic nature of some of Henry's dating. Note too that, as the title of this edition suggests, Henry's work was revised up to 1154.

[31] On relevant renaissance and modern scholars, see e.g. Ianziti, 'Humanism's New Science', 73, especially n. 40 and Godden, 'Medieval Sense', 204. Godden also explains the diversions from

Ordinary historians did exist, if ordinary is taken to mean primarily occupied with charting specific developments as opposed to explaining humanity's entire historical course. Little ordinary History was free of elements of the thought defining the philosophies/theologies, but the proportions of the ingredients varied significantly. We also need to distinguish between the philosophies/theologies of history on one side, with their claims on overall meaning and predictability, and Histories that invoked the divine in legitimation of some discrete earthly cause or other. In the latter category fall many of the medieval chronicles that will be considered in the next chapter. The point to stress is that while historiography changed in some ways with the advent of Christianity, it nonetheless retained a number of the purposes and functions that it had possessed in classical antiquity, and multiple rationales could coexist happily within the same manuscript.

On Causation: Determinism and Human Agency

When establishing distinctions between philosophies of history and ordinary History, a fundamental question is how each relates to the question of causation and the space for genuine choice and agency on the behalf of earthly individuals or groups. As we shall now see, even if determinism is accepted at one level, it need not dictate a historical account at other levels. In any case the question of determinism and its resolutions were not new to Christianity.

The philosopher Bernard Williams shows how ancient Greek poetry and tragic plays wrestled with just these issues. Sometimes, as when in Aeschylus's *Agamemnon* the eponymous king kills his daughter to appease the goddess Artemis and so produce weather fit for him to sail to Troy, necessity may present 'itself to the agent as having produced the circumstances in which he must act' and choose. In 'other cases it shapes events without presenting itself at all. It may not be known to the agent himself or known only after the event, or, most typically, it is known before the event, but in some indeterminate, ambiguous, or riddling form, and it comes to be determinately understood only afterwards.'[32] Such a 'state of affairs is very characteristic of omens and oracles', though it is not always clear what is or

---

Augustine. Further to the 'ambivalence' of Augustinian historical time, Jacques Le Goff, *Time, Work, and Culture in the Middle Ages* (Chicago: University of Chicago Press, 1980), 32. On Otto and Augustinian theology and history, and on the relevant thought of Gerhoch of Reichersberg, see Peter Claasen, 'Res Gestae, Universal History, Apocalypse', in Robert L. Benson and Giles Constable (eds.), *Renaissance and Renewal in the Twelfth Century* (Oxford: Clarendon Press, 1985), 387–417, here 403 ff. On Otto and Joachim, Reeves, *The Influence of Prophecy*, 302. On Otto as propagandist for the empire, Chenu, *Nature*, 186–96.

[32] Also Tacitus, *Annals*, Book VI.22: 'Most men...cannot part with the belief that each person's future is fixed from his very birth', yet 'some things happen differently from what has been told through the impostures of those who describe what they do not know', which 'destroys the credit of a science, clear testimonies to which have been given by past ages and by our own'.

is not an omen. In the *Odyssey* Eurymachus observes that 'lots of birds fly around under the rays of the sun, and they don't all mean something'. An oracular vision 'is usually an indeterminate prediction, or a determinate prediction that leaves it vitally unclear by what route it will come true'. Only in some scenarios are we 'told that a certain thing will happen whatever we do, although it is just the kind of thing we might hope to avoid by action. Moreover, if efforts to avoid the outcome helped in fact to bring it about, this is a reliable sign, after the event, that the supernatural has been at work.' 'So far from fatalism ruling out all effective action of any kind, its characteristic quality, on the contrary, demands that some action and decision do have an effect. It is not that people's thoughts and decisions never make a difference, but that, with regard to the vital outcome, they make no difference in the long run.'[33]

Procopius of Caesarea (*c*.500–*c*.554), widely viewed as the greatest Byzantine historian of the sixth century, showed how Christian concepts could slip quite easily into the structural role vacated either by the will of the gods or the more arbitrary fortune of the later classical period. The weight of opinion now is that Procopius was a Christian, though some still see him as a 'pagan'. While a gulf separates the religious elements of his works and those of other late antique 'secular historians' on one hand, and the work of ecclesiastical historians of the fourth and fifth centuries from Eusebius onwards on the other hand, Procopius may have emulated the ecclesiastical historians' strategic incorporation of pagan concepts. Part of the interpretative problem is that as a classicizing writer he was constrained by a Thucydidean idiom and literary style, whilst in the socio-religious context he was shaped by orthodox Christian views with a Neoplatonic influence. So fortune, *tyche*, could sometimes appear to operate separately from God's influence and even to work counter to it. On the whole, though, *tyche* seems either to have been synonymous with divine will or to have been viewed as an intermediary servant of that will. The final conception is especially interesting, because it coheres with the orthodoxy that God does not intervene directly most of the time, and that 'his' will is mysterious. Given this mysteriousness, it was quite consistent at once to submit to divine will but also to rely on one's virtue (*Arete*) in the negotiation of things that seem to be 'up to us'.[34]

[33] Bernard Williams, *Shame and Necessity* (Berkeley: University of California Press, 2008), 139–41.
[34] On Procopius's Christianity, Averil Cameron, *Procopius and the Sixth Century* (Berkeley: University of California Press, 1985), especially 118–19 on conflicting religious and literary contexts, and also harmonization of *tyche* and Christian divinity. Anthony Kaldellis, *Procopius of Caesarea* (Philadelphia: University of Pennsylvania Press, 2004) claims paganism. See especially his pp. 217–18 on *tyche* coming 'close to usurping the place of God', on the tension between god and *tyche*, as in the claim that *tyche* 'never acts in the interests of justice'. Further to Christianity and the Neoplatonic colouring that allowed for supernatural entities below god, like demons, see Treadgold, *Byzantine Historians*, 210–11 and James Murray, 'Procopius and Boethius: Christian Philosophy in the Persian Wars', in Christopher Lillington-Martin (ed.), *Procopius of Caesarea: Literary and Historical Interpretations* (New York: Routledge, 2018), 104–19, here 106–7. Murray also includes the point about *Arete* and the things that are 'up to us'. On the blending of Christian and pagan motifs, and the

A common feature of Christian and pre-Christian scholarship was the presence of portents. Medieval chroniclers evinced the uncertainty sometimes evident in Homer about what it was that portents portended and whether they were indeed portents after all. There were similar problems of establishing the scale of time against which the meaning of portents could be gauged. In a passage that could almost have come from Bernard Williams's pen, we are told that medieval chroniclers

> hardly ever claimed personally to have foretold anything; they were simply making, *in retrospect*—a fact which they made no effort to conceal—what appeared to them or others to be reasonable connections between certain significant events. Preternatural phenomena, after all, were *evidence*—like documents, or like the personal testimony of reliable witnesses—and evidence was what a good historian was meant to be interested in.[35]

The only real generalization that can be made is that the presence and role of the divine hand was variable within works and between authors, as the following rather random assemblage of scholars attests. The *Ecclesiastical History of the English People* by the Northumbrian monk Bede (672/3–735) combines many accounts of miracles—manifestations of the divine in human affairs—with more mundane explanations of causation and accompanying human responsibility. The courtier Einhard's biography of his late patron, Charlemagne, testifies more in form and rhetorical content to Suetonius's panegyric to Augustus Caesar than to any other influence (despite claims to the effect that such influences were minimal until the Renaissance rediscovered classical literary styles). In Einhard's *Vita Caroli*, composed between 829 and 836, there is certainly no divine controller directing Charlemagne's actions.[36] This is very different to the hagiographies, which replicate in microcosm Christian philosophies of the historical process as they illustrate the saint's relationship to god.[37] William of Tyre, the historian of the First Crusade and the resulting Latin eastern kingdoms from c.1095 to 1184, drew through Einhard on Suetonius for many of his character sketches. While his subject matter and his own ecclesiastical standing meant that he gave God a commanding overall presence in history, William was parsimonious in

debt in this respect to the ecclesiastical historians of the fourth and fifth centuries, from Eusebius to Theodoret, see Chesnut, *The First Christian Histories*, 190 n. 77.

[35] Chris Given-Wilson, *Chronicles: The Writing of History in Medieval England* (London: Hambledon, 2004), 31, emphasis in original, and more generally ch. 2.

[36] Einhard and Notker the Stammerer, *Two Lives of Charlemagne*, trans., with introduction, Lewis Thorpe (London: Penguin, 1969), 19–20; Edbury and Rowe, *William of Tyre*, 43. On the claim about Renaissance historians as opposed to medieval ones, Burke, *Renaissance Sense*, 131.

[37] Peter Damian-Grint, *The New Historians of the Twelfth Century Renaissance* (Woodbridge: Boydell, 1999), 189.

identifying specific moments of divine intervention, and gave ample credit to human achievement and blunder, as in the logistical inadequacies of the crusader–Byzantine expedition to Egypt in 1169.[38] Polybius had attributed only otherwise ostensibly inexplicable things to *tyche*, and Geoffroi de Villehardouin (1160–*c*.1212), a knight in and chronicler of the Fourth Crusade, and as far as we know the author of the first historical prose narrative in French, reached for the hand of God with equal parsimony, as in accounting for military successes against all the odds.[39] The *Chronik* of the priest Jakob Twinger von Königshofen (1346–1420) contained a universal History but also a local History of Strasbourg. It addressed the 'Black Death' and the great massacres of scapegoated Jews that ensued across Europe in 1348–9. Yet rather than blaming the Jews, as would have been the easiest course religiously and politically, Jakob implied that their confessions had only come about because of torture. As to the mass immolation of Strasbourg Jewry on St Valentine's Day 1349, he offered a mundane and highly plausible explanation: 'if the feudal lords had not been in debt to them, they would not have been burned'.[40]

It is a modern stereotype that in 'pre-modern' Christendom everything from politics to historiography was subordinated to theological concerns. As applied to historiography the stereotype implies overly sharp lines of division between the historianship of classical antiquity on the one side of medieval historical writing and 'early modern' historianship on the other. It is a stereotype undermined by the historiographical evidence and by the principles of human agency and 'secondary causation' to which many theologians subscribed (p. 92). Such myths die hard, though.

[38] Edbury and Rowe, *William of Tyre*, 39–43.
[39] Jeanette Beer, *Villehardouin: Epic Historian* (Geneva: Droz, 1968), 58–65.
[40] Jakob's account excerpted and contextualized in Jacob Rader Marcus and Marc Saperstein, *The Jew in the Medieval World: A Sourcebook, 315–1791* (New York: Hebrew Union College Press, 2015), 154–7. Quote from 157.

3

The 'Middle Age'

Introduction

This chapter, like all the chapters to one degree or another, is concerned with the balance of continuity and novelty that shows how arbitrarily delineated a 'period' of history is. The balance did not just change over time but also differed between contemporaries. There was not just one medieval sense of the past or rationale for studying it, because the 'medieval mind' was no more homogeneous than that of any other time. Sometimes it is difficult to establish what is novel and what continuity, given that on the whole those in search of origins of 'the modern' have started in modernity and worked backwards. That approach can well mean stopping when some precursor or ostensible caesura is located, without going yet further back to ascertain whether the precursor had precursors or the caesura was real. Since an element of what follows is to date some developments further back it may be that this work falls into just the same trap, and ignores yet earlier developments that confound or at least heavily qualify its claims about novelty in period X. If this process of correction and qualification is taken back as far as it can go, it may be that there just is not anywhere near as much novelty—whensoever dated—as most Histories of historiography suggest, only a changing balance of emphasis distributed between strands of thought that were there in the earliest historical accounts. All we are left with are fine judgements about the relative significance of certain developments, and an awareness that old wine can appear in new stylistic skins, while the endurance of old forms can conceal novelty in content.

The first two sections of the chapter illustrate considerable continuity with elements of late antique and classical historiography in the areas of History as Identity, History as Memorialization, and History as Lesson. Remaining sections show that within historically oriented medieval thought there were three tendencies for which the medieval world is not generally renowned: the conceptualization of human cultural difference over time, with its associations of an awareness of anachronism and accompanying debates over the relevance of the past to the present; a literal sense of the past, with its associations of specificity and accuracy; and the capacity for often quite sophisticated source criticism. This is not to say that such tendencies denoted dominant trends, because dominance is relative to interest, and interests varied.

As we traverse time and place, alongside the inheritance of multiple historiographical types from classical antiquity and the patristic age, distinctions between Latin and vernacular Histories also become relevant, as do distinctions between, say, monastic Histories and urban Histories, or baronial and royal genealogies.[1] Each of these sorts of History had the potential to imply a different scale and periodization of time—a different 'temporality'—as did technical and economic developments that affected the structure of the working day and diminished the significance of the natural, seasonal cycle. Some of the Histories were also important in making claims on legitimacy, which puts them into the bracket of History as Identity. But other epistemic, didactic, and socio-political considerations come in to play in shaping the purposes and means of historical enquiry.

A section is devoted to religious hermeneutics and theological-philosophical shifts, some of which cohered with Christian History as Speculative Philosophy, some of which ran separately to it, and some of which stood in tension with it. In the eleventh–thirteenth centuries, as in, say, the sixteenth–eighteenth centuries, technical developments in source evaluation were just as important to the shaping of History as were beautifully written narratives. To the former developments, across all of that time, the clergy made a disproportionate contribution in pursuance of History as Communion, and increasingly their endeavours took account of the different contexts in which the sacred texts had been written and those in which they were read.

Like preceding chapters, this one intersperses its main thematic and empirical studies with discussion of particular conceptual points as they arise. Specifically, it addresses the question of how historical change is conceived and measured, and asks what is required for a historical account to be considered relativistic when it addresses human variety across place or time.

Annals and Ancestry

Where the ancient Greeks had chronographies, Christian civilization, like pre-Christian Rome, had annals. We are straight into muddy terminological waters because at varying points, late antique (like Cassiodorus), medieval, and modern writers have distinguished in different ways between annals, chronicles, and Histories. For some, annals and chronicles were identical, with both terms being used for long lists of yearly dates next to some of which successive, mostly anonymous scribes listed events in a *pro forma* fashion. However, especially in the

[1] For some of the new range see the early chapters of Sharon Dael, Alison Williams Lewin, and Duane J. Osheim (eds.), *Chronicling History* (Pennsylvania: Pennsylvania State University Press, 2007). For the inheritance from classical antiquity and the patristic age, Shami Ghosh, *Writing the Barbarian Past: Studies in Early Medieval Historical Narrative* (Leiden: Brill, 2016), 27–38.

first half of the second millennium CE, the kind of works we are now apt to term Histories—substantial prose accounts recounting some event or development or polity—were also apt to be called chronicles by their authors. The definitional blur is appropriate because the genres were often far from distinct, but the initial focus is on the simplest, 'ideal type' annal form.

In a faulty 'orthodox view', 'the development of early medieval historical forms [is] an evolutionary process in which the annal is forever portrayed as a primitive specimen'.[2] To be sure, at first glance one can imagine why uninitiated contemporary readers would find bewildering entries like that for 776 in the *Anglo-Saxon Chronicle*: 'Here a red sign of Christ appeared in the heavens after the sun's setting. And that year the Mercians and the inhabitants of Kent fought at Otford; and snakes were seen extraordinarily in the land of the South Saxons [Sussex].' It does seem curious that serpents and skies merit more attention than the outcome of the battle at Otford. Such laconic, apparently disconnected entries can appear even for the first year of any given annal, where one might expect some sort of introduction. These entries would fit only the most expansive definitions of a narrative and adding consecutive ones together might well not make any difference given that yet other ostensibly disconnected issues were apt to be discussed in following years, often with no attempt to refer to previous entries. Furthermore, the annal has no proper ending in the sense of a conclusion, thus no ostensible overall explanatory purpose.[3]

The first thing to be said to redress misunderstandings is that snakes and heavenly phenomena were presumed to have meaning, even if the chroniclers were not certain what the meaning was. In any case such symbols do not dominate the majority of annal entries, and are absent from many. Nor are all entries as terse as the *Anglo-Saxon Chronicle*'s for 776. Different, even if now unknown, authors within the same series could bring their own styles. Sometimes, especially when working backwards to fill in years from before the beginning of their own contributions, as was the case with all of the *Anglo-Saxon Chronicle*'s entries for before the end of the ninth century, the recorders import prose wholesale from more 'conventionally' historical accounts, or even from sagas. Eyewitness accounts are occasionally included. And manifestly some annalists refused to be constrained by the small, single-line spaces originally drawn on the manuscripts.[4] The following is from the entry for 858 in the *Annales Fuldenses*, the *Annals of Fulda*,

[2] Sarah Foot, 'Finding the Meaning of Form: Narrative in Annals and Chronicles', in Nancy Partner (ed.), *Writing Medieval History* (London: Hodder Arnold, 2005), 88–108, here 93.

[3] Discussion of the 776 entry and the annals form in Foot, 'Finding the Meaning of Form', 88 ff.; the entry itself as used here is taken from the slightly different translation in *The Anglo-Saxon Chronicles*, ed. Michael Swanton (London: Phoenix, 2000), 50.

[4] Swanton, 'Introduction' to his edition of the *Anglo-Saxon Chronicles*, pp. xi–xxxv, here pp. xvi–xviii; Cecily Clark, 'The Narrative Mode of the Anglo-Saxon Chronicle before the Conquest', in Peter Clemoes and Kathleen Hughes (eds.), *England Before the Conquest: Studies in Primary Sources Presented to Dorothy Whitelock* (Cambridge: Cambridge University Press, 1971), 215–35. For much

that concerned the Kingdom of the East Franks, one of the portions of the now-divided Carolingian empire. It concerns the background to the invasion of West Francia by East Francian King Louis the German (Louis II). I did not choose it quite at random, but nonetheless there are enough entries of similar quality that it cannot be said to be unrepresentative of the *Annals*:

In July, after the armies had been gathered together and formed up and were about to set out, suddenly the king [Louis] was burdened with a great weight of troubles. For messengers came from the west, Abbot Adalhard and Count Odo, asking him to comfort with his presence a people sore pressed and in peril. If he did not do this swiftly and they were denied hope of liberation at his hands, they would have to seek protection from the pagans with great danger to the Christian religion, since they could not get it from their lawful and orthodox lords. They declared that they could no longer bear the tyranny of Charles ['the Bald']. Anything that was left to them, after the pagans from outside had plundered, enslaved, killed and sold them off without even a show of resistance being made to them, the king destroyed from within with his evil savagery. There was now no one left in the whole people who still believed his promises or oaths, and all despaired of his good faith. Hearing these things, the king was very disturbed, and found himself in a dilemma. If he acceded to the request of the people, he would have to move against his brother, which would be wicked. If, however, he spared his brother, he would have to turn back from liberating the people in danger, which would be equally wicked. Besides this there was the not negligible consideration that the people in general would suspect that all that was being done in this matter was not done out of concern for the people's well-being but simply out of a desire to extend his kingdom, although the matter was quite different from the vulgar opinion, as all those who knew of the king's plans truly testify. Thus placed beneath a weight of cares, he at length agreed to the advice of his wise men and relied on the purity of his conscience, preferring to act for the good of many rather than in agreement with the obstinacy of one man. He yielded to the prayers of the legates and promised according to the people's wishes that with God's help he would come to those who longed for his presence.[5]

Here we have the ingredients of an explanatory narrative that is internal to, and largely independent of, the overall form of the annal as such.[6] The same applies to

the same point as regards another set, see the editor's introduction, *Annals of St-Bertin* ed. Janet Nelson (Manchester: Manchester University Press, 1991), 1–19, here 1–2.

[5] *The Annals of Fulda*, ed. Timothy Reuter (Manchester: Manchester University Press, 1992), 41–2 (year 858).

[6] The idea of narrative internal to and separable from the annal as a whole needs to be taken into account in assessing the credence of Hayden White's claim that annals can have no plot because they have no meaning-revealing ending: White, *The Content of the Form*, 20–1.

many lengthy accounts of events that occurred within the parameters of a year. The 858 narrative, written with due literary concern, tells of how a king came to a decision to move against his brother in light of weighing moral issues and likely outcomes. While Louis supposedly acts in the interests of the Christian religion and the 'good of many', there is no divine determinism and no divine intervention, only hope for God's endorsement of a decision already made, which is a common feature of such accounts.

Sometimes in the annals, as in Sulpicius Severus's hagiographic *Life of Martin* (*c*.397), we see allusions the like of which the late antique secular historians were proud: Sallust and Tacitus are invoked *en passant*.[7] However 'Christian' the author or the story, throughout the medieval world it would continue to be acceptable to invoke classical authors and events from classical antiquity, as when the twelfth-century historian of the crusades Bishop Guibert de Nogent used analogies with the Trojan War.

Further to the Roman connection, the works of Sallust, Tacitus, and Livy all corresponded more or less obviously to the year-by-year annalistic form, despite the sometime mockery of this convention by Cato and Cicero. Thus within a few pages, amidst some protracted descriptions of the events of particular years, Livy's *History of Rome from its Foundation* 2.15–2.19, moves through a number of consular years in swift succession: 'The consuls for the following year were Marcus Valerius and Publius Postumius. During the year there were successful operations against the Sabines...'; 'The consuls of the following year, Opiter Verginius and Spurius Cassius, proceeded at once to attempt the reduction of Pometia...'; 'In the following year Postumus Cominius and Titus Lartius were elected consuls'; 'Nothing of importance occurred the following year, when the consuls were Servius Sulpicius and Manlius Tullius; but the year after that, when Titus Aebutius and Caius Vetusius were in office, saw the siege of Fidenae, the capture of Crustumeria, and the secession of Praeneste from the Latins to Rome.'[8] Organizationally speaking, such was the case with very many Histories since the annalistic form had been pioneered in prose in the *Annales* of Calpurnius Piso (born *c*.180 BCE, consul 133 BCE), and some of the reasons for the organization are closely analogous to some of the Christian reasons.[9] These commonalities are especially noteworthy in anticipation of the next chapter, and the formative impact on 'Renaissance' historiography of Livy and Tacitus, which is the sort of influence so often contrasted to that of Christian chronicle.

---

[7] e.g. *Annals of Fulda*, 59 (year 869), 78 (year 875). On the literary qualities of the Annals and the absence of supernatural overtones, see Timothy Reuter's introduction to the *Annals*, 1–14. On Sulpicius Severus see *Sulpicius Severus' Vita Martini*, ed. Philip Burton (Oxford: Oxford University Press, 2017).

[8] At pp. 106–9 of de Sélincourt's translation, Livy, *The Early History of Rome*.

[9] Walter, 'Annales and Analysis', 284–7 on Roman reasons, including reference to similarities in content like mention of omens.

The formal similarities between the Roman works and Christian annals suggests that on one axis of comparison we are better off conceiving of a continuum from the sparsest annal on one end to the most obviously History-like work at the other end. For a Christian example around a mid-point on this continuum, consider but the most important single source about the Merovingian dynasty up to the 590s, the *Ten Books of Histories*, a.k.a. *The History of the Franks*, by Gregory of Tours (538–95). Its essays focus especially on the Christianization of Gaul that had begun in the third century, then the conversion to Nicene ('Catholic') Christianity of Clovis I in 496, then the history of Merovingian rule in the Frankish empire that Clovis in particular had expanded.[10] Book V is illustrative. A number of its chapters seem like random interspersions linked to others by nothing other than their simultaneity (though had they been written in classical antiquity we might describe this feature as a rhetorically attractive break from dense narrative[11]). So we have: '6. In this year [576], the year in which Sigibert died and his son Childebert began to reign, many miraculous cures were performed at the tomb of saint Martin...'; '7. I must now record the names of the men who were summoned home by God this year...'; '11. Since our God is ever willing to give glory to His bishops, I will tell you what happened this year to the Jews in Clermont-Ferrand...'. But we also have: '13. I must now return to my subject', with that subject being the major theme of the book, which concerns developments in the dynasty relating to the kings Childebert and Chilperic.[12]

Another example is Part I of the sermon *De Excidio et Conquestu Britanniae*, *The Ruin and Conquest of Britain*, written by the British monk Gildas at some point in the first half of the sixth century. This relatively short account is polemical in its denunciation of the leaders of the Britons, yet it is nonetheless 'properly historical' in its presentation of an extended account purporting to provide a literal explanation of a real set of developments. It deals with the period from the Roman conquest to the Roman departure and then the parlous state depicted in Gildas's present, as the post-Roman Britons were engaged in warfare with Picts and then the ultimately victorious Saxons.[13] Gildas was not England's Gregory, however; Bede (c.672–735) was. He completed his *Ecclesiastical History of the English People* in 731, and with it popularized the dating system of the Anno

---

[10] Gregory of Tours, *History of the Franks*, ed. Lewis Thorpe (London: Penguin, 1974).

[11] Note that while on one hand the yearly annalistic structure of (for example) Livy might mean it was easier to address the relationship between simultaneous events in multiple location (Walter, 'Annales and Analysis', 286), it can also hinder 'setting out a logical sequence of events; [Livy's] reader sometimes feels as though he were reading a serial novel by Dickens, where several groups of characters all have to have their quote in each new instalment, and must keep turning back to remind himself how things stood. Sometimes we cannot see the wood for the trees.' Betty Radice, 'Introduction' to Livy, *The War with Hannibal*, trans. Aubrey de Sélincourt (London: Penguin, 1987), 7–22, here 12–13.

[12] Walter, 'Annales and Analysis', 263–7.

[13] Gildas, *The Ruin of Britain, Fragments from Lost Letters, The Penitential, Together with the Lorica of Gildas*, ed. Hugh Williams (London: Bedford Press, 1899); for analysis, Karen George, *Gildas's De Excidio Britonum and the Early British Church* (Woodbridge: Boydell, 2009).

Domini (AD) era, which in this book and elsewhere now is called the Common
Era (CE).[14] Bede is relevant in illustrating that the same author could produce
works at different points on the History–annal continuum. He compiled a major
chronographic account, *De ratione temporum*, as well as a multi-book prose
History, much as had Eusebius, whose *Historia Ecclesiastica* inspired Bede's title,
and whose *Chronicon* had been such a major influence on the proliferation of
annals from the fourth century.

   Above all, even if elaborate prose entries did not exist, and all annals comprised
the barest and most laconic recordings, the progressivist view would still be
wrong in seeing these works as rude approximations to later, 'proper' History.
Equally, the intellectual historian Hayden White, while correct in rejecting the
view of the annals as an 'infantile' form of discourse, was incorrect, at least in one
important sense, in his alternative assessment. He came to see annals as a sort of
competitor to 'proper History', and possibly a superior one at that given that, in
his view, Histories impose a spurious continuity by their linkage of events across
time whereas the annals reflect and encourage a vision of discontinuity attendant
upon a sensibility of the sublime, with any order as there might be in the world of
events inaccessible to human cognition.[15] White's view is already weakened by
entries such as that in the Fulda annals of 858, which display 'proper' Histories,
meaning complete if brief narratives, within a particular year, but viewing the
annal form as a whole—rather than any given entry—through either the prism of
immature History or as a competitor to it in its grasp of the nature of 'reality' in
the earthly realm obscures a major function. The open-endedness of the annals is
a strong clue here, because of the association with ongoing chronology. The dates
are markers on a continuum that began with the incarnation and continues until
the end of all earthly affairs. The years are a story in themselves, as they had been
for Hecataeus, the Atthidographers, and the Roman annalists.[16] What differs is
the biblical timeline and the religious lineage, but the purpose and form of the
annal genre are similar. For the Roman annalists, the time was Roman, traceable
to Rome's deep origins, dictated to Rome's dominions and associated with successive annual magistracies who at once embodied and vouchsafed freedom for the
citizenry. The annalistic form was associated with the Roman tradition since
Fabius Pictor of writing *ab urbe condita*, from the foundation of the city, and drew
in turn on the Greek chronographic project. The name *Annals*, as in Tacitus's
work, links the historian's *libri annales* with the *tabula annalis*, annual pontifical

[14] The AD system was invented by Dionysius Exiguus (*c.*470–544) though Eusebius's chronologies
were an important step in that direction. Note that Dionysius used it to identify Easters in Easter
tables. One of the tributary origins of the Christian annals was probably marginal notes in Easter tables,
which helps explain why the annal entries were often small, especially early on.
[15] White, *Content of the Form*, chs. 1–3, 'infantile' at 9.
[16] This being a major argument of Foot, 'Finding the Meaning of Form'.

lists of important events 'attested for pre-literary sacred record keeping'.[17] For the Christians Christ's birth is one obvious point of originary interest, the creation another. Thus, differing slightly from Julius Africanus's estimates, the 6 BCE entry of the *Anglo-Saxon Chronicle* records that 5,200 years have passed since the beginning of the world, and occasionally thereafter the reader is reminded of the current tally.

Annals also had a political role for Christian rulers, as they did for Rome. They provided historical or historio-religious legitimation, with genealogical and figural functions intertwined.[18] Wars and the deaths of kings and bishops are a regular feature. The marking of holy days gives a sense of reassuring continuity alongside linear unfolding (much the same had been achieved in Roman annals by recounting rituals like consular inauguration, the priests' work of expiation, and sacrifices[19]), and serves to indicate the piety of favoured subjects, namely royal families. The *Royal Frankish Annals* of 741–829—predecessor of the *Annals of Fulda*, though covering the whole of the Carolingian empire—constitute a story of the Frankish people since the death of Charles Martel, as embodied in the Carolingian dynasty. It is these rulers and their people who become associated with the temporal framework measured from the incarnation, and thus associated with God's design.[20]

The precise proportions of political and religious legitimation could vary. If the *Royal Frankish Annals* constitute an especially clear-cut example of annal-writing as a vehicle for expressions of the identity of a 'national' people, it is a matter of debate as to the role of the *Anglo-Saxon Chronicle* vis-à-vis the *Angelcynn*, i.e. the English. The *Anglo-Saxon Chronicle* was begun in the early 890s but recorded back to 60 BCE and the advent of the Romans, and continued to be updated in one version well into the twelfth century. Probably initiated under the auspices of

[17] On which, including the quotation, see Timpe, '*Memoria* and Historiography in Rome', 163–4. Walter, 'Annales and Analysis', 286–7 considers additional factors, including the relation to consular years and elections. (Note that even under the principate elections were still held for the key magistracies.) Moreover while Tacitus wrote with reference to imperial reigns, he also used consular years—ibid. 284–5.

[18] On the figural element of the *History of the Franks*, Martin Heinzelmann, *Gregory of Tours: History and Society in the Sixth Century* (Cambridge: Cambridge University Press, 2001).

[19] Walter, 'Annales and Analysis', 286.

[20] For such reasons one needs to take issue with White (*Content of the Form*, 8) when he writes of the *Anni Domini* in the left-hand column of most annals that 'We should not too quickly refer the meaning of the text to the mythic framework it invokes by designating the "years" as being "of the Lord", for these "years" have a regularity that the Christian mythos, with its hypotactical ordering of the events it comprises (Creation, Fall, Incarnation, Resurrection, Second Coming'), does not possess. The regularity of the calendar signals the "realism" of the account, its intention to deal in real rather than imaginary events. The calendar locates events, not in the time of eternity [what, one asks of the point of departure implicit in '*Anno Domini*'?], not in *kairotic* time, but in chronological time, in time as it is humanly experienced.' To reiterate the point of the main text here and of Foot, 'Finding the Meaning of Form', what is inconvenient for White's argument is the way that earthly political concerns can fuse with concerns about divine legitimation through the association of temporal and *kairotic* time.

Alfred the Great, it was the first effectively continuous History in the vernacular (Old English) of any European population group. In one school of thought the *Chronicle* illustrated the agenda of unifying Anglo-Saxon 'England' out of its diverse kingdoms.[21] The alternative view is that while the *Chronicle* was clearly keen on showing the triumph of the West Saxon dynasty from which Alfred came, it was less concerned with promoting a vision of pan-English unity.[22] If the latter view is correct then it highlights a tension with Bede's eighth-century vision of a unified England. Now for Bede, properly observed Christianity was the force that would unify all the inhabitants of the island.[23] Indeed since his loyalties finally lay with Rome, the real significance of the deeds of kings was tied up with conversion to and maintenance of a disciplined Roman Christianity. For kings themselves, and for many of their chroniclers, the dictates of the Church were not insignificant but they were not the only major considerations. Looking forwards, for twelfth-century historians like Henry of Huntingdon, William of Malmesbury, and Geoffrey of Monmouth, the kings were at the centre of the picture as the genealogical, even genetic thread linking the state through history.[24]

When thinking of biological connections, we should not allow accounts of the modern construction of nationhood and the modern provenance of biological racism to blind us to earlier iterations of nation and race: religious and civilizational genealogies might well be fused with kinship associations of a more genetic type. *Origines gentium*, tales of the foundational moment of discrete groups, were known in post-Roman Europe from the sixth century at the latest. Along with the Old Testament, which was a repository of inspiration in early medieval Europe given the story of the flight of the tribes of Israel from Egypt, the fall of Troy inspired tales of ethnogenesis as the result of the defeat and dispersal of a people, with the hope of redemptive triumph as a new Rome.[25] More than this, Trojan antecedence was claimed for some non-Roman peoples,[26] and would continue to be in certain circles for the best part of a thousand years

[21] Foot, 'Finding the Meaning of Form', 96–102; Sarah Foot, 'The Making of *Angelcynn*: English Identity before the Norman Conquest', *Transactions of the Royal Historical Society*, 6th ser. 6 (1996), 25–49. Swanton, 'Introduction', p. xx. Further on the issue of national consciousness, Patrick Wormald, 'Engla Lond: The Making of an Allegiance', *Journal of Historical Sociology*, 7:1 (1994), 1–24.

[22] The most substantial critique of the *Angelcynn* argument is George Molyneaux, *The Formation of the English Kingdom in the Tenth Century* (Oxford: Oxford University 2015), ch. 5, esp. pp. 201–6, with a salient contrast on p. 206 to the *Royal Frankish Annals*.

[23] Bede, *Ecclesiastical History of the English People*, ed. Leo Sherley-Price and D. H. Farmer (London: Penguin, 1990). On unity from diversity, see Farmer's introduction, 19–38, here 27; Foot, 'Finding the Meaning', 100–1.

[24] Given-Wilson, *Chronicles*, 163–4.

[25] Len Scales, 'Central and Late Medieval Europe', in Donald Bloxham and A. Dirk Moses (eds.), *The Oxford Handbook of Genocide Studies* (Oxford: Oxford University Press, 2010), 280–303, here 284–5; Charles F. Briggs, *The Body Broken: Medieval Europe, 1300–1520* (London: Routledge 2011), 284; Joseph H. Lynch and Phillip C. Adamo, *The Medieval Church* (London: Routledge, 2014), 206–7.

[26] Rosamond McKitterick, *History and Memory in the Carolingian World* (Cambridge: Cambridge University Press, 2004), 7–8, 208–9; Gabrielle M. Spiegel, *The Past as Text: The Theory and Practice of Medieval Historiography* (Baltimore: Johns Hopkins University Press, 1997), 96–7, 106.

thereafter. Important in the Frankish embrace of the Trojan myth was quite widespread embrace of the *Chronicle of Fredegar*, which did for a people what the Atthidographers did for cities.

As is common in the genre, the Fredegar chronicle (or annal, depending on precise definition) accepted and continued earlier chronicles, whose authors had done the same in their turn. Eusebius had been translated and continued by Jerome, who was built on by Hydatius and Gregory, who were then incorporated alongside other earlier chronicles into the *Chronicle of Fredegar*. Just as interesting as the entries after Gregory's account and up to 642 are the 'interpolations' or additions. In this case the additions made to the incorporated chronicles of the *Liber Generationis*, Jerome, and Hydatius are unsourced. They served to fuse Judeo-Christian and classical-Trojan ancestry, whereas Gregory had only established the former lineage. The Trojan King Priam is depicted as the first king of the Franks, himself descended from one of Noah's three sons, Japeth. The Trojans supposedly split into two major groups of which one, the Frigii, under King Francio, ended up between the Rhine and the Danube, where, along with the Saxons, they provided the only successful resistance against the Romans. Ultimately the author of the additions established the harmony of kinship between Franks and Latins by claiming Friga, of Priam's house, as the brother of Aeneas. Thus the Franks gained historical independence amongst, but also connection to, the other major influences in Christendom, namely the Papacy and Byzantium. Modifications to established chronicle narratives build a 'bridge between universal history into which Frankish matter is interpolated and Frankish history into which universal matter is interpolated'. The ego of the Franks was stroked. 'Fredegar' promoted the *gens Francorum*, via its elite, to the status of binding element in the Merovingian *regnum* of the time, bringing together political and ethnic considerations.[27]

Exemplarity, Allegory, and the Presence of the Past

Complex prose rarely falling into one genre alone, many of the Histories with a genealogical identity function also had an exemplary purpose. In the use of

---

[27] J. M. Wallace-Hadrill, 'Fredegar and the History of France', *Bulletin of the John Rylands Library*, 40 (1958), 527–50, quote from 539; 97–114; Ghosh, *Writing the Barbarian Past*, 97–114; Robert Flierman, *Saxon Identities*, AD 150–900 (London: Bloomsbury, 2017), 74–5. For an extensive recent treatment of Fredegar in connection with the universal History and ethnicity questions, see Helmut Reimitz, *History, Frankish Identity and the Framing of Western Ethnicity* (Cambridge: Cambridge University Press, 2015), ch. 7, especially p. 174 to the effect that the Fredegar chroniclers 'were aiming to underscore the fact that the name of the Franks did not represent a local identity or a single region at the edge of the *regnum*. It stands for the governing class, which from the start had preserved the destiny and continuity of the gens Francorum and bound the different areas and populations of this *regnum* to each other.'

History as Lesson we see significant continuity in historians' practices across the classical–Christian divide. Gregory opened the *History of the Franks* with the resonant reflection that 'many things keep happening, some of them good, some of them bad'.[28] In 844 Lupus of Ferrières, to whom Einhard had devoted one of his works, enjoined Charles the Bald, king of the west Franks, to read about the Roman emperors in order to learn 'what you should imitate or what you should avoid'.[29] In the century after Gregory, Bede dispatched a copy of his *Ecclesiastical History* to King Ceolwulf with the reflection: 'Should history tell of good men and their good estate, the thoughtful listener is spurred on to imitate the good; should it record the evil ends of wicked men, no less effectually the devout and earnest listener or reader is kindled to eschew what is harmful and perverse'.[30] Four hundred years later, Henry of Huntingdon's *Historia Anglorum* similarly averred that 'The recorded deeds of all peoples and nations, which are the very judgements of God, clemency, generosity, honesty, caution, and the like, and their opposites, not only provoke men of the spirit to what is good and deter then from evil, but even encourage worldly men to good deeds and reduce their wickedness'. Henry also drew on the classical tradition, citing Horace's praise of Homer's work for its superiority over the abstruse tomes of systematic philosophers.

> Whereas Crantor and Chrysippus sweated to produce many volumes of moral philosophy, Homer showed, as clearly as in a mirror, the prudence of Ulysses, the fortitude of Agamemnon, the temperance of Nestor, and the justice of Menelaus, and on the other hand, the imprudence of Ajax, the feebleness of Priam, the intemperateness of Achilles, and the injustice of Paris.[31]

And so on and so forth, through the 'middle ages' and beyond. Writing at the close of a fourteenth century riven with Anglo-French conflict, Jean Froissart provided the standard justification for his endeavour: the hope 'that the honourable enterprises, noble adventures and deeds of arms which took place during the wars waged by France and England should be fittingly related and preserved for posterity, so that brave men should be inspired thereby to follow such examples'.[32]

With the continued deployment of History as Lesson came the familiar range of levels of truth and meaning:

> There is no doubt that chroniclers, who included numerous accounts of military engagements in their works, were concerned to present the 'facts' of those

---

[28] Gregory of Tours, *History of the Franks*, 63.
[29] McKitterick, *Carolingian World*, 208; Einhard and Notker the Stammerer, *Two Lives of Charlemagne*, 15.
[30] Bede, *The Ecclesiastical History of the English People* (Oxford: Oxford University Press, 1999), 3.
[31] Henry of Huntingdon, *The History of the English People 1000–1154*, prologue, 3–4.
[32] Jean Froissart, *Chronicles*, ed. Geoffrey Brereton (London: Penguin, 1978), 37.

engagements—numbers on each side, the principal manoeuvres and tactical decisions, captures, casualties, terrain and so forth—as correctly as they could. There is, however, a troubling sameness about many of their descriptions… Victorious armies, for example, are usually shown maintaining strict discipline on their way to battle, arriving in good order under unified and purposeful command, devoutly committing their cause to the arbitration of God…Armies about to be vanquished, on the other hand, behave in an ill-disciplined fashion before the battle (they pillage the countryside, seize provisions without payment, commit atrocities), arrive at the battlefield in confusion, and suffer from irresolution and divisions between their leaders.[33]

The words are those of historian Chris Given-Wilson. His work on medieval chronicles makes important contrasts between what medieval chroniclers did and modern conceptions of History. Accordingly, implied in the second half of Given-Wilson's passage is a moral explanation for success, which contains a 'universal truth' about fighting battles as much as a point about any particular battle. The 'classical' concept of truth as plausibility (see p. 27) was also deployed in medieval chronicles, as for example by the Thucydidean use of invented speeches.[34]

Medieval historians also followed their classical forebears in parading their qualifications as authorities about the past in order to impart the quality of trustworthiness to their accounts. Sometimes this was achieved by the rhetorical device of admitting ignorance. Eyewitness testimony—of the author or suitably accredited informants—remained of great importance throughout the middle ages, though the bureaucratic revolution of the central middle ages provided a larger supply of written records than hitherto and produced a number of historians who inserted reference to documentary sources as well as other Histories into their text. A position of giving credence to earlier accounts appears to have been the default one, as with Herodotus vis-à-vis orally transmitted memory, and sometimes truth was actually conceived as the faithfulness of one text to another, earlier one.[35]

Significant continuity across the centuries can also be traced in the sex of most historians and the sexed and gendered nature of their subject matter. Nevertheless, beside wealthy women patrons of male historians there were a few renowned female scholars like the Ottonian Hrotsvitha of Gandersheim (c.935–c.1002), author of a History of the Ottonian dynasty up to 965 and a History of the Gandersheim house monastery, and, assuming she actually wrote what is attributed to her, the Byzantine Anna Komnēnē (1083–1153).[36] Christine de Pizan's

---

[33] Given-Wilson, *Chronicles*, 2.   [34] Ibid., ch. 1; Damian-Grint, *New Historians*, 37.

[35] Given-Wilson, *Chronicles*, ch. 1; Damian-Grint, *New Historians*, 197–200 and *passim* on the source-references of the twelfth-century Anglo-Norman *estoires*.

[36] Elisabeth van Houts, 'Women and the Writing of History in the Early Middle Ages: The Case of Abbess Matilda of Essen and Aethelweard', *Early Medieval Europe*, 1 (1992), 53–68; van Houts (ed.), *Medieval Memories: Men, Women and the Past, 700–1300* (New York: Longman, 2001); Janet L. Nelson,

Book of the City of Ladies (1405), a study of exemplary female lives drawn from across time and from myth, was in its subject-matter an exception to a pretty firm rule, though not unprecedented: she took inspiration from Giovanni Boccaccio's *Concerning Famous Women* (composed 1361–2), most of whose biographical subjects came from the history and mythology of classical antiquity. Meanwhile even if chroniclers were reluctant to identify them as eyewitness informants, it is probable that not a few women nonetheless featured in that capacity.[37]

Of broader sociological import in the relationship between present and past was the involvement of many more women and girls in a range of day-to-day memorial practices, such as preserving family genealogical information or participating in communal exercises, like the ninth-century dancers of the *farandole* to celebrate the *gesta* of the likes of King Clothar II and Bishop Faro of Meaux two centuries earlier.[38] In Carolingian society as in others, women, especially of the elite, were not merely supposed to pass on instruction but were also expected to embody moral examples in their everyday lives, partly because of gendered doctrines stemming from Jerome, partly because they had wider access than did clerics to other women, children, and social 'inferiors'. At once this role enhanced their social significance and opened them further to criticism should they be perceived to fall short.[39]

Illiterate populaces as a whole were likely to encounter some version of the past via the compendia of *exempla* used for sermons by preachers who realized the efficacy of philosophy by example.[40] For the commonality, the orally transmitted epics also provided a storehouse of metaphors just as well stocked as the scriptures and the hagiographies of saintly lives. The composition of these popular *chansons de geste* was not always insulated from the officially sanctioned charters and chronicles.[41]

As for the literate orders, while a healthy circulation of undetected documentary forgeries points to the limits of a certain sort of critical concern, this does not

---

The Frankish World, 750–900 (London: Hambledon Press, 1996), ch. 11. In terms of focus on women in historically minded works, it is interesting that pictorial miniatures in a number of late medieval vernacularizations of the *Aeneid* depict women—Dido, Camilla—in ways that challenge conventional gender roles: Christopher Baswell, *Virgil in Medieval England* (Cambridge: Cambridge University Press, 1995), 25–8.

[37] Given-Wilson, *Chronicles*, 12–13.
[38] Nelson, *Frankish World*, 185; more generally Elisabeth van Houts, *Memory and Gender in Medieval Europe, 900–1200* (London: Palgrave, 1999).
[39] Valerie L. Garver, *Women and Aristocratic Culture in the Carolingian World* (New York: Cornell, 2009), esp. ch. 3.
[40] See generally on religious literature and exemplarity Jean Thiébaut Welter, *L'Exemplum dans la littérature religieuse et didactique du moyen âge* (Paris: Occitania E. H. Guitard, 1927). Apparently this exemplary literature reached its peak in the thirteenth century, partly because of its use by mendicants.
[41] Bloch, *Feudal Society*, 88–102. On the historical references and variable historical quality of the chansons, see Joseph Duggan, 'Medieval Epic and History in the Romance Languages', in Konstan and Raaflaub (eds.), *Epic and History*, 280–92.

detract from the historically oriented belief system that the stories sustained. Moreover there is evidence that when it really mattered to them, clerics were competent in distinguishing forgeries, just as they were in, for instance, question-ing the Frankish myth of Trojan antecedence or rejecting stories about the legend-ary Merlin.[42] Geoffrey of Monmouth's grand fantasy *Historia Regum Britannie* (1136), *History of the Kings of Britain*, which was replete with tales of Merlin, Kings Arthur and Lear, and 'Old King Cole', back to the arrival of the mythical Trojan Brutus in the twelfth century BCE, met with specialist scepticism within a few decades. Nonetheless, its main lines of interpretation were absorbed into col-lective historical memory and resurfaced in subsequent Histories, partly because it provided a useful origin story and chimed with general assumptions about the origins of peoples in principle, partly because it fitted with prevailing literary fashion and helped idealize the present in the same manner as it did the past.[43]

Especially when it came to allegorical or analogical reading, it was not neces-sarily a question of medieval people's lacking a sense of the past's difference, or being blind to matters of source criticism. Rather, such interpretative practices were oriented to the historian's and reader's self-understanding as actors in the present. The point of allegorical reading was to reveal the eternal or necessary beneath the chaff of the contingent; Aristotle's criticism of History as opposed to poetry was thereby rebutted. The imagery is that of the linguist rendering some-thing from a foreign or archaic idiom into the language of the present in order to preserve what merited preservation. Such a conception still had its adherents until at least into the eighteenth century, with the philosopher-historian Henry St John, Viscount Bolingbroke (1678–1751) citing the poet Nicolas Boileau-Despréaux (1636–1711) on the art of translation:

> To translate servilely into modern language an ancient author phrase by phrase, and word by word, is preposterous: nothing can be more unlike the original than such a copy. It is not to shew, it is to disguise the author...A good writer...will jouster contre l'original, rather imitate than translate, and rather emulate than imitate: he will translate the sense and spirit of the original into his own work, and will endeavour to write as the ancient author would have wrote, had he writ in the same language.[44]

By definition of translation between idioms, it was impossible to separate the his-torical from the rhetorical. The importance of rhetoric lay not just in how the past was contemplated, but in judgements about what was worth contemplating, and

---

[42] McKitterick, *Carolingian World*, 25, 210. On forgery detection and myth criticism, Andrew Jotischky, *The Carmelites and Antiquity: Mendicants and their Pasts in the Middle Ages* (Oxford: Oxford University Press, 2002), 319–20; Damian-Grint, *New Historians*, 206.

[43] Given-Wilson, *Chronicles*, 3–6; Damian-Grint, *New Historians*, 195–6.

[44] Henry St John, Lord Viscount Bolingbroke, *Letters on the Study and Use of History* (London: T. Cadell, 1779), 51.

what the rewards of contemplation were. Equally relevant, therefore, is the Aristotelian–Ciceronian conception of topics, *topoi*, literary formulae that present the subject matter in the form of 'arguments that can be transferred to many cases'. The topical framing of historical examples must promote the capacity for active reflection rather than entailing a level of literalist contextualization that renders the examples non-transferable, rote-learned instances.[45] *Inventiones* were frequently oriented to highlighting the revealed truths of Christianity rather than to establishing the truths of physical reality present or past. This was a choice, ideological and practical, not a poverty of faculty. Sometimes the two sorts of truth-seeking ran in parallel. When push came to shove the allegorical truth was generally more important than the other, though in the coming centuries that balance would shift gradually.[46] The historians engaged in the exercise were in their own minds exponents of the true verisimilar (see p. 26).

In her landmark work *Ancient and Medieval Memories* the medievalist Janet Coleman claims that a difference between medieval and renaissance conceptions of history on one hand and modern conceptions on the other is that moderns see the past as 'over and done with'.[47] Whether she is correct about moderns is a matter for later on, and it depends on the sense in which the claim is interpreted. As for medievals, we can certainly see a replication of Orosius's achievement in reconciling secular shifts with some sense of continuity. Hans-Werner Goetz's work on 'historical consciousness' in the high middle ages and Bernard Guenée's broader survey recount the ongoing depiction of a past in which mutability was reconciled with stability. In the Jena manuscript of Otto of Freising's chronicle, for instance, the Roman Augustus, the Frankish Charlemagne, and the Germanic Otto I are depicted in chronological order but the reassuring continuity of tradition—the genealogical element that complements the figural element—is denoted by similarities in their garb and posture, much in the way that in the *Grandes Chroniques de France*[48] the monks of Saint-Denis mirrored the monarchical succession inscribed in the sculptures on the western face of Notre Dame. On that face, the ancient Hebrew kings were dressed in the clothes of the Capetian monarchs.[49]

---

[45] Wendy Olmstead, *Rhetoric: An Historical Introduction* (Oxford: Blackwell, 2006), 54–5; on the medieval inheritance of the classical device of *topoi*, see Justin Lake (ed.), *Prologues to Ancient and Medieval History: A Reader* (Toronto: University of Toronto Press, 2013), pp. xiii–xiv.

[46] Monika Otter, *Inventiones: Fiction and Referentiality in Twelfth-Century English Historical Writing* (Chapel Hill: University of North Carolina Press, 1996).

[47] Janet Coleman, *Ancient and Medieval Memories: Studies in the Reconstruction of the Past* (Cambridge: Cambridge University Press, 2005), 582.

[48] These were vernacular translations of the chronicles produced in Latin by the monks of Saint-Denis. In the thirteenth century the monks were official historiographers to the French monarchy.

[49] Hans-Werner Goetz, *Geschichtsschreibung und Geschichtsbewußtsein im hohen Mittelalter* (Berlin: Orbis mediaevalis, 1999); cf. Bernard Guenée, *Histoire et culture historique dans l'Occident médiéval* (Paris: Aubier Montaigne, 1980), especially ch. 8. See also Hans-Werner Goetz, *Die Geschichtstheologie des Orosius* (Darmstadt: Wissenschaftliche Buchgesellschaft, 1980). On Notre Dame and the *Grandes Chroniques* see Spiegel, *The Past as Text*, 105–7.

The more cyclical, liturgical aspects of medieval historical consciousness were, as Gabriel Spiegel describes, concerned with resurrecting select parts of the past rather than merely representing it.[50] We can identify two senses of liturgical, each derivable from the root of 'communion', and each thus relevant to History as Communion. Liturgical means forging a vertical connection with the divine, or the cosmic order; it also means establishing a horizontal community of values with other liturgists. In a modern idiom, we might also contrast a professional academic historiography with 'heritage', whose job, in the vein of the second sort of liturgical History, is to keep some version of the past alive for the community that 'owns' it, as when one historian of collective memory describes museums as cathedrals for an age of many religions and none.[51] This sort of liturgical History fits the definition of a very important strand of History as Identity.

Periodization and the Conceptualization of Change

We owe the stereotype of the 'middle ages', as we owe the epithet itself, to the 'Renaissance', which was in turn a term coined by Jules Michelet in the nineteenth century that captured the sense among sixteenth-century Italians of there having been in recent centuries a *rinascita* or rebirth of learning and artistic skill that harked back to the classical past. Among the motivations of a few notable inhabitants of the fourteenth and fifteenth centuries to reinvent their present we might count disillusion in the face of protracted warfare, long-term conflict between papacy and Holy Roman empire, papal scandal and the Great Schism of 1378–1417, and the Black Death—a series of crises whose cumulative force ultimately exceeded the cohesive power of the metaphor of the body of Christ that notionally held Christendom together. 'Italian' states in particular were set at odds from the twelfth century in the battle between Guelphs and Ghibellines and competing factions within those states.

An especially famous expression of disaffection with elements of the prevailing culture was the 'Letter to Posterity' of Boccaccio's older contemporary Petrarch (1304–74), who has variously been dubbed 'the first modern man of letters', 'the first modern writer of autobiography', and, almost inevitably, 'the first modern man'. He wrote:

> Among the many subjects which interested me, I dwelt especially upon antiquity, for our own age has always repelled me, so that, had it not been for the love of those dear to me, I should have preferred to have been born in any other period

---

[50] Ibid.184.
[51] Jay Winter, 'Museums and the Representation of War', *Museum and Society*, 10:3 (2012), 150–63. On heritage see Lowenthal, *The Past is a Foreign Country* and *The Heritage Crusade*.

than our own. In order to forget my own time, I have constantly striven to place myself in spirit in other ages, and consequently I delighted in history.

Petrarch has also been called the first modern tourist, which may allude to the capacity to objectify his world about him as if a tourist rather than an indigene. It also concerns his trading in the metaphorical as well as literal dimensions of travel, as a wide-ranging wanderer in time and space.[52] But whatever the innovations of Renaissance humanism, European self-reflection was aided by events that can only be excluded from the definition of 'medieval' by sleight of hand.

Let us mention the 'twelfth-century Renaissance', of which the monastic 'reformation' of that century was an integral part, and before that the 'Carolingian renaissance' of the eighth and ninth centuries. As the Carolingian renaissance had synthesized aspects of Roman, Christian, and Germanic tradition for its own purposes, restored Latin as a language of literature, and preserved much Roman prose and poetry in its copying-schools, so the twelfth-century Renaissance leant on the recovery of more of Aristotle's oeuvre, as well as borrowings from Arabic mathematics, medicine, and astronomy with their Platonic influence. Under some of these influences nature could be 'read' as a self-sufficient, seamless 'text' of physical revelation with its own internal, horizontal relations, as opposed or in addition to the vertical relations stressed in the patristic approach as it linked natural entities to higher spiritual truths.[53]

The sense of secular periodization that broke up the flow of the chronicler's continuous time is famously attributed to the post-Petrarchian Renaissance,[54] though the idea of a 'middle age' (*medium aevum*, *Mittelalter*) may have been popularized more by sixteenth-century Lutherans, especially Philip Melanchthon, to stigmatize the period between their present and a purer, pre-medieval Christianity, thereby distinguishing between the papacy that they disliked and the early church.[55] Whatever the novelty of this particular periodization, tripartite

[52] Petrarch passage from Kenneth R. Bartlett (ed.), *The Civilization of the Italian Renaissance: A Sourcebook* (Toronto: University of Toronto Press, 2011), 28. For the epithets, and an effective endorsement of them, see Arthur Augustus Tilley, *The Dawn of the French Renaissance* (Cambridge: Cambridge University Press, 1968), 4. For the tourism issue, see Henk van Oort, *The Inner Rainbow: An Illustrated History of Human Consciousness* (Sussex: Temple Lodge, 2014), 56–7 and Theodore J. Cachey, Jr, 'Petrarchan Cartographic Writing', in Stephen Gersh and Bert Roest (eds.), *Medieval and Renaissance Humanism: Rhetoric, Representation and Reform* (Leiden: Brill, 2003), 73–92, here 74 ff.

[53] Charles Homer Haskins, *The Renaissance of the Twelfth Century* (Cambridge, MA: Harvard University Press, 1927). On the hermeneutic implications, Peter Harrison, *The Bible, Protestantism, and the Rise of Natural Science* (Cambridge: Cambridge University Press, 1998). See also the useful review of this book by James Altena, 'Secular Hermeneutics', *Touchstone* 14:6 (2001), 50–5, some of which I have paraphrased here.

[54] From at least Wallace K. Ferguson, *The Renaissance in Historical Thought* (New York: Houghton Mifflin, 1948) onwards.

[55] Harold J. Berman, *Law and Revolution II: The Impact of the Protestant Reformations on the Western Legal Tradition* (Cambridge, MA: Belknap Press, 2003), 22.

divisions were scarcely unknown to a civilization whose dominant religion was based on a threefold conception of the divine: see the work of Joachim of Fiore discussed previously (p. 56). Putting aside the periodizations stemming from the book of Daniel, the Bible alludes to three periods in the existence of humankind: before the Flood; from then until Christ's first coming; and from that point to Christ's second coming.[56] The twelfth-century Renaissance brought its own intimations of periodization, notably in the changing valence of a distinction—again, not a distinction original to that period—between 'ancients' and 'moderns'.

Perhaps the earliest recorded distinction between *antiqui* and *moderni* was made by Cassiodorus under Ostrogothic rule, but since his Byzantine contemporary the historian Procopius made a similar one we can assume it had wider purchase. It may be that only the arbitrariness of documentary survival prevents us from locating an earlier iteration. The following excerpt from Procopius, who accompanied the Byzantine general Belisarius on various campaigns in former imperial provinces, including against the Ostrogoths in Italy (535–54), is especially noteworthy for its insistence on the superiority of some elements of the present, given the author's general veneration of the classical past. From the prologue to his *History of the Wars*:

It will be evident that no more important or mightier deeds are to be found in history than those which have been enacted in these wars,—provided one wishes to base his judgement on the truth. For in them more remarkable feats have been performed than in any other wars with which we are acquainted; unless, indeed, any reader of this narrative should give the place of honour to antiquity, and consider contemporary achievements unworthy to be counted remarkable. There are those, for example, who call the soldiers of the present day 'bowmen,' while to those of the most ancient times they wish to attribute such lofty terms as 'hand-to-hand fighters,' 'shield-men,' and other names of that sort; and they think that the valour of those times has by no means survived to the present,—an opinion which is at once careless and wholly remote from actual experience of these matters. For the thought has never occurred to them that, as regards the Homeric bowmen who had the misfortune to be ridiculed by this term derived from their art, they were neither carried by horse nor protected by spear or shield. In fact there was no protection at all for their bodies; they entered battle on foot, and were compelled to conceal themselves, either singling out the shield of some comrade, or seeking safety behind a tombstone on a mound, from which position they could neither save themselves in case of rout, nor fall upon a flying foe. Least of all could they participate in a decisive struggle in the open, but they always seemed to be stealing something which belonged to the men

---

[56] The concept of the 'three ages of man' preceded Christianity.

who were engaged in the struggle. And apart from this they were so indifferent in their practice of archery that they drew the bowstring only to the breast, so that the missile sent forth was naturally impotent and harmless to those whom it hit. Such, it is evident, was the archery of the past. But the bowmen of the present time go into battle wearing corselets and fitted out with greaves which extend up to the knee. From the right side hang their arrows, from the other the sword. And there are some who have a spear also attached to them and, at the shoulders, a sort of small shield without a grip, such as to cover the region of the face and neck. They are expert horsemen, and are able without difficulty to direct their bows to either side while riding at full speed, and to shoot an opponent whether in pursuit or in flight. They draw the bowstring along by the forehead about opposite the right ear, thereby charging the arrow with such an impetus as to kill whoever stands in the way, shield and corselet alike having no power to check its force. Still there are those who take into consideration none of these things, who reverence and worship the ancient times, and give no credit to modern improvements.[57]

So much for the elucidation of change via content; Procopius's work made the same point by form, in much the same way as earlier Atticists like Cassius Dio. Procopius was careful not to confuse with terms like *ekklesia*, given its earlier Athenian meaning, when he was talking about a Christian church building. Ironically, here, his use of the antiquated 'high style' of Attic Greek, as exemplified in Thucydides, at once put him at a disadvantage in terms of communicating with a contemporary audience with a somewhat differing grammar and vocabulary, and kept him and the audience attuned to the fact of the changing referents of certain linguistic signifiers by a forced self-distancing from the present. So we have 'one of the priests whom they call "bishops"', and so forth. While it modified itself somewhat, this tradition of writing endured to the very end of the Byzantine empire.[58]

Procopius's content and form pose problems for a common modern conception of the medieval sense of the past, a conception illustrated by Reinhard Koselleck's reflections on Albrecht Altdorfer's 1529 painting *Alexanderschlacht*, which depicted the Battle of Issus in 333 BCE. Altdorfer had tried scrupulously to obtain information as to the number of combatants, dead, and prisoners. Nonetheless, the armies could be taken for medieval fighters, with the Persians looking like the Ottoman forces who had besieged Vienna in the year of the picture's painting. Koselleck holds these features to support his argument that in the middle ages the 'present and the past were enclosed within a common historical

---

[57] Procopius, *History of the Wars*, trans. H. B. Dewing (London: Heinemann, 1914), I. i. 6–17.
[58] Ibid. II. ix.14; J. A. S. Evans, 'The Attitudes of the Secular Historians of the Age of Justinian towards the Classical Past', *Traditio* 32 (1976), 353–8, here 357.

plane', that temporal 'distance was not more or less arbitrarily eliminated; it was not, as such, at all apparent'.[59] Yet alternative explanations of Altdorfer's approach are possible. One is that, as in so much pre-modern History, Altdorfer was knowingly blending different sorts of truth, literal (combatant numbers) and otherwise, and thus the anachronism was quite conscious given the belief that for specific purposes the differences between 333 and 1529 were less important than the similarities.

Cassiodorus made his ancients–moderns distinction not to embrace change but rather to ensure maximal preservation of Roman culture under the new conditions of Ostrogothic rule.[60] This is the same sort of thinking evinced by the Romans who had themselves venerated the established even while innovating furiously. There is a sense in which someone can be instrumental in huge novelty even whilst professing renewal, just as one can think oneself a revolutionary whilst actually carrying forward much of the inheritance of the past. The ancient Greek rhetorician Isocrates had it about right: he tacitly recognized that it would always be a matter of some blending of continuity and change when he wrote about the effect of talking of old things in new ways or vice versa.[61]

In understanding 'medieval' attitudes to change two tendencies are noteworthy, and while in some ways they dovetailed, in other ways they sat in tension. On one hand was the distinction between a conception of change as creation *ex nihilo*, out of nothing, and the conception of change as creating something out of something else. From at least Augustine the assumption was that only God could create *ex nihilo*, though the belief may be traced to the Aristotelian tendency to consider humans and the human soul as part, albeit a privileged part, of the natural order, such that human laws should imitate natural laws rather than aspire to complete originality.[62] This assumption led to an idea of a basic ontological stability outside periods of divine intervention. On the other hand there was an idea, expressed from Hesiod through Virgil's contemporary, Ovid, and translated fairly straightforwardly to a medieval view of early Christianity, of an ideal past order of which the present was merely a degenerate version.[63] Both tendencies encouraged fidelity to what had gone before, either because what had gone before still pertained or because it provided an ideal standard, yet the latter doctrine contradicted the former in portraying real change rather than basic continuity.

[59] Koselleck, *Futures Past*, 9–10.
[60] Tilo Schabert, 'Modernity and History I: What is Modernity?', in Athanasios Moulakis (ed.), *The Promise of History: Essays in Political Philosophy* (Berlin: de Gruyter, 1986), 9–21, here 9.
[61] Isocrates cited in Atack, 'The Discourse of Kingship', 339.
[62] Ernst Kantorowicz, 'The Sovereignty of the Artist: A Note on Legal Maxims and Renaissance Theories of Art', in Millard Meiss (ed.), *De artibus opuscula XL. Essays in honour of Erwin Panofsky*, vol. I (New York: New York University Press, 1961), 267–79.
[63] On Ovid, *The Metamorphoses of Ovid*, trans. Allen Mandelbaum (New York: Harcourt Brace, 1995).

If one side of the coin was fighting the tide of the new with innovations, the other side was modifying the old dispensations in recognition of the new. The Benedictine cleric Regino of Prüm (died 915) was author of a famous chronicle that continued the *Royal Frankish Annals*, and a collection of canons on ecclesiastical discipline, *Libri duo de synodalibus causis et disciplinis ecclesiasticis*. He warned that he had felt obliged to incorporate newer provisions in the latter work, 'things which I have deemed more pertinent to these our perilous times', because of a range of new offences 'which were unheard of in olden times because they were not committed and thus were not written and condemned in established rulings'.[64] With the spread of individual confession some three hundred years later we encounter concerns about priestly laxity in the imposition of penance as against the harsher penances prescribed by the early church fathers. Alain de Lille's late twelfth-century *Liber Poenitentialis* argued that the relaxation of standards was legitimate on the grounds that 'human nature used to be stronger once', which meant that his contemporaries could not bear what had once been thought necessary.[65]

By Regino's time the inflection of 'modern' had already changed somewhat in influential strands of thought. The historian and theologian Walafrid Strabo (808–49) announced the arrival of 'saeculum modernum' ('the modern age') in the era of Charlemagne.[66] Antiquity, as opposed to modernity, was at that point understood in different ways; sometimes it was conceived as including 'pagan' classical antiquity plus the time of the early church fathers, though Augustine himself had announced the Christian era as 'new'. Equally modernity could be conceived as a more longstanding state or the description of the immediate present.[67] In his biography of Charlemagne, Walafrid's contemporary Einhard recorded the life of 'the greatest man of all those living in his own period', one whose achievements could 'scarcely be matched by modern men'.[68] The palm was still offered to the past, but it was conceivable that exceptional 'moderns' were worthy of their forebears, and by Alain's time in the twelfth century a more extensive re-evaluation of the modern was well in train, even if not everyone could agree on how to periodize it.

Sometimes 'modernity' was designated by the period for which historians could rely on evidence before their own eyes, rather than on books written by others. In the prologue to his *Abbreviationes chronicum*, Ralph of Diceto

---

[64] Zubin Mistry, *Abortion in the Early Middle Ages, c.500–900* (York: York Medieval Press, 2015), 205.

[65] Alexander Murray, *Conscience and Authority in the Medieval Church* (Oxford: Oxford University Press, 2015), 75; Thomas N. Tentler, *Sin and Confession on the Eve of the Reformation* (Princeton: Princeton University Press, 1977), 17–18.

[66] Elisabeth Gössmann, *Antiqui und Moderni im Mittelalter: eine geschichtliche Standortbestimmung* (Paderborn: Schöningh, 1974), 35–6; Chenu, *Nature*, 317.

[67] Gössmann, *Antiqui und Moderni*, 35, 37.

[68] Einhard and Notker the Stammerer, *Two Lives of Charlemagne*, 52. On Notker as well as Einhard see Gössmann, *Antiqui und Moderni*, 36.

(1148–1202) divided historical events into three: the oldest, pagan times, *vetustissima*; old times, the Christian era, *vetera*; and modern times, *moderna*, since the year of his birth. Ralph's contemporary Walter Map (1140–c.1210) identified the most recent one hundred years as *modernitas*.[69]

As to the glorification of 'modern' men by History as Memorialization, it was certainly in Map's interest as a courtier of Henry II of England to petition for literary recognition of the king's 'generosity', and to bolster his case with reference to the 'reverence' accorded to the Roman emperor Nero, despite Nero's 'tyranny'. But Map also made the broader point that while the deeds of the ancients were preserved, the same was not true of the achievements of recent times, even those achievements that offered 'something not unworthy of "the buskin of Sophocles"'. The problem was not, indeed, a dearth of 'the illustrious deeds of modern men of might', but rather a dearth of poets in an age where blame came more easily than veneration.[70] As was the case with Arrian (pp. 25–6), whose work Map invoked, writers were as important in memorialization as the great men that constituted their subject matter. Indeed Map recognized the creative element of the writer's task generations before Dante and Plutarch noted the complementarity of Caesars and poets, *arma et litterae*, whereby eternal recognition was attained 'by both war and ingenium', *tam bello quam ingenio*. This is important since the self-consciousness of creation from the original mind of the author is another of those things attributed to the Renaissance 'mind' as it supposedly departed from its 'medieval' predecessor.[71]

The twelfth-century biographer of Alexander the Great, Walter of Châtillon, bemoaned that 'we moderns stray from the footsteps of our ancestors', rather as Eusebius had vilified those whose 'yearning for innovation' drove them to 'error' (p. 52), but by Walter's time his was but one side in a dispute about whether modern ways were superior to the ancient. The dispute might be characterized by the competing propositions from Job (12:12) that 'with the ancient is wisdom' and from Paul's call for the Ephesians (4:22–4) to 'put off the old man, and put on the new man, who has been created according to God'. Paul certainly removed some of the stigma of 'newness' or novelty, redolent as that was of *novissima*, the end of the world, indicative of the move to the last of 'man's' three phases of life. Within the theological realm the church fathers were denied a monopoly on doctrinal interpretation and the twelfth century saw a telling juxtaposition of the fathers and their adherents to the *magistri moderni*, monkish 'masters' who were not cloistered, but were teachers in the new universities.[72]

[69] Chenu, *Nature*, 190.

[70] Walther Map, *De Nugis Curialium (Courtier's Trifles)*, ed. and trans. Frederick Tupper and Marbury Bladen Ogle (London: Chatto and Windus, 1924), 254–5.

[71] On Dante and Petrarch, Kantorowicz, 'The Sovereignty', 276–7, and *passim* on the relationship between canon law jurists and Renaissance conceptions of the artist as creator *ex nihilo*.

[72] Ernst Robert Curtius, *European Literature and the Latin Middle Ages* (Princeton: Princeton University Press, 1991) 254 ff.; Kwame Gyekye, *Tradition and Modernity: Philosophical Reflections on the African Experience* (Oxford: Oxford University Press, 1997), 268; Goetz, *Geschichtschreibung*, 235;

It remains fashionable to date philosophies of tradition-disavowing progress only to the time of Europe's scientific, political, industrial, and philosophical revolutions, i.e. the seventeenth and eighteenth centuries. The historically minded political theorist Hannah Arendt gave heft to this belief when she dated to Francis Bacon's time (he lived from 1561 to 1626) the salient 'shift in the understanding of Time, the emergence of the Future to the rank formerly occupied by the Present or the Past'.[73] It is surely true that it was only in the late seventeenth-century 'querelle des Anciens et des Modernes' that 'Anciens' like Boileau-Despréaux were overwhelmingly on the losing side, and that the attacks on precedent knowledge and the whole Aristotelian–scholastic framework by the likes of Bacon became especially, self-consciously aggressive. It may also be true that, in contrast to 'the' Renaissance, the renaissance of the twelfth century had a sense of renewal of what was already there rather than having been lost. But as we have been at pains to illustrate, twelfth-century 'reform', as the word suggests, was both retrospective to an original ('authentic') ideal and prospective to change, which had pretty much been Cassiodorus's situation. Whichever way the cake is cut, 'the relationship between tradition and innovation is also what the monastic "reformation of the twelfth century" was about'.[74] Thus, for instance, members of (then) new religious orders like the twelfth-century Augustinian canon Anselm of Havelburg sought, against the Benedictines, to vindicate innovation as indicating growth and flourishing rather than decadence and confusion.[75]

Theology, Religious Hermeneutics, and History as Communion

The disputes between 'ancients' and 'moderns' from the twelfth to the fourteenth centuries were not primarily historians' disputes; they were much more important. They were mainly conducted between theologian-philosophers, though they

especially Jacques Le Goff, 'What Did the Twelfth-Century Renaissance Mean?', in Peter Linehan and Janet L. Nelson (eds), *The Medieval World* (Oxford: Routledge, 2001), 635–47. Albert Zimmermann and Gudrun Vuillemin-Diemand (eds.), *Antiqui und Moderni: Traditionsbewußtsein und Fortschrittsbewußtsein im späten Mittelalter* (Berlin: De Gruyter, 1974), contains essays on most salient aspects of the advent of the *moderni*.

[73] Arendt, *The Life of the Mind*, 152. See also 154, 214.

[74] Jotischky, *The Carmelites and Antiquity*, 306; Giles Constable, *The Reformation of the Twelfth Century* (Cambridge: Cambridge University Press, 2002), introduction; Beryl Smalley, 'Ecclesiastical Attitudes to Novelty, c.1100–c.1250', *Studies in Church History* 12 (1975), 113–31; and for the relationship between tradition and reform in an area of direct relevance to this book, see Joachim Ehlers, 'Monastische Theologie, historischer Sinn und Dialektik. Tradition und Neuerung in der Wissenschaft des 12. Jahrhunderts', in Zimmermann and Vuillemin-Diemand (eds.), *Antiqui und Moderni*, 58–79.

[75] R. W. Southern, *History and Historians: Selected Papers of R. W. Southern*, ed. R. J. Bartlett (Oxford: Blackwell, 2004), 42–3.

extended into the realm of legal hermeneutics, at this time of the codification of canon law.[76] They were disputes about ways of justifying knowledge in the deepest sense. In fact they are fundamental in a long-term shift in the development of philosophy, away from ontology, which is, remember, the study of what exists in the most basic sense, to epistemology, which is the study of what/how we can know about what exists. The History practised by Christian chroniclers was in one of its functions an auxiliary science to the study of religion, just as chronicle was a lower activity than biblical hermeneutics: the main science is more significant than the auxiliary, but the relationship means that changes in the nature of religious authority and scriptural exegesis were related to changes in the arts of reading past religious texts, which should be set alongside secular, political influences on and changing popular uses of History. We may thus diverge slightly from Anthony Grafton, one of the most brilliant contemporary intellectual historians, when he differentiates humanists from scholastics by endorsing claims for the 'modernity', in the form of the 'fundamentally historical approach', of the Renaissance philologist and poet 'Poliziano' (1454–94):

[U]nderstanding of earlier thought must rest on textual exegesis—on an exegesis the exponents of which read the texts in the light of the fears and aspirations of their authors and the prejudices and assumptions of their first readers. The scholastics had read their texts as structures, systems of interlocking propositions that they tested for coherence as an engineer tests the load-bearing parts of a building. The humanists read theirs as clouded windows which proper treatment could restore to transparency, revealing the individuals who had written them. The scholar could thus come to know dead men as they had really been, and the serious effort to obtain that sort of knowledge became the first characteristically modern form of intellectual life.[77]

It would be foolish to deny any innovations to Poliziano or others around his time. Yet a more extensive examination of the legal and theological scholasticism that humanism occluded might more deeply contextualize humanism's innovations, suggesting that they were matters of technique and emphasis more than philosophy. The blanket contention is wrong that 'the medieval conception of history as a self-consciously literary and textual artifact' differed from 'the later idea that it was a transparent medium through which one could view past realities in a

[76] Janet Coleman, *Piers Plowman and the Moderni* (Rome: Edizioni di Storia e Letteratura, 1981), 20; Andrea Padovani and Peter G. Stein (eds.), *The Jurists' Philosophy of Law from Rome to the Seventeenth Century* (Dordrecht: Springer, 2007), 143.

[77] Anthony Grafton, *Defenders of the Text: The Traditions of Scholarship in an Age of Science, 1450–1800* (Cambridge, MA: Harvard University Press, 1991), 8–9; see also 55.

quite different way from the genre of fiction'.[78] Prominent scholastics sometimes maintained the coherence of their systems by historical enquiry, not just by logic.

Arguably the greatest mind of high medieval Christendom, Thomas Aquinas (1225–74), who tried to fuse Hellenic naturalism with monotheistic supernaturalism, endorsed the hermeneutic quadriga but insisted that the literal sense was foundational.[79] Here Aquinas was consistent with a trend that began with Anselm in the eleventh century and was especially evident in the work of the legal thinker Ivo of Chartres (c.1040–1115). Ivo set off along the path that would be followed in the first half of the twelfth century by Peter Abelard (1079–1142) and the Bolognese monk, Gratian. Gratian's Decretum is regarded as the foundation-stone of canon law, and was itself composed from biblical sources, writings of the early church fathers, the decrees of the papacy and church synods and councils, and Roman law, as passed down primarily through the Digests compiled under Justinian in the sixth century, and rediscovered in 1070. Abelard's competitors at the Abbey of St Victor in Paris, Hugh (1096–1141) and Andrew (c.1110–75), pursued their own line of historical-theological exegesis which pointed towards historical literalism, though in a slightly different way to that taken up by Aquinas. In this process, they and other Augustinian canons at St Victor were greatly aided by the renewal of contact with Jewish exegetical traditions, through the work of Joseph Karo, Samuel ben Meir, and in particular Rashi (acronym of Rabbi Shlomo [Y]Itzhaki, 1040–1105),[80] who also influenced Aquinas's influence, Moses Maimonides (1135–1204). The wider twelfth-century circulation of commentaries by or attributed to the fourth-century father John Chrysostom was also relevant— Chrysostom's 'Antiochene' tradition of more literal exegesis differed from the allegorizing 'Alexandrian' tradition which was better known to that point in Latin Christendom.[81]

Hugh of St Victor claimed that 'our task is to commit history to memory, as the foundation of doctrine'. Hugh was a teacher, tasked with ensuring that his

---

[78] In an otherwise highly stimulating piece: Alexandra Walsham, 'Migrations of the Holy: Explaining Religious Change in Medieval and Early Modern Europe', Journal of Medieval and Early Modern Studies 44:2 (2014), 241–80, here 265. In places this piece does show sensitivity to the significance of high medieval developments for what are often thought of as Reformation questions.

[79] Christopher Ocker, Biblical Poetics before Humanism and Renaissance (Cambridge: Cambridge University Press, 2002), 40.

[80] Sara Lipton, Images of Intolerance: The Representation of Jews and Judaism in the Bible moralisée (Berkeley: University of California Press, 1999), 73; Beryl Smalley, 'L'Exégèse biblique du 12e siècle', in Maurice de Gandillac and Edouard Jeauneau (eds.), Entretiens sur la renaissance du 12e siècle (Paris: Mouton, 1968), 273–83, here 273–5; Rainer Berndt (ed.), Schrift, Schreiber, Schenker: Studien zur Abtei Sankt Viktor in Paris und den Viktorinern (Berlin: Akademie Verlag, 2005), 97 ff. on discerning authorial intentions; passim on the intellectual context and antecedents of Andrew's work. On differences to Aquinas, Ocker, Biblical Poetics, 40.

[81] On differences between Alexandria and Antioch, Wilhelm Dilthey, 'The Development of Hermeneutics', in Dilthey: Selected Writings, ed. H. P. Rickman (Cambridge: Cambridge University Press, 1976), 246–63, here 252.

students learned deeply and properly. The capacity to memorize was highly valued then, and for a few centuries to come. It was sometimes contrasted with the act of committing things to paper, which might retard the ability to internalize, and was thus a species of forgetting, which is one further reason why it is not helpful to look only to chronicles to understand medieval engagements with the past.[82]

While Hugh was not greatly successful in stimulating historical study in general, his *Chronicon*, or *Liber de tribus maximis circumstantiis gestorum, id est personis, locis, temporibus* (*Book of the three main circumstances of history, namely persons, places, times*) had manifold significance. It fed into Helinand of Froidmont's (*c.*1160–*c.*1237) and Vincent of Beauvais's (*c.*1190–1264) later chronicles of known world history from Adam onwards. For Hugh's own students, this detailed set of lists, plus his 'glosses' to the historical books of the Old Testament, became a cardinal aid in establishing the literal meanings of scripture. Hugh's and Andrew's commentaries, along with Walafrid Strabo's *Glossa Ordinaria* and Josephus's *Antiquities*, underpinned Peter Comnestor's (died 1179) *Historia Scholastica*, a comprehensive running literal commentary on the historical books of the Bible which, in its establishment as a standard text for the teaching of sacred scripture in the schools, furthered Hugh's goal of entrenching biblical History as the ground for biblical reading. This achievement aroused the ire of affiliates of the ecclesiastical reform movement, who emphasized the practical pastoral and orthodox theological instruction of clerics over Hugh's goal of developing the contemplative mind. Thus Peter the Chanter (died 1197) decried a tendency that sounds to have something in common with the more prosaic of today's Histories of material culture as it supposedly encouraged the examination of

> superfluities, such as the exact location of places, the number of years and periods, genealogies, the mechanical dispositions in building, such as the disposition of the tabernacle, the temple, even the imaginary temple [i.e. the temple vision of Ezekiel]. Holy Scripture is not given to us to search for idle and superfluous things in it, but to search for faith and moral lessons...[83]

[82] On Hugh, Frans van Liere, *An Introduction to the Medieval Bible* (Cambridge: Cambridge University Press, 2014), 159; Franklin T. Harkins, 'Fundamentum omnis doctrinae: The Memorization of History in the Pedagogy of Hugh of St. Victor', *Pecia. Le livre et l'écrit 14: Texte, liturgie et mémoire dans l'Église du Moyen Âge* (2012), 267–93. On the principles of memorialization, Given-Wilson, *Chronicles*, 58.

[83] Southern, *History and Historians*, 41–2; cf. van Liere, *An Introduction to the Medieval Bible*, 158–63, which provides most of the material on Hugh and his influence—see also p .142 on Chrysostom and Origen as different sorts of hermeneut. On Origen and Josephus, and the extent of Comnestor's debt to Josephus and other Jewish sources, plus the significance of Comnestor's work: Louis H. Feldman, *Studies in Hellenistic Judaism* (Leiden: Brill, 1996), 302, 317–26, 343–4. On Hugh, Andrew, and Josephus, Mark Somos, *Secularisation and the Leiden Circle* (Leiden: Brill, 2011), 345–6.

For Andrew of St Victor, sometimes called 'the second Jerome', literal reading had meant an increasing focus on grammar, on recovering original wording, and on the surface meaning of words, even to the point at which he produced a non-Christological reading of books of the 'Old Testament'.[84] The author's inferred intention should also determine what counts as a figurative meaning, which is where Andrew's and Hugh's debt to Rashi is perhaps most obvious. For Rashi, the literal sense meant recapturing what the authors of scripture had intended to communicate to their primary, contemporary audiences. This quest required historical contextualization, as with his endorsement of *peshat* (literal, contextual reading) over homiletic *midrash* traditions.[85] Ironically, it may be that Hugh had turned to Jewish scholarship in the first place to further his own literal-ist interests precisely because of the enduring Christian stereotype, attributable to Paul and Augustine, that literal reading without deeper symbolic understanding was all that the benighted Jews were capable of.[86]

While, as Coleman observes, the *sensus historicus* of medieval hermeneutic was often identical with the *sensus grammaticus*, with the historical truth of what was written being accepted as literal truth once the grammatical meaning of it had been established,[87] ascertaining authorial intention demanded contextual understanding that looked beyond individual texts in a non-figurative sense: it could be History in today's sense of the word, as the medievalist biblical scholar Frans van Liere observes.[88] Checking text against text, setting one authority against another, was also a form of source criticism, as Abelard showed in a con-troversy over the biography of the first-century convert to Christianity, Dionysius the Areopagite.[89] Comparison of the original Hebrew of the Old Testament could reveal inaccuracies in later translations. By extension, such inaccuracies could affect the figural relations established between episodes in Old and New Testaments.[90] Further, as Abelard and Peter Lombard demonstrated via their dialectic methods,

---

[84] Smalley, 'L'Exégèse biblique du 12e siècle'.

[85] Timothy Ward, *Word and Supplement* (Oxford: Oxford University Press, 2002), 31–4; Olson, *World on Paper*, 149–54; Patricia K. Tull and Claire Mathews McGinnis (eds.), 'As Those Who Are Taught': The Interpretation of Isaiah from the LXX to the SBL (Atlanta, GA: SBL, 2006), 173–7; Kelber, 'The Quest for the Historical Jesus'.

[86] For this suggestion, see the 'The 12th century' part of the entry 'Hebraists, Christian', in the Jewish virtual library at http://www.jewishvirtuallibrary.org/jsource/judaica/ejud_0002_0008_0_08624.html

[87] Coleman, *Ancient and Medieval Memories*, 574.

[88] Indeed, van Liere, *An Introduction to the Medieval Bible*, 171, actually distinguishes the gram-matical sense and historical sense in some connections. The major point is that the historical sense is a literal one in terms of establishing what original authors meant, which means putting utterances in contexts including but not limited to the grammatical one.

[89] Denis/Dionysius the Areopagite, who is said had been converted by Paul, was patron saint of the monastery of St Denis. In a heated debate as to his personal History, Abelard returned to Jerome and Eusebius to refute Bede whilst also refusing to rely on the other St Denis monks' preferred authority, Hilduin. Peter Abelard, *Letters IX–XIV*, ed. Edmé Renno Smits (Groningen: Bouma, 1983), 138 ff.

[90] R. N. Swanson, *The Twelfth-Century Renaissance* (Manchester: Manchester University Press, 1999), 131; Nikolaus M. Häring, 'Commentary and Hermeneutics', in Benson and Constable (eds.), *Renaissance and Renewal*, 173–200, here 195–7.

comprehension of the differing 'gestalts', the differing psychological and political context-structures to which conflicting statements by various authorities—fathers, popes, and synods—belonged, was the key first step in the desired project of harmonizing underlying meanings.[91]

How far meanings could be harmonized is an interesting question to which the twins of legal and theological hermeneutics had dedicated anxious attention not just since Ivo, but in fact since at least the eighth and ninth centuries in reflection on Augustine's teaching, notably his theory of historical 'accommodation', which meant accommodation not just of the 'ignorant' but of those living in different circumstances.[92] In Contra Faustum, Augustine had asserted 'that all things written in the books of the Old Testament are to be received with approval and admiration [...] and that those precepts which are no longer observed outwardly are to be understood as having been most suitable in those times, and are to be viewed as having been shadows of things to come'.[93] This is standard Christian supersessionism, whereby the New Testament superseded the Old. However in Contra Faustum Augustine also explains why even some of the New Testament laws of the apostles should be understood as historically specific, and no longer applicable to the time of his writing, c.400 CE. The laws he has in mind are from Acts, in which the apostles agree to lift many of the Old Testament prohibitions on foodstuffs, and reduce the old rules down to just four prohibitions: 'abstain from food polluted by idols, from sexual immorality, from the meat of strangled animals, and from blood' (Acts 15:19–29). In accounting for the apostles' retention of some of these prohibitions, Augustine pointed to prevailing political conditions in the first century; his argument was that now the relationship between Jews and Christians was different from previously, the relevant prohibitions were anachronistic. Thus:

[When] the apostles did on that occasion require Christians to abstain from the blood of animals, and not to eat of things strangled, they seem to me to have consulted the time in choosing an easy observance that could not be burdensome to any one, and which Gentiles might have in common with the Israelites, for the sake of the Cornerstone [i.e. Christ], who makes both one in himself [...] But since the close of that period during which the two walls of the circumcision and the uncircumcision, although united in the Cornerstone, still retained some distinctive peculiarities, and now that the Church has become so entirely Gentile that none who are outwardly Israelites are to be found in it, no Christian feels

---

[91] Paul Tillich, A History of Christian Thought, ed. Carl E. Braaten (New York: Touchstone, 1968), 169–70.

[92] On elements of Augustine's theory of accommodation, Levitin, 'From Sacred History to the History of Religion', 1131; Betty Jo Teeter Dobbs, The Janus Faces of Genius: The Role of Alchemy in Newton's Thought (Cambridge: Cambridge University Press, 1991), 59–60. However, for the point about eighth- and ninth-century thought, and indeed for my entire discussion of Augustine here, references to Augustine's work and all, I am indebted completely to Rick Sowerby.

[93] Augustine, Contra Faustum, 32.14, repr in Augustine, The Works of Aurelius Augustine: A New Translation, ed. Marcus Dods, vol. 5 (Edinburgh: Clark, 1872), 541.

bound to abstain from thrushes or small birds because their blood has not been poured out, or from hares because they are killed by a stroke on the neck without shedding their blood. Any who still are afraid to touch these things are laughed at by the rest.[94]

Returning to the topic of the central middle ages, the legal scholar Gabriel Le Bras noted that the early canonists marked 'off from principles of eternal validity the variable elements of the law, which had been suggested by particular circumstances, whether of time, place, or persons', and he concluded on 'the relativity of rules'. More strongly, Donald R. Kelley detects 'geographical and historical relativism' in their thought, amid a 'process of "historicization"' in the interpretation of canon law, and a third scholarly authority, R. L. Benson, sees 'historical relativism' in the thought of Gratian and his immediate successors, the decretists.[95] It is difficult to detect relativism in this train of thought: all the medieval thinkers in question insist on distinguishing unchangeable elements of the law from variable parts. Gratian, for instance, was prepared to countenance the revision of ancient law, but only in order that it align more closely with divine law, which no human law might contradict. Ultimately his goal was dispensing with customs that did not correspond to reason and conscience. Focusing on the variable elements of law, Benson alludes to Gratian's dictum that 'if among the several things which were done by our predecessors and ancestors there are some things which were able to be [done] without guilt, and afterward turned into error and superstition, then without hesitation and with great authority, they ought to be destroyed by those who come later'.[96] As much as anything this passage illustrates the balancing act between recognition of past and present papal legislative legitimacy. Such diplomatic phrasing does not mean that 'what once was good can turn bad as a result of the changing of the times'.[97] Saying that something might have been done without guilt is not the same as saying it was good, only that the doer was not culpable. The limited circumstance in which two contradictory rules could be true, according to Gratian's prologue to the Concordance of Discordant Canons, was when they related to a law which was variable and the contradiction stemmed from a

[94] Augustine, Contra Faustum, 32.13, repr in Augustine, The Works of Aurelius Augustine: A New Translation, vol. 5, 540–1.
[95] Gabriel Le Bras, 'Canon Law', in C. G. Crump and E. F. Jacob (eds.), The Legacy of the Middle Ages (Oxford: Clarendon Press, 1943), 321–61, here 326; Kelley, Foundations of Modern Historical Scholarship, 154. Benson cited in Achim Funder, Reichsidee und Kirchenrecht: Dietrich von Nieheim als Beispiel spätmittelalterlicher Rechtsauffassung (Freiburg: Herder, 1993), nn. to pp. 292, 334. Note that Kelley also claims strains of cultural relativism in the work of the twelfth-century bishop and philosopher of History Otto of Freising: Kelley, Faces of History, 129. I cannot see relativism in Otto but obviously that does not mean it is not there.
[96] Stanley Chodorow, Christian Political Theory and Church Politics in the Mid-Twelfth Century (Berkeley: University of California Press, 1972), reproduces this passage and contextualizes it on p. 140.
[97] Funder, Reichsidee, 292: 'was einmal gut gewesen ist, kann sich durch die Veränderung der Zeiten zum schlechten wenden'.

dispensation allowed in a special case.[98] Relativism this was not, but Gratian does evince that sense of anachronism, i.e. the sense of not applying standards and perspectives to past people who did not have them, that is so often held to be a post-medieval attitude.

Another contextualizing exercise by Maimonides has led some scholars to talk of historicism and historicization in relation to his work, especially passages in his *Guide for the Perplexed* (c.1190 in Judeo-Arabic, translated into Hebrew in 1204).[99] Those scholars do not equate historicism or historicization with a relativistic view, but since historicism is sometimes given those connotations, and in light of the previous paragraph, a brief digression on relativism is merited. Relativism is a philosophical outlook predicated upon recognition of multiple, perhaps infinite accounts of the good and right (moral relativism), and/or the beautiful (aesthetic relativism), and/or the true (epistemic relativism). In its simplest 'descriptive' form relativism just acknowledges the fact of the diversity of systems of value or belief. It is doubtful that 'descriptive relativism', as it is called, really qualifies as relativism, because one could easily contend that some or all or all-but-one of these manifold systems of belief is faulty. More properly relativist is the argument that there is no standpoint or yardstick external to all cultures that provides an ultimate vindication for different belief/value systems or renders their differing terms mutually commensurable (see p. 326). Accordingly, any claim to universal standards of judgement is a form of self-deceit, a spurious universalization of one culture's standards. The only standards of, say, good and bad are those that develop within cultures, in the plural. Maimonides clearly does not hold such a position.

Like Aquinas, Maimonides was concerned with reconciling Aristotle with scripture, or at least with creating some insulation where conflict was likely. He also tried to interpret some of the apparently more arcane biblical injunctions, without allegorization, for a contemporary Jewish readership. Thus he accounted for initial divine approval of sacrifice as a concession to 'the custom which was in those days general among all men, and the general mode of worship in which the Israelites were brought up'. It was a concession to reality, much as in Islamic jurisprudence—which may have been one of the many Islamic influences on Maimonides—the Koran's acceptance of polygamy was seen as a concession to pre-Islamic practices. And just as more recent Muslim exegesis has argued that Koranic limits on the scale of polygamy suggest a tendency towards the reduction

[98] Harold J. Berman, *Law and Revolution, the Formation of the Western Legal Tradition* (Cambridge, MA: Harvard University Press, 1983), 145–6 on this point and on Gratian weeding out problematic custom.
[99] Levitin, 'From Sacred History to the History of Religion', 1131, including extensive notes to relevant scholarship. Note that Maimonides' historical thinking plays an important role in Funkenstein's thought about the origins of modern historicist thinking—see Moyn, 'Amos Funkenstein'. It should be clear that I would argue that Maimonides' contribution to a sense of acculturated human difference across time is only one among many such contributions in and around his period.

and eventual elimination of the practice, so for Maimonides the concession was a transitional measure. Manifestly there is here a sense of acculturated difference and cultural change across time. Maimonides' idiom is at once of an anthropological psychology in which it is in 'the nature of man, who generally cleaves to that to which he is used', but also of tutelage from infancy to adulthood, as Maimonides talks of young mammals being weaned from milk to solids.[100] So such tolerance as exists of the earlier practice may be sympathetic, but it is also paternalistic and provisional, as one might indulge a child. It is this psychological contextualization that distinguishes Maimonides' account from Augustine's theory of accommodation with its more circumstantial focus. (See pp. 122–3 for elaboration.)

The focus on literalism and historical contextualism as opposed to allegorical meaning in reading practices was accompanied by an increased attention to literary quality as a constituent of the written account and as an index of interest in the human author. The concept of the *auctor* shifted its meaning somewhat between the eleventh and thirteenth centuries. Sharing a root with *auctoritas*, meaning approximately authentic truth, it implied authority that commanded respect, and was the sort of thing that historians and others strived to achieve. Conventionally, God was seen as the author of the sacred texts, and the scribe merely as conduit, but as—especially under the influence of the Victorines— questions turned to matters of how, where, when, and from what materials the scribe had compiled his account, they also considered why. The 'why' concerned the personal ends of the flesh-and-blood writer, which had to be considered as an additional causal factor alongside the ultimate divine 'causes' of the work.

The concept of 'four causes' which systematically elucidated different types of influence was, by the way, a major part of the thirteenth century's Aristotelian inheritance.[101] His *Physica* and *Metaphysica* entered university curricula at that time, having mostly been translated into Latin by around 1200, while the Latin occupation of Constantinople (1204–61) facilitated a further engagement with its treasures. Aristotle's concepts had been only partially retrieved before then. Now they proved valuable not just for hermeneutics but for hermeneuts, who could become *auctors* themselves, as Walter Map had obviously aspired to be in the realm of secular History (p. 83), rather as latter-day literary theorists have been able to market their criticism as literature. The idea of a writer as an 'author' can be contrasted with the label *compilator* or compiler that medieval chroniclers often applied to themselves. For the interpreting reader, the idea of multiple causal influences also meant that it was possible to be more explicitly critical towards canonical texts, since one was not criticizing the word of God so much

---

[100] Moses Maimonides, *The Guide for the Perplexed*, trans. M. Friedländer (New York: Dover, 1956), ch. XXXII at 322–7, all quotes from 322–3.

[101] On Aristotelian categories and causation, William J. Connell, 'The Eternity of the World and Renaissance Historical Thought', *California Italian Studies* 2:1 (2011), 1–23.

as a human-influenced amalgam.[102] Scholars who study the sixteenth and seven-teenth centuries should be careful in arrogating to their period the innovation of debates on how to reconcile the biblical authority, 'which was divine, with its his-tory, which was more and more evidently human'.[103] When Grafton writes of 'humanists' reading their texts 'as clouded windows which proper treatment could restore to transparency, revealing the individuals who had written them', he makes a vital point about the recognition that texts reveal as much about their own authors and origins as about their explicit subject-matter.[104] But however much humanists may have developed this critical principle any sharp contrast with prior scholasticism does not quite work, for reasons already provided.

If Aquinas was merely one hugely influential part of a longer movement in the direction of prioritizing literalism, a further step in the subjective reading not just of actual texts but of the world as a text was provided by William of Ockham (c.1287–1347). He was not the earliest but he was the most famous medieval 'nominalist'. The debate between nominalists (formerly 'vocalists') and 'realists' corresponded to some instantiations of the debate between *moderni* and *antiqui*, and had begun in the twelfth century, especially in the crucible of Abelard's thought. While Aquinas was not of the *moderni*, he was clearly influenced by them. As ever beneath the headline bifurcation, the lines of distinction between travellers on the *via antiqua* and *via moderna* vary very much from person to person. Perhaps the most important crack that Aquinas created in Catholic orthodoxy, the crack that nominalism forced much wider and deeper, was his contention that while God was of course immediately certain for himself, he was not immediately certain to humans.[105] The nominalist challenge brought epis-temological and metaphysical questions together.

Let us open the discussion of nominalism with the dispute concerning God's role in allocating salvation. In an answer to the question, which had distinct echoes of Plato's asking whether the gods will what is just/reasonable or is the just/reasonable what the gods happen to will, the *antiqui* banked on the regulata-ble certainties of the former. Nominalism effectively reversed the order of priority. Only if God's will was supreme could 'his' power be truly unlimited, truly free.[106] This conclusion also militated against any notion emerging from the study of

---

[102] Michel Zimmermann (ed.), *Auctor et auctoritas. Invention et conformisme dans l'écriture médiévale* (Paris: École des Chartes, 2001); A. J. Minnis, *Medieval Theory of Authorship: Scholastic Literary Attitudes in the Later Middle Ages* (London: Scolar, 1984), ch. 1 but also pp. 190–210 on how 'compilation' became a literary form of its own; Sara S. Poor, *Mechthild of Magdeburg and her Book: Gender and the Making of Textual Authority* (Philadelphia: University of Pennsylvania Press, 2004), 2–4.

[103] Noel Malcolm, 'Hobbes, Ezra, and the Bible: The History of a Subversive Idea', in Malcolm, *Aspects of Hobbes* (Oxford: Clarendon Press, 2002), 383–431, here 420, cited and endorsed by Levitin, 'From Sacred History to the History of Religion', 1126–7.

[104] Grafton, *Defenders of the Text*, 8–9.   [105] Tillich, *Protestant Era*, 71.

[106] Lauri Haikola, *Gesetz und Evangelium bei Matthias Flacius Illyricus: eine Untersuchung zur Lutherischen Theologie vor der Konkordienformel* (Lund: Gleerup, 1952), 32 ff.; Jörg Dierken, *Selbstbewusstsein individueller Freiheit: religionstheoretische Erkundungen in protestantischer Perspektive* (Tübingen: Mohr Siebeck, 2005), 135–6, 203–4.

Greek naturalism that God might have to be reconciled with the laws of nature. As against a metaphysically 'realist' position that one could know the universe in itself as the manifestation of a divine, hierarchical order, nominalists believed that the human mind was left with articulating its own systems on the fragmentary evidence of experience and reason. For the same reasons nominalists conducted a cull of those atemporal, abstract entities that metaphysical/ontological realists like Plato had called eternal 'forms'—the sorts of entities that for prior theologians had divinely vouchsafed the interlinked order of the natural world. Words were increasingly seen as arbitrary signs allocated to contingent entities and linked to each other by grammatical convention—and as the tool of human *auctores* rather than anything else. They were not indicators of spiritual realities or divine natural order. Religious hierarchs were in no better position to determine the higher meaning behind the literal word than any other literate person proficient in the use of reason. Logic of thought and grammatical logic of written and spoken language were the only reliable tools of analysis at human disposal, but they were uncoupled from metaphysics. Everything else was at God's unknowable disposition, leaving the individual human with faith alone, and a terrifying freedom to choose his or her way in the world during those times when God did not intervene. Concrete, mundane individuals existed on their own, albeit in virtue of God's omnipotence and in some way in 'his' image, certain only of their own inner states.[107]

The development of nominalism as a theological position prior to and through William's early fourteenth-century work was accompanied socially by a thirteenth-century evangelical explosion in which men and a growing number of women took on the roles of *auctores*, seeking to embody and disseminate the principles that Christ had exemplified in his life, disavowing worldly goods and preaching in the vernacular.[108] Intellectually, a particular sort of subjectivism was enhanced, with the emphasis on the human mind rather than the accumulated authority of institutions and the all-encompassing order of the divine which intellectual systems were supposed to map. For related reasons, nominalism was an essential precursor of the Reformation since the Protestant belief that salvation comes from faith and God's grace alone (the meeting of the two comprising the *kairos*), not from the good works of man, stems from the rejection of inferable divine reason. For the nominalists as for Luther, one side of the interpretative coin was a recognition of how much could be inferred, unassisted, by the application of human reason to texts, and the other side of the coin was a claim about how much must remain obscure without the aid of revelation and grace.[109]

---

[107] Coleman, *Ancient and Medieval Memories*, 530–6 and *passim*; Gordon Leff, *William of Ockham: The Metamorphosis of Scholastic Discourse* (Manchester: Manchester University Press, 1975), 54–5.

[108] Poor, *Mechthild*, 4.

[109] Robert B. Pippin, *Modernism as a Philosophical Problem: On the Dissatisfactions of European High Culture* (Malden, MA: Blackwell, 1999), 19.

Socio-Economic Change and the Function of Genealogies

The new dispensations of philosophy and theology emerged roughly in tandem with Europe's high medieval commercial revolution.[110] The changing relationship between 'man', nature, God, and given hierarchy was mirrored in a changing relationship between people and money, and, relatedly, between people and time. The expansion of the cash nexus and the development of a merchant class brought with it a challenge to the prejudice against wealth that had not been acquired by inheritance or labour. Profiting from the products of others' labour, or from money itself, which was conventionally considered wealth dishonestly acquired, started to fire a system in which money and goods circulated widely rather than being consumed, exchanged, or gifted in local markets or in the context of subsistence or client–protector relationships. In the developing system, new human networks cut across established social hierarchies and configured time less around events divine or mundane than around activities.[111] As late as the fourteenth century, one Franciscan decreed that it was wrong to demand greater payment from he who could not settle his account immediately than he who could, lest the merchant profit from time itself, which belonged not to him but God. But credits and loans, investment, and purchase for future resale all hinged on a profane sense of the value of time. If, as one theorist of late capitalism has suggested, a humanistic sense of history, awareness of anachronism and all, presupposed 'a sundering of secular time from sacred time', the social and economic developments of the eleventh century onwards had long since helped in breaking this link.[112] Nevertheless, barely any of the studies of the 'modern' conceptions of time take cognizance of the medieval emergence of 'merchant time' and its challenge to church time, with trading hours gaining some of the significance of the hours of prayer and of natural, seasonal rhythms. In particular the historian Jacques Le Goff shows how work bells became as common as church bells in fourteenth-century Flanders' cloth-producing towns, at the centre of the export business. Work bells marked the beginning and end of the working day, and interval breaks. Many cloth workers were solely wage earners, not disposing of any of the products of their labour and being reliant only on the wages that could be negotiated *pro rata*—hence ensuing arguments about just how long a working day should be.[113]

---

[110] On some interesting conceptual linkages between theological debates and economics, see Siegfried Van Duffel, 'From Objective Right to Subjective Rights: The Franciscans and the Interest and Will Conceptions of Rights', in Virpi Mäkinen (ed.), *The Nature of Rights* (Helsinki: Societas Philosophica Fennica, 2010), 63–91.

[111] A distinction identified by Moishe Postone, Louis Galambos, and Jane Eliot Sewell, *Time, Labor, and Social Domination: A Reinterpretation of Marx's Critical Theory* (Cambridge: Cambridge University Press, 2003), 211.

[112] Dipesh Chakrabarty, 'The Death of History? Historical Consciousness and the Culture of Late Capitalism', *Public Culture* 4:2 (1992), 47–65, here 56.

[113] Postone et al., *Time, Labor*, 209–11.

Manifold were the background factors against which such ostensibly technical developments might be ascribed significance, but among those factors were the increasing scepticism of the 'moderns' about divine time-schemas devised by 'ancients', and the nominalist relegation of time to the realms of the unpredictable dispensations of the divine. Mundane time was freed up along with much of the natural world as a resource for individuals and their managers, at around the same point as Christendom's sense of space was being expanded by encounters at its margins, with both developments being conducive to commerce.[114] Neither of these changes coheres with Michel Foucault's claim that it was only in the seventeenth and eighteenth century that a 'new mechanism of power' was invented 'which permits time and labor, rather than wealth and commodities, to be extracted from bodies'.[115] Neither coheres with anthropologist Johannes Fabian's claim that 'Enlightenment thought' (for there is apparently only one such kind, like the 'medieval' equivalent) breaks with 'a conception of time/space in terms of a history of salvation to one that ultimately resulted in the secularization of Time as natural history'.[116] Both are obscured by studies of high medieval historiography that focus on the new eschatological speculative philosophies written in the high middle ages by Otto of Freising and Orderic Vitalis amongst others. As ever, these speculative philosophies are not categorically different in all respects to other more 'secular' Histories of the period, but their different emphases and purposes mean that they cannot be considered representative of the mass of historically oriented scholarship in the period, far less of the historical thought investigated in the previous section.[117]

The label 'renaissance' was applied to the twelfth-century crucible of nominalism and so much else, by twentieth-century medievalists keen to undo some of the damage done to the name of the middle ages by the propagandists of the better-known Renaissance. The 'monastic reformation' of the twelfth century also anticipates 'the' fifteenth- and sixteenth-century Reformation. Such labels may serve merely to antedate the origins of 'the modern' to the twelfth century, but that would be insufficient. Instead, as Le Goff and others have posited, the language of culmination may be more appropriate in highlighting the development of 'medieval' Christian civilization by its own lights. After all, it was only at the outset of the twelfth century that 'Christendom' arrogated that name to itself, after Gregorian reform and at a time of centralization and state-building. This sort of thinking prompts a reassessment of the nature of distinctions between

---

[114] Le Goff, Time, Work, and Culture, 29–41.

[115] Michel Foucault, Society Must be Defended, ed. Mauro Bertani and Alessandro Fontana (New York: Picador, 2003), 35–6.

[116] Johannes Fabian, Time and the Other, 26.

[117] e.g. the first two sentences of Ray C. Petry, 'Three Medieval Chroniclers: Monastic Historiography and Biblical Eschatology in Hugh of St. Victor, Otto of Freising, and Ordericus Vitalis', Church History 34:3 (1965), 282–93. The main focus of the article is on Orderic and Otto. Otto is also the supposedly representative medieval historian in Connell, 'The Eternity of the World', 6.

'modern' and 'pre-modern' or 'medieval', as of symmetries between humanism and antiquity, since it puts the origins of some humanist, 'modern', and indeed post-modern developments in the very heart of modernity's 'other', the middle ages.

What one does with thoughts about the relationship between 'the medieval' and 'the modern' at the normative level is a good question. In light of the conventional pejorative caricature of the middle ages, it is interesting to note the recent reversal of fortunes whereby scholars of modernity are at pains to stress modernity's violent, exclusionary potential and the problematics of its professed 'rationality' just as some medievalists are attempting to de-brutalize and contextually rationalize their period. On one plane this just shows how recent thought on 'modernity', especially by 'postmoderns', has sustained the clichéd medieval–modern distinction even if inverting some of the valences attached to it. Nevertheless we need to bear in mind that, alongside the 'enlightenment' and 'renaissance' of high medieval Europe the eleventh and twelfth centuries also saw a surge in the violent 'othering' of Jews, Muslims heretics, and even lepers, as tainted Christians whose bodily deficiencies betrayed something of their spiritual condition. This upsurge in intolerance, expropriation, and sometimes mass murder did not stand in contradiction to the flowering of medieval Christian civilization. It was part and parcel of the process of sharper self-identification that came with both the assertiveness of Rome and monarchical policies of centralization.[118] This process was in train well before the clampdown on certain strains of thought that had been unleashed by the twelfth-century 'enlightenment' contributed to the dogmatism of which humanists were so critical.[119]

The attempted expansion of papal power and the growth of more centralized monarchies, especially in England, during the high middle ages entailed a proliferation of bureaucracy and thus involved the widening of the circle of the literate, as well as the growth of the archival record. Furthermore historically oriented literature proliferated in the vernaculars. Most medieval *chansons de geste*—*geste* was the old French form of the Latin *gesta*, deeds, but increasingly meant 'narrative'— are dated from the eleventh–twelfth centuries and after, even though their subject matter is generally drawn from the eighth and ninth centuries.[120]

Always significant, *gestes* were deployed in important new discursive contexts at a time of socioeconomic change and political contestation. Where the predominant kinship system from the fall of the Roman empire had been cognatic or bilineal, this was overlaid and complicated from the eleventh century onwards by the agnatic or patrilineal system. The bilineal system was 'ego-focused', in the

---

[118] R. I. Moore, *The Formation of a Persecuting Society: Authority and Deviance in Western Europe, 950–1250* (Oxford: Blackwell, 2007).

[119] Le Goff, 'What Did the Twelfth-Century Renaissance Mean?'; Peter von Moos, 'Das. 12. Jahrhundert—eine "Renaissance" oder ein "Aufklärungszeitalter"?', *Mittellateinisches Jahrbuch*, 23 (1988), 1–10. See also the *locus classicus*, Haskins, *The Renaissance of the Twelfth Century*.

[120] Bloch, *Feudal Society*, 99–107; Damian-Grint, *New Historians*, 189.

sense that kinship was determined by relative distance from the living person (man or woman, both of whom had inheritance rights), with salient distances measured in degrees from that person. The patrilineal system was 'ancestor-focused'; it posited an absolute anchorage in the past and a line of ever-growing if now purely male extension into the present and beyond. Connection to the past was announced by the adoption of the agnatic family name, alongside coats of arms, and mottoes, with the systematic use of heraldry emerging in the mid-twelfth century. The new emphasis on patrilineage was attributable on one hand to the partial success of the church's push from the Gregorian reform period to enforce monogamy and a new marriage ethic on the nobility, and on the other hand to the matter of land resources. In an increasingly delineated Europe, neither the fruits of pillage nor new land were easy to come by, and in the interests of maintaining extant landholdings, rights of inheritance were limited, with females being most adversely affected.[121] A reciprocal relationship developed between nobles organizing themselves patrilineally and the literary genre of genealogy that expressed the lineage's self-consciousness. This new ordering principle shaped the narrativization of the past by fusing the chronography of the chronicle with the *vita* or biography. While legitimating hereditary rule by projecting it as an unbroken chain into the distant past (a continuity principle), in a way similar to the origin myths of Christianity in which Eve sprang from Adam and Christ from the Father (a religious principle), genealogical narrative also established the most important periodization (a discontinuity principle) with reference to human generational change (a secularity principle). Altogether, this produced a fusion of religious-literary tradition with the demands of new social realities. In place of the chronicler's time or a divine scheme inferable by figural thought, dynastic or political time now became more pronounced as an organizing principle for the histories of kingdoms, fiefdoms, and abbeys, along with the requisite acts of procreation, marriage, and heroism. Spiegel explains that

> Genealogy enabled chroniclers to organize their narratives as a series of *gestes* performed by the successive representatives of one or more *lignages* [lineages], whose personal characteristics and deeds, extensively chronicled in essentially biographical modes, bespoke the enduring meaning of history as the collective action of noble lineages in relation to one another and to those values to which their *gestes* gave life.[122]

---

[121] David Herlihy, *Women, Family and Society in Medieval Europe* (Oxford: Berghahn, 1995), 143–7; on heraldry, but also on the plurality of agnatic and cognatic lineages into the twelfth century and beyond, see David Crouch, 'The Historian, Lineage and Heraldry 1050–1250', in Peter Coss and Maurice Keen (eds.), *Heraldry, Pageantry and Social Display in Medieval England* (Woodbridge: Boydell, 2002), 17–37.

[122] Spiegel, *The Past as Text*, 104–110, quotation from 108–9; Given-Wilson, *Chronicles*, 87, 157.

THE 'MIDDLE AGE' 99

Clearly *gestes* were supposed to provide eternally valid *exempla*, but the sense of time measured by human life and experience, and of that life in turn being illuminated by purposive action, provides further evidence against assertions like that by Benedict Anderson of a medieval 'conception of temporality in which cosmology and history were indistinguishable'.[123]

History and Developments in Political Identity

Moments of secular rupture like the Norman Conquest stimulated greater interest in secular cultural changes within Christendom and effected fundamental shifts in the periodization of English and British Histories. More broadly, a cursory glance at the History of Europe in the eleventh and twelfth centuries reveals great developments in state formation, centralization, and colonization in which emperors and popes fought over whether primacy was to be accorded to the priestly sword or the royal one. Shared legal systems were a key source of individuating collective identity against other collectives, too. The growing pan-state influence of Roman law, the *ius commune*, while competing in some ways, favoured secular authority as against ecclesiastical law.[124] That was but one of the ways in which the secular past was increasingly imbricated in the mundane regulative structures of life: while canon law was predicated upon the ancient texts, secular law depended upon secular precedent, if also on Roman law texts, hence the importance of jurists in the early development of European historiography, and the continued influence of historians of laws and constitutions even into the modern period. All of this was in place from hundreds of years before Anderson allows the development of any patriotism distinct from a non-territorialized Christendom.[125] In fact some of these politico-legal developments, which had roots in the post-Roman sixth and seventh centuries, pre-dated the very concept of Christendom, and were not eradicated by that concept during its relatively brief and never unchallenged dominance.

The very concept of the body politic that would be so central to early modern theories of state was a twelfth-century invention even if it was disguised as being classical in origin. John of Salisbury (1120–80), a product not of the Empire but of a Chartres education and the 'modern' Anglo-Norman kingdom, propagated a positivist science of the state whose administration was based on functions and elements of meritocracy rather than feudal oaths. He helped pave the way for the

[123] Benedict Anderson, *Imagined Communities* (London: Verso, 2006), 36.
[124] Briggs, *The Body Broken*, 92–4; Joseph Canning, *The Political Thought of Baldis de Ubaldis* (Cambridge: Cambridge University Press, 1987), 131.
[125] Anderson, *Imagined Communities*, 12–19, 36.

thirteenth-century reception of Aristotle's newly translated moral philosophy, which further disseminated the idea of men—and especially of princes and kings—as political animals, animals of the polis, rather than just men of individual conscience or soul. Why would medieval rulers not heed 'the philosopher', the man who had advised the greatest of all ancient monarchs, Alexander? Aristotle's Ethics and Politics became incorporated into the most important instruction manuals, the 'mirrors for princes', that proliferated in the later Middle Ages.[126]

Secular political and administrative considerations did not have to conflict with religious precepts, especially when one could identify God's will with the fortunes of peoples under administration. Where the chronicle of the crusades Gesta Francorum (c.1100-1) pertained to all of the Franks, Guibert de Nogent's slightly later Gesta Dei per Francos, 'God's deeds through the Franks', focused on that subset of Franks who would later be called the French, i.e. the inhabitants of what had been West Francia, which had been ruled by Carolingians until 987. Since then, under the Capetian dynasty, West Francia had gained a separate identity, and was known more often as simply Francia—in 1190 Philip II called himself King of France, and the name stuck. We should note that the moment of Guibert's writing—c.1108-12—was a propitious one to make a claim for divine approval as against those other 'Franks' of the Germanic Empire, given the conflict between empire and papacy that had been in train for decades.

The late eleventh and twelfth centuries saw a more intensified, overtly political use of origines gentium not just for kingdoms but also for barons and monastic orders.[127] These competitive claims to antiquity were temporal in various senses of that word, seeking as they were the earthly legitimation and veneration that came with the greatest longevity. In a latter-day idiom, the claims were at least as much neo-conservative as properly conservative, with their proponents looking forwards while harking backwards. Often, those proponents simply invented useful pasts, as was the case with that late medieval English historiography that sought to establish royal lineages, the origins of parliament, and thus the English 'constitution', in a far remote time. Such pedigrees proved useful in the fourteenth century in substantiating claims for the independence of the Ecclesia Anglicana from the Roman Curia, which marks the beginning of the process that culminated in Henry VIII's proclaiming himself head of the Anglican Church.[128]

Returning to the twelfth century, roughly from the 1140s to the 1190s the Anglo-Norman kingdom was the scene of a very particular historiographical

---

[126] Briggs, The Body Broken, 93–7; Chenu, Nature, 196–7; S. H. Rigby, Wisdom and Chivalry: Chaucer's Knight's Tale and Medieval Political Theory (Leiden: Brill, 2009), 13–14 on the pseudo-Aristotelian Secretum Secretorum. For references as to how Aristotle's works were known at second hand before the thirteenth century, see pp. 15, 85–6.

[127] Susan Reynolds, 'Medieval Origines Gentium and the Community of the Realm', History, 68:224 (1983), 375–90; on origines ordinum, Jotischky, The Carmelites and Antiquity, 305–11.

[128] Given-Wilson, Chronicles, 179–85.

movement reflecting an equally particular issue of political identity. The *estoires* were vernacular verse Histories written in Old French. They appeared before the first vernacular prose History in that language (Villehardouin's) and before developments of a similar type elsewhere in Europe. The development of this genre, whose prime exponents were Geffrei Gaimar, Wace, and Benoît de Sainte-Maure, owes much to the vernacular tradition of the *Anglo-Saxon Chronicle* and the translation of Bede and of Orosius's *Historia contra paganos* from the Latin during the Alfredian revival. It also bespeaks a thirst for something more authoritative in the vernacular than the epic *chansons de geste*, and Gaimar et al. were studious in stressing the distinction between the two verse forms, as notably by their source-references. One of the purposes of the *estoires* appears to have been to provide second- and third-generation Anglo-Normans with historical accounts which, whilst being written in their main language (French), nonetheless spoke to their increasing sense of Englishness. Thus the verse historians picked up on extant origin stories. Gaimar's *Estoire des Engleis* rendered the *Anglo-Saxon Chronicle* to those unversed in archaic Old English; Wace's *Roman de Brut* was ultimately more successful as it developed Geoffrey of Monmouth's tale of deep Trojan ancestry.[129]

In terms of prose History, in one key respect high and late medieval England was an exception to a wider rule. In the abbey of Saint Denys on Paris's outskirts, from the 1120s generations of Benedictine monks sought to write French history from a royalist perspective which, in identifying monarchs with the realm and in twinning the story of the latter with the lineal successions of the former, tried to inculcate an 'idea of France' *avant la lettre*. In the next century in Iberia, Alfonso the Wise of Castile, and James the Conqueror of Aragon both commissioned histories of their realms with similar purposes. However in England through the fifteenth century there was no real equivalent of these prose Histories or of the earlier *Anglo-Saxon Chronicle*. Given-Wilson plausibly suggests that this pattern reflects the relative post-invasion stability, territorial integrity, and centralization of the English state vis-à-vis other states and England's own past. Accordingly, England's monastic chroniclers enjoyed significant interpretative freedom and evinced great diversity in their accounts of the past, often displaying deep scepticism about the actions of England's kings.[130]

'Others' Present and Past

As providential Histories were gifted to a range of peoples, some of these narratives inevitably clashed with others, but when it came to physical clashes the most

---

[129] Damian-Grint, *New Historians, passim.*   [130] Given-Wilson, *Chronicles*, 152–4, 211–12.

extreme European violence tended to be enacted where ethnic difference coincided with religious difference. While the crusades encouraged a notion of Latin Christendom acting in unison, they also enhanced the sense of shared 'Frenchness' of those Normans and Burgundians brought together in common martial endeavour. Arabic and Turkic Muslims, like Slavic and other eastern and north-eastern European pagans, were the 'others' against whom various collective 'selves' could be defined. 'Others' also included the widely imagined and utterly imaginary 'dogheads'—the name is self-explanatory—to the east and possibly in Scandinavia, as depicted on various high medieval *mappae mundi*.[131]

The existence of an Islamic presence to Europe's east and south-east seemed to confirm the prophecy of 'civilization's' westward movement. At the same time, the thirteenth-century experience of Mongol invasion in eastern Europe, and the subsequent trading opportunities through central to east Asia facilitated by the *pax Mongolica*, further expanded Christendom's spatial and cultural horizons, and with that came new historical re-imaginings. The way for some of this had already been paved in the Anglo-Norman kingdom by twelfth-century vernacular translations of classical sources, which evince interest in the

> *merveilleux*—not, by and large, the other-worldly marvels of the Breton
> legends...but rather the exoticism of the East, with its fabulous wealth and its
> strange plants and animals (and humans), together with a depiction of techno-
> logical marvels in connection with Byzantium (mechanical statues, artificial
> lighting, hot and cold running water) and Alexander (submarines, engines of
> war producing poison gas, waterproof doors to close the Caspian Gates).[132]

The thirteenth-century Berlin *Eniet* (*Aeneid*) manuscript of Heinrich von Veldeke symbolizes geographical distance with exotic creatures and alerts the reader to some continuities between past and present as if continuities had to be argued for rather than simply assumed; a stretcher is made for a corpse 'just as we still do today' (an echo, probably unwitting, of Herodotus's 'even still today'—p. 22). Aeneas is distinguished as an ancient leader by his outer cloak, the *chlamys*. The mid-fourteenth-century illustrations of Guido delle Colonne exoticize distances of time *via* distances of space. The Trojan War is relocated to an exotic east. The Greeks and Trojans are no longer depicted as medieval Europeans but as 'orien-tals' with flowing hair and beards. Such 'visual exoticism' continued to indicate 'imaginative distance', as later in Sebastian Brandt's illustrated *Virgil* of 1502:[133] the past as foreign country, as one might say.

---

[131] Robert Bartlett, *The Natural and the Supernatural in the Middle Ages* (Cambridge: Cambridge University Press, 2008), ch. 3.

[132] Damian-Grint, *New Historians*, 4.

[133] Baswell, *Virgil*, 28–9; on the broader context, Chenu, *Nature*, ch. 5. On Herodotus, Baron, *Timaeus*, 237 f.

As to conceptualizing foreign countries as the past, let us conclude with Giraldus Cambrensis, Gerald of Wales (c.1146–c.1223), archdeacon of Brecon and clerk to Henry II.[134] Bearing in mind Dionysius of Halicarnassus's categories of 'space' and 'time' as competing organizational principles for historians, and Petrarch's twinned 'tourism' and historicization, note that Gerald's historical reflections on Ireland appeared in his *Topographica Hibernia*, Topography of Ireland (1186–7). Written more than a century before Petrarch's birth, and a few years before Maimonides' *Guide for the Perplexed*, this series of sketches fuses many familiar themes. Gerald saw his writings as a route to fame and ingratiation with the monarch who had led the recent invasion of Ireland, and the account of the Irish is as prejudicial as accounts of the colonized by the colonizer generally are. The theory of *translatio imperii* is incorporated in the 'civilizing' solution: Henry, 'our Alexander of the West', 'stretched out [his] arms from the Pyrenean mountains to the farthest and most western borders of the ocean'.[135] Most importantly for present purposes, the theory of westward movement was reinforced with a self-consciously modernizing rationale for conquest, and while Gerald found support for the rationale in scripture there was much more to it than that.

Warming to Ephesians (p. 83), Gerald found that 'putting off the old man, and putting on the new ... is the highest pitch of excellence, when the former acts are surpassed by being followed by those which are better'.[136] None should 'condemn anything because it is new, which, as time passes on, while it is accused of novelty, ceases to be new. Let there be found here both what the present age may blame, and posterity applaud; what the one may rail at, the other read; what the one may condemn, the other love; what the one may reprove, the other approve.'[137] By contrast the Irish comprised

> a people that has not yet departed from the primitive habits of pastoral life. In the common course of things, mankind progresses from the forest to the field, from the field to the town, and to the social condition of citizens; but this nation, holding agricultural labour in contempt, and little coveting the wealth of towns, as well as being exceedingly averse to civil institutions, lead the same life their fathers did in the woods and open pastures, neither willing to abandon their old habits or learn anything new.[138]

Note 'learn', for, alongside a description of 'progression' that would not have been out of place among eighteenth-century stadial theories of human socio-economic

---

[134] On the significances of Gerald, including the ethnographic ones, see Robert Bartlett, *Gerald of Wales, 1146–1223* (Oxford: Clarendon Press, 1982). On the imperial context, see John Gillingham, 'The Beginning of English Imperialism', *Journal of Historical Sociology* 5 (1992), 392–409.

[135] Gerald of Wales, *Giraldus Cambrensis The Topography of Ireland*, trans. Thomas Forester, rev. and ed. Thomas Wright (Cambridge, ON: In Parentheses, 2000), Distinction III, ch. XLVII.

[136] Ibid., Distinction I, ch. XIII.   [137] Ibid., introduction to Distinction II.

[138] Ibid., Distinction III, ch. X.

development (Chapter 5), Gerald had the rudiments of an explanation for that progression. He wrote that 'habits are formed by mutual intercourse'. The supposed problem for the Irish was that they 'inhabit a country so remote from the rest of the world, and lying at its furthest extremity, forming, as it were, another world, and are thus secluded from civilized nations, they learn nothing, and practise nothing but the barbarism in which they are born and bred, and which sticks to them like a second nature'.[139]

For Gerald, to look west was to look back in time. The same attitude has been identified in other actors, and the anthropologist Fabian called it the 'denial of coevalness', the 'tendency to place the referent(s) of anthropology in a Time other than the present of the producer of anthropological discourse'.[140] Yet this attitude has been associated with much later developments, developments perhaps beginning with Europe's embarkation on transatlantic colonialism and encounter with the 'new world' three centuries after the *Topography of Ireland*, and crystallizing in the Enlightenment.[141]

There is an irony in Fabian's work, and it relates to his aforementioned claim that 'Enlightenment thought' breaks with 'a conception of time/space in terms of a history of salvation to one that ultimately resulted in the secularization of Time as natural history'.[142] Fabian's *Time and the Other* is a fine study of the role of 'modern' concepts of time as they have influenced anthropological thinking and shaped constructions of 'others' as backward. Yet in order to establish these concepts as distinguishing marks of modern thought, Fabian performs that now familiar construction of a contrasting, monolithic medieval mindset by his characterization of 'the' medieval comprehension of time; to highlight the supposedly distinct quality of Enlightenment thinking, he conflates the medieval and the Christian and reduces both to a single and exclusive temporal sense related to 'a history of salvation'. By Fabian's account it would have been impossible for Gerald of Wales to have written what he wrote.

---

[139] Ibid.   [140] Fabian, *Time and the Other*, 31—in the original this sentence is italicized.
[141] Ibid. 146–7.   [142] Ibid. 26.

4
Renaissances and Reformations

Introduction

This chapter concerns the time from around 1400 to around 1700. If the title gives a clue as to some of the major intellectual influences on historical thinking during the period, we ought not ignore additional cultural shifts and political and technical developments.

On the political side, conquest and sovereignty change remained as important as ever in stimulating new thinking, but the designs of monarchs with increasingly absolutist tendencies added a further element. Overtly political factors chimed with different regional strains of humanism and the religious movements of Reformation and Counter-Reformation insofar as all three clusters of thought pertained to History as Identity, in the sense of a profound concern with origins and legitimation.

Technically, the invention and diffusion of printing stands above all else. The growth of literacy which it presupposed was greatest in the Italian city-states where mercantile wealth brought education well beyond ecclesiastics and the nobility. With an expansion of readers came an expansion of writers, resulting in a significantly greater widening of perspectives than had come in, say, late medieval Britain, as secular clergy broke the previous monastic monopoly on historianship. Even though churchmen continued to play a major role over the next few centuries, there was now something of a return to the classical convention whereby men of political experience asserted their authority on what mattered in the study of the present and of the past. All these developments help explain a greater scholarly focus on the study of human achievement in the mundane sphere, the *studia humanitatis*, from which we get *umanisti*, humanists, and, at one further remove, the 'humanities' as a group of disciplines. As the printing press supplied the reading market it also supplied scholars with copies of texts ancient, medieval, and contemporary, that thitherto only existed as scarce manuscripts in limited circulation. A proliferation of scholarly materials facilitated the acquisition of erudition and the comparison of sources.

Publications also catered to existing preferences, however, and it would be misleading to think that what was held to be interesting or politically important changed abruptly or completely. In 1476–7, the *Grandes Chroniques de France* became the first French-language work to be printed in Paris, and other annalistic accounts recent and more venerable, including the work of Gregory of Tours, were reproduced and read for at least a century thereafter. In the Germanic lands, the same went for the Fredegar chronicle and its ilk.[1] Social stratification mattered here, whether in terms of purchasing power or assumptions of propriety. Putting aside that of which we know least, that which Markus Völkel calls 'wild historical knowledge' produced from below rather than above, there were major differences in the sort of historical product to which people might be exposed. In the Germanic context from the Reformation to the Enlightenment, Völkel indicates the prominence of 'the broadsheet, the pseudohistorical romance, or the even more unconsolidated form of the "yearly reports" drawn from the periodical press'.[2]

On the cultural level, the fifteenth and sixteenth centuries saw widespread encounter with more 'new' worlds, whether via more expansive commercial engagement, further Iberian exploration of Africa, or the invasion of the Americas with their particular human cultures and strange animal and vegetable species. Jean Bodin (1530–96), that embodiment of the French Renaissance, mused 'Who can doubt that the Christian religion is the true religion or rather the only one?...Almost all the World.'[3] The transatlantic venture in particular altered the mental map characterized by the *mappae mundi* by showing that Jerusalem was not the centre of the world and that the landmass of Asia, Africa, and Europe was not the only one. At the same time, though, if French literature is any indication, in the sixteenth century more was produced and consumed about European encounters with the 'Near' and 'Far East' than with the Americas, and the discrepancy only increased over time.[4]

In the interplay of spatial and temporal thought, the informative encounter with foreign worlds in the present was matched by learning from prior worlds, including via the ancient geographical descriptions of Ptolemy. Encounters with the past were perforce historical in the broad sense, and they demanded particular interpretative skills. In specialist historiographic terms, the literary forms and style of classical works of History were at least as influential as their content: hence the term 'renaissance of letters'. Other innovations with knock-on effects in historiography came in the fine arts, literature and poetry, political philosophy, and through re-engagement with a wider range of Platonic texts than had been

---

[1] On Florentine literacy and other elements of the Italian context, William J. Connell, 'Italian Renaissance Historical Narrative', in José Rabasa, Masayuki Sato, Edoardo Tortarolo, and Daniel Woolf (eds.), *The Oxford History of Historical Writing 1400–1800* (Oxford: Oxford University Press, 2015), 347–63, here 348–9; on French publishing, Chantal Grell, 'History and Historians in France, from the Great Italian Wars to the Death of Louis XIV', in the same volume, 384–405, here 384–5. On the Fredegar Chronicle's printing, Wallace-Hadrill, 'Fredegar', 528–9.

[2] Markus Völkel, 'German Historical Writing from the Reformation to the Enlightenment', in Rabasa et al. (eds.), *The Oxford History of Historical Writing 1400–1800*, 324–46, here 327.

[3] Jean Bodin, *Colloquium of the Seven about Secrets of the Sublime* (Princeton: Princeton University Press, 1975), 163. See also Auerbach, *Mimesis*, 282.

[4] Denys Hay, *Europe: The Emergence of an Idea* (New York: Harper, 1966), 99.

available earlier to the bearers of the Neoplatonist flame at Chartres and the Dominican School of Cologne.

Running in a different direction to Platonism and Neoplatonism, radical 'pyrrhonian scepticism' was also resurrected along with the works of Sextus Empiricus (160–210 CE). Pyrrhonian scepticism affected humanist more than scientific thought in the sixteenth century, and its influence was supplemented in the following century by René Descartes's assessment of History: amongst other things Descartes wrote of exemplar historians that the omissions they make in the interests of relevance ensure that 'the remainder does not appear as it really was'— *le reste ne paroît pas tel qu'il est*—and those who model their behaviour on such exempla 'are prone to succumb to the extravagances that ail the Paladins of our romances, and to conceive designs which exceed their powers'.[5] Ironically, the humanist Francesco Robortello (1516–67) may have helped promote Sextus by trying to dismiss him when, in his *De historica facultate disputatio* (1548), Robortello penned a not entirely coherent defence of History against his yet relatively obscure opponent. Latin translations of two of Sextus's major works in the 1560s brought him squarely into public view.[6] Bodin's influential *Methodus ad facilem historiarum cogitionem* (Method for the easy comprehension of History) of 1565/6 addressed scepticism about History's reliability by providing readers with criteria for discernment and writers with a manifesto on content.[7]

The main body of this chapter begins with general reflections on History's place within the wider intellectual developments of Renaissance Italy. Then it shows how the historiographies of various states, as well as their political doctrines, were to one degree or another influenced by particularistic tendencies in Italian humanism, as well as by the impact of the Reformation. France is accorded particular attention, and then more briefly England and parts of the Holy Roman Empire. Then the chapter addresses the central historiographical battles that corresponded to the religious conflicts of the sixteenth and seventeenth centuries. These were battles of ecclesiastical History, centring on ancient sources. The polemical nature of some of the disagreements and the accompanying instrumentalization of the documentary record reinforced existing scepticism as to History's 'epistemic' status, which means that they buttressed doubts about the reliability of historical knowledge claims. Yet an increasingly bipartisan critical methodology developed, based on a combination of humanist philology and new

---

[5] Descartes, *Discourse on Method*, 40.

[6] On the reception of Sextus, Luciano Floridi, 'The Rediscovery and Posthumous Influence of Scepticism', in Richard Bett (ed.), *Cambridge Companion to Ancient Scepticism* (Cambridge: Cambridge University Press, 2010), 264–87; Duncan Pritchard, 'Doubt Undogmatized: Pyrrhonian Scepticism, Epistemological Externalism and the "Metaepistemological" challenge', *Principia*, 4:2 (2000), 187–214. On Robortello, points 5–6 of Carlo Ginzburg, 'Paris, 1647: un dialogue sur fiction et histoire', *Vox-poetica*, 25 March 2011, and points 8 and 9 of his first chapter in *Threads and Traces: True False Fictive* (Berkeley: University of California Press, 2012), 13–14.

[7] Jean Bodin, *Method for the Easy Comprehension of History* (New York: Octagon, 1945).

palaeographical techniques, with established religious hermeneutics playing their part. Here the dictates of self-serving confessional History as Identity sometimes stood in tension with the demands of a proceduralist History as Methodology even as all sides agreed on the importance of History as Communion. The chapter concludes by considering the place of historical thinking in a 'scientific' seventeenth century for whose dominant intellectual figures historical enquiry supposedly had little use.

Like previous chapters, this one addresses conceptual concerns of a general nature as they arise. Especially important are issues of context and contextualiza-tion. Different sorts of contextualization are considered, along with their varying implications for thinking about the past. In particular there is the question of how a heightened attention to historical contextualization could be reconciled with ongoing demands for the relevance of History as Lesson for the present. Topical reading was one established solution, but another was resurrected with the ancient doctrine of *similitudo temporum*.

Re-Encounters

The most immediately evident influence of humanism on historianship was in the form of philology. Indicative is the fact that one of two men with claim to being the greatest historian of the early Quattrocento, the bestselling author Leonardo Bruni (1370–1444), was once a disciple of Coluccio Salutati, Chancellor of the Florentine Republic. Amongst other things, Salutati charted changes over time in the Latin language and tried to revive its Ciceronian form.

We can trace the revival of Roman literature, classical Latin, and the classical world as a whole to before Petrarch's time,[8] nevertheless, there is a good case that it is 'the return of *Greek* to western Europe' that 'overshadows all other advances in the Renaissance and more than anything else entitles it to that name'.[9] The 'return' in question is that of the Greek language, specialist Greek scholarship, and ancient texts, but again we need to think in terms of degrees of scale rather than absolute novelty since there were well-established trading contacts between Italy and Constantinople, which facilitated a general circulation of ideas and cul-ture, and the Venetians had ruled tracts of Byzantine territory through most of the thirteenth century as a consequence of the Fourth Crusade. Salutati had a hand to play in facilitating the return of Greek, and with it the return of Platonism,

---

[8] Schiffman, *The Birth of the Past*, 152; Christopher Celenza, 'Humanism', in Anthony Grafton, Glenn W. Most, and Salvatore Settis (eds.), *The Classical Tradition* (Cambridge, MA: Harvard University Press, 2010), 462–7, here 463.

[9] Michael D. Reeve, 'Classical Scholarship', in Jill Kraye (ed.), *The Cambridge Companion to Renaissance Humanism* (Cambridge: Cambridge University Press, 1996), 20–46, here 32, emphasis added.

but this was a matter of seizing an opportunity. The opportunity came from another instance of cross-cultural encounter, as more classical texts washed up on 'Europe's' shores, along with the experts in their interpretation, in the face of the Ottoman annexation of Greece and the threat, and then, in 1453, the actuality, of the conquest of Constantinople.

In 1390 the classical scholar Manuel Chrysoloras led a Byzantine delegation to Venice to beg the assistance of Christian powers against the Ottomans, whereupon he impressed the Italian cognoscenti enough for Salutati later to invite him to Florence to teach Greek literature and grammar. Chrysoloras's grammar of ancient Greek, later to be published courtesy of Gutenberg's press, became a basic text of the proliferating humanist scholars of that language, while his sometime student Bruni translated a number of Plato's *Dialogues* and letters. His archaeological insights into ruins, as in his *Comparison of Old and New Rome* (1411) are said to have marked 'a significant step beyond Petrarch', one 'fundamental to the Renaissance recovery of classical culture' in the sense of reading 'the remnant as signifying an ideal whole'. Reliefs on statues, columns, and tombs revealed, in Chrysoloras's words 'how things were in past times and what the differences were between peoples', offering 'eyewitness knowledge [*autopsía*] of everything that has happened'.[10] Another influence was Georgius Gemistos 'Plethon' who arrived as part of the Greek delegation at the councils of Florence–Ferrara in 1438–9, which took abortive steps towards the reconciliation of Eastern and Western churches in the context of the Ottoman rise and the Hussite wars. When not in session Plethon gave a number of lectures contrasting Aristotelian and Platonic philosophy, which stimulated the Florentine Platonist intellectual movement.

Shortly before the Florence–Ferrara gatherings, Nicholas of Cusa (1401–64), or Cusanus, met Plethon in a formative visit to Constantinople. Cusanus had been exposed to humanist ideas during his education in Padua and had also been educated at the Neoplatonist stronghold of Cologne. He shared Plethon's desire for a harmonious *unitas ecclesiae*, but we should not see this as yet another Romano-Christian wish for the development of unity out of initial diversity, as earlier seen in Eusebius's chronography and Bede's vision of the unifying of pagan Britons under Christianity. Rather, Cusanus's thought had connotations, within limits, of unity-in-diversity, diversity as a descent from an initial unity in 'the one'.[11]

---

[10] Patricia Fortini Brown, *Venice and Antiquity: The Venetian Sense of the Past* (New Haven: Yale University Press, 1996), 76–7. Brown also tells us that the idea of ancient artifacts and images offering 'unmediated testimony—"autopsía"...would become one of the fundamental tenets of modern archaeology'.

[11] Jasper Hopkins, *A Concise Introduction to the Philosophy of Nicholas of Cusa* (Minneapolis: University of Minnesota Press, 1978), 4, and *passim*; Marica Costigliolo, 'Organic Metaphors in "De concordantia catholica" of Nicholas of Cusa', *Viator* 44:2 (2013), 311–21, here 312, 314. See also (for some suggestive oppositions between Cusanus and the humanists on one hand and nominalism on the other) parts 10–11 of the 'Sequence on Political Ontology' of John Milbank, *Beyond Secular Order: The Representation of Being and the Representation of the People* (Hoboken, NJ: Wiley, 2013).

His *On the Peace of Faith* (1453), written at the time of the fall of Constantinople, was an imagined dialogue between different Christian confessions, representatives of Islam, Judaism, and even of religions that would have been conceived as 'pagan'. While clearly prejudiced in favour of Christianity, and sometimes dismissive of the beliefs of Jews, it sought to remove grounds for antagonism by casting religious disagreements as misconceived on the basis that behind their different 'rites' each religion tacitly shared the same assumptions and thus paved the way to the higher truth. Within constraints, 'diversity' is accepted and even welcomed.[12] Such ideas influenced Marsilio Ficino (1433–99), who published the *Complete Works of Plato* in translation in 1484.

Ficino, who was the first significant philosopher to win fame during his lifetime as a result of the printing press, subsequently produced translations of major Neoplatonists including Plotinus, whose rethinking of Plato was central to the Neoplatonic revival. Ficino also translated the work of one 'Hermes Trismegistus', supposedly an Egyptian priest who some accounts dated to around Abraham's time. We now know that the major texts of hermeticism were written at some point in the first to third century CE, but the relevance is that 'hermeticism' may well have helped draw humanists to Plato and Neoplatonism, linking Plato to the ancient Hebrews, substantiating the idea that Platonic doctrine prefigured the revelation of Christianity, and portraying Hermes as the medium of God's revelation to Jews and pagans. Obversely, Florentine hermeticism was of a distinctly Platonic tinge. Ficino gave the name *prisca theologia* to the single true theology that is supposedly to be found within every religion. Hermeticism was also bound to Neoplatonism in the work of Ficino's student Gianfrancesco Pico della Mirandola, author of the famous *Oration on the Dignity of Man* (1486). Neoplatonists of following generations included Giordano Bruno and the Augustinian biblical scholar Agostino Steuco (*On the Perennial Philosophy*, 1540) who wrote that Jews, Egyptians, and Chaldaeans had bequeathed to the ancient Greeks doctrines chiming with Christianity, like the creation of the world and the immortality of the soul. The space for this sort of thought would be radically reduced over the sixteenth century with the advent of Reformation and Counter-Reformation demands on orthodoxy, but it survived nonetheless, and had an important role to play in later historiography (see Chapters 5–6).[13]

[12] Translated text of *De Pace Fidei*, in Jasper Hopkins, *Nicholas of Cusa's De Pace Fidei and Cribratio Alkorani: Translation and Analysis* (Minneapolis: The Arthur J. Banning Press, 1994), 633–70: see especially Part XVIII, §66 and Part XIX, §§67–8 of *De Pace Fidei* at pp. 68–70. On Cusanus's 'pluralism', see Markus Riedenauer, *Pluralität und Rationalität: Die Herausforderung der Vernunft durch religiöse und kulturelle Vielfalt nach Nikolaus Cusanus* (Stuttgart: Kohlhammer, 2007).

[13] On hermeticism, see Florian Ebeling, *The Secret History of Hermes Trismegistus* (Ithaca: Cornell University Press, 2007), esp. ch. 3. For other material see Frederick Purnell Jr, 'Concord, Philosophical', in Anthony Grafton, Glenn W. Most, and Salvatore Settis (eds.), *The Classical Tradition* (Cambridge, MA: Harvard University Press, 2010), 233–4, and ch. 4 of Richard H. Popkin (ed.), *The Pimlico History of Western Philosophy* (London: Pimlico, 1999). On the Greek influence in particular, see Marios

Romans, Greeks, Goths

While boosting a religious philosophy of harmony in diversity, the engagement with Greek thought was also characterized by more culturally narcissistic tendencies. The Italian relationship to contemporary Greece could be interpreted as a classical Roman relationship to classical Greece, with all the connotations of cultural competition as well as indebtedness that that entailed. Salutati's 1396 invitation letter to Chrysoloras recalled the ancient Romans' admitting

> through the mouth of their greatest authors that from the Greeks they received all aspects of knowledge: the verdict of our own Cicero confirms that we Romans either made wiser innovations than theirs by ourselves or improved on what we took from them, but of course, as he himself says elsewhere with reference to his own day: 'Italy is invincible in war, Greece in culture'.[14]

In virtue of their language and knowledge, the 'Byzantines' were being cast as Greeks by their world-historical successors, even though the Byzantines generally regarded themselves as eastern Romans. They claimed heritage of an unbroken imperial-cultural tradition from classical antiquity—and of a powerful strand of Christianity.

An intriguing adjunct to the story is Plethon's influence, via one of his students, in the self-redefinition of Byzantines as Greeks rather than Romans. The classicizing *Histories* (1450s) of Laonikos Chalkokondyles (c.1430–c.1465) imitated Thucydides in language and Herodotus in content, depicting the triumph of oriental forces—now Ottoman Muslims rather than Persians—over occidental ones. Chalkokondyles wrote in a secular vein, with no polemical hostility towards Islam or 'Turks', and propounded a cultural–linguistic more than religious or institution-based sense of Hellenism, which was appropriate at a time when the 'Byzantine' political structure had come crashing down. This sort of thinking would be useful for members of the Greek émigré community in Italy, although Chalkokondyles himself did not emigrate, as they tried to retain their cultural distinctiveness and resist Italian condescension, while hoping that 'westerners' might some day retrieve Anatolia from the Ottoman grasp.[15]

Philippides and Walter K. Hanak, *The Siege and the Fall of Constantinople in 1453: Historiography, Topography and Military Studies* (Farnham: Ashgate, 2011), 194–5.

[14] Reeve, 'Classical Scholarship', 33.
[15] Laonikos Chalkokondyles, *The Histories*, 2 vols., ed. Anthony Kaldellis (Cambridge, MA: Harvard University Press, 2014); Anthony Kaldellis, *A New Herodotus: Laonikos Chalkokondyles on the Ottoman Empire, the Fall of Byzantium, and the Emergence of the West* (Cambridge, MA: Harvard University Press, 2014); Han Lamers, *Greece Reinvented: Transformations of Byzantine Hellenism in Renaissance Italy* (Leiden: Brill, 2016), 44–52.

In a sentiment that has been held to embody a Renaissance sense of classical renewal and authorial creation, Salutati wrote 'I must imitate antiquity not simply to reproduce it, but in order to produce something new.' The idea is that one can only talk about antiquity in this way when first one realizes that it has in fact passed away—this is the sort of realization that some suppose was unavailable to medieval thinkers. Whether it constituted imitation or innovation, Salutati was certainly interested in associating his Florence with ancient Rome as a matter of genealogy and thus identity: hence his reference to 'we Romans'. With the same concern for primacy amongst Italian cities, but different reference-points, the later *Praise of the City of Venice* (*Laus urbis Venetae*, 1493) by the Venetian historian Marin Sanudo emphasized the superiority of Venice because it was founded by Christian aristocrats, while Rome was merely the work of pagan shepherds.[16] As an archival historian Salutati silenced doubters about Florence's Roman provenance, while proclaiming that the city had been founded before the Roman Republic was subjected to autocratic rule. In any case the Roman Republic was still an empire even if it had no monarch, a nicety that allowed Salutati, and Bruni in his *Panegyric to the City of Florence* (1403–4), to wax on the twin themes of republican liberty and imperial liberty-bringing expansion.

The *Panegyric* is explicit about the enduring significance of origin stories. 'As one usually does in discussing an individual, so we want to investigate the origins of the Florentine people and to consider from what ancestor the Florentines derived and what they have accomplished at home and abroad in every age. As Cicero says: "Let's do it this way, let's begin at the beginning."' To begin with, then, 'the fact that the Florentine race arose from the Roman people is of the utmost importance. What nation in the entire world was ever more distinguished, more powerful, more outstanding in every sort of excellence than the Roman people?' As an heir of Rome, to Florence 'belongs by hereditary right dominion over the entire world and possession of your parental legacy. From this it follows that all wars that are waged by the Florentine people are most just, and this people can never lack justice in its wars since it necessarily wages war for the defence and recovery of its own territory.' To a quasi-legal claim on inherited rights was added claim to an almost genetic inheritance of virtue, whence the significance of the timing of Florence's birth:

> when Florence was founded the city of Rome flourished greatly in power, liberty,
> genius, and especially with great citizens. Now; after the Republic had been

---

[16] Marin Sanudo, 'Praise of the City of Venice, 1493', in David Chambers, Brian Pullan, and Jennifer Fletcher (eds.), *Venice: A Documentary History, 1450–1630* (Oxford: Blackwell, 1992), 4–21, with reference to shepherds at 4 and primacy at 5 and 16–17. Thanks to David Laven for this reference.

subjected to the power of a single head, 'those outstanding minds vanished,' as Tacitus says. So it is of importance whether a colony was founded at a later date, since by then all the virtue and nobility of the Romans had been destroyed; nothing great or outstanding could be conveyed by those who left the city.[17]

Bruni's verbiage deliberately conflated Florence's regional influence with Rome's imperial influence. By allusive anachronism he used the same classical terms—*socii* and *amici*—to denote Florence's allies and otherwise friendly states as had once been used to indicate the 'free states' under Roman suzerainty. As Rome had presented itself as the *communis patria* of all Italians, so other Italian states in the present would retain a sort of semi-independent status with citizenship for their peoples if they agreed to follow the rightful heir. Much the same idea had also been propounded by thirteenth-century Guelphism, which had set itself against the Holy Roman Empire and for the Rome of the papacy, and of which the city-state of Florence had been a major proponent.[18]

The twentieth-century scholar of the Renaissance, Hans Baron, claimed novelty for Bruni's historical scholarship, especially the twelve-volume *History of the Florentine People* (1442) on the grounds of its having broken with any superhistorical, medieval concept of *Roma aeterna*. Bruni dealt in secular terms with the History of an *ethnos*, a people with a culture, and with the story of Florence *ab urbe condita*, from its foundation. He sometimes deployed a naturalistic idiom to encapsulate the suffocation of ancient Rome and the draining of its vital *virtù* on the sack of Rome. Conversely, some breathing and growing space had been created for northern Italians after the ejection of the Germanic Lombards (who had ruled from 568 to 774 after the Byzantine defeat of the Ostrogoths) and the establishment, initially under the overall authority of the Holy Roman Empire, of increasingly autonomous communes-then-city-states, which had finally produced the likes of Petrarch.[19] While Bruni differed from Petrarch on the relationship of the present with ancient Rome, the two were united in their attitude to the interim period, and that attitude was the opposite of the historico-religious orthodoxy prevailing since Orosius. It rejected the conception of unity and continuity embodied in the *translatio imperii* theory, cutting directly across the idea of an enduring fourth kingdom of Rome. This is the basis of Petrarch's implicit and Bruni's explicit tripartite division of history, the division that has led to

[17] All quotes from the translation of Bruni's *Laudatio Florentinae Urbis or Panegyric to the City of Florence* (c.1403–4), online at https://www.york.ac.uk/teaching/history/pjpg/bruni.pdf
[18] Mikael Hörnqvist, 'The Two Myths of Civic Humanism', in James Hankins (ed.), *Renaissance Civic Humanism: Reappraisals and Reflections* (Cambridge: Cambridge University Press, 2000), 105–42, here 121–9.
[19] Hans Baron, 'Das Erwachen des historischen Denkens im Humanismus des Quattrocento', *Historische Zeitschrift* 147 (1932–3), 5–20, here 11–16.

Bruni's also unhelpfully being dubbed the first modern historian.[20] Bruni's third historical phase began in the year 1250, which remains a popular point of departure for Histories of the 'late medieval' or 'early humanist' periods. It was the year of the death of Emperor Frederick II, which brought to an end the struggles between the Hohenstaufen dynasty and northern Italian cities, permitting the consolidation of the latter's independence.

Bruni's periodization suggests that for all the novel elements in his work it has that familiar quality whereby concepts of temporal and cultural difference are interwoven. While Salutati mixed respect for 'Greeks' with his condescension towards them, both Petrarch and Bruni, so aware of the role of the historian in fostering a cultural consciousness, ended up constructing and 'othering' a historical period by their scorn for the foreign cultures with which they associated it. Indeed, this cultural stigmatization drove the periodization. Thus, whereas Orosius had the Visigothic King Ataulf opting to develop *Romania* instead of replacing it with *Gothia*, for Bruni this was just sophistry: if anything of the old Rome endured, it was the name alone.[21] In Petrarch's *Africa*, the epic that made this scion of Tuscany into Rome's poet laureate, Petrarch has Scipio Africanus the elder prophesying the downfall of Rome, whereupon 'strangers of Spanish and African extraction will steal the sceptre and the glory of the Empire founded by us with great effort. Who can endure the thought of the seizure of supreme control by these dregs of the people, these contemptible remnants, passed over by our sword?'[22] The 'African' and Spaniard he had in mind were probably the emperors Septimus Severus and Theodosius. Spaniards and Africans were, however, not the major targets of Petrarch or Bruni; 'Goths' were. By the sixteenth century at the latest, the pejorative 'Gothic' was attached to high medieval architecture ('irrational') and art, but it was used in the fifteenth century in relation to architectural ornaments and 'barbarous' handwriting. 'Goth' was a catch-all category for 'Germanic', or, still more broadly, 'northerner', which in turn denoted anyone from the Visigoths through the Ostrogoths, the Lombards, the Franks, and the inhabitants of much of the Holy Roman Empire latterly.[23] Successive emperors were not really Roman at all, and thus arguably not even legitimate emperors: in a letter of 1333 Petrarch wrote of Charlemagne as 'King Charles who, by the cognomen of "the Great", barbarous peoples dare to raise to the level of Pompey and Alexander.'[24]

---

[20] On the origins and endurance of this label, Gary Ianziti, 'Leonardo Bruni: First Modern Historian?', *Parergon* 14:2 (1997), 85–99.

[21] Baron, 'Das Erwachen', 14.

[22] Theodor E. Mommsen, 'Petrarch's Conception of the "Dark Ages"', *Speculum* 17 (1942), 226–42, here 234–5.

[23] On usages and referents, see variously Nick Groom, *The Gothic* (Oxford: Oxford University Press, 2012), ch. 2; E. P. Goldschmidt, *The Printed Book of the Renaissance* (Cambridge: Cambridge University Press, 1950), 2.

[24] Mommsen, 'Petrarch's Conception', 235.

Developments in Source Criticism?

The fight against barbarisms, and by extension the 'othering' of barbarians, underpinned perhaps the most famous Renaissance work of critical historical philology, by Lorenzo Valla (1407–57). Valla may well have been the first to have used 'Gothic' to stigmatize a form of handwriting, in the preface to his Latin handbook, *On the Elegancies of the Latin Language* (*Elegantiae linguae Latinae*, 1444), which he wrote 'to restore the language of Rome to the Romans'.[25] He also helped undermined the papacy's temporal authority by exposing the so-called Donation of Constantine as a forgery in a treatise of 1440.

Since its fabrication, probably in the eighth century, the Donation had authorized papal rule over vast territories in the southern, eastern, and northern Mediterranean, on the supposed authority of the converted Roman Emperor Constantine. Valla, who had vainly sought employment under Pope Eugenius, then found patronage from King Alfonso of Aragon and Sicily, who as it happens was contesting the papacy's client, the house of Anjou, for control of Naples. Valla proved beyond reasonable doubt that Constantine could never have written the Donation.[26] Yet, despite the great significance conventionally attributed to Valla's work, suspicion of the Donation's authenticity well preceded him. Moreover, Valla's work had few immediate political ramifications: it was not even published that century (see p. 139) Just as important for the present narrative is the nature of Valla's interrogation of the Donation, which is often presented as a quintessentially historical, and thus supposedly novel, form of philology. In that popular view of Valla, awareness of anachronism is the founding principle of his text. But a competing argument can be made that the founding principle is actually the same principle as that underpinning the later *Elegantiae*, namely restoring to the Roman language 'the purity that was its glory before the barbarian corruption'.[27]

Before elaborating on Valla's text, we need to understand the varieties of anachronism. The simplest is the failure to recognize that event Y happened before event Z. We might say of societies that evince this failure that they lack an interest and/or facility in establishing the temporal order of Y and Z. Clearly, given the classical and medieval preoccupation with chronography, ancients and medievals had both the interest and the facility, even if the facility was not infallible. That Valla evinced this capacity, as for instance in his recognition that temples mentioned in the 'Donation' were only built after Constantine's death, is unremarkable. Another form of anachronism is the failure to recognize that

[25] Goldschmidt, *Printed Book*, 2; de Grazia, 'Anachronism', 24.
[26] Valla, *On the Donation of Constantine*, ed. G. W.Bowersock (Cambridge, MA: Harvard University Press, 2007).
[27] De Grazia, 'Anachronism', 21, 24, 25. The interpretation hereafter is taken from De Grazia's essay, which also provides references to those who have praised Valla for his acute awareness of anachronism.

things of the sort Z could not have happened/been said/been thought at time Y because of different cultural or socio-economic contexts, differing linguistic idioms, and so on. It is the alleged failure of medieval thought in this second respect that Valla is supposed to have overcome. Now on one hand we have already seen that medieval scriptural exegetes had earlier developed something of that which is attributed to Valla. On the other hand, it seems that whilst Valla clearly possessed a sense of linguistic-cultural difference in his juxtaposition of linguistic 'barbarisms' and classical purity, this awareness was associated less with matters of temporality, asynchronicity, and anachronism than with cultural issues that still pertained in the present, however much they also obtained in the past. Germanic 'barbarians' still exist and write barbarically as they did before. The major juxtaposition is not Constantine's fourth-century-ness and the forger's likely eighth-century-ness. Parenthetically, partly because some of his assumptions about classical purity were just assumptions, Valla ended up deploying the critical standard of probability and likelihood which was familiar to medieval chroniclers as much as to Herodotus.[28]

One major historian with a great historical interest in language but less of a concern for rhetorical self-presentation was Flavio Biondo (1392–1463), to whom Valla may well owe some of his critical insight.[29] Biondo authored the massive *Decades historiarum ab inclinatione Romanorum imperii* (*Decades of History from the Deterioration of the Roman Empire*). Its title and span, from the sack of Rome in 410 up to his present in 1440, indicate Petrarchian preoccupations. Given his suspicion of partisan eyewitness testimony, a central concern of Biondo's was comparing and contrasting earlier narratives and other sources, to the point where much of his writing was more of a disquisition on evidence and the work of other historians than a continuous narrative. (This exercise in 'showing one's working' in the final written product rather than the seminar debate would periodically resurface in popularity, most recently from the late twentieth century.) Tacitus, Sallust, and Orosius all fell grist to his critical mill. Among his critical-linguistic concerns was the impossibility of channelling the vogue for classical Latin into an accurate account of post-classical history. Thus, whilst 'imperator' had once signified a supreme military commander, now, in Biondo's day, it meant the Holy Roman Emperor. Gary Ianziti sees this sort of attention to language as a new historiographical feature.[30] It does not delegitimate all of Ianziti's arguments to point in qualification to Procopius's excursus on the different sorts of combatant indicated across time by the common term bowmen (pp. 79–80).

The critical use of a wide range of often conflicting sources was a signal feature of Bruni's work as much as Biondo's, though in this respect we should only measure the distance of either from previous historiography in relatively fine degrees not

---

[28] Ibid. 20–4 (quotation from 23–4.   [29] Ianziti, 'Humanism's New Science', 61–2.
[30] Ibid. 64–9, 82–4.

nature.[31] In Bruni's case his critical endeavours were not purely the expression of commitment to rigour in principle so much as a matter of casting the net widely to substantiate new historical interpretations which had their own political connotations. As with the twelfth- and thirteenth-century barons who shaped new genealogical Histories, novelty was born of necessity. But a blow had still been struck against the partly observed norm of accepting the verdicts of previous generations of historians—this blow was the historiographical equivalent of the earlier changes in the concept of *auctoritas* in scriptural exegesis. The earlier 'convention' had permitted many students of contemporary history to assume a solid foundation upon which to construct their own edifices, which would in turn be accepted as given. The revisionist attitude had the potential to keep everything permanently open, as regards the past at least: the ever-moving present was a different matter. Implicit in Bruni's work, and more clearly in that of his follower Matteo Palmieri and of Biondo, is the sense that the contemporary cannot be written of in the same register as the past. Partly this is to do, as Valla noted in the context of inscribing the deeds of his patron King Ferdinand, with the extra pressures involved in writing about the living and the still-influential. (Nothing new there: see Polybius, Cassiodorus, and Henry of Huntingdon plus a long tradition of criticism by allegory.[32]) But just as much, this problem arose from the fluidity of the present and the sense that one does not have the same perspective on it as one has on the past. For Biondo this sense was supposedly enhanced by rapid change in the public and private spheres as well as technologies of warmaking.[33] Here again, Procopius's 'bowmen' are relevant to the historiographical debate.

Changed Circumstances, Contested Purposes

One development in History's purposes from the fifteenth and sixteenth centuries onwards was the deployment of historically oriented exemplarity in the service of a more fully fledged theory of autonomous political ethics. Bruni's *vitam et mores et res gestas* of Cicero preceded Machiavelli in separating questions of personal

---

[31] As to 'innovations' in source criticism, bear in mind that the likes of Abelard had already done some source-comparison work—p. 88. Additionally on medieval source criticism, Haskins, *Renaissance*, 236; Charles C. Rozier, 'Repairing the Loss of the Past: The Use of Written, Oral and Physical Evidence in the *Ecclesiastical History* of Orderic Vitalis (*c*.1113–42)', *Historical Research*, 92:257 (2019), 461–78.

[32] Henry of Huntingdon devoted close attention to Henry I (r. 1100–35) much of it while Henry was still on the throne. Around five years after the king's death (*c*.1140), the historian wrote: 'As usually happens when a man dies, the frank opinions of the people came out.' In his frank opinion he was critical of the erstwhile monarch's greed and cruelty. That opinion was radically revised later in a substituted passage when it became apparent that the present king, Stephen, would be succeeded by Henry's grandson (Henry II). See Henry of Huntingdon, *The History of the English People*, 65, 134.

[33] For all the themes of this paragraph, Ianziti, 'Humanism's New Science', especially 64–5, 68–9, 74–80.

morality from the political morality of the man of power: thus was History as Lesson adapted to what the sociologist Max Weber would call the ethics of responsibility of office. Like Machiavelli later, and Polybius long before, Bruni was aware of the potentially advantageous or disadvantageous elements of his own political context and the advancement his work might bring: Books VII–XII of his *History of the Florentine People* accordingly served to vindicate the Medici oligarchy which had come to power by the time of their writing or publishing. This context might help explain his attitude to the exercise of political power. Previous mirrors of princes had prioritized secular authority, but the extent of moral leeway here (as judged against Christian teaching) was new. Unlike Plutarch, Bruni did not see Cicero as failing because of personal shortcomings like excessive ambition, and unlike Petrarch he did not see Cicero as innately flawed by his ignorance of Christ. Rather, he saw that political struggles have their own rules, the moral parameters of which are governed by matters like state survival.[34] This vision need not entail atheism. For Bruni, who influenced Machiavelli more than did the theorist Valla, God provided an ultimate parameter, but that parameter was a long way in the background. The ends of politics had not necessarily changed, but in Bruni's theory the means had.

By Machiavelli's time, the political context had changed again, and it was above all this context, in particular the 'Italian wars', also called the 'Habsburg–Valois wars', that gave his work its urgency and edge. These wars lasted on and off from 1494 to 1559 and involved most of the Italian states in changing alliances with the others and with one or other of the great powers, France, Spain, and the Holy Roman Empire, that invaded parts of the peninsula at various points. At a time of gross violence and destruction in Italy, it seems rather perverse that one of the early consequences of the French invasion was an enhanced French Italophilia, even if this could take the form of grand theft from Italian libraries. Another expression of Italophilia was the royal patronization of an Italian, Paolo Emilio, to write a celebratory *History of France* (*De rebus gestis Francorum*, 1516–19) in the best humanist style.[35] While interventions and attempted interventions in Italian internal affairs by France and the Empire were by no means unprecedented, the 'Italian wars' shattered the relative peace northern Italy had enjoyed for a few decades, and threatened Bruni's vision of Florentine ascent.

---

[34] Gary Ianziti, 'A Life in Politics: Leonardo Bruni's *Cicero*', *Journal of the History of Ideas*, 61:1 (2000) 39–58, here 50–1, 56–8. Ianziti, *Writing History in Renaissance Italy: Leonardo Bruni and the Uses of the Past* (Cambridge, MA: Harvard University Press, 2012), Part II on the Florentine Histories. On classical and medieval views of the connection between elite ethical conduct and the wellbeing of the state, see Briggs, *The Body Broken*, 94.

[35] On Italomania and plunder, Grell, 'History and Historians in France', 386–7, 394; on the phenomenon of Italian humanists writing national histories for foreign monarchs, Markus Völkel, 'Rhetoren und Pioniere. Italienische Humanisten als Geschichtsschreiber der europäischen Nationen. Eine Skizze', in Peter Burschel, Mark Häberlein, and Volker Reinhardt (eds.), *Historische Anstöße* (Berlin: Akademie, 2002), 339–62.

Political and military affairs could not be anywhere but at the centre of a scholarly attempt to get to grips with the Italian situation, and while Machiavelli wrote an orthodox historical work, the vernacular *Florentine Histories*, he is best known today for crossing the line that divides exemplar History from political theory grounded in historical thought. Machiavelli's attitude to religion is a matter of controversy. In separating political from Christian morality, or at least Christian morality as interpreted by the church, he at once felt himself to be describing elements of how 'princes' had actually behaved and encouraging clearer thought about how they should behave. As constituted, Christian other-worldliness was unsuitable as a basis for civic *virtù* or political theory in a brutal world.[36] While the *de facto* situation had changed in the middle ages with the growth of secular papal power, the *de jure* status of Christian morality remained, creating a problematic tension. Machiavelli was actually true to a longstanding tradition of trying to separate church and politics.[37] In that sense he was also not far from his contemporary Luther: both fancied themselves realists about worldly politics, and, in their desire to end illusions about how government was run and how it ought to be run—i.e. free from supervening ecclesiastical influence—both gave secular governance the honour due to it.[38] All this in turn reminds us of the strength of the arguments that draw parallels between Machiavelli's thought and thought influenced by nominalism: theologically realist 'ideas' and conceptions of divinely bequeathed order were replaced with rediscovered, capricious *fortuna*; God-given moral rules gave way to flexible, prudential, and strategically immoral leadership. One had to fall back on the mental synthesis of sensual experience backed up by and systematized in historical enquiry—enquiry, that is, into the way other humans had handled the world.[39]

In one sense Machiavelli's work had the project of historical contextualization at its core. It was predicated on the idea that the highest good, order, stemmed not from fiat of higher authority but from the efforts of rulers in particular situations

[36] Christian veneration of 'humility, abnegation and contempt for mundane things' were to be contrasted with the 'magnanimity, bodily strength' and boldness encouraged in pre-Christian Rome. Niccolò Machiavelli, *The Discourses of Niccolò Machiavelli*, vol. 1, ed. Leslie Walker (London: Routledge, 2013), II.2.6–8 (at p. 364).

[37] Paul-Erik Korvela, 'Machiavelli's Critique of Christianity', in Kari Palonen (ed.), *Redescriptions: Yearbook of Political Thought and Conceptual History*, vol. 9 (Münster: LIT, 2005), 183–213, which also invokes the work of Victoria Kahn on rhetoric. On new political means and old ends, Quentin Skinner *The Foundations of Modern Political Thought*, vol. 1 (Cambridge: Cambridge University Press, 1978), 134–5.

[38] R. H. Murray, *The Individual and the State* (London: Hutchinson, 1946), ch. 4; Quentin Skinner, *The Foundations of Modern Political Thought*, vol. 2 (Cambridge: Cambridge University Press, 1978), 143.

[39] Brian Harding, *Not Even a God can Save Us Now: Reading Machiavelli after Heidegger* (Montreal: McGill-Queen's University Press, 2017), ch. 3; for the nominalist connection, Michael Allan Gillespie, *The Theological Origins of Modernity* (Chicago: University of Chicago Press, 2008), 134–8; at the nexus of nominalist influence and historiography, Janet Coleman, 'Machiavelli's *Via Moderna*: Medieval and Renaissance Attitudes to History', in Martin Coyle (ed.), *Niccolò Machiavelli's The Prince: New Interdisciplinary Essays* (Manchester: Manchester University Press, 1995), 40–65.

in which their judgement as to the dictates of necessity was paramount. Yet he expounded some of his own philosophy of statecraft in a commentary on Livy, and in *The Prince*—that new mirror of princes, that 'typology of innovators and their relations with *fortuna*'—he spoke on Moses and Cyrus in the same breath as the Renaissance states. Here is testament to his belief that beneath shifting political discourses lay historically derivable precepts of political behaviour (rather than strict laws) which it was immoral as well as unwise to ignore, even when obeying those precepts demanded immoral means. He was concerned that, if superficially conducted, comparative study would reveal only difference across time and place at the expense of important similarities and continuities. Above all, examples must be very carefully chosen and if necessary—here the delicate balance that had to be struck—they must be manipulated to reveal the deeper truth.[40] This was effectively a response to Aristotle's criticism of History as revealing only the contingent, not the necessary, but it was not the same reply as Polybius's rejoinder, which had been to try to make History into a science of universal connections (pp. 36–8). In Machiavelli's work, as with the *inventiones* of religious history, the ragged edges of literal truth sense could be trimmed to whatever *topos* (topic/theme) was seen to be essential. At the same time, while princes could learn prudence from reading and imitating, with changing circumstances such imitation must also be innovative. Here, too, there are echoes of Aristotle on the problem of applying general moral rules to particular cases. The topical framing of historical cases in this version of History as Lesson must promote the pragmatic capacity for present-oriented reflection rather than entailing a level of literalist contextualization that renders the examples into pointlessly imbibed historical stories (p. 76).[41]

It was a difference of emphasis that set Machiavelli off from his friend, critic, and fellow member of the 'generation of 1500', the lawyer-historian-statesman Francesco Guicciardini (1483–1540). Guicciardini's psychological approach led him to judgement on the characters and motives of his historical objects, but he doubted the broad applicability of Machiavelli's assumptions. Like Aristotle, he viewed the future as fundamentally unpredictable, whatever one's knowledge of the past. He was deeply concerned with the problem of contextualization in exemplarity, and drew deflationary conclusions that also had an element of Aristotle's view on History: 'governing oneself by examples is undoubtedly very

---

[40] On Machiavelli see M. C. Lemon, *Philosophy of History* (London: Routledge, 2003), 96; Ernst Cassirer, *The Myth of the State* (Hamburg: Meiner Verlag, 2007), 126–8; Robert Kocis, *Machiavelli Redeemed: Retrieving his Humanist Perspectives on Equality, Power and Glory* (New Jersey: Associated University Presses, 1998); Eugene Garver, 'After *Virtù*: Rhetoric, Prudence and Moral Pluralism in Machiavelli', in Robert Hariman (ed.), *Prudence: Classical Virtue, Postmodern Practice* (University Park, PA: Pennsylvania State University Press, 2003), 67–97, here 89; Grafton, *What was History?*, 214; Coleman, *Ancient and Medieval Memories*, 585. For the parenthetical quote about *The Prince*, which is originally from J. G. A. Pocock, see Olmstead, *Rhetoric*, 55.

[41] Olmstead, *Rhetoric*, 54–5.

dangerous if similar circumstances do not correspond, not only in general but in all particulars, and if things are not managed with similar judgement, and if, aside from all other fundamentals, one does not have similar good fortune on one's side.[42] This passage is from his masterwork, written at the end of his life, the *Storia d'Italia* (*History of Italy*, NB: Italy, not of any particular state therein), in which Guicciardini focused on the politics and wars of the peninsula from 1490 to 1534, finding relevance in proximity and drawing together the stories of different Italian states. The governing construct 'Italy' builds on Biondo's *Italia Illustrata* (*Italy Illustrated*, 1458), but the particular temporal focus of Guicciardini's History constitutes a riposte to Biondo about the possibilities of contemporary History. The ample documentation available to Guicciardini, plus his own memories of the conflicts in question, facilitated an account in which temporal flow and the threading of causality from event to event have been noted as pathbreaking features. The influence of Biondo-esque source criticism marks this work, even if by the time of the final draft successive stages of composition had smoothed away the artisanal elements of 'working' into an artistic narrative.[43]

Here seems to be the rub for those working from Guicciardini's principles: if exemplarity was compromised by contextualization, wherein lay its practical utility? Given topical thinking, we might ask whether the choice was really that stark. With subsequent debates about the development of critical historiography in mind we might also ask whether the exemplar versus contextualist 'dilemma' mapped on to the dilemma of misleading anachronism versus useless antiquarianism.[44] Even today, when the greatest influences on the historical profession have come down firmly on the side of particular sorts of contextualism, 'we' have not as a collective disavowed the idea of the past's relevance, and so we do not view ourselves as 'antiquarians' in the pejorative sense. We merely continue to work out different iterations of the relevance of History to the rationale 'philosophy by example'—a process of adjustment that is ongoing. Of the situation a century or so after Guicciardini, in light of further source-critical advances, Grafton writes:

> Writers and practitioners of the ars historica claimed that they knew how to walk the tightrope that stretched between practical application and pure historicism. In fact, however, they could not explain even to themselves how the

---

[42] From Guicciardini, *Storia d'Italia* (1537–40), cited in Mark Phillips, *Francesco Guicciardini: The Historian's Craft* (Toronto: University of Toronto Press, 1977), 27. More generally on Guicciardiani, Nicolai Rubinstein, 'The "Storie fiorentine" and the "Memorie di famiglia" by Francesco Guicciardini', *Renascimento* 4 (1953), 171–225.

[43] Woolf 'From Hystories to the Historical', 43–4; Ianziti, 'Humanism's New Science', 67; Connell, 'Italian Renaissance Historical Narrative', 360.

[44] For the phrasing of the latter dilemma, see the editor's introduction to Frederick Beiser (ed.), *The Cambridge Companion to Hegel and Nineteenth Century Philosophy* (Cambridge: Cambridge University Press, 2008), 7.

modern reader was supposed to go about both setting his texts back into their own times, with all the skill of a philologist, and making them relevant to his own day, with the bravura of a rhetorician.[45]

We should perhaps take 'historicism' here in the limited sense of being historically contextualized and thus non-transferable, rather than as having the connotations of relativism that some latter-day historicisms do. But the distinction is not always an easy one to make, as further reflection on the concept of 'contextualization' shows.

An oddity of a profession whose practitioners so regularly invoke the practice of contextualization is how rarely that practice is subject to conceptual scrutiny.[46] Consider two main sorts of contextualization: functional and cultural. The proposition underlying functional contextualizations is 'If I were in their situation I would act as they do', as for instance when one considers the extremity of human behaviour in wartime or other situations of duress. This approach posits a basically shared human rationality and value system. If functional contextualization concerns 'people like us' albeit in particular situations, cultural contextualization concerns people who are 'just different to us' in their rationality and/or value system. Cultural contextualization is involved when historians talk about 'understanding people in the context of their own time' and it is implicit in the description of the past as a 'foreign country'. Thinking back to the previous chapter, Maimonides' theory of accommodation has more of the element of 'cultural' contextualization whereas Augustine's theory is based more on a 'functional' contextualization in terms of its focus on political conditions (p. 89–92). But the distinction between these two forms of contextualization is not always clear-cut and what at first glance looks like a cultural argument may in fact be a functional argument. Thus if one observes that different societies can have very different birthrates one might automatically lean to a cultural interpretation, only to factor in more functional thought when the correlation is revealed between birthrate and poverty. Conversely, if one is exposed to new (functional) circumstances for long enough, one becomes acculturated/socialized into/by those circumstances. Since a certain amount of confusion still reigns about the nature of contextualization and since the above sorts are only entirely distinct in their ideal types, one who searches for perfect clarity in contextualization now or previously is on a

---

[45] Grafton, What was History?, 228.

[46] For relatively rare historians' forays see E. P. Thompson, 'Anthropology and the Discipline of Historical Context', Midland History 1 (1972), 41–55; Peter Burke, 'Context in Context', Common Knowledge 8:1 (2002), 152–77. Intellectual History has produced more explicit work on the concept of context than other fields, with a debt to Quentin Skinner: for relevant recent references and its own contentions on the limitations of the work, see Daniel Wickberg, 'Conclusion: The Idea of Historical Context and the Intellectual Historian', in Raymond Haberski Jr and Andrew Hartman (eds.), American Labyrinth: Intellectual History for Complicated Times (Ithaca: Cornell University Press, 2018), 305–21, with references especially at n. 1 on p. 318. For an influential essay by a non-historian, see Jacques Derrida, Margins of Philosophy (Chicago: University of Chicago Press, 1982), 307–30.

fool's errand. The matter is yet further complicated when one factors in contrasting historical interests that produce focuses on different aspects of the past.

One especially salient contrast concerns focuses on the 'external' element of action in the world as against focuses on the internal element of thought and spirit. To explore this contrast, let us juxtapose Roman annals and medieval chronicles with scriptural hermeneutics. The relevant distinction concerns the emphasis on elucidating *gestae* (deeds), with its associations with genealogical and exemplar History, versus the emphasis on interpreting meaning, with its associations with History as Communion. Again, the distinction is of an ideal nature, since the elucidation of events and the interpretation of meaning can go together, in the sense of understanding the motive that led to a deed or the significance that the historical actor attributed to the deed, just as one can devote intensive hermeneutic endeavour to divining the meaning of some event described in the scriptures. Nonetheless there can be a significant difference of emphasis between the more 'exterior' and more 'interior' approaches and it has ramifications for what 'contextualization' is taken to mean. For instance, a focus on the visible externalities of events might serve to immortalize actors and monumental deeds in a way that renders irrelevant the passage of time, whereas a focus on the internal 'Gestalt' of some ancient mind or church synod requires some distancing historicization in the first place even if just as a prelude to locating what is really relevant today after the historicization has been conducted.

Ultimately, we have four poles at the respective ends of two axes—interior versus exterior interest, functional versus cultural contextualizations—and can produce various permutations. Since these axes have any number of points between the poles the number of potential permutations when we move away from ideal forms is limitless. Any given permutation could produce a History that was novel, but that is very often the case with combinations, and novelty in this sense is not necessarily profound. What we may safely say is that all four 'poles' were present in historiographical thought for centuries before Guicciardini and his successors, and, accordingly, the potential for all manner of different permutations had also existed even if not all those permutations had been realized.

To turn the same point around, if the potential for conflict between different interests and contextualizations pre-dated the Italian Renaissance, then the ability to reconcile or at least ameliorate such conflict was also present, and continued to be so. In the period covered by this chapter, whether or not the choice between emphasizing contextualization or exemplarity was really a choice between assumed opposites, exemplarity did remain one of the major rationales for historical scholarship.[47] And as we shall now see, Polybius's cyclical doctrine

---

[47] For the opposition, Grafton, *What was History?*, 228 and Ianziti, 'Humanism's New Science', 60, though there Ianziti also stresses the general reaffirmation at the time, contra Guicciardini, of the 'paradigmatic nature of past experience' and thus the idea that *historia magistra vitae*. On the latter,

of History, *anacyclosis* (p. 36), and its close relation, the stoic concept of *similitudo temporum*, which was associated with Tacitus, provided one way among others to square exemplarity with at least some sorts of contextualism.

The Return of *Similitudo Temporum*

Without naming Polybius, more and more of whose work had become available in translation since its rediscovery at the start of the fifteenth century, Machiavelli's work reveals the influence of the *anacyclosis* concept, while Book I, chapter 2 of the *Discourses on Livy* draws extensively on Polybius's sixth book. Machiavelli was less interested in tracing historical cycles than in apprehending Polybius's lesson in how human actors might intervene to influence the cycle—as in Polybius's example of the creation of the mixed Roman constitution.[48] *Similitudo temporum* was explored by Bodin, the Flemish jurist and historian François Baudouin (1520–73), and other influential contemporaries in the sixteenth century. The concept helped move the focus away from individuals, whether in the classical and medieval garb of *res gestae* or the late medieval and early humanist clothing of biography and 'life-writing', and towards other times as a whole, especially crisis moments.[49] With the rebirth of *similitudo temporum*, as it were, one could acknowledge historical periodization and past–present contextual difference in principle while, in practice, also availing oneself of those select bits of the past that were deemed relevant to the present. Alternatively, as with the later Lutheran theologian Georg Calixtus (1586–1656), one could use the birth of Christ as a mirror point, with each numbered century working back from him finding some reflection in the events of the corresponding century working forward.[50] By the lights of *similitudo temporum* Tacitus could be appropriated as an effective contemporary, as in a number of seventeenth-century images that depict him as an early modern scholar.[51] It was indeed Tacitus, whose *Annals* and *Histories* were brought to Florence in the 1390s and became increasingly widely known from the 1420s, who became the greatest classical beneficiary of the classical theory, though uses of him were often intertwined with uses of Polybius.

Rüdiger Landfester, *Historia magistra vitae: Untersuchungen zur humanistischen Geschichtstheorie des 14. bis. 16. Jahrhunderts* (Geneva: Droz, 1972).

[48]   Brian C. McGing, *Polybius' Histories* (Oxford: Oxford University Press, 2010), 212–15.
[49]   On life-writing, Ianziti, 'A Life in Politics', 39.
[50]   Christian Thorsten Callisen, 'Scientia temporum & rerum: History or Antiquarianism? The Collection of Examples in Georg Calixtus' De studio historiarum oratio (1629)', in *Historiography and Antiquarianism*, 12–14 August 2011. Available online at https://eprints.qut.edu.au/45909/1/Callisen%2C_Scientia_temporum_et_rerum.pdf
[51]   Saúl Martínez Bermejo, *Translating Tacitus: The Reception of Tacitus's Works in the Vernacular Languages of Europe, 16th–17th Centuries* (Pisa: Edizioni Plus, 2010), 92 ff. on images and rhetoric.

Montaigne was taken with Tacitus's psychological approach, dubbing his work 'a seminary of moral, and a magazine of politique discourses for the provision and ornament of those that possess some place in the managing of the world', whilst Francis Bacon borrowed from his style as well as his History.[52] Tacitus fell into that select category of historians whom Montaigne felt had 'a right to assume the authority for moulding our beliefs on theirs', who could infer the motives of princes from their 'characters and humours', and who 'put appropriate words into their mouths'. (In Montaigne's view those lesser historians who were aware of their own limitations stuck to the compilation of facts, while the commonest sort of historian made judgements but with insufficient wisdom to justify their presumption to judge.)[53] The catastrophic conflict scarring the mostly Protestant Netherlands—the Dutch Revolt from 1568 to 1648 against Spain under the Habsburg Philip II—provided the classicist Justus Lipsius with the justification of historical analogy to publish a major edition of Tacitus's work in 1574. The doctrine of *similitudo temporum* led Lipsius to compare the prevailing political context to that of imperial Rome, hence his view of Tacitus as *velut theatrum hodiernae vitae*, 'in sum, a theatrical representation of life today'.[54] Polybius provided substantive advice to go with the historical analogy. Book 6 of his *Histories* was not just applicable to Machiavelli's preoccupations with governance, but owing to its detail on the Roman military, prompted Lipsius to write the *Five Books on the Roman Army. A Commentary on Polybius* (1595) that shaped the military reforms of William of Nassau who went on to end Spanish hegemony in the Netherlands.[55] Christopher Watson's English translation of Polybius in 1568 picked out the Greek historian's 'holsome counsels and wonderful devices against the inconstances of fickle Fortune'.[56]

As with any instance of History by analogy, all manner of opportunities presented themselves to the skilled rhetorician, and if the truth be known, Lipsius sometimes forewent the principle of careful comparison between periods in the interests of self-serving example-grabbing.[57] His *Tacitus* was dedicated to the Holy Roman Emperor Maximilian II and he had taught Maurice, Prince of Orange, whereas two centuries later Orangists were denouncing the use of

---

[52] Montaigne cited in J. H. M. Salmon, 'Stoicism and Roman Example: Seneca and Tacitus in Jacobean England', *Journal of the History of Ideas*, 50:2 (1989), 199–225, here 210; on Bacon, Francis Bacon, *Essays* (London: JM Dent and Sons, 1972), pp. xvii–xviii.

[53] Michel de Montaigne, *Essays*, ed. J. M. Cohen (Harmondsworth: Penguin, 1976),169–70.

[54] Daniel Simhon, '*Similitudo Temporum*: Agrippine et Medea, Marie et Médéé', in Richard G. Hodgson (ed.), *La Femme au XVIIe siècle* (Tübingen: Gunter Narr, 2002), 97–114, here 114 for the quote and 97 and *passim* for Lipsius's general significance.

[55] McGing, *Polybius' Histories*, 215.   [56] Polybius, *The Rise*, introduction, 19.

[57] On this variation, see Harro Höpfl, 'History and Exemplarity in the Work of Lipsius', in Erik De Bom, Marijke Janssens, Toon Van Houdt and Jan Papy (eds.), *(Un)masking the Realities of Power: Justus Lipsius and the Dynamics of Political Writing in Early Modern Europe* (Leiden: Brill, 2010), 43–73, here 70–1; Bermejo, *Translating Tacitus*, 92 ff.

similitudo temporum by Republicans seeking historical legitimation for *their* cause.[58] Jesuits like Famiano Strada saw Tacitus as subversive: in Strada's opinion the historian was a witness and as such should provide testimony (*testimonium*) not judgement (*iudicium*). If Strada's fears would be confirmed by Tactitus's popularity among Puritans, and then Parisian and Bostonian republicans, there was also an alternative Tacitus, 'black' rather than 'red'. This duality befits a man who wrote so ambiguously on Nero's persecution of Christians and was selective in which emperors he criticized. Unlike the revolutionary red Tacitus the black Tacitus could be seen as offering some succour to tyrants.[59]

No clear dividing line separated genealogical from exemplary uses of the past. Either, or both together, could serve political purposes: the special power of *similitudo temporum* was that as well as making the past relevant by analogy it could provide a secularized version of figural reading, linking the generally classical past to a self-consciously post-medieval present. The act of 'contextualization' could actually help in making such connections. At the same time, even when contextualization manifestly indicated disconnection, the idea of the irrelevance of the salient past did not necessarily follow. A case in point is a sixteenth-century French historiography noted for its sensitivity to differing historical contexts, which emerged from a young tradition of legal exegesis known as the *mos gallicus*, or 'French way', as opposed to the Italian way, the *mos italicus*. The 'national' orientation of these schools of thought is itself important and allows us to work in the next section from the issue of legal-historical interpretation to the more general patterns and preoccupations of French humanist historianship.

Sixteenth-Century French Historiography

Florentine humanist philology was a central influence on the practitioners of the *mos gallicus*, so it is ironic that the French way should end up being contrasted with the Italian. The *mos italicus* had connotations of medieval scholasticism, and was specifically associated with the University of Bologna, which had been the centre of Roman law exegesis since its founding shortly after the rediscovery of Justinian's *Digest* in 1070. A common but misleading characterization of the Italian tradition has led to the conclusion that: 'throughout the Middle Ages the Code of Justinian... was regarded as the quintessence of human law, applicable in virtually every situation'.[60] In such readings the Code was the basis of a conception of law as a 'timeless philosophy': apparently 'the medieval approach to

---

[58] On the eighteenth century Dutch debates, Wyger R. E. Velema, *Republicans: Essays on Eighteenth Century Dutch Political Thought* (Leiden: Brill, 2007), 69–70; Bermejo, *Translating Tacitus*, 92 ff.

[59] Tutino, *Shadows of Doubt*, 62; Ronald Mellor, *Tacitus* (New York: Routledge, 1994), 145; Momigliano, *Classical Foundations*, 117.

[60] Zoe Lowery, *Historiography* (New York: Britannica Educational Publishing, 2016), 34–5.

Roman law was, like so much else, completely ahistorical, with no awareness of the many differences between Roman and medieval society.[61] In correcting such views one first needs to recall the historical endeavour that had already gone into harmonizing legal-moral thought in the twelfth century (p. 90), prior to the production in the early thirteenth century of the collection of legal interpretations (*glossae*) known as the *Glossa ordinaria*. But much more needs to be said by way of nuance and partial rebuttal.

An important context is that Roman law of any sort was only thought to endure with force of law in parts of Italy and southern France; beyond those areas it could only ever exercise influence on the legal systems that were in place prior to the rediscovery of the *Digest*, and thus always existed in tension with other precepts, whatever the desire for jurisprudential harmony. This tension helps explain the evolution of the 'post-glossators', pre-eminently Bartolus de Sassoferrato (1313–57), who certainly did not treat 'Roman law as an internally consistent body of universal law, to be freely interpreted for application to the modern world'. (Note that the label *mos italicus* applies to both the glossators and the post-glossators in whose ranks Bartolus figured.) Bartolus opened the door to compromises with customary legal systems in a way that actually made some version of 'applied'—as opposed to 'pure'—Roman law quite attractive to codifiers of customary law, ensuring that it retained wide influence for a long time to come, even in Britain which had no 'continental' civil law tradition. Roman law would also influence the Code Napoleon of 1804, which standardized the legal system in France and is not generally thought of as an instance of medieval anachronism.[62]

Furthermore, to contrast the post-glossators or their predecessors with a pointedly named 'historical school' of jurisprudence[63] obscures the fact that some of the thinkers generally placed in the historical school by no means jettisoned all Bartolist precepts. The man sometimes identified as the pioneer of the anti-Bartolist historical study of the law in France, Guillaume Budé (1468–1540), seems on closer inspection not to fit that picture either.[64]

---

[61] Stephen Davies, *Empiricism and History* (Basingstoke: Palgrave Macmillan, 2003), 15.

[62] The 'universal law' quote from Schiffman, *On the Threshold*, 19, as contrasted with Daniel R. Coquillette, *The Civilian Writers of Doctors' Commons, London* (Berlin: Duncker and Humblot, 1988), 42–3; Walter Ullmann, *The Medieval Idea of Law as Represented by Lucas de Penna* (Routledge, 2010), ch. 1 and the introduction by H. D. Hazeltine; Michèle Ducos, 'Legal Science in France in the 16–17th Centuries', in Gerald N. Sandy (ed.), *The Classical Heritage in France* (Leiden: Brill, 2002), 297–314, here 312.

[63] As for instance Schiffman, *On the Threshold*, 18; Davies, *Empiricism and History*, 16.

[64] See generally the discussion in Ducos, 'Legal Science in France'; Ullmann, *The Medieval Idea of Law*, pp. xxvii–xxix; J. G. A. Pocock, *The Ancient Constitution and the Feudal Law* (Cambridge: Cambridge University Press, 1987), 23–5, on Jean Bodin and 'neo-Bartolism'. On Budé, Douglas J. Osler, 'Budaeus and Roman Law', *Ius commune: Veröffentlichungen des Max-Planck-Instituts für Europäische Rechtsgeschichte*, vol. XIII, ed. Dieter Simon and Walter Wilhelm (Frankfurt am Main: Klostermann, 1985), 195–212.

Finally, some of those who did set their faces against Bartolus were effectively just claiming to do the same thing better. Take Andrea Alciato (1492–1550), an Italian lawyer who spent much of his career teaching in France and helped introduce the new humanist-critical style that came to characterize the *mos gallicus*. For Alciato, the purpose of the philological exercise was to clear away latter-day accretions from the Roman law in order to access the purified original, rather than engaging extensively with glosses that merely confused the issue further. He was just as presentist as the scholastic hermeneuts in the quest for relevance, merely disagreeing about what it was that needed to be rendered relevant.[65]

The most extensive historicization of law—here meaning the contextualization of legal doctrines according to the different historical junctures at which they were established—was triggered almost by accident, and its fullest ramifications were not widely accepted. The critical skills wielded by Budé and Alciato, who were themselves indebted to Valla's and Poliziano's philology, were passed down to the next generation, including Bodin and Baudouin, but for such scholars the intellectual implications of the analysis were negative as much as positive, for reasons that ought now to be familiar: if the *Digest* was a product of its times, which were far removed, what interest did it have for anyone other than the antiquarian? Some legal theorists like Jacques Cujas (1522–90) may have been prepared to accept the basic irrelevance of Roman law, but that was not the prevailing view, and since some Roman law continued to hold influence in parts of France the matter could not be ignored. There was a more general principle at stake about the relationship between past and present. Ostensibly the most fervent historicizer of Cujas's and Baudouin's generation of *mos gallicus* students, François Hotman (1524–90), wrote at length in his *Anti-Tribonian* (1567)[66] about the unreliability of the Justinian Code as a guide even to anything ancient, as well as denying its transferability to the present. Yet he concluded the work commending something like Plato's project in his third book of the *Laws* (p. 33) in much the same way as Bodin had done very recently in the *Methodus*: putting aside specific regulations, Hotman felt one ought to study Roman and other law codes in the search for general underlying principles 'founded on a natural justice, reason, and equity'.[67] Here, 'contextualization' meant contextualizing in order to arrive at a point beyond contextualization.

Baudouin's *Institutio historiae universae* (*On the Institution of Universal History and its Conjunction with Jurisprudence*, 1561) also sought to understand the past

---

[65] Ducos, 'Legal Science in France', 300–1.

[66] Tribonian (c.485–542 CE) had overseen the production of the *Digest* for Justinian. The process of selection from and harmonization of earlier texts was seen by Hotman and others as one of the major causes of confusion in latter-day legal exegesis.

[67] Pocock, *The Ancient Constitution*, 11–14. The quote is from Schiffman, *On the Threshold*, 21, though Schiffman's interpretation of Hotman is different to Pocock's. For Bodin's view, Bodin, *Method*, 2–8.

on its own terms and as fully as possible in order to establish what principles from the past still obtained in the present, and what was historically variable. Baudouin viewed the marriage of history and jurisprudence as the way to provide lessons for the running of a state. He therefore endorsed the 'classical' notion of 'pragmatic' history as 'the form of history that exerts itself to explain and wisely and usefully demonstrates what it narrates, so that it describes not only events, but their causes, and gives events with their counsels'.[68] His work was more a guide to the researching of History than the writing of it as he weighed and distinguished between primary and secondary sources, examining eyewitness evidence and other historical scholarship. The conjunction of his opus and Bodin's *Methodus* only five years later underlines the continuing advances in the *ars historica*.

Bodin advocated a vastly ambitious study of human affairs, including geographical, climatic, and even cosmological influences, down to social and governmental arrangements, and how they changed over time. In his quest for causes and deep principles and patterns, which suggests the influence of Polybius's theory of cycles, he was influential, though not original, in rejecting the 'four monarchies' theory of *translatio imperii* (p. 53). His prescriptions for the content of historical enquiry presupposed the capacity critically to appraise the historianship upon which one was reliant in all of these wide-ranging investigations. He emphasized some critical historiographical principles, including the process of comparing and contrasting existing works of History, and reflecting on the subject-position of authors.

Universalistic and particularistic elements both appeared in Bodin's work as much as they did in Italian humanism, and while they sometimes jostled they could also complement each other. The element of cultural nationalism in the *Methodus* marks Bodin as a 'man of his times', times which included not just the wars of religion of 1562–98 but also the spread of Lutheranism and Calvinism into France from 1520 that supplied much of the tinder—the 'French Reformation' is said to have begun in 1534. A more specific context was the atmosphere after France's decisive defeat by the Habsburgs in the Italian Wars at Pavia in 1525. Hispanophobia waxed; Italophilia waned. Rabelais might still try to distance himself from 'the Goths, who had dealt all literature a death blow', but the equally humanist Etienne Pasquier (1529–1615) was stung by Italian scorn for the 'barbarian' French into trying to raise the cultural level of French vernacular letters.[69] Legislation about the official use of French evinced a determination to replace Latin as a language of culture, and the distancing of Roman law paved the way for

---

[68] Grafton, *What Was History?*, 70–2; Jacques Bos, 'Nineteenth-Century Historicism and its Predecessors: Historical Experience, Historical Ontology and Historical Method', in R. Bod, J. Maat, and T. Weststeijn (eds.), *The Making of the Humanities*, vol. 2 (Amsterdam: Amsterdam University Press, 2012), 131–47, here 136.

[69] On Rabelais see Schabert, 'Modernity and History I', 10. On Pasquier, Schiffman, *On the Threshold*, 39.

a stress on the relevance of French customary law, which fed into a growing interest in the particularity of French customs and culture *tout court*.[70]

A new myth of national origins replaced that one associated with classicism. Its first point of reference was ancient Gaul, with Julius Caesar's *Commentaries on the Gallic Wars* being a prime source of both History and inspiration. Gallic culture, portrayed as enduring under Roman rule, providing a supposedly unbroken if sometimes subterranean line to the French present.[71] The link is explicit in the title of Hotman's 1574 book *Franco-Gallia*. Pasquier's *Recherches de la France* (1560) began not, as per medieval convention, with mythic diasporic Trojans, but with Gauls.[72] There are elements of prefiguration in the story, as in so many genealogical accounts where links are made across large tracts of time, but the story was ethno-national rather than religious in content, which may explain why moderate Huguenots like Hotman and self-styled independent minds like Pasquier were prominent in propounding it.[73] Where confession divided, custom might unite. The characteristics of custom, as in customary law, also made it more relevant to historians shaped by the precepts of the *mos gallicus*, who might otherwise historicize the deeper past into oblivion. Indeed while the *mos gallicus* denoted a particular French school of thinking about law, we can associate it with a wider set of customary concerns that included but were not limited to law.

Custom, as studied in Pasquier's pathbreaking collection of essays in the historical ethnography of his own country, complicates any sharp 'othering' of the past. The logic went that, unlike written law, which can be pinned to specific meanings of time and place, customary law develops with the society bearing the custom. As almost a living, evolving force in Hotman's depiction, custom creates a conduit from past and present, discarding what is no longer needed, preserving that which is necessary: what exists, what remains, has proved its worth.[74] In the narrower terms of the development of historiography, a concern with custom was married to a concern with causation. It was no longer enough just to establish a lineage from deep past to present. Now one had also to explain how state of affairs A developed into state of affairs B and so on down to the present.

This building-block method of linking past to present, with a focus on culture and institutional structures rather than 'accidental' events, is well exemplified in

[70] Ducos, 'Legal Science in France'; Peter Stein, *Roman Law in European History* (Cambridge: Cambridge University Press, 2012), 77–9; Schiffman, *On the Threshold*, 19, 39.

[71] Claude-Gilbert Dubois, *Celtes et Gaulois au XVIe siècle: Le développement littéraire d'un mythe nationaliste* (Paris: Vrin, 1972).

[72] Étienne Pasquier, *Les Recherches de la France d'Estienne Pasquier* (Paris: Pierre Menard 1643), 3 ff. On the Trojan question, 37.

[73] On some of the contrivances of Pasquier's image, Catherine Magnien-Simonin, 'Étienne Pasquier (1529–1615) ou la dissidence discrète', *Les Dossiers du Grihl* (online) (January 2013): http://journals.openedition.org/dossiersgrihl/5748

[74] Pocock, *The Ancient Constitution*, 15.

the work of the Huguenot Lancelot Voisin de la Popelinière (1541–1608).[75] His preoccupation with origins as a first cause matches that of Bruni on the founding of Florence, as if the *Urpunkt* were a seed that contained and constrained all the possibilities of a culture or *polis* as it developed over time. 'Origin' and 'cause' become synonyms in some usages, and that was effectively the case here. The self-imposed demands of La Popelinière's historical coverage forced a break with the literary conventions of humanistic scholarship, even as he contrasted his causal explanation most starkly with chronicles. Whatever the scale of his literary talent, there is principle in the way he, like Pasquier, subordinated style to substance, suasion to substantiation. Narrative flow was almost inevitably hindered by the quotation of original documents, sometimes in their entirety, and the production of references in support of claims, as well as an expanding, perhaps undiscerning concern for detail.

In the spirit of nigh infinite expansion and regress, La Popelinière also penned a manifesto for a History that contemplated all peoples and times. In the historiographical volume *Histoire des Histoires* (1599) he defined History as 'the narrative of times, preserved in the memory of all things and a true collection of everything that pertains to every form of state: and particularly a narrative of everything that relates to all human orders and conditions'. As such History ought to 'comprehend the diverse nature, habits, customs and ways of doing of the people about whom she talks. Specifically the origin, progress, changes and all other notable occurrences that happened to them.'[76] This agenda feels like a natural extension of the interest in the deep History of one unique people, but it also chimes with the hermetic–Neoplatonic tradition whose cosmopolitanism coloured humanist thought and leavened its more culturally particularist aspects.

Quite how or how far hermeticism and Christian Neoplatonism shaped any given thinker is not always easy to establish, given that, like so many intellectual influences, each could be inchoate and incomplete. The 'cult of ancient wisdoms' and the idea of *prisca theologia* are given a Gallic twist in one historical work that appeared near the heyday of the 'new History': the 1570s. Guy Lefèvre de la Boderie's epic poem *La Galliade ou la Révolution des Arts et Sciences* has as its hero the fictitious ancient Gomer Gaulois, who provides a link between Noah and the subjects of the first book of Pasquier's *Recherches*, namely the ancient Gauls and their priestly druidic class. The poem details the passage of the wisdom originating in early teaching through a range of civilizations, Egyptian, Hebrew, Greek, and Roman, back to its point of departure in now-contemporary France.[77]

---

[75] See Schiffman's *On the Threshold*, 31–3 and *passim*, for most of the analysis in this paragraph.

[76] La Popelinière, *L'Histoire des histories: L'Idée de l'histoire accomplie*, cited in Costas Gaganakis, 'Thinking About History in the European Sixteenth Century: La Popelinière and his Quest for "Perfect History"', *Historein*, 10 (2010), 20–7, here 23.

[77] On La Boderie and the hermetic and Neoplatonic connection, including the popularity of such thinking in particular French intellectual circles, Frances A. Yates, *Ideas and Ideals in the North*

The association of Gomer with Noah shows a link to the monotheisms that is also posited by the Egyptian 'Hermes" alleged contemporaneity with Abraham and by Plato's supposed knowledge of Jewish scripture.

Bodin's *Methodus* combines French boosterism and respect for Jewish antiquity. Bodin was also taken with druidic wisdom, but where La Boderie saw a divine light being passed from discrete civilization to discrete civilization, and where La Popelinière advocated a culture-by-culture accounting, Bodin, like Gerald of Wales before him, stressed the interaction of civilizations as they learn from and mingle with each other. Jewish primacy comes from Bodin's conviction that only Jews 'can boast about the antiquity of their origin and the great age of their race'.[78] Elements of advance through interaction/exchange and of *prisca theologia*-type belief in the inner truth of different (but still broadly occidental) traditions are both present in Bodin's *Colloquium of the Seven About Secrets of the Sublime*, manuscripts of which were circulated after its completion in 1588. In the vein of Cusanus's *On the Peace of Faith* in the previous century, Bodin's conversing seven are: a Catholic, a Lutheran, a Calvinist, a Jew, a Muslim, a sceptic, and a philosophical naturalist.[79]

Modern Contextualization?

In modern scholarship on sixteenth-century French historical thought it has tended to be the more apparently forward-leaning or emergent aspects that have taken centre-stage at the expense of the ostensibly more esoteric Neoplatonic and hermetic components.[80] This is often the case given the search for the origins of the modern in historiography, as in other fields, and is not intrinsically problematic (anachronistic), since all historians have perforce to pursue some particular interest. As in all other areas, the conclusions from such investigations need to be assessed on their own merits. Now the overall combination of elements culminating in the work of Pasquier and La Popelinière does indeed deserve the epithet 'new' applied to it by the latter at the close of the sixteenth century, but we have already posited that combinations are frequently novel. Latter-day historians as acute as J. G. A. Pocock and Zachary Schiffman have, however, each singled out one particular element as new in a significant way.

In Pocock's words the novel element comprises 'reconstructing the institutions of society in the past and using them as a context in which, and by means of

---

European Renaissance (London: Routledge, 1999), 117–18, quote on 'cult of ancient wisdoms' from 117. See also Henry Hornik, 'Guy Lefèvre de La Boderie's La Galliade and Renaissance Syncretism', *Modern Language Notes*, 76:8 (1961), 735–42.

[78] Bodin, *Method*, ch. 9, quote from p. 362.   [79] Bodin, *Colloquium*.
[80] As noted by Yates, *Ideas and Ideals*, 117–18.

which, to interpret the actions, words and thoughts of the men who lived at that time'; 'postulating that there existed, in the past of their own civilization, tracts of time in which the thoughts and actions of men had been so remote in character from those of the present as to be intelligible only if the entire world in which they had occurred were resurrected, described in detail and used to interpret them'.[81] Certainly, the degree to which the contexualizing approach was then practised does appear to be different to anything previous. But however extensive contextualizing History was in the sixteenth century, or is now, it could not meet Pocock's exacting standard whereby an 'entire world' is reproduced in order to shed light on meanings and deeds. Who is to decide if enough relevant settings from the past have been described and whether they have been described in sufficient 'detail', especially since before this level of contextualization was applied historians did not unreasonably think themselves capable of rendering certain actions and deeds 'intelligible'? A standard of proper History is being invoked by Pocock, but in the absence of a total contextualization, which might be a description that never stopped, there will always be arguments about which aspects of which contexts ought to be emphasized. It is manifestly not the case that no pre-sixteenth-century History took a concern to contextualize anything at all since some act of contextualization is inextricable from the act of explanation and thus an account of causation. In fact there is no difference between a context and a cause; they are names we pragmatically give to different parts of an explanation. Saying that Jill kissed Jane out of love is to say that love belongs to the causal explanation of Jill's kiss, but we might just as well call love a context for the kiss. As soon as a historian offers any causal (part) explanation for anything she is providing a (part) contextualization.

Schiffman's concern to identify what is 'modern' is more philosophical than methodological. He talks of a culturally relativistic outlook amongst the 'new historians' of the sixteenth century who were informed by the *mos gallicus*. More precisely he sees them as having 'the experience of relativism' without going the whole hog and embracing the 'doctrine of relativism'. In fact he portrays a retreat from the implications of relativism on the part of the historians concerned, without making clear whether this was a conscious or unconscious reaction. For all the brilliance of his textual exegesis, he provides little evidence for the claim that it was just too much for the sixteenth-century historians to follow through with the relativistic implications of their findings. His reasoning is hamstrung from the outset in that he never defines relativism in a precise fashion. It is difficult to see what is meant by the 'experience of relativism' as separate from the 'doctrine' of it, since relativism is nothing if not a doctrine. Schiffman describes the experience of relativism as 'an awareness of the human world as being filled with unique

---

[81] Pocock, *The Ancient Constitution*, 1.

historical entities, such as laws, institutions, and states', but such an awareness has no logical consequences for relativistic doctrine-building from which a retreat had perforce to be beaten if the consequences were too much to bear. To think otherwise is to elide 'is' and 'ought': awareness of uniqueness might provide the grist for relativism but it might also provide the grist for scepticism about values or a neutralist withholding of any value considerations or an attempt to prove one set of unique institutions superior to another.[82] Indeed it would require some extensive argument to reconcile La Popelinière's position with relativism. He has a distinctly 'progressivist' view, stating that his present civilization ought to be 'superior in all things' to earlier versions partly because of its own historical knowledge. Furthermore, one rationale for his studying the indigenous peoples of the Americas is that they are on the same 'primitive' level as ancient civilizations.[83] The wider importance of the point is that Schiffman sees a later, more complete embrace of relativism as being the moment when historical thought became fully modern. To borrow from the title of his first book, *On the Threshold of Modernity*, the sixteenth-century historians refused to cross the threshold. The title of his second book, *The Birth of the Past*, purports to show how scholars of the seventeenth and eighteenth centuries took this decisive step. Now it is true that strands of relativism—here meaning moral–cultural relativism—have been important in shaping important historiographical norms in recent centuries, much more so than the epistemological relativism that has been much discussed in recent decades. Here Schiffman displays more self-awareness than many practising historians of recent generations, who if they ever discuss the matter may distance themselves from relativism even while tacitly endorsing it in the name of a certain interpretation of 'historicization'. But other influences have also shaped modern historiographical norms, such as the pressure for neutrality or impartiality (see Chapter 6), and these tendencies are not the same as relativism even if sometimes they appear to promote a similar outlook. In his imprecision about the conditions and meaning of relativism Schiffman actually epitomizes a disciplinary confusion that still reigns about how we do, and should, orientate ourselves towards the pasts on which we write (see Chapter 8).

Montaigne

'Relativist' is not the correct epithet for Michel de Montaigne (1533–92), who is far better known than the new historians of the sixteenth century and just as concerned with human diversity. The major classical influence on his moral thought

[82] Schiffman, *On the Threshold*, p. xii.
[83] Brian Brazeau, *Writing a New France, 1604–1632: Empire and Early Modern French Identity* (London: Routledge, 2016), 78–9.

was scepticism: Sextus Empiricus's concerns were at least as much about ethical convictions as knowledge. The doctrines of scepticism and relativism are actually not good bedfellows, since relativism is one of those strong conclusions that the sceptic is chary of endorsing, or at least endorsing strongly. It is scepticism that underpinned Montaigne's anti-dogmatism. While recognizing the strong attachment to belief that acculturation brings, he professed uncertainty about any specific belief-system. To explain his stance, we might look to the context of burgeoning religious strife and also his stint as Mayor of Bordeaux, holding the city for Henri III, France's most sexually controversial monarch, who could not but have benefited from Montaigne's elaboration of varying sexual mores from around the world. Looking backwards in time, Montaigne approved of Ammianus Marcellinus as a 'pagan', classicizing historian who was nonetheless fair to Christians and critical of the religious policies of the emperor Julian. Looking out to the wider world Montaigne's argument for religious toleration went hand-in-hand with reflections such as his *essai* 'On Cannibals'.

On the whole, Montaigne seems to have viewed the differences between peoples as being superficial rather than deep, and thus at some level reconcilable. He also tacitly subscribed to some moral absolutes, and, alongside proposing arguments that appealed to 'nature', he believed in a superior rationality. His admiration of the martial courage of indigenous south American peoples was less an instance of taking them on their own terms than finding commonality with the Greek culture that he so admired. He identified with the 'cannibals'' viewpoints when that helped in rendering self-criticism of French and European society. At the same time, in 'On Cannibals' the opposed categories of 'barbarian'/'savage' *are* revealed to be a matter of perspective rather than objective judgement. 'Savages'' mechanisms of leadership selection might compare favourably with allowing children to accede on the basis of heredity alone, while European inequalities exceeded anything that the old inhabitants of the 'new world' had to offer. It was not obviously worse to eat other men than to eat one's own god by way of communion; in any case, eating the bodies of the dead was better than torturing the bodies of the living. Overall, self-reflection is Montaigne's point—self-reflection as an ethos, making an enemy of dogmatism and blind assumptions of superiority or rectitude in light of agonizing schisms in his own civilization. The reversal of the gaze at the end of 'On Cannibals', where French society is seen through the eyes of indigenous Americans, indicates the capacity to estrange one's own 'mores', to see them from the perspective of an outsider to them.[84]

[84] Montaigne, *Essays*, 113, 114, 118–19, 184; Edwin M. Curley, 'Skepticism and Toleration: The Case of Montaigne', *Oxford Studies in Early Modern Philosophy*, 2 (2005), 1–33; Ann Hartle, 'Montaigne's Accidental Moral Philosophy', *Philosophy and Literature* 24:1 (2000), 138–53; Katherine Crawford, *The Sexual Culture of the French Renaissance* (Cambridge: Cambridge University Press, 2010), pp. ix–xii. Finally, thanks to Felicity Green for her thoughts on these matters.

Church, State, and Historianship: A Comparative Perspective

Some of Montaigne's overtly political pronouncements led him to be associated with the 'politiques'.[85] Badouin and Bodin were also politiques, which was the name given to a loose grouping largely comprising moderate Catholics and Huguenots (like Hotman) who sought the unity of the state as a means to religious coexistence. Membership of the tendency did not determine one's specific prescription for peaceful order. In the face of the fragmentation of French political power during the wars of religion, Bodin came to advocate something like absolutism, based in part on his reading of the black Tacitus; a ruler placed above the fray would alone have the power to end it. An alternative model was provided by the historians of customary law for reasons already given: while Roman law emphasized the ultimate decision of the sovereign lawgiver, customary law was not based on any sovereign decision. It was, perforce, an inherited constraint on the prerogatives of any leader. Its premises dovetailed with the Calvinist belief in the limits of royal authority, a conviction shared by contemporary Scottish Presbyterians. The case was given great force amongst Calvinists in France by the implication of King Charles IX in the St Bartholomew's Day massacres of Huguenots in 1572, in the aftermath of which Hotman's *Franco-Gallia* was published. But customary law principles had a wider appeal, including to nobles seeking to preserve their prerogatives in the face of royal centralization. Their failure and the success of the absolutist agenda from the end of the century correlated with the decline of France's 'new history', which meant a move back from the history of culture and society to that of the crown.[86] Parenthetically, Huguenots did gain some rights and peace under nascent absolutism, at least for a few generations, under the terms of the Edict of Nantes (1598).

The Reformation caused somewhat fewer ructions in church and state in sixteenth-century England than in contemporary France or Scotland because royal authority was not really challenged over either institution. Historiography mirrored the situation. When English historians from the mid-sixteenth century addressed religious questions, as most famously in John Foxe's *Acts and Monuments* (1563), they sought on the whole to buttress the lineage of the independent English church under the monarch. In this vein Elizabeth I (r. 1558–1603) cast herself, rather than Sylvester (Pope 314–35 CE), as a direct successor to the 'champion' of Christianity, Constantine, who had been proclaimed emperor at York in 306. Thereby the English church was heir to a purer early church.

---

[85] Philippe Desan (ed.), *Montaigne politique* (Paris: Honoré Champion Éditeur, 2006), contains essays exploring all sides of the issue, including the central question of the tension between Montaigne's public role and his role as a private intellectual.

[86] This explanation for the decline of the 'new history' is broadly George Huppert's in *The Idea of Perfect History: Historical Erudition and Historical Philosophy in Renaissance France* (Urbana: University of Illinois Press, 1970).

A similar propagandistic function was served by 'King Lucius', a fictitious monarch of the first or second century who had been brought to Christianity by Pope Eleutherius of that selfsame primitive, uncorrupted *ecclesia*. Such lineages had become more useful than the myths of Trojan ancestry propagated by Geoffrey of Monmouth et al.[87] So, like the 'new' French historiography of about the same time, we have a revision of deep historical antecedents, in both cases away from Trojans, but whereas the French alternative, the Gauls, bespeaks a more demotic interest in culture, the English alternative, early monarchs, indicates dynastic and institutional concerns, underlining the more extensive *political* centralism already achieved in England.

Only in the seventeenth century, after Charles I's absolutist aspirations threatened the *economic* prerogatives of the landed class while his religious stance antagonized puritans, do we see an English version of the 'new' French historians' interest in custom in earlier societies. A concern with supposed Anglo-Saxon arrangements prior to the imposition of the Norman 'yoke' now served arguments for limiting monarchical power. It was particularly relevant during monarchical restoration after regicide (1649) and republic (1649–60), given fears of a renewed absolutism that would wrest sovereignty back from the nation's parliamentary representatives.[88] During the English civil wars themselves, waged on and off from 1642 to 1651, the earlier coherence of most English historianship disintegrated along with the efficacy of clerical and governmental censorship, as all sides, religious and political, sought to vindicate themselves by book as well as pamphlet.[89] As the parliamentary side in the civil wars constituted the embryo of the English Whig party, against the Tories with their Royalist antecedence, so the anti-absolutist scholarly emphasis on a deep and continuous if sometimes threatened strand of customary authority comprised a key element in what would come to be called Whig History, even as the function of the Norman conquest varied in that History, mirroring its role at different stages in the historical thinking of William of Malmesbury centuries earlier (see p. 198).

The Holy Roman Empire could not centralize in the fashion of England or France because it was not a state. It was an idea and tradition more than a polity, and a powerful idea too when one thinks of its title and the theory of *translatio imperii*. Yet it became the epicentre of military as well as religious strife from 1522 to 1648 for reasons directly related to the multiplicity of political forms existing within it. In the decades prior to the 1520s, the influence of humanism plus a

---

[87] De Grazia, 'Anachronism', 24–5. Daniel Woolf, 'Historical Writing in Britain from the Late Middle Ages to the Eve of Enlightenment', in Rabasa et al. (eds.), *The Oxford History of Historical Writing 1400–1800*, 473–96, here 478–81.

[88] Pocock, *The Ancient Constitution*. On William of Malmesbury, see R. M. Thompson, 'William of Malmesbury's Diatribe against the Normans', in Martin Brett and David A. Woodman (eds.), *The Long Twelfth-Century View of the Anglo-Saxon Past* (Farnham: Ashgate, 2015), 113–22.

[89] Woolf, 'Historical Writing', 482–3.

reaction against Italian Renaissance arrogance had produced a cultural origin story that transcended myriad Germanic state boundaries. Where France's Gallic myth drew on Julius Caesar's writing, the Germanic myth drew on Tacitus, whose writings adverted attention to the fact that the Roman Empire had never conquered *Magna Germania*, stopping at the Rhine. As in France's myth, Tacitus's account aroused cultural 'memories' of Germanic liberties and egalitarianism as against Roman imperial authority and hierarchy. The attitudes thus engendered partly cut across and partly reinforced attitudes towards Rome-as-papacy, attitudes which were also shaped by the established idea of the empire as protector of the ungrateful Roman church, but they did not determine orientations towards Catholicism in the coming schism. In the first instance, Lutheranism spread by top–down reform as Luther gained the support of the rulers of various northern states. Then, after ensuing warfare between Protestant principalities and the forces of the Catholic Emperor Charles V, the Peace of Augsburg (1555) decreed that princes could align the confessions of their realms with their own religious consciences. Amongst many other things, the Augsburg dispensation established the deepest cleavage in 'German' historiography over the next two centuries. It is not that all historiography developed a preoccupation with religion, but rather that it reflected the general confessionalization of politics and culture.[90] Nonetheless, historical scholarship on religion was a central issue at the time and, by no coincidence, was important in the technical development of the discipline of History.

Ecclesiastical History and Source Criticism

At the same time as History was enjoying a mutually beneficial relationship with philology, via jurisprudence, it continued to be shaped in tandem with an older partner: religious hermeneutics. Baudouin features in both relationships, for he was sometime collaborator of the man often viewed as the father of 'modern' or at least Protestant hermeneutics—Matthias Flacius Illyricus.[91] Like Luther, Flacius (1520–75) was a traveller on the *via moderna* first paved centuries earlier by men such as Ockham, who, for Luther, was 'magister meus', 'mein lieber

[90] Markus Völkel, *Geschichtsschreibung: eine Einführung in globaler Perspektive* (Cologne: Böhlau, 2006), ch. 10.2–10.4; Völkel, 'German Historical Writing', 324–46; Völkel, 'The "Historical Consciousness" of the Holy Roman Empire of the German Nation (Sixteenth to Eighteenth Centuries)', in R. J. W. Evans, Michael Schaich, and P. H. Wilson (eds.), *The Holy Roman Empire, 1495–1806* (Oxford: Oxford University Press, 2011), 323–45. On the general reaction of German humanists to Italian cultural condescension, A. G. Dickens, *The Age of Humanism and Reformation* (London: Prentice Hall, 1977), 133.

[91] On Baudouin and the doctrine, see Gregory B. Lyon, 'Baudouin, Flacius, and the Plan for the Magdeburg Centuries', *Journal of the History of Ideas*, 64:2 (2003), 253–72, here 263–71. See also Bos, 'Nineteenth-Century Historicism and its Predecessors', 136.

Meister'.[92] Flacius provided theological heft to an exegetical style that drew on the Humanist *ars critica*. Emblematic of the contribution of the *ars critica* to the Protestant cause is Luther's use of Valla's work on the Donation of Constantine after it was finally published in 1517, the same year Luther advertised his 95 theses. Flacius contributed to the mix his version of traditions of reading that go back to the school of Antioch, via medieval hermeneuts such as the Victorines, with their particular grammatical-historical slant.[93] Though the nominalist-influenced trend towards literal reading is evident in their thinking,[94] note that neither Flacius nor Luther reduced Christian hermeneutics to the bare literalism often associated with 'modern' historiography. How could they, given that one of the abiding conceits of Christianity vis-à-vis Jews, and of Luther vis-à-vis 'papists', was the hermeneutic concern for the 'spirit' as well as the 'letter'? For the Lutherans the literal-historical and the prophetical still ran together, with God's purpose being the sinew that linked past, present, and future. The theologian Kelber tells us that

A gospel, for example, was perceived to be a story narrated by an evangelist and representing the history of its subject matter. There was a coherence between the narrative depiction and the reality it referred to. The narrative plot and the narrative's assumed historicity were still united in [Luther's] literal sense which for believers was the Word of God.[95]

Talk of gospels reminds us what was so important about Lutheran hermeneutics: exegesis was applied directly and principally to scripture. Rome's claim to cumulative institutional interpretative authority on the tenets of the faith was based on an assertion of the obscurity of meaning in the faith's founding documents, so scriptural ambiguity could only be reconciled by churchly pronouncement. Now one could undermine ecclesiastical authority by consulting the scriptures anew, armed with new devices for critical comprehension that aided discovery of 'true' biblical meanings for oneself.

The challenge to the institutions of the church was not supposed to render the fabric of Christendom asunder but rather to construct a new narrative in which evangelism was revealed as the true if hitherto unrecognized expression of Christianity. In order to perform this grand exercise in persuasion, hermeneutics—the art of *reading* texts—was not enough. History was needed, in the sense of *writing* a text about the past. Where Hugh of St Victor had written that 'our task is

[92] Matthias Kossler, *Empirische Ethik und christlicher Moral* (Würzburg: Königshausen und Neumann, 1999), 312.
[93] Dilthey, 'The Development of Hermeneutics', 252–3.   [94] Kelber, 'The Quest', 80.
[95] Ibid. 82. On continuities between Luther and trends from the high middle ages, Dierken, *Selbstbewusstsein*, 203–4; Ward, *Word and Supplement*, 32–3; on Flacius and the *via moderna*, Haikola, *Gesetz und Evangelium*, 32 ff.

to commit history to memory, as the foundation of doctrine', Flacius cut out the middleman of 'memory', which was easier to do in the age of the printing press, and essential when one was not just in the business of training other clerics: *historia est fundamentum doctrinae*—'History is the foundation of doctrine':

> I wish then, that a church history would be written in which would be shown in definite order and according to chronology, how the true church and its religion gradually fell from its original purity and unity in apostolic times into evil ways, this partially from the negligence and ignorance of its teachers and also partly through the wickedness of the godless. It should also be shown how the church now and then has been reinstated by several truly pious men...until finally in these our times, when the truth appeared almost completely wiped out, true religion in its purity has once more been established through the immeasurable goodness of God.

Here was a mission statement for the great collaborative research project Flacius led, the thirteen-volume History of the church popularly known as the *Magdeburg Centuries* (1560–5).[96] The endeavour set in motion a historiographical battle against which the tremors caused by chapters 15 and 16 of Gibbon's *Decline and Fall* two centuries later paled in comparison.

The major Catholic riposte to the Lutheran challenge came courtesy of the cardinal and ecclesiastical historian Cesare Baronio, in the form of the twelve-volume *Annales ecclesiastici a Christo nato ad annum 1198* (*The Ecclesial and Secular Annals from the Birth of Christ until the Year 1198*, 1588–1607). As well as their impact, with sales constituting 13 per cent of the Plantin Press's income in 1590–5, the *Annales* further buttressed historical literalism with the antiquarian's concern for minutiae and precision in the interests of grander projects of persuasion.[97] Ecclesiastical History was utterly bound to original principles, which is why 'the sources' might connote not just 'the evidence' but 'the origins'. (Centuries later the philosopher Jacques Derrida made play of the relationship between 'the archive' and the *arche*, or origin.) The analogy of 'cause' and 'origin' was strong for humanist historians from Bruni to La Popelinière. Since the Universal Church—which all parties to the Reformation and Counter-Reformation believed in, differing only on what its essential principles were—had historical beginnings,

---

[96] *Magdeburger Zenturien* (Jena, 1560–5): for the intellectual origins and thematic-cum-rhetorical shaping of the project, which is by no means only organized by centuries and shows Baudouin's input, see Heinz Scheible, *Die Entstehung der Magdeburger Zenturien. Ein Beitrag zur Geschichte der historiographischen Methode* (Gütersloh: Gerd Mohn, 1966). The lengthy quotation from Flacius in the main text is in Wilhelm Preger, *Matthias Flacius Illyricus und seine Zeit* (Erlangen, 1859), vol. 2, 416–17, cited, contextualized, and translated in Earle Hilgert, 'Protestantism—Revolt or Reform?', *Ministry Magazine* (July 1953), online at https://www.ministrymagazine.org/archive/1953/07/research
[97] On sales statistics, Levitin, 'From Sacred History to the History of Religion', 1118. Levitin's article more generally considers the historiographical significance of the ecclesiastical History debates.

then re-establishing principles and recreating origins, i.e. metaphysical and chronological-empirical concerns, ran together. Teams of historians returned to whatever documentary sources could be located, to Eusebius, and to Jewish historians of the early church period, in order to assess matters like St Peter's position and the evolution of ecclesiastical hierarchy and certain sacraments. In the battle for title, rhetoric was scarcely dispensed with but the bona fides of documentary substantiation, when documents were not simply reproduced, came in the form of notes—marginal notes rather than footnotes, as it happens, but the principle is the same. If, as the discussion of the middle ages above implies, the mid to late sixteenth century was not *the* moment at which *enargeia/evidentia* as vividness was supplanted by *evidentia* as evidence in the more recent sense, it clearly was *a* hugely important moment given the stakes involved as western Christianity was split into competing confessions and History became a key battleground in the theological struggle.[98]

While Thomas Carlyle later claimed that the Reformation brought 'a return to Truth and Reality in opposition to Falsehood and Semblance', in reality the 'Protestant' hermeneutics of early modern Europe produced champions just as dogmatic as those propounding the dogma they fancied themselves to have discredited.[99] Just like Baronio's *Annales*, the *Magdeburg Centuries* was more critical of the positions it attacked than it was of the evidence on which its own position was based. Each fuelled an ideological conflict and, in virtue of providing an especially prominent example of the relationship between current agenda and reading of the past, encouraged sceptics in their critique of all History. The priesthood of all believers, printed, vernacular bibles in hand, were given only limited space in which to draw their own inferences either about churchly or secular powers, as new orthodoxies tried to force the genie back into the bottle.[100] On the technical front this was because the stress on authoritative literal interpretations demanded that exegetes advert to Greek and Hebrew original texts, which perforce excluded the great majority who could not read those languages. No more than pre-Tridentine and Tridentine Catholic hermeneuts did Lutheranism propose a radical social agenda of self-instruction as far as moral, religious, and

---

[98] Momigliano, *Classical Foundations*, ch. 6; Tutino, *Shadows of Doubt*, 67–70; Ginsburg, *Threads*, 20–3; Levitin, 'From Sacred History to the History of Religion'. For Derrida's contribution on 'the archive', see Jacques Derrida, *Archive Fever: A Freudian Impression* (Chicago: University of Chicago Press, 1996).

[99] Thomas Carlyle, *Heroes and Hero Worship*, repr. in Carlyle, *Sartor Resartus, Heroes and Hero-Worship, Past and Present*, ed. G. T. Bettany (London: Ward, Lock and Co., 1892), 93; cf. Kelber, 'The Quest', 80; Jean Grondin, *Sources of Hermeutics* (New York: SUNY Press, 1995), 19–21.

[100] For examples of attempted usages of the scriptures in a political-critical spirit by the Reformation writers Anne Askew, Anne Lock, and Anne Dowriche, see Elaine V. Beilin, '"The World reproov'd": Writing Faith and History in England', in Margaret Mikesell and Adele Seeff (eds.), *Culture and Change: Attending to Early Modern Women* (Newark: University of Delaware Press, 2003), 266–80.

political conduct was concerned. Luther was notorious for relegating problematic biblical passages to secondary status within the canon, and for writing prejudicial commentaries and introductions to the scriptures—as well as for disavowing Thomas Müntzer's militant 'peasants' who mistakenly thought that the reformers' message might have some relevance for their existence outside their souls and before their deaths.

Nevertheless, critical historical scholarship did gain its own momentum during this period within small but important communities of scholars of a range of confessions. This is very far from a stereotype whereby 'Protestants wrote histories of the church's corruption by the papacy, Roman Catholics of its unchanging adherence to papal tradition, and both of the ancient Jews as God's unique chosen people', and whereby 'real' non-dogmatic, critical History only appeared under the influence of seventeenth-century deism or of eighteenth-century Enlightenment as represented by works such as David Hume's 1757 *Natural History of Religion*.[101] (How alike in condescension is the Enlightenment caricature of rigid orthodoxy in prior 'early modern' History to the Renaissance depictions of medieval scholasticism!) Sixteenth and seventeenth-century religious scholarship incorporated the study of ancient Judaism, and paganism, including pre-Islamic Arabic History, and was facilitated by the circulation of many documents and manuscripts that had been torn from cathedrals and monasteries during the Wars of Religion. It was fired by the likes of the revolutionizer of ancient and biblical chronology, Joseph Justus Scaliger (1540–1609) and his fellow Huguenot, the Hebraist Isaac Casaubon, whose 'spiritual quest', in the words of Joanna Weinberg and Anthony Grafton, 'knew no denominational boundaries'. The philosophical point at stake is that these scholars were not just involved in the politics of the period but were also engaged in a search for what they conceived as literal truth. In the aforementioned scholarly communities, historians of all confessions were recognized only as historians by other members of the communities if they subscribed to critical precepts. And if ideology could influence historical enquiry, some of the scholarly developments of the period showed that the reverse could also be true as clerics drew on the interpretative skills of humanists of the *respublica litteraria*. All this is what historiographical disputes typically tend to produce, and this was one of the most important such disputes in occidental history, and the most sophisticated thitherto. The result was what the intellectual historian Dimitri Levitin calls 'a sociology of knowledge that transcended both politics and confessions'. Indeed some of the eighteenth-century *philosophes* realized their scholarly debt to those who had disdainfully been dubbed mere *érudites*, but were too embarrassed to declare it in light of the

---

[101] Levitin, 'From Sacred History to the History of Religion', 1119–20, who rightly criticizes this vision.

belief that French neo-classicism was intellectually superior to and different from all that had gone before.[102]

Catholic and Protestant scholars differed amongst themselves as much as with each other: Jesuits, for instance, might be set against Jansenists. Most embraced historical literalism, as well as some Jewish exegetical assistance, as long as they could keep hold of some typological/figural thought. Thus the Jesuit 'Bollandists' embraced the spirit of criticism in defence of the Catholic Church, and in so doing, via the *Acta Sanctorum* (*Deeds of the Saints*) project initiated in 1607, acknowledged as a starting point the fictitious nature of almost all saints' lives produced thereto. The quest as they saw it—and still see it, since Bollandism continues to this day in Brussels—was to establish such historical reality as could be gleaned from beneath the embellishments of hagiography.[103]

A relatively late entrant to the scene was one of the most influential players. The Benedictine monk Jean Mabillon (1632-1707) worked in the traditions of the 'Maurist' school which was active from 1618-c.1730. He was at least as concerned to combat pyrrhonian scepticism and criticize Bollandist works as he was to engage in the battle against Protestantism for which his school had actually been set up. In a trio of works, the most famous of which is *De re diplomatica* (1681), in which the word 'diplomatic' pertained to 'diplomas', meaning official documents, he all but founded the modern discipline of palaeography. Where philology is concerned with the internal, linguistic features of texts, which may have connotations for ageing and verification related to authorship, palaeography is the study of scripts, which includes their materiality as well as their textual content. Mabillon's external criteria of criticism demanded expertise in parchments, ink, and paper. Of the text itself, alongside language and internal coherence, he stressed coherence with other texts, a.k.a. evidence.

The intellectual courage of some of the aforementioned figures may be inferred from the disapprobation with which their work was received by the churches whose ends they nominally served. In 1695 the fourteen volumes of the Bollandists' *Acta Sanctorum* published to that point were condemned by the Inquisition. The *Histoire critique du Vieux Testament* (*Critical History of the Old Testament*) of the Oratorian Richard Simon (1638-1712) antagonized his fellow French Catholics as well as Protestants: he was expelled from his order. It did not help Simon's case that he was associated with the thought of the excommunicate Jewish philosopher, Baruch—Benedictus—de Spinoza (1634-77). Spinoza had declared that much of what appeared to be prophetically divined morality was not actually written by

---

[102] Ibid. 1160; on Casaubon, Grafton and Weinberg with Alastair Hamilton, '*I have always loved the Holy Tongue*': *Isaac Casaubon, the Jews, and a Forgotten Chapter in Renaissance Scholarship* (Cambridge, MA: Belknap Press, 2011), 43. See also Grafton, *Joseph Scaliger: A Study in the History of Classical Scholarship*, 2 vols. (Oxford: Clarendon Press, 1983, 1993).

[103] On the Bollandists, Raymond E. Wanner, *Claude Fleury (1640-1723) as an Educational Historiographer and Thinker* (The Hague: Martinus Nijhoff, 1975), 79.

the prophets and was more in the way of a social code for a specific society, the ancient Hebrews, than a general code for all peoples. Spinoza mirrored Hobbes, Grotius, and yet others in arguing that the Pentateuch had not been written by Moses, though some doubts about Mosaic authorship had been raised as early as the tenth century by the Jewish Neoplatonist Isaac ben Suleiman. One of Spinoza's major hermeneutic tools was the awareness of anachronism, a word that unbeknownst to him probably entered the English language during his lifetime, amid the ruptures across the channel from the Netherlands. The principle was applied in a way that had many precedents in legal-historical thought. In order to detach the necessary from the contingent, the transcendent from the transient, one had first to historicize in order to establish the immediate contexts of enunciation that needed to be stripped away.[104]

Shortly after Spinoza, another member of a minority whose beliefs had caused him trouble with authorities published his *Dictionnaire Historique et Critique* (1697). Pierre Bayle was a Huguenot, who had fled France for the Netherlands, and like his sixteenth-century predecessors thus had personal cause to promote irenic thought. His dictionary deployed detailed historical study alongside strict reasoning and a highly sceptical spirit in order to argue against inherited theological tenets and thus religious dogma, and in favour of religious toleration. Both Bayle and Spinoza influenced the eighteenth-century Scottish philosopher Hume; Spinoza has been described as writing a 'natural history of religion' (i.e. not a supernatural or dogmatic one), and one Hume expert opines that without him Hume would not have been able to write his influential treatise of that name.[105] Now we know that the picture is more complicated, and the intellectual debts yet wider and deeper. Spinoza's commendation that the Bible be read like any other text had *secularizing* overtones but these need to be distinguished from *irreligious* overtones, not least because he obviously perceived a god of sorts and had a long Jewish hermeneutic tradition on which to draw—in this connection we might note the publication and popularity of Maimonides in the seventeenth-century Dutch Republic.[106] Furthermore, some of Spinoza's conclusions had been anticipated in detail by the likes of yet another Huguenot, Isaac La Peyrère (c.1596–1676), and the Quaker Samuel Fisher (1605–65).[107] Spinoza's premise that Adam was

---

[104] J. Samuel Preus, *Spinoza and the Irrelevance of Biblical Authority* (Cambridge: Cambridge University Press, 2001), 37, 182–3; on 'anachronism', Christopher Hill, *Reformation to Industrial Revolution*, vol. 2, *1530–1870* (Harmondsworth: Penguin, 1976), 198. On Isaac ben Sulieman and Ibn Ezra: John H. Hayes, 'The History of the Study of Israelite and Judaean History from the Renaissance to the Present', in V. Philips Long (ed.), *Israel's Past in Present Research* (Winona Lake, IN: Eisenbrauns, 1999), 7–42, here 19.

[105] Steven Nadler, *Spinoza: A Life* (Cambridge: Cambridge University Press, 2001), 271; Richard H. Popkin, 'Hume and Spinoza', *Hume Studies*, 5:2 (1979), 65–93, here 70.

[106] Aaron Katchen, *Christian Hebraists and Dutch Rabbis* (Cambridge, MA: Harvard University Press, 1984).

[107] Travis L. Frampton, *Spinoza and the Rise of Historical Criticism of the Bible* (New York: T&T Clark, 2006), 15–16, 41–2.

not the first man was actually the founding assumption of La Peyrère's 'polygenetic' theory of multiple human origins, as expressed in his *Praeadamitae* (1655): the Jewish people might be 'Adamite' but since the Bible was only the History of the Jewish people, no one else was.[108] Recent scholarship has suggested we can go significantly further back than these for similar critical comment on the Old Testament,[109] though it is still reluctant to accredit the relevant high medieval thinkers. In other words, we should see Spinoza as pouring oil on living flame rather than putting spark to tinder. The strength of the reaction against him is explained less by the novelty of his historical and scriptural interpretations than by how much of a premium was put on the literal truth of the scriptures at the time of his views gaining notice, and perhaps above all by the fact that his general religious views were so radically heterodox, when hitherto more critical historical methods had been developed and adopted largely independently of heterodox belief.

History in the Scientific Seventeenth Century

Since one object of this book is relating historical thought to other intellectual-cultural trends, and since the seventeenth century is associated with the Scientific Revolution more than any historiographical turn, it is interesting to recall the role of some medieval thought in this apparently least medieval of developments. Nominalist hermeneutics, and elements of nominalism's aftermath in Reformation thought, provide a cultural bridge between the Renaissance humanist focus on the human sciences and the later sixteenth- and seventeenth-century developments in natural science. Nominalism moves towards non-symbolic readings of the natural world. Protestantism, while stridently insisting on the marriage of the spirit and the letter in interpretation, nonetheless created a sharper dualism between the cities of man and of god. Accordingly it paved the way for a contraction of 'the sphere of the sacred, forcibly stripping objects, natural and artificial, of the roles they had once played as bearers of meaning', and opening the way for what are in hindsight more recognizably scientific, mechanistic explanations and models of relationships. Purged of immanent spiritual meaning, nature was rendered more fully as the servant of human material needs.[110] All of this constitutes a significant series of steps down the road to what its most influential theorists would later depict as quintessential characteristics of 'modernity'— namely a 'mathematical-scientific desire to understand and relate to what there is

---

[108] Richard H. Popkin, *Isaac La Peyrère* (Leiden: Brill, 1987), ch. 9.
[109] Malcolm, 'Hobbes, Ezra and the Bible'.
[110] Quote from Harrison, *The Bible*, 117; Altena, 'Secular Hermeneutics'; Nisbet, *Progress*, 127. On the twelfth century, see Le Goff, 'What Did the Twelfth-Century Renaissance mean?', 643–6.

in terms that are expressive not of revelation but of empirical verifiability, instrumental reason, and formal...models of thought.'[111] In the move from contemplation and veneration of the world to its practical mastery, the subject should not address the object in the attempt to come to know it as it was 'in itself', but know it in a way that permitted possession and exploitation so that humans might become 'the lords and masters of nature'.[112] Knowledge, as that devout Protestant Francis Bacon had it, was power, and by knowledge Bacon meant the sort that had recently produced gunpowder, the printing press, and the nautical compass— those things which the seventeenth-century *modernes* held up to the *anciens* in evidence of the superiority of new ways over old. This was the authentic voice of inquiry as *technē* rather than *theoria*. It represents the consummation of a long-evolving shift from the Platonic, Aristotelian, and theologically 'realist' conception of a *physis* that is basically benign and accommodating to humans, and revelatory of the divine, to a conception of a more neutral but ultimately malleable world that can be rendered into a more perfect fit for humankind.[113] The shift also complements the tendencies, at least to the west of the Elbe, of movement from local to national economies; the emergence of the calculating and recording practices of early modern capitalism; and the centralization of proto-industry and the expansion of pure wage labour (partly driven by mid-sixteenth-century inflation).[114] But the fact that so many of these intellectual developments were congruent with theological enquiry rather than necessarily a rejection of it helps explain why the Scientific Revolution easily coexisted with a seventeenth-century religious resurgence. Whatever their misgivings, many ecclesiastics realized it was in their interests to accommodate to new thinking rather than engage in a confrontation in which they were not certain of victory. Galileo had helped forced the question, but once his findings gained acceptance, it could be convenient to consecrate the separation of the realm of religion and spirituality from that of science and empirics. Alternatively, clerics could ally themselves with the likes of Bacon and Newton, who saw themselves as explaining the works of God, not explaining 'him' away.

In many of these developments historical enquiry was downgraded in the same measure as the wisdom and authority of the past was downgraded. Empiricism and rationalism flourished. Whatever their differences, both placed the emphasis on the individual subject as separate from the world, and in that sense were embedded in a long Augustinian tradition, though both had decidedly

[111] Espen Hammer, *Philosophy and Temporality from Kant to Critical Theory* (Cambridge: Cambridge University Press, 2011), 71.

[112] Descartes, *Discourse on Method*, editor's introduction 1–32, quote on 'lords' at 10.

[113] On changing views of the world Philip J. Kain, *Nietzsche and the Horror of Existence* (Lanham, MD: Lexington, 2009), 10.

[114] Richard W. Hadden, *On the Shoulders of Merchants: Exchange and the Mathematical Conception of Nature in Early Modern Europe* (Albany: State University of New York, 1994).

anti-traditional implications. Empiricism now stood against inherited precept and dogma in its emphasis on individual learning by experience of the phenomenal world, and gained from the heft of Newton in practice and Locke in principle. Rationalism, with Descartes's authority behind it, based its claims to superiority on the capacity of the intellect to establish systems like mathematics that owed nothing to traditional metaphysics or fallible experiential taint. Whatever its merits, History, along with other 'human sciences', was considered insufficiently rigorous and systematic anyway, hence Descartes's judgement in *Discourse on Method*.[115] Then we have the application of scientifically influenced materialist philosophies to the arena of human motivation and political organization, as with Hobbes. Whether or not it is correct to think of Hobbes as the first bourgeois philosopher,[116] it is certainly true that seventeenth-century philosophy was unprecedented in its sharp focus on freedom and its dialectical twin, determinism, and the thought of Hobbes, Spinoza, and Locke 'coincided' with the battle of moneyed men for liberation from the constraints not just of absolutism but of certain conventional mores, whatever the different directions in which the philosophies pointed.[117] Most importantly, the major developments in political theory in the sixteenth and especially the seventeenth centuries, namely arguments to the 'divine right of kings', social contract theories, and claims on the force of natural law, were each in some sense arguments to a basic principle. They were not arguments about historical origins, and strictly speaking their 'proof' required no historical argument, which seems to reflect the emergence of novel international and intra-state arrangements from the Peace of Augsburg in 1555 to the Treaty of Westphalia in 1648. All of this, along with enduring scepticism about historians' biases and sources, helps explain why, as one influential historian has it, 'the vogue for politics dwarfed that for history' in seventeenth-century universities.[118]

Whether the downgrading of History was so extreme is debatable, especially if the claim were to be extended to the 'public sphere' more generally. Indeed, in the British case, Daniel Woolf actually charts a significant *increase* in the social circulation of historical knowledge through 1700.[119] This should not surprise since while non-historical reasoning could influence political theory it could not

---

[115] Gerard Delanty, *Social Science: Philosophical and Methodological Foundations* (Maidenhead: Open University Press, 2005), 15–16.

[116] Peter Hayes, 'Hobbes's Bourgeois Moderation', *Polity*, 31:1 (1998), 53–74.

[117] Theodor W. Adorno, *History and Freedom: Lectures, 1964–1965*, ed. Rolf Tiedeman (Cambridge: Polity Press, 2006), 193–4; Herbert Marcuse, *Reason and Revolution: Hegel and the Rise of Social Theory* (Boston: Beacon, 1960), 226.

[118] The final quote from Grafton, *What was History?*, 230. For some of the other reasons mentioned in this paragraph as regards Britain and the Italian *mezzogiorno* in the early 1700s, see Pocock, *The Ancient Constitution*, 235–45 and Pocock's notes on pp. 16 and 18. On scepticism about bias and forged 'sources', Peter Burke, 'History, Myth, and Fiction: Doubts and Debates', in Rabasa et al. (eds.), *The Oxford History of Historical Writing 1400–1800*, 261–81.

[119] Grafton, *What was History?*, 230, cf. Woolf 'From Hystories to the Historical', 35–6.

touch the areas of identity reached by genealogical and figural History. Even at the level of specialist political and legal argumentation the evidence is more nuanced, beyond cases like that of Locke, whose political theory evinced a lack of interest in History, even as his *Essay on Human Understanding* set out some arguments about differing levels of certainty that would have aided historians in their fight against pyrrhonian scepticism.[120] For Spinoza, say, 'reason' alone could reveal knowledge of a god and should promote the golden rule of loving it and one's neighbour as oneself, but we have seen that he deployed complementary historical-hermeneutic enquiry.[121] Similarly, if the Dutch humanist lawyer Hugo Grotius (1583–1645) was one of the major seventeenth-century legal-political theorists, he too, like the later jurist-philosopher Samuel Pufendorf (1632–94), wrote works of History alongside his better-known theoretical tracts. In support of his theoretical contentions, he followed the well-trodden path of working through the historical and geographically variable 'positive' laws of human groups in order to identify a universalist core in 'natural law'. He has been accused of historical cherry-picking to this end, though that scarcely distinguishes him from Lipsius or Machiavelli, and if anything it reminds us of the ongoing significance of some version of historical exemplarity.[122] Consider for instance the use of Thucydides, whose pedigree in influencing the classically educated is as well established as that of Tacitus, and who has been deployed with equally varied results. Among students of the *Peloponnesian War* we can count the English philosopher Hobbes and the American statesman John Adams. Hobbes translated Thucydides in 1629 and there are notable similarities between Hobbes's description of the 'state of nature' and Thucydides' account of the Corcyraean revolution (427 BCE) whose bloodshed Hobbes used to illustrate anarchy and to substantiate his argument for a Leviathan-absolutism. Later, Adams (1735–1826) used the same events to illustrate the atavism of 'human nature' in order to substantiate his argument for a republican regime in which warring influences would hold each other in check by the separation of powers.[123] Finally, let us dwell for a moment on the 'Glorious Revolution' of 1688 and the 1689 Bill of Rights, of which Locke is seen as effectively the official philosopher. The events do seem to have reduced 'Whig' reliance on deep historical accounts of English liberties, but while they can be interpreted as an interpellation of reason divorced from tradition, the turn from deep History could just as well be explained by an interpretation of 1688 as a new foundational moment, a sort of year zero, in the lexicon of later

---

[120] For the nuance and Locke's exceptionality, see Pocock, *The Ancient Constitution*, 235–42. On Locke and degrees of certainty, Burke, 'History, Myth, and Fiction', 274–5.

[121] Preus, *Spinoza and the Irrelevance of Biblical Authority*, 37, 182–3.

[122] Grafton, *What was History?*, 222.

[123] Marshall Sahlins, *The Western Illusion of Human Nature* (Chicago: Prickly Paradigm Press: 2008), 8–11.

revolutions. Such moments, as in the Roman preoccupation with dating *ab urbe condita*, are themselves manifestly historical, even if they happen to be recent.[124]

So some caveats need to accompany claims to the effect that 'the founding myth of seventeenth-century political thought—the state of nature—emerged from accounts of travel rather than study of history and historians'.[125] Besides, rather than their being recent arrivals on the scene which jockeyed for attention with historical study, travel accounts had themselves served a quasi-historical purpose from Herodotus and Thucydides through Gerald of Wales, Bodin, and La Popelinière. Jumping forward a little in time to another state-of-nature thinker, 'quasi-historical' is perhaps the best way to describe the arguments in Jean-Jacques Rousseau's *Discourse on the Origin of Inequality* (1755). Its concern with origins is also a concern with development, since inequalities of wealth, status, and by extension disparities in people's estimation of their self-worth, are not seen by Rousseau as part of any given, natural state of affairs, but rather a product of human combination in society. The *Discourse* is quasi-historical in that it does not follow the likes of La Popelinière in establishing how state B emerged out of state A in any particular society, but instead conjectures as to how state B might have emerged in societies-in-general out of a hypothetical state A. In that sense it coheres quite strongly with one still healthy trend of philosophical enquiry, the sort of 'genealogy' undertaken by, say, the twentieth-century philosopher Bernard Williams as he reflected on the development of truthfulness as a corollary of the need for cooperation between humans.[126]

While Rousseau implied that the disagreeable qualities he identifies in European society are a strong possibility in all societies, he nonetheless did identify actual other societies with different practices and arrangements and as such illustrated that likelihood is not inevitability. It was not a matter of seeing 'Caribs' and 'Hottentots' as living in some pre-social situation or an early form of society, as La Popelinière had done, but rather of seeing them as having undertaken historically different paths of development. In this sense Rousseau comes closer to the sort of genealogy conducted by Theodor Adorno and Max Horkheimer in their *Dialectic of Enlightenment* (1944/47) which pathologizes long-term developments in occidental thought of which in some way both capitalism and fascism are seen as characteristic outcomes. The point of this sort of critique—and Rousseau may be seen as one of the progenitors of 'critical theory'—is to diagnose a malaise and if not to prescribe a cure, then at least to raise awareness that alternatives are possible precisely because the established way is not the only or the natural way. As Rousseau wrote to Voltaire, he 'showed men how they bring their

---

[124] Pocock, *The Ancient Constitution*, 235–42, contains much of the evidence on which I make these assertions, though Pocock bears no responsibility for any errors in my rendering.

[125] Grafton, *What was History?*, 231.

[126] Bernard Williams, *Truth and Truthfulness: An Essay in Genealogy* (Princeton: Princeton University Press, 2002).

miseries on themselves and hence how they might avoid them'.[127] Little under the sun being entirely new, there were antecedents to Rousseau's agenda of what Marxists would call 'de-reification', the denaturalization by examination of their aetiology of arrangements assumed to be natural. In 1453 Nicholas of Cusa wrote that 'the earthly human condition has this characteristic: viz., that longstanding custom, which is regarded as having passed over into nature, is defended as the truth'.[128] But in any case in Rousseau's letter we have the fundaments of the justification for studying the past that this book dubs History as Emancipation.

Since science and religion did not necessarily stand in tension, religious views of History were not necessarily threatened by science any more than non-religious views of History were threatened by philosophy. Sometimes religious views were even reinforced. Puritans, with their apocalyptic philosophies of History, contributed disproportionately to the scientific endeavour. For some puritans, 'Progress in the arts and sciences [was] held to be at once a *sign* of the imminence of the golden age of the spirit on earth and a *cause* of this imminence', thus fusing the Greek concept of advancement through the arts and sciences with theological millenarianism.[129] History also performed an exemplar function in the basic Reformer conviction that scripture provides reconstructable historical models for forging the commonwealth in the here and now. Even when that design was thwarted in Europe it might still be pursued across the Atlantic.[130]

Elsewhere, views of the course of history long endorsed by Rome were reproduced or renovated. While medievals had more than just the great theologies of history available to them to understand the past, many inhabitants of the 'early modern' world were still exposed by book and tutelage to those selfsame theologies of history that we think of as quintessentially pre-modern. In Italy, where the forces of Catholic orthodoxy were especially strong for much of the sixteenth and seventeenth centuries, secular historiography having retreated somewhat since Machiavelli and Guicciardini, the Jesuit Antonio Foresti reproduced the tenets of sacred History, divine interventions and all, in his *Mappamondo istorico* (*Historical Map of the World*, 1690–4). The work was translated into German, and reproduced by a Venetian printer as the opening part of a more global History featuring volumes on the Islamic world and China as well as Europe.[131] Most of

---

[127] Frederick Neuhouser, *Rousseau's Critique of Inequality* (Cambridge: Cambridge University Press, 2014), esp. 5–8, 210–12. Quote at 212.

[128] *De Pace Fidei*, Part I, §4, in Hopkins, *Nicholas of Cusa's De Pace Fidei*, 634.

[129] Nisbet, *Progress*, 127.

[130] On the biblical template for the contemporary commonwealth, see Beilin, ' "The World reproov'd" ', 269–70.

[131] William J. Bouwsma observed of Italian historianship after Machiavelli and Guicciardini that it 'moved from the *piazza* into the *studio*, detached itself from active politics and reflected a steady decline in human confidence': cited in Woolf 'From Hystories to the Historical', 34–5. For the rest of the material up to this point in this paragraph, see Edoardo Tortarolo, 'Italian Historical Writing, 1680–1800', in Rabasa et al. (eds.), *The Oxford History of Historical Writing 1400–1800*, 364–383, here 372–3.

all we need to consider the popularity of the work of Bishop Jacques-Bénigne Bossuet (1627–1704), who amongst other things bears some responsibility for the seizure of Richard Simon's *Histoire critique du Vieux Testament* (see p. 143). Bossuet's *Discours sur L'Histoire Universelle* appeared almost simultaneously with Mabillon's methodological opus; the contrast is marked. A vigorous Counter-Reformation Gallican apologetic, it was written for the son of Louis XIV. Edifying the Dauphin with *exempla*, this modified princes' mirror met Simon, Spinoza, and the other biblical historicists with a trenchant multi-stage restatement of providential history that leaned on the book of Daniel's prophecy of the succession of kingdoms. Regnal and sacerdotal blades were smelted into one as Bossuet pronounced:

> It is the progress of these two particulars, I mean that of religion, and that of empires, that you ought to imprint upon your memory; and as religion and political government are the two hinges, whereon all human things turn, to see whatever concerns those particulars summed up in an epitome, and by this means to discover the whole order and progression of them, is to comprise in thought all that is great among men, and to hold, so to say, the thread of all the affairs of the world.[132]

Bossuet's was the last great explicitly religious philosophy of history, with elements of Augustine and his concept of the 'two cities', but the *Discours* was notable for its incorporation of humanist sentiments and aspects of civic morals, and its general attempts at fairness to a range of parties, so it was not entirely antithetical either to Baudouin's earlier work or to the 'modernizing' religiosity of the puritans.[133] It was admired by some 'Enlighteners' for its range and its account of causation. While it was concerned with God's relationship to humanity, Bossuet's concept of 'secondary causes' meant that God's direct influence did not always need to be established, which kept the linkage between sacred and profane history whilst simultaneously opening the way for a more secular analysis of change for those not interested in or sceptical of the divine side of things.

If Bossuet's passion was winning Protestants back to Catholicism, one of his correspondents, Gottfried Wilhelm Leibniz (1646–1716), sought to end religious antagonism with a philosophy of tolerance and he produced a novel metaphysics to match. In Bossuet's 1688 tome *Histoire des variations des Églises protestantes* (*History of the Variations of the Protestant Church*), with the evidence of different Protestantisms already before his eyes, he had argued that once a dissident church

---

[132] Quotation from the English translation of the 13th edition of Bossuet's original: *An Universal History from the Beginning of the World to the Empire of Charlemagne* (New York: Robert Moore, 1821), 13; on Daniel e.g. 77 f.; 174–87.

[133] Nisbet, *Progress*, 141–2.

had rejected the idea of a worldly sovereign interpreter of scripture, that church was apt to continue fragmenting in exegetical dispute. Leibniz effectively welcomed diversity and gave it a philosophical justification in his *Theodicy* (1710) and *Monadology*, which was published in 1714 but conceived in the 1670s–1680s, when religious warfare was fresh in the memory and Louis XIV was breaking the international peace and ending religious toleration at home, via the Revocation of the Edict of Nantes (1685). Leibniz had tried to effect reconciliation between Protestants and Catholics before concentrating on intra-Protestant relations. In these works, like Cusanus, Ficino, and Bodin before him, he sought to identify the unity that could be traced through diversity.[134]

Leibniz was influenced by the Neoplatonic theory of emanationism, in which all things issue and descend—with decreasing perfection and increased concreteness—from one perfect/divine source. Of particular importance for subsequent conceptualization of the diversity of religions, nations, and individuals is his reworking of the ancient concept of the monad as part of a new metaphysics of existence. For Leibniz, God was 'the primitive unity' (*Monadology*[135] §§47–8), and each of the monads he created had the quality of a sort of soul, or 'entelechy'. There was no direct conversation between the monads; they 'have no windows' (§7). Each had its own integrity as part of a whole that was nonetheless in some way connected: as 'the same city viewed from different directions appears entirely different' there are 'as many different universes, which are, nevertheless, only perspectives on a single one' (§57). Or, as Leibniz put it in another work, each monad represents the universe from 'its point of view'.[136] While each monad itself comprised smaller monads (§§65, 67), some types of monad had a higher conceptual character than others—if 'each living body has a dominant entelechy' (§70), some elect 'souls are elevated to the rank of reason and to the prerogative of minds' (§82). Unlike ordinary entelechies/souls, 'minds' are 'images of the divinity itself, capable of knowing the system of the universe, and imitating something of it through their schematic representations of it, each mind being like a little divinity in its own realm' (§83). The idea of reasoning monads of the same level coexisting side by side legitimated varying conceptions of god—varying confessions—but could easily be adapted to pertain to varying social orders aligned with different confessions and ways of viewing the world, and to different cultures more generally. Such an elaboration need not entail relativism, since in the Leibnizian scheme diversity was reconciled in the ultimate unity of God, but given that the God's-eye

---

[134] On some of the context, Nicholas Rescher, *G. W. Leibniz's Monadology: An Edition for Students* (Pittsburgh: University of Pittsburgh Press, 1991), 5, 8, and C. A. van Peursen, *Leibniz* (London: Faber and Faber, 1969), 9. On Protestant and Catholic relations and theology see Irena Backus, *Leibniz: Protestant Theologian* (New York: Oxford University Press, 2016).

[135] Leibniz, 'Monadology', in Steven M. Cahn (ed.), *Classics of Western Philosophy* (Indianapolis: Hackett, 1990), 604–13.

[136] Leibniz, 'Principes de la nature et de la grâce fondé en raison', in Leibniz, *Oeuvres de Leibniz*, ed. M. A. Jacques (Paris: Charpentier, 1846), 479–87, here 480. Emphasis added.

perspective was not available to any person, or any people, the doctrine was one further step down the road to relativism in the sense of human unfitness to judge other ways of living and believing. As we shall see in Chapter 6, in the German idealist tradition towards which Leibniz's thought contributed, a tradition which reached its heights in the eighteenth and nineteenth centuries and found its historiographical expression in German historicism, discrete peoples, ultimately nation-states, were accorded the attributes of higher-level monads in their supposedly self-sufficient wholeness and their moral integrity as reflections of the divine.

As far as the next chapter is concerned, just as important as Leibniz's views on synchronic diversity was his account of diachronic change. In recognition of change over time, but in fidelity to his idea that monads were windowless, Leibniz claimed that each monad must be moved by an 'internal principle'. Monads must have some internal plurality of properties even in their unity: 'since all natural change is produced by degrees, something changes and something remains' at any one time. Given 'every present state of a simple substance is a natural consequence of its preceding state', he claimed, in words that would ring down the centuries, 'the present is pregnant with the future' (*Monadology* §§10–13, 22). Leibniz's theory of change was not a fully fledged philosophy of history, but it had dialectical overtones.

5
Society, Nature, Emancipation

Introduction

This chapter is predominantly concerned with the thought tendencies grouped under the heading 'the Enlightenment', with regulation caveats about variations in character, national and otherwise, of the intellectual traditions denoted by the term. The chapter works from Montesquieu and his contemporaries to Marx, which gives a reasonable idea of the conceptual as well as chronological span. The unifying theme is the relationship between historical and philosophical thought.

The thinkers addressed here tended to have their eyes on a broad horizon, as they tried to make sense of the broad sweep of human variety and development. Some cast their net very wide indeed, which was appropriate enough in the context of an eighteenth century that saw yet more colonial, commercial, and intellectual interaction across the globe, as Spanish, Mughal, and Ottoman power declined and European competitors came in to fill the gaps. Some believed that the development of human societies was a law-governed process. Accordingly, in the absence of evidence they were apt to make assumptions as to how things had probably been in the past, as they came up with stadial theories of human development and proposed motors of change from one state of civilization to the next. In circular fashion, those assumptions sometimes served as a criterion of relevance and plausibility in the deployment of such evidence as was deemed relevant; confirmation bias remains an investigative problem, if not an insoluble one.

When explaining the broad sweep, providential accounts of the course of human History were replaced by secular accounts, but in some instances the secular accounts were structurally similar to the religious ones and also fall under the rubric of History as Speculative Philosophy. We also encounter 'philosophical Histories' that perceived a grand historical process, and invited the reader to see herself within it, without claiming that this process had a point of culmination towards which it was working. They purported to identify motors of historical change rather than metahistorical 'meaning', and they illustrate the influence of scientific upon historical thought. Their heirs today are the likes of the historical sociologist Michael Mann, author of the multi-volume, multi-epochal *The Sources of Social Power*: indeed, as indicated by David Hume's 1739 call for a 'Science of Man', their creation is contemporaneous to, and linked with, the early development of the social sciences. With exceptions like Rousseau, or at least the 'quasi-historical' Rousseau of the *Discourse on the Origins of Inequality* (p. 149), most of the thinkers under consideration had a view of history as progress. On one hand, as already implied, this sort of thinking was not necessarily teleological—one could imagine a never-ending process of civilizational improvement without some culmination—and indeed it need imply no causal determinism either—it could just reflect optimism, or a sense of what would happen were human potentialities fulfilled. Yet on the other hand it could tend towards the self-congratulatory and was easily bowdlerized for popular consumption into some partisan claim on destiny, as a species of History as Identity.

On the whole the scholarship under examination evinced a liberal and peaceable spirit as regards confessional and national differences, though it was frequently marked by a partiality to occidental civilization, and traces of national bias may often be detected. The dynastic and religious wars of the sixteenth and seventeenth centuries had induced suspicion about dogmatism and scepticism as to the motivation of great men. This helps explain a shift away from the study of religious and political institutions and towards—or back towards, insofar as there was some crossover with the French 'new History' of the sixteenth century—civic morals, culture, and the structural conditions of social life. History expanded further from being an instruction in statecraft for public men to proffering more rounded edification in the form of vicarious experience of different spheres of life, which had the effect of producing more female historians and readers.[1]

At the same time, the injection of new ideologies into politics from the sixteenth and seventeenth centuries meant that it was possible to recast wars between states as conflicts between political systems rather than peoples. Whereas certain medieval chronicles and the French 'new historians' had focused on deep ethnic origins as an index of national difference and particularity, at least one strand of British historiography in the eighteenth century reflected on the common 'gothic' roots of different European peoples, such that 'the craven, despotic and Roman Catholic "other" of the Continent was not wholly alien, but a deformed and corrupted version of the hardy libertarian Goth'. While the likes of the 'Whiggish' historian Catharine Macaulay evinced an ethno-cultural chauvinism to go with her radical politics, for others the problem was not ethnic so much as political in the broadest sense, and accordingly could be solved by political changes.[2]

The interpretative battles in which Macaulay and her interlocutors engaged reminds us that there is no clear line separating (for shorthand) Enlightenment historiography from its predecessors and that equally fruitful lines of enquiry persisted and developed alongside the 'archetypal' Enlightenment sort. The

---

[1] On the last sentence, Karen O'Brien, 'English Enlightenment Histories, 1750–c.1815', in Rabasa et al. (eds.), *The Oxford History of Historical Writing 1400–1800*, 518–35, here 521–2, 531–2.

[2] Colin Kidd, *British Identities Before Nationalism* (Cambridge: Cambridge University Press, 1999), ch. 9, quote from p. 211. This may simply reflect the fact that the British historiographical tradition was less deeply rooted in ethnic thought than its French or German equivalents, for aforementioned reasons of focus on dynastic rather than ethnic matters up to the seventeenth century.

Académie Royale des Inscriptions et Belles-Lettres, founded in 1663, produced historical works such as Joseph de Guignes's *History of the Huns, Mongols, and Tartars* (1756–8) as part of a programme that was less concerned with stadial thought and universal categories than tracing genealogies and migration patterns from antiquity onwards. This programme had as much in common with Bodin as with the *philosophes*, though de Guignes published a pair of essays in 1758–9 which focused on Egyptian rather than Judaic civilizational primacy.[3]

Macaulay's eight-volume *History of England* (1763–83) is proof that national Histories continued to be written, but even as a more 'Enlightenment' interest in 'manners' as opposed to high politics infused other sorts of History, the latter did not necessarily have the conjectural nature of the 'classic' Enlightenment Histories. From the late eighteenth century, indeed, we see the production of works with the attention to source and detail that we associate with nineteenth-century professionalization, and a diversity of focus that we think of as the pre-serve of twentieth-century cultural History: works on medieval and Icelandic literature, Histories of the novel, art, domestic life, women, sports and pastimes.[4] On the whole, such work is absent from this chapter because of the governing concern with the most theoretically self-conscious attempts to establish the utility of History as a general way of understanding the human experience in light of influential concepts like *Volksgeist*, *circonstance*, *esprit général*, *représentations*, and even 'relations of production', that elucidated human diversity across time and place. So attention is not devoted to, say, the medievalist Ludovico Muratori (1672–1750), one of the greatest eighteenth-century historians in the more con-ventional sense, and a man whose short- and long-term influence on the historian's practices, within and outside Italy, was much greater than that of Giambattista Vico, who is addressed below.

The chosen thinkers alternately placed themselves within and beyond the flow of human life and interaction. Variously they prescribed, described, schematized, abstracted, incorporated, and in some cases relativized ways of life. Differences in orientation may sometimes be explained by the varying political circumstances in which they worked—from the relative peace of the early eighteenth century after almost unbroken European warfare from 1688 to 1714 to the resurgence of general hostilities in the War of the Austrian Succession (1740–8) and the Seven Years War (1756–63), then the French Revolution and Napoleonic wars, and, relevant for Marx in particular, the beginnings of industrialization—though political and military strife could stimulate pacific, cosmopolitan sentiment just as often as inflaming partisanship. Marx, however, not only produced a theory of

<hr />

[3] Guido Abbattista, 'The Historical Thought of the French *Philosophes*', Rabasa et al. (eds.), *The Oxford History of Historical Writing 1400–1800*, 406–27, here 413–14, 424–5.
[4] O'Brien, 'English Enlightenment Histories', 531–2.

history based on a particular sort of conflict—class conflict—but gave a tremendous boost to History as Emancipation.

While the thinkers collected here fully discredit any notion that the 'age of reason' was uninterested in the past, they were historical thinkers rather than historians in the more parochial sense. Then again, today's intellectual division of labour did not yet obtain and few university scholars had 'historian' as their title. Only gradually throughout the nineteenth century did discrete academic departments of History develop, with the exception of Germany, where Göttingen had blazed a trail in the eighteenth century. To that exception the present chapter attends, to show amongst other things how the agenda of the Göttingen historians was but a variant of a wider pattern of philosophical History.

Prelude: Bolingbroke and Vico

The Tory politician and political philosopher Henry St John, Viscount Bolingbroke (1678–1751) set some of the terms of the intellectual debate with which this chapter is concerned. He married a generalized classical view of History as 'teacher of life' (magistra vitae) with a particular conviction, perhaps shaped by his own fraught endeavours to promote Anglo-French peace in the last years of Queen Anne (d. 1714) and Louis XIV (d. 1715), that History could help extinguish 'those national partialities and prejudices that we are apt to contract in our education.'[5] A preacher of confessional tolerance, in the tradition of Montaigne he also used the wider world to challenge prevailing assumptions of superiority, as when he suggested that 'the Mexican with his cap and coat of feathers, sacrificing a human victim to his god, will not appear more savage to our eyes, than the Spaniard with a hat on his head, and a gonilla around his neck, sacrificing whole nations to his ambition, his avarice, and even the wantonness of his cruelty.'[6] His historical scepticism—perhaps with a nod to Descartes he once suggested that much History was just 'authorized romance'—was reflected in the fact that his best-known contribution to the discipline is a series of letters and thoughts rather than a historical narrative. We may also detect some of the influence of the new English political settlement of 1688–9 in his belief that remote areas of History were not only difficult to know but also useless to learn about because of their irrelevance to the problems of his present day. 'An application to any study, that tends neither directly nor indirectly to make us better men and better citizens, is at best but a specious and ingenious sort of idleness... and the knowledge we acquire by it is a creditable kind of ignorance, nothing more.'[7] If this was a rather unforgiving standard it once more pressed the question of the utility of historical

---

[5] Ibid. 522, 493.   [6] Bolingbroke, Letters, 26.   [7] Ibid. 12–14.

enquiry given contextual differences across time and given the challenges of philosophy which worked from principles rather than precedents. Secular philosophy of History was one answer to that question.[8]

The road from theology to secular philosophy of History passes through the work of a pious Catholic, Vico (1688–1744). While not much acknowledged at the time, Vico's work anticipated the themes of many of the other scholars we are to encounter, while sharing some elements with Leibniz's thought. It was written in conversation with Descartes, whose thought dominated Latinate philosophical circles in the seventeenth century and whose politely dismissive opinions on History we have already encountered: Descartes was also suspicious of rhetoric as something that obscured the 'clear and distinct' ideas that formed the foundations of reliable systems of belief, or, worse, provided false promise as to same.[9] Vico was additionally engaged with social contract theories.

Against Hobbes and Locke and in line with David Hume, Vico observed that humans were more likely to be joined in sociability by shared emotional ties, pasts, and associated myths, than by rational agreement. Enculturated similarity was a precondition of the capacity for rational agreement, which meant that what was considered rational would vary from culture to culture. As opposed to the rationalist students of the natural world, he claimed that humans could not bracket this sensual quality in their consciousness. Working from the claim that certain knowledge could be achieved only in mathematics, he observed that this was because principles, postulates, geometrical forms, and so on, were of human creation, and so were more like human social and cultural institutions than was the natural world—note the difference with Platonic thought in which ideal, universal forms like perfect circles had higher (metaphysical) reality than mere 'concrete' reality. Only that which 'man' had created could he know, in a way beyond utilitarian acquaintance such as he had with the natural world. The philosophical thrust was that there was no clear Cartesian distinction between investigating subject and object in the human sciences; self-understanding and historical understanding illuminated each other given the appropriate 'historical consciousness'. Historical enquiry could not be modelled on the paradigm of the natural sciences and could not rely on a concept of explanation modelled on scientific principles of causation. In such 'scientific' thinking, ancient myths were dismissed as simple misunderstandings of the way the world worked, or 'at best' seen as allegorical ways of expressing accurate knowledge of the world. For Vico, this was the high road to an anachronistic misunderstanding of the cultural worldviews that these myths had created. It also resulted in a mistaken view of the way in which the present had developed out of the past in question, which was for the

[8] I owe to Pocock, *The Ancient Constitution*, 246–8, this link from Bolingbroke to Vico and other philosophers of history.

[9] Giambattista Vico, *On Humanistic Education* (Ithaca: Cornell University Press, 2003), 25–6; Isaiah Berlin, *Vico and Herder: Two Studies in the History of Ideas* (London: Chatto and Windus, 1980).

historian a misunderstanding of 'himself' as a creature-in-time. For Vico myths were poetic in the sense of being creative; they construed the world in a way that called for hermeneutic investigation into their meaning and meaning could not be reduced to some better or worse approximation to a universal functionality. Moreover, unlike the study of series of events, myths bequeathed something about collective consciousness, shared meanings, internal life (though not just of individuals), and concepts of the transcendent. Insofar as Vico clarified and codified these distinctions he helped to shape the concept of the *Geisteswissenschaften* or human/spiritual sciences as opposed to the natural sciences, though the sort of contextualized understanding at issue was roughly what the French sixteenth-century 'new historians' and even others before them had been attempting. What Vico added was a strong element of discursive/linguistic constructivism, wherein the creative power of language, particularly in narrative form, had to be taken seriously as a causal/contextual strand in any account. Indeed, when one was working oneself 'back' into the thought-worlds of past peoples, a grasp of the way they used language, or, rather, the way they thought-through language, was vital.[10]

Vico certainly admired the mathematical and scientific thought of his age, but he addressed it within the context of human systems of meaning, asking not whether any mathematical claim was accurate but what mathematical thinking told the observer about contemporary human life. One conclusion was that, as a quintessentially human-cultural product which was geared to human purposes, such thinking actually represented just the sort of alienation from the spiritual world and the god-given natural world that occurred with the Fall of humanity. In a primordial, prelapsarian state, he posited on the basis of mythological readings, humanity was at home in the natural world, seeing itself as continuous with it, rather than seeing the world as something to be worked on via abstracting thought. Here Vico shares affinities with Adorno's and Horkheimer's twentieth-century vision of the rise to social dominance of a form of exploitative instrumental rationality, and with Martin Heidegger, who feared the alienating impact of technological civilization. For Vico the development of this sort of abstract thought within Christian civilization was nonetheless redolent of crises in the life-courses of other peoples. It is part of what we have good reason to call the dialectical quality of Vico's thought (just as Adorno and Horkheimer called their most famous work *Dialectic of Enlightenment*), that a civilizational advance like that of the sciences—and he did see it as an advance—should also contain the seeds of civilizational crisis.[11]

---

[10] Joseph Mali, *The Rehabilitation of Myth: Vico's New Science* (Cambridge: Cambridge University Press, 1992); Robert C. Miner, *Vico: Genealogist of Modernity* (Notre Dame: University of Notre Dame Press, 2002).

[11] Ibid.; on the Heidegger comparison Ernesto Grassi, *Vico and Humanism: Essays on Vico, Heidegger, and Rhetoric* (New York: Peter Lang, 1991).

Vico's reflection on the development of human institutions in the book *Scienza Nuova* (*The New Science*: editions in 1725, 1730, 1744) led him to blend some of the prescriptions of classical antiquity with those of Christian theologians including Augustine, Isidore of Seville, and Joachim of Fiore, and the proponents of *similitudo temporum*, as he suggested a universal pattern of historical development. He called it 'a system of the natural law of nations' based on the 'common nature of nations' which highlights his jurisprudential qualifications and his debts to Grotius. All peoples passed upwards through three 'ages'—Vico claimed the concept of three ages could be traced back to ancient Egypt—if at different speeds and in light of unique cultural modalities: the ages of gods, heroes, and men. First, in the age of the gods, 'the gentiles believed they lived under divine governments, and everything was commanded them by auspices and oracles, which are the oldest institutions in profane history'. Then, in the next age, the heroes 'reigned everywhere in aristocratic commonwealths, on account of a certain superiority of nature which they held themselves to have over the plebs'. Finally, in the age of men, 'all men recognized themselves as equal in human nature, and therefore there were established first the popular commonwealths and then the monarchies, both of which are forms of human government'.[12] One stage is succeeded by another as certain tendencies of friction develop from within, and then the chain starts again although it as unclear as it is in some of the Greek theories of history whether this is a never-ending circle of repetition or whether there is a spiral of gradual improvement with each cycle.

Vico's is specifically a study of the 'gentile nations', i.e. of non-Jews, and is modelled with reference to the experience of the Roman Empire and other antique cases.[13] Like Bodin, Vico believed the Hebrews to be the first people, and like Bodin his thought evinces Neoplatonic and hermetic influences.[14] But there is also a more orthodox Augustinian strain in the exception he made for Jews among the nations. He thought that they were the subject of sacred, providential history, divine revelation meaning that they did not have to experience the 'ideal eternal history' of all other peoples. It may be that the focus on gentiles meant Vico was freer to develop his basic claims about humans creating their own history by their poetic capacities, which fitted with his humanism, whereas the activities of the Inquisition in the Naples of his day rather militated against considering a biblical people in this context. This interpretation is bolstered by the fact that elements of the *New Science* do seem to pertain to Christians and pagan peoples are sometimes depicted as receiving a sort of revelation. At the same time,

---

[12] Giambattisa Vico, *New Science*, §31 in Giambattisa Vico, *The New Science of Giambattista Vico: Unabridged Translation of the Third Edition (1744)*, trans. Thomas Goddard Bergin and Max Harold Fisch (Ithaca: Cornell University Press, 1984), 20.

[13] Ibid.

[14] Giuseppe Mazzotta, *The New Map of the World: The Poetic Philosophy of Giambattista Vico* (Princeton: Princeton University Press, 1999), 115–19.

Jews and by extension Christians provide a standard against which 'gentiles' are measured.[15]

Vico's social theory moves away from a monist model, in which a universal or a best/ideal human character is posited, to a pluralist paradigm in which culture and its varieties occupy the centre ground. But this move is not complete. Since all people shared the same basic capacities, all societies had the potential finally to achieve a fully developed, rational sort of human, with past cultural arrangements being deemed better or worse in terms of their role in developing those capacities. The concept of the three ages was hierarchical, with only the age of men containing the potential for realization of the 'immutable law of the rational humanity, which is the true and proper nature of man'—an idea which had a direct influence on the early Marx. Christianity was the true religion because of its spiritualism and rationality, as opposed, say, to the outlook of classical Greece (too much rationalism) or of Islamic societies (too much dogmatism):

religions alone can bring the peoples to do virtuous works by appeal to their feelings, which alone move men to perform them; and the reasoned maxims of the philosophers concerning virtue are of use only when employed by a good eloquence for kindling the feelings to do the duties of virtue. There is, however, an essential difference between our Christian religion, which is true, and all the others, which are false. In our religion, divine grace causes virtuous action for the sake of an eternal and infinite good. This good cannot fall under the senses, and it is consequently the mind that, for its sake, moves the senses to virtuous actions. The false religions, on the contrary, have proposed to themselves finite and transitory goods, in this life as in the other (where they expect a beatitude of sensual pleasures), and hence the senses must drive the mind to do virtuous works.[16]

The French Enlightenment

Although the approach adopted by Montesquieu (1689-1755) was similar to that of Vico in terms of its stress on comparative social analysis, Montesquieu's analysis extended to a far wider range of societies than Vico's focus on ancient societies of the eastern Mediterranean, and his work has great significance in terms of its economics and anthropology. In the spirit of Bayle and with some British empiricist influence too, his *On the Spirit of the Laws* (1748)—he had once

---

[15] Joseph Mali, *Mythistory: The Making of a Modern Historiography* (Chicago: University of Chicago Press, 2003), 68–70; cf. (on contrast to the standards of the monotheists) Miner, *Vico*.

[16] Quotes from Vico, *New Science*, §§973 and 1110, in Vico, *The New Science of Giambattista Vico*, 359 and 426 respectively. For the reflections on monism and implicit hierarchies: Bhikhu Parekh, *Rethinking Multiculturalism* (Basingstoke: Macmillan 2006), 50–5.

been a practitioner of law—was a significant theoretical step towards understanding codes of law and morality purely as products of human societies rather than as emanations of the divine. In other words what Vico and Leibniz (and after them Hamann and Herder: pp. 173–8) did for the study of myths, religions, and languages, what the historian J. J. Winckelmann (1717–68) did for art, and what the theorist Anne-Louise Germaine de Staël (1766–1817) was to do for literature (p. 218), Montesquieu did for laws. He interpreted laws not just as influences on collective life but expressions of the same, windows into collective thought and imagination.

On the Spirit of the Laws also produced yet another tripartite classification: government by monarchy, republic, and despotism. The triad indicates the centrality in his work, as later in Edward Gibbon's, of the relationship of individual liberty to politico-legal structures. The point of such classifications is on the whole to abstract from a range of scenarios. Some historians today would regard such abstraction as a problem, but it is just one of the things that now distinguishes social science from History. Furthermore, Montesquieu did pour a great deal of empirical content into his concepts, especially the sort of concepts that historians tend now to refer to when they invoke 'the context of the times'. The Marxist theorist Louis Althusser traced back to Leibniz, through Montesquieu and Hegel, a sort of social theory that he dubbed 'expressive'. By this he meant that the theory proposed a sort of internally generated social essence that suffused the whole, meaning that all socio-cultural, economic, and political institutions had a similar basic orientation. Individual humans were more like expressions of the systems rather than being architects of them. In these systems, according to Althusser, 'the structure of historical existence is such that all the elements of the whole always co-exist in one and the same time.' However far Montesquieu's secularism was from Leibniz's religious metaphysics, both were strongly holistic in their conceptualization of internally coherent mini-worlds.[17]

Like Montaigne, Montesquieu used the perspectives of non-occidental cultures to bring his own under critique, notably in his Persian Letters of 1721. His earnest desire to understand foreign practices rather than to evaluate them led him to be accused by contemporaries of endorsing unchristian customs such as polygamy. That mischaracterization is as enduring as its nominal opposite, the assumption that comprehension and judgement are incompatible. Montesquieu's assessment of different practices as being 'juste' within their system was more likely an acknowledgement of their 'aptness' for such-and-such a society at such-and-such a stage, rather than their normative 'rightness' simpliciter. In any case, Montesquieu was no cultural relativist, however much he advocated sympathetic understanding.

---

[17] Louis Althusser and Étienne Balibar, Reading Capital (London: New Left Books, 1970), 94–7, 186–9; Althusser, For Marx (Harmondsworth: Penguin, 1969), 103.

Like Bodin before and Winckelmann after, Montesquieu saw peoples as shaped by their geographical and climatic contexts—temperatures, resource endowments, and so forth. However, some peoples had managed to emancipate themselves from these determinations. Only these latter sorts of people—and here the bias towards the occident—had 'proper' histories of change, and thus of politics which arbitrated change. Non-European peoples, while sharing the 'innate' love of 'liberty' (as defined in a rather European way) common to all humans, had not yet produced the genius lawgivers who could facilitate the fulfilment of their desires by liberating them from that great Other of the occident: 'oriental despotism'. In that sense, Montesquieu's main modern points of reference were European, and more specifically Anglo-French, as he reflected on the Glorious Revolution and the improvement in Anglo-French relations after Louis XIV's death.[18] Montesquieu's main point of ancient reference was Rome, with his *Considerations on the Causes of the Grandeur and Decadence of the Romans* (1734) constituting his major strictly historical work. The power that the Roman experience continued to wield over the imagination of Europe's most innovative social thinkers is remarkable indeed, if we but think that alongside Vico, Edward Gibbon (1737–94), William Robertson (1721–93), and Adam Ferguson (1723–1816) all devoted historical attention to it as a source of analogy and an anvil on which to hammer out their more general theories of history and human behaviour.

Voltaire (1694–1778) was Montesquieu's rival for the title of France's most influential historian of the eighteenth century, and their competition also extended to political outlook. Voltaire called his *Essai Sur L'Histoire Universelle Depuis Charlemagne* (1756)—translated into English as *An Essay on Universal History, the Manners, and Spirit of Nations*—a philosophy of history. It was the first work to attach that name to itself, in order to contrast it with Bossuet's 'theology of history'. Voltaire was Spinoza's heir in his quest for a rational political order freed of arbitrary customary power as well as his deism/theism, but he also desired a systematic, general History that would replace Christian teleology and self-referentiality. His earlier *Le Siècle de Louis XIV* (*The Century of Louis XIV*, 1751) had deployed a version of *similitudo temporum*, with France constituting a modern Rome to the Renaissance states' Athens as self-aware, dynamic human polities, emerging out of the voids of stagnation. But Voltaire's work was also noteworthy for its attempt at a general History in which the narrative of the west was decentred amid examinations of a wider range of empires and cultures, beginning with China rather than Egypt or the ancient Hebrews. At points various of these cultures are at the forefront of humanity's progress. A principal goal was to discredit Christian 'universal history' in favour of l'histoire de l'esprit

<hr>

[18] Parekh, *Rethinking Multiculturalism*, 55–67.

humain'. At the same time, certain formal similarities between his and Bossuet's work are undeniable:

> parallel to the providential presence of the Holy Spirit was the intramundane *esprit humain*; parallel to the apocalyptic transfiguration of the end of days was the ecumenic spread of *politesse*; the historical extinction, rebirth, and progress of the human spirit were the secular equivalent to the Christian drama of the fall of humanity in the story of Adam, the redemption of humanity in the story of Christ, and the transfiguration of humanity in the evocation of the Last Judgment.[19]

Voltaire encapsulates the difference between the French and German Enlightenment, the former being more political, rationalist, anti-clerical, and critical of revealed religion, the latter more contemplative and coloured by Lutheranism. Voltaire sometimes wrote in criticism of the Christian and medieval institutions from which he saw his own epoch as emancipating itself—a sort of History as negative Moral Lesson directed at a civilization rather than an individual historical actor. In this criticism he found allies in France and in Britain, some of whose traditions of thought he helped to introduce to France. The Scottish philosopher Dugald Stewart (1753–1828) wrote of 'a long night of Gothic barbarism' before the dawn of the eighteenth century'. The historian John Pinkerton (1758–1826) invoked an earlier Scotland overrun by a tide of 'weeds and vermin, which its ebb has left on the shore'.[20] Like the philosopher and historian Hume, Gibbon was especially scathing of the dogmatism of institutionalized monotheisms; he wrote of 'the triumph of barbarism and religion' at the end of the Roman empire, with Christianity's erosion of classical culture facilitating the 'barbarian' triumph and the fracturing of the Roman empire. By extension the subsequent 'dark' and 'middle' ages were indicted too.[21] Unlike Hume, Gibbon never professed an epistemology that differed from his historical method. Gibbon fancied himself to have discovered historical laws, including the principal law that the loss of civic liberty leads to civilizational decay. The subject of his opus *The Decline and Fall of the Roman Empire* (1776–88) contrasted with the majesty of the English constitutional settlement of 1688–9.[22]

In the same contrastive vein, Condorcet (1743–94), author of *Sketch for a Historical Picture of the Progress of the Human Mind* (1793–4), described History

[19] Barry Cooper, *Eric Voegelin and the Foundations of Modern Political Science* (Columbia: University of Missouri Press, 1999), 218–19.
[20] Quotes from David Allan, 'Scottish Historical Writing of the Enlightenment', in Rabasa et al. (eds.), *The Oxford History of Historical Writing 1400–1800*, 497–517, here 514.
[21] Edward Gibbon, *The History of the Decline and Fall of the Roman Empire*, ed. David P. Womersley, vol. 3 (Harmondsworth: Penguin, 1995), 1068.
[22] Michael Bentley, 'Introduction: Approaches to Modernity', in Bentley (ed.), *Companion to Historiography*, 395–506, here 403–5.

as 'man's confession' of bygone fanaticism and superstition.[23] The strength of Condorcet's convictions may be inferred from the fact that he penned this panegyric to anticipated human emancipation while in hiding from the Jacobin Committee of Public Safety. He tended more to the prophetic than the apocalyptic mode of philosophy of History (see pp. 55–6), presenting his world as standing on the cusp of utopia: 'how welcome to the philosopher is this picture of the human race freed from all its chains, released from the domination of chance and of the enemies of its progress, advancing with a firm and sure step in the path of truth, virtue, and happiness! How this spectacle consoles him for the errors, crimes, and injustices that still defile the earth, of which he is often the victim!' At the same time, he embodied a scientistic or 'positivist' approach to human affairs: 'The only basis for belief in the natural sciences is the idea that, whether we know them or not, the general laws governing the phenomena of the universe are necessary and constant. Why should this same principle be less true for the development of the intellectual and moral capacities of humankind than for other natural processes?'[24] While anticipating an age of enlightened equality across the globe, and critical of foregoing European imperialism, Condorcet was thoroughly Eurocentric in his idea of who was to lead the liberating charge, and rather unoriginal in his focus on Greece as the point at which occidental civilization had departed from the norm of serried backward, obscurantist peoples.[25] His work sometimes deployed a ten-part schema in which human history progresses from a state of nature to the one Condorcet foresaw. Ten stages are more appropriate than three for the atheist who favoured decimal classification in a number of spheres, but tripartite divisions would nonetheless continue to exert a peculiar hold over 'progressive' French social theorists, notably Henri de Saint-Simon (1760–1825) and, under his influence, Auguste Comte (1785–1857).[26]

Condorcet's 'social science' was one of a number to evolve in the generations around the French Revolution. The veneration of natural science certainly helps explain this development, but so too does the establishment of the nation-state with its break with tradition and its provision of a veritable social experimentation chamber. As had been the case with myths earlier, the relationship between social world and the social sciences was not one way: the theories influenced societies as well as analysing them.

[23] Breisach, Historiography, 207.
[24] Condorcet, 'Sketch for a Historical Picture of the Progress of the Human Mind: Tenth Epoch', trans. Keith Michael Baker, Daedalus, 133:3 (2004), 65–82, here 65, 81—see also 82 on 'paradise'.
[25] Ibid. 67–71; Breisach, Historiography, 205–7; David Allen Harvey, The French Enlightenment and its Others: The Mandarin, the Savage, and the Invention of the Human Sciences (London: Palgrave Macmillan, 2012), 197 ff.
[26] On the social sciences, see Harvey, French Enlightenment; for the whole text and other supporting documentation, including particular elaborations of some of the ten-stage periodization: Condorcet, Tableau historique des progrès de l'esprit humain: projets, esquisse, fragments et notes (1772–1794), ed. Jean-Pierre Schandeler and Pierre Crépel (Paris: L'Institute National d'Études Démographique, 2004).

The Scottish Enlightenment

The significance of the earlier Hume (1711–76) in these connections was not his faith—he had none—in grand interpretative historical schemes or linear developmentalism, but his reflection on psychology within the 'science of man'. Psychology was a central element in any systematic thinking about causation in human affairs and linkages between people across time and place. For Hume, as for Vico, the science of man was a foundation for considering the other scientific investigations on which 'man' embarked, but Hume perceived a more thorough-going constancy in human nature. It was this, perhaps, that allowed him to sub-scribe to most of the Greek rationales for writing History simultaneously. At one point he averred that 'the advantages found in history seem to be of three kinds, as it amuses the fancy, as it improves the understanding, and as it strengthens virtue',[27] and at another time that 'History, the great mistress of wisdom, furnishes examples of all kinds; and every prudential, as well as moral precept, may be authorized by those events, which her enlarged mirror is able to present to us'.[28] He also suggested that whoever wanted to know 'the sentiments, inclinations, and course of life of the Greeks and Romans' should study 'the temper and actions of the French and English'.

> Mankind are so much the same, in all times and places, that history informs us of nothing new or strange in this particular. Its chief use is only to discover the constant and universal principles of human varieties of circumstances and situations, and furnishing us with materials from which we may form our observations and become acquainted with the regular springs of human action and behaviour. These records of wars, intrigues, factions, and revolutions are so many collections of experiments, by which the politician or moral philosopher fixes the principles of his science, in the same manner as the physician or natural philosopher becomes acquainted with the nature of plants, minerals, and other external objects, by the experiments which he forms concerning them.[29]

To use the terms deployed earlier (p. 122) this is a more functional 'men of their place' argument than a culturally-oriented 'men of their times' stance, but Hume was aware that other cultures and times held divergent values, and insisted that people should only be judged by the standards prevailing locally, even if one disapproves of those standards. Because he believed that relatively superficial

---

[27] S. K. Wertz, 'Moral Judgments in History: Hume's Position', *Hume Studies*, XXII:2 (1996), 339–68, here 342.

[28] David Hume, *The History of England, from the Invasion of Julius Caesar to the Revolution in 1688*, vol. VII (London: T. Cadell, 1778), 150.

[29] David Hume, *On Human Nature and the Understanding*, ed. Antony Flew (New York: Macmillan, 1962), 94–5.

differences could be reduced under inspection to commonalities, he certainly did not adopt a relativistic position. Even for those with a more variegated understanding of culture, the psychological approach was central to explaining, for instance, the mythical origins of religion. This mode of explanation provided basic building blocks for further non-religious accounts of human institutions and history.[30]

Hume's *History of England* (1754–62) was deflationary in that psychological explanations undermined grander ideological explanations for political actions. He also sought to 'refute the speculative systems of politics advanced' in Britain, which is one of the hallmarks of the conservative, mistrustful of the capacity of grand designs to do justice to the messy complexity of real life, and aware of the rule of unintended consequences. That aim reflects his emphasis, common to other Scottish Enlightenment thinkers, on the importance of custom in social evolution, as opposed to great lawgivers and individual intentions. Hume was similarly opposed to mythologies of the past for their distorting, polarizing effects on political discourse. Given the historical success of variants of Protestantism in Britain and the success of Protestant powers in the Seven Years War, it tended to be Protestant claims on legitimacy and providence that sounded most stridently, such that Hume's friend William Robertson, who was at once Edinburgh University's principal and a leader of the Church in Scotland from the 1760s, found himself combating Protestant dogmatism in his historical scholarship.

At the same time Robertson played his own part in sublimating Protestant philosophies of history into a secular theory of stadial development built on universalistic precepts, most notably in the prologue to *The History of the Reign of the Emperor Charles V* (1769) and in *A History of America* (1777), which detailed pre-Columbian American history and then the collision of 'old' and 'new' worlds.[31] One wonders how much of the inspiration for such a study, as for the general fecundity of Scottish historical philosophizing around this time, was due to the great social and economic changes wrought on the country following the '45, the failed Jacobite rising against the Hanoverian dynasty. Robertson wrote that a 'human being, as he comes originally from the hand of nature, is every where the same...the talents he may afterwards acquire, as well as the virtues he may be rendered capable of exercising, depend entirely upon the state of society in which he is placed'. This view combined egalitarian universalism as regards a general human condition with the potential for prejudice against actual human societies. Indeed it seems to have been premised on the familiar assumption that

---

[30] Frank Edward Manuel, *The Eighteenth Century Confronts the Gods* (Cambridge, MA: Harvard University Press, 1959); Peter Melville Logan, *Victorian Fetishism: Intellectuals and Primitives* (Albany: State University of New York, 2009), ch. 1.

[31] Allan, 'Scottish Historical Writing', 504–6.

indigenous Americans were effectively living in a state of nature that could be observed, and out of which they could be cultivated given appropriate institutional arrangements. This is not to suggest that he in any way endorsed the violence of the invading Europeans.[32]

Robertson's contemporary Adam Ferguson made the contrary point that the state of nature was a myth, one designed to cover gaps in a theory and justify some arrangement preferred by the 'social contract' theorist. On one hand this implied the improbable assumption that no contract theorist realized the artificiality of their heuristic exercise; on the other hand, it pointed to the inherent sociality of people, the fact that when conceiving some actual person or set of people as without culture one is just showing oneself to be blind to their acculturation. As his *Essay on the History of Civil Society* (1767) unfolded, Ferguson also claimed to have identified the motor of historical development, in the human ingenuity brought forth to satisfy material needs. Ferguson did not see this as a contradiction, a return to a pre-cultural depiction of the human, because even if certain needs were clearly universal, the human capacity for invention in order to meet them was indicative of the broader capacity for different human groups to constitute themselves historically, and thus culturally: 'of all the terms we employ in treating of human affairs, those of *natural* and *unnatural* are least determinate in their meaning'. So 'we speak of art as distinguished from nature, but art itself is natural to man', and 'man' is 'in some measure the artificer of his own frame, as well as his fortune'. It would be left to Adam Smith to elaborate a theory of why there were qualitative as well as quantitative changes over time in the way of meeting needs—changes from hunter-gatherer society to a pastoral mode, then an agrarian one, and then 'commercial society'. These Smith attributed to necessity stemming from population growth, with the accompanying 'invention' not issuing from the genius of any one individual, but rather from the self-interested and basically short-sighted actions of the many.[33]

Robertson, Smith, and Ferguson are characteristic of so much Enlightenment historical thought in moving away from the conscious designs of gods and great men and towards the significance of what was known among their French contemporaries as 'circonstance': circumstance. Acting at the interface of needs, impulses, mores, collectives, and institutions, their work also showed how hard it can be after a point to distinguish between a 'functional' and a 'cultural' contextualization.

---

[32] Ibid. 506.
[33] Roger Smith, 'The Language of Human Nature', in Christopher Fox, Roy Porter, and Robert Wokler (eds.), *Inventing Human Science: Eighteenth-Century Domains* (Berkeley: University of California Press, 1995), 88–111, here 104; Craig Smith, *Adam Smith's Political Philosophy: The Invisible Hand and Spontaneous Order* (Abingdon: Routledge, 2006), *passim* on Smith and, on Ferguson, 26–33; Allan, 'Scottish Historical Writing', 507–9.

The German Enlightenment and Early Romanticism

Arguably the greatest Enlightenment philosopher, Immanuel Kant (1724–1804), addressed the same contextualization problem in his lectures on anthropology when he observed that the ability to create different natures is part of the general human endowment. But when he entered the lists of 'pragmatic' History—really a speculative venture which he explicitly distinguished from empirical historical inquiry—in his 1784 essay *Idea for a Universal History from a Cosmopolitan Point of View*, the result was teleological and its 'universalism' Eurocentric.[34] The implication of his theory of knowledge was that individuals everywhere partook of a 'psychic unity', and he did not subscribe to the polygenetic theory. Nevertheless, at points he clearly believed in distinctions within the human race, correlated with skin colour and sometimes—as in the thought of Montesquieu and Bodin—with climatic conditions. Some of this was straightforwardly racist, and even at the end of his life he did not approve of 'race-mixing', though alas that scarcely puts him in an extreme position at the time. He was not consistent in many of his views, which may be explained by the clash of personal and cultural prejudices with his theoretical propositions about the nature of cognition. Sometimes he described Africans or indigenous Americans as pre-moral, sometimes as accessible within the moral universe if on its peripheries, but over time he grew firmer in his commitment to including all within his theory of cosmopolitan right (*Weltbürgerrecht*) in a world of ever-greater connectivity. His *Towards Perpetual Peace* (1795) and *The Metaphysics of Morals* promoted criticism of colonial practices and the slave trade, and played on the concept of 'savages' in much the same way Montaigne did.[35] Proposing that all people effectively shared the same

[34] Immanuel Kant, *Idee zu einer allgemeinen Geschichte in weltbürgerlicher Absicht*, trans. in *Kant: Political Writings*, ed. Hans Reiss (Cambridge: Cambridge University Press, 1991), 41–53. For wider contextualization, Thomas Sturm, *Kant und die Wissenschaften vom Menschen* (Paderborn: Mentis, 2009) chs. VI–VII. On Kant's particular understanding of 'pragmatic', and its place in his scheme, see John H. Zammito, *Kant, Herder and the Birth of Anthropology* (Chicago: University of Chicago Press, 2002), 348–9.

[35] For changes over time and inconsistencies and consistencies, including the difference between Kant's personal prejudices and the implications of his theories: Sturm, *Kant und die Wissenschaften vom Menschen*; Robert B. Loud, *Kant's Impure Ethics: From Rational Beings to Human Beings* (New York: Oxford University Press, 2000), 99, 195, 209; Pauline Kleingeld, 'Kant's Second Thoughts on Race', *The Philosophical Quarterly*, 57:229 (2007), 573–92; and Amélie Oksenberg Rorty and James Schmidt (eds.), *Kant's 'Idea for a Universal History With a Cosmopolitan Aim': A Critical Guide* (Cambridge: Cambridge University Press, 2011), 184. On 'race-mixing', Mark Larrimore, 'Antinomies of Race: Diversity and Destiny in Kant', *Patterns of Prejudice*, 42:4/5 (2008), 341–63. For anti-colonialism and the entry of the world's peoples 'in varying degrees into a universal community' in the light of connectivity in *Towards Perpetual Peace*, see the reproduction of the essay in *Kant: Political Writings*, ed. Reiss, 93–130, here 106–7, and, for the Montaigne-like quotation on 'savages', 103: 'the main difference between the savage nations of Europe and those of America is that while some American tribes have been entirely eaten up by their enemies, the Europeans know how to make better use of those they have defeated than merely by making a meal of them. They would rather use them to increase the number of their own subjects, thereby augmenting their stock of instruments for conducting even more extensive wars.'

capacities for reason, Kant nevertheless suggested in *Towards Perpetual Peace* that how explicit those categories are in the mind, and thus how they are actualized, varies according to time and place.[36]

Just as important as Kant's reflections on history and diversity were his thoughts—and, as we shall shortly see, the reaction to those thoughts—about how people conceived themselves in time and in regard of reason and the world beyond the mind. Against the pure rationalism of Descartes (in one of his modes), Baconian and Newtonian empiricism soon showed how experimental observation of the world could confound deductive theory, but likewise it was apparent that the mind was not a blank slate on which the truths of empiricism were inscribed—instead the mind had a synthesizing quality. The very act of 'making sense' undermined the concept of mental perceptions as uncomplicatedly mirroring the world as it was, being then elucidated by transparent language. But rather than concluding that strong scepticism was therefore vindicated, Kant rejected it along with rationalism and empiricism in his 'transcendental idealism'. Kant's 'Copernican revolution' required seeing the subject as actively constituting its experience by means of a synthetic activity that it undertakes. Such a synthetic activity, according to Kant, operates by means of the 'forms of intuition', i.e. space and time, which give experience a temporal and spatial order, and by means of *apriori* conceptual categories like quantity, quality, and relation that allow that experience to be subsumed under judgements. It is only through the judging activity of the subject that it comes to have any experience of objects in the first place. Human thought was no longer to be assessed for its capacity as a more or less leaky vessel for knowledge whose origin lay beyond the subject (in God, in the world, or whatever). Rather, the mind itself was the origin of knowledge. Human subjectivity, in that sense, was the grounding of objectivity, but this is subjectivity in the sense of a general human capacity, not a unique possession of one individual. Note that what Kant called the transcendental (not transcendent) ego is to be distinguished from what he called the empirical ego. The empirical ego was the expression of unique, individual character. The transcendental ego was a characteristic of every subject, but as the very basis of subjective thought, it could only be approached by philosophical reflection not empirical enquiry. Moral philosophy too relied on the capacity to create and access a generalizable structure of reason.

Kant combined the sovereign quality of the self as legislating to itself with a rationally constituted social glue whose generally recognized legitimacy would replace that provided by revealed religion. In Kant's view, all agents of sufficient rationality could come to articulate the moral law for themselves, by virtue of reasoning that they themselves were prepared only to live with norms that they

---

[36] Michael N. Forster, *Hegel's Idea of a Phenomenology of Spirit* (Chicago: University of Chicago Press, 1998), 363.

would themselves be prepared to legislate for all rational beings. This position he termed the 'categorical imperative'. In principle, all inherited and otherwise external sources of moral or interpretative authority were supplanted by human reflection on the finite world of experience and appearance, and the capacity for reason. While the *apriori* categories were the structuring condition of thought and understanding, the exercise of the latter faculties was an achievement in human spontaneity, giving both freedom and responsibility to the subject. This was at once uplifting—transient mortal existence need no longer be contrasted with the uncorrupted and superior version—and salutary—for the soul's immortality had conventionally alleviated the burden of physical finitude, and furthermore responsibility for identifying the moral life for the sake of that life itself now lay absolutely with the human. Another nail was driven into the coffin of human orientations towards the ancestral-traditional past or the eternal. Though Kant himself was still committed to a 'rational theology', in subsequent thought humans were now oriented towards an open-ended future in which their projects needed no sanction from inherited meanings and, as long as the projects respected other rational beings, could be pursued with the deployment of fungible natural resources exploited for their instrumental value against clock time as that determined everyday secular activity.[37] A perfect philosophy, then, for a bourgeois-capitalistic modernity in which community dissolves into self-directed individualism, bonds into contracts of exchange, technological control obviates natural rhythms, and accelerated change demands prediction and control of the future?[38] If Kant would not have endorsed these conclusions, and if they are in many ways an absurd reduction of his magnificent achievement, for travellers on the *via antiqua* they would have seemed but a logical extension of the process by which the productive mystery of the Bible had been obliterated in construction of the *via moderna*.[39]

Consonant with a world of predictable rhythm, one of whose historiographical expressions was the increased circulation of History in Britain identified by Woolf (p. 147), eighteenth-century Germany witnessed a gradual and uncertain shift in the concept of 'pragmatic history', though Polybius, the historian who had coined that term, had anticipated most of the variations on the theme. While in a manifesto of 1714 Johann David Köhler associated pragmatic History with orientation in civic life, especially political affairs, Johann Christoph Gatterer (1727–99), of Göttingen's influential Royal Institute for Historical Sciences, understood it as developing 'the whole system of causes and effects, of means and

---

[37] On this aftermath, Martin Shuster, *Autonomy after Auschwitz: Adorno, German Idealism, and Modernity* (Chicago: University of Chicago Press, 2014), ch. 2; Hammer, *Philosophy and Temporality*, 71–5.
[38] Ibid. 41–53, chs. 3 and 4. For the relation to historical consciousness, see Koselleck, *Futures Past*, *passim*.
[39] Kelber, 'The Quest', 81.

intentions...Nothing should hinder [the historian] or lead him astray in this undertaking, neither the distance between areas, nor the intervals in time, nor the different types of events themselves.' We might call Gatterer's 'pragmatic' History *conjunctural*, as opposed to the *conjectural* sort of the Enlightenment's philosopher-historians. Gatterer's quest to locate historical enquiry in the 'overall connection of things in the world', '*nexus rerum universalis*', whereby no incident anywhere was an insular matter, shows the debt that a burgeoning 'science of man' owed to the mechanistic conception of the world. It also evinces similarities to the aims of Jean d'Alembert, co-editor of the great *Encyclopédie* that appeared in the 1750s–1760s.[40]

In terms of a realized History, one French comparator is the project to which Diderot contributed, but which was mainly written by Guillaume Thomas Raynal, a *Philosophical and Political History of the Settlements and Commerce of the Europeans in the two Indies* (1770–80). This work considers the role of overseas colonialism and trade in influencing far-flung places and in turn influencing the interactions of European states. While looking through European eyes, and seeing European civilization as pre-eminent, it also evinces a dialectic-of-Enlightenment quality, in that it was critical of the violence, enslavement, deceit, and greed by which European actions were marked, and European morals undermined. It was concerned with charting a path to pacific exchange, which highlights the centrality of global connections to the work.[41]

Like other historians before and after them the Göttingen historians were keen to rebut the deprecation of History by rationalists like Descartes and Christian Wolff, and to prove History an equal 'science' to the natural sciences, albeit one that had its own aesthetic principles and inductive methodology. A claim to general explanatory utility was seen as crucial to this disciplinary self-validation. Gatterer's conception of pragmatic History matches the latter side of a distinction made by Walter Schmitthenner between 'theoretical' and 'practical' universal History. Schmitthenner describes the practical variety as 'concerned with causality, relating dispersed occurrences, where possible, by determining their interdependence and establishing priorities in time'.[42] It is not primarily concerned with establishing meaning and overall direction, and so may be 'universal' in aspiration without constituting a 'speculative philosophy of history', whether religious or secular.

---

[40] On 'Nexus rerum universalis': Wolfgang Proß, 'Die Begründung der Geschichte aus der Natur— Herders Konzept von "Gesetzen" in der Geschichte', in Hans Erich Bödeker, Peter Hanns Reill, and Jürgen Schlumbohm (eds.), *Wissenschaft als kulturelle Praxis, 1750–1900* (Göttingen: Vandenhoeck und Ruprecht, 1999), 187–225, here 194; other quotes and analysis from Peter Hanns Reill, *The German Enlightenment and the Rise of Historicism* (Berkeley: University of California Press, 1975), 42–3 and Sturm, *Kant und die Wissenschaften*, 309–32, esp. 313–15. On the 'science of man', see Zammito, *Kant, Herder*, 336 ff.

[41] On which see Cecil P. Courtney and Jenny Mander (eds.), *Raynal's 'Histoire des deux Indes'* (Oxford: Oxford University Press, 2015); Abbattista, 'French *Philosophes*', 420–4.

[42] Walter Schmitthenner, 'Rome and India: Aspects of Universal History during the Principate', *The Journal of Roman Studies*, 69 (1979), 90–106, here 90.

As important a distinction divides practical 'Universalhistorie' of Gatterer's sort from the 'Geschichte der Menschheit', or History of humanity, practised by Johann Gottfried Herder (1744–1803) and in a different way by his contemporary Christoph Meiners. Quite unlike Hume's interests in events as experiments and Gatterer's interest in events within broader causal relationships, Meiners's and Herder's studies were concerned with matters like language, belief systems, forms of law and government, eating habits, education of children, family life, senses of honour, shame and communal obligation, along with theories of the relationship between geography, climate, technology, and aspects of physical and psychological constitution. Both were comparative thinkers with broad interests in a worldwide range of peoples, and both were interested in the nexus of culture and 'nature', but Meiners was a racist and a polygenist. Herder was not, though his ideal conception of differently acculturated peoples living in discrete places meant that he was either ambivalent or outrightly hostile to diasporic peoples like Jews, Romanies, and 'Turks' in Europe. On the whole he disavowed human hierarchies and the ethnocentrism characteristic of much philosophy of history and much of the anthropology that was to come later on.[43] Part of the German *Frühromantik* tradition, Herder was a product of the Enlightenment who felt that many of its thinkers had gone insufficiently far in self-critique. His *This too a Philosophy of History for the Formation of Humanity* (1774) criticizes self-regarding teleological philosophies of moral progress, the selection of favoured bits of the past by historians, and imperialism and 'civilizing missions'. As with other thinkers of human diversity, spatial-cultural and temporal elements were intertwined in his thoughts. In *This too a Philosophy* he wrote both that 'Each nation has its *centre* of happiness *in itself*, like every sphere its centre of gravity!' and that each age 'has the *centre* of its happiness *in itself*!'[44] He drew deeply on the thought of Johann Georg Hamann (1730–88), who at once shared Luther's scepticism about the prospects for human reason and rejected dualistic Kantian distinctions between the world of human affect and experience on one hand and the world of reason on the other. To Hamann we must first attend, as a seminal thinker in the 'early romantic' or so-called 'Counter-Enlightenment' tradition of which it has been said that 'no other intellectual initiative has played so great a role in fashioning attitudes to modern historical thinking'.[45]

[43] The contrast between Meiners's and Herder's approach to History on one hand and Gatterer's approach on the other from Proß, 'Die Begründung der Geschichte aus der Natur'. For Herder's attitude to diasporic groups, Karol Sauerland, '"Die fremden Völker in Europa": Herder's unpolitische Metaphern und Bilder zu den höchst politischen Begriffen Volk und Nation', in Gesa von Essen and Horst Turk (eds.), *Unerledigte Geschichten: Der literarische Umgang mit Nationalität und Internationalität* (Göttingen: Wallstein, 2000), 57–71.

[44] Johann Gottfried von Herder, *Philosophical Writings*, ed. Michael N. Forster (Cambridge: Cambridge University Press, 2002), 297 and 299 (emphases in original).

[45] Michael Bentley, 'Introduction: Approaches to Modernity', 406.

Applying Paul's concepts in 2 Corinthians, and consistent with Luther's view on consubstantiation, in which Christ's body and blood and bread and wine were all present in the Eucharist, Hamann disavowed any opposition between the spirit and the letter in the interpretation of language. The same went in Hamman's thought for the interpretation of the world of nature and the flesh as 'texts' more broadly defined—he had something akin to a 'realist' medieval view of the world as a divine text, the 'book of god'. Language had a symbolic quality as well as referential and straightforwardly communicative capacities; it was embedded in everyday life as well as having formal properties; and the spiritual and cognitive elements were irreducibly intertwined.[46] Before the Fall Adam and Eve had direct access to divine or 'angelic language'. Afterwards humans were forever engaged in a form of interpretative translation 'out of angel-speech into human language, that is, thoughts into words,—things into names,—forms into signs'. This was not, however, interpretation *ab initio*. Regarding the material world, the imagination and cognition worked on the experience of the senses. Authorial intent of, say, scripture, meanwhile, might be inferred and argued over, while the letter remained as a guide. When Hamann wrote that 'man' must 'take his external sense as a help, must be attentive to the given letter as the only vehicle of the Spirit which can be grasped' we can see the Neoplatonic element of his thought by which the divine and the human sphere are not entirely separate even while humans can never be certain of their interpretative ground. While language distances the user from original, divine meanings it is also still somehow a trace of the same, providing an oblique, mediated insight, like 'a solar eclipse which is looked at through a glass of water'.[47] Any attempt to subjugate language in the name of complete human autonomy and control was akin to the hubristic attempt to build the Tower of Babel. Reason presupposed a language in which it could be expressed, and language was unavoidably interpretative, making the reader or speaker into a participant in the construction of meaning as they operated from contexts that were irreducibly social and historical as well as sensuous.[48] 'In the language of every people we find the *history* of the same... The invisible being of our souls is revealed through words.'[49]

There is a Vico-like quality to much of this thought, especially the reflection on humankind's prelapsarian state, but within the German tradition Leibniz had already emphasized language as a generator of meaning as well as a condition of reflective thought. Leibniz had written: 'I really believe that languages are the

[46] Kenneth Haynes, *Hamann: Writings on Philosophy and Language* (Cambridge: Cambridge University Press, 2007), pp. xiii–xviii; Robert Alan Sparling, *Johann Georg Hamann and the Enlightenment Project* (Toronto: University of Toronto Press, 2011), 93.

[47] Ibid. 48–9, 81, 93; quotes from W. M. Alexander, *Johann Georg Hamann, Philosophy and Faith* (The Hague: Martinus Nijhoff, 1966), 84.

[48] Gwen Griffith Dickson, *Johann Georg Hamann's Relational Metacriticism* (Berlin: de Gruyter, 1995), 170.

[49] Alexander, *Johann Georg Hamann*, 85.

best mirror of the human mind, and that a precise analysis of the significations of words would tell us more than anything else about the operations of the understanding.'[50] Hamann had linked events in the Garden of Eden and in 'Babel' rather as they are linked in the book of Genesis. In Genesis, Adam's and Eve's rebellion, then the attempt to build a tower as a monument apart from god, each resulted in dispersal and alienation, first of people from god, then of peoples from each other.[51] For his part, Herder saw the linguistic-cultural diversity that supposedly resulted from the Babel episode as something to be celebrated, with any future conceptualization of human unity having first to take account of diversity.[52] The religious references were more by the way of adornments than architecture in the work of this erstwhile clergyman, however.

Herder replaced Hamann's historical-theological admixture with an account of historical-social evolution in which environmental factors and human reflection on sense-data also played a role, and differing religions were the products of those different circumstances.[53] He also deployed the classical concept of *humanitas/Humanität* to express a basic human commonality to set alongside his awareness of rich and very deep human cultural-linguistic differences. All groups must, he felt, have possessed some concept of humanity as a ground for social obligation: 'The human heart has always remained the same in inclinations, just as the mind has in abilities.'[54] He sought 'to gather historical examples of how far the diversity of human beings can extend, to bring it into categories, and then to try to explain it', for the history of diverse creatures is 'the history of our nature'.[55] There was no way to short-circuit the process of historical and ethnographic enquiry by some process of rational deduction, and presentism went hand-in-hand with ethnocentrism as an obstacle to thought on the human condition. 'People who, ignorant about history, know only their own age believe that the current taste is the only one and so necessary that nothing but it can be imagined.' 'Time has changed everything so much that one often needs a magic mirror in order to recognise the same creature beneath such diverse forms.'[56]

Herder's conception of the relation of culture to nature is expressed by his comment: 'How different is the world in which the Arab and the Greenlander, the soft Indian and the rock-hard Eskimo, live! How different their civilization, food,

---

[50] Leibniz quote from John Leavitt, *Linguistic Relativities: Language Diversity and Modern Thought* (Cambridge University Press, 2011), 51–2.

[51] James Austin, *The Tower of Babel in Genesis* (Bloomington: Westbow, 2012).

[52] Michael Morton, *Herder and the Poetics of Thought* (University Park, PA: Pennsylvania State University Press, 1989), 34–6, 62, 65–6.

[53] Ibid. 34–6; John R. Betz, *After Enlightenment: The Post-Secular Vision of J. G. Hamann* (Chichester: Blackwell, 2012), ch. 6; Proß, 'Die Begründung der Geschichte aus der Natur'.

[54] Herder, *Philosophical Writings*, ed. Forster, 268. See also 213–14: 'Humanity is the noble measure according to which we cognize and act'. On *Humanität* more generally: Hans Adler and Wulf Koepke (eds.), *A Companion to the Works of Johann Gottfried Herder* (Rochester, NY: Camden House, 2009), 104 ff.

[55] Herder, *Philosophical Writings*, ed. Forster, 249.   [56] Ibid. 255.

education, the first impressions that they receive, their inner structure of sensation! And on this structure rests the structure of their thoughts, and the offprint of both, their language.'[57] Mental reflection (*Besonnenheit*) on the sensual, reflection which is coextensive with language, permits abstraction within the limits of given conditions. Historical and sensual conditions account for the heteronomy of human value-systems.[58]

Herder's views on morality sometimes reached the level of proper, thorough-going relativism of the sort sometimes described today as meta-ethical moral relativism (see p. 326). There was no common denominator or yardstick outside the very general parameters set by the yet-to-be established 'nature' by which to assess differing moral outlooks. Of 'moral virtue and human beings' happiness', he wrote that

> For both of these we not only still lack a correct criterion, but it could even per-
> haps be that human nature had such a flexibility and mutability as to be able to
> form out for itself in the most diverse situations of its efficacy also the most
> diverse ideals of its actions into what is called *virtue* and the most diverse ideals
> of its sensations into what is called *happiness*, and to be able to maintain itself
> therein until circumstances change and further formation occurs.[59]

External evaluation not only seemed to make no sense, it also missed the point about something akin to what Althusser called 'expressivism' in relationship to Montesquieu's thought. Laws and norms could not be transferred piecemeal from one society to another because those societies were tightly interconnected wholes that had developed organically together and set their own, incommensurable criteria of right and wrong. 'Shortcoming and virtue always dwell together in one human hut', Herder wrote, and 'good and evil are only relational terms.'[60] The one depends on the other, and they both stem from the same *Volksgeist* or folk-national-spirit. What we see here is the transposition of a certain burgeoning Enlightenment conception of individual *people* as self-contained, consistent subjects to the conceptualization of human *collectives*. The result, for Herder, was a cultural essentialism that sits easily with his cultural relativism: essences-of-peoples were not unchanging, but at any one time they are there, which also explains Herder's difficulty with diasporic minorities that sat amongst otherwise supposedly discrete peoples.

---

[57] Ibid. 220, Herder's text from editor's note.
[58] On Spinozan questions: Proß, 'Die Begründung der Geschichte aus der Natur', and Mack, *Spinoza*, 60–3. On Besonnenheit, Helmut Gipper and Peter Schmitter, *Sprachwissenschaft und Sprachphilosophie im Zeitalter der Romantik* (Tübingen: Narr, 1979), 72–3, 151.
[59] Herder, *Philosophical Writings*, ed. Forster, 270.
[60] Ibid. 295, and similar sentiments about internal relations on 294.

Herder's cultures and linguistic communities have the quality of Leibniz's 'monads' (pp. 152–3), and that legacy endured in subsequent German historical scholarship that linked human groups to folk 'spirits'.[61] Herder saw multiplicity as an intrinsic good in Leibnizian fashion. Commerce and contact between peoples were to be applauded as a way to broaden sympathies and enhance mutual and self-understanding, but this did not justify interference by one culture in another's affairs. 'Providence itself is the best converter of peoples', he wrote, meaning changes in 'sensations, needs, and situations'.[62] Herderian relativism is what one gets when one removes the religious metaphysics from Leibniz: without the deity in whom all otherwise-incommensurable monadic perspectives are reconciled, 'meta-ethical moral relativism' is what is left.

Herder was a progenitor of important strands of latter-day anthropology, notably that of Franz Boas in the late nineteenth century. Boas's anthropology is often described as 'historicist' owing to its focus on the internal development of human groups 'on their own terms', as opposed to the diffusionist or social evolutionist (Comtean) strands of social scientific that had dominated hitherto. Perhaps it is no mere happenstance that German late Enlightenment thought should be so important in the development of the study of culture. After all, it was distinguished from French and British thought by its institutional context, namely the lack of correspondence between *Volk* and state. As Laonikos Chalkokondyles (p. 111) had started to think in more purely ethno-cultural terms as the Byzantine state disappeared, leaving only a nascent and partly diasporic 'Greekness', so Herder lived in a world where Germandom was subdivided across innumerable states, in some of which Germans were in the minority. At the same time we should note that Herder was keen to encourage national consciousness; this was a matter for Historians who could depict the journey of the *Volk* through time, but others would have to join in the distinctly political work of 'promot[ing] the unity of the territories of Germany through writings, manufactures, and institutions'.[63]

Of great importance for the human sciences subsequently was Herder's— and Hamann's—linkage of language-study to the hermeneutic method of comprehension. Insofar as other cultures were of the past, deciphering their texts was vital. The salient technique Herder called *Einfühlung*, 'feeling the way into' the mental structures that generated the verbal traces. It pursued an idiomatic

---

[61] A heritage made explicit for instance in Ernst Troeltsch, *Der Historismus und seine Probleme: Erstes Buch*, ed. Friedrich Wilhelm Graf and Matthias Schlossberger (Berlin: de Gruyter, 2008 [orig. 1922]). 402–3, 987–9. On the links between Herder and Leibniz's monadological thought: Ulrich Eisel, 'Individualität als Einheit in der konkreten Natur: Das Kulturkonzept der Geographie', in Parto Teherani-Krönner (ed.), *Humanökologie und Kulturökologie* (Opladen: Westdeutscher Verlag, 1992), 107–52, here 118 ff.; Samuel Fleischacker, *Integrity and Moral Relativism* (Leiden: Brill, 1992), 217.

[62] Herder, *Philosophical Writings*, ed. Forster, 221.

[63] Paul Bertagnolli, *Prometheus in Music: Representations of Myth in the Romantic Era* (London: Routledge, 2007), 146.

understanding born of extensive immersion in the language, history, culture, and geography in which texts were produced. The goal was not that of sharing the feelings or sensations of distant authors, but rather of engaging in painstaking historical and philological study, often by textual comparison, of the range of meanings that authors were likely to bring to their work and evince by their expressions, based on the principles of contextualization beyond the text and holism within it (i.e. a sense that one could only understand the parts in the context of the whole). Herder warned against hostility towards the people and cultures that had produced specific texts but also against over-identification with them, since both dispositions were liable to distort the 'feeling' necessary for authentic interpretation.[64] His torch was carried forward by the hermeneutic philosophers from Friedrich Schleiermacher (1768–1834) through Wilhelm Dilthey (1833–1911), as well as by opponents of positivism within sociology such as Georg Simmel (1858–1918).

Hegel

Georg Wilhelm Friedrich Hegel (1770–1831) may for present purposes be seen as fusing Kant's thought with the holism of Herder, Montesquieu's interest in institutions, and elements of Aristotelian teleology. The concept of *esprit* was central to his philosophy but it did not have the same connotations as Voltaire's. Hegel saw 'spirit', or *Geist* in his German, not as something that had to be liberated from institutions and the hold of history, but as something that developed across time in tandem with 'circonstance' and institutions. Hegel's importance to this volume is partly indirect, in the reactions which his work provoked in thinkers as different as Marx and Leopold von Ranke, but it is also direct, in that Hegel was not only deeply interested in the History of philosophy but tried to do philosophy in a way that related it to historical change. He was a significant early contributor to and product of a general historical infusion of many non-historical disciplines, though most historians would come to regard him as not being historical enough, given the teleological element in his philosophy. He was wary of History as Lesson and scorned Hume's comparisons of ancient Greeks with modern Frenchmen: 'No difference could be greater than that between the nature of those ancient peoples and our own time.'[65] One purpose of his work was nonetheless to link ancient Greeks and occidental moderns through an analysis of the entire 'historical process' that drew on inductive-empirical historical scholarship but was underpinned by a speculative philosophy whose subject was *Geist*.

[64] Editor's introduction to Herder, *Philosophical Writings*, ed. Forster, pp. xiv–xxi.
[65] G. W. F. Hegel, *Introduction to the Philosophy of History with an Appendix from The Philosophy of Right*, trans. Leo Rauch (Indianapolis, IN: Hackett, 1988), 8–9.

In common with the wider *Frühromantik* movement, Hegel sought to reconcile rationalism, with its anti-historical, anti-traditional connotations, with the world of experience and stabilizing convention. The French Revolution and Revolutionary Wars gave increased urgency to Hegel's quest, but his project was in genesis prior to Napoleon's conquest of Prussia and consolidation of many German statelets. Elements of the fusion had been established in Prussia in the age of 'enlightened absolutism' but, as a member by birth of Württemberg's professional stratum, in the 1780s–1790s Hegel was at once first-hand witness to the belated, destabilizing impact of 'enlightening' reform in that more 'backward' state, and saw himself as being qualified to suggest a remedy for its malaise. While Kant provided inspiration for radical reform amongst those prepared to build an earthly 'Kingdom of Ends' in which people made their own laws, Kant's philosophy also seemed part of the problem, given that it was based on various dualisms, including mind:world dualism and the dualism of the transcendental ego and the empirical egos of individual humans. Kant had purchased an austere, disembodied morality of conduct—an 'empty formalism', in Hegel's words—at the expense of an embedded ethics of living and an Aristotelian pursuit of fulfilment in which one did the right thing gladly, increasingly spontaneously, rather than out of a calculation as to duty.[66] If the goal was to actualize 'man's essence as an autonomous subject...with the revolutionary task of creating an integrated ethical community in the sphere of concrete natural and historical existence', Kant's emphasis on formal reasoning only spoke to half of the matter. What of the *gemeinsame Sittlichkeit*, or shared ethical sensibility of a civil society which mediated between individual morality and the law? Indeed Kant's reasoning contained a paradox. If to be an agent (on Kant's reckoning) requires that someone gives themselves the moral law (autonomy), then it becomes mysterious how someone could give themselves the law without first being an agent. Hegel's solution to this problem involved the Aristotelian concept of upbringing and a focus on how one is formed.[67] For Hegel, the tools of reason were to be employed to effect a reconciliation between the situated, finite self and the 'others' of nature and society, i.e. between subject and object of subject's attentions. In a variation on Vico's claims on the prelapsarian state, Hegel and others believed that the desired harmony had naturally existed in pre-Socratic Greek thought. Harmony had been fractured by later philosophical and theological developments, as humans started to see themselves as radically separate from nature and each other. Such developments represented a conceptual advance in terms of *Geist*'s growing 'consciousness' of its

---

[66] G. W. F. Hegel, *The Philosophy of Right*, trans T. M. Knox (Oxford: Clarendon Press, 1952), quotation from 89–90.

[67] See John Edward Toews, *Hegelianism: The Path toward Dialectical Humanism, 1805–1841* (Cambridge: Cambridge University Press, 1985), chs. 1–2, quote from 34. On 'The Kantian Paradox', Terry Pinkard, *German Philosophy 1760–1860: The Legacy of Idealism* (Cambridge: Cambridge University Press, 2002), 59–60, 227.

own nature, Hegel thought, but—and here the omnipresent dialectical element of his doctrine—it had come at the cost of *Geist's* alienation. The alienation from the world beyond the mind was expressed through objectifying that world.[68]

Since Hegel claimed that philosophy 'has no other object but God and so is essentially rational theology' it is not surprising that *Geist* can be interpreted as either a spiritual or a rational, almost social-scientific, concept, but in either case it is supra-personal.[69] Let us explore the social-scientific valence first, which is also the reading that has been most influential recently. Recall Adam Smith's idea of an invisible hand that makes sense of an infinite number of often competing and dissonant human actions and interactions: in the social scientific reading of Hegel, *Geist* pertains to the subject of humankind in the same way. To be sure, Hegel did identify 'world-historical' characters—invariably occidental—like Socrates, Jesus, Caesar, or Napoleon whose exceptional thoughts and deeds embodied the shift from one epochal order to the next rung of *Geist's* ascent, but the actors were not necessarily aware of the deep meaning of their own actions: they were simply especially prominent vessels of *Geist*. Thus, just as Smith's self-interested trader unwittingly consolidates the capitalist order even though he has no comprehension of economic theory so the historical function of individual actions is to embody and consolidate some particular stage of *Geist*. Accordingly, such 'progress' as humans make can only be assessed at the level of humankind, not of individual people. Throughout history, *Geist* has been embodied in the dominant political, legal, social, religious, and cultural institutions of social orders. Thinking along Aristotelian lines, these institutions provided the forms for the social content of human interaction. They were objectifications of *Geist*, familiar representations of the social order to its inhabitants, and they could be 'read' by later generations with the help of the hermeneutic method that provided empirical complement to speculative reflection. At any given time, particularly insightful thinkers—especially philosophers like Hegel himself—could give individual expression to the nature of *Geist* at that phase of its existence, becoming its spokespersons as it were, but even they were generally incapable of exceeding its general structural parameters, and so were better at divining what had already become manifest than predicting the future as one order ended and another began as the result of some world-historical act or change in interactive patterns. (This is the meaning of Hegel's famous claim that 'the owl of Minerva spreads its wings with the coming of the dusk'.) Thus, for Hegel, whatever constitutes the structure of reason, and so of society, at any one time is a social, historical construction, not an individual one or a metaphysical one.[70]

---

[68] Toews, *Hegelianism*, chs. 1–2.

[69] Cited in Paul Redding, *Continental Idealism: Leibniz to Nietzsche* (London: Routledge, 2009), 198.

[70] On the final sentence, Pinkard, *German Philosophy*, 249.

Periods of relative or apparent stasis exist betwixt epochal advances, all the while building up forces that are ready to be unleashed at the next 'phase transition', or revolution. Individuals may suffer in this process, because it is not an even upward march, but, in dialectical fashion, may feature ostensible setbacks. At one point Hegel categorically states, in contradiction of one of Kant's iterations of the categorical imperative, that flesh-and-blood individuals 'come under the category of means' rather than ends-in-themselves. History is 'the slaughter-bench, upon which the happiness of nations, the wisdom of states, and the virtues of individuals were sacrificed'. By one contested reading of Hegel this suffering is not just necessary for the final outcome, it is redeemed by that outcome, 'the ultimate goal for which these sacrifices were made'.[71] Before attending to the end-state, talk of redemption prompts us to see how that state might be approached in accordance with the more religious reading of Hegel.

When exploring the developmental elements of Hegel's thought the link between reason and religion is provided by Neoplatonism, though Hegel also evinces broader pantheistic influences. Hegel's *Geist* has much in common with Plotinus's *nous*, as something that may be translated as 'spirit' but also connotes reason, which is why some also translate *Geist* as 'mind'. Contrary to the dominant Christian metaphysics, for Hegel the universe was not voluntarily created by God in a one-off act. God cannot exist separately from the universe, which is an emanation of himself—while impersonal, 'he' exists in all aspects of his creation and must reveal himself in it. Dialectically, that creation is necessary for God to become aware of, and so to perfect, himself. Hegel differed from Augustine, who also saw struggle as movement, because for Augustine divine redemption was not the direct consequence of historical development. For Hegel, enlightenment was the point at which humankind realized that it had the answer to humankind's questions—at this point it was a creation reaching its own state of self-aware perfectibility. This was the moment of *Geist*'s self-conscious reach for reason, as opposed to previous orders under which people had looked to external divine forces for guidance, or invoked quasi-divine entities like the extra-mental Kantian 'noumenal' world that still somehow conditioned human reason even if it could never be apprehended by the mind. In Hegel's vision reason triumphed at the point of nothing more and nothing less than the free exchange of reasoned arguments, untrammelled by mistaken metaphysical considerations. At the same time the 'right' metaphysical thought is that the ultimate unity of subject and object are revealed by human subjects contemplating themselves as elements in a holistic world, parts of a unifying *Geist*. Scientific categories and law may not be inherent

---

[71] Hegel, *Introduction to the Philosophy of History*, 23–4, 32–8, 70, 101; Marcuse, *Reason and Revolution*, 227–34. For contestation see Shuster, *Autonomy after Auschwitz*, ch. 4 and Terry Pinkard, *Does History Make Sense? Hegel on the Historical Shapes of Justice* (Cambridge, MA: Harvard University Press, 2017).

in the object but creating those categories and laws furthered the self-knowledge of *Geist*. This is Hegel's update of the old idealist idea that knowledge of laws is knowledge of the thought of God: one knows God because one knows oneself. The advance of reason was thus intrinsically bound up with knowledge of the state of human freedom, for only under those circumstances was it possible to have the equal, intersubjective discussion whereby one could reach agreed norms via reasoned exchange. Where in the apocryphal oriental despotisms from which the Greeks had advanced the state of *Geist* was such that only the despot was known to be free, and where in Greco-Roman antiquity only the citizens were known to be free, after the Reformation with its doctrine of spiritual freedom, all were known to be free. What was then needed were the social institutions in which this freedom could be expressed, which brings us back to the more secular and sociological Hegel.[72]

In Hegel's thought the state should be understood as an organic entity housing the modern-day *ecclesia*, rather than a string of bureaucratic institutions for which Hegel had some fetish. The state actualizes the freedom of the people.[73] Some states—most obviously German ones in his time—had a role as world-leaders, Hegel thought. What he called 'world-historical national spirits' took the lead among the community of national spirits, in promoting freedom and awareness thereof. A reading of the Reformation as spiritual liberation and the progression of equality and freedoms enshrined in law were essential for the claim to German primacy, for by the early 1820s post-Napoleonic reforming Prussia had come for Hegel to symbolize the substantial, though certainly not complete, reconciliation of rational rule and communal sensibility, form and substance, particular and universal. But the deeper point about modern states as such is that they supposedly provide sites for something like the institutionalization or materialization of self-aware *Geist*. In his examination of the balance of and interrelation between personal rights, property rights, and state rights, and between different social structures from the family to the social 'estates' to the world of contractual exchange, we see Hegel at his most sociologically acute. Giving systematic form to social life, these arrangements prompt individuals to identify their own freedom with the substantial order of which they were part—again, reconciling subject and object.[74]

---

[72] Hegel, *Introduction to the Philosophy of History*, 17–18, 20–1, 99–103. John Laughland, *Schelling versus Hegel: From German Idealism to Christian Metaphysics* (Aldershot: Ashgate, 2007), 142–3; Thomas Albert Howard, *Religion and the Rise of Historicism* (Cambridge: Cambridge University Press, 2000), 84–5; Adorno, *History and Freedom*, 147–9. On *nous*, Bertrand Russell, *History of Western Philosophy* (London: George Allen and Unwin, 1947), 312–13. Also Anthony Kenny, *The Rise of Modern Philosophy* (Oxford: Clarendon Press, 2006), 113–16, 163–4, and, on intersubjective agreement and reason-giving, Pinkard, *German Philosophy*, 359–62.

[73] See Alan Patten, *Hegel's Idea of Freedom* (Oxford: Oxford University Press, 1999).

[74] Hegel, *Introduction to the Philosophy of History*, 26, 40–56; Toews, *Hegelianism*, ch. 3; Marcuse, *Reason and Revolution*, 236–9.

Despite caricatures of his thought, Hegel did not see his contemporary world as constituting history's culmination, even if he did regard it as having reached the highest point so far. Whatever the teleological element in his philosophy of history he was decidedly pessimistic about the possibility of attaining true harmony between individual and whole. He was also aware of how tenuous the Prussian political synthesis was and perceived threats to it from populist nationalism and unreflective political reaction, while his intellectual world was under constant threat of impingement by committee intervention and censorship. Consciousness of freedom, and the thought that went with such consciousness, would have always to be active, and so might well come into conflict with the very state whose existence facilitated that freedom in the first place. With an eye to continuities across the millennia, he squarely replicated a sense of the westward movement of History, from 'the Orient' through Greece, and Rome. The Mediterranean comprised the 'centre of world history', but the 'land of the future' was not Germany: it was the westernmost outpost of the occident, America.[75]

So much, then, for the conservative Hegel, or the statist patriot, or the Olympian justifier of all suffering in the name of progress. There were other visions of him at the time, as is appropriate for one whose name is synonymous with dialectic thought. If, as he famously said 'the real is rational', then rulers might fear that only what is rational is actually real in the philosophical sense, and that the self-conscious mind might adjudge contemporary realities as irrational and therefore ephemeral—there was more than enough autonomous reason in Hegel's system for that outcome. If individual events from terrible suffering to heroic triumph were vectors of deeper processes, then what seemed concrete and given at any one time might turn out to be merely fleeting. In the more sociological reading of Hegel, the 'negative' element in his thought pertains to the ways in which various configurations—forms of life, shapes of spirit—break down under their own weight and contradictions. In the more metaphysical reading the 'negative' element in his thought existed precisely to question what actually existed at any given moment, in line with the basic ontological problem of why some things existed but not others. Here, indeed, we witness echoes of Leibniz's so-called esoteric philosophy, which is by no means as favourable to the status quo as his conventionally understood position which Voltaire mocked as 'Panglossian'. Certain entities, Leibniz wrote, are not 'compossible'—they cannot coexist, so it is a matter of either-or, which is to be decided metaphorically speaking in a sort of competition between possibles after god has made the choice to create something. Similarly, for Hegel, the establishment of that which is, is also an alienating repression or repulsion of that which is not (but might have been

---

[75] On Hegel's misgivings, Toews, *Hegelianism*, ch. 3; on contingency, Pinkard, *German Philosophy*, 361; on matters geographical, Hegel, *Introduction to the Philosophy of History*, 83–91.

and might yet be). In Hegelian terms, that which is purports to constitute an organic whole but is in fact mutilated, incomplete. Negative thought is not negative in the sense of unconstructive, but in the sense of subversive, in the way that the literature and poetry of the avant-garde sought to establish a new language uncontaminated by the 'facticity' of a certain brand of realism, and modernist art rejected mimesis and classical concepts of representation, as well as Christian concepts of incarnation. Not for nothing did Friedrich Wilhelm IV of Prussia condemn Hegel as sower of the 'dragon seed' of revolution.[76]

One response to Hegelian negative philosophy, as to French revolutionary rationalism and scepticism, was positive philosophy—'positivism'. For Comte in restoration France, see the legal theorist F. J. Stahl in Germany. The 'universalism' of Comte and the nationalist-particularism of Stahl are different: the former espoused a tripartite stadial theory of 'social evolution' that supposedly applied to every people, at the final, highest, 'scientific' stage of which (his present) social thought would be governed by analogy to physiology; the latter was embedded in the specificity and historical prerogatives of the state, had debts to idealism, and set itself against universalistic concepts like natural law. But both opposed the 'insubstantial', speculative element of Hegelian dialectical thought.[77]

Marx

Whatever else he was, Karl Marx (1818–83) was a child of the Enlightenment, bringing together German, Scottish, and French influences. He ultimately disagreed that the historical process evinced any intrinsic rationality or meaning in Hegel's sense, but at all times he felt it could be rationally understood, which was essential to intervening in it. His very claim to scientific status entailed rejecting moral judgement as an obstacle to analysis, prediction, and emendation, even as moral outrage coloured so many of his deliberations. In his mode as speculative philosopher of the historical process Marx's was the obviously apocalyptic counterpart to Hegel's *ostensibly* prophetic view of history, and he rejected the redemptive aspects of Hegel's theory as obscenely complacent in the face of what they were held to redeem. He replicated Hegel's conception of successive historical stages but replaced the idealist conception of *Geist*'s self-actualization with aspects of Adam Smith's materialist stadialism. The product of all this, at least as indicated in his early *Economic and Philosophical Manuscripts* (1844), was a historical subject that only attained its fullness at the last historical stage. What Marx called alienation denoted the perversion and frustration of many potentialities.

---

[76] Marcuse, *Reason and Revolution*, pp. vii–xi, 231, 325–6; Norman Levine, *Marx's Discourse with Hegel* (Basingstoke: Palgrave Macmillan, 2012), 9. The Leibniz connection is my own.

[77] Marcuse, *Reason and Revolution*, 323–74.

Wage-labourers, despite having freely, contractually entered into employment, were alienated from the final product of their work by the division-of-labour principle and the fact that that product belonged to someone else. They were each alienated from their fellow humans by being placed into competition with them in relations determined by structures beyond their vision. There is no proper intersubjectivity within a shared Hegelian ethical order here, but rather a variant on the estrangement which Vico had identified. The structures also impaired the quintessentially human quality of creativity. Overall, we can detect the influence of Rousseau's dictum about the destruction of human self-esteem.

In his earlier work Marx foregrounded the relationship between mind-subject and natural world-object. Nature was important to Hegel's scheme, in the sense of seeing humankind within the natural order, but he had been less interested in the reciprocal or mediated relationship between humankind and the material world. Marx and Engels wrote in *The German Ideology* (1845–6) that while one may 'look at history from two sides and divide it into the history of nature and the history of men', both 'sides are, however, inseparable: the history of nature and history of men are dependent on each other so long as men exist'.[78] Labour fuses the natural and social worlds. The continuation of social life depends upon the exchange of the products of labour and so upon the laws and mechanisms of that exchange. Labour is the mechanism of the worker's emancipation from the Kantian realm of necessity to his world of freedom, a world of shared material bounty. On this point of the development of truly human potentials after needs had been more easily satisfied, there is nothing between Marx, Smith, and, later, John Maynard Keynes. Whereas from Aristotle's Greece through the feudal ages labour had signified ignobility, the creative capacity to harness the natural world was now, at least potentially, a sign of man's dignity as well as his power. Though Marx himself did not put it like this, consider the shift from *laboratores*, the working order beneath *oratores* and *bellatores* in the medieval social pile, to *laboratories*, those modern nerve-centres of technological progress. It should never be forgotten that Marx saw in capitalism a progressive force of a certain sort, one of vast power that unleashed a number of potentials and achieved notable rational outcomes. Marxism as a vision of the future is a post-capitalist ideology rather than an anti-capitalist ideology, albeit that Marxism as a social critique is preoccupied with criticism of capitalism's tendencies.

The philosopher and social scientist Helmut Fleischer usefully distinguishes three aspects of Marx's thought. One, the 'anthropogenetic' sort, is more characteristic of the earlier writings, especially the 1844 *Manuscripts*. The 'anthropogenetic' Marx has as his concern the process of the realization of the human *qua* human. It is in these works, where a species-essence is invoked, that the idea of

---

[78] Karl Marx with Friedrich Engels, *The German Ideology, including Theses on Feuerbach and Introduction to the Critique of Political Economy* (Amherst, NY: Prometheus Books, 1998), 34.

alienation has its broadest existential meanings. The other two aspects of Marx's thought Fleischer calls 'pragmatological' and 'nomological'. The essence of the pragmatological type is encapsulated in the famous claim of Marx's most famous historical essay, *The 18th Brumaire of Louis Napoleon* (1852), that 'Men make their own history, but they do not make it just as they please. They do not make it under circumstances chosen by themselves but under circumstances directly encountered, given and transmitted from the past.'[79] The pragmatological approach is context-sensitive and allows for divergent paths, albeit that—and here few historians of any stripe would disagree—the range of possible paths is constrained by paths already taken. Marx and Engels had arrived at this approach by the time of *The German Ideology*, where they criticized Hegelian philosophy of history for its determinism and mocked his dialectics. It was later, from the late 1850s, that they sometimes deployed what came to be called (by others) a dialectical materialist philosophy of history of the sort Fleischer calls nomological. As its name suggests, the nomological (i.e. law-making) form does present an overarching, unilinear theory of history.[80] Whatever the weaknesses of the nomological interpretation, many left-wing workers and intellectuals took inspiration from its optimistic sense of inevitability, just as many Protestants took inspiration from the idea that God was on their side. But scientific and pseudo-scientific developments related to the theory of evolution also seemed to push in the same direction, as with the Lamarckianism evinced in the thought of Karl Kautsky and Georgi Plekhanov in the Second International of 1889–1914. Plekhanov was the man who introduced the term 'dialectical materialism' to Marxist theory, and that was taken up and 'refined' by Joseph Stalin, though Leon Trotsky claimed to be a dialectical materialist too.[81]

While it is impossible to reconcile the nomological and pragmatological strands in their purest forms and in their entirety, it is possible to reconcile elements of each, and after all we must recall that each is only a tendency in Marx's thought rather than the all-controlling element at any given stage. Here is one attempt at partial reconciliation.[82] In the case of capitalism, Marx did see inevitability in the development of crisis, thus in Leibnizian terms the present was pregnant with the future, but not necessarily in the direction of resolution of

[79] Karl Marx, *The Eighteenth Brumaire of Louis Bonaparte* (New York: International Publishing, 1969 [orig. 1852]), 15; Helmut Fleischer, *Marxism and History* (New York: Harper, 1973); Alvin W. Gouldner, *The Two Marxisms: Contradictions and Anomalies in the Development of Theory* (Basingstoke: Macmillan, 1993).

[80] S. H. Rigby, *Engels and the Formation of Marxism* (Manchester: Manchester University Press, 1992), 81–3, 97, 187–98.

[81] On naturalism and the Second International, see Alex Callinicos, 'Marxism and the Status of Critique', in Brian Leiter and Michael Rosen (eds.), *The Oxford Handbook of Continental Philosophy* (Oxford: Oxford University Press, 2007), 210–39, here 212. For Stalin's 1938 'Dialectical and Historical Materialism', see J. V. Stalin, *Problems of Leninism* (Peking: Foreign Languages Press, 1976), 835–73, online at https://www.marxists.org/reference/archive/stalin/works/1938/09.htm

[82] I draw heavily here on Marcuse, *Reason and Revolution*, 310–19.

crisis. Dialectical thought, with its emphasis on rise and fall, stresses and strains in a Leibnizian interconnected whole, was predicated upon the emergence of internal contradictions, or the self-negation of capitalism. The contradiction springs from ever-increasing capital accumulation and concentration to the point where monopoly displaces competition. Paralleling that development is ever more intensive, competitive labour exploitation. At the same time technological advance means the value of human labour depreciates. Reduced popular purchasing power, but especially the rising 'organic composition of capital',[83] reduced the rate of profit of the surviving industries which, trapped in the logic of constant accumulation through utilization of capital, overproduce, and the search for new resources and markets prompts international warfare and expansion. Meanwhile, domestically, political repression is needed to complement workplace 'discipline' as discontent arises. Thus far, the emphasis is all on the 'objective' factors rather than on human agency and consciousness. The introduction of 'subjective' factors is key for the transition to a socialist order—here again the Hegelian synthesis of subjective and objective, which we might also call the conjunction of agency and structure—in the form of the working class's awareness of its own predicament and opportunity and of self-conscious proletarian organization in the *political* sphere. But the advent of that subjective factor is not inevitable, as stressed by Marx at points and by that notable applied theorist Lenin.

Different Marxist thinkers are free to pick-and-mix between different Marxes, but we can make some rough generalizations as to affinities. Historian Steve Rigby observes that the split between pragmatological and nomological Marxisms tends to be linked to whether, within the general Marxist emphasis on the economic *base*, they emphasize the role of *productive forces* as the key determinant of historical change or the *relations of production*. The productive forces are the technological and other skills and equipment available at any one time, say the hand-mill before it is replaced by the water-mill and that in turn by the steam-mill. The 'relations of production' means the way in which primary, technical, and human 'resources' are arranged, and thus includes class structure. Emphasis on relations of production corresponds more with pragmatological consideration of the divergence of paths and the role of class-oriented political action at specific 'under-determined' historical conjunctions. Emphasis on the causal primacy of society's growing productive forces tends to be associated with a nomological account of history as an inevitable process.[84]

Moving from the constituents of the economic base to that of what Marxists call the political and ideological superstructure, Marxism has often been seen as a

---

[83] S. H. Rigby, *Marxism and History* (Manchester: Manchester University Press, 1998), 49–50.

[84] Ibid., chs. 3–6 on the first tendency and chs. 7–8 on the second. See also on divergence Robert Brenner, 'Agrarian Class Structure and Economic Development in Pre-Industrial Europe', *Past and Present* 70 (1976), 30–74, and on underdetermined conjunctions, Althusser, *For Marx*, 228–9.

claim that there is a one-way determination of the former by the latter ('vulgar Marxism'), even though Engels went out of his way to correct this conception and even though Marx's own historical writings, most notably the *18th Brumaire*, display an awareness of the active historical role played by politics and ideas.[85] Many of Marx's balder statements about the historical primacy of base-material factors should be seen in the polemical context of his struggle with the powerful German idealist tradition. Certainly, important later Marxists have distanced themselves from vulgar Marxism, as when Antonio Gramsci (1891–1937) invoked the concept of 'hegemony' as part of his argument that proletarian ('subaltern') submission was the product not just (sometimes not even) of coercion but was also achieved at the cultural level, through which workers came to acquiesce in the moral authority of those above them. Base and superstructure might also interpenetrate, as for instance with laws affecting economic activity, meaning that they are not really separable in the first place for one to determine the other. As the Marxists Maurice Godelier and Ellen Meiksins Wood have argued, feudal law, which 'vulgar Marxism' might see as a part of the superstructure, is actually central to the definition of feudal classes by which the base is constituted.[86]

   If one wanted to identify continuities in Marx alongside the changes, one could look to the focus on *unmasking*, which is also central to the project of undermining cultural dominance/hegemony shared later by Gramsci and his contemporary György Lukács (1885–1971). Unmasking, which also fits some definitions of 'de-reification', is what the introduction to this chapter alluded to when associating Marxist historiography with the agenda of History as Emancipation. It is a matter of removing illusions of naturalness or ordained-ness. In his 1843 essay 'Contribution to the Critique of Hegel's *Philosophy of Right*', Marx wrote that 'The abolition of religion as the illusory happiness of men, is a demand for their real happiness... The criticism of religion disillusions man so that he will think, act and fashion his reality as a man who has lost his illusions and regained his reason.' In the *German Ideology* of 1845–6 he wrote that communism 'overturns the basis of all earlier relations of production and intercourse, and for the first time consciously treats all natural premises as the creatures of hitherto existing men, strip[ping] them of their natural character'.[87] Denaturalization was one of the major themes of Marx's Introduction to *A Contribution to the Critique of Political Economy* (1859) while the Preface to that work contained Marx's most famous criticism of any Kantian idea of a self-authoring sovereign subject: 'The mode of production of material life conditions the social, political and intellectual life process in general. It is not the consciousness of men that determines their being,

---

[85] Rigby, *Engels and the Formation of Marxism*, 165–9.

[86] For references and the summary of the argument, see S. H. Rigby, 'Marxist Historiography', in Bentley (ed.), *Companion to Historiography*, 889–928, here 911–12.

[87] Marx with Engels, *The German Ideology*, 89.

but on the contrary, their social being that determines their consciousness.'[88] And again, in *Capital* (1867): 'the advance of capitalist production develops a working class, which by education, tradition, habit, looks upon the conditions of that production as self-evident laws of Nature.'[89] The raising of consciousness about the artificiality of the whole set-up was a precondition for the reversal of 'self-estrangement'.

At the same time Marx's views did develop as to precisely what it was that would be un-self-estranged or unalienated. In the more 'anthropogenetic' 1844 *Manuscripts* he talked of humans being estranged from their creative species-essence by the mechanisms of capitalism, whereas later he dropped such meta-physical talk about what humans 'really are', used 'alienation' in a more limited sense, and reflected on the variable cultural construction of ways of being. When 'man' first takes up tools, he changes the world and thus himself.[90] So while in some ways Marx becomes less historically contingent (less 'pragmatological') and more law-oriented (more 'nomological') over time as regards the analysis of social-economic change, he becomes more 'historical' over time in his under-standing of the relationship of human conditions in the plural to changing socio-economic orders and the environment.

In principle there is nothing new in Marx's agenda of denaturalization. It is implicit in anthropological ventures from Hippocrates onwards, and explicit in the words of Rousseau and of the historian of ancient Rome Barthold Georg Niebuhr (1776–1831). Niebuhr wrote that History revealed what 'even the greatest and highest spirits of our human race' do not understand, namely 'how their eyes only acquired by chance the way in which they see'.[91] Marx's older contemporary John Stuart Mill (1806–73), a positivist liberal-utilitarian, asked rhetorically: 'was there ever any domination which did not appear natural to those who possessed it?' Alongside the examples of racial and sexual repression, past and present, with which he illustrated the point, Mill wrote that 'acquaintance with human life in the middle ages, shows how supremely natural the dominion of the feudal nobility over men of low condition appeared to the nobility them-selves' and 'hardly...less so to the class held in subjection'.[92] The novelty of Marx's intervention is not critical historicization in general, but the radical nature of the agenda to which he attached it. The particular focus of his critique

---

[88] Introduction repr. in Marx with Engels, *The German Ideology*, 1–23; Preface repr. in Karl Marx and Friedrich Engels, *Collected Works*, vol. 29: *Marx 1857–61* (London: Lawrence and Wishart, 2010), 261–5, with quote at 263.

[89] Karl Marx, *Capital: A New Abridgement*, ed. David McLellan (Oxford: Oxford University Press, 1999), 372.

[90] Graeme Campbell Duncan, *Marx and Mill: Two Views of Social Conflict and Social Harmony* (Cambridge: Cambridge University Press, 1977), 55.

[91] Niebuhr, *Lebensnachrichten über Barthold Georg Niebuhr*, vol. 2 (Hamburg: Perthes, 1838), 480.

[92] John Stuart Mill, *J. S. Mill: 'On Liberty' and Other Writings*, ed. Stefan Collini (Cambridge: Cambridge University Press, 2003), 129–30.

was the current economic order and its sustaining philosophies, which brings us briefly back to Adam Smith.

To take Ockham's razor to Smith's account, 'commercial society' is a product of the 'natural' inclinations to 'truck, barter, and exchange', after a certain point and under certain conditions. Given all the necessary 'positive' developments produced by demographic pressures and sufficient 'primitive accumulation', what is needed are negative measures, the removal of restrictions that inhibit and distort the 'natural' inclinations. Smith had in mind as restrictions patterns of landholding and land use associated with certain classical and medieval orders plus the mercantilism of the age of absolutism. Their removal would produce a 'spontaneous order' much more economically effective and respectful of freedoms than any that could be manufactured: realized, indeed, is the principle of the 'system of natural liberty'. For Marx, clearly enough, the capitalist order is anything but the outcome of natural tendencies unleashed in the right circumstances—it is a distinctly historical achievement, a cultural development in the broadest sense of culture. Marx also saw that capitalism had more far-reaching connotations than Smith allowed. It does not leave intact the sort of 'natural' ties of sympathy that Smith saw as the restraining moral context for the exercise of self-interest: Smith's *Wealth of Nations* should always be read against the backdrop of his earlier *Theory of Moral Sentiments*. For Marx, conversely, capitalism creates a concept of the human by its own particular 'laws' of motion, principles of competitive production, reinvestment, and profit maximization. The social serves the economic not vice versa. 'Primitive accumulation' may be necessary for this cultural shift but is by no means sufficient.[93]

Marx's conception of false consciousness and exploitative relations of production posed a full-frontal challenge to the romantic-idealist conception of society, replacing it with one of competing class interests and identities. This set him at odds with most other sociology of the nineteenth century, as well as with the dominant German historical school of his time, which rejected Hegel's overarching philosophy of History but kept the element of Herderian social holism.

---

[93] Ellen Meiksins Wood, *The Origin of Capitalism: A Longer View* (London: Verso, 2002), 21–5, 34–7; on 'spontaneous order', Smith, *Adam Smith's Political Philosophy*, with 'system of natural liberty' at 90.

6

Nationalism, Historicism, Crisis

Introduction

The relationship of the most influential nineteenth-century History to the classic eighteenth-century Enlightenment historical theories recapitulates that between French royalist historiography of the seventeenth century and the 'new' History of the sixteenth century. In both instances the horizons of enquiry narrowed after expanding, which once more shows us how misleading it is to conceive any unilinear trajectory of historiographical change. In the nineteenth century the trend was away from grand comparative stadial theories and towards particularist accounts in which the world beyond Europe—save sometimes for the 'ancient civilizations' of Asia and Egypt—was accorded less attention. Histories of and for the nation dominated especially in the second half of Europe's nineteenth century and the early twentieth century, as they did in areas beyond Europe that evinced European influences. Whether tracing genealogical linkages to the deep past, documenting monumental achievements, charting high political developments, or providing collective 'self-knowledge', the dominant historical rationale of the age was that of History as Identity, specifically national Identity.

Inevitably, as with earlier historiographical turns, not everything changed and that which did change did not do so all at once. Walter Scott is a name synonymous with the romantic reaction to Enlightenment thought. His first novel *Waverley* (1814), manifestly romantic in style, nonetheless evinced elements of 'Enlightenment' stadialism as he addressed the interface of less 'advanced' highland culture and its lowland and English counterparts around the Jacobite rising of 1745.

There is no European nation which, within the course of half a century or little more, has undergone so complete a change as this kingdom of Scotland. The effects of the insurrection of 1745,—the destruction of the patriarchal power of the Highland chiefs,—the abolition of the heritable jurisdictions of the Lowland nobility and barons,—the total eradication of the Jacobite party, which, averse to intermingle with the English, or adopt their customs, long continued to pride themselves upon maintaining ancient Scottish manners and customs,—commenced this innovation. The gradual influx of wealth and extension of commerce have since united to render the present people of Scotland a class of beings as different from their grandfathers as the existing English are from those of Queen Elizabeth's time.[1]

An 'Enlightenment' scope and a disregard for recent methodological advances was evinced in the multi-volume *World History* (*Weltgeschichte*) of one of Germany's most popular (and populist) historians of the first half of the nineteenth century, Friedrich Christoph Schlosser (1776–1861).[2] Some of the temper of Enlightenment historiography also endured in the work of the Hungarian noble and historian József Eötvös. At a time of heightened, resentful Hungarian nationalism after the Russian and Habsburg crushing of the Hungarian revolution/war of independence in 1848–9, his *The Influence of the Dominant Ideas of the Nineteenth Century on the State* (1851–3) sought to reconcile nationalism with equality as well as liberty.[3] Sometimes we see the adaptation of certain Enlightenment concepts rather than their outright rejection: while nineteenth-century historians tended to disavow grand philosophies of world history alongside the universalism of their Enlightenment forebears, a teleological element was nonetheless evident in the work of not a few, with the end-point being nation-statehood or some particularly conducive version thereof. In each successive generation French historians could be found declaring that the July Monarchy (1830–48), the Second Republic (1848–52), the Second Empire (1852–70), and the Third Republic (1870–1940) respectively represented the proper culmination of the historical process.[4] If few historians embraced Hegel's particular concept of world-spirit many embraced Herder's concept of *Volksgeist*, national-spirit.

Turning to emergent challenges rather than continuities from the eighteenth century, historical approaches modelled on the social and even physical sciences grew in influence, especially from the mid-point of the nineteenth century. Nonetheless, even where such positivist influences were strongest, as in France with its Comtean legacies, especially during the 1860s–1880s heyday of Ernest Renan (1823–92) and Hippolyte Taine (1828–93), the new Histories did not dominate until well into the twentieth century. In Britain, with the major exception of Henry Thomas Buckle's *History of Civilisation in England* (1858–61) their ethos barely threatened at all until after 1945. The intellectual conservativism of the increasingly professionalized British and American disciplines meant that the German *Methodenstreit* (conflict over method) of the late nineteenth century was

---

[1] Walter Scott, *Waverley, or 'Tis Sixty Years Since* (Edinburgh: Adam and Charles Black, 1854), 316.

[2] Alongside Friedrich Christoph Schlosser's famous biographies, note his *Weltgeschichte in zusammenhängender Erzählung*, 4 vols. (Frankfurt am Main: Varrentrapp 1815–41); *Weltgeschichte für das deutsche Volk*, 19 vols. (Frankfurt am Main: Varrentrapp 1844–57).

[3] Monika Badr, 'East-Central European Historical Writing', in Stuart Macintyre, Juan Maiguashca, and Attila Pók (eds.), *The Oxford History of Historical Writing 1800–1945* (Oxford: Oxford University Press, 2015), 326–48, here 335–6.

[4] Pim den Boer, 'Historical Writing in France', in Macintyre, Maiguashca, and Pók (eds.), *The Oxford History of Historical Writing 1800–1945*, 184–203, here 190–1, 201.

largely ignored. In Germany the story was of a certain 'historicist' thought affecting other disciplines like economics much more than those disciplines affected the work of historians. There the method conflict was decisively won by the political-institutional tendency of historiography over competing tendencies associated today particularly with Karl Lamprecht (1856–1915). The victory owed less to intellectual vindication than weight of numbers and institutional position and to the broader political and cultural climate in Germany.

The first section of this chapter addresses the general political context of so much historical thought across the Continent, with the French Revolution and its aftershocks especially prominent in the explanation. It seeks to draw connections between different sorts of national situation and different sorts of national Identity History, paying particular attention to British and French historiographical trends.

The second section narrows the focus as it examines the dominant trends of German historiography in the nineteenth century. Why Germany? Because German thought was especially significant in fostering 'national consciousness' in central, eastern and south-eastern Europe. As well as Herder, the geographical breadth of the Göttingen historian August Ludwig von Schlözer's (1735–1809) interests was an important source of inspiration in eastern Europe and indeed beyond the Continent, while it is worth noting, for instance, the intellectual debt accrued in Berlin to Leopold von Ranke by the historian, ideologue of the 1848 Moldavian Revolution, and later Prime Minister of Romania, Mihail Kogălniceanu (1817–91).[5] Moreover, German historianship was the first to professionalize in Europe and indeed the world, and what happened in the German academy shaped institutional development elsewhere. At the same time, we have already hinted at challenges to the prevailing German model of historiography. Key challenges in the 1860s from Switzerland and France are examined in the third section.

Given the grand fluctuations in German political fortunes in the nineteenth and early twentieth centuries, and the accompanying turmoil in historical philosophy, Germany also features quite heavily in most of the remaining sections of the chapter. Here we examine how the particularizing, relativizing, tendency of a brand of historical thought turned in upon itself from around 1870, as some of the ontological certainties of the nation-through-history were undermined by the effects of modernization and world conflict, and the social function of the

[5] Gyula Szvák, 'The Golden Age of Russian Historical Writing: The Nineteenth Century', in Macintyre, Maiguashca, and Pók (eds.), *The Oxford History of Historical Writing 1800–1945*, 303–25, here 305–6, 308; Badr, 'East-Central European Historical Writing', 330, 336, 340–1 (though note exceptions to the generalizations about *Geist* as regards Poland, with its more monarchical-based nationalism), 345. As mentioned, among the imitators of the *Monumenta Germaniae Historica* were the *Monumenta Hungariae historica* (*Magyar történelmi emlékek*) and the *Monumentae Historiae Bohemica*. On the circumstances of the founding of the *Monumenta Germaniae Historica* see Ian Wood, *The Modern Origins of the Early Middle Ages* (Oxford: Oxford University Press, 2013), 156–7.

historian became the subject of renewed debate. One upshot was a series of manifestos for scholarly neutrality, and a proceduralist emphasis on History as
Methodology alone.

As the influential German model of national History was weakened in the first
half of the twentieth century, more space was created for competing methodologies within Germany too, especially those associated with the social sciences. The
final section of this chapter considers some of the alternative German models as
they developed in relationship to their forebears.

Nationalism, Romanticism, Whiggery

It would be beyond the scope of the present book to rehash well-rehearsed
debates on the origins of nationalism, but they cannot be entirely ignored because
nineteenth-century historical scholarship, along with twentieth- and twenty-first-
century critiques of it, are at the forefront of some of the debates. Put bluntly,
nineteenth-century historianship has been accused of creating spurious narratives of continuity across time, producing teleological and otherwise distorted
readings, especially of the medieval period. Instead of identifying some pre-existing
essence of the nation, we are told that this essence was actually constructed in
the historiography of the nineteenth century, with prior history being shaped to
fit the narrative. Hence the idea of the modern construction of the nation in
the name of nationalism, and, by extension, the idea of the modernity of
nationalism.

Nineteenth-century Histories certainly did more than reflect the ideology of
nationalism; they helped to constitute it, as Herder had commended. The most
famous Greek historian of his generation, Konstantinos Paparrigopoulos, author
of *History of the Greek Nation* (1850–74), wrote that 'the first condition for the
salvation of nations is an exact knowledge of their true state', and he believed this
knowledge could only be gleaned historically. In his address at the opening of the
course on national History at the Mihăileană Academy in Iaşi in 1843,
Kogălniceanu opined that 'History makes us spectators of the battles and revolutions that have taken place since the beginning of time; it unearths our ancestors
and shows them to us alive, with their virtues, passions and traditions.' History
'connects us to eternity, establishing communication between the past and us and
our offspring, with whom we share our deeds'.[6]

Of at least equal significance in the construction of identity were proliferating
historical artworks and monuments, and the fact that many of the major museums
founded in the nineteenth century were explicitly designated as national

---

[6] Marius Turda, 'History Writing in the Balkans', in Macintyre, Maiguashca, and Pók (eds.), *The Oxford History of Historical Writing 1800–1945*, 349–66, here 349–50, 361.

museums. Historian Stefan Berger reminds us that grand national narratives were produced beyond the precincts of universities and the circles of trained historians. 'In many parts of Europe, it was civil servants, members of the clergy and the aristocracy, middle-class writers, and intellectuals as well as politicians who were the authors of key historical national narratives. These "amateur" historians formed historical associations and museums and edited journals as well as major source editions.'[7] Document editions included the *Monumenta Germaniae Historica*.[8] This publication series of primary sources pertaining to all places of Germanic influence from the end of the Roman Empire through the medieval period was established in 1819. The motto of the series, which encouraged Czech and Hungarian imitations, was *Sanctus amor patriae dat animum*, 'holy love of the fatherland gives spirit'. The first volume of what are now more than 300 was printed in 1826. The Russian interior minister from 1809, N. P. Rumiantsev, initiated the publication of official documentation, and one of his recruits, Pavel Mikhailovich Stroiev, copied and catalogued a vast corpus of non-state sources to complement the central archives. The first series of the *Complete Collection of Russian Annals* were published under the auspices of the Ministry of Education in the 1830s and publication has continued to the present day.[9] In the same decade, that in which, under the July Monarchy, historical instruction was formalized in French schools and teacher-training instituted, the Committee for Historic and Scientific Works was formed and began publishing the *Collection of Unpublished Documents on the History of France*.[10]

For all that, it is consistent with earlier warnings about sharp distinctions between 'modernity' and the pre-modern to advise caution about attributing too much of the 'invention of national traditions' to the nineteenth century. Invention there surely was, but not a little of it had happened much earlier. From a millennium and more before the nineteenth century, remember, *origines gentium* tales had served the purposes of political legitimation by genealogical pedigree. Even when they furthered elite interests they were often ethno-cultural, even quasi-racial, in reference, whether in the widespread invocation of Trojan roots or the construction of the Angelcynn or the Franks as chosen people. There was more to the political ideology of nationalism—the claim of a 'nation' of people to exclusive ownership of a territorial state, i.e. a nation-state—than this, but these older elements were nonetheless congruent with many modern nationalisms and they constituted the raw materials on which those nationalisms depended. Much the same

---

[7] Stefan Berger, 'The Invention of European National Traditions in European Romanticism', in Macintyre, Maiguashca, and Pók (eds.), *The Oxford History of Historical Writing 1800–1945*, 19–40, here 38.

[8] Now searchable online at https://www.dmgh.de/

[9] Szvák, 'The Golden Age of Russian Historical Writing', 306–7.

[10] *Collection des documents inédits sur l'histoire de France*: den Boer, 'Historical Writing in France', 189. The collection is searchable online at https://cths.fr/ed/liste.php?monocrit=c&collection=18

went for the association of particular ethnic groups with particular confessions, and, within broad confessions, particular churches; the nineteenth century saw a multiplication of the 'national churches' whose origins can be traced not just to the Reformation but the earlier establishment of increasingly distinct English and French Catholic churches.

The French Revolution interacted in different ways with existing philosophies of differentiation between peoples owing to its own combination of universalism and particularism. A movement that invoked a general will rather than a dynasty accentuated the tendency, inherent in pre-existing contract and natural law theories and in Anglo-Saxon constitutional developments, to move the locus of sovereignty from the crown. 'We the people' was the formula for reconfiguring the basis of legitimate authority, however the 'we' was defined. The revolutionaries and then Napoleon threatened to generalize this conceptual model through conquest and the stimulation of insurgence against existing rulers elsewhere in Europe—however tyrannical revolutionary and Napoleonic rule was in practice. Constitutions were exported alongside other 'modernizing' and 'rationalizing' reforms abroad, such as Napoleonic educational policy in the short-lived French protectorate of Illyria which ignited national-historical interests amongst Croat and Slovene scholars. Constitutions unleashed tendencies that could not just be forced back into the genie's bottle by the 1815 settlement. Nor did post-Napoleonic rulers desire to force them all back in—including French rulers, especially from the overthrow of the restoration regime in 1830. Rather, the rulers wished to exploit these new tendencies while controlling them, with memories fresh as to the potency of a revolutionary 'nation in arms'. The logic and the result could be much the same whether one embraced the inspiration of French reforms or reformed oneself in order that one was strong enough to resist conquest by the likes of France (both apply in some way to Prussia) or (as in the case of Russia or in its own way Britain) where one's 'national consciousness' had been 'enhanced' by resisting France. The key was to project, via some balance of rhetoric and policy, the idea that the interests of elites and broader swathes of the population were roughly the same. The project became especially important as the century progressed, and with it the upheavals and potential for class conflict attendant upon industrialization. Of particular symbolic use was the emphasis on shared history, culture, and language which we associate with romanticism.

Whatever else it was linked with, the revolutionary era was linked with French intrusion into other peoples' affairs. The fact that intrusion came in the name of universalism and issued forth from France prompted a rejection of universalism along with French dominance in favour of philosophical and ethno-national particularism. Disruption in the lives of Europe's states and peoples (including in France) then and during industrialization brought forth an emphasis on the continuous and the historical. This helps explain nineteenth-century medievalism, which was very different in character from the disdain for the middle ages evident in some French and British Enlightenment historiography. The medieval world was seen as the incubator of modern peoplehood, and the depth of bonds thereby intimated stood in contrast to the supposed shallowness of Enlightenment rationalism. There was functional and patriotic value to such an outlook, given the invocation of universal, natural law by the French revolutionaries. The failure of Prussian arms at Jena and Auerstadt need have no metaphysical significance if set against a theory positing the difference but not inferiority of Germanic traditions against French. What was needed to put things right, in the commendation of the philosopher Johann Gottlieb Fichte (1762–1814), was the consolidation of Germany's own folk-consciousness, the awakening of the German nation, whose political iteration was the drive for a solely German state. Indeed it was the Prussian reformer vom Stein who, fresh from disappointment that the 1815 Congress of Vienna did not promote German unification, set up with his own funds the society that produced the *Monumenta Germaniae Historica* in order to instruct Germans about their past. He was also instrumental in establishing Berlin University, as if acting under Herder's injunction to 'promote the unity of the territories of Germany through writings...and institutions' (p. 177). In principle an anti-universalist outlook was at least pluralistic, and possibly relativistic. This may appear ironic when one considers how German traditions were later promoted to the status of inherently superior after success against France in Bismarck's final war of unification. Yet Fichte himself had intimated that Germany's inherently cosmopolitan and spiritual outlook gave it a privileged place in leading the European peoples forward now that the French had forfeited their right to leadership.[11]

Emphasizing civilizational depth might entail focusing on longstanding institutions or on ethnic commonality. Sometimes these foci complemented each other, as in England, where there was extensive and enduring overlap between the territorial state and its institutions and the *ethnos* in question. The concept of 'Anglo-Saxon liberties' connoted the ethnic and the institutional at once, and such a concept underlay some of the most famous statements of 'whig' history, as did an ethos of Anglicanism. When one talks of the 'whig' tendency in English historiography the immediate associations are of constitutional History, bringing together the political and the legal across large tracts of time in an optimistic story of progressive change whereby underlying continuities are given their due and the wrong sort of change is repelled. Neither explicitly cultural nor explicitly social in approach, whig History nonetheless clearly felt itself to be bringing out something of the national 'character', and it was nationalist in its sense of English exceptionalism. The joinder of this exceptionalism with universalism is also no

---

[11] On vom Stein, Wood, *Modern Origins*, 156–7.

contradiction. The development of English liberties under law, with associated property rights and economic arrangements, arrangements all seemingly validated by imperial and economic hegemony from the second quarter of the nineteenth century, cast England as the pioneer and unique embodiment of a form of polity to which all should aspire.

One ought to stress England and English rather than Britain and British. This is relevant not just because of the ethnocentric nature of whig History but because the nature of relations between England and its insular neighbours in the nineteenth century had been settled, insofar as they were settled, more recently than many of the major touchstones of the whig account. In modern history the whigs focused particularly on the civil war era, 1688–9, and the early years of George III's reign, which began in 1760, during which the principles of 1688 were felt to be under threat. Thomas Babington Macaulay (1800–59) saw the 1688 revolution as 'restorative', 'a vindication of ancient rights'. 'It is because we had a preserving revolution in the seventeenth century that we have not had a destroying revolution in the nineteenth.' The failure of the 1848 revolutions on the European continent confirmed Britain's unique path of stable development and reinforced the ideal of continuity.[12] John Mitchell Kemble (1807–57), E. A. Freeman (1823–92) and William Stubbs (1825–1901) cast their nets wider, Kemble's *History of the Anglo-Saxons in England* (1849) appearing the year after Macaulay's *History of England from the Accession of James the Second*. The medievalist Freeman compared two Williams: the Norman Conqueror and William III, England's 'deliverer' in 1688. We can perhaps detect the traces of a figural reading (cf. p. 49) when he wrote: 'In one case the invader came to conquer, in the other he came to deliver; but in both cases alike the effect of his coming was to preserve and not to destroy; the Conqueror and the Deliverer alike has had his share in working out the continuous being of English law and of English national life.'[13]

As to yet another William, the rigour of William of Malmesbury's eleventh-century historical investigations was not its only attraction for Freeman (p. 5). Whatever William had had to say in criticism of the Norman conquest he had leavened with praise as he prided himself, a man of mixed Norman and Anglo-Saxon heritage, on historical balance. Not least among the Norman achievements, apparently, had been a religious resurgence in England. We have seen that in medieval historiography in the centuries after William, the relative stability of England meant that historians could be more critical of monarchs, less indentured to the royal perspective, than was the case in, say, Spain (p. 101). In the seventeenth century and into the eighteenth the absolutist threat was met with arguments invoking the Norman 'yoke' as against established liberties. In the nineteenth century the Normans were integrated into the narrative of liberty even

---

[12] P. B. M. Blaas, *Continuity and Anachronism* (The Hague: Martinus Nijhoff, 1978), 111, 117.
[13] Freeman cited in Bentley, 'Introduction: Approaches to Modernity', 437.

if sometimes by the reaction that their advent excited. Stubbs's *Constitutional History of England* (1874–8) claimed that Norman rule had 'invigorated the whole national system; it stimulated the growth of freedom and the sense of unity, and it supplied...a formative power which helped to develop and concentrate the wasted energies of the native race'.[14]

Prior to 1789 France could also boast continuity in core territory, population, and institutions, but the revolution precipitated a debate about French identity that raged into the second half of the twentieth century. In the introduction to his *Histoire de la Révolution Française* (1847), Jules Michelet (1798–1874) set Christianity and Revolution against each other, and taken on its face that was not an unfair explanation of the basic political tension for generations after his death. As royal and ecclesiastical reaction from 1815 relied on History and the invocation of tradition, so the bearers of the revolutionary flame scoured the past for their own discursive weapons. Familiar themes like the impact of the Franks on Gaul and the precedent of early 'national' assemblies were given another working-over, while Augustin Thierry (1795–1856) influentially illuminated the origins of the 'third estate' in medieval History as a counterweight to the historiographical and political weight of the first and second estates. Which part of the third estate received most attention varied according to the political inclinations of respective anti-Restoration historians, however, and after 1830 and the advent of the July Monarchy, different strands of the revolutionary tradition were set against each other. Liberals like Thierry and Francois Guizot, the statesman and historian responsible for many of the innovations in historical education and document publication in the 1830s, became apostles of the Orléanist constitutional monarchy. Against those with increasingly radical republican agendas were the likes of Michelet and his fellow historian Edgar Quinet (1803–75), whose respective translations of Vico and Herder had been published in France in 1827. The introduction of universal manhood suffrage upon the 1848 revolution echoed Michelet's and Quinet's concern for 'the people' as a whole rather than just the bourgeois elements of the third estate.[15]

While juxtaposing Christianity and Revolution Michelet did not mean that he saw the forces as distinct. Rather, the revolution ultimately promised an order in which justice and liberty were in balance, producing a society that embodied the ideal attributes of religion as it replaced previous societies that had been more overtly religious yet had embodied a diminished Christianity. Michelet drew on Vico's historical philosophy and fused it with elements of the old theory of *translatio imperii*, plus Montesquieu's concern with the relationship between culture and geography. Civilization advanced across time from east to west in a tale of

---

[14] William Stubbs, *The Constitutional History of England in its Origins and Development*, vol. 1 (Oxford: Clarendon Press, 1874), 247.

[15] Den Boer, 'Historical Writing in France'.

ascending liberty and consciousness as it gradually emancipated itself from an 'oriental' identification of the divine with the natural to a focus on the realm of pure mind and spirit. At the same time, this focus on the spiritual became distorted in the history of Christian civilization to bear overwhelmingly on the matter of grace, that arbitrary divine favour which Michelet equated with injustice—injustice that he saw as incarnated in the society of the ancien régime. The revolution marked the return of justice, which, as an essential element of love and the original Christian ideal, also restored grace by breaking its association with repression. France self-consciously authored itself in accordance with the principles of freedom and harmony and was a light unto all other nations. 'O France, you are saved! O World, you are saved', Michelet wrote in nationalist-exceptionalist vein of 1789. In light of events in revolutionary History after 1789—Michelet was writing in 1847—one can imagine how Fichte would have taken these words had he been alive to read them.[16]

Michelet is generally classed as a romantic historian along with Thierry and likewise Carlyle and Macaulay in Britain. If romanticism could therefore coexist with a range of political views, binding its exponents together was a concept of History as a creative and consciously interpretative as well as investigative endeavour. Literary style served to evoke and reanimate, and the reader was further engaged by details of individual agency, whether that be, as in Carlyle's later work, the agency of the 'hero' or great man, or, as in the work of Michelet, the agency of a collective 'people'. Events, in all of their stark, glorious, and bloody detail, assumed a dimension that they had lost under some of the broader-brush Enlightenment History, and as with Michelet their study could be based on extensive archival research. Nonetheless, as with Romantic art, Romantic historians sought to locate the greater transcendent reality of forces and collective ideas behind the immediate event or object, which is where narrative emplotment and symbolism played as large a role as specific argument. Romanticism's heyday in and beyond France was the second quarter of the nineteenth century.

As the short-lived Second Republic became the Second Empire (1852–70) via *coup d'état*, Catholic and imperial historiography was reinvigorated. The republican historiography of the 1789 revolution, ascendant in the 1840s, was forced to confront a new triumphal national teleology with an alternative vision of historical progress. Beyond this particular disorientation for the philosophy of revolutionary progressivism (a disorientation that did not impede Michelet's writing!), romanticism *tout court* was under challenge by artistic naturalism and realism, and by the pervasive influence of mid-century scientific developments. Comte's

---

[16] Ceri Crossley, *French Historians and Romanticism: Thierry, Guizot, the Saint-Simonians, Quinet, Michelet* (London: Routledge, 1993), 193–204; Tom Conner, 'Writing History: Michelet's *History of the French Revolution*', in Gail M. Schwab and John R. Jeanneny (eds.), *The French Revolution of 1789 and its Impact* (Westport, CT: Greenwood Press, 1995), 13–22.

Course in Positive Philosophy had appeared between 1830 and 1842, and the final two volumes concerned the prospect of a social science that would remove the 'theologico-metaphysical philosophy' with which he felt the theorizing of even the finest minds of his day was still suffused. In Comte's own tripartite stadial analysis, a social science would properly be based on the empirical principles of positive science.[17] The experimental method gained in prestige subsequently via the achievements of Marcellin Berthelot in chemistry and Claude Bernard in medicine. In France, romanticism's literary and philosophical pretensions were cast as suspect in a shift much more accentuated than the rejection of Macaulay's romanticism by later English whig historians.[18] The application of more scientific methods to History as the century progressed promised—spuriously—to obviate or transcend divisive politics.

Unlike France and England, in most 'national' cases early in the nineteenth century there was no even approximate coincidence of *ethnos* on one hand and territory or institutions on the other hand. Ultimately the wish to reconstitute borders and institutions to correspond to supposedly discrete ethnic groups triumphed in the period 1866–1923, though all manner of political and military contingencies paved the way. Beyond the twisted paths to Italian and German 'unification', especially significant was the First World War that shattered the multinational Romanov, Habsburg, and Ottoman empires.[19] Certainly the major nationalist thinkers of the early nineteenth century did not think in quite such apocalyptic terms. We know that political nationalism was initially conceived in relation to liberalism and Enlightenment ideas of equality, partly based on the analogy of collective to individual self-determination, partly because of the connection between broadened political representation and recognition of 'the people' as a source of authority. Following Herder, the vision could be of self-authorizing collectives living in harmony with each other. Elements of the flowering of vernacular literature and serried cultural renaissances of the nineteenth century did indeed evince that spirit. But since that self-same 'flowering' indicated vigorous efforts to create the nation as much as to express it, we ought to remember that creation involved definition as well as a great deal of archaeological excavation in the name of 'recovering what had been lost', be that through

[17] Comte, *The Positive Philosophy of Auguste Comte*, vol. 2, ed. Harriet Martineau (London: Trübner, 1875), 1.

[18] On these challenges see Ceri Crossley, 'Historiography: France', in Christopher John Murray (ed.), *Encyclopedia of the Romantic Era, 1760–1850* (London: Fitzroy Dearborn, 2004), 505–7; den Boer, 'Historical Writing in France', 195–6.

[19] On the matter of contingency, it is also important to stress that nationalism was not always the dominant discursive framework of discontent in the multinational empires. In the Habsburg case, for instance, many of the challenges to Vienna's authority that used History were not national, but local in character. Equally, the Habsburgs were perfectly capable of annexing the Histories of their subject peoples to the History of the multinational empire. The statue of Jan Hus in Prague was erected under the Habsburgs; the Titian memorial in the Frari church in Venice was used to stress the harmony of Venetian, Italian, and Austrian interests. Thanks to David Laven for these thoughts.

Histories of folklore, or recreations of 'pure' languages and tales of earlier civiliza-tions as well as great deeds and leaders. Creation might involve Histories that were so keen to single out the nation that they ignored other peoples, as with the disregard of the German-speaking population of Bohemia in František Palacký's influential *The History of the Czech Nation in Bohemia and Moravia* (1848–76).[20] It might involve claims like those by Bulgarian nationalists that all Slav-speaking Macedonians were really Bulgarians, or the competing claim that southern and eastern Macedonians were closer to Serbs.[21] In other words, one might seek either to excise or to assimilate, which in practice meant dominate—imperialism thus resulting from nationalism. One of the most important ways of maximizing verti-cal integration across classes was to minimize horizontal integration across real or conceptual borders, to sharpen a sense of 'otherness' as a way of consolidating 'us-ness'. In Russia, for instance, especially after the French Revolution and the Polish Rebellion of 1830–1, autocracy was justified as a part of a national trad-ition, alongside Orthodoxy, as against 'western' rationalism and secularism. At the same time Britain defined itself against illiberal, Orthodox Russia much as in the previous century its 'other' had been Catholic, authoritarian France.[22]

Sometimes boundaries were created between ethno-religious-linguistic groups within the same polity as groups nursed grievances, real or imagined, of historical dispossession and exploitation along collective lines. Slovak subjection by Magyars was a significant theme in Slovak nationalist historiography, for instance. Such grievances were magnified as increasingly literate populations consumed the products of the vernacular efflorescence, and by the internal policies of multi-national empires as they sought to sustain themselves in the face of novel pres-sures by varying combinations of 'modernizing' reform and anti-liberal repression. The failure, from a nationalist and liberal perspective, of the rebellions and revolutions of 1830 and 1848 was key to the development of historical schol-arship amongst some national groups in the Russian and Austrian empires, as it was amongst those Germans who sought unification. In Russia, as had occurred at points with Habsburg policies of 'Germanization', and as would occur later on in the Ottoman empire, the state response itself could take the form of 'nationali-zation': 'Russification' of non-Russians, as in Poland after the crushing of the 1863 rising, squared Russian nationalism with imperium. Such policies were more than just linguistic and cultural—they also affected the material interests and pre-rogatives of elites of the minority ethnic group, giving the latter a stake in nationalism.

[20] Badr, 'East-Central European Historical Writing', 333–4.
[21] Turda, 'Historical Writing in the Balkans', 355–6.
[22] Linda Colley, *Britons: Forging the Nation, 1707–1837* (New Haven: Yale University Press, 2005); Szvák, 'The Golden Age of Russian Historical Writing', 307–8.

One should not just focus on the multinational empires in this connection, however, for no state was without grievances or divisions that titular elites feared might thwart the project of national unification. The nation-state was, and remains, an ideal rather than a reality. The 'differences' that had to be transcended or eradicated in the nation-building process were not just ethnic or ethnoreligious ones, though these tended to be the ones over which most blood was to be shed outside of the USSR. Differences of regional dialect and local loyalties could be just as problematic, and extant peasant culture was as much of an obstacle as any nascent 'class consciousness' in the creation of unity and more integrated and 'rationalized' national economies, as the project of 'making peasants into Frenchmen' in late nineteenth-century France revealed. Even after 'unification' in nineteenth-century Italy or Germany, and 'liberation' in Bulgaria (1878) or Poland (1919), states had to try to foster the national consciousness, loyalty, and togetherness that unification was supposed to express. In one sense this indicates a contradiction, but in another sense it reinforced the sense of continuity-in-process over time, as when American politicians invoke the ongoing effort to create the 'more perfect union' of which the Constitution speaks.

Historicism and Developmental Thought

For better or for worse, Leopold von Ranke (1795–1886) has become synonymous with the mainstream tradition of nineteenth-century German historiography, the tradition known as historicism—*Historismus* in German. Ranke's prefaces, like those of Tacitus or Thucydides, contain some of the most quoted manifestos of the discipline, although, as with his classical forebears, if one relies on the prefaces to characterize the historian, one is apt to miss a great deal. Ranke's vast scholarly output includes volumes-worth of source discussions to underpin some of the historical narratives that precede them, while an appendix to his first monograph, *Histories of the Latin and Germanic Peoples [Völker], 1494–1535* (1824), is his best known methodological contribution. Ranke taught many students and pioneered the Berlin seminar with its focus on archival documents and source criticism, which was used *inter alia* as the model for the first US History PhD programme at Johns Hopkins University.

While Ranke conducted extensive research, often in hitherto closed archives, not everything he wrote was in accordance with his own strictures; more importantly, given that few of us are innocent of hypocrisy on that score, many of these strictures were not new. What Ranke supposedly did for the study of modern sources, Barthold Georg Niebuhr had already done for Roman sources. Putting aside the contributions to critical historical scholarship of scholars in other countries and before the eighteenth century, and focusing only on the immediate

German hinterland, mention should be made of luminaries like Justus Möser (1720–94), Johann Martin Chladenius (1710–59),[23] the Göttingen scholars (pp. 171–2),[24] and late eighteenth-century German historical-critical treatment of the Bible and the life of Jesus.[25]

Ranke was a conservative incrementalist whose outlook was coloured by Romantic idealism with its religious tint. He reacted against 'enlightenment' historiography alongside aspects of the French Revolution but nevertheless felt that revolutions could be midwives to a reshaped order of peoples that better reflected their differing traditions and outlooks, hence his obvious sympathy for Serbia in *The Serbian Revolution* (1829).[26] He was not a German nationalist but a Prussian patriot who appreciated the Holy Roman Empire's aspiration to embody a civilizational ideal. His *Histories of the Latin and Germanic Peoples*, which assured him of his appointment to Berlin University in 1825, concerned the two major groups of peoples in the empire. It claimed, in a way that chimed with the relevant interpolations in the *Chronicle of Fredegar* (p. 71) but contradicted centuries of differentiation between Italians and northerners (or Romans and Goths), that 'Latins' and 'Germans' really comprised an 'Einheit' or unity. This twinning had the effect of distinguishing the two groups from Slavs and Magyars in particular, and helps explain why, whatever Ranke's interest in the European state system, he did not find 'Europe' (which included Balkan 'Turks') or 'Christendom' (Latin or otherwise) to be entirely satisfactory categories. After a whistle-stop introductory chapter beginning with the Visigoth Ataulf in Rome, and Orosius appearing in its first footnote, the book addressed, as Ranke put it, 'on one hand, the founding of the Spanish monarchy, the loss of Italian freedom, and on the other hand, the formation of a dual opposition—a political opposition through France and a religious opposition through the Reformation: in sum, that division of our peoples into two hostile camps upon which all modern history [*neue Historie*] is based.'[27] He also thought that the Latin and Germanic peoples were possessed of a particularly strong 'ascending spiritual force' that some 'Asian' peoples had lost and that was not present in all peoples at all times—which brings him close in this respect to Hegel and anticipates Engels on the contrast between 'historical' and 'unhistorical peoples'.[28]

---

[23] Beiser, *The German Historicist Tradition*, ch. 1 on the significance of Chladenius.

[24] On the general significance of the Göttingen historians for the later historicist movement, see Ulrich Muhlack, *Geschichtswissenschaft im Humanismus und in der Aufklärung: Der Vorgeschichte des Historismus* (Munich: Beck, 1991).

[25] Howard, *Religion and the Rise of Historicism*.

[26] Leopold von Ranke, *Die Serbische Revolution. Aus Serbischen Papieren und Mittheilungen* (Hamburg: Perthes, 1829).

[27] Leopold von Ranke, *Geschichten der romanischen und germanischen Völker von 1494 bis 1535* (Leipzig: Reimer, 1824), pp. iv–v, xvii.

[28] Ranke invoked 'eine von Stufe zu Stufe sich entwickelnde geistige Macht': 'Auszug aus Rankes Vorlesungen zur Weltgeschichte (1854)', repr. in Leopold von Ranke, *Über die Epochen der neueren*

Ranke's name is often associated with the idea of History as a science, but this is apt to induce confusion if it is not appreciated that the German *Wissenschaft* has broader connotations than the natural sciences and applies to any body of systematic enquiry. The term does not merit the specific interpretation given to it by many scholars outside Germany. Not for the last time, ideas originating on the European continent found less critical application when applied in the Anglo-Saxon world.[29] The translator of the 1887 English edition of the *Histories of the Latin and Germanic Peoples* not only singularized Histories to History, thus removing Ranke's gesture to modesty, he only saw fit to reproduce the following sentence from Ranke's original—1824—preface, nourishing the idea of Ranke as a naïve fact-fetishist: 'A strict representation of facts [*Thatsache* in the original], be it ever so narrow [*bedingt*; better translated as conditional or contingent, as opposed to the philosophically 'necessary'] and unpoetical [*unschön*], is, beyond doubt, the first law.'[30] But in Germany too lesser minds reduced the thoughts of their heroes to what they themselves found most palatable—or manageable—and Ranke's emphasis on source criticism and validation became for some the alpha and omega of his message. Consider the following, written at the turn of the 1880s by George Prothero, not yet professor at Edinburgh University, of erstwhile hosts in Bonn who evinced a 'tendency to stop at a collection of facts, to let the facts speak for themselves, or rather remain dumb... They don't seek enough to get at the great laws of history, development of nations, differences of national character... One wants a people with more imagination... to extract the *essence* from the material they collect...'[31] This is actually one version of Ranke criticizing another. While encapsulating aspects of his method, the scholars whom Prothero depicted had failed to address Ranke's more philosophical concerns.

Establishing a 'regulative ideal' rather than praising his own Olympian viewpoint may well have been Ranke's own meaning when he wrote that historians should try to efface themselves from what they wrote, and that his work on the Latin and Germanic peoples 'will bloss sagen wie es eigentlich gewesen'. This line, written in the proximate context of Ranke's use of Venetian archives, means that Ranke 'wants/seeks merely to tell how it [i.e. the past] actually/essentially was',[32] though invariably the phrase is repeated or modified without the initial modal 'wants/seeks' or the adverb 'merely'. Certainly the interpretation to modesty is

Geschichte. Historisch-kritische Ausgabe, ed. Theodor Schieder and Helmut Berding (Munich: Oldenbourg, 1971), 53 ff.

[29] See for instance the reception of 'Rankean' ideas in the USA: Peter Novick, *That Noble Dream: The 'Objectivity Question' and the American Historical Profession* (Cambridge: Cambridge University Press, 1999).

[30] Leopold von Ranke, *History of the Latin and Teutonic Nations from 1494–1514*, trans. P. A. Ashworth (London: George Bell and Sons, 1887), p. vi.

[31] Cited in Michael Bentley, *Modernizing England's Past: English Historiography in the Age of Modernism* (Cambridge: Cambridge University Press, 2005), 99. Emphasis added.

[32] Ranke, *Geschichten der romanischen und germanischen Völker*, p. vi.

supported by Ranke's stated aspiration elsewhere 'to see with unbiased eyes the progress of universal history and in this spirit to produce beautiful and noble works[:] Imagine what happiness it would be for me if I could realize this ideal, even in a small degree.'[33] What exactly is denoted by 'eigentlich' remains a matter of some debate, as indicated. The differing interpretations 'actually' and 'essentially', in the sense of 'in essence', can both be justified if one holds to the view that Ranke leaned on the 1821 paper of the philosopher and educational theorist Wilhelm von Humboldt, 'On the task of the historian' (Geschichtsschreiber), for that address implies each meaning at different points.[34] This volume's contention, given how rationalists had fostered an inferiority complex among so many historians, is to place Ranke and probably Humboldt too in relation to that passage in The Discourse on Method in which Descartes writes of exemplar historians that the omissions they make in the interests of relevance ensure that 'the remainder does not appear as it really was' and who thus mislead by their partial exempla. Ranke might well have agreed with Descartes's criticism but wanted to render it redundant by his own approach to History.

As relevant as the content of Ranke's aspiration to tell the past 'wie es eigentlich gewesen' was that with which he juxtaposed the aspiration. He prefaced the famous words by a resignation from other tasks that had been conferred on History over the previous centuries, including the 'office of judging the past, of instructing the present for the benefit of future ages'. Humboldt was just as sceptical of the exemplary rationale.[35] In fact Ranke was not entirely consistent on the matter of exemplarity—elsewhere he also wrote of the guidance that might be provided by discrete 'examples of ancient and modern times'—and, as we shall see, he did think History could instruct in some way.[36] But there were reasons pragmatic as well as philosophical for disavowing History as Lesson, so we should by no means think of Ranke as purely an advocate of the procedural rationale of History as Method, whatever his insistence on scholarly rigour. Like Humboldt he had his own substantivist rationales related to his own ontology or concept of fundamental reality.

When he avowed an interest in 'der Sinn jede Epoche an und für sich selbst', i.e. in the meaning/significance of every epoch on its own terms, and wrote that all

---

[33] Final sentence cited in Leopold von Ranke, The Secret of World History: Selected Writings on the Art and Science of History, ed. Roger Wines (New York: Fordham University Press, 1981), 259.

[34] Wilhelm von Humboldt, 'On the Historian's Task', History and Theory, 6:1 (1967), 57–71, especially the opening pages. For the influence of the Humboldt essay see Georg G. Iggers, 'The Intellectual Foundations of Nineteenth-Century "Scientific" History: The German Model', in Macintyre, Maiguashca, and Pók (eds.), The Oxford History of Historical Writing 1800–1945, 41–58, here 43–4.

[35] For contextualization see Ulrich Muhlack, 'Leopold von Ranke und die Begründung der quellenkritischen Geschichtsforschung', in Jürgen Elvert and Susanne Krauß (eds.), Historische Debatten und Kontroversen im 19. und 20. Jahrhundert (Stuttgart: Steiner, 2003), 23–33, here 27–8. On Humboldt's views, Humboldt, 'On the Historian's Task', 60–1.

[36] Leopold von Ranke, The Theory and Practice of History, ed. Georg G. Iggers (London: Routledge, 2011), 82.

ages were equidistant from eternity, or 'umittelbar zu Gott', immediate unto God, Ranke was opposing the idea, associated with Hegel, that epochs or peoples were merely vectors of some progressing general spirit.[37] In his lectures to Ludwig II of Bavaria in the 1850s he anticipated Nietzsche in criticizing the 'Hegelian' idea that 'each generation surpasses the preceding one, so that the latest is always the most favoured and the preceding generations are only the bearers of those that follow.'[38] Contrary to historian Charles Bambach's claims, Ranke did not generally think in terms of a 'Hegelian pageant of world history', and while he professed thoughts tantamount to the idea that 'universal history was organized according to providential design' he did not claim to decipher the design. He did not conceive of a 'unitary narrative' or 'a historical continuum with equally measured intervals where one can...''see with unbiased eyes the progress of universal history''' (how misleading these partial quotations can be), and he did not envisage time 'as pure temporal succession' in a way that supposedly 'undergirds...the modernist logic of overcoming' and 'opens the path for...the "end of history"'.[39] While Ranke did talk of progress in a rather unclear way, and while in his very long career and intellectual development he sometimes invoked spiritual tendencies as underlying motors of visible change, most of Bambach's assertions are explicitly disavowed in Ranke's lectures on World History of 1854 and his notes on History and Philosophy in his World History of 1881–8.[40] To be sure, his uncompleted, multi-volume work on world History was Eurocentric, not least because it was interested in the impact of powerful Europe on the rest of the world, but this was a study of connections and influences between states and peoples, not a tale of rational global advance to destiny. Whatever Ranke's reservations about the approach of the earlier Göttingen historians, the philosophy of his world History owed more to Gatterer, even Bodin, than Hegel's concept of historical development, even if he and the great philosopher are bound together by some idealist precepts.[41]

---

[37] Quotes from Daniel Fulda, *Wissenschaft aus Kunst: Die Entstehung der modernen deutschen Geschichtsschreibung, 1760–1860* (Berlin: de Gruyter, 1996) 183–4.
[38] Cited in Lionel Grossman, *Basel in the Age of Burckhardt: A Study in Unseasonable Ideas* (Chicago: University of Chicago Press, 2000), 216.
[39] All quotes from Charles R. Bambach, *Heidegger, Dilthey, and the Crisis of Historicism* (Ithaca: Cornell University Press, 1995), 8–9.
[40] From the 1854 lectures, in Ranke, *The Secret of World History*, 160–1: 'We can assume in the areas of material interest an absolute progress, a highly decisive ascent which would require an enormous upset to bring about a decline. But we cannot find a similar progress in moral affairs....From the viewpoint of the divine idea, I can think of the matter only this way: humanity contains within itself an endless variety of developments which come to view from time to time, according to laws which are unknown to us, more mysterious, and greater than we can conceive.'
[41] For the philosophy of his world History see Leopold von Ranke, *Weltgeschichte*, ed. Alfred Dove and Georg Winter, vol. IX, part II (Leipzig: Duncker and Humblot, 1888), pp. vii ff. Generally on Ranke's world history, François Hartog, 'Von der Universalgeschichte zur Globalgeschichte? Zeiterfahrungen', *Le Débat*, 154 (2009), 53–66, here point 14; Ulrich Muhlack, 'Das Problem der Weltgeschichte bei Leopold Ranke', in Wolfgang Hardtwig and Philipp Müller (eds.), *Die Vergangenheit der Weltgeschichte: Universalhistorisches Denken in Berlin 1800–1933* (Göttingen:

Though Ranke was not much of a practitioner of History as Speculative Philosophy in the sense of deciphering a suprahistorical process, elements of his thought accord with the classical desire to apprehend the structure of the universe. If Rankean particularism sat uneasily with Enlightenment *universalism* as well as judgementalism, the evidence of his thoughts on world History suggests that he was certainly concerned with the *universal*. Friedrich Meinecke (1862–1954), who was both a historian of 'historicist' thought and one of its last major practitioners, hinted at the difference in approach when he defined the 'core' of historicism as 'compensation, through individualizing reflection, for a generalizing view of historical-human forces'.[42] The conservative Geoffrey Elton (1921–94) showed historicism's more than residual influence later in the twentieth century: 'All good historical writing is universal history in the sense that it remembers the universal while dealing with part of it'.[43] He also echoed Ranke in writing that 'no argument exists which successfully establishes a hierarchy of worth among historical periods or regions as such'.[44] Balance between the particular and the universal is at issue here, but Ranke and others meant that they believed the universal could only be approached via the particular. Ranke believed that God's light was refracted through the multiplicity of cultures; God's design could be beheld, if only indirectly. Thus understood, History was a species or *theoria* different to that envisaged by Polybius in his rebuttal of Aristotle; it was also a species of History as religious Communion different to that practised by the interpreters of sacred texts. The viewpoint stemmed from a variety of panentheism, of which Meinecke also partook, namely the basically Plotinian belief that the universe is contained within god or is an emanation of god. Panentheism is different to pantheism in which the universe and god are one and the same thing. The outlook chimed with Leibniz's monadological thinking and with the longer-standing Christian hermeneutic concern for the reciprocal illumination gained from considering parts and wholes in their relations. It combined the precepts of idealism and the established religious belief that individuals carried within them the spark of the divine. If nations are thoughts of god, and if, as with Spinoza, the mind's highest good is the knowledge of god, then one aspired to see the world *sub specie æternitatis*, from the perspective of eternity.[45] As Ranke put it, 'instead

Vandenhoeck & Ruprecht, 2010), 143–72. On reservations about the Göttingen approach by Ranke and Herder, see Fulda, *Wissenschaft aus Kunst*, 183 ff.

[42] Cited in Robert A. Pois, 'Two Poles Within Historicism: Croce and Meinecke', *Journal of the History of Ideas*, 31:2 (1970), 253–72, here 253.

[43] Geoffrey Elton, *The Practice of History* (Sydney: Sydney University Press, 1967), 16.

[44] Ibid. 13.

[45] On Spinoza, Russell, *History of Western Philosophy*, 597. On Ranke's panentheism, Carl Hinrichs, *Ranke und die Geschichtstheologie der Goethezeit* (Gottingen: Musterschmidt, 1954)—thanks to Reinbert A. Krol for the reference. On Meinecke's panentheism, Krol, 'Friedrich Meinecke: Panentheism and the Crisis of Historicism', *Journal of the Philosophy of History*, 4 (2010), 195–209, here 206 ff.

of the fleeting conglomerations that the [social] contract theories invoke like cloud formations, I perceive spiritual essences, original creations of the human spirit—one might say thoughts of God'.[46]

From this perspective we can also understand why historicists developed a particular focus on the state and a particular attitude towards its power. The focus, by no means all-consuming—after all, Ranke wrote not only histories of multiple major European states at key periods of their development and the papacy as a political as well as religious force, but also on Italian poetry[47]—was partly a matter of the availability of sources, partly of elitist concerns. It was also a reflection of the times themselves, in which successive European revolutions and processes of state formation seemed to indicate the overwhelming importance of politics and warfare.

The idealist legacy is apparent in Ranke's idea of public institutions as the locus of something like 'objective spirit'. The state had a will and character of sorts, and both were shaped not just by the people comprising the body politic at any one point, but by the traditions that had developed over time. The state guaranteed the liberty and expressed the individuality of nations on the stage of world history. As such, not only was it owed loyalty, it was itself a moral entity, as Samuel Pufendorf and Hegel also maintained. This is not to say that Ranke felt that the state could do no wrong: in keeping perhaps with the Neoplatonic elements of his thought, the purest entities were the highest up the chain of being, the least coloured by the mundane and the physical. But precisely because states and their leaders had to act in an imperfect world it would be wrong either to expect perfection of them or to denigrate them for their imperfection. It would, he wrote, 'be infinitely wrong to seek only the effects of brutal forces in the struggles of historical powers... no state has ever existed without a spiritual basis and a spiritual content. A spiritual essence appears in power itself, an original genius with its own particular life'.[48]

Since the state was a moral entity, its prerogatives were not easily limited by recourse to the concept of external wills and moralities; its duty was at once to protect the people and express its 'moral energy'. This was the thrust of Bismarck's emphasis on the primacy of foreign policy, the arena in which the state preserved its existence—hence the nineteenth-century resurgence in popularity of the Renaissance high priest of *raison d'état*.[49] Equally, the true statesman should imbibe History in order to acquaint himself with the appropriate way to act

---

[46] 'Statt jener flüchtigen Konglomerate, die sich dir aus der Lehre vom Vertrag erheben wie Wolkengebilde, sehe ich geistige Wesenheiten, originale Schöpfungen des Menschengeists,—man darf sagen, Gedanken Gottes': Ranke, 'Politisches Gespräch', *Historisch-politische Zeitschrift*, ed. Leopold Ranke, vol. 2 (1833–6), 775–807, here 794.

[47] Leopold von Ranke, 'Zur Geschichte der italienischen Poesie', *Abhandlungen der Königlichen Preußischen Akademie der Wissenschaften zu Berlin* (Berlin: Duncker und Humblot, 1835), 401–85.

[48] Ranke, *Weltgeschichte*, vol. IX, part II, p. xi.   [49] Cassirer, *The Myth of the State*, 125.

within national traditions and the potentialities of the age. This was one way in which the statesman, like anyone else, might benefit from the enhanced sense of his own historicity, his own nature as a being-in-time and as a product of historical forces, that he might also act with such forces. In this sense historicist thought was political through-and-through, even though its proponents saw themselves as above mere party politics. Historians working in this tradition of History as political-cultural rather than religious Communion might lay claim to divining the normative order of their state, establishing its 'common-sense', and nowhere is such a tendency clearer than in the inaugural issue of the journal the *Historische Zeitschrift*, which was first published in 1859 and spawned imitators internationally in the following decades.[50] The editor, Heinrich von Sybel (1817–95) claimed to:

> plan a historical periodical, not an antiquarian or political one. On the one hand, it is not our aim to discuss unresolved questions of current politics, nor to commit ourselves to one particular political party. It is not contradictory, however, if we indicate certain general principles, which will guide the political judgment of this periodical. Viewed historically, the life of every people, governed by the laws of morality, appears as a natural and individual evolution, which—out of intrinsic necessity—produces the forms of state and culture, an evolution which must not arbitrarily be obstructed or accelerated, nor made subject to extrinsic rules. This point of view precludes feudalism, which imposes lifeless elements on the progressive life; radicalism, which substitutes subjective arbitrariness for organic development; ultramontanism, which subjects the natural and spiritual evolution to the authority of an extraneous Church.[51]

Ranke and his successors saw themselves battling for interpretative supremacy in the human sciences as a whole. History could take its place as the cardinal humanistic discipline by making a virtue of the diverse particularities that conventional philosophy was not equipped to consider, while the spiritual-idealistic side of historicism ensured that a concern with empirics did not degenerate into a preoccupation with detail for its own sake. To this day, individual historians may spend so much time on 'the facts' because some are theory-shy, but History the discipline as such remains especially concerned with the particular, either alone or, as with Ranke, as a component and reflection of the universal. (In this line of thought the primary importance of fact is its expression of *particularity*, albeit that many latter-day arguments about the nature of History have focused upon

---

[50] Margaret F. Stieg, *The Historische Zeitschrift: The Origin and Development of Scholarly Historical Periodicals* (Tuscaloosa: University of Alabama Press, 1986).

[51] Editorial trans. and repr. in Stern (ed.), *The Varieties of History*, 171–2.

the fact's role as guarantor of *truth* interpreted as 'correctness'.[52]) Ranke wrote: 'From the particular, one can carefully and boldly move up to the general; from general theories, there is no way of looking at the particular.'[53] By no coincidence, such empirical work was also the way that the judicious—i.e. moderately conservative—politician was supposed to reason, unlike the reckless radical reformer (or the Hegelian philosopher!) who worked from abstract universals to rough reality or even downplayed existing reality in the pursuit of 'negative' thought.[54]

This particular historical philosophy exerted far wider influence than the History seminars in which documentary sources were the entry point into the hermeneutic circle linking evidence with an empathetic understanding for the accultured minds that had produced such deposits. It characterized a general historical inclination across a range of disciplines, from linguistics through law and economics. The common factor in all was the rejection of an abstract-theoretical approach predicated upon, say, the posited general truths of David Ricardo's economics, or the universal applicability of social contract theory, in favour of one illuminating how different cultural traditions shaped economic and social behaviour in different ways. In this sense it was a more descriptive tradition, which is not to say that it was antediluvian or lacking in sophistication. Whatever the peculiarities of German historiography in this period, whatever elements have been discarded along the way, it has left a vastly influential legacy in this prioritization of a particular conception of context—especially cultural—in its consideration of human diversity. The name 'historicism' came to be applied to the Rankean tradition, but it is still applied, if loosely, to denote an approach to any given past that focuses upon its 'difference' from other pasts and from the present, and can have relativist connotations.

Historicism also stressed temporal concepts like growth or development. Where Otto of Freising had followed Augustine and Aristotle in contrasting the *mutabilitas rerum* (or *miseriae mutationum*)[55] of earthly life with the atemporal plane, historicism sought to establish growth, change, flourishing, as the nature of reality at the most basic level. As with Vico and Herder, the historicist's way of understanding his or her unique object was through its internal development across time. History became a species of process philosophy, and Christlieb Julius Braniss (1792–1873) was one philosopher to merge his idealistic philosophy with

---

[52] Nathan Rotenstreich, 'From Facts to Thoughts: Collingwood's Views on the Nature of History', *Philosophy*, 35:133 (1960), 122–37, here 129. My point may or may not be an adaption. For an interrogation of the narrow conception of truth as correctness, Robert Piercey, *The Uses of the Past from Heidegger to Rorty* (Cambridge: Cambridge University Press, 2011), 53–7.

[53] Cited in Peter Koslowski (ed.), *The Discovery of Historicity in German Idealism and Historicism* (Berlin: Springer, 2005), 42.

[54] Beiser, *The German Historicist Tradition*, 278–9.

[55] Claasen, '*Res Gestae*, Universal History, Apocalypse', 401.

a species of historicism.[56] In place of what the philosopher E. A. Burtt called 'the logico-mathematical world-view', historicism implanted a worldview that was genealogical.[57] A rudimentary justification for this is the analogy of the seed or the acorn, cross-sectional analysis of which will not reveal what the plant will look like that emerges from it. Only the passing of time tells.[58] During the nineteenth century evolutionary thought drew the bio-sciences towards developmental models as opposed to the mechanistic-causal models associated with physics. Recall that evolutionary thinking preceded Darwin in the nineteenth century—his genius was to identify the motor of evolution. The conjunction of historicism and evolutionism gave vast intellectual and cultural power to a new metaphysics of existence—a new ontology—in which development, or 'becoming', became more important than atemporal 'being', revising Plato's ontological hierarchy.

While History contributed to and benefited from this intellectual atmosphere, it was not just trying to redefine its relationship to the moral, political, and social sciences, but trying to distinguish itself from literature, in which, for instance, the didactic *Bildungsroman* was also concerned with development over time. Perhaps it is not chance that one of the most prominent opponents of Ranke's insistence on archival rigour, Schlosser's student Georg Gottfried Gervinus (1805–71), was a historian of literature and its relationship to politics and morality. Gervinus's five-volume *History of the Poetical National Literature of the Germans* (1835–42)[59] was stimulated by the desire to render 'art fruitful for the present situation'. Ranke's rejoinder, shortly after Gervinus's death, was that in order for *Wissenschaft*/science to be relevant to life,

[56] Gunter Scholtz, '*Historismus' als spekulative Geschichtsphilosophie: Christlieb Julius Braniss* (Frankfurt: V. Klostermann, 1973). Braniss was a convert from Judaism, but we should note that the German-centred Jewish Enlightenment (*Haskalah*) itself evinced elements of idealism similar to Ranke's, while the developmental element of Hegelian and then historicist thought gave a new twist to the historical character that had never been absent from Jewish theology. Thus Immanuel Wolf in his 1822 'On the Concept of a Science of Judaism' (which reflected the thought of the Society for the Culture and Science of Judaism established by Hegel's student Eduard Gans (1797–1839)): 'man needs time in order to raise himself from the world of the physical and the many to that of the universal unity, the all-embracing and all existing Monas' (Monas stemming from the Greek *monos*, from which we also get 'monad'); 'peace and permanence are alien to the realm of the spirit, which is truly living. It is in the nature of the spiritual world to be in constant motion, and never to cease development'; 'It is manifest everywhere that the fundamental principle of Judaism is again in a state of ferment, striving to assume a shape in harmony with the spirit of the times.' See also Nahman Krochmal (1785–1840): 'just as the king of a nation binds it together and unifies it with regard to readily visible externals, so too the manifestation of the divine which it contains unifies and binds it together internally with regard to place and time, from generation to generation'. Wolf and Krochmal contextualized and excerpted in Davis Biale (ed.), *Judaism* (New York: Norton, 2015), 514–23, quotes from 518, 519, 521.

[57] D. Villemaire, *E. A. Burtt: Historian and Philosopher* (Dordrecht: Springer, 1992), 19.

[58] Randall, *Nature and Historical Experience*, 15; 72 ff.

[59] Georg Gottfried Gervinus, *Geschichte der poetischen National-Literatur der Deutschen*, 5 vols. (Leipzig: Engelmann, 1835–42).

it must, first and foremost, be Wissenschaft, for it is impossible to adopt a point of view in life and then carry it over into scholarship, because then it is life that is influencing scholarship, and not scholarship life.... We can only have a real influence on the contemporary world if we first turn our eyes away from it and lift ourselves to the plane of free objective scholarship.[60]

As we approach the end of this section, reflection on quite what objectivity might mean brings us to Gustav Droysen (1808–84), who also disapproved of Gervinus's approach. One of Droysen's significances it that he contributed to a shift in emphasis away from the idea of History as high art or literature to that of it as a form of *scientific* labour with a unique and rigorous methodology; any given individual specialist was but one contributor to a wider progressive process of understanding.[61] His concept of *Historik*, or 'historics', as in the title of his methodological work *Grundriß der Historik* (*Outline of the Principles of History*, 1857/8), had been deployed, *inter alia*, in an earlier work of Gervinus's where it stood in relation to History much as Aristotle's *Poetics* (*c*.335 BCE), in German *Poetik*, stood to literature.[62] The contrast, from Droysen's perspective, of *Historik* and *Poetik* is as significant in its own way as is Droysen's criticism from a hermeneutic perspective of Thomas Buckle's positivist historianship.[63] Yet for all of his emphasis on empirical research as opposed to Hegelian speculation, Droysen was much influenced by Hegelian concepts of deep historical forces, and both his philosophical reflections on History and his historical works evince teleology: while contributing to methodical debates, Droysen also sought to systematize and encourage a specific, disciplined historical way of thinking to enable historians to place their present in relationship to the past and to the future with reference to the deeper unfolding forces.[64]

Droysen is as deserving as Ranke of the epithet 'great man' historian, though there is a clear Hegelian sense of some of his great men as bearers of world-historical *Volk*-spirits (pp. 180–2). His precocious breakthrough work was his *History of Alexander the Great* (1833), shortly followed by his *History of Hellenism*. The link between the achievements of Alexander's father and Philip II in 'unifying' Greece under the Macedonian kingdom, then Alexander in expanding

---

[60] Gordon A. Craig, *The Politics of the Unpolitical: German Writers and the Problem of Power, 1770–1871* (Munich: Beck, 1993), 146, 154.

[61] Wolfgang Hardtwig, 'Geschichtsreligion—Wissenschaft als Arbeit—Objektivität. Der Historismus in neuer Sicht', *Historische Zeitschrift*, 252:1 (1991), 1–32, here 19 ff.

[62] Christiane Hackel, *Aristoteles-Rezeption in der Geschichtstheorie Johann Gustav Droysens* (Berlin: de Gruyter, 2019), 147.

[63] On Buckle see Johann Gustav Droysen, 'Erhebung der Geschichte zum Rang einer Wissenschaft', *Historische Zeitschrift*, 9 (1863), 1–22, which was reproduced in the 1882 edition of *Grundriß der Historik* (Leipzig: Veit, 1882), 47 ff.

[64] Arthur Alfaix Assis, *What Is History For? Johann Gustav Droysen and the Functions of Historiography* (New York: Berghahn, 2016), ch. 2; Beiser, *German Historicist Tradition*, ch. 8.

the reach of Greek civilization, provide a clue to Droysen's scholarly future.[65] Despite the title of the tradition he initiated, the 'Prussian school', Droysen's nationalism represents a step away from Ranke's brand of Prussian patriotism, and the political issue is relevant for understanding Droysen's opposition to what he saw as Ranke's conservative and arid concern with source criticism at the expense of a more active embrace of one's historicity that clarified one's choices and capacity for agency. For Droysen, as for many German *Bildungsbürger*, not to mention socialists, the end of revolution in 1848–9 brought frustration and disappointment. He had entered the revolution, during which he served as a politician in the revolutionary Frankfurt parliament, pushing a *kleindeutsch* unification under Prussian auspices as opposed to the *grossdeutsch* option of German unification in which the 'reactionary' Habsburg empire would be so obviously prominent. For the likes of Droysen, Prussian-led unification meant that there was no contradiction between Prussian patriotism and German nationalism. (It was not unusual in nineteenth-century historiography for particular regions to be allocated a special, 'chosen' role in national unification projects—Piedmont in Italy is another example.) To the displeasure of that different historicist, Ranke, Droysen's *History of Prussian Politics* (1855–86), was marked by teleology, as if the Hohenzollern dynasty from the fifteenth century were somehow inveigled in grand Prussian designs from before the state of Prussia actually existed.[66]

When Droysen mocked 'eunuch-like objectivity', he had Rankeans in mind, but he was not attacking shared scholarly standards, and in his lectures and writings on *Historik* he went further than Ranke in systematizing critical principles. Nor was he propounding a subjective approach in the sense of a romantic orientation springing uniquely from the creative ethos of an individual investigating subject. At the simplest level, a vast but fragmentary and contradictory source-base, combined with the need for the historian to come to it with ready-made questions and interests, meant that the order thus imposed would be of the historian's making, rather than being inherent in the past. Moreover, since interests and concepts were the products of acculturation, the History that was written according to the most impeccable professional standards would reflect the perspective of that acculturation and would be as accurate a 'take' on the past as another account written with the same care from within a different acculturated historian—in keeping with earlier monadological thought, such a perspective would contribute one facet of the 'truth' among others, rather than constituting a

[65] Droysen, *Geschichte Alexanders des Grossen* (Hamburg: Perthes, 1833); *Geschichte des Hellenismus*, 2 vols. (Hamburg: Perthes, 1836–43).

[66] Droysen, *Geschichte der preussischen Politik*, 14 vols. (Leipzig: Veit, 1855–86). For Ranke's view, Wilfried Nippel, *Johann Gustav Droysen: ein Leben zwischen Wissenschaft und Politik* (Munich: Beck, 2008), 287.

God's-eye view.[67] But Droysen went further still, actively embracing this perspectivalism: 'Insofar as I consider the past from my standpoint, from the thoughts of my nation and state, from my religion and past, I stand high above my individual ego. I think, as it were, from a higher ego, in which the slag of my little person has been melted away.' Thus we encounter not Ranke's famed (and caricatured) aspiration to self-effacement before the past, but self-effacement before the cultural traditions through which the particular historian investigates the past, the individual only ever being a less complete whole than the greater and higher whole of the collective.[68]

If we can abstract a little, moving away from Droysen's particular preoccupations, and focusing on the logic of such pronouncements, we see that they raise as many questions as they answer. Hippolyte Taine implied the superfluity of the Romantic artists' injunction *il faut être de son temps*, 'one ought to be of one's times', since one was 'of one's times' whether one liked it or not.[69] The same presumably went for one's own nation, state, religion. Furthermore, in the event that one tried consciously to embrace the relevant context(s), by that very effort one would actually be adding something over-and-above general acculturation and thus would have done the opposite of melting away the slag of one's own personal idiosyncrasies. One might add that there is no way a reader could establish whether any given historical interpretation was an authentic expression of the acculturated author or of something else altogether, irrespective of what the author claimed, not least because no culture or 'time' produces a monolithic expression of itself. Droysen's prescription was either unactualizable, meaningless, a recipe for creating uncertainty in the reading audience as to whether they had been misled about the historian's agenda, or a pseudo-philosophical justification of his nationalist position.

This debate also shows how historicism could progress from an ontological claim about the relationship between particulars and universals to an epistemological claim, a claim about the nature of knowledge. The argument would go like this: if peoples are different from each other in some fundamental way with their outlooks being set by their national 'essence' or at least their national 'experience', then they are not capable of taking a perspective from above the fray, and indeed members of one people are not really capable of grasping the perspective of

---

[67] For varying contextualizations and interpretations of Droysen on 'eunuch-like objectivity' and related matters, see Beiser, *German Historicist Tradition*, 305–7; Assis, *What Is History For?*, 66–71; White, *The Content of the Form*, ch. 4.

[68] Droysen quote from Beiser, *German Historicist Tradition*, 307; further from Droysen: 'Der einzelne wird nur relative Totalität; verstehend und verstanden ist er nur wie ein Beispiel und Ausdruck der Gemeinsamkeiten, deren Glied er ist und an deren Wesen und Werden er teilhat...'. Cited in Christian-Georg Schuppe, *Der andere Droysen: neue Aspekte seiner Theorie der Geschichtswissenschaft* (Stuttgart: Steiner, 1998), 25. All the works cited in this and the previous note are also relevant to the exegesis of these quotes, and thus also to my discussion in the following paragraphs.

[69] Linda Nochlin, *Realism* (Harmondsworth: Penguin, 1971), 104–5.

members of another people. Even in the event that competing group perspectives are believed to be perspectives on a higher truth, which is rather less popular as an idea today, there is no way of accessing that truth, so all we have is perspectives that are irreconcilable by human beings (and by extension potential ethical problems in writing about other groups than one's own for those who are not interested in celebrating their own perspective). This reasoning is one of the tributary streams to the 'crisis of historicism' that we will turn to shortly.[70]

Alternatives to the Dominant German Model in the 1860s

The tension between what we might call the 'longitudinal' and 'latitudinal' elements of historicism contributed to the 'crisis' too, which brings us to the Swiss Jacob Burckhardt (1818–97). Like his teacher, Ranke, Burckhardt had once been a theology student. He felt that a growing emphasis on laborious research as the basis of understanding threatened the aesthetic qualities of historical understanding and the poetic status of History, reducing it to a specialist guild science rather than an element of a rounded cultural education.[71] With Ranke he repudiated 'theorists' who used History to advocate or accuse, and was as vociferous in his rejection of any mechanistic 'laws' of the historical process. But where Ranke's dissertation had concerned Thucydides, Burckhardt's interest was in Herodotus, and this showed in his masterpiece, *The Civilization* (or *Culture: Cultur* in the first edition, *Kultur* in subsequent editions) *of the Renaissance in Italy* (1860). The high cultural elements of his interests, married to his social elitism, were some distance from the 'cultural turn' of late twentieth-century historians, but much less alien was his Herodotean and Vico-like interest in the importance of myths to the understanding of society, and his concerns with festival, popular religion, and mores.[72]

Burckhardt's was a departure in emphasis from the political focus of so much German historicism, though one does not wish to exaggerate the point since his initial chapter established political and structural developments as a condition of possibility for what he characterized as the Renaissance. Perhaps more important on the political front was his implication that the state might be a potentially suppressive/repressive element in aspects of socio-cultural life, as well as an expression and protector of cultural tendencies. Further, within Burckhardt's interest in

---

[70] On connections between Droysen and the 'crisis of historicism' see Beiser, *German Historicist Tradition*, 320–1.

[71] John R. Hinde, *Jacob Burckhardt and the Crisis of Modernity* (Montreal: McGill-Queen's University Press, 2000), 212. On the significance of Burckhardt's theological training, Howard, *Religion*, 110 ff.

[72] On 'theorists', Jacob Burckhardt, *The Civilization of the Renaissance in Italy* (London: Penguin, 2004), 271. On Thucydides and Herodotus and myths, Richard Franklin Sigurdson, *Jacob Burckhardt's Social and Political Thought* (Toronto: University of Toronto Press, 2004), 78 ff.

historicization, in the sense of integrating beliefs and tendencies into greater wholes in which they made unique sense, the emphasis on a specific moment in Italian development, a moment with its own dynamics, products, and internal architecture, tended less towards diachronic cultural holism, or to development over time, and more towards synchronic holism.[73] In other words, he was concerned with *Zeitgeist*, or the 'spirit' of some particular historical moment, as well as *Volksgeist*, the spirit of a people. The psychological element of his examination of the *Zeitgeist* was to be a significant influence on the cultural and comparative work of Karl Lamprecht in later decades.

On *Volksgeist* Burckhardt wrote:

> It may be possible to indicate many contrasts and shades of difference among different nations, but to strike the balance of the whole is not given to human insight. The ultimate truth with respect to the character, the conscience and the guilt of a people remains for ever a secret; if only for the reason that its defects have another side, where they reappear as peculiarities or even as virtues.[74]

These were grounds for his conclusion that 'the people of Europe can maltreat, but happily not judge one another', which intimates the clash of irreconcilable national perspectives discussed just now, and illustrates how a relativistic outlook on values is itself no obstacle to conflict with those bearing other perspectives.[75]

Almost simultaneously to Burckhardt, Fustel de Coulanges was working on *The Ancient City* (1864), which in a more overtly sociological fashion explored another *Zeitgeist*, in the form of the relationship between political institutions and religion in those 'foreign countries', the Greek and Roman city states. With his focus on the regularities of institutions rather than on variable actions or 'events', and in his analysis of the socio-political function of religion, Fustel was to be one of the major influences on his student, the great sociologist Émile Durkheim.[76] Fustel defined the 'true object' of history idealistically as 'the human mind: it should aspire to know what this mind has believed, thought and felt in the different ages of the human race'.[77] Other scholars in the nineteenth-century French historiography of society and culture went further than Burckhardt or Fustel in their attempts to codify the relationship between longitudinal and latitudinal factors, crosshatching changes over time with differences in national and

---

[73] Daniel Fulda, 'Historicism as a Cultural Pattern: Practising a Mode of Thought', *Journal of the Philosophy of History*, 4 (2010), 138–53.

[74] Burckhardt, *Civilization*, 271.

[75] Ibid.

[76] Steven Lukes, *Emile Durkheim, his Life and Work: A Historical and Critical Study* (Stanford: Stanford University Press, 1985), 60–4.

[77] Fustel, *The Ancient City*, 76.

other characteristics. In this project they could draw on romantic and positivistic influences.

The intellectual hinterland included Germaine de Staël's *On Literature Considered in its Relations to Social Institutions* (1800), which had set itself the task of examining 'the influence of religion, morals and laws on literature', and conversely 'the influence of literature on religion, morals and laws'.[78] Charting changes in this relationship in what from today's perspective is a fairly orthodox series of periodizations from Homer through Christianization and the Renaissance to her present, she also divided literature in what she called the modern period—with its particular characteristics including the specific nature of its consideration of women—according to different national-cultural and regional tendencies in Europe, and furthermore she factored in political ideologies. Her imprint, as well as that of Comte, can be detected on Hippolyte Taine's work on the psychology of art and the History of English literature in the 1860s. In the latter Taine ascribed the qualities of literature at any one moment not to the originality of the individual mind but to the nexus of three different contexts—'la race, le milieu et le moment'—whose weights of influence could be calculated.[79] Painting with too broad a brush, Taine claimed that Enlightenment thinkers believed 'men of every race and century were all but identical: the Greek, the barbarian, the Hindoo, the man of the Renaissance, and the man of the eighteenth century'. 'They did not know that the moral constitution of a people or an age is as particular or as distinct as the physical structure of a family of plants or an order of animals.'[80]

In German historiography, as in historically influenced German economics, there was less space for social-scientific or comparative approaches and the politically oriented historicist tradition remained supreme through the later nineteenth and early twentieth century. In the generations after Ranke's period of pre-eminence, the philosophy of historicism was embodied in Droysen, whose influential reaction against positivism indicated its growing strength beyond Germany, in Ranke's student von Sybel, and Sybel's editorial successor at the *Historische Zeitschrift*, Heinrich von Treitschke (1834–96). Parenthetically, all three taught Meinecke at points and so it was no surprise when he received the baton of the journal in the 1890s.

Sybel introduced the Rankean seminar to the University of Munich on his arrival in 1856, before his anti-Catholicism and pro-Prussianism prompted a departure from Bavaria, to Bonn. His major works of modern History addressed

[78] Germaine de Staël, *De la littérature considérée dans ses rapports avec les institutions sociales*, vol. 1, 2nd edition (Paris: de Crapelet, n.d.), 27.

[79] Hippolyte Taine, *Histoire de la littérature anglaise*, 5 vols. (Paris: Hachette, 1863–4), vol. 1, preface, part V; cf. Taine, *The Philosophy of Art* (New York: Holt and Williams, 1873), 180–5.

[80] Cited in Kenan Malik, *The Meaning of Race: Race, History and Culture in Western Society* (New York: New York University Press, 1996), 142–3.

the French Revolution and *The Founding of the German Empire under Wilhelm I* (1889–94), while he bound together his medieval and modern interests with the short 1862 work *The German Nation and the Empire [Kaiserreich]*, which explored the relationship between the universalist elements of the Holy Roman Empire, the polynational character of the Habsburg polity, and the particular story of the German people.[81]

Treitschke had been taught by the historian and politician Friedrich Christoph Dahlmann (1785–1860), agitator of the 'Schleswig Holstein question' and author of Histories of the English and French Revolutions, which had given him a privileged position to proselytize for constitutional monarchy as well as Prussian-led German unification.[82] Treitschke's own major historical work was the *History of Germany in the Nineteenth Century*,[83] but his philosophy of History may be inferred from his essays on contemporary politics. He rather personifies the terminal point of the shift in German nationalism (and other nationalisms too) from early and mid-nineteenth-century liberalism to later nineteenth-century chauvinism; from the nationalism of self-determination to the nationalism of imperialist self-assertion; from cosmopolitan nationalism to intolerant ethnocentrism, meaning in Treitschke's case anti-Semitism, anti-Catholicism, and anti-Polonism. The Rankean sense of the state as a moral power remained, but it was coloured by 'social Darwinism'.

Reactions to Historicism

The attitude to power of Treitschke's British contemporary, (Lord) John Dalberg-Acton (1834–1902), is summed up in his best-known aphorism: 'power tends to corrupt, and absolute power corrupts absolutely'. Acton combined an admiration for Rankean rigour with a healthy appreciation of perspectivalism in writing the past. 'The difficulty', he stated in a way that rather disarms caricatures of him as a naïve believer in objectivity, is 'to select from the mass of information, and of course there are not two men who would choose alike'.[84] When he declared that his discipline could be scientific, he was not being scientistic/positivistic. Rather, the science to which he referred was a moral science, which also set him against

---

[81] Heinrich von Sybel, *Die Begründung des deutschen Reiches durch Wilhelm I*, 7 vols. (Munich: Oldenbourg, 1889–94); von Sybel, *Die deutsche Nation und das Kaiserreich* (Düsseldorf: Buddeus, 1862).

[82] Friedrich Christoph Dahlmann, *Geschichte der englischen Revolution* (Leipzig: Weidmann, 1844); Dahlmann, *Geschichte der französischen Revolution bis auf die Stiftung der Republik* (Leipzig: Weidmann, 1845).

[83] Heinrich von Treitschke, *Deutsche Geschichte im Neunzehnten Jahrhundert*, 5 vols. (Leipzig: Hirzel, 1878–94).

[84] John Emerich Edward Dalberg-Acton, *Historical Essays and Studies* (London: Macmillan, 1908), 491. See also 352–6, 427 for praise and criticism of Ranke.

speculative philosophies of history: 'the marrow of civilised history is ethical not metaphysical, and the deep underlying cause of action passes through the shape of right and wrong'.[85] It is 'the office of historical science to maintain morality as the sole impartial criterion of men and things, and the only one on which honest minds can be made to agree'.[86]

Because he believed that God's purposes were not discernible in the study of particular events, Acton was suspicious of any History that promised to promote historical success as the main criterion of praise.[87] Such was the belief embodied in Schiller's phrase—popular in an age of increasingly unrestrained international power politics, where antagonistic conceptions of international relations had replaced Newtonian conceptions of balanced harmony—that *das Weltgeschichte ist die Weltgerichte*, the history of the world constituted the world's tribunal. Hegel used the expression at least three times.[88] In its most powerful terms the idea was that the *fait accompli* was the measure of morality, success was predicated upon providential destiny, God's blessing was inferred from that which 'he' tolerated on earth. Conversely, spurning such a doctrine placed an important duty in the hands of the historian to ensure that powerful historical actors were not exonerated by default of their position as arbiters of worldly affairs. The Actonian historian should act as the conscience of humanity, since upholding the 'inflexible integrity of the moral code is...the secret of the authority, the dignity, the utility of History'.[89] Acton's approach thus differed from Tacitus's view that it is 'from the experience of others...that most men learn to distinguish right and wrong'.[90] Nevertheless he would have concurred with Tacitus's belief 'in a historian's foremost duty to ensure that merit is recorded, and to confront evil deeds and words with the fear of posterity's denunciations'.[91] And he certainly believed that this duty should be fulfilled 'without anger or partiality' (p. 42). For Acton the judgement conventionally associated with History as Moral Lesson was intrinsic to the proceduralist ethos of History as Method. Judging past actors was important for the moral fibre of the judge, lest the historian act as 'the weaker man with the sponge' following 'the strong man with the dagger'.[92] By extension, judgement was important for the society that historians wished to help into being, since

---

[85] Ibid. 362.   [86] Ibid. 437. See also 354–5.   [87] Ibid. 437.

[88] I can take no credit for the counting: see Carlo Ginzburg, *The Judge and the Historian* (London: Verso, 1999), 123 n. 10.

[89] Acton, *Historical Essays and Studies*, 436–7, 504–6. Lord Acton, *Lectures on Modern History* (London: Fontana, 1960), 38: 'I exhort you never to debase the moral currency or lower the standard of rectitude, but to try others by the final maxim that governs your own lives, and to suffer no man and no cause to escape the undying penalty which history has the power to inflict on wrong.'

[90] Tacitus, *Annals*, 4.33.   [91] Ibid. 3.65.

[92] Lord Acton, *Lectures on the French Revolution* (London: Macmillan, 1920), 92. See also Acton, *Lectures on Modern History*, 30: 'It is by solidity of criticism more than by the plenitude of erudition, that the study of history strengthens, and straightens, and extends the mind.'

without their discernment, that society might fall into the error of worshipping false idols who were successful at the cost of moral rectitude.[93]

The author of *Thus Spake Zarathustra*, Friedrich Nietzsche (1844–1900), makes a curious bedfellow for Acton, but this is so only up to a point. After all, the ascent of Hegelian immanent reason was one target of both and Christian teleology another. Acton's point about holding power to account was also close to Nietzsche's belief that Rankean anti-Hegelianism, while it could lead to respect for all forms of life rather than just the final one, might also lead to automatic self-validation of any present, a sort of self-immunization against the criticism of posterity. Both men advocated taking the responsibility implied in judgement, and both were aware of the hold of the past on the present, and thus of the historian's social influence. Nietzsche's penchant for talking about History may obscure the fact that his is more a tale of the impact of historical thought on philosophy than vice versa.

Nietzsche's interest in what historical thinking could fruitfully instil, and when it was a burden from which humans needed to be liberated in order to flourish, led him to describe different forms of History and prescribe particular combinations of these. The emergence of the state of Germany stimulated one of his 'untimely meditations', entitled 'On the Uses and Disadvantages of History for Life' (1874), which is his most cited pronouncement on History.[94] It was shaped in the particular context of his reaction against the public (ab)uses of History in the immediate, triumphalist aftermath of war-driven unification. Those reservations were shared by Gervinus, and in fact when representing Nietzsche's attitudes to History, it is important to appreciate how much his thinking at the time of this piece was characterized by an animus to a general sub-Hegelian, propaganda-fuelled sense of riding history's wave from glory unto glory. Nietzsche also feared an overly historical disposition among moderns whose consciousness could no longer integrate past and present in a beneficial way, who wished to live in the present alone but could not find the wherewithal to forget or otherwise discard the past: in short, he feared, in Goethe's words, that 'even the best history always has something corpse-like, the smell of a tomb'.[95] He argued for a delimitation of History's purview, and at the same time stipulated the directions it might take. The past could be used for inspiration, focusing specifically on 'monumental' History that dwelt on moments of past significance as a way of making use of

---

[93] Ibid. 20, 38.

[94] Friedrich Nietzsche, 'On the Uses and Disadvantages of History for Life', in Friedrich Nietzsche, *Untimely Meditations*, ed. Daniel Breazeale (Cambridge: Cambridge University Press, 2003), 56–123. On the significance and context of that essay, and its relationship to Nietzsche's wider oeuvre, see Thomas H. Brobjer, 'Nietzsche's View of the Value of Historical Studies and Methods', *Journal of the History of Ideas*, 65:2 (2004), 301–22; Christian J. Emden, *Friedrich Nietzsche and the Politics of History* (Cambridge: Cambridge University Press, 2010).

[95] Nicholas Rennie, *Speculating on the Moment: The Poetics of Time and Recurrence in Goethe, Leopardi, and Nietzsche* (Göttingen: Wallstein, 2005), 65–6.

'memory'. 'Antiquarian' History was self-affirmative in establishing one's own antecedents and heritage. 'Critical' History was a way of escaping tradition by undermining it. He moved from advantage to disadvantage for each sort of History before moving on to the next, and his own recommendation for a balance of historical philosophies was Aristotelian in seeking harmony and moderation between extremes. Little was new in his typology of historical practice, though it provides some interesting variations on the typology presented in Hegel's intro-duction to his Philosophy of History. Nietzsche's Monumental History combines History as Lesson and History as Memorialization. Antiquarian History involves the sort of genealogical thinking that spans medieval noble family biographies on one hand and Droysen's work on the other; most of its articulations fall into the category of History as Identity. Critical History is a variant on Marxist consciousness-raising, i.e. History as Emancipation.

In a perspective that takes into account Nietzsche's entire oeuvre, thus includ-ing his later writing, he appears as historically minded in a relatively orthodox, contextualizing way.[96] He was respectful of rigorous historical thinking just as he was respectful of the rigour of the natural sciences, reserving his ire for those who fell into scientism as a philosophy of life or who adopted History as a secular substitute for the spurious providential reassurance of religion. He had himself trained as a classical philologist, was acquainted with heirs of the critical his-torical school, admired Taine, and was a friend as well as a cheerleader of Burckhardt, whose influence is manifest in The Twilight of the Idols (1888) when Nietzsche invoked historical grounds for the belief that 'culture and the state' were 'antagonists: "Kultur-Staat" is merely a modern idea'. A number of works were historical or, as with Rousseau, quasi-historical in approach. His On the Genealogy of Morality: A Polemic (1887), the successor to Beyond Good and Evil (1886), criti-cized earlier, especially 'English' psychological philosophers, including the intel-lectual descendants of the Scottish Hume, for inadequate historical sense.[97]

In Human, All Too Human (1878) Nietzsche had claimed 'everything has become: there are no eternal facts, just as there are no absolute truths. What is needed from now on is historical philosophizing, and with it the virtue of modesty [sic]'. 'Everything has become'—Alles ist geworden—was a central pillar of his Lebensphilosophie. In the same vein, he declared in the Genealogy of Morality that 'only something which has no history can be defined'.[98] 'Man' has history, and so

---

[96] Brobjer, 'Nietzsche's View'; Emden, Friedrich Nietzsche.
[97] Friedrich Nietzsche, On the Genealogy of Morality, ed. Keith Ansell-Pearson (Cambridge: Cambridge University Press, 2006), First Essay, §§1–2, at pp. 10–12, to be read against Ansell-Pearson's clarification at p. xvii. Quote from Twilight of the Idols at: Friedrich Nietzsche, The Portable Nietzsche, ed. Walter Kaufmann (Harmondsworth: Penguin, 1983), 509-10.
[98] Quotes from R. J. Hollingdale, Nietzsche (London: Routledge, Kegan and Paul, 1973), 61, with emphases in Nietzsche's original, and Nietzsche, On the Genealogy of Morality, Second Essay, §13 at p. 53. See also Jos de Mul, The Tragedy of Finitude: Dilthey's Hermeneutics of Life (New Haven: Yale University Press, 2004), 210.

may shape 'his' own character in his present, though that cannot be achieved by mere fiat. To enable the relative freedom of choice by which humans, or at least the best among them, could fulfil their creative potential, the critical work of liberation was necessary vis-à-vis inherited frameworks of thought and meaning, especially morality. Nietzsche concerned himself with 'the question of *what origin* our terms good and evil actually have', with 'the *descent* of our moral prejudices'.[99]

In rudimentary terms some of the argument of the *Genealogy of Morality* can be compared to what is today known as the 'just world fallacy'. The just world belief, that the world is basically fair—i.e. good—in its allocation of outcomes is popular in the same measure that arbitrariness is unpalatable. It promises to render the world potentially controllable given the 'right' behaviour, and thus appeals to a desire for cognitive mastery. One consequence of the idea of personal controllability is to rationalize inequalities, without questioning the way the world is and how it might be altered, by proposing that the less well situated (rather than, say, structured inequalities) are to blame for their situation. That belief is not just entertained by the powerful or well-to-do, since even for the victims of misfortune, there is a certain reassurance of orderliness in the idea that remediable behaviour brought about their situation. It has also been the province of a range of religions to inculcate a sense of sin or imperfection twinned with the promise of next-life improvement consequent on a certain mode of behaviour in this world, thus implying ultimate controllability beyond death, alongside quietism in this life. Indeed Nietzsche ties the development of a particular concept of morality as meek, ascetic self-denial to the Judeo-Christian tradition, especially in light of the historical weakness of Jews and early Christianity. The Judeo-Christian values which occidental civilization claims as its own were, he believes, defined against the self-assertive strength and nobility of Rome, and as such were shaped by that repressed envy and hatred which internalizes itself under the name 'conscience'. Nietzsche's is a story of group psychology as a particular human culture cooks up something that it calls morality, then persuades itself that this is the only true morality, while forgetting its contingent origins and development and traducing alternative value systems. Occidentals forgot the violence involved in establishing rules of law, the violence involved in domesticating human beings to observe a set of precepts, and the fact that punishment only gradually came to mean something more 'profound' than vengeance. They forgot that guilt was invented where once the concept of debt (*Schuld*) alone had existed, even as they conceived themselves beholden—indebted—to god. All this was concealed beneath a glorious origin story, but was nonetheless carried forward within the structure of the whole system of belief and value. Now despite the book's subtitle,

---

[99] Nietzsche, *On the Genealogy of Morality*, Preface, §§2–3, at p. 4. Emphases in original.

it was not just a polemic: Nietzsche believed that the Judeo-Christian 'slave revolt' in morality made humans more interesting since it somehow fostered their subjectivity and it was in some ways to be respected since it gave otherwise weak creatures power over physically stronger creatures. As at once a measure of humans and a limit on them, however, Nietzsche found this morality unsatisfactory, and he was especially concerned to ask what humans would do in an age in which religious faith, which was fundamental to the whole moral framework, was in question.

While Nietzsche used a species of historicization as a tool of existential liberation he also tried to work through the possible problems of such historicization. He feared its capacity, if followed through to one of its possible relativistic conclusions, to replace faith in the transcendent, or in a given historical 'character', with faith in nothingness, i.e. with nihilism, which was just as problematic. Moreover, whatever his thoroughly immodest claim that there are no eternal facts or absolute truths, there was still enough of a conventional, dare one say it Enlightenment, philosopher in Nietzsche for him to resist all of the implications of contextualist historicization—indeed this was implicit in his agenda of emancipation from established precepts, moral and otherwise, and embracing new values. In 1888 he wrote that the philosopher's duty was to try to 'overcome his age in himself, to become timeless', by way of trying to establish some capacity to assess one's times as if from beyond them.[100] Earlier, in 'On the Uses and Disadvantages of History for Life' he talked of the suprahistorical (*überhistorisch*) powers of art (and interestingly of religion), with the implication that some residue remained in great art once one had exhaustively historicized all that could be historicized in it. 'I call "suprahistorical" the powers which lead the eye away from becoming towards that which bestows on existence the character of the eternal and stable.'[101] Some of his historical heroes and their deeds have a timeless quality too, while he appears to have seen a generally desirable disposition in the Homeric Greeks. He had a certain philosophy of history of his own—not a stadial or teleological one, but one in which civilizational tendencies that were already present in ancient Greece circulated across time in different combinations and with different expressions.[102] All this is Nietzsche's structural alternative to matters like the 'universal' or the highest 'one' that Neoplatonism and Rankean historicism had invoked.

For a more systematic attempt to work through the implications of variety, historicity, and flux for thought about 'the human condition', we need to turn to the

---

[100] Daniel Conway, *Nietzsche and the Political* (London: Routledge, 1997), 63–4. The quotation is from Nietzsche's *Der Fall Wagner* (1888).

[101] Nietzsche, 'Uses and Disadvantages', 120.

[102] Otto Gerhard Oexle, *Geschichtswissenschaft im Zeichen des Historismus* (Göttingen: Vandenhoeck und Ruprecht, 1996), ch. 3; F. R. Ankersmit, 'The Ethics of History: From the Double Binds of (Moral) Meaning to Experience', *History and Theory*, 43:4 (2004), 84–102, here 102; Katrin Meyer, *Ästhetik der Historie: Friedrich Nietzsches 'Vom Nutzen und Nachteil der Historie für das Leben'* (Würzburg: Königshausen und Neumann, 1998), 131–3.

NATIONALISM, HISTORICISM, CRISIS   225

thought of yet another erstwhile theology student, and son of a Lutheran pastor, Wilhelm Dilthey (1833–1911). For Dilthey, when one was trying to understand oneself, Cartesian introspection or Kantian regressive analysis towards the *apriori* categories concealed the historical conditions of one's existence. All being was being in time (*Zeitlichkeit*), which also meant being-in-relation-to a range of external influences present and past. At the same time, he did not accept that these influences were determinant. They shaped the pre-conscious hypotheses that are necessary for any initial encroachment on an infinitely complex reality, but could be reduced in significance by the products of induction from empirical study. In other words, an investigator is culturally and temporally situated, but is not inevitably constrained to reproduce her own cultural thoughtworld or, when acting as an historian, to project that thoughtworld onto the historical-cultural others that she studied.[103]

Dilthey owed some conceptual debts to Droysen's emphasis on understanding one's own historicity and his elaboration of the way in which hermeneutic techniques could be expanded from the reading of texts to the contemplation of wider human worlds, including the relationship of the historian to his or her own contexts. For Dilthey, however, the major flaws of historicism à la Droysen were its overly subjective elements and its abiding emphasis on uniqueness that prohibited systematic comparative study, and thereby cut historicists off from pasts that were not the pasts of 'their own', their monad. One key way of thinking outwards and comparatively was through contemplating some of the shared ways in which life was expressed and structured. Just as in everyday life the individual gains a sense of self from interaction with others around her, so, at a higher level of reflection, the historical thinker learns to appreciate the particular character of her own niche in space-time by communing with other times. Past mental worlds could be inferred from the hermeneutic interpretation of the material products or 'objectifications'—art, architecture, but especially literary products—created by minds from those ages. Where Hegel focused on institutions as reason-bearers, Dilthey was concerned with all creative manifestations of human interaction with the natural world as expressive of human value. Moreover, he was as concerned with

---

[103] My account of Dilthey in this and the following two paragraphs is distilled, doubtless to the dissatisfaction of any given one of them, from the insights of: Rudolf A. Makkreel, 'The Productive Force of History and Dilthey's Formation of the Historical World', *Revue internationale de philosophie*, 226 (2003/4), 495–508 and more generally Rudolf A. Makkreel, *Dilthey: Philosopher of the Human Sciences* (Princeton: Princeton University Press, 1992); Eric S. Nelson, 'Empiricism, Facticity, and the Immanence of Life in Dilthey', *Pli: Warwick Journal of Philosophy*, 18 (2007), 108–28; Hajo Holborn, 'Wilhelm Dilthey and the Critique of Historical Reason', *Journal of the History of Ideas*, 11:1 (1950), 93–118; Thomas Teo, 'Karl Marx and Wilhelm Dilthey on the Socio-Historical Conceptualization of the Mind', in C. Green, M. Shore, and T. Teo (eds.). *The Transformation of Psychology: Influences of 19th-Century Philosophy, Technology and Natural Science* (Washington, DC: APA, 2001), 195–218; Jacob Owensby, *Dilthey and the Narrative of History* (Ithaca: Cornell University Press, 1994); Reinhold Niebuhr, *Faith and History: A Comparison of Christian and Modern Views of History* (New York: Charles Scribner's Sons, 1949), 18–20.

the literally individual mind as with what Hegel would have called the objective, or social-institutional mind. Dilthey's individuals were constituted at the meeting points of various social, cultural, economic, and political institutions and influences. So while agreeing with Marx that the division of labour differentiated people in one way, Dilthey believed many other inputs also needed to be considered. Just as importantly, individuals did not give the entirety of themselves to their various societal roles, so those roles in turn did not exhaust the content of their individuality. It might be impossible for the historian to penetrate to that excess of absolute individuality once relational, contextual thought had been exhausted, but from working 'inwards' from general cultural patterns that were evident even in the most original thinkers, down through the mid-range institutional influences, one was nonetheless establishing a logic of individuation. Hermeneutic understanding was realized when one recognized something of the self in the historical or cultural 'other'. This was History as Communion, not in a religious or nationalist sense, but in the broadest humanist sense.

One could use the hermeneutic understanding of the intersection of different contexts to think in a way that was both historical and existential. The enquiring subject, aware of her own structured existence in time, transcends some of the given-ness of the present by recalling the choices and changes that had led to the present. Some of these choices were hers, which illustrate her capacity to influence the future in new ways; some were not hers, which illustrates the influence of larger conceptual and situational structures. At the same time the enquirer expanded her own horizons, as she conceived of herself within ever-larger and more inclusive historical contexts up to the point of a universal, shared humanity.

Dilthey's thought seemed at the time to fall between a number of stools. The philosopher Martin Heidegger (1889–1976), whose concept of historicity, of being in time-and-culture—his most famous work was *Sein und Zeit, Being and Time* (1927)—shows clear commonality of interest with Dilthey, nonetheless criticized him for being too close to the Cartesian–Kantian aspiration to ascend to some point outside history.[104] Dilthey scarcely satisfied those Kantians who still thought in terms of the transcendental, self-authoring subject. And he was considered methodologically problematic and too relativistic by Ernst Troeltsch (1865–1923), who wrote of the 'crisis of historicism' and was itself one of its products as he struggled to reconcile his historian's belief in the historical development of competing religions and sects with his theologian's reluctance to accept the relativity of Christian truth.[105]

---

[104] Bambach, *Heidegger*, 13–17, 165.

[105] Troeltsch, *Der Historismus*; Fritz, *Ethos und Predigt*, 54; Johann Heinrich Klaus, *Die Jesus-Deutung von Ernst Troeltsch im Kontext der liberalen Theologie* (Tübingen: Mohr, 1997), 53. On Troeltsch and Dilthey, Gregory Baum, *The Social Imperative* (New York: Paulist Press, 1979), 247–8; cf. Peter Ghosh, *Max Weber and the Protestant Ethic* (Oxford: Oxford University Press, 2014), 105 n. 8.

Whether the crisis of historicism is a good name for one of the many 'crises' in this period depends on what we take the subject of the crisis of historicism to be. The crisis was one in which historicism suffered, if by historicism one means the hegemony of the German critical historical school, and the agendas of some of its key members, wherein the past was a source of meaning and an assurance of a certain existential coherence. Abetted by growing intra-societal tensions, the sense of mutability across time and place became increasingly detached from speculative philosophies of the historical process, or at least progressive ones, and any sense of the ontological security that some had found in the *Volksgeist* and others in religion. But in the broader sense of the abidingly influential particular-istic historical outlook that this book calls neo-historicism, the crisis—dating approximately from the 1870s through the interwar period—was one to which historical thought contributed, even though historians were not prominent in working through its philosophical ramifications. The crisis gained its purchase from the late nineteenth century because of the wider 'crisis of liberalism' and theology with which it intersected, plus associated material and political change.[106] The primary protagonists of the crisis were increasingly philosophers, Jewish and Christian theologians (like Troeltsch), and some nationalists, because these were the people primarily concerned with the justification of absolute, metaphysical, originary, or essentialist positions.[107] This is not to say that nation-alism itself dwindled during this period—quite the opposite, it reached an aggres-sive crescendo in which there was an obsession with internal loyalty and unity in the face of outside forces.

Classical historicism of the Rankean sort was threatened by fractures within the *Volk*, or national community, and/or the state. In the later nineteenth century, fears of degeneration and the destruction of traditional values multiplied amid population growth, industrialization and urbanization, the rise of the organized left, and demands for new forms of representative politics. The 1870s, with its stock market shock, the beginnings of repeated rural depression, and the 'second industrial revolution', instituted what the Marxist historian Giovanni Arrighi later dubbed the long twentieth century, which superseded the era of British world

---

[106] On the importance of the collapse of liberal Protestant thought in stimulating new reflection at this time, see A. James Reimer, *Paul Tillich: Theologian of Nature, Culture and Politics* (Münster: LIT, 2004), 162. On the many tributaries and differing manifestations of the 'crisis of historicism', see Herman Paul, 'Religion and the Crisis of Historicism: Protestant and Catholic Perspectives', *Journal of the Philosophy of History*, 4 (2010) 172–94. On the 'crisis of historicism' and the success of professional historianship: Beiser, *German Historicist Tradition*, 24–6.

[107] Paul, 'Religion and the Crisis of Historicism'; David N. Myers, *Resisting History: Historicism and its Discontents in German-Jewish Thought* (Princeton: Princeton University Press, 2003); Troeltsch, *Der Historismus*. Herman Paul, 'A Collapse of Trust: Reconceptualizing the Crisis of Historicism', *Journal of the Philosophy of History*, 2 (2008), 63–82, notes the important distinction between doubts about universal or objective value and doubts about being able to justify such value in the light of the collapse of historical certainties in this period. He is surely right that the latter tendency was more prevalent.

financial and commercial hegemony. Arnold Toynbee's relativistic, rhythmic philosophy of History identified the onset of 'post-modernity' in that decade;[108] others see the very advent of high modernity. Between that time and 1914 medievalism reached new heights in European culture, where the triumphalism of empire and industrial growth were accompanied by enhanced apprehension about what was being lost, and a critique of empty or degenerate bourgeois civilization. The romantic drive for preservation renders the study of the past 'for its own sake' something more than a banality.[109] Growing appreciation of Gothic art, architecture, and literature found their sociological parallel in the work of Émile Durkheim and Ferdinand Tönnies, with their distinctions between the 'traditional' sentimental bonds of community, or *Gemeinschaft*, and the contractual bonds of 'modern' society, or *Gesellschaft*. The critique of modernity was especially strong in Germany, as a 'nation' of people that had but a few decades ago been bound by culture alone across manifold lines of different state jurisdictions, and whose image as a land of idealists and philosophers had been somewhat compromised since around 1848 by material(ist) factors, i.e. industrialization. The incremental, evolutionary model of change proposed by classical historicism could not easily accommodate rapid change. Then the likes of Lamprecht tried to turn the focus away from the symbols of political unity and towards economic and social conditions and mass movements and mentalities—just the sort of thing that the powerful German socialists wished to focus on.[110]

The Franco-Prussian war signalled a major power shift, while the violent collapse of the Ottoman Empire in south-eastern Europe in 1875-8 changed the political map drastically and brought what the diplomat and historian George Kennan saw as a caesura in European diplomatic relations. Thereafter, the scramble for Africa and a *fin de siècle* explosion of competitive imperialism elsewhere projected European tensions outwards in murderous fashion. Such tensions were enhanced by the unpredicted socio-economic impact of widespread adoption of the gold standard and the rise of protectionism in Europe. The lines of the First World War military alliances were established by the 1890s.

If, with all the ruptures of the period in Europe, we see an increasing sense of the foreignness of one's own past, as in the writings of 'post-whig' historians like the great legal historian Frederic William Maitland (1850-1906),[111] actual foreign countries once again contributed to the process of disorientation. On the eve of

---

[108] Arnold Toynbee, *A Study of History*, abridgement of vols. I–VI by Robert Somervell (Oxford: Oxford University Press 1946), 39.

[109] Coleman, *Ancient and Medieval Memories*, 593.

[110] Paul, 'A Collapse of Trust', 79–80. The most relevant of Lamprecht's works in this connection is his *Deutsche Geschichte*, 12 vols. (Berlin: Gaertner, 1891–1909), but see also his earlier *Deutsches Wirtschaftsleben im Mittelalter*, 4 vols. (Leipzig: Dürr, 1885–6).

[111] Patrick Wormald, *Legal Culture in the Early Medieval West* (London: Hambledon, 1999), 58–60.

the First World War, Lord Bryce recorded the expansion in the recent scope of enquiry in historical studies, as broadly conceived.

> We have now come to regard history as a record of every form of human effort and achievement, concerned not any more definitely with political events and institutions than with all the other factors that have moulded man and all the other expressions his creative activity has found...[T]he historian, who in the days of Thucydides needed to look no further than to Susa on the east and Carthage on the west, must now extend his vision to take in the whole earth.[112]

The new wave of intellectual endeavours accompanying imperial expansion buttressed the impact of Darwin in furthering European scepticism about the truth of western religious beliefs, as well as encouraging biological racism as a way of framing the difference between peoples.

The special theory of relativity contributed to a general intellectual-cultural discombobulation by undermining what had appeared axiomatic, namely Newtonian physics' absolute concepts of time and space. In the interwar period the reconceptualization of quantum theory detracted from ideas of deterministic predictability at the minutest physical level and blurred scientific distinctions between investigating subject and investigated object by showing how the act of observation could affect the behaviour of observed phenomena. Though the thinking involved only applied by the very loosest of analogies to reflection on historical and cultural affairs, in the general climate of intellectual revolution shaped by the new discoveries the 'New Physics' found nominal kinship with the American James Harvey Robinson's presentist, revisionist *The New History* (1912), and with Robinson's fellow 'new historians' like Charles Beard (see pp. 238–40).[113]

New Philosophies of Historical 'Neutrality' from the Later Nineteenth Century

In much of Europe, and to an extent even in Germany itself, the 1880s saw an anti-historical 'synchronic turn' in the study of linguistics and languages, though historicism veritably flourished in the area of German cultural studies. Historically influenced philosophy in Germany was somewhat moderated by the temporary

---

[112] Cited in Teggart, *Theory*, 79–80.
[113] H. I. Rodgers, 'Charles A. Beard, the "New Physics," and Historical Relativity', *Historian*, 30 (1968), 545–60. Further to cultural ramifications of developments in physics, Paul Forman, 'Weimar Culture, Causality, and Quantum Theory', *Historical Studies in the Physical Sciences*, 3 (1971), 1–116. James Harvey Robinson, *The New History: Essays Illustrating the Modern Historical Outlook* (New York: Macmillan, 1912).

ascension to academic supremacy of neo-Kantianism from around the 1870s, even as some neo-Kantians moved away from Kant's concern with critical-transcendental principles of epistemology to consider matters from a more empirical—anthropological and historical—perspective. New statistical techniques and the development of modelling as a useful theoretical abstraction challenged historicist thought in many fields, as exemplified in Germany in the differing economic approaches of the deductivist 'Austrian School's' Carl Menger and the inductive, historically minded Gustav von Schmoller.[114] The battle between different sorts of approach—manifested in a less stark contrast between the work of a Lamprecht and a Treitschke—became known as the conflict over method, or *Methodenstreit*, to which was related the *Werturteilsstreit*, or conflict over the relationship of the social sciences to value judgements. Max Weber (1864–1920) merits special attention given his contribution to both conflicts.

Weber recognized that the human objects of the human sciences were value-bearing and value-creating entities and since varying values influenced behaviour in variable ways conceptions of causation could not easily be transplanted from the natural sciences and generalization was a precarious business. Nonetheless he did synthesize some of the principles of generalizing explanation, or *Erklären*, with interpretative hermeneutic *Verstehen*. The 'useful fiction' of the 'ideal types' was the product of this synthesis. Any given ideal type only pertained to certain sorts of society at certain times. An ideal type was devised after inference about the world of governing human purposes and meanings that had created a particular set of contingent civilizational characteristics, with its amalgam of bureaucratic, legal, spiritual, and economic tendencies. For heuristic purposes the imposition of such a scheme on social reality must entail isolation, even exaggeration, of certain factors and exclusion of others, but the whole stands or falls by the testable utility of its approximations and abstractions. Clearly Weber recognized that values vary within particular time-places as well as between them, and human scientists ought not claim the capacity to arbitrate value claims; indeed they could not call themselves scientists if they did. 'Science today is a "vocation" organized in special disciplines in the service of self-clarification and knowledge of interrelated facts. It is not the gift of grace of seers and prophets dispensing sacred values, nor does it partake of the contemplation of sages and philosophers about the meaning of the universe.'[115] This was a manifesto for scholarly neutrality underpinned by a particular ontology and an accompanying distinction

[114] Edward Sidelsky, *Ernst Cassirer* (Princeton: Princeton University Press, 2008), 167–8; Peter Uwe Hohendahl, 'The Crisis of Neo-Kantianism and the Reassessment of Kant after World War I', *Philosophical Forum*, 41:1–2 (2010), 17–39; Wotaru Koyama, 'The Rise of Pragmatics: A Historiographic Overview', in Wolfram Bublitz and Neal R. Norrick (eds.), *Foundations of Pragmatics* (Berlin: de Gruyter, 2011), 139–66, here 149 ff. On cultural studies, Otto Gerhard Oexle (ed.), *Krise des Historismus— Krise der Wirklichkeit* (Gottingen: Max-Planck-Instituts für Geschichte, 2007).
[115] Max Weber, 'Science as a Vocation', in *Max Weber: Essays in Sociology*, ed. H. H. Gerth and C. Wright Mills (New York: Oxford University Press, 1946), 129–56, here 52.

between the roles of the human scientist on one hand and the politician or citizen on the other hand.

Weber was influenced by Nietzsche on the end of religious certainty as a guarantor of values,[116] and was himself a theorist of modernization, with its implications of fracture and flux. He saw that meanings and values were made rather than located in the historical record or the objective patterns of the natural world: 'The fate of a cultural epoch that has eaten of the tree of knowledge is that it must know that we cannot learn the *meaning* of the world from the results of its analysis, however perfect that analysis may be, but must instead be in a position to create this meaning for itself.' Such a recognition entailed acknowledgement of different, potentially competing worldviews and prescriptions, with no higher criteria for deciding between them based on claims about the nature of reality.[117] In the present, human scientists could advise on the implications of this or that social policy, just as the teacher could advise the student, but it was still for the political leader to decide the policy.[118] It followed that insofar as social scientists advised on the implementation of policy, they should act in neutral terms towards that policy, irrespective of who the winners were and who the losers—while in full awareness that there would be winners and losers, in the sense of people whose interests and values were better or worse served by this or that dispensation.

Value-judgements might well be involved in one's choice of an object of study but the investigator's professional ethic of responsibility—as opposed to the politician's ethic of conviction as to the choice of governing values—was expressed through refraining from evaluation of this subject matter once it had been chosen.[119] Investigators were to remain descriptive of value-significance, not prescriptive of how that significant value should itself be evaluated. Whether pertaining to study of the present or the past, Weber observed the logical distinction between the investigator's subjective evaluation of social or historical facts and the scholarly task of relating those facts to values. As one of his contemporaries put it, 'Valuations must always involve *praise* or *blame*. To refer to values is to do neither.'[120] For Weber, 'the investigator and teacher should hold as unconditionally separate the establishment of empirical facts (including what he establishes as the "value-oriented" conduct of the empirical individuals whom he is

[116] On the influence of Nietzsche, Horst Baier, 'Die Gesellschaft—ein langer Schatten des toten Gottes', *Nietzsche-Studien: Internationales Jahrbuch für die Nietzsche Forschung*, 10–11 (1981–2), 6–33.

[117] Max Weber, 'Die "Objektivität" sozialwissenschaftlicher und sozialpolitischer Erkenntnis', *Archiv für Sozialwissenschaft und Sozialpolitik*, 19:1 (1904), 22–87, here 30. Emphasis added.

[118] Weber, 'Science as a Vocation', 151–2.

[119] On the ethic of responsibility versus the ethic of conviction (*Gesinnungsethik*), Weber, 'Science as a Vocation' should be read against Max Weber, 'Politics as a Vocation', in *Max Weber: Essays in Sociology*, ed. and trans. Gerth and Mills, 77–128.

[120] The contemporary was the neo-Kantian Heinrich Rickert, cited in Makkreel, *Dilthey: Philosopher of the Human Sciences*, 41.

investigating) and his own practical evaluations of those facts as commendable or reprehensible (including among such facts the evaluations made by empirical individuals that are the object of an investigation)'.[121]

When taking aim at 'seers and prophets', 'sages and philosophers', Weber was taking a controversial stand against an imperial German academic and bureaucratic brotherhood that viewed itself as the privileged interpreter of the supra-political, unifying *Geist* of the monadic nation-state. Perhaps this explains the inverted commas problematizing the concept of *Geist* in the 1920 title of Weber's work 'Die protestantische Ethik und der "Geist" des Kapitalismus'[122] ('The Protestant Ethic and the "Spirit" of Capitalism'; the inverted commas were lost in later versions), even as Weber deployed this idealist term against Marxist materialism. Weber was separating intellectual enquiry from politics as a corollary of recognizing the social value pluralism that he, like Troeltsch, feared as disharmonious, but that he was prepared to confront, not least to prevent Marxists exploiting it. The corollary of academics disavowing value judgements in their work, i.e. de-politicizing themselves, was that they could ask empirical questions of anything with implications for social and economic life, irrespective of whether those matters fell within the grounds of interest of the basic political consensus. Once the line had been strictly drawn between the factual and the evaluative, academics should investigate the factual without fear or favour. They should follow wherever their interests and conclusions lead, repelling along the way the political incursions of intruders from the other side of the empirical–evaluative border who in the name of value-commitments would try to ban some such investigations. Academic freedom was secured and pluralistic politics buttressed by the circumscription of what it meant to be an academic.[123]

Weber's scholar was the sort of 'researcher' who is so prevalent today and might invoke Weber to justify value-neutrality. No longer engaged in *theoria* in the grand classical sense, nor exemplary judgement, that scholar had a technical-exploratory specialist role. Insofar as Weber's disciple was a historian, she was engaged in *Forschung*, specialist research, rather than Humboldt's or Ranke's grand *Geschichtsschreibung*.[124] In decreeing the separation of enquiry from value judgements in the human sciences, Weber was automatically pushing a certain sort of historian—i.e. German historicists—back into their studied pasts anyway, cutting them off from the present to which their judgements were actually directed.

---

[121] Max Weber, 'Der Sinn der "Wertfreiheit" der soziologischen und ökonomischen Wissenschaften', in *Max Weber: Gesammelte Aufsätze zur Wissenschaftslehre. Hrsg. von Johannes Winckelmann. 6., erneut durchgesehene Auflage*, (Tübingen: Mohr /Siebeck, 1985), 489–540, here 499.

[122] Two journal essays—both in the *Archiv fur Sozialwissenschaft und Sozialpolitik*, 20:1 (1904), 1–54 and 21:1 (1905), 1–110—were grouped together under the problematizing title in Max Weber, *Gesammelte Aufsätze zur Religionssoziologie*, vol. 1 (Tübingen: Mohr, 1920), 17–206.

[123] Beiser, *German Historicist Tradition*, ch. 13.

[124] Hardtwig, 'Geschichtsreligion', 17–20, 32.

Two questions might be asked of Weber's reasoning about value-neutrality. The first, and the issue that has received most scrutiny, is whether that reasoning worked as regards social sciences like sociology or economics.[125] The second question is whether, even if the reasoning does work for social scientists, it pertains in the same sort of way to the work of historians: are the nature and ramifications of value judgements necessarily the same in History as in the social sciences? The second question is the one of major concern in this book, and it has received surprisingly little attention, especially when we consider that Weber's most extensive arguments against scholars introducing value judgements into the substance of their work came in the context of addresses where his major focus was on the social sciences.[126] Weber made no systematic analysis of the similarities and differences between the disciplines in this regard. Nor did he distinguish between the German historicist tradition and the sorts of judgements that might be made by historians in other traditions; compare his position to Acton's very different response to historicism.[127] From the perspective of the historical discipline internationally, Weber's was 'just' another important voice warning against partisanship in the name of a particular interpretation of science. In my original Greek categories of History's utility, he is the arch modern proceduralist, evangelist of History as Method, similar in his conclusions to, though often more coherent in his reasoning than, other scholars who had already adopted some similar stances elsewhere.

Distinguishing History as a new 'oeuvre scientifique' that was separate from artistic endeavours, Charles-Victor Langlois and Charles Seignobos gave the latter their due as the vocations whose products were possessed of eternal youth, eternal value. Using terms similar to those deployed later by Weber in his famous lecture 'Science as a Vocation', Langlois and Seignobos argued in their 1897 *Introduction to Historical Studies* that science was different: unlike artists or novelists, investigators would find no celebrity in posterity, but only the gratification of 'their research, corrected or even transformed by subsequent research, being incorporated into the body of knowledge that constitutes the scientific heritage of humanity'. The problem, so long as History was conceived as a branch of literature, was that the public would prefer its literary form over its substantiated

[125] On social science, neutrality, objectivity, and value judgements, see John Lewis, *Max Weber and Value-Free Sociology* (London: Lawrence and Wishart, 1975); Colin Loader, *The Intellectual Development of Karl Mannheim* (Cambridge: Cambridge University Press, 1985), 98–100; Jay A. Ciaffa, *Max Weber and the Problems of Value-Free Social Science* (Cranbury, NJ: Associated University Presses, 1998), 63 ff.

[126] The social sciences figure in the full titles of Weber, 'Die "Objektivität"' and Weber, 'Der Sinn der "Wertfreiheit"'; note also that Weber began 'Science as a Vocation' (p. 129) by referring to himself as a 'political economist'. For dissent from Weber's arguments about value neutrality in History, see Donald Bloxham, *History and Morality* (Oxford: Oxford University Press, 2020).

[127] The concluding pages of the present book address the difficulties historians face in removing all intimations of value judgement, and they question the desirability of such a divestment (pp. 353–7).

contents. Thus Thierry, Carlyle, and Michelet were read long after their death, despite having been interpretatively superseded. Conversely, the public would read on the natural sciences whatever the author's style, since there the content was what mattered.[128] This does not mean that Langlois and Seignobos were (social) scientific positivists in the search for social laws: they were not, and indeed the political paradigm for historiography that they adopted was one of the objects of critique and modification in the establishment of the journal *Revue de synthèse historique* (1900) and in the work of Lamprecht's friend Henri Pirenne (1862–1935). What Langlois and Seignobos had in mind was a particular, ascetic approach to research which eschewed speculation and focused on the empirically verifiable.

Well before this point romantic style and literary quality had been associated with rhetoric in the sense of illegitimate persuasion, as we know, but there were now additional political reasons for distancing oneself from the work of a Thierry. Whatever the specifics of his own role as cheerleader of the July Monarchy, Thierry's anti-clerical, pro-revolutionary stance, first established in print in the teeth of the Restoration regime, drew the intellectual focus towards class conflict. With the downfall of the Second Empire in 1870, then further defeats at Prussian hands, and the advent and crushing of the Paris Commune in early 1871, the social and ideological divisions that had never disappeared in French society gained the significance that, beyond constituting an argument about France's path internally, they were a source of weakness in its external relations. French fragmentation contrasted with Prussian, now German, unity, and catalysed the sort of reappraisal of French institutions that Napoleonic conquest had prompted in other states at the beginning of the century.

The educational system in general, and universities in particular, were reformed, and within the universities historical research and teaching was professionalized decades after similar developments in various German states. German historiography was seen as one of the keys to German unity of historical sense and present purpose, even as Germanophobia was entrenched in so much French political discourse.[129] In *La Monarchie franque* (1888) Fustel reflected on the motto of the *Monumenta Germaniae Historica*, i.e. 'the love of the fatherland gives spirit'. 'The motto is beautiful', he wrote, 'but it is perhaps not appropriate for science', before going on to observe how in German historical scholarship of the previous fifty years historical theory and patriotism had been in striking

---

[128] Charles-Victor Langlois and Charles Seignobos, *Introduction aux études historiques*, ed. Pierre Palpant (electronic edition, 2005 [orig 1898]), 167–8: http://classiques.uqac.ca/classiques/langlois_charles_victor/intro_etudes_historiques/seignobos_etudhisto.pdf See also Weber, 'Science as a Vocation', 137–8.

[129] Isabel DiVanna, *Reconstructing the Middle Ages: Gaston Paris and the Development of Nineteenth-Century Medievalism* (Newcastle: Cambridge Scholars Press, 2008).

harmony.[130] While he proclaimed that science and patriotism ought not to be conflated, he also wrote in 1871 that 'imperfectly observed, history divides us; it is through history properly understood that conciliation must begin'. It is hard to see this desire for national conciliation as apolitical and it is equally unclear who decides what a proper understanding is, but what is clear is that Fustel's route to what he thought of as the proper understanding was circular, since it involved gaining knowledge that is 'exact and scientific, sincere and without bias'.[131] The multi-volume work in which *La Monarchie franque* appeared, Fustel's *Histoire des institutions politiques de l'ancienne France* (1874–92), pursued a conciliating agenda of sorts. Stimulated by France's recent conflict with Germany and running at odds to Thierry's *Récits des temps mérovingiens* (1840) with its story of racial subjection, Fustel rejected the narrative whereby conquering Franks had revolutionized the institutions of Gaul via the introduction of such things as feudalism. Instead, Fustel argued, the Frankish impact was minimal. The property order that endured from Merovingian times in some form up to the French Revolution was not a Germanic imposition that needed to be rejected by the sorts of high medieval freedom-seeking urban ('bourgeois') communards honoured by Thierry—it was part of the deeper historical way of doing things, with roots in Roman law. While Fustel himself was no opponent of the 1789 revolution, he was certainly opposed to ongoing arguments about the socio-economic set-up.[132]

Similar conceptual tensions about History's social role are present in the thought of Jacques Monod (1844–1912), like Fustel one of the central figures in the reorganization of the French historical academy from the 1870s. Monod founded the *Revue Historique* in 1876, partly in imitation of the *Historische Zeitschrift*—in the preface to the first issue Monod and his co-editor Gustave Fagniez noted the loss of French superiority in historical research—and partly as a liberal alternative to the royalist and Catholic *Revue des Questions Historiques*. Espousing 'impartiality' and 'severity of methodology and of criticism', the editors demanded 'original contributions, based on original sources' and rejected 'rhetoric' and the work of scholars who used 'history as a weapon in defense of their religious or political ideas'; contributors should 'avoid contemporary controversies'. Yet the editors also recognized the 'national importance' of 'the study of France's past' and sought to give to France 'the unity and moral strength she needs

---

[130] N. D. Fustel de Coulanges, *Histoire des institutions politiques de l'ancienne France*, vol. III: *La Monarchie Franque* (Paris: Hachette, 1905 [orig. 1888]), 31.

[131] N. D. Fustel de Coulanges, 'L'Organisation de la Justice dans l'antiquité et les temps modernes', *Revue des Deux Mondes*, 94 (July 1871), 536–56, here 538.

[132] N. D. Fustel de Coulanges, *Histoire des institutions politiques de l'ancienne France*, 6 vols. (Paris: Hachette, 1874–92); Augustin Thierry, *Récits des temps mérovingiens précédés de Considérations sur l'histoire de France*, 2 vols. (Paris: Tessier, 1840).

by revealing her historical traditions and, at the same time, the transformations these traditions have undergone'.[133]

In Britain politics was somewhat less pressured but some of the foregoing themes are recognizable. In his 1903 inaugural as Regius Professor of History at Cambridge, J. B. Bury reinforced the notion that History was not a branch of literature and should also disavow 'her old associates, moral philosophy and rhetoric'.[134] The prefatory note to the first issue of the *English Historical Review* in 1886 laid out the journal's philosophy in order to 'avoid the suspicion of partisanship in such political or ecclesiastical questions as are still burning'. It is a bit of a hodge-podge:

> Some topics it will be safer to eschew altogether. In others fairness may be shown
> by allowing both sides an equal hearing. But our main reliance will be on the
> scientific spirit which we shall expect from contributors likely to address us. An
> article on the character and career of Sir Robert Peel will be welcome, so long as
> it does not advocate or deprecate the policy of protective tariffs; and President
> Andrew Jackson may properly be praised or blamed if the writer's purpose be
> neither to assail nor to recommend, with President Cleveland in his eye, the sys-
> tem of party appointments to office. Recognizing the value of the light which
> history may shed on practical problems, we shall not hesitate to let that light be
> reflected from our pages, whenever we can be sure that it is dry light, free from
> any tinge of partisanship.[135]

Fear of political division and the accusation of partisanship in the reflection thereof could reinforce a common worldview that was the enemy of certain forms of critical thought while presenting itself as the acme of critical thought. Peter Novick highlights the problem in his study of the American historical profession at the turn of the twentieth century. He illustrates a shared political outlook stemming from a shared sociocultural milieu and evolutionist worldview amongst the relatively small number of practitioners, and shows how their philosophy of history functioned to minimize tensions over, say, the causes of the American Civil War. Eager to bolster their discipline and their individual reputations with it, these historians found mutual reinforcement in the common projection that they were actually apolitical avatars of a new, objective scholarship which involved downplaying clashes in the past.[136] They constitute an instance of what

---

[133] Text of preface trans. and repr. in Stern (ed.), *The Varieties of History*, 172–4, with quotes from 173–4. Stern's introductory remarks on the journal at p. 171.

[134] Doris S. Goldstein, 'J. B. Bury's Philosophy of History: A Reappraisal', *The American Historical Review*, 82:4 (1977), 896–919, here 897.

[135] Preface repr. in Stern (ed.), *The Varieties of History*, 176.

[136] Novick, *That Noble Dream*, chs. 2–4.

sociologists of knowledge call 'epistemic communities', akin to that of successive editor-gatekeepers of the *Historische Zeitschrift* in their claim to arbitrate what was objective, and to render the 'objective' normative. As with the editors of the *Historische Zeitschrift*, validating certain views of the past in the interests of the present was also a process of marginalizing in the present the dissenting perspectives that might otherwise be identified from within the past.

Much depended upon whether one had in mind a national audience or the international forum. The national unity approach to historiography presupposed international competition; what of those who wished to create an alternative model of relations? If the past was a country to be approached with care, relations with other countries in the here and now had to be borne in mind. The French chemist Jean-Baptiste Dumas had called science 'this neutral and pacific ground of Natural Philosophy, where defeats cost neither blood nor tears';[137] in Bury's vision historical study provided a similar forum for nations to come together in common enterprise. Of his own ambitions for the multi-volume, multi-author *Cambridge Modern History* (1902–12), Acton asked: 'Can an Englishman or an Irishman, a German or a Frenchman be expected to emancipate himself from his national predilections, and write history that gives no hint of national affiliations or loyalties?' The answer was obviously supposed to be in the affirmative, which also meant that the chosen authors were expected to live up to Acton's strictures on writing without fear or favour. The work was intended as a synthesis of perspectives in the fullest sense, though Acton did not clarify how that was to work when matters of contested moral purport were under examination. 'Contributors will understand... that our Waterloo must satisfy French and English, Germans and Dutch alike; that nobody can tell, without examining the list of authors, where the Bishop of Oxford laid down the pen and whether Fairbairn or Gasquet, Liebermann or Harrison, took it up.'[138]

Bury's ambitions could not be said to have been realized before 1914, but they were completely undermined when Europe descended into war. Historians cleaved to national camps in much the same way as most other intellectuals and most members of the supposedly international movements of workers and feminists. They pitched in on either side of the war guilt question and of what historian Herbert Butterfield ironically dubbed the 'war for righteousness', with some British scholars eagerly anticipating the end of the 'age of German footnotes' and of the 'dry chaff of [German] historical research and criticism'.[139]

---

[137] Dumas quoted in René Vallery-Radot, *The Life of Pasteur* (London: Constable, 1928), 251.

[138] Acton quoted in Breisach, *Historiography*, 284.

[139] Herbert Butterfield, *Christianity, Diplomacy and War* (London: Epworth, 1953), 4. On footnotes, Niall Ferguson, *The Pity of War* (New York: Basic Books, 1999), 233.

'Progressive' History

In the interwar years the American historian Charles Beard (1874–1948) drew out some of the self-deceptions of the neutralists, including those among his compatriots. He noted that historians were apt to be 'disturbed, like their fellow citizens, by crises and revolutions occurring in the world about them', and drew explicitly on the work of the Italian philosopher historian Benedetto Croce, the sociologist Karl Mannheim, and the theologian and author of *The Crisis of Historicism* (1932), Karl Heussi, in observing that 'so-called neutral or scientific history reached a crisis in its thought before the twentieth century had advanced far on the way'. These crises affected different countries in different ways, largely dictated by their relationship to the course of the First World War and the interwar order. At the time of speaking, the outset of the New Deal period in 1933, Beard was optimistic enough to foresee history's 'forward' movement to a 'collectivist democracy'.[140]

Beard was one of the foremost members of the 'Progressive' American historical movement, alongside Robinson, Carl Becker, and Mary Beard. Becker was waxing Weberian when he averred that the historian's own concept determines the choice of facts, not vice versa, and observed the difficulty of distinguishing 'facts' from 'theories'.[141] Beard: 'no historian can describe the past as it actually was' (a dig at a vision of Ranke) and 'every historian's work—that is, his selection of facts, his emphasis, his omissions, his organization, and his methods of presentation—bears a relation to his own personality and to the age and circumstances in which he lives'. Despite the notoriety of his remarks about the historian's situatedness, the reformist-socialist Beard stressed that he was only repeating the received wisdom of 'a century or more that each historian who writes history is a product of his age, and that his work reflects the spirit of the times, of a nation, race, group, class, or section'. It is just that such opinions had not tended to receive much of an airing in previous presidential addresses to the American Historical Association, many of whose members were still in thrall to the 'scientific' Ranke. As it happens, Beard approved of the 'scientific method', seeing in it, in the fateful year of Hitler's ascent but from a safe distance, 'the chief safeguard against the tyranny of authority, bureaucracy, and brute power'—but he felt in rather Nietzschean fashion that 'science', while a good servant, was a poor master.[142] Some of his own historical investigations look more like orthodox leftist critiques based on an orthodox process of inference from evidence, so we could take his views on perspectivalism as descriptive rather than necessarily prescriptive of a

---

[140] Charles A. Beard, 'Written History as an Act of Faith', *American Historical Review*, 39:2 (1934), 219–31, here 221, 228. See also Karl Heussi, *Die Krisis des Historismus* (Tübingen: Mohr, 1932).
[141] Carl Lotus Becker, *Detachment and the Writing of History* (Ithaca: Cornell University Press, 1958), 24, 10–11.
[142] Beard, 'Written History', 227.

new way of writing History. His earlier *An Economic Interpretation of the Constitution of the United States* (1913) pointed to the entrenchment of vested material interest in the civil structure of a supposedly egalitarian society. It was anti-idealist in both the philosophical and commonplace sense of 'idealism', and in many places straightforwardly materialist in the Marxist sense, with a doctrine of base and superstructure, interest and exploitation. Thus: 'party doctrines and "principles" originate in the sentiments and views which the possession of various kinds of property creates in the minds of the possessors; class and group divisions based on property lie at the basis of modern government; and politics and constitutional law are inevitably a reflex of these contending interests.'[143]

Other Progressivists, or New Historians, were prepared to prescribe historical content: it has been said that for them 'history became a parade of human solutions to temporal problems of existence'.[144] In a 1918 article on the need to create a 'Usable Past' the historian and literary critic Van Wyck Brooks urged a new generation of writers to turn away from current interpretive hegemony in literary criticism and search for alternative traditions that had temporarily been submerged. The 'spiritual past has no objective reality', yielding 'only what we are able to look for in it', he wrote. 'It yields up, now this treasure, now that, to anyone who comes to it armed with a capacity for personal choices.'[145] At the same time Brooks had already argued in rather historicist fashion that 'all true originality immediately reconciles itself with tradition, has in itself the elements of tradition, and is really the shadow of tradition thrown across the future'.[146] Just as the past provided the opportunities from which the present selected so the present would always be linked with the past no matter what. One ought not fear change.[147]

It was an important difference of nuance whereby Robinson, in the words of one of his admirers, believed that 'to give meaning to the present, history must be treated as an ever-continuous genetic development in which the present is illuminated by perceiving anachronisms or the often-irrational origins of our ideas and institutions'.[148] There is an element of Nietzsche here but it also suggests another turn of the wheel as regards the utility of historical thought. From scholastic reading practices onwards, identifying anachronism meant jettisoning irrelevant accretion to the kernel of real truth, up to the point of reinterpreting that truth for present conditions. Gradually anachronism also—and ultimately instead—came to mean a fear of applying contemporary values retrospectively. For Robinson anachronism did not denote misrepresenting the past by presentist

[143] Charles A. Beard, *An Economic Interpretation of the Constitution of the United States* (New York: The Free Press, 1965 [orig. 1913]), 15–16.
[144] Villemaire, *E. A. Burtt*, 15–19.
[145] Van Wyck Brooks, 'On Creating a Usable Past', *The Dial*, 64:7 (11 April 1918), 337–41, here 338–9.
[146] Van Wyck Brooks, *The Wine of the Puritans* (London: Sisley's, 1908), 138.
[147] Villemaire, *E. A. Burtt*, 15–19.   [148] Ibid. 18–19, quoting Harvey Wish.

interpretation so much as preventing the past's unwarranted intrusion into the present. The emphasis was less on the interpretation of truth than its replacement.

The Decline of Historicism and the Rise of German Social History

The interwar atmosphere was altogether more extreme in Germany, the country whose intellectuals had helped set the American 'new historians'' thoughts in train and whose cultural crisis was aggravated by the economic crises of the era. Shortly after Brooks's essay appeared, and only a year after Weber had written along similar lines about the creation rather than the location of meaning, the German-Jewish pacifist Theodor Lessing published his once-censored *Geschichte als Sinngebung des Sinnlosen*. The title translates as 'History as the conferral of meaning on the meaningless' and is a characterization of the discipline that became one of Hayden White's clarion calls about half a century later.[149] Lessing's work dissected self-serving dealings with the past, especially teleological readings.

It was overshadowed within a year by the best-selling work of philosophy of History in the twentieth century: Oswald Spengler's two-volume *Der Untergang des Abendlandes*, *The Decline of the Occident*, which fused the portentous tone of the medieval theologians of history with the assumptions of epistemic and cultural relativism. Like Toynbee's later twelve-volume *A Study of History* (1934–61), Spengler's work become something of a case study in the sort of cherry-picking historians ought not to engage in. This should not obscure its immense popularity at the time. While it had been substantially completed before the war, giving it a prophetic character, it appeared between 1918 and 1923, thus chronologically bracketing Troeltsch's *Der Historismus und seine Probleme* (1922). Many among Spengler's German audience read *Untergang* as 'downfall' or collapse, and inferred from the book a pessimism that Spengler himself purported not to share. Yet the work had broader implications than for German nationalists and anti-democrats. It was a species of monadology modified for a godless moment, decentring the occidental experience and removing any fixed point of reference beyond the lives of peoples. Spengler regarded a unilinear ancient–medieval–modern developmental conception of History as analogous to the discredited Ptolemaic, earth-centred view of the physical universe. He compared himself to Copernicus as a revolutionizer of thought and perspective, again illustrating the cultural significance of revolutionary scientific thinking in that era.

---

[149] Theodor Lessing, *Geschichte als Sinngebung des Sinnlosen* (Munich: Beck, 1919).

For Spengler, cultures were not linked in some developmental chain; they enjoyed their own isolated and apparently predetermined patterns of birth, life, and death. Where Toynbee contrived to reduce the 'major civilizations' of the past and present world to 21–23 in number, and attributed monadic qualities to them, he, like Troeltsch, denied that such entities were *windowless* monads, or *Ganzheiten*, self-enclosed wholes.[150] Spengler, whose 'high' or 'mature' world-historical cultures numbered precisely eight, leaned more towards Leibniz in that insofar as his *Ganzeiten* came into contact with each other, they only left superficial impressions, one never influencing the other's essence. Spengler sought to illustrate the contention of radical difference with an example from the most logical of disciplines: for the ancient Greeks, mathematics was about magnitude; for modern Europeans living with the insights of Euclidean geometry, mathematics was a matter of function. Thus, while a modern German might be able to learn the ancient Greek word for 'mathematics', she would not understand the same thing by it as the ancient Greeks did—the concepts were *incommensurable*, and the idea of incommensurability hangs over Spengler's book in tandem with that of relativism, though he only occasionally used the term itself.[151] Common to most of 'incommensurability's' definitions is the absence of a common denominator or external standard of measurement, which associates the concept with relativism. There is no set of higher co-ordinates on which, say, different ethical values or mathematical precepts can be plotted, probably because their functions within their respective systems are just different. For Spengler, a culture's essence lay in its relationship with its environment, and, in the absence of any aperspectival notification of the relationship, discerning this relationship was a matter of the historian's subjective judgement. The historian should not be a moralist and, in her striving for understanding at the level of essence, she should not forget that she was an aesthete more than a scientist. Spengler's work was admired by some of Dilthey's followers and the first volume of *Untergang* was awarded a prize by the Nietzsche archive.[152]

If the collapse of the 'Third Reich' sounded the death-knell for classical historicism as a national German approach to History, the statist and high political focus had been influentially challenged in the interwar period from further to the right. The catastrophe of the First World War fed competing waves of German nihilism and cultural despair, dialectical materialism, and aggressive organicist nationalism that broke in the intellectual ferment of the Weimar Republic.

---

[150] Toynbee's position in Michael Palencia-Roth, 'On Giants' Shoulders: The 1961 Salzburg Meeting of the ISCSC', *Comparative Civilizations Review* (Spring 2010), 142–58. Troeltsch, *Der Historismus*, 987.

[151] Spengler, *Der Untergang des Abendlandes* (Munich: Beck, 1998), 87 ff. on Euclid and the 'inkommensurable'.

[152] Eugene F. Miller, 'Positivism, Historicism, and Political Inquiry', *American Political Science Review*, 66:3 (1972), 796–817, here 799 n. 9. William Dray, *Perspectives on History* (London: Routledge and Kegan Paul, 1980), part 3, has influenced my discussion here.

A range of philosophies took concepts like *Volksgeist* and rebirth and, like Martin Heidegger, applied them in highly political ways 'appropriate' to Germany's situation during and after the conflict.[153] Germany's territorial diminution in the Versailles peace treaty, and this so soon after the vast eastward expansionist agenda set forth in the March 1918 treaty of Brest-Litovsk, highlighted the misfit between the boundaries of the state and of the Germanic people, or *Volk*. As had been the case in the historiography of other peoples before they had gained statehood, or in Chalkokondyles' case after the state had been lost, the historical focus shifted directly to the *ethnos*, as opposed to the political entity that housed it. This emphasis on the *Volk* was also thoroughly characteristic of Nazism, so practitioners of the new *Volksgeschichte*, like Werner Conze (1910–86) and Theodor Schieder (1908–84), and of the related *Landesgeschichte*, like Otto Brunner (1898–1982), found an especially conducive political environment after 1933. If not necessarily outright Nazis, such historians were generally of the hard conservative right, whose agenda of territorial revisionism, ethno-nationalism, and anti-socialism dovetailed with Nazism in many respects. The *Ostforschung* of the *Volks*-historians, including work on 'lost territories', ethnic Germans in eastern Europe, and the legitimacy of German empire over 'inferior' peoples, provided intellectual sustenance for Hitler's imperialism, and indeed some of these scholars acted as direct advisers to the Nazis.[154]

As to historicists in the older vein, Germany's experience in both world wars and under Nazism even caused Meinecke to recant his faith in the moral primacy of the nation-state. He now criticized the idealization of power that had drawn German away from the ideals of Goethe to those—allegedly—of Machiavelli. He defected from Ranke to Burckhardt. Meinecke was followed in his disenchantment with statist moral-legal positivism by a number of colleagues, especially after Nazi Germany's decisive defeat at Stalingrad at the turn of 1942–3. To be sure, Meinecke did not desist from seeking solace in his historical interpretations. Having earlier reflected in rather Weberian form that the principal concerns of the historian were values and causation, and that these two were intrinsically linked, by the time of *The German Catastrophe* (1946) causation, in terms of the rise of Nazism, had become for Meinecke a matter of sheer (mis)fortune.

---

[153] Forman, 'Weimar Culture, Causality, and Quantum Theory'; Sidelsky, *Ernst Cassirer*, 167–8; Hohendahl, 'The Crisis of Neo-Kantianism'.

[154] For distinctions and relations between *Volksgeschichte* and *Landesgeschichte*: Willi Oberkrome, *Volksgeschichte: Methodische Innovation und völkische Ideologisierung in der deutschen Geschichtswissenschaft, 1918–1945* (Göttingen: Vandenhoeck und Ruprecht, 2011), including 22 ff. on the anti-Versailles agenda and 56 ff. and 211 ff. on 'Ostforschung'. Extensively on Conze: Thomas Etzemüller, *Sozialgeschichte als politische Geschichte: Werner Conze und die Neuorientierung der westdeutschen Geschichtswissenschaft nach 1945* (Munich: Oldenbourg, 2001), including 70–89 on Otto Brunner.

Germany's crimes beyond Germany were marginalized; the 'catastrophe' was one that Nazism may have produced but Germany experienced.[155]

The trope of Nazism as an aberrant interlude was a popular one, especially for nationalist conservatives. Included in that number was Meinecke's student Hans Rothfels (1891-1976). A Jewish convert to Lutheranism, Rothfels, like his own student Conze, had opposed the Weimar republic and endorsed German imperialism in eastern Europe. He reluctantly fled Germany in 1938 under pressure of racist persecution. His 1948 work *The German Opposition to Hitler* embodied his view that the conspirators involved in the July 1944 plot on Hitler's life represented the essence of German conservative and militaristic traditions, whereas Nazism was an interloping force. The non-Nazi conservative nationalist historian Gerhard Ritter (1888-1967), who had actually been incarcerated for his membership of the circle involved in the 1944 plot, had a similar vision of the true Germany, one he had developed before the war. He conceived a fundamental break in 1918, which introduced an unwelcome era of 'mass democracy' that included the Weimar and the Nazi periods, and could be traced back to the foreign influence of the French Revolution. Nonetheless Ritter sensed enough of a problem in the longstanding traditions of German historianship that in 1949 he urged the convention of the German Historical Association to stop taking reality for granted. He seems to have meant this in the sense of not giving normative status to the powers that be simply because they be, which is one implication of Ranke's claim that each epoch is immediate to god—he equally rejected the Rankean view of war as a 'struggle of moral energies'. Instead historians should be prepared to apply political and moral judgement to discern between more and less appealing options in any given historical context.[156]

In light of the decline of classical historicism, it is one of History's and history's little ironies that the post-war decade was the incubation period for a vital late development in the hermeneutics that had bound philosophy to historicism. Where some hermeneuts had prided themselves that they might know the authors of historical texts better than those authors knew themselves, and Humboldt suggested that one's understanding of the objects of one's investigations would always be deficient, Hans-Georg Gadamer, erstwhile student of Heidegger, came to a third conclusion. He wrote that 'there is no understanding or interpretation in which the totality of this existential structure [the structure shaping the consciousness of the investigator] does not function, even if the

---

[155] Meinecke, *Burckhardt und Ranke* (Berlin: Deutsche Akademie der Wissenschaft, 1948); Meinecke, *Die Deutsche Katastrophe* (Wiesbaden: Brockhaus, 1947), *passim*, but see especially comments on p. 125; Hardtwig, 'Wissenschaft als Arbeit', 10.

[156] On Rothfels's pre-war scholarship and thought, Oberkrome, *Volksgeschichte*, 132 ff.; Etzemüller, *Sozialgeschichte*, 24-5. On Ritter: Klaus Schwabe, 'Change and Continuity in German Historiography from 1933 into the Early 1950s: Gerhard Ritter (1888-1967)', in Hartmut Lehmann and James Van Horn Melton (eds.), *Paths of Continuity: Central European Historiography from the 1930s to the 1950s* (Washington, DC: German Historical Institute, 2003), 83-108, esp. 104 ff.

intention of the knower is simply to read "what is there" and to discover from his sources "how it was".'[157] This did not mean that the hermeneut merely read the present into the past. Such meanings as historical texts evince will be the *fusion* of the horizons of meaning of the contemporary interpreter with the meanings of a text that was produced against a different horizon. That fusion, rather than the comprehension of the 'original meaning', is not a misunderstanding; it is just what 'understanding' is. It is not clear from Gadamer that he thought the subject could fuse horizons with the pasts, or, one assumes, the presents, of significantly different human groups, and this may be another area in which he differs from Dilthey as from Herder. Thinking within the boundaries of one's 'own', however, a philosophy of fusion across time implied that even when revolution or defeat—in 1789, 1918–19, or 1945—appeared to have established a clear break with the past, there were always points of inheritance, and thus continuity. For German liberals and leftists, conversely, the inherited traditions of 'life' were precisely what needed to be brought under critique.

Left-leaning German intellectuals, many sociologists among them, had been decimated under Nazi rule, leaving little in the way of more radical opposition voices. For a revolution in West German historianship generational change was needed, and a related shift away from two decades of post-war political domination by the conservative Christian Democratic Union. The propitious cultural environment of the later 1960s coincided with the intellectual diversification attendant upon the expansion of the German university system, with academics and students more than quadrupling in numbers from 1960 to 1975.[158] The year 1975 also saw the first edition of the journal *Geschichte und Gesellschaft*, whose title, 'History and Society', indicates the sort of History in question. Whatever has subsequently been said about it, though, this historiographical 'revolution' inhered more in the political philosophies of the new historians than in their methods and focus; the latter were only new when contrasted with the Rankean model that had already been brought into question.

Hans-Ulrich Wehler (1931–2014), arguably the pre-eminent social historian of Germany's later twentieth century, acknowledged his debt to the interwar economic historianship of Hans Rosenberg (1904–88) and Eckhart Kehr (1902–33), and their identity as marginalized émigrés from Nazi Germany bolstered the 'critical' credentials of his project, yet in terms of method and approach he owed as much to Conze. In 1957, from a chair in Heidelberg, and along with another former *Volks*-historian, Eric Maschke, Conze established an Institute for Economic and Social History and was a key player in the simultaneous creation of the Working Group for Modern Social History. Conze's anti-socialist

[157] Hans-Georg Gadamer, *Truth and Method* (London: Sheed and Ward, 1979 [orig. 1960]), 232.
[158] For the statistics and elements of the context, David Blackbourn, *Populists and Patricians: Essays in Modern German History* (Abingdon: Routledge, 2014), 10.

philosophy of social or, as he called it, 'structural' History prompted work on the transformations of German society since the eighteenth century at the agrarian and industrial levels. Many of the supposed innovations of post-war social History can be traced to the interwar period; the *Volks*-historians' multi-dimensional concern with society necessitated engagement with folklorism, demography, geography, ethnology, and sociology.[159] Conze had even reflected on an attenuated sense of common historiographical revisionism with the French Annales school, which is considered on its own terms in the next chapter.[160]

Where Wehler would presumably have displeased his doctoral supervisor Schieder was in the political thrust of his work and that of the whole 'Bielefeld school' of social History with which he became synonymous. Another leading Bielefeld light, Jürgen Kocka (1941–), once mused that there might have been more friction between Germany's historical profession and Nazism had the former been more suffused with the cosmopolitan, comparative, indeed 'Enlightened' outlook of the likes of Gatterer, Vico, Voltaire, and Adam Ferguson, rather than the heritage of nineteenth-century historicism with its emphasis on national particularity.[161] The historical project of Kocka, Wehler, and others means that both they and their conservative protagonists were very obviously fighting battles of their present by the discussion of its immediate Nazi, Weimar, and Wilhelmine historical background. Rejecting not just the organicist thrust of historicism but the hermeneutic approach that could serve merely to comprehend the dominant forces of the nation-state-monad on its own terms, the more social-scientific approaches of the new German social History were aligned to emancipation and national self-critique as much as explanation, even as they focused more on longer-term processes and structures than individual agents. Key goals included exposing social structures that might still dominate suppressed social groups and identifying continuities between Nazism and the Kaiserreich that problematized the comforting view of Nazism as aberration. This was the 'negative *Sonderweg*' thesis, i.e. the counterpart to the complacent, self-regarding conservative view of German History that had emphasized the superiority of German institutions and spirituality.[162]

---

[159] Peter Lambert, 'Social History in Germany', in Peter Lambert and Phillipp Schofield (eds.), *Making History* (Abingdon: Routledge, 2004) 93–108, here 93–6; and Etzemüller, *Sozialgeschichte*.

[160] For the nature and limits of these links, see Etzemüller, *Sozialgeschichte*, 1, 54–9; Traian Stoianovich, *French Historical Method: The Annales Paradigm* (Ithaca: Cornell University Press, 1976), 45–6; Peter Schöttler, 'Das "Annales-Paradigma" und die deutsche Historiographie (1929–1939)', in Lothar Jordan and Bernd Kortländer (eds.), *Nationale Grenzen und internationaler Austausch* (Tübingen: Niemeyer, 1995), 200–20.

[161] Jürgen Kocka, *Geschichte und Aufklärung* (Göttingen: Vandenhoeck und Ruprecht, 1989), 142–4.

[162] Arguably the cardinal document of the negative *Sonderweg* theory was Wehler, *Das Deutsche Kaiserreich, 1871–1918* (Göttingen: Vandenhoeck und Ruprecht, 1973). For a succinct summary of the positive and negative *Sonderweg* debates, see Blackbourn, *Populists and Patricians*, 1–12.

7
Turns to the Present

Introduction

The work of Wehler and others in Germany was part of the broader north Atlantic ascent of social History from the later 1950s to the peak of the 1970s and early 1980s. Social History took different forms in different countries depending on their political constellations and the relative significance of related disciplines. From the 1980s social History was gradually supplanted in prominence by a cluster of related historiographical developments concerned with language and culture. In the last fifteen years or so newer fashions have waxed, and to those too this chapter will attend, but in terms of major new lines of occidental historiography with consequences in justifications for History, social History and what for shorthand we may call the linguistic and cultural turns remain of particular importance.

In a broader historical perspective, the oscillation between social and linguistic-cultural concerns looks like a reprise of the eighteenth-to-nineteenth-century battles between 'German' culturalism and 'French' sociological thought. There is truth to the comparison, but such dyads obscure as much as they reveal, since by no means all social History was conducted with the social science method, and by no means all cultural History focused on the more internalized understanding and exploration of subjective meaning that we associate with hermeneutics. Social History, especially History 'from below', as the French socialist politician and historian Jean Jaurès (1859–1914) may have been first to call it,[1] could be just as interested in matters of 'subjective' individual and social 'consciousness' as matters of 'objective' social 'existence', and it could focus on the interpenetration of material and cultural elements rather than the determination of one level by the other. Cultural History could be concerned with culture as a separate sphere to 'the social' or 'the economic', but it could be just as all-encompassing in its approach as social History had sometimes attempted to be. Under precepts influenced by the linguistic and cultural theory of structuralism and its descendants, cultural History could be conducted according to 'scientific' (scientistic?) principles of explanation at least as much as hermeneutic principles of interpretative understanding.

---

[1] See Georges Lefebvre, *The Coming of the French Revolution*, ed. and introduced by Timothy Tacket (Princeton: Princeton University Press, 2005), p. xi.

Claims for the utility of History varied according to practitioner but a few sub-stantivist rationales stand out. Social-scientific social historians were more apt to assert History's predictive value or at least its pragmatic contemporary import-ance at a time of industrialization beyond the north Atlantic—this was an update of History as Practical Lesson. More methodologically 'traditional' qualitative social historians were more likely to be found revising prevailing conceptions of the past with a view to altering politics in the present—disturbing 'whiggish' nar-ratives, or inserting the marginalized into the historical record to fortify their voices now. This was a species of History as Identity fused with History as Emancipation. 'New cultural historians' specialized in a version of History as Travel as they invoked exotic worlds past. They, like the many historians under the influence of Michel Foucault, who addressed culture through the prism of power, might adapt the Travel rationale, contrasting past ways of doing things with present ways in order to underline/unmask the conventional, made and remade, character of social relations and of human-being, and thus the possibility of changing them. This was a Marxist agenda of History as Emancipation adapted for a post-Marxist philosophy. Its proponents discarded Dilthey's definition of hermeneutic understanding as recognizing the self in the historically distant Other, and focused more exclusively on the differences. The element of History as Communion that had underlain so many hermeneutic approaches to the evi-dence of the past was abandoned in this philosophy.

Like History as Emancipation, the other relatively new rationale for History in the period, 'History as Therapy', owes more to thought incubating in the nine-teenth century than to any of the self-conscious theoretical radicalism of the later twentieth century. Since History as Therapy is less popular a rationale than History as Emancipation or indeed any of the other rationales, further discussion of it is postponed until the final chapter where all are revisited. The words of the sociologist Pierre Bourdieu (1930-2002) nonetheless illustrate how closely the therapeutic and emancipatory agendas can be associated as he broadened the associations of the 'unconscious' from those in Schelling's philosophy and psy-choanalysis. He used it in relation to his concept of the 'habitus', the set of norms, skills, and, tastes that we each develop according to our socialization:

In practice, it is the habitus, history turned into nature, i.e. denied as such, which accomplishes practically the relating of these two systems of relations [i.e. the relations between objective structures, subjective practices, and the uncon-scious], in and through the production of practice. The 'unconscious' is never anything other than the forgetting of history which history itself produces.[2]

---

[2] Pierre Bourdieu, *Outline of a Theory of Practice* (Cambridge: Cambridge University Press, 2003), 78.

Note that each of the three uses of 'history' has a different meaning. The 'history' that is forgotten is the way that the present emerged contingently from the past. The 'history' that induces the forgetting of the past is a sort of official account, a realization, perhaps of what the Marxist theorist György Lukács (1885–1971) conceived as the aim of 'bourgeois' thought: 'an apologia for the existing order of things or at least the proof of their immutability' as supposedly 'eternal laws of nature'. 'As Marx points out,' Lukács wrote, 'people fail to realise "that... definite social relations are just as much the products of men as linen, flax, etc."'[3] Bourdieu's solution to that second sort of 'history'—i.e. his recommended device for reversing the 'denial' of the contingency of historical developments and their presentation as given 'nature'—was a third form of history, which is my upper-case History, that which in some instantiations has claim to be called critical enquiry into the past. Thus, in Bourdieu's words:

> All sociology should be historical and all history sociological. In point of fact, one of the functions of the theory of fields that I propose is to make the oppos-ition between reproduction and transformation, statics and dynamics, or struc-ture and history, vanish... [W]e cannot grasp the dynamics of a field without a historical, that is, a genetic, analysis of its constitution and of the tensions that exist between positions in it, as well as between this field and other fields.[4]

If this chapter is mainly concerned with what was added to History's tapestry in the north Atlantic centres of professional historiography, we must as ever acknowledge that which was not new but which was retained from the past, i.e. political History and related areas of elite interest like diplomatic History and 'traditional' international History. Especially from the 1960s the popularity of political History dwindled signally among professional historians, though much less so amongst general reading publics. Along with many other strands of his-toriography it has reinvented itself, as we shall see at the end of the chapter.

Structures and Superstructures

The First World War shook what was left of the stuffing from the British 'Whig' tradition that had developed out of the progressivist confidence of the eighteenth century and peaked during Britain's mid-nineteenth-century world dominance. The power of the whig narrative had been waning for at least a generation by

---

[3] Georg Lukács, *History and Class Consciousness: Studies in Marxist Dialectics* (Cambridge, MA: MIT Press, 1971 [orig. 1922]), 48.
[4] Pierre Bourdieu and Loïc Wacquant, *An Invitation to Reflexive Sociology* (Cambridge: Polity, 1992), 90.

1914, consistent with 'crisis-thinking' across the Continent, and now it was criticized by a new breed of 'modernist' historians who rejected its 'picturesqueness'
and rhetorical tendencies in the name of a forensic discipline.[5] Some of their
barbs were not a world removed from the criticisms which the later nineteenth-
century whigs had directed at Macaulay before them. In 1929 the historian of
Anglo-Saxon England Frank M. Stenton (1880–1967) wrote sniffily of Stubbs's
Constitutional History of England (1874–8; pp. 198–9) that 'the details of medieval
finance [and] law are frequently interrupted by moral reflection in which a literary purpose is powerfully present'.[6]

The epithet 'modernist' has been applied to the likes of Stenton by the historian
Michael Bentley and it helps to understand what Bentley means to read the label
as denoting contrast both to 'whigs' beforehand and 'postmodernists' afterwards.
Alongside a conviction that secure atomic facts could be established by archival
research and then used as firm bases on which to construct or test interpretations,
these modernists rejected speculation and suasive prose—and in the process they
rather rejected reflection on their own subject-positions and the literary and
otherwise creative ('poetic') nature of their own products. Bentley writes of a general sensibility, 'the modernist feel for realizable truth and a consistent implication that the past was out there as a visitable place'.[7] Arguably these scholars did
come close to the barest historical literalism, the diminution of the already
reduced Lutheran hermeneutics to half of its purpose, but this literalism was not
the same as credulity. The 'modernists' were skilled in source criticism—as such
they were a world away from literalists as pejoratively understood—and while
they may have fancied themselves to be detached students of the past, there was
no general subscription to any simplistic liberal theory of context-free human
being as regards the people they studied. In that sense they were guilty of the
same sins of self-exemption or performative contradiction (where one's practice
gainsays what one preaches) that marks a huge number of historians. Whilst
ditching some of the self-conscious narrative tendencies of historicism they
maintained and even enhanced its contextualism.

Most august of these modernists, Lewis Namier (1888–1960) was what the
social historian E. P. Thompson called an 'inverted Marxist': a man of the political
right who believed interests shape values. Namier also commended his friend
Freud's insight into non-rational and unconscious motivations. Above all, he may
be said to have tied high politics to social History. His parliamentary History
assumed that the political behaviour of members could only be understood with

---

[5] Bentley, *Modernizing*, 98, citing Tout.   [6] Ibid. 107.
[7] Ibid., and Bentley, 'Approaches to Modernity', 488. See also Mark Bevir, 'The Contextual
Approach', in George Klosko (ed.), *The Oxford Handbook of the History of Political Philosophy* (Oxford:
Oxford University Press, 2011), 11–23, here 12.

reference to their biographies, social backgrounds, class interests, and so forth.[8] The titular 'structure' of Namier's magnum opus, *The Structure of Politics at the Accession of George III* (1929), was firmly contrasted to 'narrative'; he called his a 'static' History, redolent of Burckhardt's historical cross-sections. In this study of the composition and functioning of the House of Commons around 1760 he warned the reader that between eighteenth-century politics 'and the politics of the present day there is more resemblance in outer forms and denominations than in underlying realities' and illustrated his contentions in the fashionable idiom of scientific revolution:

> A system of non-Euclidean geometry can be built up by taking a curve for basis instead of the straight line, but it is not easy for our minds to think consistently in unwonted terms; Parliamentary politics not based on parties are to us a non-Euclidean system, and similarly require a fundamental readjustment of ideas and, what is more, of mental habits.[9]

Along with other 'modernists', Namier performed a task which postmoderns would endorse, as they combated cultural essentialism across time and the conception of unity in the past. A phobia of anachronism became almost a watchword as the modernists broke down grand narratives to reveal just how little continuity there might be in—say—the British constitutional past, once sufficient attention was paid to the changing meaning of similar-sounding legal concepts. 'While ideas outlive reality, names and words outlast both', creating 'an illusion of stability... which is apt to give rise to wrong inferences.'[10] Namier's scientific analogy and his 'static', synchronic cross-section suggested that Spengler's 'incommensurability' might be applied across eras as well as across nations; the past as foreign country.

The point is made clearer if we jump a few decades ahead for a moment, to the early work of Foucault (1926–84), whose sometime title—'Professor of the History of Systems of Thought'—gets at the heart of the matter. Foucault wrote of successive 'epistemes', the Renaissance, Classical, and Modern epistemes, which were conceptual structures that gave a characteristic form to what was held to be scientific knowledge in any given era. One episteme was incommensurable with another, which was important in a broader sense as regards the philosophy of history; while he embraced the sort of epochal categorization characteristic of

---

[8] The 'history of parliament' project was the grandest expression of this philosophy. On Thompson's description, and Freud, Kevin Passmore, 'History and Historiography since 1945', in Roger E. Backhouse and Philippe Fontaine (eds.), *A Historiography of the Modern Social Sciences* (Cambridge: Cambridge University Press, 2014), 29–61, here 34.

[9] Lewis Namier, *The Structure of Politics at the Accession of George III* (London: Macmillan, 1973), pp. x–xi.

[10] Lewis Namier, 'History' (1952), excerpted in Stern (ed.), *The Varieties of History*, 373. More generally on anachronism see Blaas, *Continuity and Anachronism*.

stadial History, Foucault did not present one stage as an advance on previous ones. His famed project of creating a 'historical ontology of ourselves', i.e. a historical picture of successive human conceptions of what it was to be human, is a sharpened elaboration of the nineteenth-century Francophone History in the tradition of Taine, whose message was that 'Each epoch of history...had its distinctive institutions. Men were molded and remolded by these changing social forms. Thus men could not be regarded as the same throughout history'; each period had its 'peculiar institutions and...corresponding psychology'.[11] In the first edition of Foucault's *Folie et déraison: Histoire de la folie à l'âge classique* (1961), the later English version of which was called *Madness and Civilization*, he talked of producing 'a structural study of an historical ensemble—notions, institutions, juridical and police measures, scientific concepts'.[12] Overall, there is a Namier-esque quality both to the 'static' analysis of some of Foucault's work and the determination to show discontinuity across time in matters like scientific concepts. When objecting to 'the philosophical myth of history' as a 'grand and extensive continuity', he repeatedly credited practising historians in general with having destroyed this myth, and when he identified any particular historians, he noted not just some of his own French predecessors but 'the English historians'. 'Modernist' historians like Namier, with their preoccupation with anachronism and suspicion of Whiggery, were, I propose, precisely the English historians he had in mind. Others of the same stripe included Maitland (pp. 228–9), who in turn bears the influence of the philosopher Henry Sidgwick, of whom it has been said that he used the past 'not to construct patterns of historical dynamics but to discredit them' along with 'grand schemes of social evolution'.[13]

Namier's title, like some of Foucault's aforementioned vocabulary in *Folie et déraison*, also hints at affinities with the structuralism that was fashionable in interwar Continental linguistic theory and is most associated with the Swiss Fernand de Saussure (1857–1913). Saussure rejected the conception of language as relating the mind directly to the things of the external world. Thus far he was consistent with romantic theories of language since Leibniz, and with nominalism. However he also opposed the conventional historical approach to language that seemed irrelevant to the actual lived experience of the language community and the psychological reality of the language user at any given moment. He made

---

[11] Martha Wolfenstein, 'The Social Background of Taine's Philosophy of Art', *Journal of the History of Ideas*, 5 (1944), 332–58, here 337.

[12] Translated and criticized in Jacques Derrida, *Writing and Difference*, ed. Alan Bass (London: Routledge, 2005), 53.

[13] Thomas R. Flynn, *Sartre, Foucault and Historical Reason*, vol. 1 (Chicago: University of Chicago Press, 1997), 246–7. For further remarks as to the role of artisanal historians in undermining the myths of philosophical History, see Michel Foucault 'Discourse on Language' (1971) published as appendix to Foucault, *The Archaeology of Knowledge* (New York: Pantheon, 1972), 215–37, here 230; and the quotations in Flynn, *Sartre, Foucault and Historical Reason*, vol. 2, (Chicago: University of Chicago Press, 2005), 50–51, 115–16. On Maitland and Sidgwick, Wormald, *Legal Culture*, 60–1.

the comparison between economic and linguistic systems that were not just transactional but value-creating. Meanings are generated by language itself, by syntax (word order), grammar, and relations of opposition (left versus right, etc.). Given the highly contextual, web-like quality of meaning-production, one could not actually dissociate the expression of an ostensibly simple 'matter of fact' or a 'truth of reason' from all of the other conventional understandings that structured the intelligibility of the proposition.[14]

Why spend so much time on a linguistic theory? Because structuralist principles were later adopted in the human sciences well beyond the discipline of linguistics: indeed they were adopted there even as they were being challenged in linguistics. Saussure himself had thought to develop a general theory of semiotics on the principle that language was only the most obvious system of signs by which humans made sense of the world and oriented their behaviour. A more general semiotics (the study of sign-systems) sheds light on the unspoken but omnipresent set of taboos, prompts, and community-specific forms of expression, from facial markings to eating rituals to architectural forms, that make up the thing we call a culture. The anthropologist Claude Lévi-Strauss asked this question, to which his answer was positive: 'Although they belong to *another order of reality*, kinship phenomena are *of the same type* as linguistic phenomena. Can the anthropologist, using a method analogous *in form* (if not in content) to the method used in structural linguistics, achieve the same kind of progress in his own science as that which has taken place in linguistics?'[15] This marked the advent of structuralist anthropology, as against Boas's historicist anthropology. Moreover, structuralism fed a general intellectual atmosphere that was already receptive to broadly similar ideas. Structuralism has some similarities with, and possibly roots in, the side of Kant's thought that dealt with the transcendental ego, with its focus on structures shaping the cognitive faculties that were brought to bear on the phenomenal world. Forms of psychology bear comparison to structuralism too, in the idea of a subconscious influencing conscious behaviour. Structuralism can also be seen as analogous to the Marxist concept of relations of production defining social (class) arrangements, i.e. the economic base determining the socio-cultural superstructure, but also in the mutually constituting nature of oppositions/relations (left–right, bourgeoisie–proletariat). In each case some subterranean force shapes surface enunciations, as when Herbert Butterfield criticized Namier for explanatory resort to a vague but determinant underlying 'structure of politics'.[16]

---

[14] On truths of fact and truths of reason see Willard Van Orman Quine, 'Two Dogmas of Empiricism', *The Philosophical Review*, 60 (1951), 20–43.

[15] Claude Lévi-Strauss, *Structural Anthropology* (New York: Basic Books, 1963 [orig 1958]), 34. Emphases in original.

[16] Butterfield, *George III and the Historians*, cited in Paul Franco, *Michael Oakeshott: An Introduction* (New Haven: Yale University Press, 2004), 138.

However, such analogies only work so far. Kant's transcendental ego has to go by the board along with anything else resembling a universal structure of reason: under structuralism, while there is a purely formal similarity of law-giving structures across all cultures and language, substantively there is no way of comparing language X or culture Y with an overarching supracultural standard. Structuralism therefore has strong relativist connotations, and indeed from the mid-twentieth century structuralist relativism reinforced the relativist connotations of classical historicism even as classical historicism was discredited by the world wars. Lévi-Strauss wrote of the role of myths, in creating a sense of cultural discontinuity 'by the radical elimination of certain fractions of the continuum'; 'a discrete [cultural] system is produced by the destruction of certain elements or their removal from the original whole'.[17] The same idea applied diachronically too, judging by Lévi-Strauss's criticism of certain sorts of History as giving a false sense of continuity across time.[18] Sharper differentiation across time as well as place is the essence of neo-historicism, as this book calls it.

Something is also lost in the analogy of psychological theory and structuralism. In order to render mental material malleable enough to accord with structuralism without remainder, Lévi-Strauss had to evacuate on one hand any element of recalcitrant individual uniqueness à la Jung, and on the other hand any of the innate, universal drives that Freud conceived.[19] Similarly, the strength of the analogy with Marxism varies according to the type of Marxism chosen. Those who think less in terms of the determination of the superstructure by the base, and more in terms of the interpenetration or reciprocal influence of the two elements, will find the analogy less satisfactory. Where Marxism of any sort (and psychoanalysis) differs from structuralism is that it purports not just to describe but to diagnose and where possible amend. Nonetheless, the spirit—less often the letter—of structuralist, psychological, and Marxist thought is in evidence in so much of what was novel in twentieth-century occidental historianship.

Marxist-inspired History made significant inroads from the margins after the Bolshevik revolution. Marx's historian followers have increasingly discarded Marx the dialectical philosopher of History but regard Marx the historian, economist, and sociologist as having created important analytical tools. In the USA the early influence of Marxism showed itself in the diluted form of the 'progressive' New History. In the UK, the development of social History was shaped in the interwar period by a group of interdisciplinary left-wing historians, social scientists, and policymakers at the London School of Economics, that product of

---

[17] Claude Lévi-Strauss, *The Raw and the Cooked* (Harmondsworth: Penguin, 1986), 52–3: my attention was drawn to this passage by Gillian Gillison, 'From Cannibalism to Genocide: The Work of Denial', *The Journal of Interdisciplinary History*, 37:3 (2007), 395–414, here 412.

[18] Claude Lévi-Strauss, *The Savage Mind* (London: Weidenfeld and Nicolson, 1966), 256–64.

[19] Gillison, 'From Cannibalism to Genocide', 411–13.

Fabian social democratic principles.[20] The cohort including the medievalist Eileen Power, R. H. Tawney, Barbara Hammond, J. L. Hammond, Beatrice Webb, Sidney Webb, and G. D. H. Cole stand comparison with any in Britain before or since.

Alongside the 'English historians', Foucault named Marc Bloch and Lucien Febvre as having dealt a mortal blow to 'history as philosophy', which brings us to the *Annales* school and its relationship to psychology and structuralism. From the 1920s–1930s under Bloch's and Febvre's leadership the *Annales* scholars embraced a whole range of intellectual approaches and methodologies that, in combination, supposedly opened the way to *histoire totale*, a History of the totality of the inputs—or contexts—shaping human experience. These early *Annalistes*, as they have been called, put particular emphasis on the deeper structures of reality, but for them these structures were not metaphysical, as with Hegel and Ranke, but were rather psychological and material, and even sometimes quite literally elemental—geological, or geographical.[21]

In exposing all these levels and their relations, the *Annalistes* could draw on an impressive new range of techniques developed in the sciences and social sciences, but it merits emphasis that Bloch and Febvre still saw a suitably revised History as the master discipline, and in that sense followed in Ranke's footsteps even though he had exemplified a different approach. This iteration of the battle between History and the social sciences had been joined well before the 1920s: around the turn of the century Paul Lacombe and François Simiand stood against Seignobos as they enjoined History to become concerned with the normal, the general, and the predictable rather than the idiographic.[22] The *Annalistes* adopted some of Simiand's proposed topics and methods, including an enhanced focus on the rule-bound and repetitive rather than the unique, the social rather than the individual, with the use of modelling and collaborative research products to gather and process the relevant data, but they worked to ensure that History remained the unifying discipline.[23]

This goal perforce implied that History and sociology could/should not be identical or otherwise it was merely a matter of semantics as to which of the two prevailed. One way in which the disciplines could sometimes be distinguished is by reflection on Durkheim's claim that once History raised itself above the study

---

[20] Maxine Berg, *A Woman in History: Eileen Power 1889–1940* (Cambridge: Cambridge University Press, 1996), 162 ff.

[21] e.g. Lucien Febvre, *Philippe II et la Franche-Comté* (Paris, Champion, 1912), esp. ch. 1 for the geographical context; Febvre, *La Terre et l'évolution humaine: Introduction géographique à l'histoire* (Paris: La Renaissance du Livre, 1922).

[22] Charles Seignobos, *La Méthode historique appliquée aux science sociales* (Paris: Alcan, 1901); cf. Paul Lacombe *L'Histoire considérée comme science* (Paris: Hachette, 1894) and François Simiand, 'Méthode historique et science sociale', *Revue de Synthèse historique*, 6 (1903) 1–22, 129–57.

[23] François Dosse, *New History in France: The Triumph of the Annales* (Chicago: University of Illinois Press, 1994) 13 ff.; Hartog, 'Von der Universalgeschichte', point 11.

of unique particularities it was already a social science. For all of their adoption of social scientific methods and suspicion of high political History it is not clear that the *Annalistes* were moving from the particular to the general in the way Durkheim commended. One might just as well say that they had larger-scale particulars in mind, since geography, geology, and deep structures of belief were not the same everywhere, and the historians in question did not seek to abstract away from those particularities so as to create a general, lawmaking science of humankind, or even of humankind at particular stages of development. Bloch himself was an early advocate of comparative History, though comparison may be concerned as much with differences as similarities. Works like his *Les Caractères originaux de l'histoire rurale française*,[24] however bold in scope, still had a high level of specificity as to the (three) types of agrarian community in France, and the influence of these patterns over centuries into the French present, with the implication that France was different in that respect to, say, the British present. Finally, however long the spans of time with which *Annalistes* concerned themselves, they still took the temporal, processual element seriously, and did not deal in the timeless models characteristic of structural linguistics or econometrics.

The *Annalistes* rejected as subjective and unsystematic any concept of History as the study of individual meaningful actions and events embedded in contingent causal sequences, phenomena whose character was only ascertainable through the lens of a potentially infinite number of actor-perceptions as to their 'meaning'. With their focus ranging from the early development of the capitalist system to topography through the full range of subjects studied by the human sciences in their broadest definitions, the *Annalistes* were above all concerned with the overarching, or perhaps underpinning, environmental, economic, psychological, technical, and social frameworks within which different peoples lived. All this helps explain Bloch's opposition to moral evaluation of individuals who partook of broader '*mentalités*', which were a creation of forces beyond their comprehension and which comprised the condition of their consciousness rather than being its creation. The contrast is sharp with the prevailing orthodoxies of the historical discipline at the outset of the twentieth century, when political History accounted for more than half of all French History theses and biographical studies for more than 30 per cent.[25] In other countries political History was yet more dominant.

The concept *mentalité*, nearer in determinative strength to 'episteme' than '*Zeitgeist*', and partly defined against intellectual 'ideas', is the product of Febvre's call for 'historical psychology', and perhaps also of Bloch's experience of collective behaviour during the First World War. As in Georges Lefebvre's *The Great Fear of 1789* (1932),[26] on popular unrest in the build-up to the French Revolution, the

---

[24] Oslo: Aschehoug, 1931.   [25] Dosse, *New History in France*, 13.
[26] Georges Lefebvre, *La Grande Peur de 1789* (Paris: Armand Colin, 1932).

notion of *mentalité* leans on positivistic concepts like Gustav Le Bon's 'psychology of the crowd' or Karl Lamprecht's *Massenpsychologie*,[27] and on Durkheim's ideas of collective psychology and collective representations. Only to a significantly lesser degree does it draw on Freud's work, and then more on his thoughts on mass psychology. We see *mentalité* at work in Bloch's *Les Rois thaumaturges* (1924),[28] where he sought to explain beliefs in medieval France and England that monarchs could cure scrofula and other diseases by their touch. Alongside examination of the rites and symbols associated with this supernatural power, and of the function of the royal claim to possess it (i.e. legitimation of royal power, including against Rome, by association with the divine), Bloch launched a critique of latter-day scholars who had sought to provide 'rational' explanations of the royal touch that made sense according to the lights of those scholars—for instance explanations to the effect that medieval people were confused in their understandings. *Mentalité* was also under investigation in Febvre's enquiry into the very possibility of atheism in the climate of thought prevailing in sixteenth-century France, *The Problem of Unbelief in the Sixteenth Century*.[29] Lévi-Strauss offered an assessment of that book's major contributions, in support of his observation that while

> the anthropologist applies his analysis primarily to the unconscious elements of social life, it would be absurd to suppose that the historian remains unaware of them... Thus any good history book (and we shall cite a great one) is saturated with anthropology... Febvre constantly refers to psychological attitudes and logical structures which can be grasped only indirectly because they have always eluded the consciousness of those who spoke and wrote—for example, the lack of terminology and standards of measurement, vague representation of time, traits common to several different techniques, and so forth. All these pertain to anthropology as well as to history, for they transcend documents and informants' accounts, none of which deals with this level, and rightly so.[30]

Lévi-Strauss also observed that economic History often dealt preponderantly in terms of unconscious, structural causation,[31] and while *Annales* scholarship was important in the interwar rise of economic History it was by no means uniquely so. The *Economic History Review*, coedited by Tawney and Ephraim Lipson, was first published two years before the initial edition of the journal *Annales d'histoire économique et sociale* (later *Annales: économies, sociétés, civilisation*). The inaugural edition of the former celebrated the fact that the International Congress of

[27] André Burguière, *L'École des Annales. Une histoire intellectuelle* (Paris: Odile Jacob, 2006), 42–3.
[28] Strasbourg: Istra, 1924.
[29] Lucien Febvre, *Le Problème de l'incroyance au XVIe siècle* (Paris: Albin Michel, 1942).
[30] Lévi-Strauss, *Structural Anthropology*, 23–4.   [31] Ibid.

Historical Studies had had an economic section for some time. The influence of German nineteenth-century historical economics was noted, alongside the work of Pirenne, French studies of the impact of the French Revolution on local economic life, and, in Britain, the work of Arnold Toynbee senior (1852–83).[32]

It may be that economic History benefited in popularity from the same tendencies that boosted intellectual History between the wars (though not in the work of the early *Annalistes*), as the study of high politics and diplomacy came under the same sort of critique as the high politicians who had led the continent into destruction.[33] But the stock market crash of 1929 guaranteed greater attention to impersonal economic forces, and by coincidence the *Annales* journal was first published in that year. In a famous 1933 book, Ernst Labrousse deployed quantitative methodology to gauge the movement of prices and revenue in eighteenth-century France,[34] and capitalized on the immediate interest in the present conjuncture and the enduring interest in the causes of the French Revolution. His was only the best known of a number of investigations into the history of economic fluctuations at the time from the very first issue of *Annales* onwards, and in the work of Simiand.[35]

Structures and Events

Labrousse juxtaposed long-term societal 'structures' with shorter-term 'conjunctures', and in so doing introduced to modern historiography a conceptual division of timespans, the most famous of which was a tripartite model proposed by Fernand Braudel. Braudel's *longue durée* was the measure of 'geographical time', measured against the glacially slow movement of the natural environment, but also against civilizations as understood in the very broadest sense: the sense by which we might speak of a Christian civilization that stretches from the patristic age to the present. Then came 'social time' of the sort indicated by Labrousse's 'structures' or Fustel's and Durkheim's institutions, measured as it was by the lifespan of socio-economic and technological structures and *mentalités*. Then we have 'individual time' measured against the doings of particular people and

---

[32] William Ashley, 'The Place of Economic History in University Studies', *The Economic History Review*, 1:1 (1927), 1–11.

[33] D. R. Woolf, 'The Writing of Early Modern European Intellectual History, 1945–1995', in Bentley (ed.), *Companion to Historiography*, 307–35, here 309.

[34] Ernst Labrousse, *Esquisse du mouvement des prix et des revenues en France au XVIIIe siècle* (Paris: Dalloz, 1933).

[35] François Simiand, *Les Fluctuations économiques à longue période et la crise mondiale* (Paris: Alcan 1932); Simiand, *Recherches anciennes et nouvelles sur le mouvement général des prix du VXIe au XIXe siècle* (Paris: Domat-Montchrestien, 1932). For the *Annales* journal, merely consult the contents pages.

groups in the sphere of 'events', happenings—the sort of thing constituting the focus of what Lacombe and Simiand called *l'histoire événementielle*.[36]

The significance of 'événements' varied slightly between *Annalistes*. Some implied that these 'events' had causal significance but only within the confines set by the structures corresponding to the longer timescales. Sometimes 'events' appeared less as causes in their own right than as symptoms of changes on the deeper levels, which is where a quite strong affinity with the subterranean causation of structuralism is evident: Braudel compared them to 'surface disturbances, crests of foam that the tides of history carry on their strong backs'.[37] Only in 1974 did the Annales-affiliated cultural historian Pierre Nora announce a concerted return to the 'event', though not loudly enough for the philosopher Jacques Rancière, who issued his own grand summons in 1992.[38] By that time, as it happens, French philosophy had developed a major specialism in the contemplation of 'events', spurred on by the unpredicted *événements* of May 1968 and the clarion call 'structures don't take to the streets'.[39]

Note the quotation-marks around 'events'. Events could only ever have disappeared from *Annales* scholarship if they were defined in a particular way, generally in the sense of something like political events of a special, ostensibly status-quo-disturbing nature, or in the sense of products of individual agency, as in what Braudel dismissed as Treitschke's 'proud and unilateral declaration: "men make history"'.[40] Yet such definitions of the event are arbitrary. Think of the concepts with which 'events', less arbitrarily defined, might be contrasted. 'Processes' is one possibility, but then we might just as well say that all events are themselves processual, and all processes can be broken down into constituent events. 'Continuity' is another, but then we should remember that continuities are not characterized by nothingness but by acts/events/processes of reproduction and repetition. 'Structures' is another, but then we see that structures are themselves constructed and modified processually, i.e. event-fully. The final possibility, and the only one that really works as a contrast, is to define events not against substantive *structures* in the sense of prisons or bureaucracies or even coastlines and climates, but against the purely formal, abstract, timeless relations idealized in the doctrine of *structuralism*. Clearly enough this is not the contrast Braudel was making. Even Braudel's *longue durée* is still a *durée*. As he well knew it was not

[36] Fernand Braudel, *The Mediterranean and the Mediterranean World in the Age of Philip II*, vol. 1 (London: Collins, 1972 [orig. 1949]), 21.
[37] Ibid.
[38] Pierre Nora, 'Le Retour de l'événement', in Jacques Le Goff and Pierre Nora (eds.), *Faire de l'histoire*, 3 vols. (Paris, Gallimard, 1974), I, 285–308; Jacques Rancière, *Les Mots de l'histoire. Essai de poétique du savoir* (Paris, Seuil, 1992).
[39] François Dosse, *History of Structuralism*, vol. 2: *The Sign Sets, 1967–Present* (Minneapolis: University of Minnesota Press, 1998), 116.
[40] Fernand Braudel, *On History* (Chicago: University of Chicago Press, 1980), 10.

timeless: coastlines erode by myriad event-ful processes; climates change likewise.[41]

Foucault stressed that 'events' had not really disappeared in the salient historical scholarship:

> We frequently credit contemporary history with having removed the individual event from its privileged position and with having revealed the more enduring structures of history....I do not think one can oppose the identification of the individual event to the analysis of long term trends quite so neatly. On the contrary, it seems to me that it is in squeezing the individual event, in directing the resolving power of historical analysis onto official price-lists (mercuriales), title deeds, parish registers, to harbour archives analysed year by year and week by week, that we gradually perceive—beyond battles, decisions, dynasties and assemblies—the emergence of those massive phenomena of secular or multi-secular importance. History, as it is practised today, does not turn its back on events; on the contrary, it is continually enlarging the field of events...[42]

If the relationship of events and structures needs clarification, confusion may also arise over the relationship of structures to structuralism, though what is at issue is merely a semantic similarity. Structuralism pertains to elements in an interrelated system; those elements may be structures in the substantive sense, but simply talking about structures is not to subscribe to structuralism, and as soon as one attends to the specificities/contents of substantive structures one has already shifted emphasis away from the precepts of structuralism with its emphasis on the productive quality of relations between elements. It does, however, help to explain the prominence of 'the event' in French philosophy in the second half of the twentieth century if we see it as something conceived as in ontological contradiction to 'the system' or whatever is seen as the underlying determinant of the social order—as if that order were not itself the product of event-ful processes, or as if there were some difference in metaphysical kind between 'the event' and those other events.

Whatever the difference between talk of structures and of structuralism, structuralism's inability to account for change is related to its lack of interest in historical analysis, but also to the coherence that it implies for any given order as it stands. On the whole, historical thought influenced by structuralism tends either to ignore change, via static descriptions, or posits some revolution-like eruption in a way that may be inspired by Marxist thought. Beyond adapting Weberian

---

[41] See Braudel's awareness of the contestableness of his definition of 'event': Fernand Braudel, *The Mediterranean and the Mediterranean World in the Age of Philip II*, vol. 2 (Berkeley: University of California Press, 1995), 1243.

[42] Foucault, 'The Discourse on Language', 230.

legal-rationalization theory in his work on disciplinary institutions,[43] Foucault was not strong at accounting for the *why* of the inception of new structures of thought and their accompanying practices even as he was preoccupied with showing the *what* of the changes that had been wrought—see *The Birth of the Clinic*, 1963; *Discipline and Punish: The Birth of the Prison*, 1975. That which A. J. Rowse said of Bolingbroke's *Letters on History* is roughly true of Foucault in his work on historical epochs: 'he thinks of successive periods as a series of water-tight compartments, with nothing to account for the transition from one to another except catastrophes or breakdowns.'[44] The same could go for talk of revolution: in the study of scientific History, Gaston Bachelard, who was one of Foucault's great influences, talked of periodic 'epistemic ruptures', prefiguring the work of Thomas S. Kuhn, whose work *The Structure of Scientific Revolutions*[45] met the challenge of a theory of change from one scientific 'paradigm' to another—say from Aristotelian to classical mechanics, or Euclidean to non-Euclidean geometry. These paradigms had more than a passing resemblance to what Foucault called epistemes, though they were more narrowly disciplinary in applicability, which also gave them some similarity to what Foucault was to call 'discourses'. Kuhn laid equal emphasis on the pull exerted on scientists by the paradigm and on the infrequent 'revolutionary' moments when one 'paradigm' was put under enough explanatory stress to lead (unforeseeably) to its replacement by another.

Associations of 'the event' with rupture, revolution, and so forth, help us to explain Braudel's turn away from the political sphere. Braudel's choice of focus was itself political, in much the same way as were Fustel's and Monod's prescriptions for the historical discipline in the aftermath of the Franco-Prussian war. While *The Mediterranean* was published in 1949, most of the work had gone into it in the interwar period in which France was concerned with sustaining peace at home and in Europe. Braudel sought unity and an end to the social antagonisms fuelled by Marxism or the event-centric political History that had traditionally been so divided over the meaning of the French Revolution. Where Bloch had issued a ban on moral judgement in historiography, Braudel cautioned distrust of that 'traditional history' of events 'with its still burning passions , as it was felt, described, and lived by contemporaries whose lives were as short and as short-sighted as ours'.[46] To contemplate the undercurrents over a long period was to perceive a world of slower, evolutionary change in which people's differences mattered less than they tended to think. This was a 'French' doctrine of

[43] John O'Neill, 'The Disciplinary Society: From Weber to Foucault', *British Journal of Sociology*, 37:1 (1987), 42–60.

[44] A. J. Rowse, *The Use of History* (Harmondsworth: Pelican, 1971), 85.

[45] Chicago: University of Chicago Press, 1961.

[46] Braudel, *The Mediterranean*, vol. 1, p. 21. On moral judgement, Marc Bloch, *The Historian's Craft* (New York: Vintage Books, 1953 [French orig. 1949]), 139, 142.

continuity that differed in certain respects from the classical historicist 'German' doctrine of the same.

Braudel realized that the broader the historical canvas upon which one wishes to paint, the less significant individual or even collective agency will seem, up to the point where the individual and even the war or revolution is erased entirely. But it is just a matter of choice as to whether one focuses most of one's energy on addressing the *longue durée* or on shorter ones, on the impersonal or the personal—neither approach reveals 'the truth about history' as a process. The answer one gets is a function of the question one has set oneself, and there is no intrinsic hierarchy of importance of such questions. Nor is there any inherent incompatibility in studying different *durées*. Bloch's study of feudalism certainly seems to have little to do with the later *microstoria* or 'microhistory' of Carlo Ginzburg and Natalie Zemon Davis, and indeed microhistory was a reaction to the vast sweep of earlier *Annales* scholarship. But the microhistorians had an eye on the bigger picture, however ostensibly small their focus, on the principle that a case study well conducted can cast wider light whether its focus is on a civilization, a sixteenth-century Friulian miller (Ginzburg, *The Cheese and the Worms*, 1976) or an impostor in a Pyrénéan village of the same period (Davis, *The Return of Martin Guerre*, 1983). Giovanni Levi, author of *The Immaterial Inheritance: Career of an Exorcist in Seventeenth-Century Piedmont* (1985), wrote of his desire to 'address a more complex social structure without losing sight of the individual's social space and hence, of people and their situation in life', noting that the 'minutest detail/ action of say somebody buying a loaf of bread actually encompasses the far wider system of the whole world's grain market'.[47] Writing in the 1990s, Hans Medick claimed that his local history of the Swabian village of Laichingen from 1650 to 1900 could be a 'micro-historically grounded' form of 'general History' (*allgemeine Geschichte*).[48] Braudel's student Emmanuel le Roy Ladurie navigated between the macro level, with his study of the peasants of the Languedoc from the fifteenth to the eighteenth centuries, and the meso level, with his account of a single village over thirty years.[49] The concept of *mentalité* guided a number of these scholars, though they would differ amongst themselves and with other microhistorians as to the relationship between *mentalité* and the individual capacity for reflection and agency. On the whole, the sharper the focus on

---

[47] Giovanni Levi, 'On Microhistory', in Peter Burke (ed.), *New Perspectives on Historical Writing* (University Park: Pennsylvania State University Press, 1992), 93–113, here 99, 104; Giovanni Levi, *L'Eredità Immaterial: Carriera di un Exorcista nel Piemonte del Seicento* (Turin: Einaudi, 1985); Carlo Ginzburg, *The Cheese and the Worms: The Cosmos of a Sixteenth-Century Miller* (London: Routledge, 1980 [Italian orig. 1976]); Natalie Zemon Davis, *The Return of Martin Guerre*, (Cambridge, MA: Harvard University Press, 1983).

[48] Hans Medick, *Weben und Überleben in Laichingen, 1650–1900: Lokalgeschichte als Allgemeine Geschichte* (Göttingen: Vandenhoeck & Ruprecht, 1996), 13.

[49] Emmanuel le Roy Ladurie, *Les Paysans de Languedoc*, 2 vols. (Paris: Mouton, 1966); *Montaillou, village occitan de 1294 à 1324* (Paris: Gallimard, 1975).

individual lives, the greater the impression of agency and of the capacity for
self-fashioning.

From Interwar to Post-War

Allied victory in 1945 ensured the continued rise of the *Annales* as an institution,
though it was only in the 1970s with English language translations of the major
works that its influence thoroughly percolated the American academy. While the
editorial philosophies of the journal changed somewhat along with personnel,
maintaining a distance from the emotions of contemporary politics was a consistent feature of the *Annales* ethos from Bloch through Braudel and Ladurie. This
ethos chimed with 'Weberian' neutralism even while it had its own distinct
genealogy. Both stances met with a full-frontal challenge in the political circumstances of the time. In France, as elsewhere, the Second World War and then the
advent of the Cold War ignited further History wars along the lines of political
identity.[50]

As around the 1914–18 conflict, the issue of moral righteousness came to the
fore for professional historians as well as politicians. In the USA in 1949 the president of the American Historical Association enjoined historians to enlist in 'total
war', supporting certain values as absolute, and censoring themselves by the recognition that some historical matters were not 'appropriate for broadcasting at
street corners'.[51] Writing in 1952, the American historian of slavery Kenneth
Stampp noted the ongoing debate within his country's historical profession
between 'scientific' and 'subjectivist-relativist-presentist' schools as to the validity
of moral judgement in works of History.[52] In Britain in the decade from 1953,
Toynbee, Isaiah Berlin, Geoffrey Barraclough, C. V. Wedgwood, David Knowles,
and E. H. Carr pitched into the same argument. Herbert Butterfield held fairly
constantly to the nuanced anti-judgementalism that he had established before the
advent of Nazism.[53] A chasm separates the agendas of Braudel's *Mediterranean* or
Laudurie's *Paysans de Languedoc* on one hand and on the other hand those of
Germany's Hans Rothfels and his British counterpart Barraclough as they set

[50] Pieter Lagrou, *The Legacy of Nazi Occupation: Patriotic Memory and National Recovery in
Western Europe, 1945–1965* (Cambridge: Cambridge University Press, 2000).

[51] Conyers Read, 'The Social Responsibilities of the Historian', *American Historical Review*, 55
(1949–50), 275-85, here 283–4.

[52] Novick, *That Noble Dream*, 351.

[53] Arnold Toynbee, 'The Writing of Contemporary History for Chatham House', *International
Affairs*, 29:2 (April, 1953), 137–40; Isaiah Berlin, *Historical Inevitability* (London: Oxford University
Press, 1954), 30–53; Geoffrey Barraclough, *History in a Changing World* (Norman, OK: University of
Oklahoma Press, 1956), 1–7; Barraclough, 'History, Morals, and Politics', *International Affairs*, 34:1
(1958), 1–15; C. V. Wedgwood, *Truth and Opinion: Historical Essays* (London: Collins, 1960), 47–54;
E. H. Carr, *What Is History?* (New York: Knopf, 1962), 75–6; David Knowles, *The Historian and
Character* (Cambridge: Cambridge University Press, 1963), 12–15.

about entrenching 'contemporary History' as a discrete object of study, building on interwar foundations set by such as the French historian Ernest Lavisse.[54] Barraclough rejected the more longitudinal cultural relativism of classical historicism and its emphasis on continuity: he was another student of rupture, of 'the fortuitous and the unforeseen...the new, the dynamic and the revolutionary, which breaks through untrammelled by the past, at every great turning-point in human history'. This view lent itself to a periodization based on 'when the problems which are actual in the world today first take visible shape'.[55] The years 1890-1960 were a whole in this respect, he felt—even if he did not reserve the title 'contemporary history' for that period. Such a periodization had a significant overlap with the era of the World Wars and totalitarianism that most of Europe's other new 'contemporary historians' took, and often still take, as their centre of historical gravity.[56] Given Rothfels's view of Nazism as a totalitarian interruption of the course of Germany history (p. 243), contemporary History for him began around the First World War, the chaotic aftermath of which provided the ground for takeover by demagoguery. Rothfels became the first director of Munich's Institute for Contemporary History, which from 1953 published the Vierteljahreshefte für Zeitgeschichte, the Contemporary History Quarterly.

Given the international context from the late 1940s onwards, the left–right division was inevitably central to so much political debate, yet the constitution of that division was in flux. The philosopher Stephen Toulmin once observed that the political dissenter in the present tends to be a moral critic, and this is borne out to some degree in the world of historians by the stance of leftwingers (broadly speaking) like R. H. Tawney alongside Toynbee.[57] Likewise there is a rough correlation on the other side of the argument with historians of conservative political persuasion warning their fellows against allowing any presentist concern to contaminate historical study or simply enjoining them, as did H. S. Commager in his The Search for a Usable Past (1967), to 'refrain from the folly and vanity of moral righteousness about the past'.[58] 'Conservatives' could be of the left or the right, however, depending on which enjoyed hegemony. Given cultural retrenchment in the north-west, wars of decolonization and imperial aggression by the capitalist states, and Soviet imperial repression in Hungary and then Czechoslovakia, both

[54] Ernest Lavisse (ed.), Histoire de France contemporaine, depuis la revolution jusqu'à la paix de 1919, 10 vols. (Paris: Hachette, 1920–2).

[55] Geoffrey Barraclough, 'The Historian in a Changing World', in Hans Meyerhoff (ed.), The Philosophy of History in Our Time (New York: Doubleday, 1959), 28–35, here 30–2; Barraclough, Introduction to Contemporary History (Harmondsworth: Penguin, 1967), 20.

[56] Kristina Spohr Readman, 'Contemporary History in Europe', Journal of Contemporary History, 46:3 (2011), 506–30.

[57] Stephen Toulmin, The Place of Reason in Ethics (Cambridge: Cambridge University Press, 1950), 171, 223.

[58] Bédarida, 'The Modern Historian's Dilemma', 339–40. H. S. Commager, The Search for a Usable Past (New York: Knopf, 1967), 316.

old left and right looked like the forces of repression to the 'revolutionaries' of the 1960s.

The social upheavals of the Sixties made due impact on the mainstreams of western professional historiography, though the themes of rights, repression, and liberation were taken up in the first instance more at the margins of the academy. As to the influence of social scientific theories, those that were most evident in the mainstream historical work of the 1960s and 1970s were precisely the ones that the conflicts of 1968 brought into question.

Social History, Sociology, Modernization

In the mid-1950s Richard Hofstadter wrote that 'the most important function which the social sciences can perform for the historian is that they provide means...by which he can be brought into working relationship with certain aspects of the modern intellectual climate'.[59] By modern thought he meant the sort of thing celebrated by his fellow historian Thomas C. Cochran around the same time when Cochran said that 'at the center of any comprehensive and meaningful synthesis, determining its topical and chronological divisions, should be the material and psychological changes that have most affected, or threatened most to affect, such human conditioning factors as family life, physical living conditions, choice of occupations, sources of prestige, and fundamental beliefs'.[60]

Hofstadter may have known that his criticism as to 'means' was not valid for *Annales* historiography of the time, and from the 1970s that French influence shaped the 'intellectual climate' of American historiography, as did American sociology. However, this was no radical hybridization since both *Annales* scholarship and US sociology had Durkheimian lineages. Furthermore, French–American intellectual cross-fertilization in the field had been encouraged in order to counter French anti-Americanism by such means as the Ford Foundation's grant for the establishment of the *Maison des sciences de l'homme* in 1959.

Hofstadter and Cochran were speaking to an American audience of historians who still overwhelmingly practised political History, though their points about absences pertained equally to mainstream British and German historiography of the time. Historicism had dealt in terms of monads rather than laws, of unique individual entities and the grandest wholes, but even as it tried to hold the part and the whole in balance, it maintained the dichotomy, leaving the middle ground to the social scientists. The 'comparatively constant' was the purview of the sorts

---

[59] Richard Hofstadter, 'History and the Social Sciences', in Stern (ed.), *Varieties of History*, 359–70, here 363.

[60] Thomas C. Cochran, 'The Social Sciences and the Problem of Historical Synthesis', in Stern (ed.), *Varieties of History*, 348–59, here 357.

of social scientists on whom historians could most fruitfully draw. This was the realm of approximate similarities and recurrences, whether in forms of governance or economy, or patterns of elite or mass behaviour. Scholars might also make lawlike generalizations delimited by temporal or cultural boundaries, building on the Weberian ideal type.[61] The American economic historian Alexander Gerschenkron, who had been trained in Austrian-school economics with its anti-historicist doctrine, described historical research as 'application to empirical material of various sets of empirically derived hypothetical generalizations and in testing the closeness of the resulting fit, in the hope that in this way certain uniformities, certain typical situations, and certain typical relationships among individual factors in those situations can be ascertained'. Cochran deployed a Braudelian idiom of political events as 'surface manifestations that are not of the highest importance' and so commended the study of threatened or realized deep 'material and psychological changes' in human patterns of life.[62] Whereas the French Revolution had once been a paradigm for political historiography and a point of contrast for the *Annalistes*, and whereas May 1968 was to become a paradigm for philosophical thought about resistance to authority, the new social historiography had 'modernization' as its paradigm.

Sociology's stock was already high in the USA as enhanced federal funding promoted a discipline that had suggested its utility during the New Deal and in wartime administration and would be needed for harmonious integration and the analysis of post-war ills. Equally important was the 'productivist' Fordism of the American economy, and its concern with societal regulation and predictability.[63] Talcott Parsons, the dominant sociologist of mid-century America, and another student of society persuaded by the utility of psychoanalysis, put his focus on the preconditions for stability, seeing abrupt or disorderly change as a sign of systemic dysfunction rather than the expression of emancipatory tendencies. In this intellectual environment, 'modernity' and 'modernization' were sociological buzzwords whereas unsurprisingly 'capitalism', dialectics, and the class struggle were not so fashionable. In some quarters 'class' was used less to denote position in the relations of production, and came to mean something more akin to the Weberian concept of 'status' in the sense of 'the relative position of actors or social groups in a subjectively defined hierarchy of honour and

[61] Helen P. Liebel, 'Philosophical Idealism in the *Historische Zeitschrift*, 1859–1914', *History and Theory*, 3:3 (1964), 316–30, here 330.
[62] Gerschenkron and Cochran quotes from Cochran, 'The Social Sciences', 348–9.
[63] George Steinmetz, 'American Sociology before and after World War Two', in Craig Calhoun (ed.), *Sociology in American: A History* (Chicago: University of Chicago Press, 2007), 314–66; Tony Judt, 'A Clown in Regal Purple: Social History and the Historians', *History Workshop Journal*, 1 (1979), 66–94, here 81; for History's interaction with social sciences in different countries, Passmore, 'History and Historiography since 1945'.

prestige'.[64] Attention was shifted from a contest-based dynamic to a sort of epochal succession with a rough similarity to Comte's or Condorcet's vision. Elements of neo-Comteanism were present in Walt W. Rostow's *Stages of Economic Growth: A Non-Communist Manifesto* (1960), which substituted nations for classes as historical actors, and industrialization for capitalism as that which demanded explanation. Rostow purported to have identified five phases through which all societies passed in the ascent from 'traditional' to 'modern' status. As it had been for Marx, Britain was an important case study for Rostow, even if he did not attribute to it quite the paradigmatic status that some historians of Britain were keen to impute to his work for the sake of validating their own interests. Whether received as evidence of Britain's pathbreaking for the modern world or further evidence that history was on the side of the USA, the modernization theory that Rostow so helped popularize allowed other developmental paths, principally of the socialist or the German *Sonderweg* sort, to be presented as unhealthy deviations from the ideal route.[65]

As it happens Britain constitutes a problematic focal point for any such study since it had been the major incubator of capitalism in the world and so, uniquely, never had to play the game of force-paced catch-up. Moreover when it came to contrasts between Britain and Germany, one had to be careful not to idealize Britain's institutional development in 'whiggish' fashion, or indeed underestimate the authoritarian qualities of any other nineteenth-century states with which Germany might be compared. Conversely, it was easy to stereotype Prussia and Germany's post-1848 trajectory as ineluctably authoritarian, to stress the alleged imbalance between the Kaiserreich's economic development and its 'pre-industrial' monarchical-aristocratic-militaristic political power structure, most of which supposedly survived into the Weimar republic, while ignoring the elements of political 'bourgeoisification' that did occur in the late nineteenth century and underplaying the novelty of the Nazi brand of right-wing politics and the circumstantial contingencies by which Hitler rose to power. Such criticisms were made by the British social historians David Blackbourn and Geoff Eley in their *Mythen deutscher Geschichtsschreibung* (1980), later revised and translated as *The Peculiarities of German History*, which questioned the very idea of a normative 'modernity' against which candidate countries should be measured.[66]

---

[64] Gareth Stedman Jones, 'From Historical Sociology to Theoretical History', *The British Journal of Sociology*, 27:3 (1976), 295–305, here 302.

[65] For Rostow's historiographical significance, Passmore, 'History and Historiography since 1945', 35–40. On misreadings of Rostow, Guy Ortolano, 'The Typicalities of the English? Walt Rostow, *The Stages of Economic Growth*, and British History', *Modern Intellectual History*, 12: 3 (2015), 657–84.

[66] David Blackbourn and Geoff Eley, *Mythen deutscher Geschichtsschreibung. Die gescheiterte bürgerliche Revolution von 1848* (Frankfurt am Mein: Ullstein, 1980); *The Peculiarities of German History: Bourgeois Society and Politics in Nineteenth Century Germany* (Oxford: Oxford University Press, 1984).

In most of the relevant sociological thought, 'modern' equated to industrial and urbanized, and 'modernizing' to industrializing and urbanizing. Given the focus on the crises and challenges of modernization, the History influenced by such sociology tended to address what Braudel called 'social time' rather than the *longue durée*, and generally sidelined the world before the middle of the eighteenth century—this was true for German as much as American historiography. The 'modern' and indeed contemporary focus also made some sense in a global perspective, since at that point new postcolonial states were trying to develop their own industries to keep afloat in a competitive international system, often from scratch. Politicians in those states, like some historians, also had their own nationalist reasons for presenting independence as a thoroughgoing caesura. Nonetheless there is a telling contrast between most of the sociological social History of the 1960–1970s and the work of Marxist historians like Rodney Hilton or Christopher Hill on the medieval and early modern periods respectively. They, and for different reasons a growing band of postcolonial theorists, would have recoiled from the traditional/modern dyad deployed by certain American social historians. In their work on women's labour and the family in nineteenth-century Europe Joan Wallach Scott and Louise Tilly used unproblematized Durkheimian concepts like 'traditional values' and 'traditional families', implicitly the binary opposite of 'modern' values and families as depicted in modernization theory.[67]

In the north-western academy, building on some *Annales* foundations, the 1960s–1970s saw a spate of modelling, regression analysis, quantification and aspirant-lawmaking that merits the epithet methodologically positivistic far more than does any Rankean History. The individual, the quixotic, and the political might find themselves submerged beneath objectively measurable trends, cohorts, and abstractions like the not always well defined 'society' and not always elaborated but scientific-sounding 'social structure'.[68] But one ought not to claim too much about methodology or for that matter political orientation—and the same goes for the historiographical tendencies against which social historians most often defined themselves.[69] The very real issues denoted by the term

---

[67] Joan W. Scott and Louise A. Tilly, 'Women's Work and the Family in Nineteenth-Century Europe', *Comparative Studies in Society and History*, 17:1 (1975), 36–64, here 42, 50. On traditional versus modern in modernization theory, Ortolano, 'The Typicalities of the English?', 658.

[68] On the final points, Jones, 'From Historical Sociology to Theoretical History', 301–2.

[69] These 'tendencies' are those of political historians. Take the case of political historians in Britain's historical profession, which had (has?) a reputation for theory-averseness. What was alleged as intellectual conservatism on the basis of focus of historical interest and method did not necessarily equate to political Conservatism—compare A. J. P. Taylor to Lewis Namier—and political Conservatives differed as much in their methods as Geoffrey Elton and Maurice Cowling. And note that in the German case, while we have seen on one hand that it was eminently possible to have very rightwing social historians, equally on the other hand it was not just social historians who took up cudgels against nationalist political historiography and the positive version of the *Sonderweg* thesis. Well before Wehler's contribution Fritz Fischer's *Griff nach der Weltmacht* (Düsseldorf: Droste, 1961), English translation *Germany's Aims in the First World War*, was amongst other things a study of political decisions, pressure groups, and decision-making resting on official documentation.

'modernization' defined much of the basic problematic, but how and with what motivations one picked up on any of the range of related topics varied greatly. One could be just as interested in explaining the social roots of rebellion as the social process of adjustment to new norms and practices.

On the methodological side, any given historian could combine competence in qualitative and quantitative skills, just as she or he might blend the approaches of *Erklären* and *Verstehen*: for one or both of these combinations see for instance the works of Ladurie, Scott and Tilly, Paul E. Johnson, William J. Sewell, Eric Hobsbawm, and George Rudé. And while quantification seemed to promise an objectivity lacking in hitherto dominant qualitative historical models, a proliferation of empirically rich 'small-N' comparisons marked the take-off of detailed comparative history after earlier prompts by Weber, Pirenne, and Bloch. A landmark in this respect was the establishment of the journal *Comparative Studies in Society and History* in 1958 by the social historian of the Middle Ages Sylvia Thrupp, a former student of Eileen Power. Theda Skocpol explained what a 'small-N' approach means, while exemplifying it in her discussion of the discontents of modernization in *States and Social Revolutions: A Comparative Analysis of France, Russia and China* (1979): 'the comparative method is nothing but that mode of multivariate analysis to which sociologists necessarily resort when experimental manipulations are not possible and when there are "too many variables and not enough cases"'. In her version of comparison, the comparativist 'looks for concomitant variations, contrasting cases where the phenomena in which one is interested are present with cases where they are absent, controlling in the process for as many sources of variation as one can, by contrasting positive and negative instances which otherwise are as similar as possible'. So the cases of Japan, Germany, and pre-1905 Russia were studied as contrasting instances of 'non-social revolutionary modernization'. For all the social-scientific verbiage, Skocpol recorded her determination to read extensively on the Histories of her chosen countries prior to engaging the sociological models of revolution, of which she was suspicious.[70] Her comparative method was influential on important historians, though we should not forget alternative comparative approaches.[71] She herself was a historical sociologist, and that breed was probably at its most influential in the 1960s–1970s by virtue of her work and that of Barrington Moore,

---

[70] Skocpol, *Social Revolutions in the Modern World* (Cambridge: Cambridge University Press, 1994), 135; *States and Social Revolutions: A Comparative Analysis of France, Russia, and China* (Cambridge: Cambridge University Press, 1979), preface.

[71] On both Skocpol's influence and alternative models, Mary Fulbrook, *Piety and Politics: Religion and the Rise of Absolutism in England, Württemberg and Prussia* (Cambridge: Cambridge University Press, 1983), 184–6. On the interface between the work of many historians and historical sociologists, and the range of comparative models, Theda Skocpol, 'Emerging Agendas and Current Strategies in Historical Sociology', in Skocpol (ed.), *Vision and Method in Historical Sociology* (Cambridge: Cambridge University Press, 1994), 356–91.

Reinhard Bendix, Shmuel Eisenstadt, Immanuel Wallerstein, Seymour Martin Lipset and Stein Rokkan, Hugo Heclo, and Charles Tilly.[72]

It is also important to stress that in the absence of a comparable quality of source material to that enabling, say, Ranke's lives of the popes, or Burckhardt's high cultural study of the Renaissance, the social historian's embracing quantitative methods entailed no necessary denial of the human element. See, for instance, the work on patterns of family life, *The World We Have Lost*,[73] by Peter Laslett, who was a founding member of the Cambridge Group for the History of Population and Social Structure. Given the available sources, often specific *meaning* could only be inferred from general patterns of social behaviour, and given disparities of power, *purposes* could only be significantly pursued in the fields of social reproduction and transformation at the level of collective agency.

At the same time, price and wage series, historical demography, and economic models were not just means to compensate for absent evidence of different sorts. When the right questions were asked of them they contributed in ways other sorts of evidence could not to the understanding of the conditions of life for large numbers of people in the past. Getting away from the idea of great figures and the paramountcy of individual agency might entail a turn from the hermeneutic approach, with its interest on the 'inside' of personalities, to a more exteriorized approach, but, as ever, it was possible to combine different philosophies just as to combine different methodologies.

As to political outlooks, the likes of Scott and Sewell were clearly on the left, and Charles Tilly's historical concerns overlapped significantly with those of the British Marxist Hobsbawm.[74] Paul E. Johnson, whose *A Shopkeeper's Millennium: Society and Revivals in Rochester, New York, 1815–1837* (1978) examined the relationship between religious revivalism and the 'market revolution', later recalled his training as a quantitative social science historian at UCLA in the late 1960s—a regime that he would later characterize as 'the last gasp of positivism'.[75]

> Much of this was acted out with mad-scientist bravado. One well-known quantifier said that anyone who did not know statistics at least through multiple regression should not hold a job in a history department. My own advisor told us that he wanted history to become 'a predictive social science.' I never went that far. I was drawn to the new social history by its democratic inclusiveness as

[72] Skocpol, 'Emerging Agendas'; James Mahoney and Dietrich Rueschemeyer, *Comparative Historical Analysis in the Social Sciences* (Cambridge: Cambridge University Press, 2003), editors' introduction, 3–40, esp. 7–9; Edwin Amenta, 'What we Know about the Development of Social Policy', ibid. 91–130.

[73] London: Methuen, 1965.

[74] Geoff Eley, *A Crooked Line: From Cultural History to the History of Society* (Ann Arbor: University of Michigan Press, 2005), 45–6.

[75] In Paul E. Johnson's preface to the 25th anniversary edition of *A Shopkeeper's Millennium: Society and Revivals in Rochester, New York, 1815–1837* (New York: Hill and Wang, 1994).

much as by its system and precision. I wanted to write the history of ordinary people—to historicize them, put them into the social structures and long-term trends that shaped their lives, and at the same time resurrect what they said and did. In the late 1960s, quantitative social history looked like the best way to do that[76]

Johnson's aim was different to that of the French and Scottish Enlightenment historians who addressed 'manners and mores' in the sense of general culture. It was not, however, altogether new. Michelet had made a great point of writing 'ordinary people' into the historical record, seeking to retrieve the memory of the 'too-forgotten dead', those 'miserabiles personae' like widows and orphans, each of whom 'leaves but a small property, his memory, and asks that it be cared for. For the one who has no friends, the magistrate must supply one.... This magistracy is History.'[77] French nineteenth-century historiography had preceded Marx in examining social classes, with Marx dubbing Thierry the 'father of the class struggle in French historiography'.[78] In the interwar period Georges Lefebvre brought Michelet's and Thierry's interests together from a Marxist perspective with his study of the northern French peasantry during the Revolution.[79] The US 'progressive' historians, like the British left-wing historians of Tawney's generation, had fused their economic interests with concerns for the lives of non-elites. In Eileen Power's case, the result was studies of the life of a Carolingian peasant, a fourteenth-century Parisian housewife, and an Essex clothier during the reign of Henry VII.[80] Alice Clark, Annie Abram, and Ivy Pinchbeck, who all wrote their doctorates at the London School of Economics, produced *Social England in the Fifteenth Century, The Working Life of Women in the Seventeenth Century,* and *Women Workers and the Industrial Revolution* in 1909, 1919, and 1930 respectively; and Lina Eckenstein published *Women under Monasticism* before any of them, in 1896.[81] African American historiography had made significant strides early in the twentieth century, as we shall see shortly. What was unprecedented from the late 1960s was the number of historians in different countries who were starting to think in this way—and further unprecedented was the range of different groups whose historical presence was to be considered.

[76] Paul E. Johnson, 'Reflections: Looking Back at Social History', *Reviews in American History*, 39:2 (2011), 379–88, here 380.

[77] Jules Michelet, *Histoire du XIXe siècle*, vol. II: *Le Directoire*, Preface, repr. in Roland Barthes, *Michelet* (Berkeley: University of California Press, 1992), 101–2.

[78] Quote in Ralph Raico, *Classical Liberalism and the Austrian School* (Auburn, AL: Ludwig von Mises Institute, 2012), 187.

[79] Georges Lefebvre, *Les Paysans du Nord pendant la Révolution française* (Lille, Camille Robbe, 1924).

[80] Eileen Power, *Medieval People* (London: Methuen, 1924).

[81] Ann Oakley, *Women, Peace and Welfare: A Suppressed History of Social Reform, 1880–1920* (Bristol: Policy Press, 2019), 12.

Social History, Experience, Identity

In the western bloc, Marxism played a greater role in British social History than American, while for specific reasons it featured barely at all in the most influential West German social History.[82] British social History also evinced international influences earlier and more markedly than US social History. *Past and Present: A Journal of Scientific History*, established in 1952, immediately incorporated *Annaliste* and eastern European scholarly approaches. The journal's subtitle, later to be changed as it became less Marxist, hinted at its embrace of social scientific methodologies, which set it apart from the mainstream of British historiography quite as much as did the political orientation of its founders. Only with the pro-liferation of British universities and the liberalization of British society from the 1960s would British social History encroach from the margins, and even then some of its leading Marxist lights found difficulty gaining conventional academic posts.

Geoff Eley gives us some of the flavour of his national context when he recalls 'the pompous and sentimentalized nationalist history delivered by conservative patriots during the first two postwar decades in Britain, for which the grandiose multipart television documentary celebrating Churchill's war leadership, *The Valiant Years*, was the epitome'. In Eley's dispiriting initiation to Oxford University in 1967 'the first term brought only Gibbon and Macaulay, de Tocqueville, Burckhardt, and—last but not least—the Venerable Bede'. There was no sense that the syllabus had been established with a view to comparing some classic models of yesteryear with more contemporary and novel approaches, since the latter went unmentioned. The Swinging Sixties this was not. For approaches that better matched his social concerns at Oxford, Eley had to look to the intellectual mar-gins of the History faculty, to historians at the new universities, and to other disciplines.[83]

If the social science with which British social historians established the closest working relationship was economics, we need to resist any assumption of a nar-row materialist doctrine. Marx was, after all, the presiding sociologist, and in both his more and less determinist modes he insisted on the connectedness of all facets of life, differing only on the causal relationships between them. Furthermore, while the influential Cultural Studies Movement associated with Stuart Hall did not include many historians, it grew out of the same post-war Marxist milieu as the Communist Party Historians Group (1946–1956/7) and shared many of the group's broad intellectual concerns. When social History fell out of fashion in the USA in the final two decades of the century it was replaced

---

[82] On the German context, including the *Berufsverbot*, see Eley, *Crooked Line*, 73–4.
[83] Ibid. 1–2 and *passim*. Additional information from personal correspondence with Geoff Eley.

by the 'new cultural History' (pp. 281-8), but many of Britain's most prominent social historians had long since transcended that divide.

The *Annaliste* concept of *mentalité* influenced the famous school of British Marxist historians but these scholars also had 'western Marxist' theory, from György Lukács onwards, to prompt and feed their interest in culture and other matters that Marxists had once consigned to a secondary, 'superstructural' status. The question of proletarian consciousness came to occupy western Marxists in light of the failure of enduring socialist revolution outside the USSR. Lukács had demurred from the economic/materialist determinism of the likes of Stalin, focusing on the importance of proletarian 'consciousness' as against bourgeois 'ideology', but the essays in his *History and Class Consciousness* (1922) had been compiled in 1917-22, against a backdrop of revolutionary success in Russia and his native Hungary, which may explain why, even while claiming that the emergence of a revolutionary consciousness was not an automatic development, he did not provide a thorough analysis of how such a consciousness actually came into being. Conversely Antonio Gramsci did his most important theorizing under fascist rule, in prison. His concept of hegemony sought to account for the strength of obstacles to the establishment of revolutionary consciousness, which drew his attention to the cultural sphere—the sphere of norms, traditions, legitimacy, and the sense of the possible. Hegemony was a function of what Lukács called the ruling classes' 'overwhelming resources of knowledge, culture and routine'.[84]

While E. P. Thompson's monumental *The Making of the English Working Class*[85] was criticized by later cultural historians for allowing too much influence to the economic 'base', it was also criticized by more materialist Marxists for being too concerned with the 'superstructure', culture and all. In a 1978 essay, Thompson sought to counter 'the notion that it is possible to describe a mode of production in "economic" terms; leaving aside as secondary (less "real") the norms, the culture, the critical concepts around which this mode of production is organised'.[86] Such concerns had already been ventilated through historical investigation in the work of the literary theorist Raymond Williams in his *Culture and Society, 1780-1950*.[87] All those historians who retained a focus on Marxist categories and concepts, including Dorothy Thompson, Victor Kiernan, Hilton, Hill, Hobsbawm, and Rudé, found the 'pragmatological', historically divergent Marx much more useful than the 'nomological', determinist Marx (pp. 186-7).[88] This was appropriate for a group of scholars who were concerned not just with social structures but

---

[84] Lukács, *History and Class Consciousness*, 197.

[85] Harmondsworth: Pelican, 1968 (orig. 1963).

[86] E. P. Thompson, 'Folklore, Anthropology and Social History', *Indian Historical Review*, 2:2 (1978), 247-66, here 262. See also Thompson, 'Anthropology and the Discipline of Historical Context'.

[87] London: Chatto and Windus, 1958. See also Williams, 'Base and Superstructure in Marxist Cultural Theory', in Raymond Williams, *Problems in Materialism and Culture* (London: Verso, 1980), 31-49. The essay was originally published in 1973.

[88] Rigby, *Marxism and History*.

with bottom–up agency, whether in the English Peasants' Revolt of 1381 or the self-constitution of the English working class from the late eighteenth century. Hilton's work on medieval peasant movements, like Rudé's work on the French Revolution, exploded the stereotype of the mindless mob that was common to anti-revolutionaries at the time of both sets of events and to some of the contemporary 'modernization'-oriented sociology.[89]

As well as straightforward historical analysis, the work of the British Marxists often fulfilled the functions of monumental exemplarity regarding the possibilities of change in the present, as they reflected on past moments of actual or frustrated change. Their work, married to a memorial commitment to the lowly and the forgotten, is marked by an interest in revolutions, civil wars, rebels, and dissenters. Thompson's *The Making* combined the functions of History as Lesson, Memorial, and Identity—in the sense of critical reflection on identity—as he revealed the social struggles and 'lost causes' that lay beneath the surface of comforting narratives of British institutional evolution.[90]

For Thompson, 'class', as in the self-manufacture of 'the working class', was a popularly generated cultural response to changing material circumstances and norms. We can see some of the same ideas at work in the Subaltern Studies Collective on South Asian History, which took off from beginnings at the University of Sussex in 1979–80. The title of the group and its anthologies indicated a debt to Gramsci.[91] The work of its first leading light, Ranajit Guha, on peasant society, 'peasant consciousness', and the associated character and underappreciated political significance of rural insurgency under imperialism, brought together now familiar elements of Marxism inflected with a concern for non-elite agency and the lives and worldviews of those so often left out of national political narratives. Quite how far the early agenda of the journal *Subaltern Studies*, first published in 1982, simply adopted the approaches and concerns of British Marxist historians is debated, but the inheritance is significant.[92] Both, in any case, intersected with the wider interest in 'History from below'.

---

[89] Rodney Hilton and Hyman Fagin, *The English Rising of 1381* (London: Lawrence and Wishart, 1950); Rodney Hilton, *Bond Men Made Free: Medieval Peasant Movements and the English Rising of 1381* (London: Routledge, 2003 [orig. 1973]). George Rudé, *The Crowd in the French Revolution* (Oxford: Clarendon Press, 1959). See also Eric Hobsbawm and George Rudé, *Captain Swing* (London: Lawrence and Wishart, 1969) and E. P. Thompson, 'The Moral Economy of the English Crowd in the Eighteenth Century', *Past & Present*, 50 (1971), 76–136. For the historiographical contextualization, Passmore, 'History and Historiography since 1945' and Eley, *Crooked Line*.

[90] Thompson, *The Making*, 13.

[91] See in particular Ranajit Guha, *Elementary Aspects of Peasant Insurgency in Colonial India* (Delhi: Oxford University Press, 1983) and, for a further tribute to the significance of Gramsian categories, Guha, *Dominance without Hegemony: History and Power in Colonial India* (Cambridge, MA: Harvard University Press, 1998).

[92] Dipesh Chakrabarty, 'Subaltern Studies and Postcolonial Historiography', *Nepantla: Views from South*, 1:1 (2000), 9–32, who contests Arif Dirlik's and Edward Said's arguments about the extent of the borrowing. Conversely, and for a position which this author sees as more persuasive, see e.g. Arif

History from below was not constrained, or certainly not necessarily, by concerns about 'the working class' as a class. The German version was *Alltagsgeschichte*, the History of everyday life. It was pioneered by the likes of Alf Lüdtke, who fought for a place for mundane experience and actor perspectives as against the structurally oriented and impersonal work—elite actors sometimes excepted—of major powerbrokers like Wehler.[93] In Britain, a pathbreaker was the History Workshop Movement, with its openness to non-academics and associations with adult education. Methodological innovations included oral History. New work in women's History consolidated the progressive legacy of Power, Abram, and Clark at the LSE.

With its more radical character, more marginal status, and broader range of interests tying 'new' and 'old left' together, British social History of the 1950s–1960s had a little more in common on the average than did sociological American social History with the historiographical developments invigorated by the US civil rights struggle. In the USA the civil rights struggle led the way as a political model for new forms of mass association and political-intellectual vocalization. The struggle was by no means limited to the 1950s–1960s—it began much earlier, albeit that those decades were important in the process of a very gradual 'mainstreaming' of African American History, which also meant that white US historians started to make a substantial critical contribution after decades when African American scholars largely worked alone, barring exceptions like the Jewish Marxist historian Herbert Aptheker (1915–2003), whose *American Negro Slave Revolts* appeared in 1943.[94] Later nineteenth- and early twentieth-century historiographical foundations had been laid by, amongst others, John Wesley Cromwell (1846–1927), author of *The Negro in American History* (1914), W. E. B. Du Bois (1868–1963), author of *Black Reconstruction in America* (1935), and Carter G. Woodson (1875–1950). From the 1910s through the 1930s Woodson wrote key Histories on aspects of African American social life and slavery in the antebellum period, and he also founded the Association for the Study of Negro Life and History in 1915 and the *Journal of Negro History* in 1916, which was renamed the *Journal of African American History* in 2002. In 1926 he established 'Negro History Week', the precursor of today's Black History Month. A conducive intellectual and political context in the 1920s was the Harlem Renaissance, with its emphasis on African American culture, while in the 1930s

Dirlik, 'The Postcolonial Aura: Third World Criticism in the Age of Global Capitalism', *Critical Inquiry*, 20:2 (1994), 328–56, here 340.

[93] Alf Lüdtke (ed.), *Alltagsgeschichte: zur Rekonstruktion historischer Erfahrungen und Lebensweisen* (Frankfurt am Main: Campus, 1989).

[94] Herbert Aptheker, *American Negro Slave Revolts* (New York: Columbia University Press, 1943). I stress 'critical contribution' as against apologetic accounts, e.g. Ulrich Bonnell Phillips *American Negro Slavery* (New York: Appleton, 1918), which influenced 'mainstream' scholarship through the 1950s, as testified to by David Brion Davis, 'Reflections: Intellectual Trajectories: Why People Study What they Do', *Reviews in American History*, 37:1 (2009), 148–59, here 157.

interest in the life of an oppressed minority dovetailed with some of the concerns of Progressive US historiography, and was fed by the slave narratives collected under the auspices of the New Deal Federal Writers' Project. Pushing into the 1940s Benjamin Arthur Quarles (1904–96) published his doctoral dissertation on the abolitionist Frederick Douglass in 1948 and went on to become one of the major African American historians of the third quarter of the century. John Hope Franklin's (1915–2009) autobiographical *Mirror to America* (2005) appeared more than sixty years after his 1943 volume *The Free Negro in North Carolina, 1790–1860*.[95]

Was the project of attending to the history of non-elites a matter of showing what the relevant group had historically experienced, or what it had done? The answer, predictably enough, is either and both. Accounts of slavery and discrimination perforce pointed to black experiences, but, especially in response to slavery Histories that caricatured slaves as passive victims, the portrayal of experience fused with that of deeds of resistance in all senses of the term—spiritual, familial, physical, political. Emphasis on deeds, whether in African American or feminist scholarship, helped combat allegations of inferiority. Uniting the study of doing and being was the political desideratum of registering historical presence. 'If a race has no history, if it has no worthwhile tradition', wrote Woodson in the inaugural Black History Week pamphlet, 'it becomes a negligible factor in the thought of the world and it stands in danger of being exterminated'. The Jamaican-born political theorist Marcus Garvey (1887–1940) likewise felt that 'a people without the knowledge of their past history, origin and culture is like a tree without roots'.[96] Towards the other end of the century, in *Staying Power: The History of Black People in Britain* (1984), Peter Fryer observed that 'traces of black life have been removed from the British past to ensure that blacks are not part of the British future' so he sought to help in 'setting the record straight'.[97]

In the date of its appearance, *Hidden from History: 300 Years of Women's Oppression and the Fight Against It* (1973), by the British feminist theorist and historian Sheila Rowbotham, was in harmony with historiographical

[95] Quarles's early publications include *Frederick Douglass* (Washington, DC: Associated Publishers, 1948) and *The Negro in the Civil War* (Boston: Little, Brown and Co., 1953). John Hope Frankin, *The Free Negro in North Carolina, 1790-1860* (Chapel Hill: University of North Carolina Press, 1943); *Mirror to America* (New York: Farrar, Straus and Giroux, 2005). John Wesley Cromwell: *The Negro in American History* (Washington, DC: American Negro Academy, 1914). W. E. B. Du Bois, *Black Reconstruction in America* (New York: Harcourt, Brace, and Co., 1935). Woodson's works include: *The Education of the Negro Prior to 1861* (New York: G. P. Putnam's Sons, 1915), *A Century of Negro Migration* (Washington, DC: Association of Negro Life and History, 1918), *The Negro in Our History* (Washington, DC: Associated Publishers, 1922).

[96] Woodson: Jeffrey Aaron Snyder, *Making Black History: The Color Line, Culture, and Race in the Age of Jim Crow* (Athens: University of Georgia Press, 2018), 96–7. Garvey, and similar sentiments by Malcolm X: Rufus Burrow, Jr, *James H. Cone and Black Liberation Theology* (Jefferson, NC: McFarland, 1994), 21.

[97] Peter Fryer, *Staying Power: The History of Black People in Britain* (London: Pluto Press, 1984), 399. Thanks to Tony Kushner for pointing me to this quote.

developments across the Atlantic. In the USA, Barbara Ehrenreich's and Deirdre English's *Witches, Midwives and Nurses* appeared in the same year; Elizabeth Gould Davies's *The First Sex* two years earlier. The 1970s were as crucial for women's History as for second-wave feminism. Rowbotham wrote of her aspiration to turn 'up the top soil in the hope that others will dig deeper', adding, 'I know already the woman's movement has made many of us ask different questions of the past'.[98] There is, again, a heuristic distinction to be made between sorts of History: on one hand writing women back into the past ('women's History') and on the other hand addressing the facts and mechanisms of patriarchy with a view to liberation in the present ('feminist History'). Clearly these agendas could be fused in any given work, as Rowbotham's title and subtitle indicate. Gerda Lerner, who, like Rowbotham and Joan Kelly, enjoined the recovery of women's pasts, made her justification for History explicit with the observation that 'patriarchy as a system is historical: it has a beginning in history. If that is so, it can be ended by historical process.'[99]

Since they were often aimed more at non-academic or only partly academic audiences, newer Histories benefited from and contributed to the rise of 'radical publishers'. Neither in the mass-sales mainstream nor the university press tradition, these publishers routinely produce some of the most stimulating intellectual output in the areas of feminist, anti-racist, and socialist scholarship. Both Rowbotham and Fryer were published by Britain's Pluto Press, founded in the 1970s.[100] *Witches, Midwives and Nurses* was published by the Feminist Press, founded as a non-profit organization in 1970.

If some of the new Histories were politically forthright, or romanticizing, this was not without good reason.[101] Sometimes their authors felt more obligation to those groups than to the national professions—not to mention states—that had marginalized them. Much more importantly, while establishments might charge these new Histories with politicization, such a response could elide distinctions between History written for political reasons, History with political ramifications, History in which uncomfortable or thesis-challenging evidence had been excluded for political ends, and History whose content was manipulated by parts of its audience for political reasons. As in all such discussions, we need to consider what this 'politicized History' was implicitly being contrasted with, and to disavow any presumption of the sort evinced in the opening editorial of the

---

[98] Sheila Rowbotham, *Hidden from History* (London: Pluto Press, 1973), p. x; Barbara Ehrenreich and Deirdre English, *Witches, Midwives and Nurses* (New York: Feminist Press, 1973); Elizabeth Gould Davies, *The First Sex* (New York: Penguin, 1971).

[99] Gerda Lerner, *The Creation of Patriarchy* (New York: Oxford University Press, 1986), 6, cited in Dorothy Ko, 'Gender', in Ulinka Rublack (ed.), *A Concise Companion to History* (Oxford: Oxford University Press, 2011), 203–25, here 207–8.

[100] Thanks again to Tony Kushner for this observation.

[101] See Barbara Ehrenreich's and Deirdre English's reflective introduction to the second edition of *Witches, Midwives and Nurses* (New York: Feminist Press, 2010).

Historische Zeitschrift (p. 210) that more established sorts of History were more objective or apolitical. Nor was romanticization the sole preserve of any group or historical school.

Nor, again, was 'identity politics' confined to any one identity group, which is important to bear in mind as the aforementioned historical tendencies are corralled under the heading History as Identity. History as Identity has been around as long as History has existed, but the term identity politics was coined and accepted into academic discourse in the 1960s–1970s. The basic idea of identity politics is similar to the Marxist idea of class consciousness as self-awareness of collective predicament, as opposed to the liberal bourgeois conception of politics as negotiation of individual self-interest. Some of the manifestations of identity politics can be described in the argot of 'political emotion', which is relevant in virtue of a shift in the meaning of 'empathy' from its nineteenth-century meaning as a form of cognition to the sort of affective/emotional valence that it often possesses today, where it has taken on some of the meaning of 'sympathy'. This shift gave an added significance to the potentially essentialist claim, which can be traced back at least as far as Gustav Droysen on the other side of the political spectrum (pp. 214–16), that only members of group X could empathize with or 'really understand' the historical experience of group X—and thus that members of other groups were actually not competent to write Histories of X.

Looking forward, a certain homogenization of within-group 'experience' and 'identity' presented problems for scholars working within the aforementioned traditions as they sought to preserve the initial emancipatory drive of their historical-theoretical project against contradictions emerging from within those traditions. *Alltagsgeschichte* sounded problematic when one got to the Nazi period, since German Jews were systematically excluded from the 'everyday' of non-Jews. Joan Scott illustrated that Thompson's *The Making of the English Working Class* was a tale of English working men as *the* rational, political actors of their class, with class given a correspondingly masculine character, and women, barring some exceptions that proved the rule, largely in domestic or support roles.[102] Equally, social and gender History in the USA and beyond could be very shortsighted on matters of 'race' as the critical social theorist bell hooks observed.[103] The postcolonial theorist Gayatri Chakravorty Spivak asked whether there really was a homogeneous 'peasant consciousness' among Indian subalterns.[104]

There is certainly a real sense in which, as historian Priya Satia notes, inclusion begets inclusion; once one goes down the path of amending omissions and

---

[102] Joan Wallach Scott, *Gender and the Politics of History, 30th Anniversary Edition* (New York: Columbia University Press, 2018), ch. 4.

[103] bell hooks, *Ain't I a Woman? Black Women and Feminism* (Boston, MA: South End Press, 1981).

[104] Gayatri Chakravorty Spivak, 'Subaltern Studies: Deconstructing Historiography', in Ranajit Guha and Gayatri Chakravorty Spivak (eds.), *Selected Subaltern Studies* (New York: Oxford University Press, 1988), 3–32.

digging down, one is more apt to be aware of hitherto unnoticed omissions and hitherto unappreciated depths.[105] But one cannot focus on everything at the same time. As often as not the 'classic' triumvirate of social cleavages—race, class, and 'gender' (which really meant 'sex' for a long time)—joined later by sexuality, competed for representational space in History books, as they do up to the present. The tensions have been ameliorated but not averted by intersectional analysis, and it is unclear that they can be averted. If one is thinking in the emancipatory vein, the prospect of a 'rainbow alliance' of the marginalized and repressed is an attractive one, but once one has transcended binary divisions of society where the lines of battle and solidarity are straightforward, one encounters criss-crossing lines of power, privilege, and prejudice that can make potential allies in one sphere into opponents in another.[106]

What we may say with safety is that the *culture* wars of the 1960s highlighted the limitations of any purely or even primarily material analysis of society, and in that sense dovetailed neatly with the cultural concerns of 'western Marxism'. The 'new left' that emerged empowered from these conflicts was at least as concerned with matters of identity as place in the relations of production. The fortunes of the old left were additionally damaged by the (further) discrediting of the USSR in Hungary and Czechoslovakia, the actions of communist parties like the PCF that opposed the '68ers just as much as did de Gaulle, by the end of Keynesianism in the early 1970s, and by the rise of neo-liberalism.

Language and Culture

Where sociology and economics had provided the main external disciplinary inputs to north Atlantic historiography in the second and third quarters of the twentieth century, the final quarter saw more extensive borrowings from linguistics, Continental philosophy, and anthropology. The ensuing historiographical developments have sometimes been described under the headings of the 'linguistic turn' and the 'cultural turn'. Rather than allowing the focus to be determined by labels that mean slightly different things to different people, the intention of this section is to probe relevant linkages and distinctions between linguistic and cultural matters, especially with regard to different elements of the historian's activities. To begin with, though, let us consider another, largely non-taken 'turn', this time of a literary-aesthetic sort. This discussion, while seeming further to complicate matters, ultimately helps in clarification.

---

[105] Priya Satia, 'The Whitesplaining of History is Over', *The Chronicle of Higher Education*, 28 March 2018, The Chronicle Review.

[106] Rainbow alliance reference and problematization: Rosalind O'Hanlon and David Washbrook, 'After Orientalism: Culture, Criticism and Politics in the Third World', in Vinayak Chaturvedi (ed.), *Mapping Subaltern Studies and the Postcolonial* (London: Verso, 2012), 191–219, here 200.

The literary-aesthetic movement can be encapsulated in a person: the intellectual historian Hayden White (1928–2018). Were this book directly concerned
with the nature of historical narrative, then it would address his contributions at
length. Yet while White's work *is* relevant to reflection on History's purposes, for
better or worse its central element has made little impact on the order of justifications most frequently offered for History. His thought on the tropological or
figurative character of language, and differing modes of narrative 'emplotment',
certainly has been fruitfully co-opted for historical research: he enhanced the
ability of historians to read different, especially non-literal levels of meaning, in
their source materials in a way not dissimilar to certain pre-modern religious
hermeneutic practices. But few historians have met his challenge when it comes
to writing, to the 'emplotment' of their own accounts, rather than reading. If, *pace*
Weber, Nietzsche, and Lessing, the only non-literal meaning to be found in a historical account is that imputed to it by the historian, White wanted historians to
embrace the responsibility of meaning creation for the present by the ways in
which they phrased and structured their accounts. He urged them to embrace the
'poetic', i.e. creative, side of their endeavour, to see their works as literary products
as well as fact-based investigations. White made his prescription on aesthetic
grounds but also on moral and political grounds, on the principle that the way
one tells a tale shapes the moral of the story.[107]

Distinguishing White's particular literary preoccupations from other phenomena under consideration does not mean that we can always make a sharp distinction between the inputs of literary theory, cultural theory, and linguistic theory.
Consider the career of structuralism: after starting out as a linguistic theory about
the nature of language, around the same time as it became a theory about cultures, structuralism was also adopted as a literary theory, i.e. a way to read literary
texts. With structuralism's emphasis on the 'internal' and conventional rather
than external and referential nature of meaning (pp. 251–2), it cohered, as previously noted, with so much pre-twentieth-century 'romantic' hermeneutics from
Leibniz to Hamann, Herder, and beyond. The symbolic cultural anthropologist
Clifford Geertz was indebted to Dilthey's hermeneutics, and he hinted at the joinder of hermeneutics and literary theory when commending reading cultures as
one would a text. The cultural historian Robert Darnton chimed in: 'one can read
a ritual or a city, just as one can read a folktale or a philosophic text'.[108]

For their part, cultural and linguistic matters can often be grouped together
insofar as cultures and languages are systems of symbols or signs. The word 'semiotics' is rooted in the Greek word for sign or mark and connotes the study of their
use and interpretation. Signs and symbols should be understood in the broadest

---

[107] Hayden White: *Metahistory*; *The Content of the Form*; and *Tropics of Discourse* (Baltimore: Johns
Hopkins University Press, 1978).
[108] On Geertz and Darnton, Burke, *What is Cultural History?*, 37–8.

sense to include images, from TV advertisements to icons, and rituals, from church processions to styles of massacring, from grammatical systems to body art. Here we may also advert to Foucault, translations of whose work from the 1970s brought him great celebrity in America especially, but elsewhere too. His conception of power as not emanating from a royal decree or any other centre of subjective human intention, but rather circulating impersonally, had a notable affinity with the operation of language, and the affinity is only underlined by his concept of 'discourses' (perforce verbal entities) that define the parameters of intelligibility and, where relevant, propriety, in any formal precinct of know-ledge.[109] Yet whatever the overlap in approaches for analysing culture and lan-guage, interpretations of the relationship of language and culture vary. Under a broad enough definition of culture, language is a subset of it; at the same time, thinking in terms of the interpretative schemes by which we interpret the world, there is a significant body of thought that places language as primary.

When it comes to the relationship between theories of culture and/or language on one hand and History on the other hand, much depends, as with the assimila-tion of White's work, on the direction in which the theories are predominantly applied. Are they applied more to the past world under investigation or to the historian herself as an acculturated being embedded in a particular set of sign systems? This may sound like a false dichotomy, given that, *pace* Gadamer on interpretation (pp. 243–4), the reading of evidence from the past may provide some 'fusion' of the historian's world of understanding and that of the world under investigation. But 'fusion' is a capacious concept and no one commended just let-ting fusion happen without the interpreter first equipping herself with all neces-sary theories and skills. There is no reason why this self-equipping cannot include the investigator's first 'theorizing' herself in the relevant sense before moving on to investigate some past world: that very project goes by the name reflexivity, or self-reflectivity, and major impetus for it was provided by anthropologists, as, aware of the implication of the earlier implication of their discipline in imperial-ism, they strove to divest themselves of preconceptions emerging from their own society to enable them to address their investigated societies non-instrumentally, and more fully 'on their own terms'.

The problem for the reflexivity agenda is that it can never be fulfilled, and one cannot know what ramifications self-reflection has actually had for one's studies. One's deepest preconceptions are the most difficult things on which to gain crit-ical purchase, and even if one does divest oneself of them this does not mean that one will be without preconceptions: they will just be different preconceptions to the previous ones. Ultimately, any interpretation of foreign countries past (as pre-sent) will be judged in relation to its use of evidence and its internal consistency,

---

[109] Jonathan Hearn, *Theorizing Power* (Basingstoke: Palgrave Macmillan, 2012), 90–2.

not in relation to the level of conscious self-theorizing in which the investigator has engaged, and it is unclear that one can establish, in non-circular fashion, a causal relationship between conscious self-theorizing and superior quality of interpretations. So it is not necessarily a wilful disregard of the reflexivity agenda that leads historians and other investigators to focus their interpretative skills on the evidence, buttressed by such interpretative techniques, hermeneutic and otherwise, as they are acquainted with. For centuries any hermeneutic theory worth its salt has already begun from the premise of at least partly different mental or cultural worlds.

Much more can be said about investigatorial uncertainty and—with the anthropologists' reflexivity agenda in mind—the investigator's power as a representer of 'others'. Some of it will be said in the next section on 'Theory and History', which is especially pertinent for those for whom History's interface with linguistic theory and Continental philosophy is captured by the term poststructuralism and the name Derrida. The rest of this section concentrates on the aims and pay-off of theories of culture and language as historians have brought them to bear directly on the study of the past.

As with social History, it helps in understanding the varied remit of semiotically oriented History to know what its practitioners defined themselves against. Some social historians defined themselves against political historians by claiming that 'the (high) political' and 'the social' were just different spheres of life; social History was just more relevant to those with more demotic, less elite interests. Other social historians, especially those with economic interests, might posit the greater importance of 'the social', seeing high political developments as an expression or reflection of more fundamental shifts in the socio-economic 'base'. Others were interested in interaction and interpenetration between the spheres. Similarly, cultural historians reacted against the materialist element of social History but this reaction could take an additive form of finding other aspects of life just more interesting, or suggesting an interesting perspective on topics old as well as new, or a corrective form as regards certain hitherto misunderstood particulars, or a general, supplantive form whereby the study of culture or language became a master approach.

Some sorts of semiotically informed work could stand in tension with other sorts. When the historian Lynn Hunt described the 'new cultural History' as centred on the 'deciphering of meaning, rather than the inference of causal laws',[110] she was presumably reacting against quantitative approaches like that of Paul E. Johnson's doctoral supervisor, but there are also points of contrast with the work of Foucault and Foucauldians. Whereas, say, the microhistorians tried to relate historical actors, as agents, to the meaning systems of their own worlds,

---

[110] Lynn Hunt, 'Introduction: History, Culture, and Text', in Lynn Hunt (ed.), *The New Cultural History* (Berkeley: University of California Press, 1989), 1–22, here 12.

Foucauldians might be concerned with the impersonal determinants of consciousness and value in any given society, in an approach with a conceptual debt to strands of Marxism and structuralist-informed History. What Foucault called the 'microphysics of power' could only be detected from 'below' in its everyday operational instantiations, and at points he prompted a sort of 'History from below' that was not concerned with people so much as the construction of their subjectivity through power-discourses.[111]

In terms of new topics, one subset of cultural Histories is 'the cultural History of X'. Here, X frequently denotes things deemed too mundane for prior historical attention or too technical or ostensibly natural for traditional consideration in a humanistic discipline.[112] Examination of the design or use of furniture, or attitudes towards it, tells us something about human values and practices at some point in the past. Histories of smell, as in the work of Alain Corbin, reveal the way in which different odours have had changing associations with social hierarchy, for instance, such that the tolerance of this or that odour changed across time.[113] The other senses have also been given due attention, likewise hair, dress, money, food, gardens, animals, and so on.[114] Again, French historiography had made some of the early running in giving a History of difference to things that might previously have been assumed to be cultural constants. Philippe Ariès's L'Enfant et la vie familiale sous l'ancien régime (1960), later translated as Centuries of Childhood, argued that prior to the seventeenth century childhood was not recognized as a discrete phase in the human lifespan. The 'modern' conception was, he argued, a function of expanding education and thus the need increasingly to segregate children according to age, which meant expanded age-specific discipline and an enhanced view of 'the child' as needing adult supervision and tutelage; it was also a function of enhanced focus on the private nuclear family as opposed to more open 'households' and extended families.[115] So pervasive has this sort of

[111]   At other points Foucault's historical agenda was comparable to that of a Cryer or a Thompson as a more orthodox form of 'History from below' that wrote particular groups and actors back into the past and generated a critical perspective on the present. Thus Foucault once wrote of the retrieval of what he called 'subjugated knowledges'. Retrieval involved taking seriously the perspectives—and by extension, contra Joan Scott (see p. 290) the experience—of 'the psychiatrized, the patient, the nurse, the doctor…the knowledge of the delinquent'. This 'retrieval' was, obviously enough, historical scholarship, leading to a 'historical knowledge of struggles.…We have both a meticulous rediscovery of struggles.…If you like, we can give the name "genealogy" to this coupling together of scholarly erudition and local memories, which allows us to constitute a historical knowledge of struggles and to make use of that knowledge in contemporary tactics'. Foucault, Society Must be Defended, 7–9.
[112]   See Jordan Goodman, 'History and Anthropology', in Bentley (ed.), Companion to Historiography, 783–804, here 792–4.
[113]   Burke, What is Cultural History?, 113 on the work of Alain Corbin.
[114]   All items in this list have been addressed inter alia by the Bloomsbury 'Cultural Histories' series. The output of Reaktion Books covers some of the same areas and in addition addresses topics including the Earth and—in the 'Objekt' series—all manner of design objects.
[115]   Philippe Ariès, L'Enfant et la vie familiale sous l'ancien régime (Paris: Plon, 1960). Ariès's work has now been superseded, especially by 'new childhood studies' scholarship which has highlighted the

approach to historical variability become that in 2018 the historian Matthew Crow dubbed it 'the duck-hunt model of critical scholarship: your task in the game as a licensed historicizer is to find something insufficiently historicized, get out your context gun, and shoot it'.[116] Whatever 'critical scholarship' might mean—after all, who would self-identify as an uncritical scholar?—the principle of 'historicization' is anything but new, as the name indicates. Indeed such duck-hunting is really just one of the longstanding intellectual trajectories of the discipline extended a bit.

In terms of new perspectives on old topics, indeed potentially almost all historical questions one could have, say, cultural Histories of political or military events. Examples include Hunt's analysis of the mobilizing force of Jacobin motifs in the French Revolution—'Revolutionary language did not simply reflect the realities of revolutionary changes and conflicts, but rather was itself transformed into an instrument of political and social change'[117]—and a study that addresses the intersection of popular culture and politics in the 'naval theatre' of ship launches, fleet reviews, and other such displays in the pre-1914 Anglo-German naval race.[118] From 'cultural' approaches to historical arenas not normally described under that rubric we get concepts like 'political culture'. Such fusions have expanded the toolkit of political historians at the same time as broadening the writ of cultural History by elaborating the unwritten rules and performative quality of debate and leadership, or trying to account for the political attitudes of particular groups when those attitudes are not accounted for by explanations to material interest.

With changed perspectives came changed rationales. As semiotic interests diverted attention from the material 'base' of society, they militated against the stadialist preoccupations of modernization theory and opened the path for a renewal of interest in distant times and places in and for themselves, rather than in a developmental relationship to some later state of being. Davis's essay 'The Rites of Violence: Religious Riot in Sixteenth Century France' (1973) on the St Bartholomew's Day massacres of Huguenots, rejected an existing class-based explanation, even as she recognized that much of the violence was demotic and lacking in governmental sanction. She noted the parallels between the conduct of

importance of recovering children's perspectives and agency, rather than perpetuating their marginalization or representation as objects of adult scrutiny. For recent work (with thanks to Louise Jackson) see Harry Hendrick, *Children, Childhood and English Society, 1880–1990* (Cambridge: Cambridge University Press, 1997); Steven Mintz, *Huck's Raft: A History of American Childhood* (Cambridge, MA: Harvard University Press, 2004). Hendrick and Mintz have also proposed that 'age' be treated as a category of analysis analogous to 'gender'.

[116] Matthew Crow, 'Context as Environment: A "Workmanlike" Approach', online at http://history-ofthepresent.org/forum/M_Crow_Context_as_Environ.pdf
[117] Lynn Hunt, *Politics, Culture, and Class in the French Revolution* (Berkeley: University of California Press, 1984), 24.
[118] Jan Rüger, *The Great Naval Game: Britain and Germany in the Age of Empire* (Cambridge: Cambridge University Press, 2007).

the killing and the church's purificatory rituals—the Huguenots were, after all, seen as pollutants. This contextualization helped explain the use of fire and water as methods of destruction and the desecration of corpses as a further 'weakening' of the spiritual threat.[119] Darnton's famous essay 'Workers' Revolt: The Great Cat Massacre of the Rue Saint-Séverin' (1984) showed why it made cultural as well as sociological sense that a group of downtrodden Parisian apprentice printers in the 1730s should find it amusing to slaughter the 'privileged' animals after a mock trial of the same.[120]

History as Travel, or 'capturing otherness' as Darnton put it, was back on the agenda. In a way that would have been familiar to the British historian Keith Thomas, who also drew on anthropology to explore the bygone exotic, Darnton wrote: 'When we cannot get a proverb, or a joke, or a ritual, or a poem, we know we are onto something. By picking at the document where it is most opaque, we may be able to unravel an alien system of meaning. The thread might even lead into a strange and wonderful world view.' 'And once we have puzzled through to the native's point of view, we should be able to roam about in his symbolic world.'[121] Getting students to 'see the world through the eyes of others', 'through the prism of another time and another place' is an avowed aim of the cultural historian of the Renaissance, Kenneth Bartlett.[122] As a mind-broadening hermeneutic pursuit this species of History as Travel had something in common with History as Communion, though its benefits were less direct and the interlocutor different. While most of the American social History of the 1960s–1970s focused on the nineteenth and twentieth century, many more new cultural Historians focused on medieval and early modern history, the better, presumably, for contrast—and here there is a marked crossover with the focus, as well as the ethos, of the microhistorians. In a 1988 work on Renaissance England the 'new historicist' literary theorist Stephen Greenblatt named his 'desire to speak with the dead'. Greenblatt coined the name 'new historicism', which constitutes a major point of intersection between literary theory and new cultural History. In terms redolent of Darnton, H. Aram Veeser described how new historicists alight 'upon an event or anecdote—colonist John Rolfe's conversation with Pocahontas' father, a note found among Nietzsche's papers to the effect that "I have lost my umbrella"—and re-read it in such a way as to reveal through the analysis of tiny particulars the

[119] Natalie Zemon Davis, 'The Rites of Violence: Religious Riot in Sixteenth-Century France', *Past and Present*, 59 (1973), 51–91.
[120] Robert Darnton, 'Workers' Revolt: The Great Cat Massacre of the Rue Saint-Séverin' is chapter 2 of Robert Darnton, *The Great Cat Massacre and Other Episodes in French Cultural History* (New York: Basic Books, 1999 [orig. 1984]).
[121] Ibid. 5, 262. Keith Thomas, 'Ways of Doing Cultural in History', in Rik Sanders, Bas Mesters, Reinier Kramer, and Margreet Windhorst (eds.), *Balans en Perspectief van de Nederlandse Cultuurgeschiedenis* (Amsterdam: Rodopi, 1991), 65–82.
[122] Kenneth R. Bartlett, 'Cultural History Advice for Students from Professor Ken Bartlett', online at https://www.youtube.com/watch?v=Px1GwHyAYXs

behavioural codes, logics, and motive forces controlling a whole society'.[123] This literary-theoretical movement forms part of the broader neo-historicist trend, and the term neo-historicism had to be coined in this book because 'new historicism' had already been taken.

The recognition of cultural difference across time—it cannot remotely be called a discovery, but it can be called a re-emphasis on particular aspects of difference and differentiation, characterized by a rebellion *inter alia* against a type of materialist thought that at its extreme dissolved questions of value or meaning into matters of interest—fuelled another pre-existing justification for History: History as Emancipation. Emancipatory History shared the premises about difference that underpinned History as mind-broadening Travel, but it had less of an orientation towards Communion with different people past and a more explicitly critical agenda towards the present. The extent to which the advocates of History as Emancipation were interested in exploring different ways of thinking 'from the inside' varied: the constant was their interest in the mechanisms whereby 'differences' are constructed and might be deconstructed. This is the school of thought associated with Foucault, though it cannot be reduced to his thinking.

The issue is fruitfully approached through Joan Scott's 1986 article 'Gender as a Category of Historical Analysis'. Gender History can be linked with new cultural History just as women's History from the 1960s onwards may be associated with the social History that explored less well covered terrains of experience, contribution, and identity. Gender History is concerned less with the study of women 'in and for themselves' than with the way in which femininity and masculinity are variably defined under different cultural dispensations. Natalie Davis first suggested to Scott that reminded us that '"women" were always defined in some relationship to men', which has a structuralist ring to it. The idea of a power agenda being involved in the construction of gendered difference also appealed to the growing number of admirers of Foucault for whom power inhered impersonally in relations, and it meant that concerns of power did not have to be discarded as materialist and class analysis was downplayed. Scott wrote that 'gender is a constitutive element of social relationships based on perceived differences between the sexes', and a 'way' of 'signifying relationships of power'.[124]

Women's History and gender History could both be written with emancipationist goals, but that did not mean that women's and gender historians necessarily approved of each others' approaches and their implications. Consider the idea

[123] Stephen Greenblatt, *Shakespearean Negotiations* (Berkeley: University of California Press, 1988) 1; H. Aram Veeser, introduction to H. Aram Veeser (ed.) *The New Historicism* (New York: Routledge, 1989), pp. ix–xvi, here p. xi.
[124] Joan W. Scott, 'Gender: A Useful Category of Historical Analysis', *The American Historical Review*, 91:5 (1986) 1053–75, here 1067. On Davis's prompt, see Joan W. Scott, 'Unanswered Questions', *The American Historical Review*, 113:5 (2008), 1422–30, here 1422. On changing historical constructions of femininity, see also the work of Scott's sometime collaborator, Denise Riley, *Am I that Name? Feminism and the Category of 'Women' in History* (Basingstoke: Macmillan, 1988).

of 'women's liberation' associated with second wave feminism. This might be taken to assume that across time and place there was a stable category, 'women', that could be liberated or liberate itself. (By no means all second wave feminism had an essentialist view: as Simone de Beauvoir wrote in 1949, 'one is not born, but rather becomes, a woman'.) A constructivist gender analysis would say that there is no such stability in the category in the first place, since different societies at different times constructed gender differences differently. As Scott put it in a later piece, 'there is no essence of womanhood (or of manhood) to provide a stable subject for our histories; there are only successive iterations of a word that doesn't have a fixed referent and so doesn't mean the same thing'. '"Women" in the Middle Ages were not "women" as we think of them today.'[125] This is a classic 'new cultural History of X'-type operation, in that it takes categories or concepts with connotations of the natural—woman, or female—and historicizes them. For some feminists, such historicization undermined feminist aspirations by dissolving the collective subject—women—whose interests feminism claimed to serve.[126] Conversely, Scott saw it as a basis for possible emancipation since historicization pointed to the socio-cultural constructedness of social relations and categories in the past, and the way those constructions changed over time, and so raised the possibility of alteration in the present. There might not be a trans-historical subject 'women' to be emancipated, but individual people currently described as women could fight in a self-emancipatory fashion for the scrapping or redefinition of the concept. Such options are what Sewell had in mind when talking about 'gaining discursive control over the shapes of our lives'.[127]

The agenda of 'denaturalization' was centuries if not millennia old, but its linkage to emancipation in the present is typically Marxist, even if it has been associated more with Foucault in recent decades.[128] Lukács, writing early in the twentieth century, praised Marx's contribution to 'a consciousness of consciousness. This critical philosophy implies above all historical criticism. It dissolves the rigid, unhistorical, natural appearance of social institutions; it reveals their historical origins and shows therefore that they are subject to history in every respect including historical decline.'[129] Relevant to the gender discussion, when Gerda Lerner argued that revealing patriarchy as a historical system brought with it the

[125] Scott, 'Unanswered Questions', 1426.

[126] By the reasoning highlighted by Mary Poovey, 'Feminism and Deconstruction', Feminist Studies, 14:1 (1988), 51–65, here 62.

[127] William G. Sewell, Logics of History: Social History and Social Transformation (Chicago: University of Chicago Press, 2005), 357.

[128] e.g. Michel Foucault, 'Questions of Method', in K. Baynes, J. Bonman, and T. McCarthy (eds), After Philosophy, End or Transformation? (Cambridge, MA: MIT Press, 1987), 101–17, here 104. Cf. Marx's statements previously quoted on pp. 187–8.

[129] Lukács, History and Class Consciousness, 47.

implication that patriarchy could 'be ended by historical process', she was building on Engels's *Origins of the Family, Private Property and the State* (1884).[130]

Semiotic analysis could affect the trappings of a social science just as much as could Marxism or structuralism, as it attempted to say something general about the way things are in the construction of human worlds. Some of the most prominent practitioners of this mode of analysis—Scott and William Sewell—were intellectually socialized as sociologically oriented social Historians, and a residual positivism can be identified in their work after they both took a semiotic turn. In his *Logics of History* (2005), Sewell wrote of extending 'radically the range and ambition of cultural history' to the point of 'specifying the codes or paradigms underlying meaningful practices that seem resistant to linguistic analysis and that might conventionally be thought of precisely as the sort of "nondiscursive social realities" that causally limit or shape discourses'.[131] He claimed that 'the social'

is best understood as, first, an articulated, evolving web of semiotic practices (this is the language metaphor) that, second, builds up and transforms a range of physical frameworks that both provide matrices for these practices and constrain their consequences...The fundamental method for understanding the social, so understood, [involves...] explicating performances by reconstructing the semiotic codes that enable their production.[132]

At points like this semiotic approaches moved from being additive to the rich blend of existing approaches, or corrective of them in some important particulars, to claiming the status of a new master approach. At such points semiotic approaches, cultural or linguistic, could be as reductive as economic or materialist determinism.

If the basic claim of, say, new cultural History at its most imperialist is that ways of thinking, seeing, valuing, etc. are culturally constructed, and thus that everyone, past and present is always already constructed to think, etc., through a particular, if changing, cultural matrix, we need to follow Peter Burke in asking after the agents, materials, and constraints of that construction.[133] If one defined culture, or meaning, or language broadly enough then it would cover everything, but the victory would be pyrrhic since nothing would then really be explained. How, if at all, did factors that could not satisfactorily be accounted for under the rubric of culture, as culture was understood by the new cultural historians,

---

[130] Friedrich Engels, *Origins of the Family, Private Property and the State* (Chicago: Kerr, 1902 [German orig. 1884]); Ko, 'Gender', 207–8, identifies the influence of Engels on Lerner and other feminists of her period.
[131] Sewell, *Logics of History*, 338.   [132] Ibid. 369.
[133] e.g. Burke, *What is Cultural History?*, ch. 5.

influence the culture? How far were people choicelessly following a cultural script or interpreting in accordance with a governing power-discourse? One among many definitions of the cultural historian's aim is 'discover[ing] the ways in which past actors sought to give meaning to their lives through symbol, ritual and narrative',[134] which suggests some active seeking by agents. As to language, Hunt's important claim that 'Revolutionary language did not simply reflect the realities of revolutionary changes and conflicts, but rather was itself transformed into an instrument of political and social change' raises as many questions as it answers. The fact that that language was 'itself transformed' suggests some extra-linguistic power doing the transforming, or some extra-linguistic change in the world that caused the language to gain new purchase.

Theoretical enquiry here has not been aided by the lack of consistency with which the case has been made by major proponents, though we must allow for the hyperbole that accompanies innovation in any field of enquiry. Just two pages before stressing the primacy of semiotics, and thus of semiotic code-breaking, Sewell noted that physical substances such as the human body and the natural and built environment are subject to 'other determinations than the semiotic', and that semiotic and non-semiotic elements of social life are intertwined.[135] Consider also Gareth Stedman Jones, who was explicit in his debts to Saussurean linguistics in his pathbreaking essays *Languages of Class* (1984). The insertions in italics within the brackets in the body of Jones's text serve to highlight the inconsistencies of the promised explanation.

> In general, whether steeped in the older traditions of labour history or the newer conventions of social history, historians have looked everywhere except at changes in political discourse itself to explain changes in political behaviour.... The implicit assumption is of civil society as a field of conflicting social groups or classes whose opposing interests will find rational expression in the political arena. Such interests, it is assumed, pre-exist their expression...
>
> In order to rewrite the political history of the 'working class' or 'working classes', we should start out from the other end of the chain. [*A strong claim.*] Language disrupts any simple notion of the determination of consciousness by social being because it is itself part of social being. [*A weaker claim: language is 'part of social being', not determinant of it.*] We cannot therefore decode political language to reach a primal and material expression of interest since it is the discursive structure of political language which conceives and defines interest in the first place. [*Back to a stronger claim, albeit with a narrower conception of*

---

[134] Dan Stone, 'Introduction: The Holocaust and Historical Methodology', in Dan Stone (ed.), *The Holocaust and Historical Methodology* (New York: Berghahn, 2012), 1–19, here 13.

[135] Sewell, *Logics of History*, 367.

language—'*the discursive structure [sic] of political language*'—*as the defining element.*] What we must therefore do is to study the production of interest, identification, grievance and aspiration within political languages themselves. [*The strong position is maintained: (political) language is the site of production of interest, etc.*] We need to map out these successive languages of radicalism, liberalism, socialism etc., both in relation to the political languages they replace and laterally in relation to rival political languages with which they are in conflict. Only then can we begin to assess their reasons for success or failure at specific points in time. It is clear that particular political languages do become inapposite in new situations. How and why this occurs involves the discovery of the precise point at which shifts occur as well as an investigation of the specific political circumstances in which they shift. [*Note now the move to 'political circumstances' as a site of production: political languages here are shaped by or in reaction to things outside language, which is not even a weaker version of the basic claim, it is a reversal of the strong claim.*] To peer straight through these languages into the structural changes to which they may be notionally referred is no substitute for such an investigation, not because there is not a relationship of some kind, but because such connections can never be established with any satisfying degree of finality. [*A bit of a fudge.*][136]

In a sympathetic and sensitive work on voices and the victims of the Inquisition John Arnold deploys the Foucauldian concept of 'discourse' and tries to explain change (or perhaps just the possibility of change) with reference only to the workings of discourse. In the process he replicates the ambiguities of Foucault's own thought on power and discourse. In the vein of History as Practical Lesson, Arnold concludes that

> Discourses construct and position us as subjects; but they also allow (or, as
> I have argued, demand) an *excess* of speech and action. In confronting that
> excess, change occurs. And where there is change, there is hope. We are not,
> as some have suggested, merely prisoners of discourse, we are also its—and
> our—guardians and servants. But if we have agency, there may be other roles we
> can choose.[137]

Discourses demand something, or perhaps they just allow it, but then that something can be used to act against the demands of discourses. We are prisoners, servants, and guardians of the same thing, with the ability to rebel and choose not

---

[136] Gareth Stedman Jones, *Languages of Class* (Cambridge: Cambridge University Press, 1984) 21–2, and 20 on Saussure. The first nine lines of Jones's p. 24 could be subjected to similar treatment.
[137] John H. Arnold, *Inquisition and Power* (Philadelphia: University of Pennsylvania Press, 2001), 228.

to fulfil any of those functions (if discourse allows it?). Inmates of supermax penitentiaries may or may not feel that the carceral metaphor is apt.

Similarly, Richard Biernacki has shown of Joan Scott's analysis of discourses on economic matters among Parisian garment makers in the 1840s that in practice, whatever her claims about the primacy of language in constituting reality, Scott ends up positing economic distress as the cause of the relevant linguistic framing. Likewise he shows that in her discussion of Chartism she ends up 'assuming the fit' between a discourse on propertylessness 'and the social positions of property-less agents', which problematizes any idea that the discourse drove the constitution of the outlook of the propertyless.[138] In works such as those examined by Biernacki, Scott is clearly trying, albeit not entirely successfully, less to subvert than to invert the determinant relationship proposed in elements of Marxist thought between the ideological 'superstructure' (now labelled discourse, culture, etc.) and the material 'base'. Elsewhere, in a famous essay 'The Evidence of Experience' Scott oscillates between stronger and weaker claims as to the causal powers of the semiotic. She brings under critique the sort of 'identity History' associated with the civil rights movement and second wave feminism, with its recounting of the experiences and agency of the groups in question. First we are given the weaker, additive claim: 'Treating the emergence of a new identity as a discursive event is not to introduce a new form of linguistic determinism, nor to deprive subjects of agency. It is to refuse a separation between "experience" and language'. Then we are confronted with the stronger, supplanting position, which better reflects the tenor of her essay: 'subjects are constituted discursively', and historians should 'take as their project not the reproduction and transmission of knowledge said to be arrived at through experience, but the analysis of the production of that knowledge itself'. (Why historians may not do both is unclear). Scott claims that the latter approach 'does not undercut politics by denying the existence of subjects, it instead interrogates the processes of their [i.e. the subjects'] creation'. But this 'clarification' comprises a distinction without a difference unless one allows that after the moment of their 'creation', subjects can somehow act upon reflection, perhaps in the light of new experiences, which would rather undermine the imperative to study the 'creation' rather than what comes after it.[139]

---

[138] Richard Biernacki, 'Method and Metaphor after the New Cultural History', in Victoria E. Bonnell and Lynn Hunt (eds.), *Beyond the Cultural Turn* (Berkeley: University of California Press, 1999), 62–92, here 68 and 86 (n. 26). See also Biernacki, 'Work and Culture in Class Ideologies', in John R. Hall (ed.), *Reworking Class* (Ithaca: Cornell University Press, 1997), 169–92, here 174.

[139] Joan W. Scott, 'The Evidence of Experience', *Critical Inquiry* 17:4 (1991), 773–97, here, in order of the quotations in my main text, 792–3, 793, 797.

Theory and History

If there are manifest problems with the wholesale importation of theoretical answers into the writing of History, the retail importation of theoretical questions has much enhanced the historian's practice. Significant contributions have been made in every area: in the realms of new approaches, new objects of study, and a greater attentiveness to the positioning and responsibilities of the historian who is engaged in the construction of accounts of the past that stand in some relation to the present. This 'theory—a capacious signifier that seems to apply to anything from interesting reflection to conceptual or methodical innovation to bodies of propositions that claim some predictive or retrodictive potential—has no single trajectory, which explains both its tremendous richness but also the difficulties into which the indiscriminate importer can run.[140] It is nonetheless worth reflecting on how much the general thrust of the most influential theorists evinces affinities with the general historical, not to say historicist, character of intellectual fashion from the later nineteenth century onwards. In that light, new historical departures leaning on some element of philosophical or social theory sometimes look like mildly conceptually enriched versions of old historical approaches that may have informed that selfsame theory or sprung from a shared root.

The most obvious sources of theoretical authority in the last forty years or so have been French, but there is no one French school, and the 'Frenchness' of any of the relevant intellectual genealogies is variable. The more purely indigenous French intellectual tradition of Durkheimian sociology had roots in nineteenth-century thought at the nexus of History and the social sciences, which were never so distinct in France as in Germany or Britain. This was the intellectual milieu in which the *Annales* was at home. *Annaliste* thinking of the eras of Bloch and Braudel obviously made its mark on Foucault but well before the 1980s and 1990s the pages of *Annales* displayed the sort of intellectual variety we now associate with the 'new' cultural History of those decades. Febvre's editorial philosophy endured alongside his fecund intellectual legacy, as new editors continued to commission pieces rather than merely await submissions. The 1960 volume included studies of Yoruba farming practices, Bosnian goldmines, the eighteenth-century Chilean economy, North African camels in the Roman era, as well as Le Goff's first foray into changing medieval conceptions of time, Lévi-Strauss on

---

[140] On the essays 'we've all read…where Freud and Foucault, Baudrillard and Booth are each and all cited as sources of analytic authority without concern for the incompatibilities among them': Bill Brown, cited in Stanley Fish, 'Theory's Hope', *Critical Inquiry*, 30:2 (2004), 374–8, here 375. Note, too, that when I use 'theory' here it is as a shorthand for the most self-conscious correctives of recent generations; all History is theory-laden in some respects, and when 'theory' is used as loosely as it is in so many of these debates, historians not persuaded by some of the new theories can claim to be deploying their own theories all the time. So it is rarely a case of theoretically-informed thought *versus* non-theoretically-informed thought.

History and anthropology, Robert Mandrou on the notion of the baroque, Roland Barthes on Jean Racine, and Lucien Goldmann on Chagall. The 1970 volume featured work on Etruscan city planning, Indian gods, Sudanese gold, Bedouins, fairy-tales, Freud, climate History, Peruvian cathedrals, brain physiology, and the '68 student movement.[141]

The key twentieth-century French theorists drew on yet more august Germanic predecessors. The *Lebensphilosophie* or 'philosophy of life' that culminated in Heidegger and thinkers of a different political persuasion like Ortega y Gasset had roots in the thought of Dilthey as well as Nietzsche, and of every hermeneut who was dissatisfied with the abstractions and formalism of Kantians and the scientism of the sociological positivists and sought to preserve other ways of knowing the human in all its cultural variety. Consider, for instance, Dilthey's conceptualization of the individual as constituted at the meeting points of various social, cultural, economic, and political influences (pp. 225–6): this conceptualization is not so very far from Foucault's vision in which the individual's consciousness is constructed at the intersection of various discourses. Like neohistoricism, the entire postmodern critique of the idealized 'Enlightenment' hermetic/punctal/self-sufficient 'subject' has debts to the contextualist theories of Hamann, Herder, and *Historismus*. Hermeneutic and historical enquiry provided one of the major routes away from traditional philosophy with its concern for abstractions and universals. The rejection of questions of 'first philosophy' prompted one thinker to label much 'continental' thought of the last 150 years or so as 'antiphilosophy'.[142] Above all else, the attention to particular contexts is one of the major ways in which Continental philosophy distinguishes itself from foregoing philosophy and contemporary analytical philosophy. 'Context', and the particularity that goes along with it, is something that historians are good with in practice even if not necessarily in theory.

Historians can also combine an interest in situated/contextualized being with an interest in becoming, as they address the relationships between context and process, structure and agency, continuity and change. 'Process philosophy', from Hegel through Nietzsche, indicates the impact of historical thought on philosophy.[143] At the same time, while in his *The Postmodern Condition* (1979) Jean-François Lyotard defined postmodernism is a matter of 'incredulity towards metanarratives' of the Hegelian sort, i.e. philosophies of history, postmodernists scarcely have claim to being the first to develop this scepticism.[144] As Foucault

---

[141] For all of which and more see George Huppert, 'The *Annales* Experiment', in Bentley (ed.), *Companion to Historiography*, 873–88, here 880, 882.

[142] Boris Groys, *Introduction to Antiphilosophy* (London: Verso, 2012).

[143] See generally David D. Roberts, *Nothing But History: Reconstruction and Extremity After Metaphysics* (Berkeley: University of California Press, 1995).

[144] Jean-François Lyotard, *The Postmodern Condition* (Manchester: Manchester University Press, 1984 [French orig. 1979]), p. xxiv.

attested, many artisanal historians had already rejected Hegel alongside all his predecessor and successor schemes (p. 251).

The emphasis on change and temporality sets History apart from some of the most influential forms of anthropology. The criticisms of structuralism by Jacques Derrida echo the words of anthropologist Edward Evans-Pritchard before him, namely that social anthropologists had been writing 'cross-sections of history, integrative descriptive accounts' depicting worlds 'at a moment of time'.[145] While agreeing with structuralism's contention about the conventional nature of language Derrida dismissed it on other grounds. Following Louis Althusser's and Fernand Braudel's ideas of different temporalities or *durées* coexisting, and criticizing the absence of a historical dimension in general from the static structuralist analysis, Derrida underlined how structuralism imputed too great a coherence to any social order and gave the observer an illusion of being able to read the order from some sort of privileged point of access.[146] Derridean poststructuralism was partly established in rejection of structuralism's scientistic pretensions.[147] It is anti-predictive in its emphasis on the interplay of structure and event/contingency/temporality. If anything, it can only work on the basis of a last instance appeal to heed specificity, incongruity, the particular that is never subsumed by the general law or theory or structural account, which would scarcely surprise the fairly conventional idiographic historian. Althusser dubbed his own theory of change, with its different 'temporalities' and all, 'matérialisme aléatoire', 'aleatory materialism':[148] 'aleatory' means dependent upon chance rather than determination, and whatever Althusser's theoretical elaboration it brings to mind nothing so much as Harold Macmillan on the disruptive power of 'events, dear boy, events'. Analogously, Derridean deconstruction demands that the reader be alive to resistances in the text, precisely so it does not assume the reductive capacity of any reading that is too keen to impose some theoretical grid on its subject matter.

Deconstruction takes a different tack from, say, biblical hermeneutics, which seeks to reconcile the particular and the general within a text, and to transcend ostensible contradictions.[149] Deconstruction is best known as a hermeneutics of

---

[145] Evans-Pritchard cited in Aletta Biersack, *Clio in Oceania: Toward a Historical Anthropology* (Washington, DC: Smithsonian Institution Press, 1991), 1.

[146] On explicit and implicit criticisms of structuralism see Derrida, *Writing and Difference*, 52–3, 197 and 351 ff.; and Derrida, *Margins of Philosophy*, 307–30. For Derrida's position on different temporalities in the Althusserian vein, Jacques Derrida, *Positions* (Chicago: University of Chicago Press, 1982), 57–9.

[147] Michael Peters, '(Posts-) Modernism and Structuralism: Affinities and Theoretical Innovations', *Sociological Research Online*, 4:3 (1999) http://www.socresonline.org.uk/4/3/peters.html

[148] Louis Althusser, *Écrits philosophiques et politiques*, vol. 1 (Paris: Éditions Stock, 1994), 21 and *passim*.

[149] For an attempt to establish relationships between Derridean hermeneutics and its more 'conventional' predecessors, John D. Caputo, *Radical Hermeneutics: Repetition, Deconstruction, and the Hermeneutic Project* (Bloomington: University of Indiana Press, 1987).

disruption, which can turn parts against the whole, and it is used in interrogating the claims to authority in legal or philosophical texts. It is alive to the constructed, conventional nature of binary oppositions, which is its debt to structuralist precepts, and it owes to psychoanalysis its attention to minor textual 'tics' that may be tantamount to Freudian slips. None of this means that deconstruction necessarily de-legitimates the argument of the text on which it operates, but it does mean that space is opened up for alternative readings than that which the author seems most obviously to be intending.[150] However indiscriminately deconstruction was applied as it reached the level of high intellectual fashion in literary theory—Derrida regretted the extent to which the interpretative 'freeplay' he had spawned had been accorded too great a status, preferring the more limited 'play', *jeu*—it engaged with many elements of a text and as such represents an advance on, say, Hayden White's reductive formalism, with its proximity to structuralism and its programmer's talk of codes.[151]

The issue of discriminate application obtains when it comes to deconstruction's relevance for works of History. Unlike philosophical or legal or theological tracts about how things 'just are', or 'must be', or 'ought to be', works of History are generally concerned with making claims on how things contingently were, or contingently came to be. Historians do not—or certainly ought not—claim for their work the same sort of conceptual completeness or closure that are often claimed for the other sorts of text. (Even in their primary task of explaining some development or illuminating some past world of experience historians should know that their work is incomplete.) In other words, Histories have none of the supposed axiomatic coherence that some might contend deconstruction exists to scrutinize.[152] Indicatively, when Derrida reviewed Foucault's *Folie et déraison* there was nothing distinctively 'deconstructive' about his essay, nothing in

---

[150] There is more to it than this of course. An excellent account is Simon Critchley, *The Ethics of Deconstruction: Derrida and Levinas* (Edinburgh: Edinburgh University Press, 1999). Thanks to Guy Halsall for discussion on these matters.

[151] To other literary analysts White claimed that the greater 'utility' of his semiological method over the utility of any content-based approach was 'quantitative—it could 'account for more of the elements of any given text'. While enjoining historians to liberate their subjectivity from a conservative historical idiom, he criticized other literary theorists for basing their analyses on 'personal taste, inclination, or ideological commitment'. Instead, he prescribed a method that sought 'to characterize the types of messages emitted [by a text] in terms of the several codes in which they are cast and to map the relationship among the codes thus identified both as a hierarchy of codes and a sequence of their elaboration'. All White quotes from Russell Jacoby's analysis of White in Jacoby, 'A New Intellectual History', in Elizabeth Fox-Genovese and Elisabeth Lasch-Quinn (eds.), *Reconstructing History* (London, Routledge, 1999), 94–118, here 100–1. For White's disparaging of deconstruction and the poststructuralist turn, see his chapter 'The absurdist moment in contemporary literary theory' in White, *Tropics of Discourse*, ch. 12, pp. 261–82.

[152] Critchley, *Ethics of Deconstruction*, 2, says that 'the pattern of reading produced in the deconstruction of—mostly, but by no means exclusively—philosophical texts has an ethical structure'. Though qualified, this statement implies that the nature of the text itself is relevant to the relevance of deconstructing it. See also Umberto Eco, 'Intentio lectoris: The State of the Art', *Differentia*, 2 (1998), 147–68, here 166. Christopher Norris, *Derrida* (Cambridge, MA: Harvard University Press, 1987), 20–7, 52–60, addresses the literature–philosophy nexus, as well as debunking the 'freeplay' element.

principle to distinguish it from an 'ordinary' critical review.[153] The question of deconstruction's relevance also pertains to historians' readings of historical evidence. Insofar as historians address past theological, philosophical, or legal texts they tend not to treat them in the way that their authors might have wished them to be treated, being more concerned with the question 'what did it mean to them in the past' than 'what should it mean to us now?'

For all that works of History are not works of philosophy, any Foucauldian would remind us that historians' products can be implicated in relations of power in the present just as that which historians treat as historical evidence might well have been implicated in relations of power in the past under historical study. In a more prosaic vein, as most historians well know, works of History and evidence both belong to worlds where certain things are assumed, expected, and elided; they reflect the influence of contexts over and above what their authors may wish to convey. As such, reading practices associated with deconstruction may be deployed by and against historians. Looking at historiographical debates and historical evidence respectively, Guy Halsall and Ethan Kleinberg both make use of the idea of constitutive silences, meaning the 'absences' that help structure what is expressed in a text or oral utterance and that can therefore be 'read' in light of what is expressed, in order to shed light on the unconscious, the taken-for-granted, or the deliberately suppressed.[154] How far such practices are original to Derrida is not always clear given the long, rich history of hermeneutics and rhetoric;[155] if deconstruction owes a debt to Heidegger and Nietzsche, the modern study of constitutive silences may be traced back to Leibniz via Hegel's dialectical recognition that that which comes into being, or receives articulation, constitutes a repression of that which does not (pp. 183–4). Those not *au fait* with the relevant theory may yet find themselves doing something tantamount to reading for constitutive silences in historical evidence when they read it 'against the grain' of the author's evident agenda.

Whatever the relevance of 'full-blown' deconstruction for historians, post-structuralism, as a proposition about the relationship of structure, genesis, and flux in any system of meaning, and thus about the instability of meaning, must have some affinity with a 'discipline of context and process', as Thompson called History. In Thompson's words, 'every meaning is a meaning-in-context, and

---

[153] Derrida, *Writing and Difference*, 36–76.

[154] Guy Halsall, 'Transformations of Romanness: The Northern Gallic Case', in Walter Pohl, Clemens Gantner, Cinzia Grifoni, and Marianne Pollheimer-Mohaupt (eds.), *Transformations of Romanness: Early Medieval Regions and Identities* (Berlin: de Gruyter, 2018), 41–58; Ethan Kleinberg, *Haunting History: For a Deconstructive Approach to the Past* (Stanford: Stanford University Press, 2017), chs. 1 and 2.

[155] For some relevant debts to the philosopher Friedrich Schlegel (1772–1829), especially in the areas of reading texts for contradictions and the significance of inferable unconscious meanings, see Michael N. Forster, 'Hermeneutics', in Leiter and Rosen (eds.), *The Oxford Handbook of Continental Philosophy* (Oxford: Oxford University Press, 2007), 30–74, here 45–8.

structures change while old forms may express new functions or old functions may find expression in new form,[156] which is not far from Nietzsche's point that 'the whole history of a "thing", an organ, a tradition can...be a continuous chain of signs, continually revealing new interpretations and adaptations.'[157] To this problematic the poststructuralist would add the uncertain stance of the interpreter in the ever-changing, multi-contextual present. Derrida equated 'there is no outside-text' (hors-texte), sometimes translated as 'there is nothing outside the text', with there is no 'outside-context', sometimes translated as 'there is nothing outside context'. Everything is interpreted through conceptual schemes rather than just apprehended, and these schemes, relating as they do to other interpretations, present, and past, are never transparent. There is no space that exists in a state of separation from context.[158] Far from negating any attempts to interpret, Derrida's point was that all that was left was interpretation, of the diverse and often conflicting elements of one's own lifeworld and of other lifeworlds.[159] This did not mean just any old interpretation, irrespective of intelligence, erudition, or procedural ethos, so we may discard the 'anything goes' idea that was sometimes associated with poststructuralism; as Derrida put it in a related connection, 'it should be possible to invoke rules of competence, criteria of discussion and of consensus, good faith, lucidity, rigor, criticism, and pedagogy.'[160] Again, contra structuralism and other positivisms, he disavowed a final master interpretation that claimed some objective grounding in semiotic codes or logics (a similar objective grounding to that once claimed by quantitative methodologists) that would situate the investigator outside the interpretative process. Derrida took it as a Gadamerian given that the interpretative process would be a fusion of the interpreter's horizon(s) of meaning—a horizon that was contextually shaped in the present—with the set of contextual meanings bound up with the object of the interpretation. That fusion is one of the reasons why the deconstructionist rejects the idea that any reading can finally establish the meaning of a text.[161]

Thinking to rationales for History and analogous interpretative acts, there is, by Derrida's thinking, always the possibility of something like an authentic encounter with another world for the interpreter who is sufficiently open to the possibility of embracing interpretation in its unknown potential. Such an event-like encounter, or 'interruption', can expand or alter the interpreter's own symbolic world. In the theoretical jargon, there is potential for the hermeneutic

[156] E. P. Thompson, Persons and Polemics: Historical Essays (London: Merlin, 1994), 213.

[157] Nietzsche, On the Genealogy of Morality, Second Essay, §12, at p. 51.

[158] Jacques Derrida, Limited Inc. (Evanston, IL: Northwestern University Press, 1988), 136. See also 9, 148, 152.

[159] John D. Caputo, The Prayers and Tears of Jacques Derrida: Religion Without Religion (Bloomington: Indiana University Press, 1997), 276–7.

[160] Derrida, Limited Inc., 146. See also 144.

[161] On Derrida's debts to Gadamer, see Michael N. Forster, 'Hermeneutics', 66–8.

sublime.[162] (The link here to the broader preoccupation of mid- and later twentieth-century French philosophy with the structure-busting 'event' is not at all coincidental—and note that Althusser also called his 'aleatory materialism' the 'matérialisme de la rencontre' or materialism of the encounter. If we wished to go further back we could trace elements of such concern to religious notions of epiphany and *kairos*.[163]) Following this reasoning as applied to History, studying the past can be a species of Travel in a stronger sense than just collecting photos for an album. If, as is now a commonplace, the practice of History tells us about the present, then studying the past can also alter us in the present, just not by handing us the decoding machine.

New New Histories

In recent generations, especially since the 'new cultural History' one supposes, it has been more professionally advantageous to be a new something than an old one. To be self-referential, I was labelled a practitioner of the 'new transnational trend' in History for a work on the international origins and aftermaths of the Armenian genocide.[164] The label captured an important aspect of what I was up to, though had I been asked at the time of writing the book I would have mumbled something about combining diplomatic, political, and social History as a contribution to 'genocide studies'—the 'studies' bit of which, as in medieval studies or queer studies, denotes an interdisciplinary approach to which History can contribute.

Sometimes I have also described my work as 'new international History'. Where the 'transnational' label captured the important regional and cross-border dynamics of my project as regards knock-on effects between developments in the southern Balkans, Anatolia, and the Russian-ruled Caucasus, the 'international' moniker worked a little better for the elements of geo-strategy, foreign policy, and diplomacy that came into play when further removed powers, including Britain, France, and the USA, were involved. As it happens transnational History owes

---

[162] Paul Patton, 'Events, Becoming and History', in Jeffrey A. Bell and Claire Colebrook (eds.), *Deleuze and History* (Edinburgh: Edinburgh University Press, 2009), 33–53, here 41–3; Derrida, *Writing and Difference*, 74: on dialogue 'between that which exceeds the totality and the closed totality' and more generally *Writing and Difference*, 193–211. The concepts of openness and the hermeneutic sublime, etc., show Derrida's debts to the work of the philosopher Emmanuel Levinas (1906–95) on the ethic of relationship to the 'Other', notably in regard of the appearance of the 'face' of the other. On this relationship see Critchley, *Ethics of Deconstruction*.

[163] This is true of Levinas (see previous note), for whom the 'face' of the other is akin to the face of god. See also on the connections between philosophy and theology in some twentieth-century Continental thought Ward Blanton and Hent de Vries (eds.), *Paul and the Philosophers* (New York: Fordham University Press, 2013).

[164] Jay Winter, review of Donald Bloxham, *The Great Game of Genocide* (Oxford: Oxford University Press, 2005), in *European History Quarterly*, 38:1 (2008), 126–8, here 126.

a significant debt to the 'older' area studies tradition, which suggests that some of the 'new' Histories are really conceptually expanded versions of prior sorts, evincing the influence of the major twentieth-century 'turns' in their additive and corrective manifestations. The new political History is a case in point.[165]

Since roughly the end of the Cold War global and world History have developed major significance. With the disappearance of the 'second world', nonaligned status also became meaningless. Much of what had been problematically called the 'third world' had already been incorporated into the economic structures of international capitalism. After the downfall of the USSR most of the rest of it was incorporated too, alongside Russia and the other formerly Soviet states. 'One world' was the result, albeit that some parts of it were 'developed' and some still 'developing'. 'Globalization' was the buzzword for the dynamic by which different parts of the world were connected. Connectivity, embodied in the rise and rise of multinational corporations, labour mobility, cheaper travel, and freer finance flows, encouraged a re-focusing away from the nation-state and towards the forces that transcended national boundaries. The History of international law and international political institutions received a boost for much the same reasons.

Historians were also encouraged to think backwards to earlier moments of globalization, such as the nineteenth-century heyday of the British empire. The old economic theory of 'hegemonic stability'—where stability referred to the operations of the international economy rather than the lives of people affected by the hegemon's actions—meant that one need not jettison the study of empire in order to partake of one of the new Histories. As to the new global hegemon, American-led armed interventions, after the successful prosecution of the 1991 Gulf war had ameliorated the 'Vietnam syndrome', and especially after the terrorist attacks of 11 September 2001, were but another sign that national destinies were not entirely in the hands of national leaders and domestic majorities, despite decolonization.

It was not just modern or 'modernizing' empires that piqued the interest. Decentring the nation-state prompted renewed attention to other sorts of polity, a range of empires included, that might previously have been deemed irrelevant to the post-1918 or post-1945 worlds in which nation-states proliferated. Conversely, with the emphasis on continuity rather than contrast, for all of the political imperative for postcolonial states to develop Histories of and for the nation-state, the border-transcending forces of the present surely also prompted scholars to

<hr />

[165] Steven Fielding, 'Political History', and Patrick Finney, 'International History', online respectively at:http://www.history.ac.uk/makinghistory/resources/articles/political_history.html http://www.history.ac.uk/makinghistory/resources/articles/international_history.html

See also Allan G. Bogue, 'United States: The "New" Political History', *Journal of Contemporary History*, 3:1 (1968), 5–27.

pierce the 'periodization blinders that prevent scholars from finding commonalities between the colonial and national periods'.[166]

Precisely what defines global and world History respectively is to some extent in the eye of the beholder, but some generalizations are possible. The journal *World History* was only established in 1990, but world History has been practised in a recognizable form since at least the Enlightenment. It treats the world as its unit of analysis and is concerned with trends and tendencies that are observable in or across the boundaries of many societies. There is some fusion between world History and global History in works that treat the world as an interconnected whole. The scholarship of William H. McNeill from the 1960s and 1970s exemplifies, as it addressed the interactions of different cultures, as opposed to painting a Spenglerian portrait of monads wending their own way through time without really influencing one another.

Global History tends to be associated more with the processes of globalization and its antecedents. We should note the paths broken by the neo-Marxist school of 'world systems theory', which set itself against the precepts of 'modernization theory', and drew in its turn on 'dependency theory' and ultimately on Lenin's and Rosa Luxemburg's theories of imperialism. Perhaps it is no coincidence that a Marxist anthropologist, Eric Wolf, should have been so prominent in illustrating the relations between different peoples across the globe while countering a stereotype of westerners and 'the west' as historical agents acting on more passive 'others'. In global History the emphasis is on connections between parts of the whole (the globe) and as such it is perfectly possible to write a global History of a village, or indeed a person, as long as one embeds that object in relation to things spatially removed. One is apt to read quite a lot about cultural exchange, explorers, commerce, and commodities from spices to opium to cotton, and, to use a term from postcolonial theory, 'hybridity'.[167]

If much global History and world History tends to be practised these days in a way that decentres the European or occidental experience, thus providing an important corrective to earlier Eurocentric accounts, this is a development more at the level of historical content than historical method or concept. Put in the terms of the postcolonial theorist Dipesh Chakrabarty, such 'provincialization' of the west as has occurred in historiography *within the global north-west* has been

---

[166] Jacob Blanc and Frederico Freitas, 'Introduction', in Jacob Blanc and Frederico Freitas (eds.), *Big Water: The Making of the Borderlands Between Brazil, Argentina, and Paraguay* (Tuczon: University of Arizona Press, 2018) 3–21, here 10.

[167] For similar distinctions between the overlapping spheres of global and world History see Diego Olstein, *Thinking History Globally* (Basingstoke: Palgrave Macmillan 2013). William H. McNeill's works, some of which do have Eurocentric aspects, include in their number *The Rise of the West: A History of the Human Community* (Chicago: Chicago University Press, 1963); *A World History* (New York: Oxford University Press, 1967). As to Eric Wolf: *Europe and the 'People Without History'* (Berkeley: University of California Press, 1982).

more a matter of empirical focus than anything else.[168] The great 'turns' of twentieth-century historiography—social, cultural, linguistic—and what were in their moment the avant-garde theories associated with these turns—Marxism, structuralism, poststructuralism, serried literary and anthropological movements— were embedded in western intellectual trends and often reflected western cultural problems. This is not to suggest a hermetic seal separating western from non-western trends; we are dealing in generalizations rather than categorical divides. And it is certainly not to suggest that only 'western' minds could have conceived of these theories. The point of dwelling on the conceptual self-referentiality of much mainstream north-western historiography is as oft before, to highlight regrettable inequality along the north-west/south-east cleavage. The matter is important because of the still-great influence in the wider world of north-western academies and their fashions.

Within north-western academies the tide of cultural History has ebbed but the 'cultural History of X' tradition (p. 282) remains influential, as in Histories of the body, bodily experiences, or emotions. Indeed, given the thoroughly historicizing thrust of the 'affective turn', it does no conceptual harm to see it as a subset of the new cultural History.[169] At the same time, it is eminently possible for the study of, say, emotions, to be fused with the enduring study of History 'from below', as is urged by the American Marxist historian and one-time student of E. P. Thompson, James R. Barrett, in his recent essay collection *History from the Bottom Up and the Inside Out: Ethnicity, Race, and Identity in Working-Class History* (2017).[170]

Within the broad ambit of semiotic analysis, the Foucauldian input is variable, but has certainly shaped 'subaltern' historical studies since the earlier Gramscian–Thompsonian days of that movement. Postcolonial theory, which is obviously not coextensive with all the History produced in postcolonial states, is deeply imbued with power theories alongside its critical concern for linguistic–cultural binaries like civilized/uncivilized. Looking at the historio-graphical traditions of the author's own country, imperial History, the 'new imperial History included', could do with a stronger dose of postcolonial theory to complement its traditional strengths in political and economic analysis and in the relevant social History of the metropole.

Intellectual History has followed the trajectory of neo-historicism characteristic of so much twentieth-century historiography, and has enjoyed something of a

---

[168] Dipesh Chakrabarty, *Provincializing Europe: Postcolonial Thought and Historical Difference* (Princeton: Princeton University Press, 2000). See also the debate between Chakrabarty and Dirlik at n. 92.

[169] Rob Boddice, 'The Affective Turn: Historicizing the Emotions', in Cristian Tileagă and Jovan Byford (eds.), *Psychology and History: Interdisciplinary Explorations* (Cambridge: Cambridge University Press, 2014), 147–65.

[170] James R. Barrett, *History from the Bottom Up and the Inside Out: Ethnicity, Race, and Identity in Working-Class History* (Durham, NC: Duke University Press, 2017), 1–2. For elements of Barrett's intellectual biography, see the book's foreword by David R. Roediger.

resurgence in recent decades. If we were to characterize, perhaps caricature, an 'older' intellectual History tradition it would have a Hegelian flavour in the sense of treating past philosophy as its own time represented in thought, and/or a 'vertical' character whereby philosophical texts address each other in a grand conversation across large tracts of time. Twentieth-century linguistic theories (not just francophone ones like structuralism, but those of the likes of J. L. Austin and Ludwig Wittgenstein) and associations with political thought and Kuhnian thought on the History of Science helped move the axis more to the 'horizontal'— see the thoughts of intellectual historian J. G. A. Pocock on what constitutes 'context' (pp. 132–3), and the vast Cambridge University Press monograph series 'ideas in context' that bears the imprint of Quentin Skinner. Tying philosophical texts much more closely into their immediate contexts of enunciation and reception is perforce to integrate them more broadly with social, political, and cultural concerns, and the thinking of 'non-canonical' intellects, and reinforces the neo-historicist orientation towards viewing intellectual History as the study of 'the intellectual life of the past in its knotty, irreducible pastness'.[171]

Two relatively recent and still relatively marginal historical approaches are noteworthy for the way in which they engage different articulations of 'culture' at very different scales and levels of enquiry. On one hand we have historians engaged in environmental History in the broadest sense, where recurrent patterns of climate change, demographic shift, disease, and natural disaster fill the places traditionally reserved for wars, cultural crises, and grand discoveries. Culture as broadly conceived does remain important here, since the climate change which we have begun to witness is human-caused—anthropogenic—and the geological epoch in which we now live has been dubbed the Anthropocene. The interactive, indeed interpenetrative culture–nature relationship in question here is similar to the one that Marx was getting at with his thought on labour. Presumably we will see more of this work as the degradation of the environment belatedly gets the attention it merits and cultural responses are formed to the huge material pressures of desertification, heat waves, sea-level rises, and resource scarcity. The other general pattern-builders also work at the interface of History and science, and are concerned with sociobiological and 'biocultural' explanations for human cognition and behaviour.[172]

---

[171] Quote from Stephan Collini, 'The Identity of Intellectual History', in Richard Whatmore and Brian Young (eds.), A Companion to Intellectual History (London: Wiley, 2016), 7–18, here 10. On the role of political thought and the History of science, see p. 9. See pp. 10–11 on the recent growth of intellectual History, and the entirety of the essay for an assessment of the state of the field. Skinner's debts to Austin's language theory, and Skinner's broader hermeneutic philosophy are outlined early in Skinner, 'Hermeneutics and the Role of History', New Literary History, 7:1 (1975), 209–32. As to 'vertical' versus 'horizontal' approaches, see Collini, 'Intellectual History' at: http://www.history.ac.uk/makinghistory/resources/articles/intellectual_history.html

[172] See, for instance, John Onians, Neuroarthistory: From Aristotle and Pliny to Baxandall and Zeki (New Haven: Yale University Press, 2007); Daniel Lord Smail, On Deep History and the Brain

Some strands of scientifically oriented History have elicited claims that cultural differentiation and associated neo-historicism have over-egged the pudding, and that a Ciceronian view of History's role as teacher of life should instead be reactivated.[173] Relevant reasons were elaborated in 2010 by the literary theorist Marshall Gregory. He based his advocacy of a new ethical turn in literary criticism partly on the 'new empiricist' work on common human 'biocultural' and cognitive heritages. In a swift summary he begins with philosophers including Mark Johnson and Richard Eldridge[174] who argue that

> instead of human beings being creatures of social construction 'all the way down', human beings have a nature in which, not very far down at all, lies a vast network of inclinations, dispositions, neural programming, and perceptual protocols that come installed in every human being's brain as a part of our evolutionary heritage....In 1991 Mary Midgley published *Can't We Make Moral Judgments?*, and in 1992 Robert Louden published *Morality and Moral Theory: A Reappraisal and Reaffirmation*, both of which argue that ethics comes neither from transcendental sources nor entirely from culture, but from intrinsic human needs that get mediated and tweaked by culture but that are not created by culture....In 1996 Steven Mithen published... *The Prehistory of the Mind*, giving readers a sense of the vastness of time in which evolutionary pressures shaped the human brain, and, thus, also shaped many features of human cognition, emotion, perception, and interpersonal protocols, such as ethics.[175]

This is a good corrective to what is indeed in parts of the humanities a scientifically illiterate 'culture-is-all historicism' as Geertz scornfully called it, but it does not close the case.[176] Viewed from enough distance cultural variations certainly look like variations on a theme, just as convulsive events lose their jarring significance, but particularists are within their rights to emphasize the variations rather than the theme. How 'far down' commonality appears is still relative to question, whatever conclusions scientists reach.

(Berkeley: University of California Press, 2008); Iain McGilchrist, *The Master and his Emissary: The Divided Brain and the Making of the Western World* (New Haven: Yale University Press, 2009). See also the list in Caroline W. Bynum, 'Perspectives, Connections & Objects: What's Happening in History Now?', *Daedalus* (Winter 2009), 71–86, here 77–8.

[173] Wolf Schäfer, 'Knowledge and Nature: History as the Teacher of Life Revisited', *Nature and Culture*, 2:1 (2007) 1–9.
[174] Mark Johnson, *The Body in the Mind: The Bodily Basis of Meaning, Imagination, and Reason* (Chicago: University of Chicago Press, 1987); Richard Eldridge *On Moral Personhood: Philosophy, Literature, Criticism, and Self-Understanding* (Chicago: University of Chicago Press, 1989).
[175] Marshall Gregory, 'Redefining Ethical Criticism: The Old vs. the New', *Journal of Literary Theory*, 4:2 (2010), online at: http://www.jltonline.de/index.php/articles/article/view/287/879
[176] Clifford Geertz, 'Anti Anti-Relativism', *American Anthropologist*, New Series, 86:2 (1984), 263–78, here 268.

For the same reasons one may also take issue with the historian of religion and postmodernist Callum G. Brown, who claims that morality's 'absence of constancy is especially noticeable for those alive in the last 60 years as western society has undergone the most dramatic shift in its sexual, racial and legal morality'.[177] Far from closing the case, Brown begs the question about variables, comparators, and the relative magnitude of the relevant differences. By way of making the contrast with a certain representation of pre-modern historical consciousness, Zachary Schiffman suggests that were we today 'to ask ourselves whether we would be different had we been born ten years earlier or later, most of us would automatically answer in the affirmative—while dismissing the question as too obvious'.[178] 'Different', certainly, but how different?

The present work has proffered particular views on change and continuity, difference and similarity, in a discipline of thought that counts the study of just those duos among its major concerns. Specifically, the objects of concern have been justifications for History, which means what the study of the past has been thought to 'do' for historians and their audiences. There is no consensus as to justification today and there never has been but interestingly enough the menu of options over which historians still argue has not changed much in two and a half thousand years. To conclude the book, let us assess the justifications head-on.

---

[177] Callum G. Brown, *Postmodernism for Historians* (Harlow: Pearson, 2005), 145. Emphasis added.
[178] Zachary Sayre Schiffman, 'Historicizing History/Contextualizing Context', *New Literary History*, 42:3 (2011), 477–98, here 496.

8
Justifying History Today

Introduction

This chapter tackles rationales for History on their own merits, in and for the here-and-now. As well as considering the relatively young rationales of History as Emancipation and History as Therapy, it returns to those that have existed for millennia, namely History as: Entertainment; Memorialization; Speculative Philosophy; Practical Lesson; Moral Lesson; Travel; Method; Communion; and Identity. It considers which rationales still have any currency, concluding in favour of all but Speculative Philosophy, Moral Lesson, and Communion in its original sense. It then assesses the ones that do have currency for their coherence, before making suggestions of its own.

Predictably enough, in most cases coherence depends upon how each rationale is interpreted and what is promised on its behalf. For instance while History as Travel can broaden the mind, as its proponents suggest, it cannot of itself foster the virtue of tolerance. Your author is less sanguine than many about the prospects for History as Emancipation, and more optimistic than many about forms of History as Practical Lesson. History as Method has something going for it but even on its own best ethical terms it needs to be bolstered by some substantivist concerns, meaning concerns related to the content of the past rather than just to procedures for researching and writing History. And when we come to the slightly less exalted claims by which History as Method translates to the historian's 'transferable skills', the vocations to which the skills are transferred often do not need or even desire the more holistic critical ethos that is supposed to underpin their deployment.

It would be better to say that coherence is addressed where necessary, as it is not in the case of History as Entertainment. One simply is or is not entertained, and it is debatable how fruitful the discussion is as to whether one ought or ought not be. The fact that many people do seem to find History entertaining, as judged by broadcasting and bookshops, might be thought rationale enough for it. In an academic world where more and more emphasis is put upon measurable results and monetary value the peculiar 'utility' of merely finding something interesting or enjoyable ought perhaps to be celebrated. At the same time it does seem, measured again in terms of broadcasting and bookshops, that people are especially entertained by particular sorts of History rather than just anything that happens to be historical in focus, so the Entertainment rationale is generally alloyed with other rationales. A theme running through the chapter and brought to the fore in the section 'Knowledge and Human Interests' involves the tricky question, arising from a rationale like Entertainment, of what it is for something to be intrinsically interesting, or important, as opposed to being more instrumentally relevant.

Given crossovers between certain classes of rationale this chapter will not allot equal or equally explicit attention to all. Thus the case of Memorialization is subsumed within discussion of the Identity and Lesson genres. History as Identity remains arguably the most important of all the substantivist rationales: it is certainly the most significant politically, which is why this chapter and thus the book is crowned with a discussion of it. History as Identity is so often at issue even when the identity question is addressed only indirectly via History as Travel, since it is difficult to get away from the matter of how one defines oneself in relation to other, different ways of being and doing. Furthermore, those historians who engage in Emancipatory History à la Foucault would be more effective if they engaged more directly in Identity History, replacing their 'crypto-normative' critiques (the expression is explained below, p. 339) and engaging normativity straightforwardly. Extending the discussion of normativity, the very final pages of the book turn to the matter of moral evaluation by the historian, suggesting that evaluation is not a category error or an anachronistic residue of the days when History as Moral Lesson was explicitly endorsed by many historians.

History as Speculative Philosophy

In the historical profession, Speculative Philosophy is at its lowest ebb for many centuries, perhaps for the entire history of History. Hayden White claimed to the contrary, but this was more by assertion than illustration. A major influence on White, the literary theorist Northrop Frye, reflected on Aristotle's distinction between poetry and History, according to which the latter only dealt with the particular whereas the former dealt with the universal. Frye claimed 'that when a historian's scheme gets to a certain point of comprehensiveness it becomes mythical in shape and so approaches the poetic in its structure'.[1] White radicalized the claim, holding at the end of his opus *Metahistory: The Historical Imagination in the Nineteenth Century* (1973) that 'proper history and speculative philosophy are distinguishable only in emphasis'. In White's view the former sort of History, the sort of History that most historians think they are engaged in, was just more surreptitious or implicit in propagating some philosophy of History beyond its explanation of some specific historical issue.[2]

[1] Northrop Frye, *Fables of Identity: Studies in Poetic Mythology* (New York: Harcourt, Brace, and World, 1963), 53–4.
[2] Hayden White, *Metahistory*, 427.

It is difficult to square White's vision with the highly contextual neo-historicist tendencies of latter-day historiography. But even in White's accounting it is unclear exactly how broad a section of 'proper' History he is referring to when making his claims. The preface *of Metahistory* makes White's distinction between on one hand historians' data, theoretical concepts for explaining and ordering the data, and so forth, and on the other hand the 'deep structural content which is generally poetic [i.e. creative], and specifically linguistic, in nature, and which serves as the precritically accepted paradigm of what a distinctly "historical" explanation should be'. Yet the preface goes on to qualify that '[t]his paradigm functions as the "metahistorical" element in all historical works that are more comprehensive in scope than the monograph or archival report'.[3] It is unclear exactly what he means by an archival report, but since he has excepted monographs, which constitute the bulk of the book-length output of most academic historians, one assumes that he is also prepared to exclude journal articles, which generally have a monographic quality and constitute much of the non-book-length output of most academics. It is reasonable to suppose that thematized textbooks or problem-oriented primers are out of the equation too. What we do not have from White is a theoretical explanation of the salient difference between the salient sorts of History, which leaves us with the tautological claim that all types of History have metahistorical elements that have metahistorical elements.

Putting aside that problem and taking White on the terms of his more unqualified claim about the relationship between 'proper' History and speculative philosophy, he failed to distinguish consistently between a philosophy of History and a theory of History. The difference is that one can lay claim to some theory about motors of historical change without having any account of history's working towards some end, or any theory of a human essence being revealed through the historical process.[4] Sometimes White did equate ordinary works of History with theories of History in this non teleological sense, but even then the equation does not work, or certainly need not, if we recall for instance Helmut Fleischer's distinction between the nomological and the pragmatological Marx (pp. 186–7). Beyond Marxist historiography, one must distinguish between the many and diverse generalizations that underpin accounts of why X happened to transpire, and firmer supposed laws of the historical process by which X had to transpire; all works of History deploy the former in some measure, while few seem to deploy the latter.[5] Finally, even in the event that we accept the unsubstantiated claim that there is 'only' a difference in emphasis between 'proper' History and speculative

---

[3] Ibid., p. ix.

[4] Alex Callinicos, *Theories and Narratives: Reflections on the Philosophy of History* (Durham, NC: Duke University Press, 1995).

[5] Peter Munz, 'The Historical Narrative', in Bentley (ed.), *Companion to Historiography*, 851–72, esp. 860–1. Similar points about generalizations in Alan Bulloch, 'The Historian's Purpose: History and Metaphysics', in Meyerhoff (ed.), *The Philosophy of History in Our Time*, 292–9, here 295–7.

philosophy of History, a large enough degree of emphasis can be rather significant. There is only a difference in degree—of consciousness—between my being asleep and my being awake but it seems useful to hang onto the distinction.

History as Method

At my university's open days for potential students, far from proclaiming the historian as oracle we employees are apt to be found extolling the 'transferable skills' developed in the practice of History. This is a benefit of History as Method. The idea of transferability appeals to historians' self-image as critical thinkers while sounding worthwhile to potential employers of History students. It promises to blend holistic and instrumental criteria—the argument goes that critical minds are good things for people and society to have in general, whilst being useful in a narrower productive sense.

Employment patterns suggest that historical training is valued in many workplaces, either directly or when refracted through conversion courses. That may be enough for those looking to 'sell' the discipline, but it only tells us necessarily about the technical side of the historian's training and its instrumental potential. It does not necessarily say anything about the whole critical-reflective disposition that a historical training is also said to foster. So let us distinguish between the thought of a rather stereotyped functionary and 'critical' thought. The distinction is between those who apply their thinking in pursuit of the already established ends of some extant set-up, and those who might apply their thinking critically towards the founding assumptions of the set-up. The values that one reflects on as a citizen might sit uncomfortably with the interests that one furthers in one's job by one's particular skillset—of course they also might not clash, but the point is that skills in the narrow sense are neutral as to the purposes they serve, whereas the critical faculty in the broader sense is not. She who lends her skills professionally to the pursuit of maximizing profit may or may not as citizen approve of the set-up that incentivizes such behaviour. She who has developed her critical faculties might appreciate that the very idea that one's work be hived off from one's life as a citizen stems from a particular worldview that is itself eligible for criticism.

A second heuristic distinction cuts across the distinction between critical thinkers and functionaries. It is a distinction based on the varying roles of truthfulness in relation to the conduct of one's activities. On one side are intellectual disciplines like History for which truthfulness is (or ought to be) a governing value. On the other side are undertakings for which truthfulness is not necessarily a governing value. The significance of this distinction is best elucidated by considering some of the specific claims made on behalf of History and other scholarly undertakings.

The historiographer John Tosh lists among the virtues that have been proclaimed for History the provision of 'a training in the rational evaluation of evidence and argument, on which democratic discourse depends', adding that this classically liberal justification 'is probably the only perspective on which all historians agree', but also that 'it amounts to no more than claiming for history a special distinction in attitudes which are found in other disciplines too'.[6] The study of literature, poetry, and pragmatist philosophy has indeed enjoyed similar endorsement from some of its advocates,[7] and we ought also to note the connection that Karl Popper drew between scientific method, openness to new conclusions, and the 'open society'.[8] In *Human, All Too Human* Nietzsche provided his own justification for systematic enquiry:

> On the whole, scientific methods are at least as important as any other result of research: for it is upon the insight into method that the scientific spirit depends...Clever people may learn as much as they wish of the results of science...[but] lack the scientific spirit...They are content to find any hypothesis at all concerning some matter; then they are all fire and flame for it and think that is enough....If something is unexplained, they grow hot over the first notion that comes into their heads and looks like an explanation—which results progressively in the worst consequences, *especially in the sphere of politics*. For that reason everyone should now study at least one science from the bottom up: then he will know what method means and how important is the utmost circumspection.[9]

Now in many of these cases an 'appropriate' contribution to the political or civic spheres is associated with procedure, i.e. with respect for a methodical process. But how well does the analogy with intellectual disciplines like History work when we move beyond questions of procedure to the ethos of truthfulness governing the procedure?

There are reasons to doubt the efficacy of the analogy at this level. Nietzsche had an intellectually conscientious politician in mind, yet whatever one thinks politics should be about, judging by the record of many successful politicians, a training in certain skills of analysis and argument might produce people who are very good at deceit, or the instrumental and selective use of evidence to bolster

---

[6] John Tosh, *Why History Matters* (Basingstoke: Palgrave, 2008), 120.

[7] J. Hillis Miller, *The Ethics of Reading* (New York: Columbia University Press, 1987), 5; Stanley Fish considers some candidates from the realms of poetry and pragmatic philosophy: Fish, *The Trouble with Principle* (Cambridge, MA: Harvard University Press, 1999), 300.

[8] Popper's contentions are considered in Nigel Rapport (ed.), *Democracy, Science and the 'Open Society': A European Legacy?* (Münster: LIT, 2005) with a summary of Popperian claims in Rapport, 'Introduction', 1–32, here 2–4.

[9] Nietzsche, *Human, All-Too-Human*, §635: Friedrich Nietzsche, *The Portable Nietzsche*, ed. Walter Kaufmann (Harmondsworth: Penguin, 1983), 64–4. Emphasis added.

sectional interest under pretence of open enquiry or pursuit of the common good. Such people we might call propagandists. If 'propagandist' sounds too prejudicial, take the adversarial stance of the lawyer in the common law system. The lawyer tries to win an argument by any means that can be gotten away with within the rules of the courtroom, rules which are by no means the same as the rules of scholarly enquiry invoked by Nietzsche et al. The lawyer honours her profession—and fulfils an important social role—by acting as a zealous advocate for a party to a dispute. When contrasting historians on one hand and lawyers and certain politicians on the other, the claim is not that historians do not succumb to advocacy or propagandistic forms of argument. Today, at least as much as before, there is a professional tendency and a commercial imperative to make one's mark by a 'strong argument', where 'strong' does not mean 'well-substantiated' so much as 'provocative'—'better to be strong and wrong', I have heard said. Alan Bennett's play *The History Boys* (2005) reported rather than invented a vision of the discipline wherein the capacity to persuade that orange is green is a virtue to be applauded. Nevertheless, there is a different balance of governing ideals in an intellectual discipline of supposedly open enquiry, as opposed to the balance pertaining in sundry official, representative, and adversary roles, however appropriate and even admirable the differing balances might be in their respective spheres.

As we move the discussion on, please note that the assertion that truthfulness ought to be a governing ideal for those in the intellectual disciplines is made in full awareness that, insofar as it has been an ideal for historians over time, the understanding of what 'truthfulness' means has varied along with concepts of truth. In this book we have encountered concepts of truth as plausibility or as capturing the way things generally are assumed to be irrespective of particulars. We have heard of historians bolstering their truth-telling authority by catering to popular belief in omens and miracles. But we have also encountered the concept of audience expectations of Histories, the greater credence audiences gave to some parts of a work than others, audience awareness of authorial tropes, and so forth. In short, we have grounds to believe that there was very often an implicit contract of trust between writer and audience as to the nature of the written product, however much the product and the expectation differed over time. We have also tracked a diminution of the types of 'truthfulness', with increasing prioritization of a certain literal, particular sort, as opposed, say, to figural truth. This diminution over time correlates roughly with the rise of specialism, then professionalism, if also with a decline in certain hermeneutic traditions. Today, on the whole, central to the contract of trust that the historian has with her audience is a stipulation as to the historian's truthfulness in this narrower sense. The contract is underwritten by a belief, right or wrong, that by their training historians are best placed to honour that particular ideal of truthfulness in the (method-ical) way in which they draw inferences from evidence, but there must be a presumed commitment to truthfulness in the first place. Indeed, irrespective of how things were in the past in the practice of historians, there are good Kantian reasons for high-lighting the significance of the contract of trust, because to abuse trust—to deceive—is to treat audience members as means for the agenda of the deceitful historian, not as ends in themselves. To deceive might also involve co-opting the denizens of the past. In the absence of a tacit commitment to fulfilling the contract of trust with the audience, the historian will step into the shoes of the zealous advocate with her different and, in the context of the discipline as it is at present, inappropriate ethic of vocational responsibility.[10]

That august body, Britain's Incorporated Association of Assistant Masters in Secondary Schools, was heading roughly in the direction of venerating truthfulness when, alongside advocating the marketability of the historian's skillset, its *The Teaching of History* (1957) noted:

> Accuracy in apprehension and statement, ability to distinguish what is relevant and to select what is important—these are at least as necessary in studying history as in other disciplines. More peculiar to history itself [!] are the weighing of evidence, the detection of bias, the distinguishing of truth from falsehood, or at least the probable from the impossible.[11]

A clarification: the focus in this section is on *truthfulness* rather than the 'truth' invoked by the Assistant Masters. Under discussion is not the ability to ascertain historical truth,[12] which, even in the event that we all accepted a common definition, will always be the subject of argument in an inferential undertaking. The idea of truthfulness as a disposition or regulative ideal rather than truth-finding as a capacity is the sort of thing the historian and political scientist Mark Bevir is getting at when designating objectivity a normative standard to which to aspire, rather than an epistemic claim about one's standpoint or achievement. Truthfulness as a parameter or ideal is implicitly honoured by the likes of the historian and historiographer G. J. Reiner who noted in 1950 that 'the morality of history-writing is exclusively methodological'.[13] It is explicit when intellectual historian John Zammito lists 'truth-telling' as chief among what he calls the 'cognitive virtues' of the scholar.[14] The medievalist Eric John made the same point.[15] One historian said of the British cohort that Bentley calls modernists (p. 249) that those 'new academic professionals' regarded accepting the principles of

[10] By 'the audience' I mean a general audience, not a particular one that might wish to have its prejudices confirmed against another part of the potential audience.
[11] Cited in D. M. Sturley, *The Study of History* (London: Longmans, 1969), 7.
[12] Williams, *Truth and Truthfulness*.
[13] Mark Bevir, 'Objectivity in History', *History and Theory* 33:3 (1994), 328-344, here 335; G. J. Reiner, *History: Its Purpose and Method* (London: Allen and Unwin, 1950), 255.
[14] John H. Zammito, review of David Carr, Thomas R. Flynn, and Rudolf Makkreel (eds.), *The Ethics of History* (Evanston, IL: Northwestern University Press, 2004) at http://ndpr.nd.edu/news/24599-the-ethics-of-history
[15] Eric John, 'Some Questions on the Materialist Conception of History', *History*, 38 (1953), 1-10.

non-partisan dispassion and method as itself 'morally elevating'.[16] The Belgian historian Jean Stengers reached much the same conclusion.[17] Nancy Streuver thinks that 'Not the past, but investigating the past is edifying. From this follows the very economical decision not to apply moral criteria to historical actions, not to stipulate morality as present or absent in historical actors, but rather apply moral criteria to the acts of investigating historical events.'[18] Streuver's fellow intellectual historian Allan Megill states that 'the epistemology of historical investigation is closely connected to the ethics of historical investigation', indeed that the obligation to 'the maximal telling of truth ... is where the only ethics of history worthy of the name is to be found'.[19] From a critical perspective, the postmodernist cultural theorist Elizabeth Deeds Ermarth notes that 'History is a method', and that 'Its method is its moral'.[20]

Zammito importantly complicates the picture when he identifies 'cultural responsibility' as another category of ethical salience alongside 'truth-telling', deliberately leaving 'cultural responsibility' vague in light of the many possible interpretations of it.[21] We should think of 'cultural responsibility' as a category that may subsume 'truth-telling' rather than standing in juxtaposition to it, given the cultural prominence of historians as 'truth-tellers', or, more properly, expert inferrers-from-evidence. Not all historians think their cultural responsibilities fully discharged by their commitment to truthfulness. Without conducting exhaustive examination of the possible variations in interpretation of 'cultural responsibility' or related concepts like 'political responsibility', one may still say this: the idea that the commitment to truthfulness must perforce be undermined if the historian writes with additional motives is a Platonic fallacy. One cannot judge the validity of people's claims by their motives for making them. Take the historian who wishes to write the History of group X 'back into the historical record' out of some sense of injustice, or fidelity to group X in the present. Obviously the writing 'back' can be done in better and worse ways in the procedural sense but if one has evidentiary warrant to infer that group X has been the subject of an enduring cultural stereotype, or suffered historically, or made some contribution hitherto ignored in the historiography, then undermining the stereotype or recording the suffering or contribution can serve the non-procedural motives of the historian while honouring procedural precepts.

[16] John Kenyon, *The History Men* (Pittsburgh: University of Pittsburgh Press, 1984), 283.
[17] Jean Stengers, 'Quelques réflexions sur le jugement moral en histoire', *Bulletin de la Classe des Lettres et des Sciences morales et politiques de l'Académie Royale de Belgique*, 5th ser., 58:5 (1972), 189–205.
[18] Nancy Streuver, 'Philosophical Problems and Historical Solutions', in Bernard P. Dauenhauer (ed.), *At the Nexus of Philosophy and History* (Athens: University of Georgia Press, 2010), 73–93, here 85.
[19] Megill cited in Zammito review of Carr et al. (eds.), *The Ethics of History*.
[20] Ermarth, 'Ethics and Method', *History and Theory*, 43:4 (2004), 61–83, here 63.
[21] Zammito review of Carr et al. (eds.), *The Ethics of History*.

We can also approach the issue from a different direction. Truthfulness is obligatory when one embarks on a historical investigation but one has first to choose what to investigate. The simple fact one believes something to be true is no reason to say it. One needs a line of enquiry to which it is pertinent. In the choice of questions one may ask about the past there is no parallel to the precepts that govern procedure in the answering of those questions. (And even if all historians embodied the proceduralist ethos no two of them would come up with exactly the same answers to the same question.) If we are to have any History we need people with motives to study bits of the past. Political motives, including motives emerging from the general, holistic critical attitude to which an education in History might itself contribute, are as good as any other motives assuming that they do not override the procedural commitment about the way one answers a question.

Overall, the justification History as Method is a slightly odd one when it stands alone, even in the event that its promise is realized – and we have provided reasons why the promise of 'transferability' may often not be realized in important senses. In its purest form the procedural rationale is divorced from any concern with the content of the past, which is peculiar for a discipline whose claim to distinction is the study of the past. Since other disciplines also teach critical thought and presuppose a commitment to truthfulness, proceduralism is a rationale for studying the past but, equally, for studying something other than the past.

Knowledge and Human Interests

Unsurprisingly, advocates of History as Method tend to augment it with other rationales, just as they did in classical antiquity. For Acton as for Tacitus judging without fear or favour was itself an exercise in civics: methodological proceduralism was married to a concern with the content of the past, i.e. to a (moral) substantivism. Elton struggled to reconcile his general proceduralism with his substantive determination that politics was what the historian should study on grounds of its particular importance.[22] Those British historians invoked by Kenyon also had distinct hierarchies of significance in subject matter to go alongside their method-asceticism. Streuver's claim that it is not the past itself but rather the act of 'investigating the past [that] is edifying' (p. 311), turns out over the course of her essay not to be a paean to pure proceduralism. Her position is substantivist in its concern to engage the dialogic or conflictual elements in the past, as opposed to just any part of the past. Thus 'the usefulness of history lies in its

[22] Quentin Skinner, 'Sir Geoffrey Elton and the Practice of History', *Transactions of the Royal Historical Society*, 6th ser., VII (1997), 301–16.

reconstitution of our memory of specific controversy, bitter quarrel, endless debate'.[23]

Substantivist rationales for History are numerous indeed, and historically have been the most prominent. Let us start with the most general, the idea of knowledge for knowledge's sake. That idea, roughly speaking, was the object of the French Enlighteners' scorn as they contrasted themselves with the *érudites*.

It has been intimated with reference to historical coverage in any bookshop that certain bits of the past just do attract more attention than others. Taking the next step, it is difficult to show that anything in the past or indeed the present is *intrinsically* interesting, because that means that it is interesting in and of itself, objectively interesting as it were, rather than being an object of someone's interest, where that interest is subjective. Investigating or obtaining the object of the interest is a way of satisfying some need or desire. Again, there is nothing necessarily sinister in identifying interests. Interests are endlessly diverse and the interests in question could be products of the merest whim, rather than, say, the interests of the ruling class—though for those seeking strong justifications for History whimsy could be just as problematic!

For some professional historians, knowledge for knowledge's sake can be a petition to be allowed to follow their own interests, however tightly defined, whilst still drawing a salary; that would be an argument to narrow interest. But when people invoke 'knowledge for knowledge's sake', it is to be hoped that they do not really mean 'knowledge for my sake, and very possibly no one else's'. There is a difference between a reason some particular person might be interested in the study of the past and a reason why the past might be deemed a thing worth encouraging people in general to take an interest in. 'Knowledge for knowledge's sake' implies that knowledge is in some way a good thing, and one assumes that this is a general good.

One way of conceiving this broader conception of good is to reflect on what it might be defined against, which brings us to those early nineteenth-century artists who talked of 'art for art's sake'. Those artists were opposed to utilitarian conceptions of human activity, the reduction of everything to some marketplace logic or instrumental function. Through their art—and this is also Adorno's and Horkheimer's view of the role of 'authentic' works of culture—they wished to

---

[23] Streuver, 'Philosophical Problems and Historical Solutions', writes that 'The history of the use of casuistry is interesting, the history of employed moralisms is not' (p. 88). However, she goes on to relate to the substance of the past not just in the form, say, of past argumentative strategies but as regards the moral weight of that substance. It becomes not just a matter of History of the *use* of casuistry, but History of the impact of issues about which casuistic arguments are used. In insisting on 'history as constituting a shared memory of our confections of moral identity', she sees the constraint 'to positive as well as negative considerations of past manifestations of moral competence' (p. 89), which implies nothing less than moral assessment of things past. If 'even negative thoughts about the past are ethically viable', paving the way for the 'uses of a bad past' (p. 90) then judgement is presupposed. This is little distance from exemplary History.

prompt people to explore wider dimensions of human experience and diverse sorts of meaning, encouraging imagination and creativity rather than just reflecting a pre-packaged mundanity. In a typology of intellectual undertakings called *Knowledge and Human Interests*, whose title has been purloined for the heading of this section, Adorno's and Horkheimer's student Jürgen Habermas associated History, or at least the sort of History informed by hermeneutics, as a discipline of 'communication' with others.[24] As with the visions of Vico and Dilthey, this sort of knowledge was of a different sort, with different purposes and potentials, than knowledge of the natural world or instrumentalizing technological know-how. Insofar as History as Communion in its conventional religious sense has declined, the nub of what Habermas calls communication is a rough secular equivalent. When communication pertains to past versions of the present We, the relevant rationale is History as Identity, but that rationale finds a complement in the serious versions of History as Travel, when communication stretches to those of obvious cultural distance.

Nevertheless, whatever the claims made for a mind-broadening, non-utilitarian utility under the rubric 'knowledge for knowledge's sake', questions may always be raised about how far the principle can be taken. Is there literally nothing in the past whose study cannot be vindicated by the claim 'History for History's sake'? How far does study of X really open our eyes, or help us reflect on our condition? Depending on perspective the arguments in favour of 'knowledge for knowledge's sake' could produce the conclusion that it is an unassailable rationale for History or a weak one. The arguments have similar strengths and flaws to the argument that one cannot put a price on the study of the past. That argument, which is supposed to undermine market-based justifications for History, might end up raising public investment in the study of the past. It might also justify reducing History's allocation from the public purse, since if a price cannot be put on History then a small price is no more inaccurate a quantum of its value than a large one.

History as Practical Lesson

Reaching even a loose consensus as to the substantive value of studying the past is not made easy by the fact that some academic historians often trade on a general sense of History's relevance while rather belittling the sorts of reasons that non-academics might espouse. There are also different ways of honouring oneself. For every popularizer who rides to celebrity on the back of the hard-won findings of archival scholars, there are several cosmopolitan-but-protectionist historians, self-appointed gatekeepers of esoteric knowledge: 'it's more complicated than

---

[24] Jürgen Habermas, *Knowledge and Human Interests* (Cambridge: Polity Press, 1987), 309–10.

that, as you would know if you had read the sources in four languages and twenty archives'.

The tension between 'relevance' and 'specificity' has grown with academic specialism and with the ever finer differentiations characteristic of neo-historicism. It has been highlighted in Britain by successive governments' demands that academics in all fields show the social, political, or economic 'impact' of their research. ('Impact' is a separate category of measurement to quality, so in the overall reckoning one can offset a jamboree of impact against a deficit of 'excellence'.) Since there are funding and ranking connotations that set institution against institution by way of marketizing the sector, some historians are increasingly concerned to show some quantifiable relevance of History even while others fight an anti-utilitarian rearguard under the banner of 'knowledge for knowledge's sake' or 'holistic critical faculty'. Putting to one side inane and/or pernicious British higher education policies, the underlying intellectual issues have concerned serious thinkers since at least the time of Aristotle.

How, given the focus on knowing more and more about less and less during one's training, is one to answer the PhD examiner's 'so what' question? The very asking of the question renders ineligible a 'knowledge for knowledge's sake' defence. The implication is that some knowledge is more valuable/relevant/significant than others. Over-interpretation can be one way of responding to the question, with hard-earned empirical precision accompanied by conceptual overstretch, as if one's chosen topic were a microcosm of a larger homogeneous whole, or a case study of one among a standardized class of entities. In order to justify their study, particular signs and texts must embody wider systemic logics or discourses, or, the reverse, be the signs of deep conflict within the historical meaning-system from which they sprang.[25] If one cannot claim wider empirical or heuristic relevance for one's subject matter one may hope alternatively to hone an investigative method of more general utility. The frenzy to coin terms that one hopes will catch on, with appropriate footnotes to their progenitor, is the most obvious instance of this tendency; the kingdom is yours if your name ends up being associated with a 'turn'.

The risks of over-interpretation are the price often paid for conceptual and methodological innovation, so one should not be too harsh on over-interpreters. But it does need to be noted how much the generalizing tendencies of over-interpretation can militate against the neo-historicist logic with which the gatekeepers of esoteric knowledge try to police their empirical bailiwick. Student and examiner alike also need to recognize that measurements of significance are relative to scale and interest. The work of the examiner who asks 'so what?' may fall foul of allegations of irrelevance when the focus is moved up an order of

---

[25] Raphel Samuel, 'Reading the Signs II: Fact Grubbers and Mind-Readers', *History Workshop Journal*, 33 (1992), 220–51, here 243–4.

magnitude, and there is likely a difference between what the examiner—a particular specialist professional—will find significant and what other historians, not to speak of members of the general public, will find significant. So while the 'so what' question derives from a substantive rationale for History stronger than own-sake-ism, it rarely carries a stipulation as to who the substance of the past is supposed to be important for.

The History-reading public has been moved rather less profoundly than the academic profession by the 'turns' of the last four decades. This is partly because of the rise of an alienating jargon, a tendency which at once stems from and reinforces a wider tendency: most historians write primarily for other historians. A minority of popularizers attend to the tastes and needs of the reading public, which is itself relatively diverse owing to the spread of literacy. Unlike in classical antiquity and beyond, only a few historians of any stripe today see elite decision-makers as the major target audience, which is also an outcome of the turf-war over the centuries between History and other disciplines, notably political philosophy and then the social sciences. History has ceded ground in some areas while having more fall-back positions than these other disciplines have. So while History as Travel, Entertainment, Memorialization, and Identity remain influential, History as Practical Lesson in the classical form of elite instruction is rarer than it used to be.

As with other rationales, History as Practical Lesson has metamorphosed rather than disappearing. It has softer and harder types. Lessons can come in more and less literal form, and, in the shape of History as Emancipation, in 'negative' form. Some relatively hard lessons are inferred by readers even when not necessarily propounded by historians. The story of war-waging politicians fighting present wars through the lenses of the memory of previous wars is among the most unfortunate and important of such cases—a blend of imagined exemplarity and the *similitudo temporum* that has for centuries acted to reduce the historical distance between relevant pasts and present, in a way that runs against the distancing tendency of 'modern historical consciousness'.[26] Not that there is any shortage of historians trying to cash in on anniversaries with stronger arguments as to the relevance of the memorialized event than the fact that past and present moments are linked by calendrical digits.

Tosh has a 'soft' practical rationale in mind when he suggests that 'historical re-creation' offers 'vicarious experience to writer and reader alike'.[27] Vicarious experience was identified as a benefit of History by Carl Becker and, slightly more

---

[26] On exemplarity in policymaking, Ernest May, *'Lessons' of the Past: The Use and Misuse of History in American Foreign Policy* (New York: Oxford University Press, 1975); Yuen Foong Khong, *Analogies at War: Korea, Munich, Dien Bien Phu, and the Vietnam Decisions of 1965* (Princeton: Princeton University Press, 1992).

[27] John Tosh, *The Pursuit of History*, 2nd edition (Harlow: Longman, 1993), 29.

recently, the historian of late antiquity Henri Marrou.[28] The historian of science Thomas Söderqvist rejects the connotations of the sociologically oriented social constructionist approach to the History of science, which he sees as downplaying the creative agency and individuality of particular scientists. He commends writing detailed biographies that empower readers to make their own existential choices by showing how historical figures made theirs. This is a form of practical inspiration without any accompanying template for action.[29] Foucault implied a rather harder lesson when he wrote of retrieving 'subjugated knowledges' buried beneath dominant thought systems (pp. 280–81), and at points in his work on ancient Greece he subscribed to something not so very distant from exemplarity.

Foucault's views shifted as to the balance of similarity and difference across time, which reflected amongst other things the difference between his sedimenting horizontal-structural 'archaeological' approach and the diachronic biopsy of his 'genealogical' approach. When trying to establish his position on the relationship between past and present, and thus the use of History for life, there is also a tension between his detailed, monographic 'analytical' historical work about regimes of power-knowledge and his 'diagnostic' and prescriptive thinking about resisting power in the present, which was to be found in the form of short essays and interviews. It is said by one of Foucault's enthusiasts of his late career lectures at the Collège de France that 'nowhere more clearly than [here] do we see the balancing, the alternation, and the overlapping of these two poles'. Carefully chosen words; 'reconciliation' is not among them.[30] In what turned out to be his final years, Foucault had not achieved a consistent view on History's utility, but it is clear that on occasions he was far *less* ruthlessly (neo-)historicizing than many of the historians influenced by his early and mid-career work. When asked in 1983 whether ancient Greek ethics offered a plausible alternative in the present his answer was emphatically negative. 'I am not looking for an alternative; you can't find the solution of a problem in the solution of another problem raised at another moment by other people. You see, what I want to do is not the history of solutions—and that's the reason why I don't accept the word *alternative*. I would like to do the genealogy of problems, of *problématiques*.'[31] Now it takes little reasoning to establish that there must be some relationship between the History of problems and that of solutions, and a little later in the same interview Foucault confirmed as much. 'Among the cultural inventions of mankind there is a treasury of devices, techniques, ideas, procedures, and so on, that cannot exactly be

---

[28] Henri Marrou, *The Meaning of History* (Dublin: Helicon, 1966), 260; Becker, *Detachment*, 61.

[29] Thomas Söderqvist, 'Scientific Biography as a Hermeneutics of Edification', *International History of Science Newsletter*, no. 3 (April 1995), 4–6. For additional references and a critique: Paolo Palladino, 'Icarus' Flight: On the Dialogue between the Historian and the Historical Actor', *Rethinking History*, 4:1 (2000), 21–36.

[30] Foucault, *Society must be Defended*, editor's introduction, pp. xvi–xvii.

[31] Michel Foucault, *Ethics: Subjectivity and Truth*, ed. Paul Rabinow (New York: New Press, 1997), 256.

reactivated but at least constitute, or help to constitute, a certain point of view which can be very useful as a tool for analyzing what's going on now—and to change it.[32] History is the teacher of life, as Cicero wrote. When asked months later whether the ancient Greek practice of personal development that he called 'care of the self' should be updated, Foucault responded enthusiastically, in the fashion of Gadamer on the fusion of horizons: 'Absolutely, but I would certainly not do so just to say, "We have unfortunately forgotten about the care of the self; so here, here it is, the key to everything."...[Conversely again, this] does not mean that contact with such and such a [classical] philosopher may not produce something, but it must be emphasized that it would be something new.'[33] In his 1984 paper 'What is Enlightenment?' he ended up somewhere in the triangular space delineated by the Gadamerian horizon-fuser, the Diltheyan historicist concerned with the balance of general and particular, and the Ciceronian topical thinker. In any case he was far from the earlier theorist of inter-epistemic rupture, which conveniently fitted his move backwards from the later 1970s from the study of modern History to his examinations of classical History:

> historico-critical investigations are quite specific in the sense that they always
> bear upon a material, an epoch, a body of determined practices and discourses.
> And yet, at least at the level of the Western societies from which we derive, they
> have their generality, in the sense that they have continued to recur up to our
> time: for example, the problem of the relationship between sanity and insanity,
> or sickness and health, or crime and the law; the problem of the role of sexual
> relations; and so on.[34]

It is hard to quantify the relevance of an issue at one point in time to a related or roughly similar issue at another point in time, but that may be more of a problem for those preoccupied with quantification than those who seek broader and richer insight. When one talks of 'shedding light' on a problem one does not necessarily mean definitively solving that problem but helping to conceive of its relevance and dimensions in a new way, apprehending its persistence across time in a way that may promote investigation of alternative or additional causal elements, and so forth.

Foucault aside, historical or at least quasi-historical analysis has served some highly influential modern philosophers, including Heidegger, Adorno and Horkheimer, Gilles Deleuze, and above all Rousseau and Nietzsche. To begin with, philosophers can gain more than just antiquarian knowledge from the historical study of their own discipline. The History of philosophy is relevant to philosophical thought because philosophy itself is a product of the evolution of

---

[32] Ibid. 261.   [33] Ibid. 294–5.   [34] Ibid. 317–18.

previous philosophies, philosophical questions the derivatives of earlier philosophical questions. Philosophy is significantly constituted by its theory of itself, and that theory evolves historically.[35] Thinking to philosophers' relationships to broader society, while the historical evolution of practices and the concepts which the practices embed is not strictly relevant to an assessment of their 'logic', efficacy, or appropriateness (see pp. 338–9), philosophy is not limited to those sorts of assessments. The explanation of how a course of developments produced some concept in its current shape fulfils a rather Hegelian role of philosophy as a mode of making sense of the practices of the philosopher's time.

From the throng of more conventional historians, an example of practically helpful scholarship is produced by Katie Barclay. It was published on the British 'History and Policy' website which, as its name suggests, was set up with the aim of influencing public policy with reference to relevant History. Barclay's piece is entitled 'Creating "cruel" welfare systems: a historical perspective'. Its introductory summary is as follows:

> Current welfare systems are coming under significant critique, not least for 'cruelty' to service users[;] Abuse and cruelty in previous welfare systems have been at significant cost to individuals and nations[;] Historical welfare policies provide useful evidence of how systems designed to care can become cruel[;] Abuse by caring institutions is not just a problem of 'isolated perpetrators', but is enabled by the ideologies around, investments in, and management of welfare systems.[36]

While Barclay's piece works by comparison/analogy, for example from the moralistic attitude to work and the deliberate harshness of welfare regimes in late eighteenth- and early nineteenth-century Ireland to the present in Britain, the work of the social historian Louise Jackson in the same online venue highlights a different relationship of relevance between past and present—the relationship of genealogy. Her piece on 'Child sexual abuse in England and Wales: prosecution and prevalence 1918–1970' points to problems with the law's response to abuse, showing amongst other things that 'Legislation developed in the nineteenth century, which reflected Victorian moral values, was adapted inadequately to deal with offences against children' which led to legal loopholes. 'It also made it impossible for politicians, policy-makers and campaigners to monitor increases in sexual offences against children using criminal justice statistics.'[37]

---

[35] On the theoretical self-constitution of theory, Kwame Anthony Appiah, *In My Father's House: Africa in the Philosophy of Culture* (New York: Oxford University Press, 1992), 142.

[36] http://www.historyandpolicy.org/policy-papers/papers/creating-cruel-welfare-systems-a-historical-perspective published 1 March 2018.

[37] http://www.historyandpolicy.org/policy-papers/papers/child-sexual-abuse-in-england-and-wales-prosecution-and-prevalence-1918–197 published 18 June 2015.

'Hardest' of all in practical aspiration was some of the quantitative sociological social History of the 1960s–1970s. While it could not be said that the likes of Paul E. Johnson's doctoral supervisor succeeded in making History into a predictive social science (p. 269), this does not mean that History has nothing to contribute in terms of informing action here and now, or, conversely, that the social and political sciences that take prediction as part of their business are as good at it as some of their more scientist practitioners claim. Note the failures of the relevant experts to see the warning signs of the USSR's collapse or the 2008 financial crisis. Conversely note the relevance of the economic History of the 1929 crash and ensuing depression to policy-choices in the last decade or so—irrespective of whether those lessons have been learned by policy-makers. That the past does not guarantee the future only means that we cannot predict the way that transformation and reproduction will interact, not that there will be no reproduction. If one wishes to go down the route of History-as-prediction, the fact that there is no way of guaranteeing the accuracy of predictions does not mean that there is no point trying to anticipate, make contingency plans, or, say, speculate on outcome distributions rather than particular instances. (I might not be able to predict the career pattern of any given one of my students but I am on firmer ground in projecting from extant data that roughly X per cent of the undergraduate History cohort will go into a particular line of work, Y per cent into another.) Prudential thought, as Aquinas knew, was a future-oriented product of reflection on the past, and the social sciences are in the same boat as History insofar as the evidence on which they rely pertains to the past, even if that is only the recent past. Based on historical experiences acquired in one decade, one could, for instance, project with a reasonable degree of confidence some of the outcomes of IMF-dictated 'structural adjustment programmes' as they continued to be imposed on 'developing economies' in the next decade.

We had better be aware that there are patterns and trajectories that exist not because of some divine will but because humans have put them in place. Carol Anderson's *White Rage* (2016) provides chapter and verse on the roll-back reactions that have followed every significant African American political advance over the last 150 years or so.[38] Historical *laws* there probably are not; historical *trends* there most certainly are. Some of these trends can be very large and long-term ones, as with 'the rise of capitalism' and 'the generalization of the nation-state form'. 'The marketisation of universities' is a shorter-term manifestation of one of those longer-term trends. If one wants to change or perpetuate trends or structures, analysing them is helpful. To the extent that understanding their evolution is helpful, then History is helpful—though it is understandable that historians, like one of their number, Ranke, might not wish to justify themselves by

---

[38] Carol Anderson, *White Rage: The Unspoken Truth of Our Racial Divide* (New York: Bloomsbury, 2016).

their value as under-labourers to the social sciences and political philosophy. And, as Nietzsche put it, one needs to exercise the utmost circumspection here, as elsewhere.

History as Moral Lesson

The stock of History as Moral Lesson has depreciated for many of the same reasons that have affected the fortunes of History as Practical Lesson. Contextualism, historicism, anachronism, relativism, neutralism: sometimes historians appeal to one of these concepts as against evaluative thought when they mean another. They can be placeholders that interchangeably vouchsafe the non-judgemental disposition one feels one ought to adopt towards the foreign country past, where they do things differently.

It is, nonetheless, not unheard of for historians today to justify their work with reference to moral edification. Michael Dintenfass recommends that History become 'a project of the should and the ought as well as the did and the was', though he would have done well to register that this was a function of History for most of its existence.[39] John Arnold thinks that examining 'what human beings have done in the past—the bad and the good—provides us with examples through which we might contemplate our future actions'.[40] This sounds old-fashioned, but who decreed that historians had to adopt a modern enthusiasm for the new? The historical theorist Jörn Rüsen once pointed out how little we really know about the way readers assimilate History, and in an attempt to help rectify the situation through an empirical study at the University of Bochum he found that students embraced exemplarity as a way of learning.[41] We have seen that the point of topical thinking, which is a few millennia old, is that it is not a form of rote-learning but an example-based exercise in honing one's thinking such that it can be deployed in new situations. One 'thinks with' real-life or hypothetical scenarios, which is why novels, with their dense, highly contextualized evocations of complex, fraught situations, can be so stimulating to the critical faculty.[42] This does not mean one expects to find a situation which mirrors one's favourite read in all particulars. No less a moral rationalist than Kant recognized that examples are the 'go-kart' of moral thought—that which gives impetus to the whole

---

[39] Michael Dintenfass, 'Truth's Other: Ethics, the History of the Holocaust, and Historiographical Theory After the Linguistic Turn', *History and Theory*, 39 (2000), 1–20, here 20.

[40] John Arnold, *History: A Very Short Introduction* (Oxford: Oxford University Press, 2000), 118.

[41] See George Kitson Clark on morality: *The Critical Historian* (London: History Book Club, 1968), 207. Jörn Rüsen, 'The Didactics of History in West Germany: Towards a New Self-Awareness of Historical Studies', *History and Theory*, 26:3 (1987), 275–86, here 282–3.

[42] This is one of the core tenets of the thought of those sometimes called literary Aristotelians. See for instance Marshall Gregory, *Shaped by Stories: The Ethical Power of Narratives* (Notre Dame: University of Indiana Press, 2009).

endeavour by illuminating the real and possible stakes, concretizing thought by reference to specifics.[43]

Even if one forswears exemplarity, that is a far cry from removing all evaluative elements from one's History. Exemplarity is a specific mode of didactics; evaluation, moral and otherwise, is an integral part of certain explanations and empirical characterizations, as we shall see later. The idea of evaluation is also inherent, despite appearances to the contrary, in the enduring doctrine that History is a teacher of tolerance.

History as Travel, History as Tolerance?

R. G. Collingwood, arguably the most influential English-language historian-philosopher of the first half of the twentieth century, stated that 'The past is in no sense whatever actual. It is wholly ideal. And that is why our attitude towards it is wholly different from our attitude towards the present, which, because it is actual, is the scene of our practical activity and the proper subject of our moral judgements.'[44] Where the historicists drew dividing lines of culture as well as time, Collingwood drew a line between those matters that were immanent to consciousness or susceptible to worldly action, and those that were inaccessible except through the traces that historians themselves had mentally to animate, as they worked their way into the mindset that motivated past *gestes*, deeds. In 1946, Collingwood established as one of his four defining criteria of History that it was 'self-revelatory', meaning that it 'exists in order to tell man what man is by telling him what man has done'.[45] This also meant telling 'man' what she was contingently not, in virtue of recognizing those historical characteristics that were incompatible with her own heritage and reflexivity. Either way, the result was a sense of shared historicity and a tolerance that Collingwood saw as the hallmark of the historical rather than the logical mind, given the latter's aspiration to singular correct outcomes. Tolerance meant 'the ability to live one's own life and yet to admire and love people who live by the systems which one rejects'. Such tolerance entailed avoidance of 'idolatrous worship of one phase of the past' at the expense of others or indeed the present, and by extension of the present at the expense of any past.[46] Collingwood's prescriptions, like aspects of his method, evoke

---

[43] Hannah Arendt, *Responsibility and Judgement* (New York: Shocken, 2003), 143–4.

[44] R. G. Collingwood, *The Idea of History*, revised edition (Oxford: Oxford University Press, 2005), 403–4.

[45] Ibid. 18.

[46] Lionel Rubinoff, *Collingwood and the Reform of Metaphysics: A Study in the Philosophy of Mind* (University of Toronto Press, 1970), 229; William M. Johnston, *The Formative Years of R. G. Collingwood* (The Hague: Martinus Nijhoff, 1968), 60; Alan Donagan, *The Later Philosophy of R. G. Collingwood* (Oxford: Clarendon Press, 1962), 246, and the review of Collingwood by Hayden White in *History and Theory*, 4:2 (1965), 244–52.

Herder.[47] If few historians then or since restricted themselves to Collingwood's conception of method, very many endorsed some variant of his rationale. The intellectual historian Arthur O. Lovejoy wrote:

> It is not impossible nor unprofitable for a rational animal—and it is imperative for the historian—to realize that his ancestors had ends of their own which were not solely instrumental to his ends, that the content and meaning of their existence are not exhaustively resolvable into those of the existence of their posterity. In these aspects of history lie not the least of its values; for it is they, especially, which make of it a mind-enlarging, liberalizing, sympathy-widening discipline, an enrichment of present experience.[48]

Similarly, Tosh writes that 'human awareness is enhanced by the contemplation of vanished eras',[49] whilst for Raymond Aron the 'never-ending discovery and rediscovery of the past is the expression of a dialectic which will last as long as the human race and which is the very essence of history: individuals and communities alike find contact with others enriching and self-revealing'.[50] Something of this attitude was present in the historian of early-modern Europe Hugh Trevor-Roper, who described historical imagination as 'the capacity to migrate into distant, foreign minds'.[51] For the social historian Richard J. Evans, History's 'most important justification lies in its less immediately tangible effects. History can teach us about other societies, other beliefs and other times, and so make us more tolerant of differences in our world.' Indeed he says that 'it can provide us with a democratic civic education to help us build a better world for the future'.[52] Alongside his pronouncements against value judgements, Butterfield also hinted at the argument to tolerance in his discussion of historians and attitudes to diversity.[53] Much the same philosophy was espoused by G. M. Trevelyan,[54] although the gist of the idea goes at least as far back as Herodotus. Perhaps the doctrine of tolerance that some have ascribed to William of Tyre in the crusader kingdoms was influenced by his historical thought (or perhaps the relationship

---

[47] Herder, *Philosophical Writings*, ed. Forster, editor's introduction, pp. xxvii–xxviii.

[48] Arthur O. Lovejoy, 'Present Standpoints and Past History', in Meyerhoff (ed.), *The Philosophy of History in Our Time*, 173–87, here 180.

[49] Tosh, *The Pursuit*, 29.

[50] Raymond Aron, 'Relativism in History', in Meyerhoff (ed.) *The Philosophy of History in Our Time*, 153–61, here 160–1.

[51] Trevor-Roper cited in H. P. Rickman, *Meaning in History: W. Dilthey's Thoughts on History and Society* (London: Allen and Unwin, 1961), 43.

[52] Richard Evans, 'What is History?', in Harriet Swain (ed.), *Big Questions in History* (London: Jonathan Cape, 2005), 1–12, here 5 and 7.

[53] Herbert Butterfield, *The Whig Interpretation of History* (New York: Norton, 1965), 95–6, cf. 109 and 117 against value judgements.

[54] Trevelyan's view summarized in Sturley, *The Study of History*, 6.

was the other way around).[55] We are on firmer ground with Bolingbroke: 'An early and proper application to the study of history will contribute extremely to keep our minds free from a ridiculous partiality in favour of our own country, and a vicious prejudice against others.'[56] Like Montaigne, Bolingbroke differs only in tone from Descartes's ever-so-slightly-dismissive conception of History as travel to broaden the mind: 'It is', wrote Descartes, 'good to know something about the manners and customs of other nations so that we may judge more sanely of our own, and may not think that whatever is contrary to our own mode of life is both ridiculous and unreasonable, as is usually the case with those who have seen nothing', although he also said that 'a man who has spent too much time in travelling becomes in the end a stranger in his own country; and a man who has too much curiosity about what happened in past centuries usually shows a great ignorance of what is happening in this one.'[57] Early in 2018 a group of senior British medievalists justified their activities in the face of assault by a government that included no small number of History graduates, concluding that studying History makes one a 'richer, better, more tolerant, better informed person.'[58] One of those had earlier written of the benefit of exploring an 'alternative world' because 'visiting the past is something like visiting a foreign country.'[59]

In the accounts of these scholars the idea of History as Travel is a non-instrumental justification for the discipline, akin to Habermas's vision of History as a form of communication (p. 314). There are some grounds for accepting the view: the basic interest in other ways of life, and how other humans experience things, clearly can exist apart from any utilitarian justification. But this is not the only reason for 'travel': what of that great British institution, the booze-cruise? Even the sort of tourism with a little more in common with 'the grand tour' may be more angled at gratification or relaxation than edification. (With the Presocratic Gorgias ringing in the ears (p. 30), one needs to reject the fallacy whereby something cannot be edifying if it is also entertaining: the question is of the nature of this entertainment.) When we come to matters like sex-tourism then self-gratification is also instrumentalization of others. In the scholarly and political realm, one only needs to reflect upon the role that historical and anthropological enquiry into the ways of 'others' has sometimes played in justifying imperialism: here Foucauldian critiques about the relationship of knowledge

[55] Rainer C. Schwinges, 'Kreuzzugsideologie und Toleranz im Denken Wilhelms von Tyrus', Saeculum, 25 (1974), 367–85; Ulrich Berner, 'Die Bibel in der mittelalterlicher Diskussion um Ketzer und Muslime', in Joachim Kügler and Werner H. Ritter (eds.), Auf Leben und Tod oder völlig egal: Kritisches und Nachdenkliches zur Bedeutung der Bibel (Munster: LIT, 2005) 11–24, here 22 ff.

[56] Bolingbroke, Letters, 27.   [57] Descartes, Discourse, 40.

[58] James Tapper, 'Is Medieval History Bunk? Not if you're a cabinet minister', The Observer, 28 January 2018.

[59] Arnold, History, 119–20.

to power cohere with Edward Said's critique of 'orientalism' and with some of the central concerns of postcolonial scholarship.[60]

The association of History as Travel with tolerance is also wrong if it comes with any presupposition of ditching the evaluative thought associated with History as Moral Lesson. The problem is identical to the liberal problem of whether to tolerate the intolerant or the intolerable. Tolerance is a principle which will have at points to compete with other principles. When, having explicitly disavowed moral evaluation, Collingwood et al. claim that History will encourage the embrace of human variety, each is prejudicing the issue. The attitude that is supposed to be inculcated by studying the past is imposed, or already possessed, prior to any particular encounter with the past, otherwise there is no guarantee of the right outcome. Here we find much the same confusion—or circularity—that we identified in the late nineteenth century when Fustel, Monod, and Fagniez decreed that History, 'properly' understood, would promote national unity and strength (pp. 235–6).

One cannot say in advance of encountering a specific practice that one will be tolerant of it. That would be to forego the possession of any other principle than tolerance, to render oneself so completely mutable as to have no identity as a value-bearing individual qualified to be tolerant. Some of us might find that studying the past makes us tolerant, others that it drives us to fury at the injustice of it all. Others might take inspiration from the evidence of so many people profiting from theft or slavery and getting away with it. Then again, surveying other forms of life past or present might produce admiration and a desire for emulation. As it happens such positively evaluative reactions are ruled out by the anti-evaluative 'tolerance' prescription in the same way that negative responses are.

Unusually for a thinker of his calibre, Collingwood ended up in something of a conceptual muddle over the tolerance question, When warning historians against thinking as if 'the massacre of Corcyra was now being enacted in the next room and we ought to break open the door and stop it' he was implying, in the same way as the philosopher Michael Oakeshott later, that such present-centric responses were category errors.[61] Why, then, is tolerance exempt from the charge of being a category error? It is, after all, a present-centric response that is (supposedly) produced in relation to some historical substance, i.e. some foreign way of thinking, being, doing. In the search for conceptual consistency ought we also to disapprove of tolerance as an upshot of History? Or ought we to rethink these prescriptions in light of the fact that people, historians included, will continue to have varying emotional, political, and evaluative responses to stories of the past? Indeed the inferred substance of the past that feeds these responses is significant in drawing people to History.

---

[60] Edward Said, *Orientalism: Western Conceptions of the Orient* (London: Routledge and Kegan Paul, 1978).

[61] Collingwood, *The Idea of History*, 404–6.

Advocates of History as Travel have something in common with Herderian students of *Volksgeist* in the sense that they invoke some generalized encounter with a whole foreign country past at the level of something like 'spirit' or *mentalité* or some concept of culture, but without the politics. One envisages a sojourner who sees the sights, eats the food, listens to some music, learns the language, but doesn't read a newspaper and so remains ignorant about what the new regime is doing to dissidents, or why the country is riven over an issue of social justice. That sojourner encounters what to him or her are peculiar cultural practices but feels 'tolerant' towards them on the assumption that they are practices approved by all parties within the foreign country. But as soon as the idea occurs of power imbalances or exploitation then 'tolerance' becomes a form of taking sides within the foreign country. At the same time, recognition of the lack of homogeneity within the foreign country reveals that an attitude of intolerance towards some practice is not the same as an attitude of intolerance towards the 'general culture' (whatever that means) or the social entirety of that foreign country, which is possibly the fear behind the advocacy of tolerance in the first place. Just the same goes in key respects for the doctrine of moral relativism.

One should rather say 'doctrines' of moral relativism. Perhaps the most intellectually powerful such doctrine is sometimes called meta-ethical moral relativism, sometimes just meta-ethical relativism.[62] It has nothing to say about what is good or bad but is rather concerned with the nature and justification of judgements about what is good and bad. The contention of this sort of relativist is that there are no rational grounds outside of societies to resolve deep-seated moral differences between societies; there are no external foundations or yardsticks for values and evaluation against which the values or the value-generating mechanisms of any given society can be measured. Let us leave this moot, because whatever power this relativist argument has in the abstract, it has little practical purchase when it comes to the way in which members of one society act and judge when they encounter members of another society. Furthermore, it is not in itself an argument against judgement across, say, cultural boundaries. The meta-ethical moral relativist could allow that judgement about some of culture B's practices was meaningful to members of culture A, and would merely claim, in a way that is irrelevant to the current argument, that such judgements have no basis to bind members of culture B.

A well-known species of moral relativism claims something like: 'we can only judge the moral rightness of a practice or value in accordance with the beliefs of the group that conducts the practice or holds the value, and if that group

---

[62] Good surveys of moral relativisms, including accounts of 'meta-ethical moral relativism' are: Maria Baghramian, *Relativism* (Abingdon: Routledge, 2004), ch. 9; Chris Gowans, 'Moral Relativism', in Edward N. Zalta (ed.), *The Stanford Encyclopedia of Philosophy* (Summer 2019 Edition), online: https://plato.stanford.edu/archives/sum2019/entries/moral-relativism/

considers the practices/values to be right, then it is wrong for external parties to criticize those practices/values'. This species of relativism is self-undermining because the stipulations about the conditions of judgement, culminating in the 'it is wrong' parts of the claim, are not themselves relativized. The sort of general, group-transcending conviction about what is right or wrong is just what the relativist in question seeks to delegitimate, so that selfsame relativist cannot appeal to a non-relativized sense of wrongness. Furthermore, this sort of relativism demands the impossible. Say that I encounter some foreign practice that brings obvious happiness or suffering to some member(s) of that society. My immediate reaction is to think how favourably or unfavourably that compares with some approximately equivalent practice to which I am accustomed, or just to think how pleasant or unpleasant the practice seems, period. Does the relativist tell me that I cannot have that initial, let us call it 'gut' reaction? If so, then she or he is whistling in the wind. Alternatively, does she tell me that I cannot progress from the immediate reaction to any further cognitive processing that might result in a more carefully formed value judgement, whether less or more favourable? If so, then even if such a dictum can really be followed in practice, it cannot remove my initial reaction, so my visceral impression will remain the same, and will merely be unadulterated by any reflection. In this case the relativist doctrine will actually hinder any understanding of the other society, as that understanding might be furthered by contextualized comprehension of the practice—comprehension of its social function, of the theories underlying it, of the attitudes to it of various practitioners, including the issue of how far those attitudes vary along power cleavages, and so forth. An agenda of sympathetic or admiring understanding is thereby excluded alongside one of condign judgementalism. Perhaps relativism permits the cognitive process up to but excluding any evaluation that I might make about the practice. Can such a dictum really be followed? Possibly, in theory, insofar as it is true that, while understanding and evaluation are not opposed—the former being a condition for the latter, as properly enacted—they are not the same thing. Yet actually no, insofar as the drive to understand in this scenario was provided precisely by the desire to progress beyond the initial judgemental reaction. Even without some formal conclusion to top off the whole business of reflection, it will be impossible to ignore the way in which the greater understanding negated, reinforced, or diluted my initial reflex-appraisal. Evaluation, positive or negative, is already upon me. The only question is whether it will be informed and reflective or uninformed and unreflective.

Whatever the relativist (and here the relativist can be of any sort) might think about the whole evaluative exercise, it cannot be said to be arbitrary, since it was stimulated by inference about happiness or misery in the foreign country. Far from being a necessarily imperialist exercise, the initial 'reflex' reaction connotes human recognition across the borders of disparate times and cultures. The further act of reflective evaluation concerning the causes of the happiness or suffering is the sort of mind-broadening experience that History as Travel is supposed to foster.

History as Therapy

The newer rationales for History are based less on the Travel and Methodology conviction that History will be *liberalizing* and more on the hope that it will be *liberating*. History as Therapy and History as Emancipation are present-centric, but since all rationales for History are present-centric in some way, that tells us nothing in itself about their proponents' commitments. Elements of both rationales are captured in Goethe's aphorism 'Geschichte schreiben ist eine Art sich das Vergangene vom Halse zu schaffen': writing History is a way of shedding the burden of the past. Like Nietzsche, who might have written the same words, Goethe regarded historians' primary responsibilities as being to themselves and their readers rather than to the past itself.[63]

Any discussion of History as Therapy must accord pride of place to the intellectual historian Dominick LaCapra. He argues that the historian is a 'secondary witness' to historical events and when those events are traumatic, the historians should, in the summary of the literary theorist Eric Kligerman, 'generate the lost anxiety of trauma in tolerable doses in order to circumvent repetition and filter the shock of history's traumas for the generations after the trauma'.[64] The alternative, by which I understand LaCapra to mean the result of standard historical practice in recounting traumatic events, is that the past might repeat itself: a traumatized individual re-enacts past traumas, as the historian forecloses on events like genocide by encapsulating them in descriptions whose claim to cognitive authority denies the capacity of the events to elude comprehension. The literary theorist Eric L. Santner suggested that conventional narrative accounts of traumatic events might constitute 'narrative fetishism'.[65] By fetishism, he means the historian's alleged desire to gain mastery of the event not through a sort of authentic psychoanalytic working-through of the trauma, or a mourning process, but by repressing the traumatic aspects and then presenting the event to readers as safe, as actually not traumatic in the first place. In the best scenario for LaCapra, 'Working through trauma brings the possibility of counteracting compulsive "acting out" through [an] explicit, critically controlled process of repetition that

---

[63] See aphorisms 193 and 191 in Johann Wolfgang von Goethe, *Goethe Werke—Hamburger Ausgabe Band 12*, ed. Erich Trunz (Munich: Beck, 2008), 390–1.

[64] Eric Kligerman, *Sites of the Uncanny: Paul Celan, Specularity and the Visual Arts* (Berlin: de Gruyter, 2007), 52–3.

[65] Eric L. Santner, 'History Beyond the Pleasure Principle: Some Thoughts on the Representation of Trauma', in Saul Friedländer (ed.), *Probing the Limits of Representation* (Cambridge, MA: Harvard University Press, 1992), 143–54, here 144.

significantly changes a life by making possible the selective retrieval and modified enactment of unactualized past possibilities'.[66]

In bringing such thinking under critique here I note that in other works I have found utility in LaCapra's thinking on counter-transference;[67] nevertheless, the basic analogy between History and psychoanalysis is too loose. More precisely, there are two analogies in play. The first is an analogy of the individual and group psyche and situation—which LaCapra actually suggests is more than merely an analogy.[68] The second analogy is that between the way the individual therapist relates to the individual patient and the way historians relates to their readerships, which is assumed to correspond to the traumatized collective. This is at least one analogy too far.

Even if one accepted the analogy between individual analysand and collective analysand, and thus the applicability of similar psychoanalytic concepts to each, then absent in the relationship between historian and collective analysand is the sort of interaction that is achieved in the relationship between therapist and patient. In the relationship between therapist and individual patient, the production of representations of the past stands constantly in conversation with the way in which such representations are consumed—sometimes producer and consumer are the same person. In the relationship between historian and collective 'patient', the production stands alone, with the nature and outcome of consumption untested and uncontestable, with no representative of the collective psyche who can be assessed or can speak to the efficacy of the cure. Besides, in LaCapra's vision it rather seems that there is just one anointed historian-therapist providing one therapeutic (or problematic) representation of the traumatic event. Perhaps all historians are supposed to confer in order to coordinate their accounts (and those of various museums, television documentaries, and so forth) in order not to confuse the analysand.

Yet there is no reason to accept the individual:collective analogy either. It is one thing to say, as LaCapra does, that there is a collective context for any therapy since it is always therapy of the socialized individual, and quite another to say that the collective has the same sort of consciousness and reflexes as the individual.[69] True, there is a shared idiom of suffering: governments and leaders can easily deploy the language of traumatization and catharsis, but this does not mean that this language refers to the same phenomena. For instance, while one can talk of both individual trauma and collective trauma, societies do not experience flash-backs and involuntary reactions.

---

[66] Dominick LaCapra, *Representing the Holocaust: History, Theory, Trauma* (Ithaca: Cornell University Press, 1996 [orig. 1994]), 173–4.

[67] Bloxham, *History and Morality*.

[68] LaCapra, *Representing the Holocaust*, 173–4; LaCapra, *History in Transit: Experience, Identity, Critical Theory* (Ithaca: Cornell University Press, 2004), 73–4.

[69] LaCapra, *Representing the Holocaust*, 173–4.

We need not concur with Lewis Namier, who made an early comparison of History with psychoanalysis and concluded that both were better at diagnosing than curing: while the jury is out on History, psychoanalysis has achieved some success. Namier was surely correct, however, that such benefits as analysis confers are not attained by reading the results of someone else's engagement with the process, but rather by participating in the process—participating intersubjectively, not one-sidedly. A somewhat better analogy would be to the writing of History as therapy for the historian, not its reading as therapy for someone else for whose particular existential dilemma the History was not composed.[70]

This is not to say that the reading of History can deliver no psychological benefit. We know from various therapies that explanations which make symptoms comprehensible may help the analysand even while not alleviating the symptoms themselves. They enable some sort of cognitive control. Shedding light on the present by explaining problems stemming from the past may help the analysand to feel less powerless, less at the mercy of incomprehensibly induced emotions.[71] With the structural substitution of socio-economic circumstances for emotions we may concur with the feminist medieval historian Judith Bennett when she argued that a historically derived understanding of reproduced structures of inequality can counteract the tendency to self-blame for 'failure' according to the inequitable rules of the game.[72] Bourdieu made the same point in regard of his sociology, even once claiming for it a quasi-psychoanalytic, or 'socioanalytic', function: sociology can help people stop looking in vain for biographical solutions to structural problems.[73]

A difference between Bennett's argument and LaCapra's is that the analogy emerging from Bennett's case is not of historical conditioning and trauma. Furthermore, while Bennett's 'therapy' might provide a stimulus for structure-changing action in pursuit of fuller social emancipation, in itself it 'only' entails subjective 'mental' emancipation vis-à-vis social structures. This is perhaps the most we can expect of any historical course of treatment, and it is no small thing though it may appear to be when set against some of the grander emancipatory promises made for History.

Varieties of Emancipatory History

History as Emancipation and LaCaprian History as Therapy are both oriented towards changing consciousness but in different ways. History as Therapy

---

[70] John Brooke, 'Namier and Namierism', *History and Theory*, 3 (1964), 331–47, here 345.
[71] Anthony Storr, 'The Concept of Cure', in Charles Rycroft (ed.), *Psychoanalysis Observed* (London: Constable, 1961), 51–84, here 73.
[72] Judith M. Bennett, *History Matters: Patriarchy and the Challenge of Feminism* (Philadelphia: University of Pennsylvania Press, 2006), 152.
[73] Michael Grenfell, *Pierre Bourdieu: Agent Provocateur* (London: Continuum, 2004), 180.

purports to help by changing attitudes to the past and reducing the hold of the past on the individual's present. History as Emancipation in its Marxist form purports to demystify the way the world is set up, as a prelude to changing that world in accordance with a specific alternative. History as Emancipation in its most popular non-Marxist form purports to disavow any claim to revealing truths about the way the world really is and really ought to be; it is concerned with paving the way to individual self-determination in the present by challenging given claims on the way things really are and ought to be—Marxist claims included.

The intellectual historian Quentin Skinner has at points talked about the utility in the present of contemplating early modern republican thought, which touches on the terrain of History as Practical Lesson.[74] More purely characteristic of History as Emancipation is his belief that 'to demand from the history of thought a solution to our own immediate problems is...to commit not merely a methodological fallacy, but something like a moral error. But to learn from the past— and we cannot otherwise learn it at all—the distinction between what is necessary and what is the product merely of our own contingent arrangements, is the key to self-awareness itself.' Insofar as Marxism had highlighted the constraints placed by society 'upon our imaginations...the historical study of the ideas of other societies should be undertaken as the indispensable and the irreplaceable means of placing limits on these constraints'.[75] Skinner was effectively reiterating the point made in 1946 by A. L. Rowse that 'freedom for a human being consists in knowing the extent to which he is conditioned, and choosing his course accordingly'.[76] Similar sentiments were expressed at the outset of the third millennium CE by the American historian of the Cold War, John Lewis Gaddis,[77] but they could have come straight from the pens of Nietzsche, Adorno, Marrou, a range of postcolonial theorists and in his own way even Lord Acton![78] Foucault's thought is also relevant here.

It has been said of Foucault that he 'does not seek the unchangeable amid the changing, but rather to identify that which can be changed in that which is presumed static',[79] which suggests a different angle to that of Skinner when Skinner talked of some necessity that might be detected behind contingent arrangements.

[74] Quentin Skinner,'The Idea of Negative Liberty: Philosophical and Historical Perspectives', in Richard Rorty, J. B. Schneewind, and Quentin Skinner (eds.), *Philosophy in History: Essays on the Historiography of Philosophy* (Cambridge: Cambridge University Press, 1998), 193–221. See also Skinner, *Liberty before Liberalism* (Cambridge: Cambridge University Press, 1998).

[75] Quentin Skinner, 'Meaning and Understanding in the History of Ideas', *History and Theory*, 8:1 (1969), 3–53, here 53.

[76] Rowse, *The Use of History*, 91.

[77] John Lewis Gaddis, *The Landscape of History* (Oxford: Oxford University Press, 2004), conclusion, especially 148–51.

[78] Marrou, *The Meaning of History*, 283.

[79] Kevin O'Brien, 'Michel Foucault's Genealogy of the Subject' (PhD Thesis: Katholieke Universiteit Leuven, 1988), 326.

When Foucault wrote of giving 'new impetus...to the undefined work of freedom',[80] he also stressed that 'we have to give up hope of ever acceding to a point of view that could give us access to any complete and definitive knowledge of what may constitute our historical limits'.[81] Foucault is correct: one cannot know what it is that one cannot know; as soon as one purports to have identified one's conceptual limits one has actually already surpassed them, but that just goes to show that they were not really one's conceptual limits after all. It is precisely that recognition that limits the possibilities for the pursuit of the 'undefined work of freedom' via the historical/genealogical approach, and here Foucault created confusion, for at times he suggested that one could after all glean insight into such limits, talking of 'excavation beneath our own feet', or the aim of showing, 'based upon their historical establishment and formation, those systems which are still ours today and within which we are trapped'.[82]

History as Emancipation in its most common form today enquires into the past to illustrate, by contrast with the present, that alternative ways of life are possible. It relies on a combination of inspiration and provocation. It tends not to look to the past for specific lessons or examples, not least because it is apt to be as critical of past orders as present ones. Its major conceptual weapon is the revelation of the contingent difference, across time and place, of ways of thinking, being, and doing, which is why it coheres so straightforwardly with the wider neo-historicist approach to History. Some Historian-Emancipators might go one step further and suggest that knowing the historical aetiology of the present is a practical tool for change of the present.

Any proponent of History as Emancipation must subscribe to the first of the following three claims, while many proponents subscribe to two or all three of them:

I. *The items X are social/cultural constructions. They were different in the past and we can change them in the present if we wish.* (Note that the claim is not unique to this school of thought. What might vary between salient schools of thought is the size of set X.)
II. *We need to change things because they are undesirable.*
III. *In order to change things, we need to understand their origins.*

The three claims will now be assessed in reverse order. My deflationary assessments are strictly related to the conceptual coherence of History as Emancipation in those areas where it can be distinguished from History as Practical Lesson, which, as argued above (pp. 314–21), can be useful in shaping thought in the present. The point of the coming argument is not to deny that evidence as to

---

[80] Foucault, *Ethics*, 315–16.   [81] Ibid. 316.
[82] Michael Mahon, *Foucault's Nietzschean Genealogy* (Albany: SUNY Press, 1992), 121.

historical mutability and contingency can sometimes help with emancipatory arguments, but rather that one cannot at all rely on the efficacy of the approach. A further contention is that the most important arguments to be had in this area are really arguments about value and evaluation, not about contingency. Those arguments are better made with their value judgements clear, which is a claim that links History as Emancipation to History as Identity, discussion of which closes the chapter and the book.

History as Emancipation III

History as Emancipation III comes closest to History as Therapy for what we might call 'social neurosis'. The idea of raising awareness of human historical conditioning by highlighting the past moments in which specific choices were made or not made, and opportunities taken or thwarted—as in the study of successful or failed revolutions—is comparable to the therapeutic process of locating the origin of longstanding behavioural patterns in earlier life. Foucault gave the name 'History of the Present' to a study of those institutional forms and conceptual parameters that are still with us, and was keenly interested in their historical inception.[83] Such a concern for historical beginnings can be traced back to Marx and Marxism, Engels's *Origins of the Family* being a case in point, but it has been incorporated into other critical traditions too. The sociologist Bourdieu claimed: 'there is no more potent tool for rupture than the reconstruction of genesis', and 'by bringing back into view the conflicts and confrontations of the early beginnings and therefore all the discarded possibles, it retrieves the possibility that things could have been (and still could be) otherwise.'[84] The Kantian liberal Jürgen Habermas wrote that 'when reflection understands the genesis of tradition from which it proceeds and to which it returns, the dogmatism of life-praxis is shaken.'[85] The sociologist of science Steve Fuller believes 'that even disappointment can be used strategically to point out better paths that were originally not taken, but that (with some adjustment) may be taken up in the future.'[86] Resonances are obvious with Joan Scott's talk of interrogating the processes of the creation of subjects

[83] Michel Foucault, *Discipline and Punish* (London: Penguin, 1991), 31, 308. See also S. Fuggle, Y. Lanci, and M. Tazzioli (eds.), *Foucault and the History of our Present* (Basingstoke: Palgrave Macmillan, 2015).

[84] Pierre Bourdieu, 'Rethinking the State: Genesis and Structure of the Bureaucratic Field', in George Steinmetz (ed.), *State/Culture: State Formation after the Cultural Turn* (Ithaca: Cornell University Press, 1999), 52–75, here 57.

[85] Jürgen Habermas, *On the Logic of the Social Sciences* (Cambridge, MA: MIT Press, 1988 [orig. 1967]) 168.

[86] Steve Fuller, *Thomas Kuhn: A Philosophical History for our Times* (Chicago: University of Chicago Press, 2001), p. xvi.

(p. 290). John Arnold enjoins studying how we came about in order 'to be made aware of the possibility of doing things differently'.[87]

In order to assess the emancipatory prospects of origin-quests we first need to distinguish between chronological and conceptual senses of 'origin'. One has to guess which meaning of origin Max Horkheimer had in mind when he wrote that 'for the little man who is turned down when he asks for a job because objective conditions make it impossible, it is most important that their origin be brought to the light of day so that they do not continue being unfavorable to him'.[88] One of Horkheimer's successors in the Frankfurt School, the Hegelian Marxist Herbert Marcuse, did not elaborate the difference between the chronological and conceptual senses of origins either, but both are present in his work. He argued that 'social theory is historical theory', and asked, 'among the various possible and actual modes of organizing and utilizing the available resources [of any given, actual society], which ones offer the greatest chance of an optimal development?'[89] Leaning towards conceptual origins in one passage, Marcuse stated that reification 'sets forth the actual social relations among men as a totality of objective relations, thereby concealing their origin, their mechanisms of perpetuation, and the possibility of their transformation. Above all, it conceals their human core and content.'[90] In another passage, Marcuse focused more on chronological origins:

> The way in which a society organizes the life of its members involves an initial *choice* between historical alternatives which are determined by the inherited level of the material and intellectual culture. The choice itself results from the play of the dominant interests. It *anticipates* specific modes of transforming and utilizing man and nature and rejects other modes. It is one 'project' of realization among others. But once the project has become operative in the basic institutions and relations, it tends to become exclusive, and to determine the development of the society as a whole.[91]

Marcuse used the term 'project' because it accentuates 'most clearly the specific character of historical practice'. That practice 'results from a determinate choice, seizure of one among other ways of comprehending, organizing, and transforming society'. Marcuse sought to 'emphasis[e] the element of freedom and responsibility in historical determination', to link 'autonomy and contingency'.[92]

[87] Arnold, *History*, 119–20.

[88] Max Horkheimer, *Dawn and Decline, Notes 1926–31 and 1950–69* (New York: Seabury/Continuum, 1978), 50–2. I thank Yiannis Kokosalakis for this reference.

[89] Herbert Marcuse, *One Dimensional Man* (London: Sphere, 1968), 10.

[90] Marcuse, *Reason and Revolution*, 280.

[91] Marcuse, *One Dimensional Man*, 14.   [92] Ibid. 174 and 14 n.

The distinction between chronological and conceptual origins merits emphasis because while investigation of either might serve, in Foucault's words, to 'breach' the 'self evidence' of arrangements in the present,[93] only in the chronological sense is historical analysis necessary. If one wishes to pinpoint History's critical utility one needs to be clear about whether the conceptual and chronological investigations really relate to one another. They may so relate in philosophical endeavours of reconstruction and critique such as Heidegger's *Destruktion* of traditional metaphysics and his 'recovering' of a particular concept of truth. Heidegger's was an exercise in reading ever further back into the philosophical tradition to trace the 'originary point' at which another concept of truth gained hegemony, and with it a certain ontology.[94] Yet that exercise was only historical in an attenuated sense. One ought not understate the sociological and intellectual challenges from within the profession to some of these attempts to rethink philosophical tradition, but those obstacles are small relative to the problems of rethinking social development. There is a 'logical' or at least genre-internal element to philosophical development that does not exist in social development. This means that for the philosopher, one can do what is roughly analogous to checking the mathematical working of the discipline, namely establishing where it went wrong (if indeed it did), and starting again from that point. We cannot, however, assume that establishing the historical origin of some *social* development has any similar emancipatory promise. Historical understanding reveals that the past is a cause of the present in a way that is rather 'thicker' than the ritual invocation of contingency may suggest. Marcuse is too simplistic in depicting historical trends as the consequence of some initial 'project' choice that can just be unmade as if by some tracing and recovery process. Unpicking, say, capitalism would lead to a post-capitalist scenario not a pre-capitalist one: the new scenario would still have capitalism in its causal history, and capitalism would influence though not determine what came afterwards.

Heidegger's historically oriented project of critical *Destruktion* was arguably only an auxiliary to his conceptual project anyway, and much the same goes for Lukács's twin endeavours.[95] When Lukács alluded to the false 'second nature' created by capitalistic arrangements, he did not think that the 'first', real nature had been lost at some point in the past; rather, it had been repressed and still had some underground existence. It could be liberated and the truth revealed about relations between person and person, people and the natural world. Since Lukács and Heidegger in his relevant thinking felt they were dealing with a live conceptual–existential problem, it was a secondary matter as to whether or not

[93] Foucault, 'Questions of Method', 104.

[94] Bern Magnus, *Heidegger's Metahistory of Philosophy: Amor fati, Being and Truth* (The Hague: Martinus Nijhoff, 1970).

[95] For comparisons between Heidegger and Lukács: Axel Honneth, *Reification: A New Look at an Old Idea* (New York: Oxford University Press, 2008), 28 ff.

they had located the actual chronological origins of the problem, whereas that is a primary concern for those who emphasize historical aetiology, moments of decision, transformation, etc.

The challenge of knowing exactly where chronological origins are to be found is a challenge amongst other things to practitioners of a Foucauldian 'History of the present'. The problem of where to begin one's critical account of 'the present' is obviously a function of establishing where the salient present began. This will seem comparatively easy for those who, like Foucault at one stage, believe that the past can be split into blocks defined by particular epistemes, discursive structures, and so forth, since one just has to look for the dividing moments like 'epistemic ruptures' or great political revolutions. Much encouragement for this sort of view has been provided by the popularity of the classical sociological concept of 'modernity' as a particular *state* or stage of human existence, as opposed, for instance, to the Marxist emphasis on capitalism as a *force* that keeps pressing and changing things, and has done either side of the supposed caesura between premodern and modern.

In the caesural view, one period of the past is effectively the present extended backward through time, while previous periods of time are properly, qualitatively past. Given a non-caesural view, in which some continuity and change coexist at all points in some shifting balance—a view substantiated by those critiques of Foucault's empirical work that show that certain medical practices do not correspond with the supposed lifespans of his epistemes[96]—then one has to be a little more circumspect. When Hayden White wrote that 'the understanding of any of [a society's] processes must always be directed at the search for origins, its relations to its time and space and socially specific contexts, and the emplotment of its transformations over time', he was, in preaching so many 'musts', just spreading his bets.[97] When engaging in historical explanation one needs to recognize the inherently pragmatic nature of all of one's starting points, the inherent contestability of the way that, by some act of initial 'contextualization', one cauterizes the open vessels of history that pass beyond the point at which one has chosen to start the story. Recognizing the possibility of a still-changing balance of change and continuity after one's chosen beginning is consonant with the version of poststructuralism in which meanings and contexts are seen as constantly interacting and modifying each other, as opposed to that stop–start view of history encouraged by the 'opposition' between 'structure' and 'event'. Evolutionary changes may be less obvious than, but as significant when accumulated over time as, the

---

[96] José Guilherme Merquior, *Michel Foucault* (Berkeley: University of California Press, 1985), 29 (see also 27): 'Foucault's epochal monoliths crumble before the contradictory wealth of the historical evidence'. Also: Ian Maclean, 'Foucault's Renaissance Episteme Reassessed: An Aristotelian Counterblast', *Journal of the History of Ideas*, 59:1 (1998), 149–66.

[97] Hayden White, 'Afterword', in Victoria E. Bonnell and Lynn Hunt (eds.), *Beyond the Cultural Turn* (Berkeley: University of California Press, 1999), 315–24, here 318.

revolutionary visions characteristic of some of the heroic French theory of recent generations. Here is also a difference between Nietzsche's genealogy and Foucault's most categorical exercises in historicization. Sometimes Nietzsche does evince a caesural view, as when writing of a 'continuous chain of signs, continually revealing new interpretations and adaptations, *the causes of which need not be connected even amongst themselves, but rather sometimes just follow and replace one another at random*', or stating that 'there is no more important proposition for every sort of history than that which we arrive at only with great effort but which we really should reach,—namely that the origin of the emergence of a thing and its ultimate usefulness, its practical application and incorporation into a system of ends, are *toto coelo* [i.e. categorically] separate'.[98] Yet Nietzsche was also concerned to show just how much had harmfully endured in Christian-occidental thought, from ancient Christianity through Protestantism and into the Kantian system of morality.

In concluding this section, let us focus upon the distinction between a general reflection on the mutability of things, and a specific reflection on the inception of a particular thing. If one is looking for some indication of the possibility of change, or an inspiration for the attempt at change, the general reflection is just as good as the specific one; that general reflection is a corollary of History or Travel and is not remotely new. If one seeks a particular subversive potential by investigating the origins of a particular matter, that specific reflection is either not primarily historical or not useful. The conditions and justifications that obtained in the past can only be changed insofar as they still obtain in the same way now, and where that is not the case, historical accounts of aetiology will be unfit as tools of change. At such points, to return for a moment to the connection between History as Emancipation and History as Therapy, any analogy to therapy may have to give way to analogy to that condition wherein analysands constantly relive some past series of events in the subconscious hope that those things will eventually turn out differently than they in fact did. Alternatively, it may have to give way to the equally fruitless 'Oedipal' analogy, whereby the subject dwells on imagined alternatives to the harmful parents that he or she actually had.

History as Emancipation II

The underlying proposition of History as Emancipation II is: we need to change things because they are undesirable. This section address the ways in which History might be drawn into the argument, with a view to clarifying some points of principle.

---

[98] Nietzsche, *On the Genealogy of Morality*, Second Essay, §12, at pp. 50–1. Emphasis added to the first quote.

Clarification is needed in view of pronouncements like Foucault's: 'In what is given to us as universal, necessary, obligatory, what place is occupied by whatever is singular, contingent, and the product of arbitrary constraints?'[99] Here, 'obligatory' is paired with 'arbitrary', and 'arbitrary' placed alongside 'contingent'. Yet 'arbitrary' is prejudicial, and establishing something as contingent has no intrinsic bearing on its desirability or legitimacy—to think otherwise is to subscribe to a form of what is known as the genetic fallacy.

The cultural theorist Fredric Jameson enjoined 'always historicize!'[100] More recently a historian wrote that 'history is the most radical of all the disciplines; contrary to its stuffy image, history destabilizes everything precisely by historicizing it'.[101] A theorist of History repeated Jameson's prescription and also wrote 'everything is relative (historicist)'.[102] But the pay-off of historicization depends amongst other things on how 'radical' one wants it to be. Is it a call to help understand the thing historicized, or is it a way of relativizing the thing historicized? If the former, then 'historicize' really just means 'explain', which incorporates 'contextualize'. If the latter, one response to Jameson would be to ask him to historicize his injunction to historicize, thus either qualifying the utility of historicization or setting off an infinite regress of historicization. Before the historicizer gets to historicize, one has to historicize the historicizer, but before that one has to historicize the admonition for the historicizer to be historicized, and so on. What if historicization is supposed to delegitimate? Historicization, in the sense of accounting for the emergence of a particular idea at a particular spatio-temporal cultural or functional point, may indeed relativize or—differently—invalidate some concepts that have seemingly unimpeachable universal authority. It certainly requires that ideas claiming self-evidence account more extensively for themselves. At the least, it asks why certain questions have obtained such urgency at certain times, with the corollary that even if the answers to those questions are universally true, the answers may not always be equally pressing or interesting. On the specific question of legitimacy, think of the contemporary warning 'check your privilege'. The warning may be important as an argument to the significance of a position's being adopted by someone—'it's easy for you to say that', or 'it's middle-class white men telling us what to do again'—or to the different degrees of difficulty implementing a prescription according to, say, socio-economic position. It may be a way of criticizing the sanguinity of someone who has not been personally affected by the thing about which they are sanguine, or of saying 'your concern is not mine, as you would know if you were in a different position'. In these cases, 'check your privilege' means, weakly, 'be aware of your subject

[99] Foucault, *Ethics*, 315–16.
[100] Fredric Jameson, *The Political Unconscious* (London: Routledge, 1983), p. ix.
[101] Dan Stone, 'Surviving in the Corridors of History or, History as Double or Nothing', in Jeffrey R. Di Leo (ed.), *Federman's Fictions* (Albany, NY: SUNY, 2011), 203–13, here 205.
[102] Keith Jenkins, *Re-Thinking History* (London: Routledge, 1991), 30, 82.

position' or, strongly, 'adjust your perspective'. It pertains to the relationship between power and argument but is not itself a question of logic of argument. It draws attention to the salience, purpose, or priority of an argument in situation X: 'why are you raising that at his juncture?'; 'it's not helpful for someone in your position/with your privileges/your track record to be making this point now'. It cannot legitimately mean 'anything you have to say is illegitimate owing solely to the fact that it is you saying it'. By analogy, the historicist argument to historical/ cultural/sectional origins cannot legitimately mean 'any concept or claim established in that context is illegitimate beyond that context, owing solely to the fact it was established in that context'. Finally, for those who wish to use a sort of historicization of the present in order to delegitimate some dispensation in the present, the argument to origins cannot legitimately mean 'current or inherited dispensations are illegitimate just because they are current or inherited'. The arguer would have perpetrated the genetic fallacy.

Philosophical arguments aside, there are social and psychological reasons why appreciation of mutability and the contingency of one's own traditions need not in and of itself generate a desire to change one's ways. Since narratives of civilizational progress across time still hold some popular sway, some people combine a recognition of the past's difference with a sense of the *superiority* of the present. Others are fond of their traditions not because they do not know that they are 'just traditions' but because they are *their* traditions. They cling to their particularity not because they have not realized that it is not the only way to be but precisely because they see it as their way of being. To be sure, many people are indentured to particular tales of the way their traditions developed; appeals to the past in modern polities of all stripes need not be categorically different to those appeals which characterized the *origines ordinum* accounts of medieval Benedictines or the *origines gentium* stories of medieval state genealogists or the agnatic lineages of the high medieval nobility. But acts of contesting those traditions, say by showing tradition to be invented more recently than generally supposed, or that the alleged founding date is a mistake, or that one is not really the heir of some thirteenth-century knight, or that the tradition is nowhere near as inclusive as it claims, are acts of showing the tradition-tales to be *incorrect*, which is not at all the same as showing the traditions themselves to be *contingent*. By the same token, if one wishes to change the present situation that traditions have shaped, then one needs an argument about their normative *wrongness* rather than their historical contingency. Sometimes, as in arguments that traditions are not as inclusive as claimed, the arguments to incorrectness and to normative wrongness are coextensive, but neither is coextensive with an argument to contingency.

Sometimes arguments about contingency do contain an unacknowledged normative thrust—these critiques we may call 'crypto-normative'. An example is some of Foucault's mid-career work in which he purports merely to be analysing how things are in the world of discursive knowledge and power whilst betraying

his distaste for modern power-knowledge regimes and going on in later scholarship
to contemplate ways of escaping them.[103] This tension is a problem in principle
for the best-known Foucauldian analyses: since they claim that subjectivity, and
any and all ideas of 'the human', are merely products of contingent socio-historical
set-ups, thus that there is no 'first nature' to be liberated from the 'second nature'
that the set-up creates, one might reasonably ask what normative grounds they
have for criticizing the set-up.

Perhaps for the Foucauldian in historical mode critiques emerge from contemplation of the past. One can imagine instances in which the historian comes
across something troubling or joyous in the past and it makes her re-evaluate
something in the present. But we have evidence that this is not always how critiques develop in the Foucauldian's mind. Take Foucault's *Discipline and Punish:
The Birth of the Prison*. By his admission in the book the project was stimulated
by contemplating the nature of contemporary prison regimes and the discontent
of the inmates.[104] This means that we have to question his later assertion that 'it
really was the appearance of historical contents' 'that made an effective critique of
the asylum or the prison possible'.[105] We have grounds to believe that before the
historical enquiry into the birth of the prison (*Naissance de la prison* in the subtitle of the French original) came a normative critique stimulated by present
arrangements. *Mutatis mutandis*, one can readily imagine feminists who were
feminists before they became critical theorists and engaged those intellectual traditions precisely because of the promise of sharper critical tools to enhance the
feminist critique which is at base a normative one. The felt necessity of feminist
critique was there prior to its application to—in this case—some historical interest. One result of these reflections is that clearly discourses of power-knowledge,
propriety, and normative correctness are not as strong in the present as suggested
by Foucauldians and sometimes by Foucault himself: just as Foucault was preceded by a long line of liberal prison-reformers unpossessed of the magic of postmodern 'critique', 'ordinary people', not least rebellious prisoners, are frequently
capable of reflecting critically on their own experience and the experiences of
others. (Whether they have the power to act effectively on that reflection is a different matter.) But the main point is that in cases when normative critique has
inspired the historical examination rather than the other way around, History is
just one weapon in a battle that has already been joined. It is a tool of emancipation
in a different sense of emancipation to that of History as Emancipation I. History
serves here not to alert people to the contingency of their ways in order to liberate
their capacity for choice but rather makes the case for emancipation from a

---

[103] On crypto-normativity and related criticisms, Nancy Fraser, 'Foucault on Modern Power:
Empirical Insights and Normative Confusions', *Praxis International*, 1:3 (1981), 272–87; Jürgen
Habermas, *The Philosophical Discourse of Modernity* (Cambridge, MA: MIT Press, 1990), 238–93.
[104] Foucault, *Discipline and Punish*, 30.   [105] Foucault, *Society Must be Defended*, 7.

specific state of present affairs that is argued to be *wrong*. We are encroaching on the fiefdoms of History as Lesson and, as below, History as Identity. These are types of History that wear their normativity on their sleeves: types of History whose presentism is of a different nature to the shadow scientism and crypto-normativity of key Foucauldian strands of History as Emancipation.

History as Emancipation I

The idea underlying History as Emancipation I was defined above in these terms: 'The items X are social/cultural constructions. They were different in the past and, and we can change them in the present if we wish.' History as Emancipation I is subject to the same qualifications and elaborations of utility as earlier applied to History as Travel, since the two justifications are in principle identical. Unlike History as Emancipation II, which involves some normative evaluation of the present, History as Emancipation I is purely descriptive of difference between now and then. If it is not original to the fashions of the later twentieth century, History as Emancipation I may nonetheless differ today in reach from earlier iterations. More tends to be seen as socially/culturally constructed nowadays than in Rousseau's or Adam Ferguson's time, or Montaigne's day before that. Any given claim about construction must be assessed on its own merits, but that is not as straightforward as it sounds given the confusing jumble of epistemological, onto-logical, moral, and political considerations often at issue.

The epistemological matter is a particular case of the general problem of distin-guishing between our concepts or perceptions of a thing and that thing to which our concepts or perceptions pertain. One form of social constructionism, the sort most relevant for the coming discussion, would deny that there is any 'way things are' apart from the way societies discuss or conceive of them. This is a species of idealism. When testing the propositions of social constructionism one always needs to ask philosopher Ian Hacking's question *The Social Construction of What?*[106] The game of tennis is manifestly a purely social creation, likewise a par-liament, but those sorts of things are not the sort of things that arguments tend to get heated about, and granting the claims of social constructionism in certain areas is by no means to mandate social constructionism as a general claim on the nature of things, i.e. a general ontological claim. Some things Hacking would call ontologically subjective, like tennis or customs or relations of production or par-liaments. (Note that when a tennis match or a parliamentary session is in process, it is still a matter of what Hacking calls *epistemic objectivity* whether player A won a set or legislation B was passed.) Other things are ontologically objective, like

---

[106] Ian Hacking, *The Social Construction of What?* (Cambridge, MA: Harvard University Press, 1999).

that mountain over there. The mountain is my example, though Hacking would probably accept it as an example of something ontologically objective. Others might or might not accept the example, and there are a host of matters in addition that some might think to be ontologically objective and others think to be ontologically subjective. Some social constructionists argue, for instance, about 'the social construction of nature', which can mean different things in different mouths.[107]

Arguments about sex and differences or similarities of sex show how politically loaded consideration of the relations between the historico-cultural and the natural can be. It is absolutely appropriate that claims about what is taken to be natural have come in for profound scrutiny in this areas since, as in the idea of 'woman's nature', such claims have often been the spurious basis for assigning social roles. So much hinges, however, on where and how and with what significance the natural is held to fit into the debate in the first place, since particular claims about the natural need have none of the social significance attached to phrases like 'women's nature'—phrases that have a metaphysical air as much as anything else. That, indeed, is the thesis that needs to be borne in mind over the following few paragraphs, prior to my argument's culmination. Over matters of sex and much else besides, more may depend on the associations culturally (religiously, philosophically, etc.) attributed to the natural than to the belief or the warranted assertion that this or that thing is partly or wholly natural. Assuming this argument holds, then if History can play an emancipatory role in the relevant debates it may be a different role to that which it currently plays.

Using debates around sex as a point of departure, let us consider Thomas Laqueur's 1990 volume *Making Sex: Body and Gender from the Greeks to Freud*. It was prominent in pressing on the distinction between sex and gender, a distinction whereby sex is seen as a biological matter and gender a matter of identity shaped at some nexus of cultural 'common-sense' and subjective orientation. Laqueur's historical enquiry showed how scientific understandings of sex difference and similarity had changed over time. In Laqueur's view 'sex, as much as gender, is made', a somewhat opaque statement qualified by his disavowal of any 'interest in denying the reality of sex or of sexual dimorphism as an evolutionary process'. He noted the distinction in his book 'between language on the one hand and extralinguistic reality on the other; between nature and culture'. He sought to navigate a separate path to 'those who would eliminate gender by arguing that so-called cultural differences are really natural' and to those who 'empty sex of its content by arguing, conversely, that natural differences are really cultural'.[108]

---

[107] David Demeritt, 'What is the "social construction of nature"? A Typology and Sympathetic Critique', *Progress in Human Geography*, 26:6 (2002), 767–90.

[108] Thomas W. Laqueur, *Making Sex: Body and Gender from the Greeks to Freud* (Cambridge, MA: Harvard University Press, 1990), pp. ix, 11–12.

Eighteen years later the historian Joan Scott placed herself in the second of these camps as she addressed the same question of the relationship between gender and sex, and put sex on entirely the same cultural footing as gender. Thus: 'differences of sex [are] not set by nature but [are] established through language'; 'sex, like gender, [has] to be understood as a system of attributed meaning. Neither [is] about nature; both [are] products of culture.'[109] As it happens, Scott also wrote of 'the admittedly different bodies of women' and approvingly quoted another schol-ar's unproblematized reference to 'female physiology',[110] but did not reconcile her belief in physiological differences with her belief in the thoroughgoing cultural construction of sex. We will stay with her claim about cultural construction, because, as with the stronger of two claims about linguistic idealism in 'Evidence of Experience' (p. 290), that is the one that gives Scott's argument its point of con-troversy and celebrity. Scott's stronger claim is of the form 'not nature but instead culture'. It is not the same as one of Laqueur's points, the important one that 'dif-ference and sameness, more or less recondite, are everywhere; but which ones count and for what ends is determined outside the bounds of empirical investigation'.[111] Scott's claim rules out the possibility, suggested by Meryl Altman and Keith Nightenhelser in response to parts of Laqueur's book, that it is 'not that "sex" is socially constructed too, but simply that we need to move the boundary a bit—that we've been calling some things "sex" that are really, after all, gender'.[112] Scott also implicitly rules out the idea that the cultural and the natural could be co-constitutive of an outcome, or that the cultural and the natural could inter-penetrate. Either of these possibilities break down the sharp nature–culture dichotomy that Scott deploys.[113]

In the same categorical not-nature-but-instead-culture vein, within a generally fascinating volume that exemplifies the power of cultural History, *Common Bodies: Women, Touch and Power in Seventeenth Century England*, Laura Gowing writes that 'the most apparently natural of bodily events and processes—like desire, labour or motherhood—are the product of culture'.[114] Putting aside

---

[109] Scott, 'Unanswered Questions', 1423, 1424.   [110] Ibid. 1426.
[111] Laqueur, Making Sex, 10.
[112] See their review of Laqueur in Postmodern Culture 2:3 (1992).
[113] On which see Anne Fausto-Sterling, Sexing the Body: Gender Politics and the Construction of Sexuality (New York: Basic Books, 2000); Fausto-Sterling, Sex/Gender: Biology in a Social World (New York: Routledge, 2012). Work on bioculture shows how seriously biologists have taken culture, including the culture of non-human animals, in recent decades. It is also worth noting that when thinking about the relationship between 'nature and nurture' we historians explicitly or tacitly embrace the well-substantiated science that rejects genetic determinism, since it allows a great deal of space for the discussion of social and cultural arrangements that we are more competent to discuss.
[114] Laura Gowing, Common Bodies: Women, Touch and Power in Seventeenth Century England (New Haven: Yale University Press, 2003), 205. Thanks to Dror Wahrman, 'Change and the Corporeal in Seventeenth- and Eighteenth-Century Gender History: Or, Can Cultural History Be Rigorous?', Gender and History, 20:3 (2008), 584–602, here 588–9, 598, for drawing my attention to Gowing's work via the cited passage. Wahrman's arguments in that article have been most influential on my account here.

Gowing's three stated examples, which need further elaboration anyway, and focusing on the general principle that 'the most apparently natural of bodily events and processes... are the product of culture', does she really wish to claim this for all of the most apparently natural bodily events and processes? As regards another statement emerging from the new cultural History, it may well be that 'smell is cultural' since 'odours are invested with cultural values' and that 'smell is historical', because its associations change over time', but that is a distance from saying that smell is *only* cultural or historical—indeed the contrasts across time and culture can only be made against an assumed parameter of a common capacity to smell.[115] Exemplifying the 'culture-is-all historicism' stance that Geertz believed 'no one of any seriousness holds',[116] the former president of the Modern Language Association Robert Scholes wrote in 2006 that 'we were natural for eons before we were cultural—before we were human, even—but so what? We are cultural now'. And, he added 'culture is the domain of the humanities'; science was apparently irrelevant to considering humans today.[117] In the vein of injunctions to historicize everything, the literary theorist Jonathan Culler wrote that 'the main thrust of recent theory' is 'the critique of *whatever* is taken as natural, the *demonstration* that what has been thought or declared natural is in fact a historical, cultural product'.[118]

One wonders about the prospects for thesis-challenging evidence in the face of Culler's determination to conclude on culture instead of nature. A note on method is in order to check such potentially illegitimate conclusions as might be reached by cultural History and related cultural theory. One certainly cannot base claims about the culturally constructed—ontologically subjective—nature of, say, sex or sex difference/similarity on consideration of historically variable discourses on sex and sex-difference/similarity, since that approach begs the question. It presupposes the culturally or linguistically determined conclusions that are supposedly reached by its deployment. In such matters it is not just ontological objectivists that might have further questions to ask, but common-or-garden sceptics too. Note that critical scepticism, with its 'negative' aspects, is not at all the same as the strong *positive* claims about the—thoroughly constructed—way of the world made by our constructionists. Both the objectivists and the sceptics are entitled to ask the subjectivists/constructionists to answer the 'how do you

---

[115] The first two quotations are reproduced in Burke, *What is Cultural History?*, 113; the third, on the same page, comprises Burke's own words. I do not accuse him of refusing to acknowledge the common capacity—he just does not discuss it. Note, though, that (p. 115) he records that his 'own inclination would be to reserve the term "cultural" for the history of phenomena that seem "natural", such as dreams, memory and time'. The same considerations would apply to dreams and memory as I have applied to smell.

[116] Geertz, 'Anti Anti-Relativism', 268.

[117] Robert Scholes, 'Reply', *Proceedings of the Modern Language Association*, 121:1 (2006), 297–8.

[118] Jonathan Culler, *Literary Theory: A Very Short Introduction* (Oxford: Oxford University Press, 1997), 14. Emphases added.

know?' question as thoroughly as the objectivists should answer it, and that may well involve engaging with the full range of competent scientific and philosophical opinion, rather than just cherrypicking conducive thinkers. With an eye to warding off circularity, sceptics or objectivists about some aspect of sex or sex-difference/similarity might advert to the genetic fallacy. They might contend that all cultures past just got their understanding of the relevant issue wrong, and/or that even if present understandings are as questionable as earlier ones that does not mean there is not something extra-cultural about some aspect of sex or sex-difference/similarity to be (mis-)understood in the first place.

For the overall argument here, it is important to establish the identity of the claimants on the natural to which the constructionists are effectively responding. Some claimants might be political authorities, perhaps backed by philosophers or theologians, who are interested in instituting or sustaining particular social orders. Others might be scientists. Perhaps the scientists and the political authorities are the same people, but that is not always the case, and scientists have as often been a threat to authorities as a buttress. Sometimes scientists have provided 'justification' for, say, claims about 'racial' inequality but they have also challenged such claims.[119] In other words, 'science' does not speak with a single transhistorical voice. Would the most thoroughgoing not-nature-but-culture constructionists present the well-corroborated scientific conclusions about the absence of innate 'racial' inferiority/superiority as really just the expression of another culturally contingent way of thinking about the so-called natural, an outlook needing immediate historicization? In practice, probably not, since on the whole constructionists see their constructionism as politically progressive, and the scientific conclusions as to innate equality are apt to be embraced in progressive politics. Yet it is not clear that the strongest constructionists could say no in principle, which illustrates that there is nothing intrinsically progressive about thoroughgoing social constructionism and its conceptual tool, historicization. Equally there is nothing intrinsically conservative, or controlling, or whatever, about claims that such-and-such a thing is partly or wholly natural. So much depends on the context in which the claims are made. Consider the debate about homosexuality and the hypothalamus triggered by Simon LeVay in the 1990s: the claim that homosexuality had an involuntary organic foundation is only 'progressive' in a culture that otherwise claims that homosexuals could and ought to change their sexual orientation, and equally in one that would not draw the

---

[119] For instance Angela Saini's works *Superior* (Boston, MA: Beacon Press, 2019) and *Inferior* (London: Harper Collins, 2018) illustrate the role of scientists' prejudices in producing racist and sexist conclusions. Her criticism of the relevant science as deficient of course appeals to a standard of relatively good science; the epistemically better science is also the less racist or sexist science. Laqueur, *Making Sex*, 9–10, also makes an appeal to the better science when he writes that 'what evidence there does exist for biological difference with a gendered behavioral result is either highly suspect for a variety of methodological reasons, or ambiguous, or proof of Dorothy Sayers' notion that men and women are very close neighbors indeed if it is proof of anything at all.'

conclusion that it would be best to exterminate such organically 'compromised' individuals.[120] And, as suggested above with regard to context, a very great deal hinges on what weight is attached in any given culture to the idea of the natural. As it happens, attempts to delegitimate any claims on the natural still attribute by default an unnecessarily great social power to pronouncements about nature. It is as if we were still in the days when nature was held to reveal the mind of God and so had a metaphysical quality from which normative implications flowed.

The claims of natural science on one hand, and religion and certain sorts of philosophy on the other hand, only appear to be of much the same sort if one makes the mistake of conflating the natural with a particular concept of the metaphysical. The 'natural' is indeed given a fearsome quality by the ancient Christian idea of nature as waystation to God, creation as the book of God, and so forth.[121] That idea is itself akin to the Platonic idea of the cosmos as something to which one ought to accommodate oneself, and the Platonic and Christian idea of transcendent forms to which earthly bodies are a rough approximation. The 'natural' is given religious-metaphysical connotation in, for instance, the Vatican's *Male and Female He Created Them* (2019), whose title is drawn from Genesis 1:27. With the shadow of god's creating mankind in his own image hanging over the discussion, this 'educational' document purports to reaffirm, in the battle against an apparently terrifying 'gender theory', 'the difference and reciprocity in nature of a man and a woman'.[122] It is only when 'nature' is associated with ideas of the god-given that expressions like 'X is natural' have the meaning 'X is good', 'X must be decisive on our thinking', and expressions like 'X is not natural', or 'X goes against nature' have the form of condemnations. One needs to jettison all such associations and recognize that whatever else normativity is, it is a concept that only exists within the realm of human culture(s). The same goes for all questions of rights, equality, and legislation, which is where the battle between progressives and their opponents is really joined.

An accompaniment to resisting the association of the natural with species of metaphysical thinking is stressing what distinguishes sciences like biology from theology and forms of speculative philosophy. One break with metaphysics was when scientists stopped thinking in teleological Aristotelian terms about nature's ultimate ends and purposes, and intervened in nature, i.e. manipulated it, via the experiment. The relevant crux of the distinction here is the difference between the natural and what metaphysicians call the necessary, and it is important further to define these terms in relation to the concept of the 'contingent', that mobilization

[120] Thanks to Jane Caplan for this point and for the references: Simon LeVay, *The Sexual Brain* (Cambridge, MA: MIT Press, 1993) and *Queer Science: The Use and Abuse of Research into Sexuality* (Cambridge, MA: MIT Press, 1996).
[121] On creation as the book of God: Rigby, *Wisdom and Chivalry*, 236 ff.
[122] Agence France-Presse, 'Vatican launches guide to tackle "educational crisis" on gender', *Guardian*, 11 June 2019.

slogan of anyone from B. G. Niebuhr to Marcuse and Foucault. 'Necessary' is the opposite of 'contingent'; 'natural' is not. Natural things like mountains are still contingent; they are not necessary. They are contingent on tectonic plate movements, volcanic activity, etc. Their ongoing existence is contingent, among other things, on their not being blown up by human-made explosives. Let us say that we agreed for the sake of argument that human bodies and their processes were in some measure natural. They are still contingent—*inter alia* on evolution. Individual bodies are also contingent on death and decay, and death can be natural or unnatural. Individual living bodies are also in some ways contingent on culture. As with the capacity of explosives to alter mountains, technology means that it is possible to make increasingly significant cultural interventions in the body, including for instance via transgender hormone therapy and reassignment/ corrective surgery. Much like actions against discrimination on grounds of sex, gender, sexuality, or any other basis, decisions as to the use of such technology are normative ones that ought to be shaped though informed, empathetic debate. While scientists may be specially qualified to advise on the scope and risks of the technology's application, they have no special qualification *qua* scientists to assess its rectitude. And what societies in the past did, or did not do, what they thought and did not think, should also be supremely irrelevant in the evaluation process.

A final thought on the deployment of critical historicization for emancipatory purposes is that so much hinges on things having been different in the past, in order to provide contrast to the present and fortify the case for cultural constructionism. What inferences would the most thoroughgoing constructionists draw were their historical investigations to find constancy in salient discourses or practices across tracts of time and space?[123] Sharon Block's study of rape in eighteenth-century America illuminates some of the conceptual issues as she wrestles candidly with the strained relationship between her research findings and intellectual socialization. She began, in her own words, 'from the assumption that sexual practices, desires, and ideologies are cultural constructs'. Consistent with the neo-historicist convention characterized by Matthew Crow as duck-hunting (p. 283), she notes that 'as a historian, I have been trained to mark the exceptionality of an era, region, or cultural group'. However she reaches the conclusion that 'rape seems widely transhistoric and transcultural'. We can perhaps detect the tension between the two positions in the sentences: 'Ultimately, I am not opposed to readers' seeing various parts of this book as transhistorical, but I also hope that they will see how sexual coercion was intricately tied to early America's specific social and cultural realities. Rape's imbrication in multiple strands of history, discourse, and popular culture makes rape both transhistoric and culturally specific.' The tension is certainly present in Block's stressing that she has avoided

---

[123] On related scenarios and associated anxieties, see Wahrman, 'Change and the Corporeal', 597–8.

'ahistoricism or essentialism',[124] because she does not elaborate any conceptual distinction between essentialism, ahistoricism, and the transhistorical. If we disregard the perennial boo-word 'essentialism', Block's separation of ahistoricist and transhistorical seems no more than performative, a reassurance to her readers that they are dealing with a *bona fide* historian. It is instructive, then, that ahistoric*ist* seems to have been taken to mean the same as ahistoric*al*. Of course it is not written in stone that History needs to show cultural difference. And, to the main point, there are no necessary normative connotations if an enquiry suggests similarity. If it transpired that rape, with whatever particular local modalities, was common to all societies of which we had knowledge this would not affect the desire to stamp it out in the here and now. And if we are determined, as we need not be, to make the issue into one of (claims about?) culture versus (claims about?) nature, then note that it is not uncommon in the history of culture to encounter normative admonitions to restrain some element of nature, a mundane example being vegetarians whose anatomy evolved for an omnivorous diet.[125]

When all is said and done, the association of the natural and the normative via the metaphysical is rather old-fashioned, and the emancipatory desire of certain strong social constructionists to dissolve nature entirely into culture looks like a new libertarian twist on an old will-to-power. Take Francis Bacon's claim that knowledge is power—the claim Foucault inverted as 'power is knowledge'. Take also what is generally referred to as Cartesian mind:world dualism, a dualism of which mind:body dualism is a subset. Together Bacon and Descartes provide the basis for an image of the human mind gaining detached technical knowledge in order to manipulate the world for its own ends. That does indeed sound powerful, but it turns out to be less powerful in key ways than the image of subjectivity that has come to replace it for some. The 'Cartesian subject', often taken together with the later Kantian transcendental ego, is the focus of postmodern but by no means only postmodern critiques of 'the Enlightenment ideal of the disembodied mind'.[126] Any criticism of a concept of subjecthood or mind as disembodied perforce prompts including study of the body (including the physical brain), its needs, impulses, etc., in the constitution of subjecthood. That looks like an argument for including some element of the natural in the aetiology of the subject.

---

[124] All quotes from Sharon Block, *Rape and Sexual Power in Early America* (Chapel Hill: University of North Carolina Press, 2006), 7, 241. Again, thanks to Wahrman, 'Change and the Corporeal', 598–9, for adverting me to the text and its relevant elements. Wahrman also provides a justly appreciative account of Block's work.

[125] Note the influence on this discussion of Robert B. Pippin, 'Natural and Normative', *Daedalus* (Summer 2009), 35–43.

[126] Ania Spyra, 'Is Cosmopolitanism Not For Women? Migration in Qurratulain Hyder's *Sita Betrayed* and Amitav Ghosh's *The Shadow Lines*', *Frontiers: A Journal of Women Studies*, 27:2 (2006), 1–26, here 1. See also Sonya O. Rose, *What is Gender History?* (Cambridge: Polity, 2010), 103 on 'disembodied white men' as a particular case of the issue.

Such an argument is supposedly rebutted if what looks like the natural (in this example, the body) is actually claimed to be a cultural construct. This keeps the study of the body as the preserve of students of the cultural, and just renders it part of the broader cultural fabric, its discourses, language, etc., that are held to constitute subjecthood. So the terms of mind:world (including mind:body) dualism are replaced with 'mind:culture' as a prelude to immediately breaking down any such dualism and replacing it, in the strongest version of the new argument, with a relationship of culture→mind determinism. This looks like a weak form of subjecthood if one is still thinking in individualistic terms, since the individual is really just a function of the cultural. But cultures are humanmade, even if not by individual persons. Accordingly, the anti-Cartesian theory is still anthropocentric and stronger in relevant respects than the Cartesian/Baconian vision, since in the latter the (individual) mind is only put in a position to perceive and alter the natural world whereas in the former, with the power of the culture substituted for the power of the mind, the culture is capable of *creating* what has hitherto been mistakenly identified as the natural world. Where the individual mind returns to the picture is in the persona of our Foucauldians and semiotic code-crackers. By the magic of their 'critique' they have managed to break out of the discursive prison, stray from the ordained script, and so forth. The power of the liberating thought of these critics correlates positively with the supposed constituting strength of the discourses from which they free themselves and purport to free others with neo-historicist reference to things like historical-cultural contingency. The idealist insight that that which is thought about the world is part of the world gets expanded to the point that thought (or in the Foucauldian case discourse) becomes the determinant of the world 'in itself'.

If you are unpersuaded of the efficacy of this sort of thinking, but nonetheless object to the role that claims on the natural play in the politics of your world, you need to be clear who your interlocutors are in any given case. This will affect the sorts of arguments you need to make against them and will provide you with strategies for playing them off against each other in the event that they form contingent alliances. We have already identified two potential interlocutors: natural scientists or some subset thereof, and socio-political authorities leaning on certain metaphysical (whether religious or philosophical) claims. When talking of politics and legitimation, these two groups must in turn be conceptually separated—whatever the overlaps that may exist in practice—from a third group, those whom we might call conservatives.

When talking of conservatives one must distinguish the classical theory of conservatism, as represented in the recent past by the likes of Michael Oakeshott, from certain usages in the contemporary British and American environments where 'conservative' is applied to the avant-garde of a revolutionary neo-liberal capitalism. Conservatives in the classical sense differ from the scientists because the natural and the metaphysical *need* play no part in their discourse (though it often has), even as the normative must. In archetype, the differences between the groups are as follows:

- Scientists make claims on the *natural* with *no necessary relevance for the normative*;
- Metaphysicians (the relevant ones) use the *natural* to substantiate claims on the *normative* based on *metaphysical* presuppositions about the natural;
- Conservatives make claims on the *normative* based on the *cultural*, or put differently, the culturally given has a normative status for them.

Conservatives are the ones whose claims on how things should be are apt most frequently to involve evaluative attitudes to the past, given the relationship between culture and history. This brings us finally to the terrain of History as Identity, which is the ground on which many exponents of History as Emancipation are actually operating anyway, whatever they might think.

History as Identity

History as Identity means that subset of historical enquiry that shapes readers', listeners', and observers' thoughts and feelings about their heritage. Some forms of History as Identity are coextensive with a secularized form of History as Communion. Identity History is widely consumed and readily recognizable, apt as it is to address particular wars, revolutions, national stories, triumphs, losses, and whatnot. It frequently forms an alliance of commercial convenience with History as Entertainment.[127] It can dovetail with History as Memorialization when the memorialized deeds are specifically the deeds of one's own claimed forebears. A touch of *similitudo temporum* (pp. 124–6) might close the historical 'gap' between the memorialized past and the present for which the past is touchstone. At that point one cannot insert a cigarette paper between inspirational, 'monumental' History (in Nietzsche's term—p. 221) and History as Lesson.

No criticism is intended by the label History as Identity. Different historians operating in the tradition operate with different political agendas and differing levels of proceduralist commitment. Different readers approach it with different expectations and minds of varying degrees of openness. Some read just to find out more about where they have 'come from', as the saying goes, based on the

---

[127] I stress 'convenience'. The commercial potential of History as Identity favours this union, but by no means all commercially successful historians are Identity historians or Entertainment historians of the more gratuitous sort; by the same token, the great mass of practising historians who have no commercial success contain within their number Identity historians. Note also that the Entertainment and Travel rationales have found just as rich a synergy.

widespread feeling that this will tell them something about who they are. Others want affirmation of a collective identity. Yet others seek substantiation for the dissent they already espouse.

The potentially significant political ramifications of History in its Identity mode mean that it has many more exponents than just academic historians, and fewer professed than actual exponents amongst the ranks of academic historians. Its practitioners could be museum curators, documentary makers, schoolteachers, architects, city planners, politicians, newspaper editors, tour guides, historical novelists, film directors, elders, parents... The list indicates how far all of us are always-already under the influence of explicit historical interpretations and meaning-laden historical imagery before we begin any enquiries of our own.

In identity History the potential for tension between '"modern" historical consciousness' and 'historicity' is greatest. By historicity I mean the *subjective* way in which one sees oneself as the product of particular historical patterns and institutions, but also the *objective* ways in which one's outlook, privileges, and disadvantages are influenced by such institutions whether one realizes it or not. It will not necessarily do, therefore, just to proclaim one's emancipation from the past because one does not feel connected to it. Recall the words of Fustel, notwithstanding his injunction to study the past as if it were a 'foreign nation': 'the past never completely dies for man. Man may forget it, but he always preserves it within him. For, take him at any epoch, and he is the product, the epitome, of all the earlier epochs. Let him look into his own soul, and he can find and distinguish these different epochs by what each has left within him'. As well as his soul, we might add, let 'him' look into his circumstances.

For those who embrace the idea, '"modern" historical consciousness' is a *subjective* awareness of an *objective* reality, i.e. an awareness of actual differences of present from past. Things are not so simple. What is taken for 'awareness' here is not the correspondence of perception to external reality but the product of variable judgements about the significance and extent of various differences across time. And what if something is adjudged to be significantly *different* under the rubric of historical consciousness, yet still *relevant* under the rubric of historicity? Establishing that something is a foreign country does not mean one has nothing to do with it except the occasional holiday. Cross-border wars, alliances, and commerce are not rarities in human history. They need not bespeak similarity between the relevant parties but they undoubtedly indicate influence from one party to another, and what goes synchronically, across place, can go diachronically, across time.

In clarifying the issues at stake in identity-arguments, it is important to recognize how many claims about the nature of the relationship of past to present and future are imbued with judgements as to the desirability of that relationship, as was the case in sundry debates across the centuries between *antiqui* and *moderni* (pp. 79–85). Why, for instance, in and beyond the nineteenth century, was there a goodly correlation between conservatives and hermeneutics and between liberals and empiricism?[128] Part of the answer is that hermeneutics—and its extension in classical historicism—sustained some sort of community with the past precisely because things were changing; after the 'rupture' of the French revolutionary era, classical historicism tried to hold historical consciousness and a sense of historicity in balance. Empiricism, conversely, was a way of breaking with the precepts of inherited wisdoms. Empiricism was not the only movement that could be set against 'tradition', however: we can also name rationalism. The conceptual differences between rationalism and empiricism are important but have been somewhat obscured by a 'postmodern' tendency to bundle the two together under the unhelpful and in this case pejorative umbrella term 'Enlightenment thought'. Postmoderns have more in common with liberal-empiricists than they might like to imagine. (Some self-proclaimed liberals may also be rationalists, but that is not hugely important when dealing, as now, in heuristic types only.) Foucault, Lyotard, and the philosopher Emmanuel Levinas come together with liberals like Isaiah Berlin and Karl Popper in rejecting the sorts of schemes of social reorganization that were inferable from rationalist thought, on the basis of their proponents' claims about some actual or ideal human 'way'. Each thinker tended to see such schemes as incipiently totalitarian. Further, in the sense that all of them reject theoretical 'foundationalism' of the rationalist (say, Kantian) sort, these liberals and postmodern thinkers share some ground with conservatives like Oakeshott. Where postmoderns depart from conservatives, but remain with liberal-empiricists, is, as said, in their *attitude* towards the customary. Conservatives put a premium on the customary: when Oakeshott spoke of the *real* complexity of social orders, he meant that those orders—their bonds of mutual understanding and affection, their evolved checks and balances—were far more sophisticated than the reductive descriptions of rationalist philosophers and grand revolutionaries, so any ensuing revolutionary prescriptions were, like contract theories, bound to fail even on their own best terms.[129] While postmoderns and liberal-empiricists reject *self-foundation* on some set of universal rationalist principles, however, they thoroughly embrace an individualistic *self-determination* as against historically and collectively given mores.[130] The agenda of self-determination has as its tool the 'critique' that postmoderns like to claim as their own as they try to divest themselves of the influences of power-knowledge 'discourses' (though in fact they resemble their liberal predecessors who tried to rid themselves of the influence of 'tradition'): hence the affinity of

---

[128] There was also a close relationship between socialists and dialectics, but I shall ignore that nexus in the interests of relative clarity in dense conceptual terrain.

[129] Michael Oakeshott, *Rationalism in Politics and Other Essays* (New York: Basic Books, 1962).

[130] Hans Blumenberg, *The Legitimacy of the Modern Age* (Cambridge, MA: MIT Press, 1999) is the source of the distinction between self-foundation and self-assertion. See also the helpful discussion in Chantal Mouffe, *The Return of the Political* (London: Verso, 2005), 10–11, 41–2.

postmodernism and the 'emancipatory' brands of neo-historicism. As established in the previous discussion of History as Emancipation II, such critiques of the historically evolved present are apt to be normative critiques, whatever their proponents might think, and wherever the critiques come from conceptually. This is just as well if the critiques are to have much political purchase.

If one disagrees with the social prescriptions that conservatives proffer, and of course one need not, there is little utility in arguments of science or shadow science, metaphysical claim and counter-claim, or abstract debates about historical consciousness. One's arguments will not win out by the identification of missed possibilities from the past, or by mourning for what might have been. The issue will not be decided by the 'revelation' that any given historico-cultural arrangement is contingent, because a certain contingency is what conservatives celebrate when they associate the empirical (not metaphysical) 'is' with the 'ought'. Conservative ranks comprise the people identified above who endorse their cultural arrangements precisely because they are *their* cultural arrangements (p. 339): arrangements that, as Heidegger might have put it, give them a sense of being at home in the world. In that preference, the sort of people most often regarded as conservatives are far from alone. They are supported in principle by many cultural relativists and by the likes of the American philosopher Richard Rorty, whose thought combined liberal and Heideggerian insights, and in whose writing recognition of the 'contingency' of one's own social arrangements is a centrally important concept alongside proclaiming the virtues of those arrangements.[131] Arguments with members of this broad church, if one wishes to argue with them, have to work on the level of normativity that underpins all political debate, and the same goes for tributary historiographical conflicts too. This much was recognized by the feminist historians of the 1970s and 1980s, the civil-rights-era historians of African America, and the likes of E. P. Thompson. Their Histories were attempts to amend something like what the sociologist Arlie Hochschild calls the 'deep story'.[132]

The deep story, with all its metaphorical elements, is the tale of one's emotional home, with accompanying connotations of endeavour, hearth, kinship, possession, and pride. If one wishes to present the matter prejudicially, one could say that the deep story is the wellspring of collective narcissism, akin to a Durkheimian view of religion as worshipping one's ideal collective self. It certainly has some of the quality of ancestor worship blended with a sense of uniqueness. One need not be a member of a societal elite to propagate a story; the identity that partaking of the story entails may be compensation for some material disadvantage and indeed a way of marking oneself off from other subalterns who otherwise seem to be in the same boat. Witness: the history of nationalism.

---

[131] Richard Rorty, *Contingency, Irony, and Solidarity* (Cambridge University Press, 1989).
[132] Arlie Hochschild, *Strangers in their Own Land: Anger and Mourning on the American Right* (New York: The New Press, 2016).

At the same time, substantial numbers of people reject particular deep stories, or want to revise them, or wish to articulate their own deep story as against another that has occluded it. Any of these endeavours is apt to be incendiary given that they strike at the identity, with all of its more and less inchoate, reflex, or reflective assumptions of the comforting, the orienting, the good. Just think of the touchiness about empire or slavery in Britain and the USA: the knee-jerk justifications, the avoidance, awkward deflection, or some reference to the 'values of the time' whose logic of distancing—it sounds like an appeal to the truths of the 'modern historical consciousness'—is contradicted by the fact that it is obviously uttered in *defence* of something that the defender's historicity renders relevant in the now. Sometimes the claim will be that one story is downright false, sometimes that it contains important omissions and is skewed to serve one part of a community more than others. Sometimes the arrangements that have proved good for one group might be shown to have been deleterious for others, which reminds us that groups rarely develop in isolation from others, and so cannot always insist on the right to be left alone to their positive feelings about their historical identity. If the deep story concerns home, what happens when it is revealed that the home was built on stolen land, by slave labour?

Debates about reparations for historical wrongs are only the tip of the conceptual iceberg, but they highlight something important about the objective element of historicity. They remind that some groups are beneficiaries of historical interactions, and whether or not any given members of such a group subjectively identify with their victor-forebears, they may still owe relatively advantageous life-circumstances to those forebears. The question then, as with affirmative action—based as it is on the principle of levelling a historically tilted playing field—is what they are going to do about it.

Deep story battles are fronts in the conflict that we ascribe to identity politics. We need, though, to remember that identity politics and identity History are not just the preserve of minorities and the weak, but of majorities and the strong too. It is an error to assume that the currently prevailing story, or the one that used to prevail prior to recent contestation, is the only non-political one. This is the error that the historian and diplomat Gerard Libaridian pinpoints when he writes that 'Historians often function not only with the benefit of hindsight but also through the recognition of [contemporary] political realities of which they are a part. In their zeal to remain "non-political" they tacitly accept the assumption underlying that same system.' Their questions are influenced by the imperative to 'interpret the past in a way that it does not challenge the rationale of the present. This mutual reinforcement between particular perceptions of the past and the present, seen as objective since it implies no critique of the present, emanates from a specific ideological perspective.'[133]

---

[133] Gerard J. Libaridian, 'Objectivity and the Historiography of the Armenian Genocide', *The Armenian Review*, 31:1 (1978), 79–87, here 83.

With identity History in mind, perhaps the most important question is not: how do vocational historians rationalize what they do? Perhaps it is: given that the past matters in questions of identity, what are we who spend our lives investigating the past going to do about it? We are not obliged to engage in identity History: interests vary immensely, and long may that be so. But what about when our interests do coincide with identity topics?

Theoretical trepidation about engaging on this terrain is relatively recent, being a product of that confluence of tributary streams named neutralism, pacifism, relativism, and so forth. The trepidation ought not be overstated, because some historiographical theorists, and many historical practitioners, would say that identity-relevant History can be conducted according to the tenets of one or more of those tributary streams in the way that any other sort of History can be. As it happens, there are reasons to disagree both with the people who worry about the potential for partisanship in the area of identity History alone and with some of those who think that it can be conducted 'unproblematically' like other sorts of History. So much depends on what the 'normal' way of conducting History is meant to involve. Having already problematized appeals to relativism and the tolerance-building capacities of History, let us now problematize 'neutrality'. By its special contemporary sensitivity, History in the Identity vein shines a bright light on unavoidable *normative* questions, and while these questions are just as unavoidable in some other areas of historical enquiry, there are obvious contemporary *political* consequences of Identity History in the way in which these evaluative questions are answered, whereas that may not be the case in others areas. The whole issue is clouded in confusion, not least because for so long evaluative thought was seen as coterminous with exemplarity—History as Lesson—and as the latter receded as a justification for History, the former was either assumed likewise to have receded or was regarded as an anachronistic vestige that proper application of proceduralist precepts would eliminate.

Remember, first, that there is no necessary contradiction between faithfulness to procedure and political engagement (pp. 311–12). A criticism of some narrative of the 'rise of X' or 'the benevolence of Y' could at once be politically motivated and more plausible—better substantiated—than the narrative under criticism. As the literature scholar Brook Thomas once wrote, 'so long as we believe that we are empowered by knowledge of our situation in the world and so long as we believe that that situation has in part been determined by the past, the most empowering study of the past will be the one that comes as close as possible to telling how it really was'.[134]

[134] Brook Thomas, 'The New Historicism and other Old-Fashioned Topics', in Veeser (ed.), *The New Historicism*, 182–203, here 201. Thomas's final—Rankean—words should not distract from his point: the concept of telling it how it was can easily be substituted for some more epistemologically respectable construction about warranted inference from evidence.

Whether or not a historical investigation is politically motivated it can have political consequences. In principle historical revelations need have no such contemporary valence: the historical 'was' has no necessary influence on contemporary value-debates. In practice the historical 'was' (very different to the metaphysical 'is') can have that valence, *given historically oriented identity commitments and historically inherited (dis/)advantage.* More than ninety years ago the economic historian Leland Hamilton Jenks wrote that the conflict of opinion between historians can itself be 'of the story of events which gave rise to it'.[135] An example would be the debate, at once historiographical, of contemporary political relevance, and with its origins in anti-imperialism at the time, over the 'Indian drain', the economic cost to India of British rule. Different communities, or parts of communities, may just remember different things but they may also remember the same thing differently. In these memory battles, certain inferences from evidence can hurt or help, whatever the reason they are adduced. Who enslaved/killed/invaded whom, and who profited, are important questions. When dealing with such matters, it is impossible to separate causal explanations from attributions of responsibility.

In the past, as now, power was wielded positively and negatively, but never neutrally.[136] It is a matter for investigation, not assumption, as to whether it was wielded legitimately. It is not alien to historians to try to establish the content of norms in foreign countries past, and then to try to establish how far actors acted consistently in relation to those norms, and so on. Even without some formal 'verdict' such exercises are of a piece with moral theory, as well as involving precisely the sort of local knowledge of which historians pride themselves as having a special understanding. The historian cannot escape the normative realm with reference to 'complexity' or nuance. Many human affairs are complex, which is why we have experts to investigate them, and complexity is not a synonym of ambiguity. Stating that something is complex is a prelude to trying to clarify it and reach conclusions, however qualified: it is not a substitute for a conclusion. If the conclusion is indeed to ambiguity, in the terms framed it must be a conclusion to evaluative ambiguity, which is a conclusion within the realms of evaluative discourse, not outside it. The same goes for conclusions that are deflationary. Trying to reduce the stakes is something that can only be done by taking some stakes into account. Mitigation of responsibility (guilt), perhaps by functional contextualization, is in the same evaluative universe as the aggravation of that responsibility. Praise—which historians are on the whole happier distributing—only makes sense if blame also does.

---

[135] Leland Hamilton Jenks, *The Migration of British Capital to 1875* (New York: A. A. Knopf, 1927), 225.
[136] Colin Richmond, 'Mickey Mouse in Disneyland: How Did the Fifteenth Century Get that Way?', in Linda Clark (ed.), *The Fifteenth Century: V: Of Mice and Men: Image, Belief and Regulation in Late Medieval England* (Woodbridge: The Boydell Press, 2005), 157–70, here 166.

Even in the event that it seems power was legitimately wielded by the lights of the wielder, this is no guarantee that the object of the power felt the same way. Differences of opinion as to legitimacy may constitute one of the major cleavages in identity History, and the absence of just one set of standards 'back then' reminds us why it is often insufficient to adopt a crypto-relativistic argument to 'the standards of the time'. Such crypto-relativist arguments may or may not affect our judgements towards individual slaveowners, imperialists, and so on, as historically situated agents acting with particular cultural assumptions, but those arguments cannot affect our normative attitudes to the institutions and practices of slavery, empire, and so on.

Remember, in the foregoing discussion of relativism, the significance for the evaluative process of historical practices themselves: the human consequences of these practices in happiness or suffering (pp. 326–8). The historian is in charge of the portrayal of such practices and/or their human consequences, and even if she refrains from explicit judgement, the way that such matters are discussed, constitutive silences and all (p. 295) has the potential to evoke some response by the reader. With this in mind, how should the historian proceed? If the answer is that her description and explanation ought to be as 'balanced' as possible, then, again, we are already in the normative universe. If the answer is that she should write in such a way that she is likely to produce no response whatsoever from the reader, might we not think that slightly strange? It is unclear that the demand for the historian's 'neutrality' must mean that the historian has to try to 'neutralize', since that term itself suggests some agenda of manipulation: 'neutralization' is not 'neutral'.

It is difficult to reconcile neutralization with the procedural requirement of truthfulness, for trying to 'get it right', since 'getting it right' might involve showing that as far as one can infer from the evidence, historical character or interest group X was responsible for whipping up hatred against group Y. If we take the act of trying to 'be fair' to relevant historical actors to be synonymous with trying to be accurate about them based on the evidence, then obviously enough 'being fair' to them is not the same thing as 'being nice' to them or treating them neutrally. It may mean treating them *impartially* but, according to definition, that can be a very different thing. Under one definition, impartiality is a position that one adopts as the way to reach the best conclusion, and so actually implies the judgement that 'neutrality' rejects. One might also think of a definition of 'impartiality' appropriate to the historian's particular ethic of responsibility. Where civil servants ought 'impartially' to implement the policies of the government of the day on recognition that that government is legitimate, historians ought 'impartially' to report their interpretations of the past with no consideration for how much they might irritate the government of the day. Historians might thus be playing a political role, even a democratic one, but it is a role whose integrity is guaranteed precisely by their not betraying their procedural ethic in the service of any constituency or regime.

It is fair to point out that historians are generally not trained in the sort of evaluative reasoning that might make any of their judgements reliable, but what is the thrust of that observation supposed to be? If it is to prompt historians to acquaint themselves better with the tenets of evaluative reasoning, that is one thing, and a rather good idea, though it ought not be thought that such training will lead to unanimity in judgement, any more than the other elements of training lead to unanimity in conclusion in any other area of historical enquiry. If, however, the point about training underpins an argument against historians making evaluations then that is also an argument against historians doing the sorts of History in which evaluations or evocative or neutralizing descriptions are unavoidable. We can argue about precisely how many categories of History that would exclude but it would likely rule out several areas of History as Identity, Travel, Lesson, Memorialization, and Emancipation, which together account for a great deal of all the History written and even more of the History that is read by the general public. To be clear: the only way historians in the relevant areas could escape normative engagement, as opposed to continuing to use evocative language and make evaluative analyses without admitting it, is not to write or speak on those areas. This would be a pity because it would remove empirically informed voices when they are most needed.

If the idea of making or consciously prompting judgements sounds presumptuous, it is really nothing more than an expression of the responsibility that historians take on when engaging in the first place with historical matters of moral significance. This responsibility is the quantum of the power historians can wield in a world where opinions about the past still have fundamental importance.

Bibliography of Works Cited

Newspapers and Journals

Abhandlungen der Königlichen Preußischen Akademie der Wissenschaften zu Berlin
American Anthropologist
American Historical Review
American Journal of Philology
American Political Science Review
Ancient History Bulletin
Annali della Scuola Normale Superiore di Pisa
Archiv für Sozialwissenschaft und Sozialpolitik
Armenian Review
British Journal of Sociology
Bulletin de la Classe des Lettres et des Sciences morales et politiques de l'Académie Royale de
     Belgique
Bulletin of the John Rylands Library
California Italian Studies
Chronicle of Higher Education
Church History
Classical Journal
Classical Philology
Common Knowledge
Comparative Civilizations Review
Comparative Studies in Society and History
Critical Inquiry
Cuadernos de Filología Clásica. Estudios griegos e indoeuropeos
Daedalus
Differentia
Early Medieval Europe
Economic History Review
European History Quarterly
Feminist Studies
Frontiers: A Journal of Women Studies
Gender and History
Guardian
Hermes
Historein
Historian
Historical Journal
Historical Research
Historical Studies in the Physical Sciences
Historiography and Antiquarianism
Historische Zeitschrift
Historisch-politische Zeitschrift

History
History and Theory
History Workshop Journal
Histos
Hume Studies
I Tatti Studies in the Italian Renaissance
Indian Historical Review
International Affairs
International History of Science Newsletter
Ius commune
Journal of Contemporary History
Journal of Historical Sociology
Journal of the History of IdeasJournal of Interdisciplinary History
Journal of Literary Theory
Journal of Medieval and Early Modern Studies
Journal of the Philosophy of History
Journal of Roman Studies
Klio
Le Débat
London Review of Books
Modern Intellectual History
Midland History
Ministry Magazine
Mittellateinisches Jahrbuch
Modern Language Notes
Museum and Society
Nature and Culture
Nepantla: Views from South
New Literary History
Nietzsche-Studien
Observer
Oxford Studies in Early Modern Philosophy
Parergon
Past and Present
Patterns of Prejudice
Pecia. Le livre et l'écrit
Philosophical Forum
Philosophical Quarterly
Philosophical Review
Philosophy
Philosophy and Literature
Polity
Postmodern Culture
Praxis International
Principia
Proceedings of the Modern Language Association
Progress in Human Geography
Public Culture
Renascimento
Rethinking History

Reviews in American History
Revue de Synthèse historique
Revue des Deux Mondes
Revue Historique
Saeculum
Sociological Research Online
Speculum
Studies in Church History
The Dial
Touchstone
Traditio
Transactions of the American Philological Association
Transactions of the Royal Historical Society
Tyndale Bulletin
Viator
Vox-poetica

Online materials

Kenneth Bartlett interview: https://www.youtube.com/watch?v=Px1GwHyAYXs
Leonardo Bruni, *Laudatio Florentinae Urbis or Panegyric to the City of Florence* (c.1403–4), online at https://www.york.ac.uk/teaching/history/pjpg/bruni.pdf
Collection des documents inédits sur l'histoire de France: https://cths.fr/ed/liste.php?monocrit=c&collection=18
Stephan Collini, 'Intellectual History' online at: http://www.history.ac.uk/makinghistory/resources/articles/intellectual_history.html
Matthew Crow, 'Context as Environment: A "Workmanlike" Approach', online at http://historyofthepresent.org/forum/M_Crow_Context_as_Environ.pdf
The Encyclopedia of Ancient History, Wiley online library 2012: https://onlinelibrary.wiley.com/
Steven Fielding, 'Political History', online at: http://www.history.ac.uk/makinghistory/resources/articles/political_history.html
Patrick Finney, 'International History', online at: http://www.history.ac.uk/makinghistory/resources/articles/international_history.html
Lloyd Gerson, 'Plotinus', in Edward N. Zalta (ed.), *The Stanford Encyclopedia of* (Summer 2014 edn.): https://plato.stanford.edu/archives/sum2014/entries/plotinus/
Chris Gowans, 'Moral Relativism', in Edward N. Zalta (ed.), *The Stanford Encyclopedia of Philosophy* (Summer 2019 edn.): https://plato.stanford.edu/archives/sum2019/entries/moral-relativism/
History and Policy: http://www.historyandpolicy.org/policy-papers/
Internet Encyclopedia of Philosophy: http://www.iep.utm.edu/origen-of-alexandria/#SH5b
Jewish virtual library: http://www.jewishvirtuallibrary.org/jsource/judaica/ejud_0002_0008_0_08624.html
Monumenta Germaniae Historica: https://www.dmgh.de/

Books

Abelard, Peter, *Letters IX–XIV*, ed. Edmé Renno Smits (Groningen: Bouma, 1983).

Acton, Lord, *Historical Essays and Studies* (London: Macmillan, 1908).

Acton, Lord, *Lectures on the French Revolution* (London: Macmillan, 1920).

Acton, Lord, *Lectures on Modern History* (London: Fontana, 1960).

Adler, Hans, and Wulf Koepke (eds.), *A Companion to the Works of Johann Gottfried Herder* (Rochester, NY: Camden House, 2009).

Adorno, Theodor W., *History and Freedom: Lectures, 1964–1965*, ed. Rolf Tiedeman (Cambridge: Polity Press, 2006).

Alexander, W. M., *Johann Georg Hamann, Philosophy and Faith* (The Hague: Martinus Nijhoff, 1966).

Althusser, Louis, *For Marx* (Harmondsworth: Penguin, 1969).

Althusser, Louis, *Écrits philosophiques et politiques* vol. I (Paris: Éditions Stock, 1994).

Althusser, Louis, and Étienne Balibar, *Reading Capital* (London: New Left Books, 1970).

Anderson, Benedict, *Imagined Communities* (London: Verso, 2006).

Anderson, Carol, *White Rage: The Unspoken Truth of Our Racial Divide* (New York: Bloomsbury, 2016).

Ankersmit, Frank, *Sublime Historical Experience* (Stanford: Stanford University Press, 2005).

Apfel, Lauren J., *The Advent of Pluralism: Diversity and Conflict in the Age of Sophocles* (Oxford: Oxford University Press, 2011).

Appiah, Kwame Anthony, *In My Father's House: Africa in the Philosophy of Culture* (New York: Oxford University Press, 1992).

Aptheker, Herbert, *American Negro Slave Revolts* (New York: Columbia University Press, 1943).

Aquinas, Thomas, *Summa Theologica* (Raleigh, NC: Hayes Barton Press, 2006).

Arendt, Hannah, *The Life of the Mind* (New York: Harcourt, 1978).

Arendt, Hannah, *Responsibility and Judgement* (New York: Shocken, 2003).

Ariès, Philippe, *L'Enfant et la vie familiale sous l'ancien régime* (Paris: Plon, 1960).

Aristotle, *On the Art of Poetry*, trans. Ingram Bywater (Oxford: Oxford University Press, 1920).

Arnold, John, *History: A Very Short Introduction* (Oxford: Oxford University Press, 2000).

Arnold, John H., *Inquisition and Power* (Philadelphia: University of Pennsylvania Press, 2001).

Arrian of Nicomedia, *Arrian*, trans. E. Iliff Robson (London: William Heinemann, 1967).

Assis, Arthur Alfaix, *What Is History For? Johann Gustav Droysen and the Functions of Historiography* (New York: Berghahn, 2016).

Auerbach, Eric, *Mimesis: The Representation of Reality in Western Literature* (New York: Doubleday, 1957).

Auerbach, Eric, *Scenes from the Drama of European Literature* (Minneapolis: University of Minnesota Press, 1984).

Augustine of Hippo, *The Works of Aurelius Augustine: A New Translation*, ed. Marcus Dods, vol. 5 (Edinburgh: Clark, 1872).

Austin, James, *The Tower of Babel in Genesis* (Bloomington: Westbow, 2012).

Backhouse, Roger E., and Philippe Fontaine (eds.), *A Historiography of the Modern Social Sciences* (Cambridge: Cambridge University Press, 2014).

Backus, Irena, *Leibniz: Protestant Theologian* (New York: Oxford University Press, 2016).

Bacon, Francis, *Essays* (London: JM Dent and Sons, 1972).

Baghramian, Maria, *Relativism* (Abingdon: Routledge, 2004).

Bakker, Egbert J. (ed.), *A Companion to the Ancient Greek Language* (Chichester: Blackwell, 2010).

Bambach, Charles R., *Heidegger, Dilthey, and the Crisis of Historicism* (Ithaca: Cornell University Press, 1995).

Baragwanath, Emily, and Mathieu de Bakker (eds.), *Myth, Truth and Narrative in Herodotus* (Oxford: Oxford University Press, 2012).

Barnes, Timothy D., *Ammianus Marcellinus and the Representation of Historical Reality* (Ithaca: Cornell University Press, 1998).

Baron, Christopher A., *Timaeus of Tauromenium and Hellenistic Historiography* (New York: Cambridge University Press, 2013).

Barraclough, Geoffrey, *History in a Changing World* (Norman, OK: University of Oklahoma Press, 1956).

Barraclough, Geoffrey, *Introduction to Contemporary History* (Harmondsworth: Penguin, 1967).

Barrett, James R., *History from the Bottom Up and the Inside Out: Ethnicity, Race, and Identity in Working-Class History* (Durham, NC: Duke University Press, 2017).

Barthes, Roland, *Michelet* (Berkeley: University of California Press, 1992).

Bartlett, Kenneth R. (ed.), *The Civilization of the Italian Renaissance: A Sourcebook* (Toronto: University of Toronto Press, 2011).

Bartlett, Robert, *Gerald of Wales, 1146–1223* (Oxford: Clarendon Press, 1982).

Bartlett, Robert, *The Natural and the Supernatural in the Middle Ages* (Cambridge: Cambridge University Press, 2008).

Baswell, Christopher, *Virgil in Medieval England* (Cambridge: Cambridge University Press, 1995).

Baum, Gregory, *The Social Imperative* (New York: Paulist Press, 1979).

Baynes, K., J. Bonman, and T. McCarthy (eds), *After Philosophy, End or Transformation?* (Cambridge, MA: MIT Press, 1987).

Beard, Charles A., *An Economic Interpretation of the Constitution of the United States* (New York: The Free Press, 1965).

Beck, Hans, and Uwe Walter, *Die frühen römischen Historiker*, 2 vols. (Darmstadt: Wissenschaftliche Buchgesellschaft, 2001, 2004).

Becker, Carl Lotus, *Detachment and the Writing of History* (Ithaca: Cornell University Press, 1958).

Bede, *Ecclesiastical History of the English People*, ed. Leo Sherley-Price and D. H. Farmer (London: Penguin, 1990), and ed. Judith McClure and Roger Collins (Oxford: Oxford University Press, 1999).

Beer, Jeanette, *Villehardouin: Epic Historian* (Geneva: Droz, 1968).

Beiser, Frederick(ed.), *The Cambridge Companion to Hegel and Nineteenth Century Philosophy* (Cambridge: Cambridge University Press, 2008).

Bell, Jeffrey A., and Claire Colebrook (eds.), *Deleuze and History* (Edinburgh: Edinburgh University Press, 2009).

Bennett, Judith M., *History Matters: Patriarchy and the Challenge of Feminism* (Philadelphia: University of Pennsylvania Press, 2006).

Benson, Robert L., and Giles Constable (eds.), *Renaissance and Renewal in the Twelfth Century* (Oxford: Clarendon Press, 1985).

Bentley, Michael, *Modernizing England's Past: English Historiography in the Age of Modernism* (Cambridge: Cambridge University Press, 2005).

Bentley, Michael(ed.), *Companion to Historiography* (Abingdon: Routledge, 2007).

Berg, Maxine, *A Woman in History: Eileen Power 1889–1940* (Cambridge: Cambridge University Press, 1996).

Berger, Alan L., and David Patterson, *Jewish–Christian Dialogue: Drawing Honey from the Rock* (St Paul, MN: Paragon House, 2008).

Berlin, Isaiah, *Historical Inevitability* (London: Oxford University Press, 1954).

Berlin, Isaiah, *Vico and Herder: Two Studies in the History of Ideas* (London: Chatto and Windus, 1980).

Berman, Harold J., *Law and Revolution, the Formation of the Western Legal Tradition* (Cambridge, MA: Harvard University Press, 1983).

Berman, Harold J., *Law and Revolution II: The Impact of the Protestant Reformations on the Western Legal Tradition* (Cambridge, MA: Belknap Press, 2003).

Bermejo, Saúl Martínez, *Translating Tacitus: The Reception of Tacitus's Works in the Vernacular Languages of Europe, 16th–17th Centuries* (Pisa: Edizioni Plus, 2010).

Berndt, Rainer (ed.), *Schrift, Schreiber, Schenker: Studien zur Abtei Sankt Viktor in Paris und den Viktorinern* (Berlin: Akademie Verlag, 2005).

Bertagnolli, Paul, *Prometheus in Music: Representations of Myth in the Romantic Era* (London: Routledge, 2007).

Berzon, Todd S., *Classifying Christians: Ethnography, Heresiology, and the Limits of Knowledge in Late Antiquity* (Oakland: University of California Press, 2016).

Bett, Richard(ed.), *Cambridge Companion to Ancient Scepticism* (Cambridge: Cambridge University Press, 2010).

Betz, John R., *After Enlightenment: The Post-Secular Vision of J. G. Hamann* (Chichester: Blackwell, 2012).

Biale, Davis (ed.), *Judaism* (New York: Norton, 2015).

Biersack, Aletta, *Clio in Oceania: Toward a Historical Anthropology* (Washington, DC: Smithsonian Institution Press, 1991).

Blaas, P. B. M., *Continuity and Anachronism* (The Hague: Martinus Nijhoff, 1978).

Blackbourn, David, *Populists and Patricians: Essays in Modern German History* (Abingdon: Routledge, 2014).

Blackbourn, David, and Geoff Eley, *Mythen deutscher Geschichtsschreibung. Die gescheiterte bürgerliche Revolution von 1848* (Frankfurt am Mein: Ullstein, 1980).

Blackbourn, David, and Geoff Eley, *The Peculiarities of German History: Bourgeois Society and Politics in Nineteenth Century Germany* (Oxford: Oxford University Press, 1984).

Blanc, Jacob, and Frederico Freitas (eds.), *Big Water: The Making of the Borderlands Between Brazil, Argentina, and Paraguay* (Tuczon, AZ: University of Arizona Press, 2018).

Blanton, Ward, and Hent de Vries (eds.), *Paul and the Philosophers* (New York: Fordham University Press, 2013).

Bloch, Marc, *Les Rois thaumaturges* (Strasbourg: Istra, 1924).

Bloch, Marc, *Les Caractères originaux de l'histoire rurale française* (Oslo: Aschehoug, 1931).

Bloch, Marc, *The Historian's Craft* (New York: Vintage Books, 1953).

Bloch, Marc, *Feudal Society* (London: Routledge, 1989).

Block, Sharon, *Rape and Sexual Power in Early America* (Chapel Hill: University of North Carolina Press, 2006).

Bloxham, Donald, *History and Morality* (Oxford: Oxford University Press, 2020).

Bloxham, Donald, and A. Dirk Moses (eds.), *The Oxford Handbook of Genocide Studies* (Oxford: Oxford University Press, 2010).

Blumenberg, Hans, *The Legitimacy of the Modern Age* (Cambridge, MA: MIT Press, 1999).

Bödeker, Hans Erich, Peter Hanns Reill, and Jürgen Schlumbohm (eds.), *Wissenschaft als kulturelle Praxis, 1750–1900* (Göttingen: Vandenhoeck und Ruprecht, 1999).

Bodin, Jean, *Method for the Easy Comprehension of History* (New York: Octagon, 1945).

Bodin, Jean, *Colloquium of the Seven about Secrets of the Sublime* (Princeton: Princeton University Press, 1975).

Bod, Rens, Jaap Maat, and Thijs Weststeijn (eds.), *The Making of the Humanities*, 2 vols (Amsterdam: Amsterdam University Press, 2010 and 2012).

Bolingbroke, Henry St John, Lord Viscount, *Letters on the Study and Use of History* (London: T. Cadell, 1779).

Bonnell, Victoria E., and Lynn Hunt (eds.), *Beyond the Cultural Turn* (Berkeley: University of California Press, 1999).

Bossuet, Jacques-Bénigne, *An Universal History from the Beginning of the World to the Empire of Charlemagne* (New York: Robert Moore, 1821).

Bourdieu, Pierre, *Outline of a Theory of Practice* (Cambridge: Cambridge University Press, 2003).

Bourdieu, Pierre, and Loïc Wacquant, *An Invitation to Reflexive Sociology* (Cambridge: Polity, 1992).

Braudel, Fernand, *The Mediterranean and the Mediterranean World in the Age of Philip II*, vol. 1 (London: Collins, 1972), vol. 2 (Berkeley: University of California Press, 1995).

Braudel, Fernand, *On History* (Chicago: University of Chicago Press, 1980).

Brazeau, Brian, *Writing a New France, 1604–1632: Empire and Early Modern French Identity* (London: Routledge, 2016).

Breisach, Ernst, *Historiography: Ancient, Medieval and Modern* (Chicago: University of Chicago Press, 2007).

Brett, Martin, and David A. Woodman (eds.), *The Long Twelfth-Century View of the Anglo-Saxon Past* (Farnham: Ashgate, 2015).

Briggs, Charles F., *The Body Broken: Medieval Europe, 1300–1520* (London: Routledge 2011).

Brooks, Van Wyck, *The Wine of the Puritans* (London: Sisley's, 1908).

Brown, Callum G., *Postmodernism for Historians* (Harlow: Pearson, 2005).

Brown, Patricia Fortini, *Venice and Antiquity: The Venetian Sense of the Past* (New Haven: Yale University Press, 1996).

Buchanan, George Wesley, *The Book of Daniel* (Eugene, OR: Wipf and Stock, 1999).

Burckhardt, Jacob, *The Civilization of the Renaissance in Italy* (London: Penguin, 2004).

Burguière, André, *L'École des Annales. Une histoire intellectuelle* (Paris: Odile Jacob, 2006).

Burke, Peter, *The Renaissance Sense of the Past* (London: Arnold, 1969).

Burke, Peter (ed.), *New Perspectives on Historical Writing* (University Park: Pennslyvania State University Press, 1992).

Burrow, John, *A History of Histories* (London: Allen Lane, 2007).

Burrow, Rufus, Jr, *James H. Cone and Black Liberation Theology* (Jefferson, NC: McFarland, 1994).

Burschel, Peter, Mark Häberlein, and Volker Reinhardt (eds.), *Historische Anstöße* (Berlin: Akademie, 2002).

Butterfield, Herbert, *Christianity, Diplomacy and War* (London: Epworth, 1953).

Butterfield, Herbert, *The Whig Interpretation of History* (New York: Norton, 1965).

Cahn, Steven M. (ed.), *Classics of Western Philosophy* (Indianapolis: Hackett, 1990).

Calhoun, Craig (ed.) *Sociology in American: A History* (Chicago: University of Chicago Press, 2007).

Callinicos, Alex, *Theories and Narratives: Reflections on the Philosophy of History* (Durham, NC: Duke University Press, 1995).

Cameron, Averil, *Procopius and the Sixth Century* (Berkeley: University of California Press, 1985).

Canning, Joseph, *The Political Thought of Baldis de Ubaldis* (Cambridge: Cambridge University Press, 1987).

Caputo, John D., *Radical Hermeneutics: Repetition, Deconstruction, and the Hermeneutic Project* (Bloomington: Indiana University Press, 1987).

Caputo, John D., *The Prayers and Tears of Jacques Derrida: Religion Without Religion* (Bloomington: Indiana University Press, 1997).

Carlyle, Thomas, *Sartor Resartus, Heroes and Hero-Worship, Past and Present*, ed. G.T. Bettany (London: Ward, Lock and Co., 1892).

Carr, E. H., *What Is History?* (New York: Knopf, 1962).

Cassirer, Ernst, *The Myth of the State* (Hamburg: Meiner Verlag, 2007).

Chalkokondyles, Laonikos, *The Histories*, 2 vols., ed. Anthony Kaldellis (Cambridge, MA: Harvard University Press, 2014).

Chakrabarty, Dipesh, *Provincializing Europe: Postcolonial Thought and Historical Difference* (Princeton: Princeton University Press, 2000).

Chambers, David, Brian Pullan, and Jennifer Fletcher (eds.), *Venice: A Documentary History, 1450–1630* (Oxford: Blackwell, 1992).

Chaturvedi, Vinayak (ed.), *Mapping Subaltern Studies and the Postcolonial* (London: Verso, 2012).

Chenu, Marie-Dominique, *Nature, Man, and Society in the Twelfth Century* (Chicago: University of Chicago Press, 1968).

Chesnut, Glenn F., *The First Christian Histories: Eusebius, Socrates, Sozomen, Theodoret, and Evagrius* (Macon, GA: Mercer University Press, 1986).

Chesterton, G. K., *Tremendous Trifles* (London: Methuen, 1909).

Chodorow, Stanley, *Christian Political Theory and Church Politics in the Mid-Twelfth Century* (Berkeley: University of California Press, 1972).

Ciaffa, Jay A., *Max Weber and the Problems of Value-Free Social Science* (Cranbury, NJ: Associated University Presses, 1998).

Cicero, *Cicero: On the Orator, Books 1–2*, trans. E. W. Sutton and H. Rackham (London: Heinemann, 1967).

Clark, George Kitson, *The Critical Historian* (London: History Book Club, 1968).

Clark, Linda (ed.), *The Fifteenth Century: V: Of Mice and Men: Image, Belief and Regulation in Late Medieval England* (Woodbridge: The Boydell Press, 2005).

Clemoes, Peter, and Kathleen Hughes (eds.), *England before the Conquest* (Cambridge: Cambridge University Press, 1971).

Cochran, Terry, *Twilight of the Literary: Figures of Thought in the Age of Print* (Cambridge, MA: Harvard University Press, 2001).

Coleman, Janet, *Piers Plowman and the Moderni* (Rome: Edizioni di Storia e Letteratura, 1981).

Coleman, Janet, *Ancient and Medieval Memories: Studies in the Reconstruction of the Past* (Cambridge: Cambridge University Press, 2005).

Colley, Linda, *Britons: Forging the Nation, 1707–1837* (New Haven: Yale University Press, 2005).

Collingwood, R. G., *The Idea of History*, revised edition (Oxford: Oxford University Press, 2005).

Commager, H. S., *The Search for a Usable Past* (New York: Knopf, 1967).

Comte, Auguste, *The Positive Philosophy of Auguste Comte*, vol. 2, ed. Harriet Martineau (London: Trübner, 1875).

Condorcet, Nicolas de, *Tableau historique des progrès de l'esprit humain: projets, esquisse, fragments et notes (1772–1794)*, ed. Jean-Pierre Schandeler and Pierre Crépel (Paris: L'Institute National d'Études Démographique, 2004).

Constable, Giles, *The Reformation of the Twelfth Century* (Cambridge: Cambridge University Press, 2002).

Conway, Daniel, *Nietzsche and the Political* (London: Routledge, 1997).

Conzemius, Victor, Martin Greschat, and Hermann Kocher (eds.), *Die Zeit nach 1945 als Thema kirchlicher Zeitgeschichte* (Göttingen: Vandenhoeck & Ruprecht, 1988).

Cooper, Barry, *Eric Voegelin and the Foundations of Modern Political Science* (Columbia: University of Missouri Press, 1999).

Coquillette, Daniel R., *The Civilian Writers of Doctors' Commons, London* (Berlin: Duncker and Humblot, 1988).

Cornford, Francis MacDonald, *Thucydides Mythistoricus* (London: Edward Arnold, 1907).

Coss, Peter, and Maurice Keen (eds.) *Heraldry, Pageantry and Social Display in Medieval England* (Woodbridge: Boydell, 2002).

Courtney, Cecil P., and Jenny Mander (eds.), *Raynal's 'Histoire des deux Indes'* (Oxford: Oxford University Press, 2015).

Coyle, Martin (ed.), *Niccolò Machiavelli's The Prince: New Interdisciplinary Essays* (Manchester: Manchester University Press, 1995).

Craig, Gordon A. *The Politics of the Unpolitical: German Writers and the Problem of Power, 1770–1871* (Munich: Beck, 1993).

Craig, Edward (ed.), *Routledge Encyclopedia of Philosophy*, vol. 7 (London: Routledge, 1998).

Crawford, Katherine, *The Sexual Culture of the French Renaissance* (Cambridge: Cambridge University Press, 2010).

Cregan-Reid, Vybarr, *Discovering Gilgamesh: Geology, Narrative, and the Historical Sublime in Victorian Culture* (Manchester: Manchester University Press, 2013).

Critchley, Simon, *The Ethics of Deconstruction: Derrida and Levinas* (Edinburgh: Edinburgh University Press, 1999).

Cromwell, John Wesley, *The Negro in American History* (Washington, DC: American Negro Academy, 1914).

Crossan, John Dominic, Luke Timothy Johnson, and Werner H. Kelber, *The Jesus Controversy: Perspectives in Conflict* (Harrisburg, PA: Trinity Press, 1999).

Crossley, Ceri, *French Historians and Romanticism: Thierry, Guizot, the Saint-Simonians, Quinet, Michelet* (London: Routledge, 1993).

Crump, C. G., and E. F. Jacob (eds.), *The Legacy of the Middle Ages* (Oxford: Clarendon Press, 1943).

Culler, A. Dwight, *The Victorian Mirror of History* (New Haven: Yale University Press, 2009).

Culler, Jonathan, *Literary Theory: A Very Short Introduction* (Oxford: Oxford University Press, 1997).

Cummings, Brian, and James Simpson (eds.), *Cultural Reformations: Medieval and Renaissance in Literary History* (Oxford: Oxford University Press, 2010).

Curtius, Ernst Robert, *European Literature and the Latin Middle Ages* (Princeton: Princeton University Press, 1991).

Dael, Sharon, Alison Williams Lewin, and Duane J. Osheim (eds.), *Chronicling History* (Pennsylvania: Pennsylvania State University Press, 2007).

Dahlmann, Friedrich Christoph, *Geschichte der englischen Revolution* (Leipzig: Weidmann, 1844).

Dahlmann, Friedrich Christoph, *Geschichte der französischen Revolution bis auf die Stiftung der Republik* (Leipzig: Weidmann, 1845).

Damian-Grint, Peter, *The New Historians of the Twelfth Century Renaissance* (Woodbridge: Boydell, 1999).

Darnton, Robert, *The Great Cat Massacre and Other Episodes in French Cultural History* (New York: Basic Books, 1999).

Dauenhauer, Bernard P. (ed.), *At the Nexus of Philosophy and History* (Athens, GA: University of Georgia Press, 2010).

Davies, Elizabeth Gould, *The First Sex* (New York: Penguin, 1971).

Davies, Stephen, *Empiricism and History* (Basingstoke: Palgrave Macmillan, 2003).

Davis, Natalie Zemon, *The Return of Martin Guerre* (Cambridge, MA: Harvard University Press, 1983).

Dawson, David, *Christian Figural Reading and the Fashioning of Identity* (Berkeley: University of California Press, 2001).

De Bom, Erik, Marijke Janssens, Toon Van Houdt, and Jan Papy (eds.), *(Un)masking the Realities of Power: Justus Lipsius and the Dynamics of Political Writing in Early Modern Europe* (Leiden: Brill, 2010).

Delanty, Gerard, *Social Science: Philosophical and Methodological Foundations* (Maidenhead: Open University Press, 2005).

de Mul, Jos, *The Tragedy of Finitude: Dilthey's Hermeneutics of Life* (New Haven: Yale University Press, 2004).

Derrida, Jacques, *Margins of Philosophy* (Chicago: University of Chicago Press, 1982).

Derrida, Jacques, *Positions* (Chicago: University of Chicago Press, 1982).

Derrida, Jacques, *Limited Inc.* (Evanston, IL: Northwestern University Press, 1988).

Derrida, Jacques, *Archive Fever: A Freudian Impression* (Chicago: University of Chicago Press, 1996).

Derrida, Jacques, *Writing and Difference*, ed. Alan Bass (London: Routledge, 2005).

Desan, Philippe (ed.), *Montaigne politique* (Paris: Honoré Champion Éditeur, 2006).

Descartes, René, *Discourse on Method*, trans. Andrew Wollaston (Harmondsworth: Penguin, 1960).

Dickens, A. G., *The Age of Humanism and Reformation* (London: Prentice Hall, 1977).

Dickson, Gwen Griffith, *Johann Georg Hamann's Relational Metacriticism* (Berlin: de Gruyter, 1995).

Dierken, Jörg, *Selbstbewusstsein individueller Freiheit: religionstheoretische Erkundungen in protestantischer Perspektive* (Tübingen: Mohr Siebeck, 2005).

Di Leo, Jeffrey R. (ed.), *Federman's Fictions* (Albany, NY: SUNY, 2011).

Dilthey, Wilhelm, *Dilthey: Selected Writings*, ed. H. P. Rickman (Cambridge: Cambridge University Press, 1976).

Dionysius of Halicarnassus, *On Thucydides*, ed. W. Kendrick Pritchett (Berkeley: University of California Press, 1975).

DiVanna, Isabel, *Reconstructing the Middle Ages: Gaston Paris and the Development of Nineteenth-Century Medievalism* (Newcastle: Cambridge Scholars Press, 2008).

Dobbs, Betty Jo Teeter, *The Janus Faces of Genius: The Role of Alchemy in Newton's Thought* (Cambridge: Cambridge University Press, 1991).

Donagan, Alan, *The Later Philosophy of R. G. Collingwood* (Oxford: Clarendon Press, 1962).

Dosse, François, *New History in France: The Triumph of the Annales* (Chicago: University of Illinois Press, 1994).

Dosse, François, *History of Structuralism: vol. 2: The Sign Sets, 1967–Present* (Minneapolis: University of Minnesota Press, 1998).

Downing, F. Gerald, *Cynics, Paul and the Pauline Church* (London: Routledge, 1998).

Dray, William, *Perspectives on History* (London: Routledge and Kegan Paul, 1980).

Droysen, Johann Gustav, *Geschichte Alexanders des Grossen* (Hamburg: Perthes, 1833).

Droysen, Johann Gustav, *Geschichte des Hellenismus*, 2 vols. (Hamburg: Perthes, 1836–43).

Droysen, Johann Gustav, *Geschichte der preussischen Politik*, 14 vols. (Leipzig: Veit, 1855–86).

Droysen, Johann Gustav, *Grundriß der Historik* (Leipzig: Veit, 1882).

Dubois, Claude-Gilbert, *Celtes et Gaulois au XVIe siècle: Le développement littéraire d'un mythe nationaliste* (Paris: Vrin, 1972).

Dubois, Claude-Gilbert, *La Conception de l'histoire en France au XVIe siècle* (Paris: Nizet, 1977).

Du Bois, W. E. B., *Black Reconstruction in America* (New York: Harcourt, Brace, and Co., 1935).

Duncan, Graeme Campbell, *Marx and Mill: Two Views of Social Conflict and Social Harmony* (Cambridge: Cambridge University Press, 1977).

Easterling, P. E., and B. M. W. Knox (eds.), *The Cambridge History of Classical Literature: Vol. 1 Part 3: Philosophy, History and Oratory* (Cambridge: Cambridge University Press, 1989).

Ebeling, Florian, *The Secret History of Hermes Trismegistus* (Ithaca: Cornell University Press, 2007).

Edbury, Peter W., and John Gordon Rowe, *William of Tyre: Historian of the Latin East* (Cambridge: Cambridge University Press, 1990).

Ehrenreich, Barbara, and Deirdre English, *Witches, Midwives and Nurses* (New York: Feminist Press, 1973; 2nd edition 2010).

Einhard and Notker the Stammerer, *Two Lives of Charlemagne*, trans., with introduction, Lewis Thorpe (London: Penguin, 1969).

Eldridge, Richard, *On Moral Personhood: Philosophy, Literature, Criticism, and Self-Understanding* (Chicago: University of Chicago Press, 1989).

Eley, Geoff, *A Crooked Line: From Cultural History to the History of Society* (Ann Arbor: University of Michigan Press, 2005).

Elton, Geoffrey, *The Practice of History* (Sydney: Sydney University Press, 1967).

Elvert, Jürgen, and Susanne Krauß (eds.), *Historische Debatten und Kontroversen im 19. und 20. Jahrhundert* (Stuttgart: Steiner, 2003).

Emden, Christian J., *Friedrich Nietzsche and the Politics of History* (Cambridge: Cambridge University Press, 2010).

Enders, Jody, *The Medieval Theater of Cruelty: Rhetoric, Memory, Violence* (Ithaca: Cornell University Press, 1999).

Engels, Friedrich, *Origins of the Family, Private Property and the State* (Chicago: Kerr, 1902).

Etzemüller, Thomas, *Sozialgeschichte als politische Geschichte: Werner Conze und die Neuorientierung der westdeutschen Geschichtswissenschaft nach 1945* (Munich: Oldenbourg, 2001).

Eusebius of Caesarea, *The History of the Church: A New Translation*, ed. and trans. Jeremy M. Schott (Oakland, CA: University of California Press, 2019).

Evans, R. J. W., Michael Schaich, and P. H. Wilson (eds.), *The Holy Roman Empire, 1495–1806* (Oxford: Oxford University Press, 2011).

Fabian, Johannes, *Time and the Other: How Anthropology Makes its Object* (New York: Columbia University Press, 2014).

Fausto-Sterling, Anne, *Sexing the Body: Gender Politics and the Construction of Sexuality* (New York: Basic Books, 2000).

Fausto-Sterling, Anne, *Sex/Gender: Biology in a Social World* (New York: Routledge, 2012).

Febvre, Lucien, *Philippe II et la Franche-Comté* (Paris, Champion, 1912).

Febvre, Lucien, *La Terre et l'évolution humaine: Introduction géographique à l'histoire* (Paris: La Renaissance du Livre, 1922).

Febvre, Lucien, *Le Problème de l'incroyance au XVIe siècle* (Paris: Albin Michel, 1942).

Feldherr, Andrew, and Grant Hardy (eds.) *The Oxford History of Historical Writing: Beginnings to AD 600* (Oxford: Oxford University Press, 2011).

Feldman, Louis H., *Studies in Hellenistic Judaism* (Leiden: Brill, 1996).

Ferguson, Niall, *The Pity of War* (New York: Basic Books, 1999).

Ferguson, Wallace K., *The Renaissance in Historical Thought* (New York: Houghton Mifflin, 1948).

Fischer, Fritz, *Griff nach der Weltmacht* (Düsseldorf: Droste, 1961).

Fish, Stanley, *The Trouble with Principle* (Cambride, MA: Harvard University Press, 1999).

Fleischacker, Samuel, *Integrity and Moral Relativism* (Leiden: Brill, 1992).

Fleischer, Helmut, *Marxism and History* (New York: Harper, 1973).

Flierman, Robert, *Saxon Identities, AD 150–900* (London: Bloomsbury, 2017).

Flynn, Thomas R., *Sartre, Foucault and Historical Reason*, 2 vols. (Chicago: University of Chicago Press, 1997 and 2005).

Fornara, Charles William, *The Nature of History in Ancient Greece and Rome* (Berkeley: University of California Press, 1983).

Forster, Michael N., *Hegel's Idea of a Phenomenology of Spirit* (Chicago: University of Chicago Press, 1998).

Foucault, Michel, *The Archaeology of Knowledge* (New York: Pantheon, 1972).

Foucault, Michel, *Discipline and Punish* (London: Penguin, 1991).

Foucault, Michel, *Ethics: Subjectivity and Truth*, ed. Paul Rabinow (New York: New Press, 1997).

Foucault, Michel, *Society Must be Defended*, ed. Mauro Bertani and Alessandro Fontana (New York: Picador, 2003).

Fox, Christopher, Roy Porter, and Robert Wokler (eds.), *Inventing Human Science: Eighteenth-Century Domains* (Berkeley: University of California Press, 1995).

Fox-Genovese, Elizabeth, and Elisabeth Lasch-Quinn (eds.), *Reconstructing History* (London, Routledge, 1999).

Frampton, Travis L., *Spinoza and the Rise of Historical Criticism of the Bible* (New York: Clark, 2006).

Franco, Paul, *Michael Oakeshott: An Introduction* (New Haven: Yale University Press, 2004).

Frank, Jill, *A Democracy of Distinction: Aristotle and the Work Of Politics* (London: University of Chicago Press, 2005).

Franklin, John Hope, *The Free Negro in North Carolina, 1790–1860* (Chapel Hill: University of North Carolina Press, 1943).

Franklin, John Hope, *Mirror to America* (New York: Farrar, Straus and Giroux, 2005).

Friedländer, Saul (ed.), *Probing the Limits of Representation* (Cambridge, MA: Harvard University Press, 1992).

Froissart, Jean, *Chronicles*, ed. Geoffrey Brereton (London: Penguin, 1978).

Frye, Northrop, *Fables of Identity: Studies in Poetic Mythology* (New York: Harcourt, Brace, and World, 1963).

Fuggle, S., Y. Lanci, and M. Tazzioli (eds.), *Foucault and the History of our Present* (Basingstoke: Palgrave Macmillan, 2015).

Fulda, Daniel, *Wissenschaft aus Kunst: Die Entstehung der modernen deutschen Geschichtsschreibung, 1760–1860* (Berlin: de Gruyter, 1996).

Fulbrook, Mary, *Piety and Politics: Religion and the Rise of Absolutism in England, Württemberg and Prussia* (Cambridge: Cambridge University Press, 1983).

Fuller, Steve, *Thomas Kuhn: A Philosophical History for our Times* (Chicago: University of Chicago Press, 2001).

Funder, Achim, *Reichsidee und Kirchenrecht: Dietrich von Nieheim als Beispiel spätmitte-lalterlicher Rechtsauffassung* (Freiburg: Herder, 1993).

Funkenstein, Amos, *Theology and the Scientific Imagination from the Middle Ages to the Seventeenth Century* (Princeton: Princeton University Press, 1986).

Fustel de Coulanges, N. D., *Histoire des institutions politiques de l'ancienne France*, 6 vols. (Paris: Hachette, 1874–1892).

Fustel de Coulanges, N. D., *The Ancient City* (Kitchener, ON: Batoche, 2001).

Gadamer, Hans-Georg, *Truth and Method* (London: Sheed and Ward, 1979).

Gaddis, John Lewis, *The Landscape of History* (Oxford: Oxford University Press, 2004).

Gandillac, Maurice de, and Edouard Jeauneau (eds.), *Entretiens sur la renaissance du 12e siècle* (Paris: Mouton, 1968).

Garver, Valerie L., *Women and Aristocratic Culture in the Carolingian World* (New York: Cornell, 2009).

Gay, Peter, *The Enlightenment: An Interpretation* (New York: Norton, 1966).

George, Karen, *Gildas's De Excidio Britonum and the Early British Church* (Woodbridge: Boydell, 2009).

Gerald of Wales, *Giraldus Cambrensis The Topography of Ireland*, trans. Thomas Forester, rev. and ed. Thomas Wright (Cambridge, ON: In Parentheses, 2000).

Gersh, Stephen, and Bert Roest (eds.), *Medieval and Renaissance Humanism: Rhetoric, Representation and Reform* (Leiden: Brill, 2003).

Gervinus, Georg Gottfried, *Geschichte der poetischen National-Literatur der Deutschen*, 5 vols. (Leipzig: Engelmann, 1835–42).

Ghosh, Peter, *Max Weber and the Protestant Ethic* (Oxford: Oxford University Press, 2014).

Ghosh, Shami, *Writing the Barbarian Past: Studies in Early Medieval Historical Narrative* (Leiden: Brill, 2016).

Gibbon, Edward, *The History of the Decline and Fall of the Roman Empire*, ed. David P. Womersley, vol. 3 (Harmondsworth: Penguin, 1995).

Gildas, *The Ruin of Britain, Fragments from Lost Letters, The Penitential, Together with the Lorica of Gildas*, ed. Hugh Williams (London: Bedford Press, 1899).

Gillespie, Michael Allan, *The Theological Origins of Modernity*, (Chicago: University of Chicago Press, 2008).

Ginzburg, Carlo, *The Cheese and the Worms: The Cosmos of a Sixteenth-Century Miller* (London: Routledge, 1980).

Ginzburg, Carlo, *The Judge and the Historian* (London: Verso, 1999).

Ginzburg, Carlo, *Threads and Traces: True False Fictive* (Berkeley: University of California Press, 2012).

Gipper, Helmut, and Peter Schmitter, *Sprachwissenschaft und Sprachphilosophie im Zeitalter der Romantik* (Tübingen: Narr, 1979).

Given-Wilson, Chris, *Chronicles: The Writing of History in Medieval England* (London: Hambledon, 2004).

Goethe, Johann Wolfgang von, *Goethe Werke—Hamburger Ausgabe Band 12*, ed. Erich Trunz (Munich: Beck, 2008).

Goetz, Hans-Werner, *Die Geschichtstheologie des Orosius* (Darmstadt: Wissenschaftliche Buchgesellschaft, 1980).

Goetz, Hans-Werner, *Geschichtsschreibung und Geschichtsbewußtsein im hohen Mittelalter* (Berlin: Orbis mediaevalis, 1999).

Goldschmidt, E. P., *The Printed Book of the Renaissance* (Cambridge: Cambridge University Press, 1950).

Gooder, Paula, *The Pentateuch: A Story of Beginnings* (London: T&T Clark, 2000).

Gössmann, Elisabeth, *Antiqui und Moderni im Mittelalter: eine geschichtliche Standortbestimmung* (Paderborn: Schöningh, 1974).

Gouldner, Alvin W., *The Two Marxisms: Contradictions and Anomalies in the Development of Theory* (Basingstoke: Macmillan, 1993).

Gowing, Laura, *Common Bodies: Women, Touch and Power in Seventeeth Century England* (New Haven: Yale University Press, 2003).

Grafton, Anthony, *Joseph Scaliger: A Study in the History of Classical Scholarship*, 2 vols. (Oxford: Clarendon Press, 1983, 1993).

Grafton, Anthony, *Defenders of the Text: The Traditions of Scholarship in an Age of Science, 1450–1800* (Cambridge, MA: Harvard University Press, 1991).

Grafton, Anthony, *What was History? The Art of History in Early Modern Europe* (Cambridge: Cambridge University Press, 2007).

Grafton, Anthony, and Megan Williams, *Christianity and the Transformation of the Book: Origen, Eusebius, and the Library of Caesarea* (Cambridge, MA: Harvard University Press, 2006).

Grafton, Anthony, Glenn W. Most, and Salvatore Settis (eds.), *The Classical Tradition* (Cambridge, MA: Harvard University Press, 2010).

Grafton, Anthony, and Joanna Weinberg with Alastair Hamilton, *'I have always loved the Holy Tongue': Isaac Casaubon, the Jews, and a Forgotten Chapter in Renaissance Scholarship* (Cambridge, MA: Belknap Press, 2011), 43.

Grassi, Ernesto, *Vico and Humanism: Essays on Vico, Heidegger, and Rhetoric* (New York: Peter Lang, 1991).

Greenblatt, Stephen, *Shakespearean Negotiations* (Berkeley: University of California Press, 1988).

Gregory, Marshall, *Shaped by Stories: The Ethical Power of Narratives* (Notre Dame: University of Indiana Press, 2009).

Gregory of Tours, *History of the Franks*, ed. Lewis Thorpe (London: Penguin, 1974).

Grenfell, Michael, *Pierre Bourdieu: Agent Provocateur* (London: Continuum, 2004).

Grethlein, Jonas, *The Greeks and their Past: Poetry, Oratory and History in the Fifth Century BCE* (Cambridge: Cambridge University Press, 2010).

Grethlein, Jonas, and Christopher B. Krebs (eds.), *Time and Narrative in Ancient Historiography* (Cambridge: Cambridge University Press, 2012).

Groom, Nick, *The Gothic* (Oxford: Oxford University Press, 2012).

Grossman, Lionel, *Basel in the Age of Burckhardt: A Study in Unseasonable Ideas* (Chicago: University of Chicago Press, 2000).

Groys, Boris, *Introduction to Antiphilosophy* (London: Verso, 2012).

Guenée, Bernard, *Histoire et culture historique dans l'Occident médiéval* (Paris: Aubier Montaigne, 1980).

Guha, Ranajit, *Elementary Aspects of Peasant Insurgency in Colonial India* (Delhi: Oxford University Press, 1983).

Guha, Ranajit, *Dominance without Hegemony: History and Power in Colonial India* (Cambridge, MA: Harvard University Press, 1998).

Guha, Ranajit, and Gayatri Chakravorty Spivak (eds.), *Selected Subaltern Studies* (New York: Oxford University Press, 1988).

Gunderson, Erik (ed.), *The Cambridge Companion to Ancient Rhetoric* (Cambridge: Cambridge University Press, 2009).

Gyekye, Kwame, *Tradition and Modernity: Philosophical Reflections on the African Experience* (Oxford: Oxford University Press, 1997).

Habermas, Jürgen, *Knowledge and Human Interests* (Cambridge: Polity Press, 1987).

Habermas, Jürgen, *On the Logic of the Social Sciences* (Cambridge, MA: MIT Press, 1988).

Habermas, Jürgen, *The Philosophical Discourse of Modernity* (Cambridge, MA: MIT Press, 1990).

Haberski, Raymond Jr, and Andrew Hartman (eds.), *American Labyrinth: Intellectual History for Complicated Times* (Ithaca: Cornell University Press, 2018).

Habinek, Thomas, and Alessandro Schiesaro (eds.), *The Roman Cultural Revolution* (Cambridge: Cambridge University Press, 1997).

Hackel, Christiane, *Aristoteles-Rezeption in der Geschichtstheorie Johann Gustav Droysens* (Berlin: de Gruyter, 2019).

Hacking, Ian, *The Social Construction of What?* (Cambridge, MA: Harvard University Press, 1999).

Hadden, Richard W., *On the Shoulders of Merchants* (Albany: State University of New York, 1994).

Haidu, Peter, *The Subject of Violence: The Song of Roland and the Birth of the State* (Bloomington: Indiana University Press, 1993).

Haikola, Lauri, *Gesetz und Evangelium bei Matthias Flacius Illyricus: eine Untersuchung zur Lutherischen Theologie vor der Konkordienformel* (Lund: Gleerup, 1952).

Hall, John R. (ed.), *Reworking Class* (Ithaca: Cornell University Press, 1997).

Hammer, Espen, *Philosophy and Temporality from Kant to Critical Theory* (Cambridge: Cambridge University Press, 2011).

Hankins, James (ed.), *Renaissance Civic Humanism: Reappraisals and Reflections* (Cambridge: Cambridge University Press, 2000).

Harding, Brian, *Not even a God can Save Us Now: Reading Machiavelli after Heidegger* (Montreal: McGill-Queen's University Press, 2017).

Hardtwig, Wolfgang, and Philipp Müller (eds.), *Die Vergangenheit der Weltgeschichte: Universalhistorisches Denken in Berlin 1800–1933* (Göttingen: Vandenhoeck & Ruprecht, 2010).

Hariman, Robert (ed.), *Prudence: Classical Virtue, Postmodern Practice* (University Park, PA: Pennsylvania State University Press, 2003).

Harris, Stephen, and Bryon L. Grigsby (eds.), *Misconceptions about the Middle Ages* (New York: Routledge, 2008).

Harrison, Peter, *The Bible, Protestantism, and the Rise of Natural Science* (Cambridge: Cambridge University Press, 1998).

Hartley, L. P., *The Go-Between* (New York: New York Review Books, 2002).

Harvey, David Allen, *The French Enlightenment and its Others: The Mandarin, the Savage, and the Invention of the Human Sciences* (London: Palgrave Macmillan, 2012).

Haskins, Charles Homer, *The Renaissance of the Twelfth Century* (Cambridge, MA: Harvard University Press, 1927).

Hay, Denys, *Europe: The Emergence of an Idea* (New York: Harper, 1966).

Haynes, Kenneth, *Hamann: Writings on Philosophy and Language* (Cambridge: Cambridge University Press, 2007).

Hearn, Jonathan, *Theorizing Power* (Basingstoke: Palgrave Macmillan, 2012).

Hegel, G. W. F., *The Philosophy of Right*, trans T. M. Knox (Oxford: Clarendon Press, 1952).

Hegel, G. W. F., *Introduction to the Philosophy of History with an Appendix from The Philosophy of Right*, trans. Leo Rauch (Indianapolis, IN: Hackett, 1988).

Heinzelmann, Martin, *Gregory of Tours: History and Society in the Sixth Century* (Cambridge: Cambridge University Press, 2001).

Hendrick, Harry, *Children, Childhood and English Society, 1880–1990* (Cambridge: Cambridge University Press, 1997).

Henry of Huntingdon, *The History of the English People 1000–1154*, ed. and trans. Diana Greenway (Oxford: Oxford University Press, 2002).

Herder, Johann Gottfried von, *Philosophical Writings*, ed. Michael N. Forster (Cambridge: Cambridge University Press, 2002).

Herlihy, David, *Women, Family and Society in Medieval Europe* (Oxford: Berghahn, 1995).

Herodotus, *Histories*, trans. George Rawlinson (Ware: Wordsworth, 1996).

Heussi, Karl, *Die Krisis des Historismus* (Tübingen: Mohr, 1932).

Hill, Christopher, *Reformation to Industrial Revolution*, vol. 2, 1530–1870 (Harmondsworth: Penguin, 1976).

Hilton, Rodney, *Bond Men Made Free: Medieval Peasant Movements and the English Rising of 1381* (London: Routledge, 2003).

Hilton, Rodney, and Hyman Fagin, *The English Rising of 1381* (London: Lawrence and Wishart, 1950).

Hinde, John R., *Jacob Burckhardt and the Crisis of Modernity* (Montreal: McGill-Queen's University Press, 2000).

Hinrichs, Carl, *Ranke und die Geschichtstheologie der Goethezeit* (Gottingen: Musterschmidt, 1954).

Hobsbawm, Eric, and George Rudé, *Captain Swing* (London: Lawrence and Wishart, 1969).

Hochschild, Arlie, *Strangers in their Own Land: Anger and Mourning on the American Right* (New York: The New Press, 2016).

Hodgson, Richard G. (ed.) *La Femme au XVIIe siècle* (Tübingen: Narr, 2002).

Hollingdale, R. J., *Nietzsche* (London: Routledge, Kegan and Paul, 1973).

Honneth, Axel, *Reification: A New Look at an Old Idea* (New York: Oxford University Press, 2008).

hooks, bell, *Ain't I a Woman?: Black Women and Feminism* (Boston, MA: South End Press, 1981).

Hopkins, Jasper, *A Concise Introduction to the Philosophy of Nicholas of Cusa* (Minneapolis: University of Minnesota Press, 1978).

Hopkins, Jasper, *Nicholas of Cusa's De Pace Fidei and Cribratio Alkorani: Translation and Analysis* (Minneapolis: The Arthur J. Banning Press, 1994).

Horkheimer, Max, *Dawn and Decline, Notes 1926–31 and 1950–69* (New York: Seabury/ Continuum, 1978).

Howard, Thomas Albert, *Religion and the Rise of Historicism* (Cambridge: Cambridge University Press, 2000).

Hume, David, *The History of England, from the Invasion of Julius Caesar to the Revolution in 1688*, vol. VII (London: T. Cadell, 1778).

Hume, David, *On Human Nature and the Understanding*, ed. Antony Flew (New York: Macmillan, 1962).

Humphrey, Chris, and W. M. Ormrod (eds.), *Time in the Medieval World* (Woodbridge: York Medieval Press, 2001).

Hunt, Lynn, *Politics, Culture, and Class in the French Revolution* (Berkeley: University of California Press, 1984).

Hunt, Lynn(ed.), *The New Cultural History* (Berkeley: University of California Press, 1989).

Hunter, Virginia J., *Thucydides the Artful Reporter* (Toronto: Hakkert, 1973).

Hunter, Virginia J., *Past and Process in Herodotus and Thucydides* (Princeton: Princeton University Press, 1982).

Huppert, George, *The Idea of Perfect History: Historical Erudition and Historical Philosophy in Renaissance France* (Urbana: University of Illinois Press, 1970).

Ianziti, Gary, *Writing History in Renaissance Italy: Leonardo Bruni and the Uses of the Past* (Cambridge, MA: Harvard University Press, 2012).

Jacoby, Felix, *Atthis: The Local Chronicles of Ancient Athens* (Oxford: Clarendon Press, 1949).

Jameson, Fredric, *The Political Unconscious* (London: Routledge, 1983).

Jenkin, Richard, *Virgil's Experience: Nature and History; Times, Names and Places* (Oxford: Clarendon Press, 1998).

Jenkins, Keith, *Re-Thinking History* (London: Routledge, 1991).

Jenks, Leland Hamilton, *The Migration of British Capital to 1875* (New York: Knopf, 1927).

Johnson, Mark, *The Body In the Mind: The Bodily Basis of Meaning, Imagination, and Reason* (Chicago: University of Chicago Press, 1987).

Johnson, Paul E., *A Shopkeeper's Millennium: Society and Revivals in Rochester, New York, 1815–1837* (New York: Hill and Wang, 1994 [orig. 1978]).

Johnston, William M., *The Formative Years of R. G. Collingwood* (The Hague: Martinus Nijhoff, 1968).

Jones, Gareth Stedman, *Languages of Class* (Cambridge: Cambridge University Press, 1984).

Jordan, Lothar, and Bernd Kortländer (eds.), *Nationale Grenzen und internationaler Austausch* (Tübingen: Niemeyer, 1995).

Jotischky, Andrew, *The Carmelites and Antiquity: Mendicants and their Pasts in the Middle Ages* (Oxford: Oxford University Press, 2002).

Kain, Philip J., *Nietzsche and the Horror of Existence* (Lanham, MD: Lexington, 2009).

Kaldellis, Anthony, *Procopius of Caesarea* (Philadelphia: University of Pennsylvania Press, 2004).

Kaldellis, Anthony, *A New Herodotus: Laonikos Chalkokondyles on the Ottoman Empire, the Fall of Byzantium, and the Emergence of the West* (Cambridge, MA: Harvard University Press, 2014).

Kant, Immanuel, *Kant: Political Writings*, ed. Hans Reiss (Cambridge: Cambridge University Press, 1991).

Katchen, Aaron, *Christian Hebraists and Dutch Rabbis* (Cambridge, MA: Harvard University Press, 1984).

Kelley, Donald R., *Foundations of Modern Historical Scholarship: Language, Law, and History in the French Renaissance* (New York: Columbia University Press, 1970).

Kelley, Donald R., *Faces of History: Historical Inquiry from Herodotus to Herder* (New Haven: Yale University Press, 1998).

Kelly, Gavin, *Ammianus Marcellinus: The Allusive Historian* (Cambridge: Cambridge University Press, 2008).

Kenny, Anthony, *The Rise of Modern Philosophy* (Oxford: Clarendon Press, 2006).

Kenyon, John, *The History Men* (Pittsburgh, PA: University of Pittsburgh Press, 1984).

Kewes, Paulina (ed.), *The Uses of History in Early Modern England* (San Marino, CA: Huntington Library, 2006).

Khong, Yuen Foong, *Analogies at War: Korea, Munich, Dien Bien Phu, and the Vietnam Decisions of 1965* (Princeton: Princeton University Press, 1992).

Kidd, Colin, *British Identities Before Nationalism* (Cambridge: Cambridge University Press, 1999).

Klaus, Johann Heinrich, *Die Jesus-Deutung von Ernst Troeltsch im Kontext der liberalen Theologie* (Tübingen: Mohr, 1997).

Kleinberg, Ethan, *Haunting History: For a Deconstructive Approach to the Past* (Stanford: Stanford University Press, 2017).

Kligerman, Eric, *Sites of the Uncanny: Paul Celan, Specularity and the Visual Arts* (Berlin: de Gruyter, 2007).

Klosko, George (ed.), *The Oxford Handbook of the History of Political Philosophy* (Oxford: Oxford University Press, 2011).

Knowles, David, *The Historian and Character* (Cambridge: Cambridge University Press, 1963).

Kocis, Robert, *Machiavelli Redeemed: Retrieving his Humanist Perspectives on Equality, Power and Glory* (New Jersey: Associated University Presses, 1998).

Kocka, Jürgen, *Geschichte und Aufklärung* (Göttingen: Vandenhoeck und Ruprecht, 1989).

Konstan, David, and Kurt A. Raaflaub (eds.), *Epic and History* (Chichester: Wiley-Blackwell, 2010).

Koselleck, Reinhart, *The Practice of Conceptual History: Timing History, Spacing Concepts* (Stanford: Stanford University Press, 2002).

Koselleck, Reinhart, *Futures Past: On the Semantics of Historical Time* (New York: Columbia University Press, 2004).

Koslowski, Peter (ed.), *The Discovery of Historicity in German Idealism and Historicism* (Berlin: Springer, 2005).

Kossler, Matthias, *Empirische Ethik und christlicher Moral* (Würzburg: Königshausen und Neumann, 1999).

Kraye, Jill (ed.), *The Cambridge Companion to Renaissance Humanism* (Cambridge: Cambridge University Press, 1996).

Kügler, Joachim, and Werner H. Ritter (eds.), *Auf Leben und Tod oder völlig egal: Kritisches und Nachdenkliches zur Bedeutung der Bibel* (Munster: LIT, 2005).

Kuhn, Thomas, *The Structure of Scientific Revolutions* (Chicago: University of Chicago Press, 1961).

Labrousse, Ernst, *Esquisse du mouvement des prix et des revenues en France au XVIIIe siècle* (Paris: Dalloz, 1933).

LaCapra, Dominick, *Representing the Holocaust: History, Theory, Trauma* (Ithaca: Cornell University Press, 1996).

LaCapra, Dominick, *History in Transit: Experience, Identity, Critical Theory* (Ithaca: Cornell University Press, 2004).

Lacombe, Paul, *L'Histoire considérée comme science* (Paris: Hachette, 1894).

Ladurie, Emmanuel le Roy, *Les Paysans de Languedoc*, 2 vols. (Paris: Mouton, 1966).

Ladurie, Emmanuel le Roy, *Montaillou, village occitan de 1294 à 1324* (Paris: Gallimard, 1975).

Lagrou, Pieter, *The Legacy of Nazi Occupation: Patriotic Memory and National Recovery in Western Europe, 1945–1965* (Cambridge: Cambridge University Press, 2000).

Lake, Justin (ed.) *Prologues to Ancient and Medieval History: A Reader* (Toronto: University of Toronto Press, 2013).

Lambert, Peter, and Phillipp Schofield (eds.), *Making History* (Abingdon: Routledge, 2004).

Lamers, Han, *Greece Reinvented: Transformations of Byzantine Hellenism in Renaissance Italy* (Leiden: Brill, 2016).

Lamprecht, Karl, *Deutsches Wirtschaftsleben im Mittelalter*, 4 vols. (Leipzig: Dürr, 1885–6).

Lamprecht, Karl, *Deutsche Geschichte*, 12 vols. (Berlin: Gaertner, 1891–1909).

Landfester, Rüdiger, *Historia magistra vitae: Untersuchungen zur humanistischen Geschichtstheorie des 14. bis. 16. Jahrhunderts* (Geneva: Droz, 1972).

Lange, Carsten Hjort, and Jesper Majbom Madsen (eds.), *Cassius Dio: Greek Intellectual and Roman Politician* (Leiden: Brill, 2016).

Langlois, Charles-Victor, and Charles Seignobos, *Introduction aux études historiques*, ed. Pierre Palpant (electronic edition, 2005).

Laqueur, Thomas W., *Making Sex: Body and Gender from the Greeks to Freud* (Cambridge, MA: Harvard University Press, 1990).

Laslett, Peter, *The World We Have Lost* (London: Methuen, 1965).

Laughland, John, *Schelling versus Hegel: From German Idealism to Christian Metaphysics* (Aldershot: Ashgate, 2007).

Lavisse, Ernest (ed.), *Histoire de France contemporaine, depuis la revolution jusqu'à la paix de 1919*, 10 vols. (Paris: Hachette, 1920–2).

Le Goff, Jacques, *Time, Work, and Culture in the Middle Ages* (Chicago: University of Chicago Press, 1980).

Le Goff, Jacques, and Pierre Nora (eds.), *Faire de l'histoire*, 3 vols. (Paris, Gallimard, 1974).

Leavitt, John, *Linguistic Relativities: Language Diversity and Modern Thought* (Cambridge: Cambridge University Press, 2011).

Lee, Kyong-Jin, *The Authority and Authorization of Torah in the Persian Period* (Leuven: Peeters, 2011).

Lefebvre, Georges, *Les Paysans du Nord pendant la Révolution française* (Lille: Camille Robbe, 1924).

Lefebvre, Georges, *La Grande Peur de 1789* (Paris: Armand Colin, 1932).

Lefebvre, Georges, *The Coming of the French Revolution*, ed. and intr. Timothy Tacket (Princeton: Princeton University Press, 2005).

Leff, Gordon, *William of Ockham: The Metamorphosis of Scholastic Discourse* (Manchester: Manchester University Press, 1975).

Lehmann, Hartmut, and James Van Horn Melton (eds.), *Paths of Continuity: Central European Historiography from the 1930s to the 1950s* (Washington, DC: German Historical Institute, 2003).

Leibniz, Gottfried Wilhelm, *Oeuvres de Leibniz*, ed. M. A. Jacques (Paris: Charpentier, 1846).

Leiter, Brian, and Michael Rosen (eds.), *The Oxford Handbook of Continental Philosophy* (Oxford: Oxford University Press, 2007).

Lemon, M. C., *Philosophy of History* (London: Routledge, 2003).

Lerner, Gerda, *The Creation of Patriarchy* (New York: Oxford University Press, 1986).

Lessing, Theodor, *Geschichte als Sinngebung des Sinnlosen* (Munich: Beck, 1919).

LeVay, Simon, *The Sexual Brain* (Cambridge, MA: MIT Press, 1993).

LeVay, Simon, *Queer Science: The Use and Abuse of Research into Sexuality* (Cambridge, MA: MIT Press, 1996).

Levi, Giovanni, *L'Eredità Immaterial: Carriera di un Exorcista nel Piemonte del Seicento* (Turin: Einaudi, 1985).

Lévi-Strauss, Claude, *Structural Anthropology* (New York: Basic Books, 1963).

Lévi-Strauss, Claude, *The Savage Mind* (London: Weidenfeld and Nicolson, 1966).

Lévi-Strauss, Claude, *The Raw and the Cooked* (Harmondsworth: Penguin, 1986).

Levine, Norman, *Marx's Discourse with Hegel* (Basingstoke: Palgrave Macmillan, 2012).

Lewis, John, *Max Weber and Value-Free Sociology* (London: Lawrence and Wishart, 1975).

Lianeri, Alexandra (ed.), *The Western Time of Ancient History* (Cambridge: Cambridge University Press, 2011).

Liddel, Peter, and Andrew Fear (eds.), *Historiae Mundi: Studies in Universal Historiography* (London: Duckworth, 2010).

Lillington-Martin, Christopher (ed.), *Procopius of Caesarea: Literary and Historical Interpretations* (New York: Routledge, 2018).

Linehan, Peter, and Janet L. Nelson (eds), *The Medieval World* (Oxford: Routledge, 2001).

Lipton, Sara, *Images of Intolerance: The Representation of Jews and Judaism in the Bible moralisée* (Berkeley: University of California Press, 1999).

Livy, *The Early History of Rome*, trans. Aubrey de Sélincourt (Harmondsworth: Penguin, 1960).

Loader, Colin, *The Intellectual Development of Karl Mannheim* (Cambridge: Cambridge University Press, 1985).

Logan, Peter Melville, *Victorian Fetishism: Intellectuals and Primitives* (Albany: State University of New York, 2009).

Long, V. Philips (ed.), *Israel's Past in Present Research* (Winona Lake, IN: Eisenbrauns, 1999).

Loud, Robert B., *Kant's Impure Ethics: From Rational Beings to Human Beings* (New York: Oxford University Press, 2000).

Lowenthal, David, *The Past is a Foreign Country* (Cambridge: Cambridge University Press, 1985).

Lowenthal, David, *The Heritage Crusade and the Spoils of History* (Cambridge: Cambridge University Press, 1998).

Lowery, Zoe, *Historiography* (New York: Britannica Educational Publishing, 2016).

Luce, T. James, *The Greek Historians* (London: Routledge, 1997).

Lukács, Georg, *History and Class Consciousness: Studies in Marxist Dialectics* (Cambridge, MA: MIT Press, 1971).

Lüdtke, Alf (ed.), *Alltagsgeschichte: zur Rekonstruktion historischer Erfahrungen und Lebensweisen* (Frankfurt am Main: Campus, 1989).

Lukes, Steven, *Emile Durkheim, His Life and Work: A Historical and Critical Study* (Stanford: Stanford University Press, 1985).

Luraghi, Nino (ed.), *The Historian's Craft in the Age of Herodotus* (Oxford: Oxford University Press, 2001).

Lynch, Joseph H., and Phillip C. Adamo, *The Medieval Church* (London: Routledge, 2014).

Lyotard, Jean-François, *The Postmodern Condition* (Manchester: Manchester University Press, 1984).

McGilchrist, Iain, *The Master and his Emissary: The Divided Brain and the Making of the Western World* (New Haven: Yale University Press, 2009).

McGing, Brian C., *Polybius' Histories* (Oxford: Oxford University Press, 2010).

Machiavelli, Niccolò, *The Discourses of Niccolò Machiavelli*, vol.1, ed. Leslie Walker (London: Routledge, 2013).

Macintyre, Stuart, Juan Maiguashca, and Attila Pók (eds.), *The Oxford History of Historical Writing 1800-1945* (Oxford: Oxford University Press, 2015).

McKitterick, Rosamond, *History and Memory in the Carolingian World* (Cambridge: Cambridge University Press, 2004).

McNeill, William H., *The Rise of the West: A History of the Human Community* (Chicago: Chicago University Press, 1963).

McNeill, William H., *A World History* (New York: Oxford University Press, 1967).

Magnus, Bern, *Heidegger's Metahistory of Philosophy: Amor fati, Being and Truth* (The Hague: Martinus Nijhoff, 1970).

Mahon, Michael, *Foucault's Nietzschean Genealogy* (Albany: SUNY Press, 1992).

Mahoney, James, and Dietrich Rueschemeyer, *Comparative Historical Analysis in the Social Sciences* (Cambridge: Cambridge University Press, 2003).

Maimonides, Moses, *The Guide for the Perplexed*, trans, M. Friedländer (New York: Dover, 1956).

Mäkinen, Virpi (ed.), *The Nature of Rights* (Helsinki: Societas Philosophica Fennica, 2010).

Malcolm, Noel, *Aspects of Hobbes* (Oxford: Clarendon Press, 2002).

Mali, Joseph, *The Rehabilitation of Myth: Vico's New Science* (Cambridge: Cambridge University Press, 1992).

Mali, Joseph, *Mythistory: The Making of a Modern Historiography* (Chicago: University of Chicago Press, 2003).

Malik, Kenan, *The Meaning of Race: Race, History and Culture in Western Society* (New York: New York University Press, 1996).

Manuel, Frank Edward, *The Eighteenth Century Confronts the Gods* (Cambridge, MA: Harvard University Press, 1959).

Map, Walther, *De Nugis Curialium (Courtier's Trifles)*, ed. and trans. Frederick Tupper and Marbury Bladen Ogle (London: Chatto and Windus, 1924).

Marcus, Jacob Rader, and Marc Saperstein, *The Jew in the Medieval World: A Sourcebook, 315–1791* (New York: Hebrew Union College Press, 2015).

Marcuse, Herbert, *Reason and Revolution: Hegel and the Rise of Social Theory* (Boston: Beacon, 1960).

Marcuse, Herbert, *One Dimensional Man* (London: Sphere, 1968).

Marincola, John (ed.), *Greek and Roman Historiography* (Oxford: Oxford University Press, 2011).

Marincola, John, Lloyd Llewellyn-Jones, and Calum Alasdair Maciver (eds.), *Greek Notions of the Past in the Archaic and Classical Eras: History without Historians* (Edinburgh: Edinburgh University Press, 2012).

Marrou, Henri, *The Meaning of History* (Dublin: Helicon, 1966).

Marx, Karl, *The Eighteenth Brumaire of Louis Bonaparte* (New York: International Publishing, 1969).

Marx, Karl, *Capital: A New Abridgement*, ed. David McLellan (Oxford: Oxford University Press, 1999).

Marx, Karl, with Friedrich Engels, *The German Ideology, including Theses on Feuerbach and Introduction to the Critique of Political Economy* (Amherst, NY: Prometheus Books, 1998).

Marx, Karl, and Friedrich Engels, *Collected Works*, vol. 29: *Marx 1857–61* (London: Lawrence and Wishart, 2010).

Matthews, John F., *The Roman Empire of Ammianus Marcellinus* (Baltimore: Johns Hopkins University Press, 1989).

May, Ernest, *'Lessons' of the Past: The Use and Misuse of History in American Foreign Policy* (New York: Oxford University Press, 1975).

Mazzotta, Giuseppe, *The New Map of the World: The Poetic Philosophy of Giambattista Vico* (Princeton: Princeton University Press, 1999).

Medick, Hans, *Weben und Überleben in Laichingen, 1650–1900: Lokalgeschichte als Allgemeine Geschichte* (Göttingen: Vandenhoeck & Ruprecht, 1996).

Meinecke, Friedrich, *Die Deutsche Katastrophe* (Wiesbaden: Brockhaus, 1947).

Meinecke, Friedrich, *Burckhardt und Ranke* (Berlin: Deutsche Akademie der Wissenschaft, 1948).

Meiss, Millard (ed.), *De artibus opuscula XL. Essays in Honour of Erwin Panofsky*, vol. 1 (New York: New York University Press, 1961).

Mellor, Ronald, *Tacitus* (New York: Routledge, 1994).

Merquior, José Guilherme, *Michel Foucault* (Berkeley: University of California Press, 1985).

Meyerhoff, Hans (ed.), *The Philosophy of History in our Time* (New York: Doubleday, 1959).

Mikesell, Margaret, and Adele Seeff (eds.), *Culture and Change: Attending to Early Modern Women* (Newark: University of Delaware Press, 2003).

Milbank, John, *Beyond Secular Order: The Representation of Being and the Representation of the People* (Hoboken, NJ: Wiley, 2013).

Mill, John Stuart, *J. S. Mill: 'On Liberty' and Other Writings*, ed. Stefan Collini (Cambridge: Cambridge University Press, 2003).

Miller, J. Hillis, *The Ethics of Reading* (New York: Columbia University Press, 1987).

Miner, Robert C., *Vico: Genealogist of Modernity* (Notre Dame: University of Notre Dame Press, 2002).

Minnis, A. J., *Medieval Theory of Authorship: Scholastic Literary Attitudes in the Later Middle Ages* (London : Scolar, 1984).

Mintz, Steven, *Huck's Raft: A History of American Childhood* (Cambridge, MA: Harvard University Press, 2004).

Mistry, Zubin, *Abortion in the Early Middle Ages, c.500–900* (York: York Medieval Press, 2015).

Molyneaux, George, *The Formation of the English Kingdom in the Tenth Century* (Oxford: Oxford University 2015).

Momigliano, Arnaldo, *Classical Foundations of Modern Historiography* (Berkeley: University of California Press, 1990).

Momigliano, Arnaldo, *Essays in Ancient and Modern Historiography* (Chicago: University of Chicago Press, 2012).

Moore, R. I., *The Formation of a Persecuting Society: Authority and Deviance in Western Europe, 950–1250* (Oxford: Blackwell, 2007).

Mortley, Raoul, *The Idea of Universal History from Hellenic Philosophy to Early Christian Historiography* (New York: Edwin Mellen, 1996).

Morton, Michael, *Herder and the Poetics of Thought* (University Park, PA: Pennsylvania State University Press, 1989).

Mouffe, Chantal, *The Return of the Political* (London: Verso, 2005).

Moulakis, Athanasios (ed.), *The Promise of History: Essays in Political Philosophy* (Berlin: de Gruyter, 1986).

Muhlack, Ulrich, *Geschichtswissenschaft im Humanismus und in der Aufklärung: Der Vorgeschichte des Historismus* (Munich: Beck, 1991).

Muntz, Charles Edward, *Diodorus Siculus and the World of the Late Roman Republic* (Oxford: Oxford University Press, 2017).

Murray, Alexander, *Conscience and Authority in the Medieval Church* (Oxford: Oxford University Press, 2015).

Murray, Christopher John (ed.) *Encyclopedia of the Romantic Era, 1760–1850* (London: Fitzroy Dearborn, 2004).

Murray, R. H., *The Individual and the State* (London: Hutchinson, 1946).

Myers, David N., *Resisting History: Historicism and its Discontents in German-Jewish Thought* (Princeton: Princeton University Press, 2003).

Nadler, Steven, *Spinoza: A Life* (Cambridge: Cambridge University Press, 2001).

Nagy, Gregory, *Poetry as Performance: Homer and Beyond* (Cambridge: Cambridge University Press, 1996).

Namier, Lewis, *The Structure of Politics at the Accession of George III* (London: Macmillan, 1973).

Nelson, Janet L., *The Frankish World, 750–900* (London: Hambledon Press, 1996).

Nelson, Janet (ed.), *Annals of St-Bertin* (Manchester: Manchester University Press, 1991).

Nielsen, Fleming A. J., *The Tragedy in History: Herodotus and the Deuteronomistic History* (Sheffield: Sheffield Academic Press, 1997).

Neuhouser, Frederick, *Rousseau's Critique of Inequality* (Cambridge: Cambridge University Press, 2014).

Niebuhr, B. G., *Lebensnachrichten über Barthold Georg Niebuhr*, vol. 2 (Hamburg: Perthes, 1838).

Nietzsche, Friedrich, *The Portable Nietzsche*, ed. Walter Kaufmann (Harmondsworth: Penguin, 1983).

Nietzsche, Friedrich, *Untimely Meditations*, ed. Daniel Breazeale (Cambridge: Cambridge University Press, 2003).

Nietzsche, Friedrich, *On the Genealogy of Morality*, ed. Keith Ansell-Pearson (Cambridge: Cambridge University Press, 2006).

Nippel, Wilfried, *Johann Gustav Droysen: ein Leben zwischen Wissenschaft und Politik* (Munich: Beck, 2008).

Nisbet, Robert A., *History of the Idea of Progress* (New Brunswick, NJ: Transaction, 2009).

Nochlin, Linda, *Realism* (Harmondsworth: Penguin, 1971).

Norris, Christopher, *Derrida* (Cambridge, MA: Harvard University Press, 1987).

Novick, Peter, *That Noble Dream: The 'Objectivity Question' and the American Historical Profession* (Cambridge: Cambridge University Press, 1999).

Oakley, Ann, *Women, Peace and Welfare: A Suppressed History of Social Reform, 1880-1920* (Bristol: Policy Press, 2019).

Oakeshott, Michael, *Rationalism in Politics and Other Essays* (New York: Basic Books, 1962).

Oberkrome, Willi, *Volksgeschichte: Methodische Innovation und völkische Ideologisierung in der deutschen Geschichtswissenschaft, 1918-1945* (Göttingen: Vandenhoeck und Ruprecht, 2011).

O'Brien, Kevin, 'Michel Foucault's Genealogy of the Subject' (PhD Thesis: Katholieke Universiteit Leuven, 1988).

Ocker, Christopher, *Biblical Poetics before Humanism and Renaissance* (Cambridge: Cambridge University Press, 2002).

Oexle, Otto Gerhard (ed.), *Krise des Historismus—Krise der Wirklichkeit* (Gottingen: Max-Planck-Instituts für Geschichte, 2007).

Olmstead, Wendy, *Rhetoric: An Historical Introduction* (Oxford: Blackwell, 2006).

Olson, David R., *The World on Paper: The Conceptual and Cognitive Implications of Writing* (Cambridge: Cambridge University Press, 1996).

Olstein, Diego, *Thinking History Globally* (Basingstoke: Palgrave Macmillan 2013).

Onians, John, *Neuroarthistory: From Aristotle and Pliny to Baxandall and Zeki* (New Haven: Yale University Press, 2007).

Otter, Monika, *Inventiones: Fiction and Referentiality in Twelfth-Century English Historical Writing* (Chapel Hill: University of North Carolina Press, 1996).

Ovid, *The Metamorphoses of Ovid*, trans. Allen Mandelbaum (New York: Harcourt Brace, 1995).

Padovani, Andrea, and Peter G. Stein (eds.), *The Jurists' Philosophy of Law from Rome to the Seventeenth Century* (Dordrecht: Springer, 2007).

Palonen, Kari (ed.), *Redescriptions: Yearbook of Political Thought and Conceptual History*, vol. 9 (Münster: LIT, 2005).

Parekh, Bhikhu, *Rethinking Multiculturalism* (Basingstoke: Macmillan 2006).

Partner, Nancy (ed.), *Writing Medieval History* (London: Hodder Arnold, 2005).

Pasquier, Étienne, *Les Recherches de la France d'Estienne Pasquier* (Paris: Pierre Menard 1643).

Patten, Alan, *Hegel's Idea of Freedom* (Oxford: Oxford University Press, 1999).

Patterson, David, and Alan L. Berger, *Jewish–Christian Dialogue: Drawing Honey from the Rock* (St Paul, MN: Paragon House, 2008).

Philippides, Marios, and Walter K. Hanak, *The Siege and the Fall of Constantinople in 1453: Historiography, Topography and Military Studies* (Farnham: Ashgate, 2011).

Phillips, Mark, *Francesco Guicciardini: The Historian's Craft* (Toronto: University of Toronto Press, 1977).

Phillips, Ulrich Bonnell, *American Negro Slavery* (New York: Appleton, 1918).

Pico della Mirandola, Giovanni, *Pico della Mirandola: Oration on the Dignity of Man: A New Translation and Commentary*, ed. Francesco Borghesi, Michael Papio and Massimo Riva (Cambridge: Cambridge University Press, 2012).

Piercey, Robert, *The Uses of the Past from Heidegger to Rorty* (Cambridge: Cambridge University Press, 2011).

Pinkard, Terry, *German Philosophy 1760–1860: The Legacy of Idealism* (Cambridge: Cambridge University Press, 2002).

Pinkard, Terry, *Does History Make Sense? Hegel on the Historical Shapes of Justice* (Cambridge, MA: Harvard University Press, 2017).

Pippin, Robert B., *Modernism as a Philosophical Problem: On the Dissatisfactions of European High Culture* (Malden, MA: Blackwell, 1999).

Pocock, J. G. A., *The Ancient Constitution and the Feudal Law* (Cambridge: Cambridge University Press, 1987).

Pohl, Walter, Clemens Gantner, Cinzia Grifoni, and Marianne Pollheimer-Mohaupt (eds.), *Transformations of Romanness: Early Medieval Regions and Identities* (Berlin: de Gruyter, 2018).

Pollmann, Judith, *Memory in Early Modern Europe, 1500–1800* (Oxford: Oxford University Press, 2017).

Polybius, *The Rise of the Roman Empire*, trans. Ian Scott-Kilvert (London: Penguin, 1979).

Poor, Sara S., *Mechthild of Magdeburg and her Book: Gender and the Making of Textual Authority* (Philadelphia: University of Pennsylvania Press, 2004).

Popkin, Jeremy D., *From Herodotus to H-Net: The Story of Historiography* (Oxford: Oxford University Press, 2015).

Popkin, Richard H., *Isaac La Peyrère* (Leiden: Brill, 1987).

Popkin, Richard H. (ed.), *The Pimlico History of Western Philosophy* (London: Pimlico, 1999).

Postone, Moishe, Louis Galambos, and Jane Eliot Sewell, *Time, Labor, and Social Domination: A Reinterpretation of Marx's Critical Theory* (Cambridge: Cambridge University Press, 2003).

Power, Eileen, *Medieval People* (London: Methuen, 1924).

Pownall, Frances, *Lessons from the Past: The Moral Uses of History in Fourth Century Prose* (Ann Arbor: University of Michigan Press, 2007).

Preus, J. Samuel, *Explaining Religion: Criticism and Theory from Bodin to Freud* (Oxford: Oxford University Press, 1996).

Preus, J. Samuel, *Spinoza and the Irrelevance of Biblical Authority* (Cambridge: Cambridge University Press, 2001).

Procopius, *History of the Wars*, trans. H. B. Dewing (London: Heinemann, 1914).

Quarles, Benjamin Arthur, *Frederick Douglass* (Washington, DC: Associated Publishers, 1948).

Quarles, Benjamin Arthur, *The Negro in the Civil War* (Boston: Little, Brown and Co., 1953).

Rabasa, José, Masayuki Sato, Edoardo Tortarolo, and Daniel Woolf (eds.), *The Oxford History of Historical Writing 1400–1800* (Oxford: Oxford University Press, 2015).

Raico, Ralph, *Classical Liberalism and the Austrian School* (Auburn, AL: Ludwig von Mises Institute, 2012).

Rancière, Jacques, *Les Mots de l'histoire. Essai de poétique du savoir* (Paris, Seuil, 1992).

Randall, John Hermann, *Nature and Historical Experience* (New York: Columbia University Press, 1958).

Ranke, Leopold von, *Geschichten der romanischen und germanischen Völker von 1494 bis 1535* (Leipzig: Reimer, 1824).

Ranke, Leopold von, *Die Serbische Revolution. Aus Serbischen Papieren und Mittheilungen* (Hamburg: Perthes, 1829).

Ranke, Leopold von, *History of the Latin and Teutonic Nations from 1494–1514*, trans. P. A. Ashworth (London: George Bell and Sons, 1887).

Ranke, Leopold von, *Weltgeschichte*, ed. Alfred Dove and Georg Winter, vol. IX (Leipzig: Duncker and Humblot, 1888).

Ranke, Leopold von, *Über die Epochen der neueren Geschichte. Historisch-kritische Ausgabe*, ed. Theodor Schieder and Helmut Berding (Munich: Oldenbourg, 1971).

Ranke, Leopold von, *The Secret of World History: Selected Writings on the Art and Science of History*, ed. Roger Wines (New York: Fordham University Press, 1981).

Ranke, Leopold von, *The Theory and Practice of History*, ed. Georg G. Iggers (London: Routledge, 2011).

Rapport, Nigel (ed.), *Democracy, Science and the 'Open Society': A European Legacy?* (Münster: LIT, 2005).

Redding, Paul, *Continental Idealism: Leibniz to Nietzsche* (London: Routledge, 2009).

Reeves, Marjorie, *The Influence of Prophecy in the Later Middle Ages: A Study of Joachimism* (Oxford: Oxford University Press, 2000).

Reimer, A. James, *Paul Tillich: Theologian of Nature, Culture and Politics* (Münster: LIT, 2004).

Reimitz, Helmut, *History, Frankish Identity and the Framing of Western Ethnicity* (Cambridge: Cambridge University Press, 2015).

Reiner, G. J., *History: Its Purpose and Method* (London: Allen and Unwin, 1950).

Rennie, Nicholas, *Speculating on the Moment: The Poetics of Time and Recurrence in Goethe, Leopardi, and Nietzsche* (Göttingen: Wallstein, 2005).

Rescher, Nicholas, *G. W. Leibniz's Monadology: An Edition for Students* (Pittsburgh: University of Pittsburgh Press, 1991).

Reuter, Timothy (ed.), *The Annals of Fulda* (Manchester: Manchester University Press, 1992).

Richter, Daniel S., and William A. Johnson (eds.), *The Oxford Handbook of the Second Sophistic* (Oxford: Oxford University Press, 2017).

Rickman, H. P., *Meaning in History: W. Dilthey's Thoughts on History and Society* (London: Allen and Unwin, 1961).

Riedenauer, Markus, *Pluralität und Rationalität: Die Herausforderung der Vernunft durch religiöse und kulturelle Vielfalt nach Nikolaus Cusanus* (Stuttgart: Kohlhammer, 2007).

Rigby, S. H., *Engels and the Formation of Marxism* (Manchester: Manchester University Press, 1992).

Rigby, S. H., *Marxism and History* (Manchester: Manchester University Press, 1998).

Rigby, S. H., *Wisdom and Chivalry: Chaucer's Knight's Tale and Medieval Political Theory* (Leiden: Brill, 2009).

Riley, Denise, *Am I that Name? Feminism and the Category of 'Women' in History* (Basingstoke: Macmillan, 1988).

Roberts, David D., *Nothing But History: Reconstruction and Extremity After Metaphysics* (Berkeley: University of California Press, 1995).

Robinson, James Harvey, *The New History: Essays Illustrating the Modern Historical Outlook* (New York: Macmillan, 1912).

Rohrbacher, David, *The Historians of Late Antiquity* (London: Routledge, 2002).

Rorty, Amélie Oksenberg, and James Schmidt (eds.), *Kant's 'Idea for a Universal History With a Cosmopolitan Aim': A Critical Guide* (Cambridge: Cambridge University Press, 2011).

Rorty, Richard, *Contingency, Irony, Solidarity*, (Cambridge: Cambridge University Press, 1999).

Rorty, Richard, J. B. Schneewind, and Quentin Skinner (eds.), *Philosophy in History: Essays on the Historiography of Philosophy* (Cambridge: Cambridge University Press, 1998).

Rose, Sonya O., *What is Gender History?* (Cambridge: Polity, 2010).

Rowbotham, Sheila, *Hidden from History* (London: Pluto Press, 1973).

Rowse, A. J., *The Use of History* (Harmondsworth: Pelican, 1971).

Rubinoff, Lionel, *Collingwood and the Reform of Metaphysics: A Study in the Philosophy of Mind* (Toronto: University of Toronto Press, 1970).

Rublack, Ulinka (ed.), *A Concise Companion to History* (Oxford: Oxford University Press, 2011).

Rudé, George, *The Crowd in the French Revolution* (Oxford: Clarendon Press, 1959).

Rudwick, Martin J. S., *Worlds before Adam: The Reconstruction of Geohistory in the Age of Reform* (Chicago: Chicago University Press, 2008).

Rüger, Jan, *The Great Naval Game: Britain and Germany in the Age of Empire* (Cambridge: Cambridge University Press, 2007).

Russell, Bertrand, *History of Western Philosophy* (London: George Allen and Unwin, 1947).

Sahlins, Marshall, *The Western Illusion of Human Nature* (Chicago: Prickly Paradigm Press: 2008).

Said, Edward, *Orientalism: Western Conceptions of the Orient* (London: Routledge and Kegan Paul, 1978).

Saini, Angela, *Inferior* (London: Harper Collins, 2018).

Saini, Angela, *Superior* (Boston, MA: Beacon Press, 2019).

Samuel, Raphael, *Theatres of Memory* (London: Verso, 1994).

Sanders, Rik, Bas Mesters, Reinier Kramer, and Margreet Windhorst (eds.), *Balans en Perspectief van de Nederlandse Cultuurgeschiedenis* (Amsterdam: Rodopi, 1991).

Sandy, Gerald N. (ed.), *The Classical Heritage in France* (Leiden: Brill, 2002).

Scheible, Heinz, *Die Entstehung der Magdeburger Zenturien. Ein Beitrag zur Geschichte der historiographischen Methode* (Gütersloh: Gerd Mohn, 1966).

Schiffman, Zachary Sayre, *On the Threshold of Modernity: Relativism in the French Renaissance* (Baltimore: Johns Hopkins University Press, 1991).

Schiffman, Zachary Sayre, *The Birth of the Past* (Baltimore: John Hopkins University Press, 2011).

Schlosser, Friedrich Christoph, *Weltgeschichte in zusammenhängender Erzählung*, 4 vols. (Frankfurt am Main: Varrentrapp 1815–41).

Schlosser, Friedrich Christoph, *Weltgeschichte für das deutsche Volk*, 19 vols. (Frankfurt am Main: Varrentrapp 1844–57).

Schuppe, Christian-Georg, *Der andere Droysen: neue Aspekte seiner Theorie der Geschichtswissenschaft* (Stuttgart: Steiner, 1998).

Schwab, Gail M., and John R. Jeanneny (eds.), *The French Revolution of 1789 and its Impact* (Westport, CT: Greenwood Press, 1995).

Scott, Joan Wallach, *Gender and the Politics of History, 30th Anniversary Edition* (New York: Columbia University Press, 2018).

Scott, Walter, *Waverley, or 'Tis Sixty Years Since* (Edinburgh: Adam and Charles Black, 1854).

Seidel, Bradley Nelson, 'Giambattista Vico and the Emergence of Historical Consciousness' (Marquette University: PhD thesis, 1996).

Seignobos, Charles, *La Méthode historique appliquée aux science sociales* (Paris: Alcan, 1901).

Sewell, William G., *Logics of History: Social History and Social Transformation* (Chicago: University of Chicago Press, 2005).

Shuster, Martin, *Autonomy after Auschwitz: Adorno, German Idealism, and Modernity* (Chicago: University of Chicago Press, 2014).

Sidelsky, Edward, *Ernst Cassirer* (Princeton: Princeton University Press, 2008).

Sigurdson, Richard Franklin, *Jacob Burckhardt's Social and Political Thought* (Toronto: University of Toronto Press, 2004).

Simiand, François, *Les Fluctuations économiques à longue période et la crise mondiale* (Paris: Alcan 1932).

Simiand, François, *Recherches anciennes et nouvelles sur le mouvement général des prix du VXIe au XIXe siècle* (Paris: Domat-Montchrestien, 1932).

Ska, Jean Louis, *Introduction to Reading the Pentateuch* (Winona Lake, Indiana: Eisenbrauns, 2006).

Skinner, Quentin, *The Foundations of Modern Political Thought*, 2 vols. (Cambridge: Cambridge University Press, 1978).

Skinner, Quentin, *Liberty before Liberalism* (Cambridge: Cambridge University Press, 1998).

Skocpol, Theda, *States and Social Revolutions: A Comparative Analysis of France, Russia, and China* (Cambridge: Cambridge University Press, 1979).

Skocpol, Theda, *Social Revolutions in the Modern World* (Cambridge: Cambridge University Press, 1994).

Skocpol, Theda (ed.), *Vision and Method in Historical Sociology* (Cambridge: Cambridge University Press, 1994).

Smail, Daniel Lord, *On Deep History and the Brain* (Berkeley: University of California Press, 2008).

Smith, Craig, *Adam Smith's Political Philosophy: The Invisible Hand and Spontaneous Order* (Abingdon: Routledge, 2006).

Snyder, Jeffrey Aaron, *Making Black History: The Color Line, Culture, and Race in the Age of Jim Crow* (Athens: University of Georgia Press, 2018).

Somos, Mark, *Secularisation and the Leiden Circle* (Leiden: Brill, 2011).

Southern, R. W., *History and Historians: Selected Papers of R. W. Southern*, ed. R. J. Bartlett (Oxford: Blackwell, 2004).

Sparling, Robert Alan, *Johann Georg Hamann and the Enlightenment Project* (Toronto: University of Toronto Press, 2011).

Spengler, Oswald, *Der Untergang des Abendlandes* (Munich: Beck, 1998).

Spiegel, Gabrielle M., *The Past as Text: The Theory and Practice of Medieval Historiography* (Baltimore: Johns Hopkins University Press, 1997).

Staël, Germaine de, *De la littérature considérée dans ses rapports avec les institutions sociales*, vol. 1, 2nd edition (Paris: de Crapelet, n.d.).

Stalin, J. V., *Problems of Leninism* (Peking: Foreign Languages Press, 1976).

Stein, Peter, *Roman Law in European History* (Cambridge: Cambridge University Press, 2012).

Steinmetz, George (ed.), *State/Culture: State Formation after the Cultural Turn* (Ithaca: Cornell University Press, 1999).

Stern, Fritz (ed.), *The Varieties of History* (New York: Meridian, 1956).

Stieg, Margaret F., *The Historische Zeitschrift: The Origin and Development of Scholarly Historical Periodicals* (Tuscaloosa: University of Alabama Press, 1986).

Stoianovich, Traian, *French Historical Method: The Annales Paradigm* (Ithaca: Cornell University Press, 1976).

Stone, Dan (ed.), *The Holocaust and Historical Methodology* (New York: Berghahn, 2012).

Stronk, Jan P., *Ctesias' Persian History: Introduction, Text, and Translation* (Düsseldorf: Wellem, 2010).

Stubbs, William, *The Constitutional History of England in its Origins and Development*, vol. 1 (Oxford: Clarendon Press, 1874).

Sturley, D. M., *The Study of History* (London: Longmans, 1969).

Sturm, Thomas, *Kant und die Wissenschaften vom Menschen* (Paderborn: Mentis, 2009).

Sulpicius Severus, *Sulpicius Severus' Vita Martini*, ed. Philip Burton (Oxford: Oxford University Press, 2017).

Swain, Harriet (ed.), *Big Questions in History* (London: Jonathan Cape, 2005).

Swanson, R. N., *The Twelfth-Century Renaissance* (Manchester: Manchester University Press, 1999).

Swanton, Michael (ed.), *The Anglo-Saxon Chronicles*, (London: Phoenix, 2000).

Sybel, Heinrich von, *Die deutsche Nation und das Kaiserreich* (Düsseldorf: Buddeus, 1862).

Sybel, Heinrich von, *Die Begründung des deutschen Reiches durch Wilhelm I*, 7 vols. (Munich: Oldenbourg, 1889–1894).

Tacitus, *Tacitus: The Annals and the Histories*, ed. Hugh Lloyd-Jones (New York: Washington Sqaure Press, 1964).

Taine, Hippolyte, *Histoire de la littérature anglaise*, 5 vols. (Paris: Hachette, 1863–4).

Taine, Hippolyte, *The Philosophy of Art* (New York: Holt and Williams, 1873).

Teggart, Frederick J., *Theory and Processes of History* (Berkeley: University of California Press, 1962).

Teherani-Krönner, Parto (ed.), *Humanökologie und Kulturökologie* (Opladen: Westdeutscher Verlag, 1992).

Tentler, Thomas N., *Sin and Confession on the Eve of the Reformation* (Princeton: Princeton University Press, 1977).

Thierry, Augustin, *Récits des temps mérovingiens précédés de Considérations sur l'histoire de France*, 2 vols. (Paris: Tessier, 1840).

Thompson, E. P., *The Making of the English Working Class* (Harmondsworth: Pelican, 1968).

Thompson, E. P., *Persons and Polemics: Historical Essays* (London: Merlin, 1994).

Thucydides, *The Peloponnesian War: The Crawley Translation* (New York: Random House, 1982).

Tileagă, Cristian, and Jovan Byford (eds.), *Psychology and History: Interdisciplinary Explorations* (Cambridge: Cambridge University Press, 2014).

Tilley, Arthur Augustus, *The Dawn of the French Renaissance* (Cambridge: Cambridge University Press, 1968).

Tillich, Paul, *The Protestant Era* (London: Nisbet, 1955).

Tillich, Paul, *A History of Christian Thought*, ed. Carl E. Braaten (New York: Touchstone, 1968).

Toews, John Edward, *Hegelianism: The Path toward Dialectical Humanism, 1805–1841* (Cambridge: Cambridge University Press, 1985).

Tosh, John, *The Pursuit of History* (Harlow: Longman, 1993).

Tosh, John, *Why History Matters* (Basingstoke: Palgrave, 2008).

Toulmin, Stephen, *The Place of Reason in Ethics* (Cambridge: Cambridge University Press, 1950).

Toynbee, Arnold J., *Greek Historical Thought* (New York: Mentor Books, 1952).

Toynbee, Arnold J., *A Study of History*, abridgement of vols. I–VI ed. Robert Somervell (Oxford: Oxford University Press 1946).

Toynbee, Arnold J., *A Study of History*, abridgement of vols. VII–X ed. Robert Somervell (Oxford: Oxford University Press, 1985).

Treadgold, Warren, *The Early Byzantine Historians* (Basingstoke: Macmillan, 2010).

Troeltsch, Ernst, *Der Historismus und seine Probleme: Erstes Buch*, ed. Friedrich Wilhelm Graf and Matthias Schlossberger (Berlin: de Gruyter, 2008).

Tucker, Aviezer (ed.), *A Companion to the Philosophy of History and Historiography* (London: Wiley, 2009).

Tull, Patricia K., and Claire Mathews McGinnis (eds.), *'As Those Who Are Taught': The Interpretation of Isaiah from the LXX to the SBL* (Atlanta, GA: SBL, 2006).

Tutino, Stefania, *Shadows of Doubt: Language and Truth in Post-Reformation Catholic Culture* (Oxford: Oxford University Press, 2014).

Ullmann, Walter, *The Medieval Idea of Law as Represented by Lucas de Penna* (Routledge, 2010).

Valla, Lorenzo, *On The Donation of Constantine*, ed. G. W. Bowersock (Cambridge, MA: Harvard University Press, 2007).

Vallery-Radot, René, *The Life of Pasteur* (London: Constable, 1928).

van Houts, Elisabeth, *Memory and Gender in Medieval Europe, 900–1200* (London: Palgrave, 1999).

van Houts, Elisabeth (ed.), *Medieval Memories: Men, Women and the Past, 700–1300* (New York: Longman, 2001).

van Liere, Frans, *An Introduction to the Medieval Bible* (Cambridge: Cambridge University Press, 2014).

van Oort, Henk, *The Inner Rainbow: An Illustrated History of Human Consciousness* (Sussex: Temple Lodge, 2014).

van Peursen, C. A., *Leibniz* (London: Faber and Faber, 1969).

Veeser, H. Aram (ed.) *The New Historicism* (New York: Routledge, 1989).

Velema, Wyger R. E., *Republicans: Essays on Eighteenth Century Dutch Political Thought* (Leiden: Brill, 2007).

Vico, Giambattisa, *The New Science of Giambattista Vico: Unabridged Translation of the Third Edition (1744)*, trans. Thomas Goddard Bergin and Max Harold Fisch (Ithaca: Cornell University Press, 1984).

Vico, Giambattisa, *On Humanistic Education* (Ithaca: Cornell University Press, 2003).

Villemaire, D., *E. A. Burtt: Historian and Philosopher* (Dordrecht: Springer, 1992).

Voegelin, Eric, *Published Essays, 1953–1965* (Columbia: University of Missouri Press, 2000).

Völkel, Markus, *Geschichtsschreibung: eine Einführung in globaler Perspektive* (Cologne: Böhlau, 2006).

von Essen, Gesa, and Horst Turk (eds.), *Unerledigte Geschichten: Der literarische Umgang mit Nationalität und Internationalität* (Göttingen: Wallstein, 2000).

Walbank, Frank W., *Polybius, Rome and the Hellenistic World* (Cambridge: Cambridge University Press, 2015).

Wanner, Raymond E., *Claude Fleury (1640–1723) as an Educational Historiographer and Thinker* (The Hague: Martinus Nijhoff, 1975).

Ward, Timothy, *Word and Supplement* (Oxford: Oxford University Press, 2002).

Warner, Rex, *The Greek Philosophers* (New York: New American Library, 1958).

Weber, Max, *Gesammelte Aufsätze zur Religionssoziologie*, vol 1 (Tübingen: Mohr, 1920).

Weber, Max, *Max Weber: Essays in Sociology*, ed. H. H. Gerth and C. Wright Mills (New York: Oxford University Press, 1946).

Weber, Max, *Max Weber: Gesammelte Aufsätze zur Wissenschaftslehre. Hrsg. von Johannes Winckelmann. 6., erneut durchgesehene Auflage* (Tübingen: Mohr/Siebeck, 1985).

Wedgwood, C. V., *Truth and Opinion: Historical Essays* (London: Collins, 1960).

Wehler, Hans-Ulrich, *Das Deutsche Kaiserreich, 1871–1918* (Göttingen: Vandenhoeck und Ruprecht, 1973).

Welter, Jean Thiébaut, *L'Exemplum dans la littérature religieuse et didactique du moyen âge* (Paris: Occitania E. H. Guitard, 1927).

Westman, Robert S. and David Biale (eds.), *Thinking Impossibilities: The Intellectual Legacies of Amos Funkenstein* (Toronto: University of Toronto Press, 2008).

Whatmore, Richard, and Brian Young (eds.), *A Companion to Intellectual History* (London: Wiley, 2016).

White, Hayden, *Metahistory: The Historical Imagination in the Nineteenth Century* (Baltimore: Johns Hopkins University Press, 1973).

White, Hayden, *Tropics of Discourse* (Baltimore: Johns Hopkins University Press, 1978).

White, Hayden, *The Content of the Form* (Baltimore: Johns Hopkins University Press, 1987).

Whitmarsh, Tim, *Beyond the Second Sophistic: Adventures in Greek Postclassicism* (Berkeley: University of California Press, 2013).

Williams, Bernard, *Truth and Truthfulness: An Essay in Genealogy* (Princeton: Princeton University Press, 2002).

Williams, Bernard, *Shame and Necessity* (Berkeley: University of California Press, 2008).

Williams, Raymond, *Culture and Society, 1780–1950* (London: Chatto and Windus, 1958).

Williams, Raymond, *Problems in Materialism and Culture* (London: Verso, 1980).

Wolf, Eric, *Europe and the 'People Without History'* (Berkeley: University of California Press, 1982).

Wolfskeel, C. W., *De Immortalitate Animae of Augustine: Text, Translation and Commentary* (Amsterdam: Grüner, 1977).

Wood, Ellen Meiksins, *The Origin of Capitalism: A Longer View* (London: Verso, 2002).

Wood, Ian, *The Modern Origins of the Early Middle Ages* (Oxford: Oxford University Press, 2013).

Woodman, A. J., *Lost Histories: Selected Fragments of Roman Historians* (Newcastle: Histos, 2015).

Woodson, Carter G., *The Education of the Negro Prior to 1861* (New York: G. P. Putnam's Sons, 1915).

Woodson, Carter G., *A Century of Negro Migration* (Washington, DC: Association of Negro Life and History, 1918).

Woodson, Carter G., *The Negro in Our History* (Washington, DC: Associated Publishers, 1922).

Wormald, Patrick, *Legal Culture in the Early Medieval West* (London: Hambledon, 1999).

Yates, Frances A., *Ideas and Ideals in the North European Renaissance* (London: Routledge, 1999).

Zacher, Samantha, *Rewriting the Old Testament in Anglo-Saxon Verse: Becoming the Chosen People* (London: Bloomsbury, 2013).

Zammito, John H., *Kant, Herder and the Birth of Anthropology* (Chicago: University of Chicago Press, 2002).

Zimmermann, Albert, and Gudrun Vuillemin-Diemand (eds.), *Antiqui und Moderni: Traditionsbewußtsein und Fortschrittsbewußtsein im späten Mittelalter* (Berlin: De Gruyter, 1974).

Zimmermann, Michel (ed.), *Auctor et auctoritas. Invention et conformisme dans l'écriture médiévale* (Paris: École des Chartes, 2001).

Index

For the benefit of digital users, indexed terms that span two pages (e.g., 52–53) may, on occasion, appear on only one of those pages.